LEAVE A
OF LIFE T

Each and every day the lives of tho
Magen David Adom, Israel's emergency medical service. MDA ambulances cover the country from coast to coast and border to border. Our casualty stations span the country. MDA alone is responsible for the storage and distribution of blood throughout Israel. A legacy to Magen David Adom will help them continue their life saving work. MDA is a non-governmental organisation and relies wholly on donations from the community.

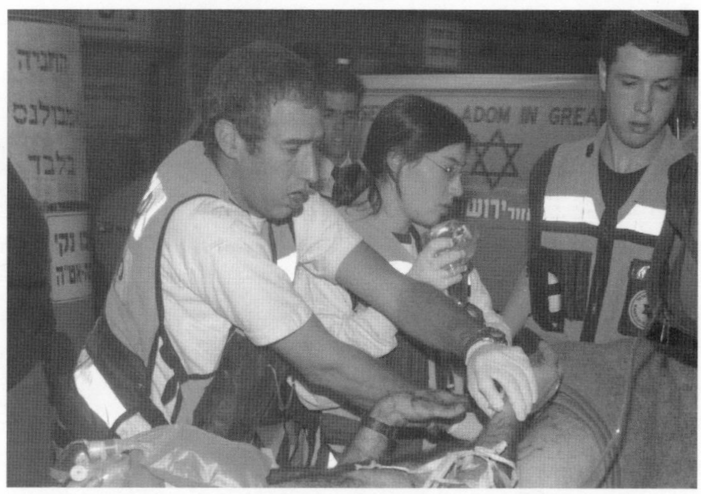

MAGEN DAVID ADOM

Contact: Eli Benson, Executive Director
Magen David Adom UK
Pearl House, 746 Finchley Road, London NW11 7TH
Tel: 020-8381 4849 Fax: 020-8381 4898
Email: info@ukmda.org www.ukmda.org

Registered Charity No. 210770

LIBRARY

THE HOLOCAUST CENTRE

"In spite of everything,
I still have hope for the future.
I'll tell you what gives me hope
for the future...
it's a place like this."

Anita Lasker-Wallfisch,
Auschwitz survivor

Museum and Gardens
Open to the general public

February - November

Wednesday - Sunday
Entry: £6.00 adults
£4.00 concessions

A visit to The Holocaust Centre is educational, moving, challenging and inspiring.
The Centre houses a permanent exhibition on the Holocaust and is set in landscaped memorial gardens. It caters for individual visitors, booked groups and school visits. It also provides a wide range of services and resources relating to Holocaust and Citizenship education.

For more information, visit www.holocaustcentre.net
Or call 01623 836627The Holocaust Centre, Laxton, Nr. Ollerton, Notts NG22 0PA

Vallentine Mitchell

Did you ever meet Hitler, Miss?

Trude Levi

Teaching the Holocaust is a difficult and sensitive task. The facts and figures are readily available but it is the individual experiences that engage and interest pupils and allow them to understand the full implications of the Holocaust. Consequently, this book by Trude Levi will prove an invaluable teaching tool. Trude tells her story with little comment, allowing the terrible facts to speak for themselves. She describes without sentiment her experiences in Hungary under the Nazis, the horrors of Auschwitz-Birkenau and Buchenwald and, finally, the death-march, during which she collapsed on her twenty-first birthday and was left for dead. This account provides the context for the main part of the book in which the author sets out some of the questions she has been asked by schoolchildren and university students from both Germany and England.

128 pages 2002
0 85303 467 2 paper £9.95/$14.45

UK: Crown House, 47 Chase Side, Southgate, London N14 5BP.
Tel: +44 (0)20 8920 2100 Fax: +44 (0)20 8447 8548

North America: 5824 NE Hassalo Street, Portland, OR 97213 3644
Tel: 800 944 6190 Fax: 503 280 8832

Website: www.vmbooks.com

C153

...gue L...

THE JEWISH YEAR BOOK
2003

Joseph Sonntag, 1905–84
(photograph copyright Peter Fisher, courtesy of *Jewish Chronicle*).

The Jewish Year Book

Published in association with the Jewish Chronicle, London

Founded 1896

2003
5763–5764

Edited by
STEPHEN W. MASSIL

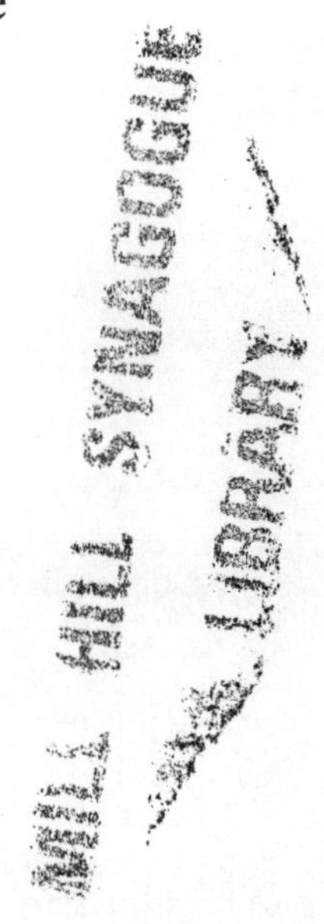

VALLENTINE MITCHELL
LONDON • PORTLAND, OR

Published in 2003 in Great Britain by
VALLENTINE MITCHELL
Crown House, 47 Chase Side, Southgate
London N14 5BP

and in the United States of America by
VALLENTINE MITCHELL
c/o ISBS, 5824 N.E. Hassalo Street,
Portland, Oregon, 97213-3644

Website: www.vmbooks.com

Copyright © 2003 Vallentine Mitchell and the Jewish Chronicle

ISBN 0 85303 466 4
ISSN 0075 3769

All rights reserved. No part of this publication may be reproduced, stored in or introduced into a retrieval system, or transmitted, in any form or by any means, electronic, mechanical, photocopying, recording or otherwise, without the prior written permission of the publisher of this book.

Printed in Great Britain by
MPG Books Ltd, Bodmin, Cornwall

Contents

Preface

The Board of Deputies moved to Bloomsbury Square at the end of 2001. The Board now joins a select group of institutions occupying heritage buildings with magnificent premises to show to visitors. It is, however, only by chance that there is a plaque (historic in itself in pre-dating the LCC blue plaques) recording Isaac Disraeli's occupancy of the building, but the area does have good associations with the years of early zionist activity in London as well. The relocation of the JFS to Kenton, after more than 40 years in Camden, is the latest in the series of moves in its long history, but a significant development nonetheless. The Ben Uri has also found a new home – it is to be hoped a permanent one – after several shifts over the years, and its current exhibition of the works of Mark Gertler coincides with a major new biography of the artist. The International Council of Jewish Women has moved its headquarters from London to Montevideo.

The uncovering of a mikveh in Milk Street in the City of London was a late attraction at the end of 2001 when, among others, Dayan Ehrentreu is reported to have descended through layers of civic detritus and the stratas of desecration and of the plague years to examine for himself this remarkable discovery; the Jewish Historical Society, imitating its founders debating the character of Moyses Hall in Bury St Edmunds in the 1890s, gave the floor to a thorough archaeological discussion of this remarkable medieval survival and a reconsideration of the Gresham Street discovery of 1986.

On the other hand, we have also to report further sales of the United Synagogue's books, a topic that was given wider treatment at Jewish Book Week in March in a session entitled 'Selling the Family Silver'. News that the Montefiore Endowment of the Spanish & Portuguese Jews' Congregation had decided to sequester its manuscript holdings at Jews' College – a collection that had been deposited at the College in 1899 'in perpetuity' – only confirmed how little attention is paid to public debate on communal responsibility. This development was seen immediately as a direct repudiation of Lauderdale Road's confidence in the future of the College. And Jews' College, itself, known since 2000 as the London School of Jewish Studies, was subsequently understood to have sought export licences for valuable parts of its own library collections, while still labouring to secure a future for itself. This news makes a sad reflection in a year reduced by the death of the former librarian of the College, Ruth Goldschmidt-Lehmann, in January.

I have had occasion this year to invite his Honour Judge Owen to insert a note into the section on UK legislation mentioning the 'Divorce

(Religious Marriages) Act, 2002', which will receive fuller treatment in next year's revision. The North-West London eruv finally took effect. We have been noting its gestation over several years and trust that the local communal organizations involved have kept pace with the requirements for access to buildings for the disabled and for children now that beneficiaries of the eruv will be keen to push, carry and ride to services under its aegis, the necessary regulations coming under the provisions of the Town and Country Planning Acts. The travail to secure its emplacement has been long and fraught with dissension compared with implementations in other cities and other countries.

In Scotland, there was news of the amalgamation of the Netherlee & Clarkston and the Queen's Park Synagogues, to be based for the future at Clarkston. The new Scottish form of prayers for the Royal Family now refers to Prince Charles by his Scottish title, the Duke of Rothesay.

There was a service for the Queen Mother at Bevis Marks in February. In June, the Chief Rabbi attended the Jubilee service at St Paul's; he provided a preface to the latest Bishop Otter Memorial paper on the Chagall glass at Chichester and Tudelay. Hyam Corney, Deputy Editor of the *Jewish Chronicle*, retired to Israel. Lord Winston demonstrated on television how descent on the y-chromosome is traced also through the male line (thus vindicating biblical genealogical practice).

The Jewish Museum, in its seventieth anniversary year, is embarking on plans for major expansion. Its programme celebrating Continental Britons strikes well with the spate of literature on the exiles and emigrés from Central Europe. Celia Rose of the Clapton Club led a session in the museum's programme accompanying its exhibition on Hackney. Frank Auerbach was exhibited at the Royal Academy last autumn, and this year a survey of Lucien Freud has been a major event at the Tate Gallery and the Queen's Galleries now feature his portrait of Her Majesty. That he is the curator of a Constable exhibition currently in Paris is a wonderful outcome to a long career, distinguished now by the receipt of the Order of Merit. Australian novelist Bernard Cohen is writer-in-residence at the Sir John Soane Museum.

In a year marking the centenary both of the Order of Merit (the first Jew to be honoured was Samuel Alexander in 1930, followed by Herbert Samuel in 1958, and there are five at the present time) and of the British Academy, the number of Jews so honoured continues to be high. It is, however, worth noting that the British Academy, while honouring Jewish scholars in many areas of study and others in the fields of semitic and oriental studies, has yet to honour Hebrew scholarship as such. The number of Jews distinguished by the Nobel prizes has also been significantly increased this year through the work of Sidney Brenner, Israeli-born economist Daniel Kahneman, and Robert Horvitz, who shared the award for medicine; the prize for literature was awarded to Imre

Kertesz. There were honours, too, for Jonathan Miller and Peter Lachmann (knighthoods), Harold Pinter (CH) and Ruth Deech (DBE), and Sir Tom Stoppard also joins the Order of Merit. Tony Blair, on the other hand, received an Honorary Doctorate from Haifa University. At the beginning of November the Prime Minister formally opened the JFS at its new premises.

Jewish music and performers were featured at the Spitalfields Festival, including works by Minna Kael and the Ne'imah Choir, to the extent that I have been able to augment the 'Who's Who' with a significant musical element this year, if only to extend recognition to chazanim and musicians at the death of Mikhail Alexandrovitch, who was briefly chazan in Manchester in his early career and was notable also as, apparently, Benjamin Gigli's last pupil. And Vlado Perlmuter died at a great age. Enesco's opera *Oedipe*, with libretto by Edmund Fleg, was performed at the Edinburgh Festival. Polonski's *The Pianist* won the Palme d'Or at Cannes. David Hare brought back his solo performance of 'Via Dolorosa'. A street in Jerusalem was named after Heine. Sir Isaiah Berlin was the presiding spirit over Tom Stoppard's trilogy *The Coast of Utopia*, on Russian and other exiles of the nineteenth century, at the National Theatre.

Books of the year include Michael Oren's *The June War, 1967*, Brenda Maddox's life of Rosalind Franklin and Ira Nadel's life of Tom Stoppard; there were two biographies of Primo Levi (by Carol Augier and Ian Thomson) and Eric Hobsbawm's autobiography *Interesting Times*. Michael Roseman's *The Villa, the Lake, the Meeting: Wannsee and the Final Solution* and Pamela Shatzkes' *Holocaust and Rescue: Impotent or Indifferent? Anglo-Jewry 1938–1945* deal with different aspects of the Holocaust; and Vallentine Mitchell have marked the tenth anniversary of their Library of Holocaust Testimonies. Kenneth Collins published a medical record of Glasgow Jewry, *Be Well! Jewish Immigrant Health and Welfare, 1860–1914*, with a foreword by the Chief Rabbi. Zui Jagendorf won the Society of Authors Sagittarius Prize for his *Wolfy and the Strudelbakers*.

Professor David Latchman has been appointed the new Master of Birkbeck College.

The deaths recorded this year include those of Ernst Gombrich, Max Perutz and César Milstein, depleting those numbered among the most highly honoured in the community; also Joseph Finklestone, Sir Lou Sherman, Tommie Gould, VC, Benny Rothman (latter-day halakhist with his concern for the right to roam); Sydney Davis of AJEX, Esther Carvalho and Baroness Serota; novelist Chaim Potok, industrialist Lord Weinstock; Neville Sandelson, Rita Rosemarine and Martin Savitt, pre-eminent among the communal leadership of the day; and David Asseo (Turkey) and Harry Rabinowicz among the rabbinate. Harry Ward, whose Zangwill Collection was safely deposited at the Hartley Library, Southampton, some time ago, has also died. Lionel Bernstein and other activists from the South African ANC movement died this year; also Rabbi Zerachya in Israel, Elie Hobeika of the Lebanese militia, Tahsein Buslin, diplomat at the Israel–Egypt peace talks, and Swedish diplomat Per Auger, whose careers have all had a significant impact on the lives of Jews.

Organizations featured for the first time in the directory include the Association of Jews from Egypt, the Jewish Literary Trust and the Jewish Police Association.

All of these matters, lives and deaths of honour, carry the edifying flow of a fruitful and notable year in the community. Our lives have, however, carried on amid a current of poisonous vindictiveness, stemming from the terrorist attacks of 11 September, the continuing Intifada in Israel, matched by the 'rooting out of terror' as the preferred Israeli option, and the shadow of imminent war over Iraq.

It is felt that antisemitism has been on the increase throughout Europe and in Britain; commentators on Israel–Palestine have been seen coming almost to blows in the *New York Review of Books* and the *London Review of Books*; there was an editorial apology from the *New Statesman* following its unseemly presentation; the temporary suspension of sales of 'Israel' products at stores including Selfridges and Harrods have brought tensions to the market-place. Israeli academics have been subjected to the type of boycott that Jews in other times and elsewhere have been adept at promoting.

The great event of communal solidarity this year was the meeting in support of Israel in Trafalgar Square in May. There had already been, however, a public stand by representatives of the Neturei Karta on a Palestinian platform, also in Trafalgar Square, in the full limelight of London politics and journalism. The Chief Rabbi gave the Templeton Lecture in Philadelphia on the theme of his book *Dignity and Difference*, which has attracted admiration from many quarters and, at the same time, communal obloquy. It appears that he is to prepare a revision for the second edition of the book under the duress of communal and Board of Deputies' pressure and the intervention of parties who elsewhere disdain his authority. Such censure and censorship is unprecedented in British-Jewish affairs. In Israel itself, the government coalition is on the verge of collapse because of disagreements over the budget, and the timing of elections for the Knesset in 2003 may open a horizon for new leadership. A prerequisite of the political process must be a change of consciousness; the cycle of recrimination and the dwelling on the causal chain, so unproductive, must give way to new thinking for a positive outcome to the inherent horror of the situation. Leadership, on both sides, seems so glaringly deficient. The trial of Marwan Barghouti began in August.

Tom Segev gave the annual Jacob Sonntag Memorial Lecture under the title 'From Balfour to Sharon: The Legacy of the British Mandate', and recorded the sweetness, no less, of life in Mandate Palestine and the sense of purpose of the final years of that epoch when, even at the siege of Jerusalem in 1948–49, optimism and a sense of achievement prevailed. The news throughout this past year has been fraught with the crazy acts of despair and the convolutions of recrimination, retaliation and counter-blows of repression and suspicion, too many to record dispassionately in the calendar of events. The Peace Process begun in Oslo has hardly been given time to work through and has been well-nigh abandoned in both Israeli and Palestinian attitudes. That there is no expectation of a change of direction in political terms but only a reliance on strategies for manipulating the media sets prospects for progress during 2003 at a nadir.

My thanks this year, as ever, are due to John Fischer, in one of the few less complicated years of calendar-making; and also to Rabbi Jeffrey Davis, Marlena Schmool, Mordaunt Cohen in his retirement, Diana Lazarus, Judith Freedman, Michael Jolles, Ronald Domb, Mrs Haria, Rabbi Plancey and Raymond Kalman, for their attention to detail which greatly improves the record here put forward. I should mention that Mrs J. Cotsen of the South Wales Representative Council has retired after many years' service, and to her and the many other communal officers of her standing I offer my thanks for the efforts that sustain this publication.

The essays that precede the substantive directory this year mark the fiftieth anniversaries in 2003 at the *Jewish Quarterly* and the Institute of Jewish Studies, and I am grateful to Professor Geller for a timely essay that also forms part of the series on Jewish educational establishments which has been a feature of the last few years; I regret that the centenary of the Oxford University Jewish Society eluded my correspondents. I am grateful to Ruth Sonntag for her personal account of her father's remarkable career and his devotion to Jewish writing, and for her efforts and to the *Jewish Chronicle* for the portrait that graces this volume. The other essays are intended to uphold the character of the *Jewish Quarterly* and are by Cecil Bloom (sustaining the musical theme for the year), Sally Berkovic on new efforts by Jewish women, and, owing to the lack of the significant figures anticipated from the 2001 census, an essay by Diana Rau on the demographic plenty offered by the opening of the files of the 1901 census for research to a generation avid for genealogical and sociological news of our forebears. Murray Freedman has taken an early view of the material with his work *Leeds Jews in the 1901 Census: A Demographic Portrait of an Immigrant Community*.

The publication of the results of the 'religious' question which appeared in the census of 2001 will be an early topic for 2003. In March 2003, Jewish Book Week will form the cornerstone and see the launch of the revived Jewish Arts Festival.

London, 23 October 2002, 17 Marcheshvan 5763 **SWM**

Jacob Sonntag: A Personal Memoir

Ruth Sonntag

In so many of the letters and articles written in tribute to Jacob Sonntag after his death, there appeared the words 'the *Jewish Quarterly* must continue'. Nineteen years later, the magazine still does exist – which is nothing short of amazing, given that the average life of a 'small' magazine is about five years. Indeed, the *Jewish Quarterly* is celebrating its fiftieth birthday this year. This is surely a tribute to the vision of its founder, Jacob Sonntag, who inspired those individuals who took up the torch and committed themselves to keeping the journal alive and vibrant.

What is its secret? What has always made it so special? First and foremost, its independence from all traditional Jewish establishments and institutions has made it possible to maintain a unique integrity. Of course, it has evolved since Sonntag's death. It is run in a more business-like fashion; there have been attempts to 'modernize', using cartoon illustrations to lighten the intellectual density; the logo has changed several times; the range of topics has expanded; and there are many more women contributors. There is also more division of labour. Notwithstanding a valued and loyal editorial advisory board, the *Quarterly* was, for 31 years, essentially a one-man show. Sonntag dealt with everything: the soliciting of material, proof-reading, copy-editing, correspondence, advertising, publicity, distribution, organization of cultural events, and so on. He worked, single-mindedly, from early morning until late at night, even when he was in his seventies. True, in later life, he had no choice but to recruit help with some of the tasks, and the Jewish Literary Trust, set up in 1975, took on some of the responsibilities, mainly financial. This not only assured the Editor a monthly, albeit meagre, salary, but enabled him to get on with the main job of piecing the *Quarterly* together year after year.

Though married with two children, the *Jewish Quarterly* took up most of Sonntag's time, energy and passion. 'Jacob Sonntag was the *Jewish Quarterly* and the *Jewish Quarterly* was Jacob Sonntag' (Renee Winegarten). This was a typical reference as to how the two entities were perceived to be inseparable. Many epithets were used by admirers to describe 'Jacob Sonntag – the man', in testimonial after testimonial: good, gentle, humble, courageous, serious, tenacious, selfless, great, single-minded, respected, a sage, heroic, amazing phenomenon, fiercely obstinate, a humanist and indefatigable. Rafael Scharf, who was very close to him during the last decade of Sonntag's life, wrote:

Ruth Sonntag is the daughter of Joseph Sonntag.

> He was one of the last of the great characters who, in his person, life and work formed a bridge between the world of East-European Jewry, which is no more, and contemporary Jewish life in Israel and in Britain … He was a self-taught *maskil*, in the mould of the great Jewish men of letters of bygone days, civilized in the widest sense of the word … A man of unswerving integrity, a sage and a rebel … he soldiered on with utter dedication and single-mindedness in the belief that an idea, a printed word, has the power to influence the course of history ... [He] felt ... a personal obligation towards Jewish culture in all its aspects, a duty to preserve continuity. The motif that often ran through his discourse was '*die goldene keyt*' – the golden chain. New links had to be forged and joined with the old. In this he succeeded better than most.

The late Chaim Bermant described him as 'brave writer with a mission'. But Moshe Dor, in the Israeli daily *Ma'ariv*, lamented the endless worry and concern that had beset his ageing friend over the very existence of the *Quarterly*, his life's work and mission, which, despite the efforts of some, was constantly threatened by insufficient funds and support from the Anglo-Jewish community: 'I know that there were many difficult hours too heavy to bear; any man of lesser persistence and steadfastness would have thrown away the yoke and the burden. But Sonntag stood firm, ground his teeth and continued to climb the foothills of a mountain which has no peak. And the *Jewish Quarterly* continued to appear.'

In relation to Israel, Dor also referred to the 'endless [painful] love and patience' with which Jacob strove to build a bridge 'that connects between the more sensitive and attentive intellectuals of the United Kingdom and the State of Israel. Israel burned like an eternal candle on the pages of the *Quarterly*.' Whereas Hyam Maccoby wrote in *The Times* obituary: 'He retained the idealism of the early Zionist movement and was a link with a great generation which sought national identity, but whose highest hopes were for cultural development and for peace.'

Sonntag, however, did agonize about how those ideals had been betrayed. In his final editorial, dictated from his hospital bed, he shared Ahad Ha-am's longing for a future Israel that would be a 'spiritual centre' for the Jewish people, accepting that the majority of Jews would remain outside Israel and that Palestine would continue to have a large Arab population. The editorial ends:

> As to the question what we could or should do in relation to Israel, there is only one answer: we should support, in every way possible, those in Israel who are working towards genuine peace and real progress. We must not shy away from criticising polices we consider wrong and ill-conceived. On another level, we should establish and

> extend cultural exchanges between our two countries and initiate a continuous dialogue between our own and Israeli writers; this can contribute to a better understanding of Jewish needs and concerns. This is indeed what the *Jewish Quarterly* has always aspired to since its foundation in 1953.

In the same editorial he concurs with views expressed by Nahoum Goldman that the State of Israel should not be a state like any other state, but – unlike any other – should be 'based on justice, genuine democracy, equality of rights of all citizens irrespective of race, origin and religious affiliation – principles which were embodied in the Declaration of Independence adopted in May 1948'.

Sonntag was known for his 'uncompromising integrity' and spoke his mind within the pages of his journal. He did not fear others' responses. Indeed, he welcomed them, as the *Quarterly* was supposed to be a forum for lively debate and creative dialogue, both within its pages and face to face on many symposium platforms in the UK and Israel. But, occasionally, certain individuals would take umbrage and withdraw their financial support if the views expressed were perceived as too much against the grain, especially concerning Israel.

On the occasion of the *Quarterly*'s thirtieth anniversary in 1983, David Herman described Sonntag as 'Brave champion of unpopular causes'. David (son of Josef Herman) was one of a younger generation who grouped around Sonntag during the latter years of his life. The purpose of this group, led by Colin Shindler, was to assure the continuity of the magazine. After Sonntag's death, Antony Lerman became editor for a short time, followed by Shindler, for some ten years, then Elena Lappin and now Matthew Reisz. Each editor has brought their own particular mark, while remaining true to the ideals of cultural pluralism and open debate, about sometimes difficult and contentious issues of concern to Anglo-Jewry – or what Sonntag felt should be of concern – including world current affairs, as well as remembering and learning from the past and building upon our great cultural heritage. It should be said that the emphasis was on Eastern and Central European heritage, and that, generally, the audience was, and probably still is, the intellectual fringe of Anglo-Jewish society.

Though his life's mission became the promotion of Jewish secular culture, Jacob was in fact born (in 1905) into an Orthodox Jewish family in Viznitz, in northern Bukovina (then part of the Austro-Hungarian Empire). He was the eldest of the five children of Benzion Singer-Sonntag and Eidel David. His father and grandfather were bookbinders. When Jacob was four, the family moved to Kosov, a small town in eastern Galicia, until the outbreak of the First World War. The family fled in 1916, before the advancing Russian invasion, and finally settled in Vienna in 1917, where Jacob completed his elementary schooling and entered grammar school, which he left at the age of 16. With the winds of change gusting across Eastern and Central Europe, he diverted his passion for Torah and Talmud to the secular pursuits of literature, philosophy, politics and socialist Zionism.

Still in his teens, he began writing (in his native German) under the name of Jakob Singer, mostly poetry and a few plays. One of his poems, 'Ich Sehne Mich', was set to music composed by Alois Kern. Between 1923 and 1925 he contributed regularly, in prose and verse, to local Viennese Jewish newspapers (*Der Tag Der Jugend* and the Jewish Youth section of the *Wiener Morgenzeitung)*.

Sonntag became a member of *Blau Weiss* and *Gordonia*, and while on *Hachshara* (preparation for Aliyah – in Zionism and agriculture) he met Berta Weinraub. They married in 1929 and went to Palestine in 1930, but they returned to Vienna after only six months. Jacob resumed his work as a freelance journalist, contributing regularly to various, mainly Jewish, newspapers and periodicals. He also acted as an occasional correspondent for Jewish newspapers in France and America. In 1935, as a result of the Fascist Putsch in Vienna, the couple fled to Czechoslovakia, where Jacob continued as a freelance journalist (first in Brno and then in Prague). In November 1938, after the 'Munich Agreement', he arrived in England, in the first group of refugees brought over with the help of the Czech Trust Fund and the National Union of Journalists. After a period of internment on the Isle of Man, he eventually resumed his freelance writing and translating, mainly from Yiddish, Hebrew and German, contributing regularly to local Jewish publications such as the *Jewish Chronicle*, the *Zionist Review*, the *Jewish Observer* and the *Jewish Standard*. He also edited, for a time, a small publication issued by the Austrian Centre, entitled *Zeitspiegel*, and became associated with a number of other small, short-lived Jewish publications. His first major professional undertaking began with his editorship of a Jewish pictorial monthly, *New Life*, which lasted for two years (1947–48). The periodical was discontinued because of the restrictions on paper at the time. He then edited two equally short-lived newspapers, the *Jewish Literary Supplement* and the *Jewish Literary Gazette.*

It was less than a decade after the Second World War; the public at large was beginning to grasp the extent of the Holocaust; it was less than five years after the State of Israel had been established; the world was in fear of the Cold War; hopes of peace were remote; and the murder of the Jewish writers in the Soviet Union had recently come to light. It was into such a world that, in May 1953, the *Jewish Quarterly* was born.

Somehow, Jacob Sonntag, with no money of his own, had managed to persuade a few friendly benefactors to support his cause: to establish an independent forum for creative writers, thinkers and artists to give voice to (among other things) what it meant to be a Jew in the post-Holocaust era. The late Josef Herman, artist and close friend, especially in the early days, wrote in his tribute: 'When … I said that this whole project of launching a magazine, without any financial resources, seems to me crazy, he thought for a while, then as though speaking to himself: "Too much sanity when attempting something creative is positively dangerous, don't you agree?".'

And so the *Jewish Quarterly* was launched. It was first registered under the Business Names Act. It was then taken over by a private limited company, Jewish Literary Publications, jointly owned by all existing Anglo-Jewish publishing houses, under whose imprint it continued until about 1975, when the Company was acquired by the Jewish Literary Trust Ltd, which continues to publish the magazine to this day. The last copy of the *Jewish Quarterly* to be edited by Jacob Sonntag was the one hundred and fourteenth issue.

The contributors throughout Sonntag's 31-year editorship were many indeed, and the following form but a fraction of the list. They include novelists, essayists, poets and playwrights, Yiddishists, philosophers, historians, scholars, academics, scientists, artists, art and literary critics, film directors and musicologists: Dannie Abse, S.Y. Agnon, Shalom Aleichem, Aaron Appelfeld, Alexander Baron, Isaiah Berlin, Chaim Bermant, Martin Buber, Paul Celan, Gerda Charles, Isaac Deutscher, Brian Glanville, Louis Golding, Nathan Goldman, Josef Herman, Arthur Jacobs, Louis Jacobs, Leo Koenig, Alexander Knapp, Lionel Kochan, Bernard Kops, Joseph Leftwich, Dan Leon, Primo Levi, Hyman Levy, Barnet Litvinoff, Emmanuel Litvinoff, Hyam Maccoby, Wolf Mankowitz, Louis Marks, Amos Oz, Harold Pinter, Chaim Raphael, Frederic Raphael, Nellie Sachs, Raphael Scharf, Ben Segal, Jon Silkin, Charles Spencer, George Steiner, A.N. Stencl, Yacov Talmon, Benjamin Tammuz, Dov Vardi, Renee Winegarten, Arnold Wesker, Robert Wistrich and Harry Zohn. Some on the list died long ago, some had their first works published in the *Quarterly* and went on to make names for themselves, and some were well known already. Many other worthy contributors are not listed here for no other reason than limited space.

In association with the *Jewish Quarterly*, Sonntag also edited several anthologies: *Caravan – A Jewish Quarterly Omnibus* (Thomas Yoseloff, 1961), *Jewish Writing Today* (Vallentine Mitchell, 1974), *New Writing From Israel* (Corgi Books, 1976) and *Jewish Perspectives – 25 Years of Jewish Writing* (Secker & Warburg, 1980). He contributed essays on Yiddish to various encyclopaedias. One of his translations from Yiddish of a narrative poem by Abraham Sutzkever, *Siberia* (first published in 1953), appeared in hardback with eight original illustrations and a preface by Marc Chagall; Joseph Sonntag wrote the Introduction (Abelard-Schuman, 1961).

In a piece called 'A Kind of Testament', written in hospital, by hand, Jacob said his 'farewell to a troubled world', stating that 'There are still some plans I had for work which is unfinished, and hope that those who will continue it will do it in the best tradition of Jewish writing of all times'. This remains the challenge for the *Jewish Quarterly* in its fiftieth year and in the years to come – in a world no less troubled.

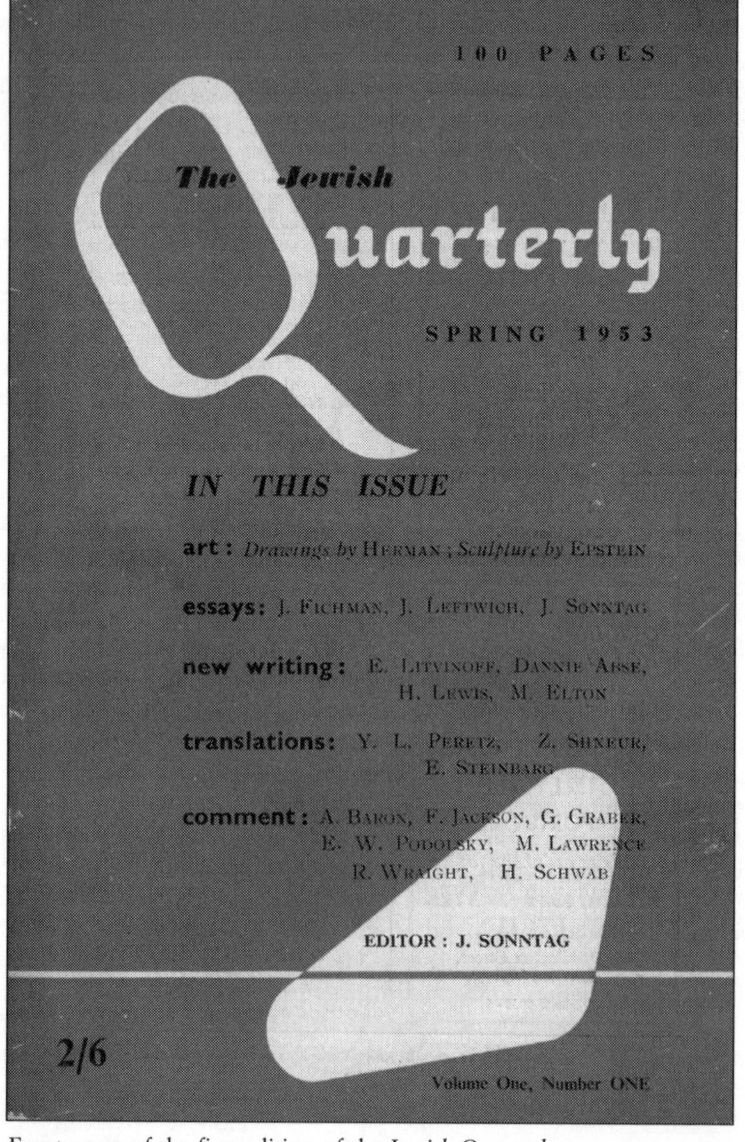

Front cover of the first edition of the *Jewish Quarterly*

Daughters of the Revolution: What Has Changed for Orthodox Women in Britain?

Sally Berkovic

I was a foreign bride. Dragged, albeit willingly, from Manhattan – a place where it is cool to be *frum* – to London – a place where being *frum* is regarded coolly. It was 1993, and one of the biggest internal challenges facing the modern Orthodox community was the growing number of dissatisfied women who wanted more than the Orthodox community was willing to give. These women wanted access to a better Jewish education, to participate in more public religious rituals without compromising *halacha* (Jewish law) and to have greater power in positions of communal responsibility. I had felt privileged to live in Manhattan. Courageous innovators in the Orthodox community were taking positive action so that determined, inspiring women could study Talmud (traditionally off-limits to women), participate in women's prayer groups or create meaningful batmitzvah ceremonies for their daughters. It was a time of great hope and vistas of possibility, with repercussions that are yet to come. Then I came to London.

Foreign brides have a bad reputation – upsetting the ecological balance, taking local boys away from the local girls, and importing foreign domestic habits such as asking direct questions and encouraging people to drop in without making formal arrangements. At times, London felt like a regression – Jewishly speaking – and all the initial tell-tale signs suggested I was doomed. But I was in the throes of newly wedded bliss so things like the centralized control of the United Synagogue, the lack of any dynamic learning programmes, the inherent conservatism of most of the women I met and their fear of change, and the seeming complacency and parochialism of the Orthodox community merely bemused me. Ironically, it was just like 'home', as I had grown up in a close-knit community in Melbourne, Australia, partly modelled on the traditions and tunes of Anglo-Jewish synagogue life.

Fortunately, and fairly soon after I arrived, I met three women who really helped me understand the dynamics of Anglo-Jewry and its relationship to women. Remember, it was 1993. The first person I met was Judith Usiskin, who at the time was a social worker and trainer at Jewish Care. She and her colleagues were aware of Jewish women experiencing domestic abuse, who needed protection from their husbands. Judith

---

Sally Berkovic is the author of *Under My Hat* (Joseph's Bookstore, 1997).

claimed that these women spanned the whole religious and socio-economic spectrum of the community. Together with other social workers from London's major Jewish social services, she launched a public awareness programme about domestic violence in the Jewish community. Some establishment figures and rabbis tried to minimize her concerns, claiming exaggeration.

The second person was Sharon Lee, who co-founded the Jewish Women's Network and the Stanmore Women's Tefillah group. She was in touch with many women who felt frustrated by their exclusion from synagogue life, yet were searching for a meaningful way to express their spirituality. She was aware of initiatives in New York and Jerusalem, but her attempts to establish a London women's prayer group and use a Torah scroll were thwarted in nearly every direction.

The third person was Sandra Blackman who had been waiting for a 'get' (document granting a religious divorce) from her husband for several years. She told me about many other Jewish women with a civil divorce who were unable to remarry in a synagogue because their husbands would not give them a religious divorce. With some other women, she had begun a campaign lobbying for the Beth Din to take action against these men with sanctions, and for a pre-nuptial agreement which states a man's obligation to grant a Jewish divorce in the event of a civil divorce. Her 'never give up' determination was impressive.

Additionally, around this time, Rosalind Preston was conducting a review, initiated by the Office of the Chief Rabbi, to articulate the concerns of women. Women all over the country were canvassed about their views on the family, education, adoption, conversion, communal life, marriage and divorce. The complexity of trying faithfully to represent all Anglo-Jewish women, while being a review conducted by the United Synagogue, an Orthodox institution, must have presented problems. Nevertheless, the results were published as *Women in the Jewish Community*, a comprehensive document that highlighted women's priorities and formulated a strategic plan of action for the following years.

Fast forward to 2003: some ten years later, and as *The Jewish Year Book 2003* goes to print, it is staggering to think what has happened in the lives of Anglo-Jewish women.

In 1997, the first (and I believe only) kosher Jewish women's refuge in Europe was opened in north London. Jewish Women's Aid, founded by Judith Usiskin, is recognized by the community and local government as the main service assisting Jewish victims of domestic violence. A helpline is open to answer calls, there are training courses and regular speaking events. The house is always full: Chassidic women from Stamford Hill mix with non-observant women from the provinces – the pain of the shattered Jewish family uniting them in a common purpose of rebuilding their lives and nourishing their children.

In 1994, the first women's prayer group at Yakar synagogue attracted Jewish and non-Jewish media attention and over 150 women. Since then, prayer groups continue to meet in Stanmore, Leeds and Manchester. Women have learnt the specific skills required to conduct a religious service. In 1995, Sharon Lee was voted a Newsmaker of the Year by the *Jewish Chronicle*, for her work in establishing prayer groups and founding the Jewish Women's Network. For the last two years, the London School of Jewish Studies (formerly Jews' College) has been hosting a Megillah reading on Purim for women by women. This would have been unimaginable when I arrived in 1993.

In 1996, Sandra Blackman finally received her religious divorce. The United Synagogue has pre-nuptial agreements in place, and sanctions to discredit recalcitrant husbands have been agreed upon. Although the Office of the Chief Rabbi has denied that the lobbying of these women made any difference to their course of action, I would suggest that it is precisely because these women have agitated that change has come in response to grass-roots behaviour. She and her colleagues have also been lobbying for a change in the civil law that would impel a man to grant his wife a 'get' as a precondition to being granted a civil divorce. In July 2002, the Divorce (Religious Marriages) Bill passed its final reading in the House of Lords and received the Royal Assent. The Bill provides for the court, when it considers it appropriate, to order that a decree of divorce is not to be made absolute until a declaration is made by both parties that they have taken the necessary steps to obtain a religious divorce. After a religious (and civil) divorce each party would be free to remarry in a religious ceremony. It will become law at the end of this or the beginning of next year.

Many of the recommendations of the Preston Report have been implemented, and others are waiting. In January 2002, a conference to consider the Preston Report was held. A small booklet, *Moving On: Jewish Women in the 21st Century*, was published and generated further discussion for action. (Readers who are interested in specific causes or documents can consult the contact list and bibliography at the end of this essay.)

You can no longer say that 'nothing happens in London'. It does – you just have to know where to look. As this essay cannot do everything to demonstrate how much the lives of Anglo-Jewish women have changed in the last ten years, it is time to narrow the focus.

I am particularly interested in the changes in the Orthodox community – partly because I am part of that community and partly because I believe these changes are the most radical. At first blush, they may seem naïve, sweet and almost flippantly irrelevant. But I would argue that they cut to the core of the future of Modern Orthodoxy. They reflect the ability of Modern Orthodoxy to grapple with the contradictions that lie at its doorstep. Women are defining the future of that community, and if we do not understand what the women want, the community is likely to lose them. The 'defection' rate from the religious community is abetted by an inability to cater to the needs of this articulate, well-educated, aspiring group of women.

Let me highlight just two examples of significant change in the Orthodox community: education for women and the batmitzvah ritual. Shortly before writing this essay, I raised these issues, among a host of others, with six women in a round-table discussion one evening. They were Tamra Wright (TW), Felicia Epstein (FE), Lindsay Simmonds (LS), Sarah Robinson (SR), Lindsey Taylor-Gutharz (LT) and Shira Lewin-Solomons (SS). (See the end of this essay for a brief biographical note about each woman.) Selections from the transcripts will give the reader a flavour of some of dynamics of the Orthodox community.

In 2000, Dr Tamra Wright founded the Susi Bradfield Women Educators' programme at the London School of Jewish Studies. It is designed to train a group of Orthodox women to teach Judaism in a range of informal settings. Women participate in weekly textual study sessions as well as researching teaching techniques. I started by asking Tamra about the impact of the course, and about the type of role models being created.

TW: The programme is only two years old, so evaluating its impact is hard. But we do see that the men who are married to women in the programme have been extremely supportive – almost 100 per cent. There's a kind of younger generation – in their late twenties – who feel that as long as the wife does things during the week while the kids are at school, things that won't impact on their lifestyle, it's OK. If we try to do things on a Sunday, we have a problem – who will look after their kids?
LS: Some men don't realise the impact this is having on the women. The self-development for the women is amazing – a world is opening up to them that they didn't know.
LT: This course will have a very interesting impact over time. There are going to be over 50 educated Orthodox women loose in the community.
TW: It's interesting to see it bringing in sisters in families, kind of pulling these people together. We've had three sisters on the course, sisters-in-law together – in one extended family; the kids will see that all their mothers learn – that it will be expected that mothers learn.
SR: It's building a community of teachers.
LS: Knowing that there are other women out there teaching, learning, having a network of people who are interested, who find learning important, who make space in their lives for learning, has a major impact.
SR: There's a common language that gives us the tools to communicate with.
LS: Coming back to England is hard. In Israel, you're just learning like everyone else. Then you're back in England – you're thrust into a role, and

people have expectations.
SB: What do you think can we take from those experiences we all have had in Israel to enliven Anglo-Jewry? What do we do with it? What about the education of our own daughters? The education system here doesn't support initiatives that are happening abroad.
LT: We have to struggle. What else can we do? For me, the question is how do you get people interested.
SR: At sensitive times, when women are looking for guidance, one of our major roles is to provide a bridge between the halachic structure and our daily practice. When we teach, we have to talk about how we decide things – bring in the process of how we get to a certain point. How we feel confident about what we do is very important ...

This led to a discussion about Batmitzvah ceremonies.

LS: Batmitzvah is an obvious target. We are encouraging girls to start learning now – not to see the batmitzvah as the end of the process – it's the beginning. It's a good age – their minds are just developing – we want to encourage them – to encourage them not to be afraid to take their emotional energy to their Judaism.
TW: We have set up a mother/daughter batmitzvah class. The ten-session course meets every two weeks. We bring in a text and some questions, there's time to look at the text, and we introduce the idea of hevruta study – studying with a partner – how to do it, to read aloud, be critical, so mothers are actively studying with their partner, their daughter. One mother told me that with her son she felt a little left out of his barmitzvah, but this allowed her to be involved for the whole batmitzvah year.
SR: I teach a lot of batmitzvah girls – and I can see how the institutions are changing. Girls are giving a 'dvar Torah' after the service ... some prefer something on a Sunday.
LS: People are looking for symbols – it's important for the girls, something different, new, special.
LT: People are looking for shape and form – they are looking and taking – finding rituals that make sense.
FE: We shouldn't have to spend time fighting to introduce something, rather we have to spend time creating exciting goals. If something inspires learning, that's where we have to be.

In Britain, a major impediment to change is the voluntary submission to rabbinic control, which is not to be confused with the importance of seeking guidance from a rabbi. Lindsey Taylor-Gutharz summed it up: 'When we tried to start our Yedidya minyan [more participatory and informal, with an option for women to hold a separate women's Torah reading] one young woman asked, "What does the Edgware rabbi say about it?", and we replied "We didn't ask him". She was flabbergasted – that we would do something like that without first asking a rabbi.'

There are other developments abroad. In Israel, women can study Talmud in a number of Orthodox institutions, and women can receive certification from the Rabbinate to advise women on issues related to divorce and family purity laws (for example, use of the mikveh). There is a 'cutting edge' Orthodox minyan in Jerusalem where men and women sit separately but women are permitted to read from the Torah for the congregation. In America, the Jewish Orthodox Feminist Alliance in New York acts as an umbrella organization for the myriad of women's interests where Orthodoxy and feminism intersect. Their recent conferences, attended by more than 2,000 women (and a few men), have firmly brought the concerns of Orthodox women into the public–halachic policy arena.

One cannot conclude an essay on Orthodox women without mentioning the growing group of single Orthodox women in their thirties and forties. 'Don't be too smart or you will never get married' is the battle cry from anxious parents in turmoil about their desire to give their Jewish daughters a university education and a career while not jeopardizing their chances for a 'successful' marriage. Despite the abundance of singles events and the growth of matchmaking services, many Orthodox (and, indeed, non-Orthodox) women have been unable to find a Jewish mate. The implications are two-fold. First, as women reach their mid-thirties, the disparity between their achievements in the working world and the expectations of creating a traditional home produce a schism that often forces women to choose between the two worlds. Naturally, there will be some women who do not want to get married, and do not want children. However, for others, finding no place in the Jewish tradition, a tradition that reveres the family unit, they are more likely to opt out of the community. Second, if and when these women do marry and have children, they are less likely to have the large families upon which the community depends for long-term growth. Interestingly, there are a small number of observant women who have chosen artificial insemination and are now single-mothers-by-choice within their own Orthodox communities. Dvora Ross has written a seminal (no pun intended) essay on the relevant halachic issues. In the interim, we have a responsibility to ensure that our religious and communal structures do not further marginalize and alienate single women (or men).

Where to next? There is an old Ethiopian saying: 'Slowly, slowly, even an egg learns to walk.' It seems to me that many Anglo-Jewish daughters are ready to run.

My thanks to the following for sharing their thoughts:

Felicia Epstein studied in Israel at the Pardes Institute, Nishmat and Matan. Before moving to the UK, she worked at the Association for Civil Rights in Israel as the International Spokesperson and Director of Development. She has just completed her legal studies in the UK.

Sarah Robinson teaches at Immanuel College, a Jewish secondary school, and for the Mother and Daughter Bat Mitzvah Programme (Kolot). She has just completed a year as a contributing panellist for the sedra column of the *Jewish Chronicle*.

Lindsay Simmonds returned to the UK four years ago after several years studying in Israel at Nishmat and Midreshet Lindenbaum. She is a women's educator in several London communities, including the Midrasha at LSJS. She lives in Edgware with her husband and four children.

Shira Lewin Solomons is an economist and is the Rebbetzin at Potters Bar and Brookmans Park Synagogue. She also plays an active role in training women to read the Megillah on Purim.

Lindsey Taylor-Guthartz is an editor and translator. After graduating from the Susi Bradfield Women Educators' programme, she began teaching Jewish subjects, and is particularly interested in making classic Jewish texts accessible to everyone.

Dr Tamra Wright is the Bradfield Lecturer in Jewish Studies at the London School of Jewish Studies. She teaches Jewish philosophy and Jewish Women's Studies as well as running the Susi Bradfield Women Educators' programme and the Midrasha.

RESOURCES

www.agunot-campaign.co.uk (for information on the recent Divorce (Religious Marriages) Bill).
www.brandeis.edu/hirjw/ Hadassah International Research Institute on Jewish Women at Brandeis University.
www.edah.org An excellent website with an on-line library resource related to Modern Orthodox issues.
Jewish Women's Aid, PO Box 2670, London N12 9ZE. Tel. (020) 8445 8060; National Helpline Freephone: 0800 591203.
www.jofa.org Jewish Orthodox Feminist Alliance. Includes information about women's tefilla groups and other resources.
www.jwn.org.uk Website of Jewish Women's Network, established in 1993

to promote dialogue and action across the religious spectrum.
www.jwn.org.uk/movingon1.html For a report on the 'Moving On' conference and proceedings of the workshops.

Ross, D., 'Artificial Insemination in Single Women' (in Hebrew), in *Jewish Legal Writings by Women*, M. Halpern and C. Safrai, eds (Jerusalem: Urim Publications, 1998).

Shapiro, M., 'Qeri'at ha-Torah by Women: A Halakhic Analysis', *Edah Journal*, 1:2 (2001) (can be downloaded from www.edah.org).

Leonard Bernstein: A Jewish Composer

Cecil Bloom

Bach, Haydn, Mozart and Beethoven may not have had Jewish contemporaries of any consequence but the nineteenth and twentieth centuries saw the emergence of many creative artists of Jewish origin, some of whom readily used Jewish subjects and motifs in their music. Ernest Bloch has been correctly described as *the* Jewish composer *par excellence*, but there were others who put deep Jewish feeling into their compositions. One of the most important was Leonard Bernstein, a musical prodigy who was given gifts in every department of music. He wrote scores for six musicals, one of which, *West Side Story*, is surely the greatest of all musicals. He was an outstanding orchestral conductor, a brilliant lecturer and a pianist of no mean talent. His career began dramatically when, at the age of 25 and at very short notice, he replaced the renowned Bruno Walter as conductor at a Carnegie Hall concert. It was a sensational debut and his success as a conductor continued up to his death in 1990 at the age of 72. As for composition, he wrote his first piece when he was 17 and went on to compose 60 or so works, including three symphonies and 14 other orchestral works. Seven of his major classical compositions use Jewish subjects. Bernstein was, unquestionably, the most influential musician in America in the second half of the twentieth century.

Bernstein's father was of Hassidic stock and the young boy heard him singing Hassidic melodies in the home. He also heard much music in the synagogue, later used to great effect in his music. His 'Jewish' compositions all show a strong devotion to Jewish tradition. Bernstein was a dedicated supporter of Israel. He had strong musical associations with *Eretz Israel* and first conducted the Palestine Symphony Orchestra in 1947. When the War of Independence broke out, he went to the newly founded state and took the now renamed Israel Philharmonic Orchestra to the front-line and to embattled villages and towns. After the Six-Day War in 1967, he conducted the orchestra on the slopes of the newly conquered Mount Scopus, in a concert described as 'the cultural opening of the united city of Jerusalem'. Less well known is the fact that he did have some connection with Begin's *Irgun Tvei Leumi* underground organization. He organized a concert on its behalf in New York and included the funeral

---

Cecil Bloom was formerly the technical director of a multi-national pharmaceutical corporation. Since retirement, he reviews books and is a freelance writer on aspects of Jewish music literature and history. He is a contributor to *Midstream*, *Jewish Spectator* and *Jewish Renaissance*, and to the book *Jewish Writers of the 20th Century*.

march from Beethoven's 'Eroica' Symphony (the same music played many years later in Munich to mourn the Israeli athletes murdered by Palestinian terrorists) 'in memory of 20 *Irgun* soldiers who had died on the beaches of Tel Aviv'. This led to a minor political storm and pickets demonstrated against him outside the hall.

His first compositional effort used a Jewish subject; he set Psalm 148 in English for voice and piano. Later, he rearranged a number of Hebrew folk songs and a few miniatures on Jewish themes. 'Simchu na' and 'Re'ena', Hebrew folk songs, were written in 1947 for voices in chorus and he set the important hymn 'Yigdal' in 1950. Another work entitled 'Silhouette', subtitled 'Galilee', is distinguished for its use of Arabic sing-song. Bernstein's first 'major' Jewish work, his first symphony ('Jeremiah'), was composed in 1942 and it consists of three movements, not the usual four. The first movement, entitled 'Prophecy', attempts to demonstrate in music the prophet's efforts to urge his people to sin no more. It contains music based on Hebrew liturgy from all the main Holy Festivals. The scherzo second movement, 'Profanation', illustrates the derangement that followed the debasement of society caused by pagan corruption, and the third movement, 'Lamentation', which contains motifs from the Tisha b'Av service, depicts Jeremiah's cry of despair as he mourned the destruction of his Holy City which he had so clearly foreseen. A mezzo-soprano sings verses from Chapters 1, 4 and 5 of the Book of Lamentations. Bernstein ignored the orthodox custom and used a female voice in the work.

Bernstein also chose a Jewish subject for his third ('Kaddish') symphony. He was orchestrating the final section of the work on the day John F. Kennedy was assassinated in Dallas and he dedicated it to him. The work is a semi-oratorio and part-dramatic monologue. A narrator holds rebellious arguments with God and, in a reference to the assassination, criticizes Him with these words: 'You let this happen, Lord of Hosts! You with your Manna, Your pillar of fire! You ask for faith. Where is Your own?' At its American premiere and in the first recording of the work, Bernstein's wife was narrator but a later version used a male voice. The symphony goes through a wide range of emotions, accomplished by having the *Kaddish* prayer recited thrice, each time set differently. The first features the troubled narrator who wants to say *Kaddish*; he has little time and is worried there may be no one else left to say it after him. A tranquil movement, which brings forth man's doubts about whether the Almighty is listening to his pleas, follows, and the third movement is exultant and full of enthusiasm. The *Kaddish* prayers are sung by a mixed choir in the first movement, by a soprano accompanied by a boys' choir in the second and by the soprano with boys' choir and mixed chorus in the third. For his father's seventieth birthday, in 1962, Bernstein had composed a song his father used to sing which he entitled 'Meditation on a Prayerful Theme my father sang in the shower 30 years ago', and he included this in the symphony.

Soon after 'Jeremiah', another composition using a Jewish subject – 'Hashkivenu' – was written. It is a setting of a prayer in the *Ma'ariv* (Evening) service. An important item in Bernstein's list of works, it is scored for tenor with chorus and organ accompaniment. Two years later he spoke (or, in his words, 'gave a sermon') at a Boston temple on the subject 'What is a Jewish composer?' using 'Hashkivenu' to illustrate his thesis. 'Chichester Psalms', one of Bernstein's most important compositions, followed in 1965. Commissioned by the Dean of Chichester Cathedral in England, Bernstein described it as 'quite popular in feeling with an old-fashioned sweetness along with its more violent moments', but it shows little sign of traditional music. Each of its three movements contains a complete psalm (Psalms 100, 23 and 131 respectively), together with one or more verses from complementary ones (Psalms 108, 2 and 133 respectively) chosen to produce contrasts. Bernstein insisted the psalms should be sung in Hebrew and he described the work as a 'simple and modest affair, tonal and tuneful', but it is far from simple. The Bishop of Chichester was said to have remarked that, in listening to the music, he had seen David dance before the Ark. The work has been scored for mixed or all-male choir with a boy alto. A ballet entitled *Psalms*, based on religious motifs and those dealing with Jewish history was later choreographed from the composition.

Another important composition takes a secular subject as its theme. S. Ansky's great Yiddish classic play, *The Dybbuk*, is a powerful drama, and it had fascinated Bernstein for many years. He eventually conceived the idea of a ballet based on its text and in this he collaborated with Jerome Robbins, the leading American choreographer of the day. A dybbuk is a ghost who enters the spirit of a living person. The story is about two young people, Leah and Chonon, whose fathers pledged they would marry when they grew up. They love each other deeply but Leah's father breaks his promise and arranges for her to marry a wealthy husband – not Chonon, who is a poor student. To win her, Chonon invokes the mystical powers of the *Kabbalah*, but he dies. At Leah's wedding he returns as a dybbuk and enters Leah's body in order to claim her. She becomes possessed; the community's elders try to exorcise him from her body, but Leah also dies so that she can join him. Bernstein then developed two suites from the ballet music. The first suite consists of ghetto-like music with two singers in *chazzan*-type roles (one bass and one tenor) and the first section is based on music used in the *Havdalah* (end of *Shabbat*) ceremony, followed by music based on the oath of allegiance between David and Jonathan. Snatches of music from the *Song of Songs* are also heard. In the second (non-vocal) suite, Bernstein used the 12-tone system which he characterized using *Kabbalistic* symbols. A new ballet entitled *Leah* was recently choreographed based on Bernstein's score.

His next 'Jewish' composition, 'Halil', came seven years later. 'Halil' is the Hebrew word for 'flute' and the work was inspired by the 1973 Yom Kippur War and by the death near the Suez Canal of a talented flautist called Yadin Tanenbaum. 'Halil' is dedicated to 'the spirit of Yadin and his fallen brothers' and is scored for strings, harp and percussion as well as flute, all in one movement. It is essentially a concerto for flute and orchestra, described by Bernstein as a 'kind of night music which is an ongoing conflict of normal images, wish-dreams, nightmares, repose, sleeplessness, night terrors and "Death's twin brother" sleep'. The final section suggests Yadin's death and ends with the flute becoming silent just before an off-platform alto flute is heard to imply the departure of the spirit from the fallen soldier.

In 1986 Bernstein composed a work called 'Jubilee Games' for the Israeli Orchestra, to commemorate its 50 years of existence. In the first of its two movements, entitled 'Free Style Events', there is a quotation from Leviticus 25:8–17 referring to the sabbatical year and the year of the jubilee, and the orchestral players are instructed to shout *sheva* (seven) seven times followed by *hamishim* (50), at which point the brass instruments stand in for the sound of the *shofar* which the biblical narrative commands to be sounded. He applied *gematria* (interpretation through the numerical values of Hebrew letters) to the second movement which he called 'Diaspora Dances'. The voices of the orchestra are used this time to whisper *hai* (alive) and *hayim* (to life). In *gematria*, *hai* has the numerical value of 18 and this number is relevant in a number of ways. Twice 18, that is 36, is significant as part of the secular year of birth of the orchestra (1936) and it is also the number of 'Just Men' (*lamed vovnik*) present in every generation, but there are a number of other references to the number 36. The 'Diaspora Dances' are free-style and eclectic in form and their musical connotations range from Middle Eastern to Central European ghetto motifs, as well as to jazz. Three years later, Bernstein added two additional movements sandwiched over 'Diaspora Dances', retitling the work 'Concerto for Orchestra'. 'Mixed Doubles', the new second movement, is a theme with seven variations and a quotation from Psalm 118 ('Give thanks unto the Lord, for He is good') ends the movement. 'Benediction' or, paradoxically, 'Opening Prayer' is the name assigned to the fourth movement, which ends with music based on traditional Hebrew benedictions sung by a baritone, using the Hebrew words of three verses from the Book of Numbers (6:24–26).

One other substantial work contains a Jewish theme. In 1988 Bernstein wrote *Arias and Barcarolles*, a cycle of seven songs for two voices depicting aspects of the life of man. One song is a setting of a Yiddish poem which tells of a *klezmer* musician who appears at a wedding and thrills his audience with the brilliance of his playing.

As a Jewish artist, Leonard Bernstein remains an enigmatic figure despite all that has been written about him. That he was a genius is not in question; that he was a Jew with a sense of Jewish history and a pride in the achievements of the State of Israel is not in doubt. The enigma relates to the inconsistencies between his personal life-style and his outlook on Judaism. His compositional output clearly shows his keen interest in and love of his faith or, at least, some aspects of it. Leaving aside his musicals, he put more into those classical works with Jewish connotations than into any other compositions, and some of these – two symphonies, 'Chichester Psalms', 'Hashkivenu', 'Halil', *Dybbuk* and 'Concerto for Orchestra' – will long remain in the repertoire of music. They may not be as fondly remembered as *West Side Story* but music lovers, especially Jewish ones, will not easily forget them. Leonard Bernstein may have gone astray in some aspects of his private life but he never forgot his roots or his inheritance and, as such, will be remembered, along with Bloch and others, as a brilliant composer who brought to the attention of music lovers many Jewish ideals and attitudes.

The 1901 Census: A Source for Demographic Research

Diana Rau

The year 2002 brings access to another of the decennial censuses of population held in this country since 1801 (with the exception of the war year of 1941). Reports and tabulations of data are available shortly after each census is taken, but the details of individuals and households are kept 'closed' for 100 years in order to guarantee privacy. These details were recorded in the census enumerators' books (CEBs), and we now have the opportunity to analyse the recently released CEBs of 1901. Research can thus be carried out into social and demographic features at the beginning of the twentieth century, using twenty-first-century computer technology and online access to study this valuable source.

Every ten years the release of these records of individuals is eagerly awaited not only by genealogists and researchers of family history, who are interested in tracing their ancestors and families, but also by historical demographers, who are more interested in the patterns and changes in population and groups revealed by the CEBs when analysed systematically. Records offices and archives have in recent years been swamped by family and other researchers using the nineteenth-century records, and it was decided to provide access to the 1901 CEBs online through the internet. They contain over 32 million individuals on 1.5 million pages, and will be sure to attract immense interest. The initial popularity of the site, however, led to its immediate breakdown, and the need for considerable technical work and extensive testing; full operation of the census online should be achieved by early 2003. There was a similar experience in 2001 when the equally popular United States Ellis Island internet site opened. As with the previous censuses, access to the 1901 CEBs is also available on microfilm in local records offices for their local areas. There have been many research studies using the CEBs from 1841 to 1891 as they have become available, but, in fact, the 1901 census is the last one which will offer analysis in this way, as in 1911 there was machine tabulation direct from the householder schedules.

Each census of population was preceded by an Act of Parliament, until the 1920 Census Act made it permanent. Each enumerator was responsible

---

Diana Rau lectures and teaches in social history and English for academic purposes. She has carried out demographic studies of parts of London using the nineteenth-century censuses and the earlier parish registers, and her paper on the 1891 Census Project in Spitalfields appears in A. Newman and S.W. Massil (eds), *Patterns of Migration, 1850–1914* (1996).

for a designated area, and the listing was of all those present in the area on census night. From 1841 onwards the householder filled in a schedule, the details of which were copied by the enumerator into his official CEB. These books were checked by local registrars and then sent to the Census Office in London, where clerks extracted information for the published tables. The marks of this clerical processing are often visible and indeed can obscure some of the details. The information that was gathered in the censuses grew gradually throughout the nineteenth century, with additional questions reflecting administrative concerns. These developed from medical, sanitary and mortality matters at mid-century to more economic and social concerns towards its end. The important category of the number of rooms occupied if less than five was introduced in 1891, in response to worries about overcrowding in the cities. The new features recorded in 1901 were more details about employment status, a homeworking question and slightly altered infirmity categories.

What does this source offer us and how can we use it? The CEBs contain a wealth of information, and by 1901 we have the enumerator's record of the following for each address: house inhabited, uninhabited or building; number of rooms occupied by the household if less than five; name and surname of each person resident; the relationship to head of family; marital status; age at last birthday; profession or occupation; and whether an employer, worker or working on own account, and if working at home. Also recorded are the place of birth and disabilities, under deaf and dumb, blind, lunatic, imbecile or 'feeble-minded'. The interpretation of the recorded information should be approached with care, bearing in mind the contemporary understanding of historical terms, particularly with occupations, and the householder's own understanding of the information required. The context of place and society should always be regarded.

The British census is considered a reliable source, although it is not without problems of accuracy and consistency. Examples include the inconsistent recording of occupations of married women in the male-dominated Victorian society, and the exact definition of a 'household' or 'room' – difficult to count even today. The difference between 'lodgers' and 'boarders' is not always clear, and there have been problems of underenumeration and mistakes with age. These have been discussed in the literature, but as a regular and national source of data the census is considered useful and valuable.

The computer access to the records through the online internet site means that one is able to consult the 1901 CEBs with relative ease. There is a very useful index, and a search of the index is free of charge, using person, address, place, institution, vessel or direct search. There is a small charge for digital images of the CEB pages or the transcribed details of an individual, with zoom facilities up to 400 per cent. The minimum charge is £5 and payment is by credit/debit card or voucher. Details may be found on www.census.pro.gov.uk. This access should make the task of analysis of the data much simpler and quicker than with the earlier CEBs. There is also much information about the census in general on www.statistics.gov.uk. These are reliable, official websites, but one should take care with information from many other websites, which can sometimes be misleading.

The censuses of 1881 to 1901 cover the period of the great influx of Jewish immigrants to Britain and their settlement from 1881. Estimates suggest that about 150,000 Eastern European immigrants came to Britain between 1881 and 1914. Much evidence of their economic and social life and organization may be studied using the CEBs, in order to ascertain a realistic rather than an impressionistic picture. I led a team which carried out a detailed study using the 1891 CEBs, building a database of a part of the Spitalfields area of Whitechapel, East London – bounded by Brushfield Street, Commercial Street, Wentworth Street and Middlesex Street/Sandys Row. This showed the patterns of settlement in this small area, differentiated between Dutch Jews and those from Eastern Europe, and pointed to the detail available of patterns of migration and occupational division. In 1901 foreigners were to give country of nationality as well as country of birth, and in both 1891 and 1901 there was an explanatory version of the census form in Yiddish and in German. There was no question about religion on the census until an optional question in 2001, so the Jewish population in the past can only be estimated using various factors for guidance.

How can we enhance our knowledge of Jewish matters from the 1901 census? On the one hand, genealogists will be able to extend their family trees, and possibly unearth some unexpected and interesting relationships on the way. On the other hand, there is massive scope for the detailed study of individuals, families and communities in general. It is now possible to carry out comparative work on the three relevant censuses, from 1881 to 1901, to look at the growth and change of the Jewish community over the period of great immigration. This is possible in various types of micro-study, such as the investigation of residential persistence or segregation, overcrowding or specialization of occupation, and at the macro-level with comparison of areas of Jewish settlement in various major British cities. A brief look at a tiny sample in Palmer Street in Spitalfields in 1891 and in 1901 finds residential persistence in the same house of one-third of the heads of family, and a slight fall in average household size and overall population. One needs to examine factors including age and family structure, occupation and birthplace in order to try to explain such behaviour and to assess how typical this might have been of Spitalfields or Whitechapel or London or other cities. At a wider level, it could be interesting to compare demographic features in areas of Jewish and non-Jewish settlement, and to follow the migration patterns of all groups, including short- and long-distance migration. In the East End of

London we have seen Spitalfields as the area of first settlement of many waves of immigrants – the Huguenots, the Irish, the Jews and now the Asians – all leaving their marks on the area, with evidence of the continuity of use of religious buildings from chapel to synagogue to mosque in, for example, the Machzik Adath in Brick Lane, and with the continuity of immigrant occupations in clothing and textiles.

Many studies have used the census tables and statistics in relation to the Jewish community, and the CEBs for 1901 offer a wonderful source for micro-studies of individuals, households, communities, streets, housing, occupations, migration patterns and other topics of great interest. Other historical records and sources, such as maps and street directories, will offer essential support in such studies. The use of computers enables a relatively easy access to the indexed material and images, and analysis at the touch of a key. It is hoped that with the proceeds of the internet access to the 1901 CEBs the Public Record Office will be able to fund the digitization of the earlier 1891 census, which will enable still further and easier online search, analysis and comparison.

The Institute of Jewish Studies, University College London: A Brief History

Mark Geller

A number of years ago, I received a telephone call from New York, from a scholar who had been invited to give a public lecture for the Institute of Jewish Studies. He was a little nervous about his lecture and wanted know what the audience would be like. Would they all be scholars, or colleagues, or students, or members of the public? 'Everyone is invited to attend, since our lectures are free and open to the public,' I answered, 'but Isaiah Berlin might come.'

This concept of the academic public lecture has been the *raison d'être* of the Institute of Jewish Studies since its founding in Manchester by Alexander Altmann in 1954. At that time, the Institute was intended to respond to an urgent post-war problem. The destruction of European academic Jewish centres had not been adequately compensated for in Britain, since very few centres of Jewish studies existed in British universities. The origins of the Institute of Jewish Studies (IJS) at University College London reflected the need to attract scholars and scholarship – at a high level of competence – to Britain, and to promote scholarship and research in Jewish Studies.

The first five years of the existence of the IJS (1954–59) in Manchester gave several important scholars their first academic position – men such as Chaim Rabin, David Patterson, Zvi Werblowsky and Joseph Weiss, all of whom went on to have distinguished academic careers. While these young scholars taught extra-mural university courses, the IJS organized major public lectures on the key areas of research at that time. For example, Yigal Yadin was invited to lecture about the Dead Sea Scrolls, S.D. Goitein on the Cairo Genizah, and Gershon Scholem on Jewish mysticism. At the same time, under the direction of Alexander Altmann, an important monograph series of six volumes appeared under the imprimatur of the IJS, as well as the *Journal of Jewish Studies*. No comparable contribution to Jewish scholarship can be found in any other British university at the time.

When Alexander Altmann was invited, in 1959, to the distinguished Professorship of Jewish Philosophy at Brandeis University, the IJS moved from Manchester to University College London (UCL), where it was joined to the Hebrew and Jewish Studies Department. The IJS's function changed

---

Mark Geller is Director of the Institute of Jewish Studies and Professor of Semitic Languages at University College, London.

dramatically with this move. The IJS had been located in an extra-mural department, but was now integrated into the centre of London University, since the Chair of Hebrew was one of ten founding chairs of University College London. However, as the Hebrew and Jewish Studies Department was involved primarily in teaching students, the IJS developed a new role for promoting scholarship and research. During this period, the Institute maintained a regular programme of seminars over the academic year, aimed at scholars reporting on their recent research to other colleagues and advanced students. The emphasis was on having a relatively small and selective audience of experts and specialists, in order to submit new academic research to critical judgment and appraisal. The IJS had by now developed a reputation in the academic community as a serious research forum.

When Raphael Loewe retired as Director in 1983, new strategies were sought to promote scholarship and research in Jewish Studies. As the newly appointed Director, I worked closely with Dr Manfred Altman (Alexander's younger brother), who had been closely associated with the IJS since its inception and had now taken over from Lord Mishcon as Chairman of the IJS. We first decided to expand the activities by having more widely publicized seminars, to which all students and members of the public would be invited. One of the most effective seminars was given by a young scholar who had recently completed his doctorate, Jonathan Sacks, speaking about Jewish philosophy. Seminars were relocated to a much larger seminar room, instead of the rather cramped quarters of the Mocatta Library. For the first time notices about the IJS seminars were circulated among other academic departments, and colleagues from other disciplines began to attend.

The next major change resulted from a chance conversation with a UCL historian, who commented on the IJS seminar series. He asked why the IJS invited one person every week to give seminars. 'Why not', he asked, 'invite them all on the same day and have a conference?' This rather casual remark resulted in a new iniative, launching international conferences. The first such conferences were organized in 1983, on a theme of 'Figurative Language in the Ancient Near East', and in 1984 on 'The Changing Character of Jewish Authority in the Modern Age', co-sponsored by the Oxford Centre for Postgraduate Hebrew Studies (as it was then called). Many mistakes were made, such as the choice of venue in 1984 – a lecture theatre for 250 people! In addition, most speakers were predominantly from the UK, whereas future IJS conferences would concentrate on bringing scholars from abroad, to introduce new faces and new research. Furthermore, Jewish Studies were, in future, to be defined in much broader terms, far beyond the parameters of either the Jewish Historical Society or the Wiener Library. However, the principle of all subsequent IJS conferences was introduced – that, in general, the event should be free and open to the public.

A future programme for the IJS began to emerge. Although Manfred Altman approved of the idea of annual conferences on different themes – from ancient, medieval and modern periods – he wanted the weekly lectures and seminars to continue as before. These lectures were no longer to be held in a seminar room, around a table, but the weekly events became public lectures, usually held in the Gustave Tuck Theatre (which has a Hebrew inscription above the podium). We now had an increasingly active programme, although audiences were very unpredictable. On some occasions only a handful of listeners would attend, while on other occasions we had a full house, as was the case when Professor Isadore Twersky from Harvard delivered the first Alexander Altmann Lecture, with the UCL Provost, Sir James Lighthill, in the chair.

Public lectures are each unique and, as time goes on, each lecture attracts different audiences. Lectures on Yiddish subjects, for instance, often have the most excitable audiences, and on several occasions the listeners did not let the speaker finish the lecture before beginning to ask questions. On one occasion, elderly listeners were rather shocked by a lady professor from Harvard reading out modern Hebrew poetry, most of which turned out to be luridly pornographic. One of the more exotic lectures was delivered by a visiting professor from China about the Jews of China, but the great majority of public lectures cover areas of cutting-edge research in fields of Jewish Studies, in the widest possible contexts, and audiences have continued to increase over the years.

Every year since 1983, the IJS has organized and sponsored at least one international conference. Each international conference has its own character and drama, and each has its own behind-the-scenes stories. The conference in 1990 on 'Government, Nationality and the Jews of Russia (1772–1990)' presaged many of the coming changes in that part of the world. I was forced to rise at five every morning in the weeks before the conference to ring the British Consul in Moscow about visas for our speakers. Until the very last day before the conference, no one knew whether the Russians would be arriving, or who would be arriving. One Soviet scholar who managed to attend, with KGB permission, could speak no English at all, but a member of the audience, Dr Tamara Dragadze, suddenly stepped forward to give a simultaneous translation of the lecture in Russian. One of the more poignant sessions of the conference, however, witnessed elderly East End Jewish Communists criticizing Russian scholars who were preparing to throw off the yoke of Soviet Communism.

Another unanticipated event occurred just before our conference on the *oeuvre* of I.B. Singer in 1993, shortly after the writer's death. A few days before the conference, we received a telephone call from Israel, from Mr Israel Zamir, who introduced himself as I.B. Singer's son. He asked to be invited to attend, and to provide his own reminiscences about his father. We agreed. Zamir was the very last lecturer in the three-day conference.

Having attended every other lecture, he introduced his own talk by saying how much he had enjoyed the academic discussion about his father. 'But now', he commented, 'I'd like to tell you what my father was really like.'

This confrontation between theory and reality had happened before. One of the earliest IJS conferences, 'Assimilation and Community in European Jewry', was held in 1985 at Hillel House. Professor Ismar Schorsch from the Jewish Theological Seminary in New York lectured about the Schocken Press and other popular Jewish publishing houses in pre-war Germany. The response came from a professor emeritus from the School of Slavonic and East European Studies, Francis Carsten, who had grown up in Berlin, the son of a German-Jewish banker. According to Carsten, his family in pre-war Berlin had had an extensive library, containing none of the books listed in Schorsch's research.

Other conferences attempted to confront or challenge existing academic positions. One conference, held in 1987 at the Warburg Institute, celebrated the fortieth anniversary of the Dead Sea Scrolls, and brought together almost all the scholars in the world who were working on unpublished Qumran manuscripts. The conference addressed the problem of slow progress in publishing the scrolls, as well as presenting new texts for the first time. BBC Radio 4 later produced a 45-minute documentary based on this conference.

Another controversial conference, 'Archaeology of Israel in the Period of the Monarchy', in April 1996, dealt with new theories regarding biblical archaeology, which later became popular themes and subjects of debate in the popular press, both in Israel and abroad. Most of Israel's best-known archaeologists were present, giving their conflicting views of biblical chronology and history.

A different kind of controversy occurred during our conference on Aramaic magic ('*Officina Magica*') in 1999. The conference chairman, Professor Shaul Shaked from the Hebrew University, received a strong letter of complaint from Lord Renfrew of Cambridge, complaining about Shaked's own lecture on unpublished Jewish Aramaic magic bowls, which Lord Renfrew considered to represent the stolen cultural heritage of Iraq. The controversy caused us to change the conference venue from the Institute of Archaeology to the Warburg Institute, and some scholars chose to boycott the conference.

In 1994, the IJS held a special conference in memory of Alexander Altmann on Jewish philosophy, later published by Alfred Ivry of New York University. The keynote speaker was Jacob Katz of the Hebrew University, who became ill the evening after his lecture, and I accompanied him to the Casualty Department of University College Hospital. The nurse on duty was taken aback when Professor Katz gave his date of birth as 1904. Jacob Katz's lecture had been one of the high points of the conference.

The IJS organizes conferences not only at University College, but also at other venues. The IJS has also co-sponsored conferences at other institutions in London, such as the Wellcome Institute for the History of Medicine (on medical history), Queen Mary & Westfield College (on Sephardic Jewry), and the School of Oriental and African Studies (on Byzantine history). In addition, the IJS has co-sponsored events abroad, such as a conference in Spain on Abraham Ibn Ezra, as well as a conference in Krakow on 'Jewish Spirituality in Poland'. Furthermore, several conferences were held in conjunction with special exhibitions at the Jewish Museum in Camden Town. The finest reception to date was hosted by the Italian Cultural Institute after our conference on 'The Jews of Italy', since special Italian-Jewish cuisine was provided by cookery writer Claudia Roden. Two conference receptions were held at the home of Mr Jack Lunzer, on which occasions Professor Chimen Abramsky discussed exemplars of early Italian and Dutch printing from the Valmadonna Trust Library, and the IJS hosted the only exhibition of rare books from the Valmadonna Trust Library ever held in London, at University College's Strang Print Room.

The IJS also hosts visiting professors for one month every year who have, so far, come from the USA, Israel, Holland and Poland, and writers such as David Grossman and Meir Shalev who have read from their own fiction. However, the most important aspect, of the Institute's work is the publication of its conference proceedings. We now have a new agreement with Brill Academic Publishers in Leiden to publish all future IJS conference volumes. To date, the IJS has published 13 volumes. However, the hundreds of public lectures and seminars have promoted countless numbers of other publications. This forms the basis for the permanent contribution to Jewish scholarship.

I am frequently asked why IJS conferences seem to be so congenial and intellectually stimulating. I always give the same answer, that if you invite the best people in the world to discuss a particular theme, you will always get good results. And that is how we plan to continue in the future.

CONFERENCES OF THE INSTITUTE OF JEWISH STUDIES

1983 'Figurative Language in the Ancient Near East'
two-day colloquium in honour of Henri Frankfort

1984 'The Changing Character of Jewish Authority in the Modern Age'
three-day conference; co-sponsor: Oxford Centre for Postgraduate Hebrew Studies

1984 'Land Tenure in Hellenistic Palestine and Babylonia'
half-day colloquium

1985 'Assimilation and Community in European Jewry, 1815–1881'
two-day conference; co-sponsor: Oxford Centre for Postgraduate Hebrew Studies

1986 'Legal Systems of the Hellenistic World'
one-day conference, preceded by a series of seven seminars on 'Legal Documents of the Hellenistic World', February–May 1986, at the Institute of Classical Studies

1987 'Symposium on the Manuscripts from the Judean Desert'
two-day conference

1988 'The Social Function of Mystical Ideals in Judaism: Hasidism Reappraised'
three-day conference in memory of Joseph Weiss

1989 'Britain and the Holy Land 1800–1914'
one-day conference and public lecture; co-sponsor: Jewish Historical Society

1990 'Government, Nationalities and the Jews of Russia 1772–1990'
two-day conference

1991 'Jewish Folklore'
one-day conference and public lecture

1991 'Aramaic and the Arameans: New Sources and New Approaches'
three-day conference

1992 'The Jews of Medieval Islam: Community, Society and Identity'
two-day conference

1993 'International Isaac Bashevis Singer Conference'
three-day conference

1993 'Patterns of Migration 1850–1914: Impact on Jewry'
three-day conference in association with the Jewish Historical Society of England in celebration of its centenary

1994 'Jewish Studies in London and New York'
one-day joint symposium, Department of Hebrew and Jewish Studies and Institute of Jewish Studies, UCL, and Skirball Department of Hebrew and Judaic Studies, NYU

1994 'Aspects of Jewish Intellectual History'
fortieth anniversary international three-day conference in memory of Alexander Altmann

1995 'The Jews of Italy: Memory and Identity'
three-day conference with the Department of Italian, UCL, and the Italian Cultural Institute

1996 'The Archaeology of Israel in the Period of the Monarchy'
two-day conference; IJS contribution to the Jerusalem 3000 celebration

1996 'Aramaic Culture, Christian and Jewish, 100–600 AD'
one-day symposium with the Department of the Study of Religions, SOAS

1996 'Concepts of Disease in Ancient Babylonia'
two-day conference; Wellcome Institute for the History of Medicine with the Institute of Jewish Studies

1997 'Jews and the Classical Tradition in the Renaissance'
two-day conference; Warburg Institute in collaboration with the Institute of Jewish Studies

1997 'Israel's Origin – Current Debate: Biblical, Historical and Archaeological Perspectives'
Irene Levi-Sala Annual Research Seminar; co-sponsor Institute of Jewish Studies (preceded by four special research seminars in February and March 1997, sponsored by the Sydney and Elizabeth Corob Charitable Trust)

1997 'The History and Culture of the Jews in the Low Countries'
three-day conference with the Centre for Low Countries Studies, UCL

1998 'Hebrew Literature – The Text and Its Context'
three-day conference

1999 'Leone Ebreo's Dialoghi d'Amore (1535)'
one-day conference, preceded by a public lecture
with the Warburg Institute and the Centre for Italian Studies, UCL

1999 'Jewish Spirituality in Poland'
three-day conference in memory of Professor Chone Shmeruk at the

Jagellonian University, Cracow; co-sponsor Institute of Jewish Studies

1999 'Public Crisis and Literary Response: Jewish Writing in the Twentieth Century'
one-day conference with the Netherlands Graduate School for Literary Studies

1999 '*Officina Magica* – The Workings of Magic'
three-day conference

2000 'In and Out of the Enclave'
one-day seminar

2000 'Reflections of Polish-Jewish Relations in Film'
one-day conference given by the Institute for Polish-Jewish Studies, in collaboration with the Polish Cultural Institute, and the Institute of Jewish Studies

2000 'Nationalism, Zionism and Ethnic Mobilization'
three-day conference; centenary of the Fourth Zionist Congress, London (1900)

2000 'London 2000: International Conference for Postgraduate Students in Jewish Studies'
five-day conference sponsored by the Jewish Historical Society of England, organized with assistance from the Institute of Jewish Studies

2001 'The Shtetl'
three-day conference

2001 'Twelfth British Conference on Judeo-Spanish Studies'
three-day conference, Queen Mary–University of London in co-operation with the Institute of Jewish Studies

2002 'Jewish Theatre'
three-day conference, concurrently with three theatre performances of the Yiddish play *Jacob Jacobson, or the Story of Creation* at the Bloomsbury Theatre, UCL

Abbreviations Used

Ad. – Address
Admin. – Administrative; administration; administrator; administer
Adv. – Advisory; adviser
AJA – Anglo-Jewish Association
Ajex. – Association of Jewish Ex-Servicemen and Women
AJY – Association for Jewish Youth
Amer. – America; American
Assn. – Association
Asst. – Assistant
Auth. – Authority; author

B. – Born
Bd. – Board
BMA – British Medical Association
BoD – Board of Deputies
Br. – Branch
Brit. – British; Britain

C. – Council
CBF-WJR – Central British Fund for World Jewish Relief
CCJ – Council of Christians and Jews
C of E – Council of Europe
Cllr. – Councillor
Coll. – College
Com. – Communal; community; commission(er)
Comp. – Company
Cttee. – Committee

Dep. – Deputy
Dept. – Department
Dir. – Director
Distr. – District

Eccl. – Ecclesiastical
Edr. – Editor, Editorial
Educ. – Education; educationist; educational
Emer. – Emeritus
Exec. – Executive

Fdr. – Founder
Fed. – Federation; federal
Fel. – Fellow; Fellowship
Fin. – Finance; financial
Fom. – Former; formerly
Fr. – Friends

Gen. – General
Gov. – Governor; governing
Govt. – Government

H. – Honorary
Hist. – History; historical; historian
HM – Headmaster
HT – Head Teacher

IJPR– Institute for Jewish Policy Research
Instit. – Institute; institution(al)
Internat. – International

JBS – Jewish Blind Society
JEDT – Jewish Educational Development Trust
JIA – Joint Israel Appeal
JMC – Jewish Memorial Council
JNF – Jewish National Fund
JWB – Jewish Welfare Board

Lab. – Labour; laboratory
Lect. – Lecturer; lecture(ship)
Libr. – Librarian; library
Lit. – Literature
Lond. – London

M. – Minister
Man. – Manager; management; managing
Med – Medical; medicine
Min. – Ministry; ministerial
MEP – Member of European Parliament
MP – Member of Parliament

Nat. – National; nationalist; nation(s)

Off. – Officer; office
Org. – Organiser
ORT – Organisation for Resources and Technical Training

Parl. – Parliament; parliamentary
Pol. – Political; policy
Princ. – Principal
Prof. – Professor
Publ. – Publication; public; publicity; publishing

R. – Reader
Reg. – Registrar; Register(ed); region(al)
Rel. – Religion; religious; relation; relief
Rep. – Representative
Res. – Research; Residence
Ret. – Retired
RSGB – Reform Synagogues of Great Britain

Sch. – School; Scholar(ship)
SDP – Social Democratic Party
Sec. – Secretary
Soc. – Society; social; sociology
Sr. – Senior
Supt. – Superintendent
Syn. – Synagogue

T. – Treasurer
TAC – Trades Advisoy Council
Tech. – Technical; technology, -ical
Tr. – Trustee; trust

ULPS – Union of Liberal and Progressive Synagogues
Univ. – University
UK – United Kingdom
US – United Synagogue

V. – Vice
Vis. – Visitation; visitor; visiting
Vol. – Voluntary; volunteer; volume

W. – Warden
WIZO – Women's International Organisation
WJC – World Jewish Congress
WZO – World Zionist Organisation

Z. – Zionist; Zionism

ANGLO-JEWISH INSTITUTIONS

REPRESENTATIVE ORGANISATIONS

BOARD OF DEPUTIES OF BRITISH JEWS

6 Bloomsbury Square, London WC1A 2LP.
☎ 020-7543 5400. Fax 020-7543 0010. E-mail info@bod.org.uk; Website www.bod.org.uk.
Board of Deputies Charitable Foundation (Reg. Charity No. 1058107)
Founded in 1760 as a joint committee of the Sephardi and Ashkenazi communities in London, the Board of Deputies of British Jews has flourished in its role as the elected representative body of the British Jewish community. It has taken part in all movements affecting the political and civil rights of British Jewry and in many cases at times of crisis in affairs overseas. It conveys the views of the community to Government and other public bodies on political and legislative matters which affect British Jewry, and provides information about the Jewish community and Israel to the non-Jewish world. The Board examines legislative proposals in Britain and the European Union which may affect Jews, and ensures the political defence of the community. It collects statistical and demographic information and undertakes research on and for the community. It maintains contact with and provides support for Jewish communities around the world and promotes solidarity with Israel. It counters bias in the media and ensures that Jews enjoy the full rights of all British citizens.

The Board plays a co-ordinating role in key issues affecting the Jewish community, and promotes co-operation among different groups within the community. The basis of the Board's representation is primarily synagogal, although the body itself has no religious affiliations. All properly constituted synagogues in Great Britain are entitled to representation, as are other significant communal organisations, such as the Regional Representative Councils, youth organisations and other communal bodies, including major charities. The Board meets most months in London, but holds one meeting a year in a provincial community. It also holds an annual conference open to the community.

President Jo Wagerman, OBE; *Senior Vice President* Henry Grunwald, Q.C.; *V. Presidents* Tony Sacker, Jerry Lewis; *Tr.* Flo Kaufmann, JP; *Dir. Gen.* Neville Nagler.

The work of the Board is channelled through four Divisional Boards, each chaired by an Honorary Officer and supported by a professional Director.

International Division: *Chairman* Tony Sacker; *Dir.* Fiona Macaulay.
Community Issues: *Chairman* Jerry Lewis; *Dir.* Marlena Schmool.
Finance and Organisation: *Chairman* Flo Kaufmann, JP; *Dir.* Sandra Clark.
Defence Policy and Group Relations: *Chairman* Henry Grunwald; *Dir.* Mike Whine, Fiona Macaulay.
Regional Council: *Chairman* Ephraim Borowski.
Community Research Unit: (Est. 1965) Compiles statistical data on various aspects of the community and prepares interpretative studies of trends. *Chairman* Robert Owen; *Dir.* Marlena Schmool.
Yad Vashem Committee: *Chairman* Ben Helfgott.
Trades Advisory Council: Affiliated to the Board of Deputies, the Council seeks to combat causes of friction in industry, trade and commerce, and discrimination in the workplace, where these threaten good relations in which Jews are concerned. The TAC offers arbitration and conciliation facilities in business disputes and

advice to employees who consider that they have suffered discrimination. *Dir.* Sandra Clark.

Jewish Community Information Desk, Communal Diary: Operated by volunteers, the Desk provides factual information on all aspects of Jewish home and community life and indicates access to the appropriate authorities to members of the public requiring expert advice. The Communal Diary is designed to avoid difficulties which often arise when dates and times of important meetings and functions clash. ☎ 020-7543 5421/5422.

Central Council for Jewish Community Services - Ombudsman, c/o The Board of Deputies of British Jews, ☎ 0 20-7543 0105 (answerphone). (Reg. Charity No: 269525) The Ombudsman is available to deal with disputes or complaints concerning Jewish community services, i.e. any institutions in the Jewish community. It is an independent service, for which no fee is charged, provided for the benefit of the community. *Tr:* the Rt Hon the Lord Woolf, Victor Benjamin, Melvyn Carlowe OBE, Dr Colin Livingston, MBE, JP; *Ombudsman* Paul Shaerf.

All Aboard Shops Limited: (Est. 1987) To manage charity shops raising income for the Board and all British Jewish charities (see p.101). ☎ 020-8361 1717 Fax 020-8361 1718; Websites www.allaboardshops.com;info@allaboardshops.com; *Officers* Stella Lucas, Monique Landau, Jeffrey Pinnick; *Admin.*

JEWISH REPRESENTATIVE COUNCILS

Berkshire Jewish Representative Council (Est. 1995). *Chairman* J. Foreman, c/o 2(B) Tilehurst Road, Reading, Berks RG1 7TN. ☎ 0118-9571167. Fax 0118-9510740.

Representative Council of Birmingham & Midland Jewry (Est. 1937). *President* Roland Diamond; *Chairman* Prof. S. Abudurham; *Hon. Sec.* Leonard Jacobs. ☎ 0121-236 1801; *Admin.Sec.* Mrs R. Jacobs, Singers Hill, Blucher St., B1 1HL. ☎/Fax 0121-643 2688. E-mail bjrepco@dircon.co.uk Website: www.brijnet.org//-birmingham.

Bournemouth Jewish Representative Council. *Co-chairs* Linda Ford-Horne, Gillian Walker; *H. Sec.* Mrs A. Sklan. (The Southampton and adjacent area is also represented).

Brighton & Hove Jewish Representative Council. *Chairman* Ivor Richards; *H. Sec.* Mrs. D. Levinson and Aubrey Milstein, P.O.B 2001, Hove, BN3 4RY. ☎ 01273 558559.

Bristol Representative Council. *Chairman* M. Romain, 7 College Fields, Bristol BS8 3HP ☎ 0117-973 9312. E-mail romain@netgates.co.uk. *Sec.* Mrs K. Balint-Kurti, 6 Ashgrove Rd., BS6 6LY. ☎ 0117-973 1150.

Glasgow Jewish Representative Council. 222, Fenwick Rd., Giffnock, Glasgow G46 6UE. ☎ 0141-577 8200. Fax 0141-577 8202. E-mail glasgow@j-scot.org; Website www.j-scot.org/glasgow. *President* S. I. Kliner; *H. Sec.* E. Isaacs; *Admin.* Mrs B. Taylor.

Hull Jewish Representative Council. *President* Prof. J. Friend, 9 Allanhall Way, Kirkella, Hull HU10 7QU, ☎ 01482 658930; *H. Sec.* Mrs. A. Segelman, 251 Beverley Road, Kirkella, Hull HU10 7AG. ☎ 01482 650288.

Leeds Jewish Representative Council. *President* I. J. Goldman, 151 Shadwell La., LS17 8DW. ☎ 0113 2697520. Fax 0113 2370851; *Hon. Sec.* Judge R. Bartfield; *Exec. Off.* Mrs M. Jackson.

Jewish Representative Council of Greater Manchester & Region. *President* David Arnold, Jewish Cultural Centre, Bury Old Road, M7 4QY. ☎ 0161-720 8721. E-mail jewishmanchester@anjy.org; Website www.anjy.org/jewishmanchester. *H. Secs* B. D. Goldstone, L. Jacobs. *Publ.* Year Book.

Merseyside Jewish Representative Council. *President* Mrs E. Morron; *Chair of C.* Mrs N. S. Kingston; *H. Sec.* B. Levene, 433 Smithdown Road, L15 3JL.

☎ 0151-733 2292. Fax 0151-734 0212. Email mjrcshifrin@hotmail.com. *Publ.* Year Book.

Representative Council of North East Jewry (Reg. Charity No. 1071515). *President* Joe Gellert; *V. Presidents* G. Pearlman, J. Slesenger; *H. Sec.* Henry Ross, 56 Southwood Gdns., Newcastle upon Tyne NE3 3BX. ☎ 0191-285 4043. Fax 0191-284 8941.

Nottingham Representative Council. 265 Wollaton Vale, Wollaton, Nottingham NG8 2PX. ☎ 0115 928 1613. Fax 0115 916 2960. Email lynnechapman@innotts.co.uk. *Chairman* D. Lipman; *Sec.* Mrs L. Chapman.

Sheffield Jewish Representative Council. *President* B. Rosenberg ☎ 0114 230 8433; *H. Sec.* M. Rose, 76 Dove Rd., Sheffield S17 3NE. ☎ 0114 236 0984 Fax 0114 235 3045; 0114 230 1125.

South Wales Jewish Representative Council. *President* Prof. David Weitzman, 41 Hollybush Rd., Cardiff CF23 6SY; *H. Sec.* Mrs R. Levene. ☎ 029-2075 2277.

Southend & District Jewish Representative Council. *Chairman* Derek Baum, MBE; ☎ 01702 343789; *H. Sec.* J. Barcan, 22 2nd Avenue, Westcliff-on-Sea, Essex SS0 8HY. ☎ 01702-343192.

Southport Jewish Representative Council. *President* Mrs S. Abrahamson ☎ 01704 540704; *H. Sec.* Lawrence Abelson. ☎ 01704 545363.

ANGLO-JEWISH ASSOCIATION

Suite 5, 107 Gloucester Place, London W1U 6BY.
☎ 020-7486 5055. Fax 020-7486 5155. Email info@anglojewish.co.uk; Website www.anglojewish.co.uk.
(Est. 1871). Membership of the Association is open to all British Jews who accept as their guiding principle loyalty to their faith and their country. Its aims are: To promote the education of Jews in the United Kingdom and elsewhere; to instruct in Jewish affairs and matters relating to the Jewish religion or race; to collect and publish information relating to the religious and social conditions of Jews throughout the world; to encourage Jews in the UK to support Jewish charitable organisations by personal service and financial assistance; to join or promote any charitable society or body in the UK or elsewhere, in order to further any of its objects and people; to use its education cultural and political experience for the promotion of good will towards Israel. *President* Michael Hilsewath; *Deputy President* Gabriel Herman; *Sec.* Cynthia Steuer, MICM.

ASSOCIATION OF JEWISH FRIENDSHIP CLUBS

26 Enford Street, London W1H 2DD.
☎ 020-7724 8100. Fax 020-7724 8203.
(Est. 1948. Reg. Charity No. 211013) An umbrella organisation for a network of 70 social clubs for men and women in the sixty-plus age group (see p. 102). *Nat. Chairman* Mrs L. Bromley; *Hon. Chaplain* Rev. G. Glausiusz.

ASSOCIATION OF JEWISH WOMEN'S ORGANISATIONS IN THE UNITED KINGDOM

4th Floor, 24–32 Stephenson Way, London NW1 2JW.
☎ 020-7387 7688. Fax 020-7387 2110.
(Est. 1965.) To further communal understanding; to promote the achievement of unity among Jewish women of differing shades of opinion, belonging to autonomous organisations with different aims. *Affiliate orgs.:* Assn. of Masorti Women; Assn. of US Women; British Emunah; Brit. ORT Women's Div.; Fed. of Women Zionists (Brit. WIZO); Frs. of the Hebrew Univ. Women's Group; Jewish National Fund 'First' Ladies Committee; Jewish Women's Aid; Jewish Women's Network; League of Jewish Women; Reform Syn. Guilds; Sephardi Women's Assn.; 35's Women's Campaign for Soviet Jewry; UJIA Women's Div.; ULPS; **Observer**

org. B'nai B'rith Women; *Chairman* S. Harris; *V. Chairmen* L. Freedman, H. Reisman; *H. Sec.* A. Elman; *H.T.* J. Rose.

COMMUNITY SECURITY TRUST

PO Box 35501, London NW4 2FZ. ☎ 020-8457 9999. Manchester: PO Box 82, Manchester M8 4AX.

(Est 1994. Reg. Charity No. 1042391) To provide security advice, training and defence research for the Jewish community.

COUNCIL OF CHRISTIANS AND JEWS

Patron: Her Majesty the Queen.

5th Floor, Camelford House, 87-89 Albert Embankment, London SE1 7TP.

☎ 020-7820 0090. Fax 020-7820 0504. E-mail cjrelations@ccj.org.uk Website www.ccj.org.uk.

(Est. 1942. Reg. Charity No. 238005.) The Council brings together the Christian and Jewish Communities in a common effort to fight the evils of prejudice, intolerance and discrimination between people of different religions, races and colours, and to work for the betterment of human relations, based on mutual respect, understanding and goodwill. It is neither a missionary nor a political organisation. *Presidents* The Archbishop of Canterbury; The Cardinal Archbishop of Westminster; The Archbishop of Thyateira and Gt. Brit.; The Moderator of the Church of Scotland; The Free Churches' Moderator; The Chief Rabbi; Rabbi Dr Albert Friedlander, OBE, PhD, DD, MHL. *Chairman, Exec. Cttee.* The Rt. Revd. C. Herbert; *V. Chairmen* The Rt. Revd. C. Henderson, VG, KCHS, R. S. Rubin; *Jt. H. Ts.* Robert G. Vincent, MA, FCA; Asher Corren, MIMGT; *Jt. H. Secs.* Revd. Eric Allen, B.D. Rosalind Preston, OBE; *Dir.* Sr. Margaret Shepherd nds, BA, MTh; *Educ. Adv.* The Revd Jonathan Gorsky, MA; *Educ. Off.* Jane Clements, MA, BD, Cert Ed; *Assistant Educ. Off.* Rabbi Rachel Montagu, MA; *Youth and Dev. Officer* Gemma Abbs, MA. *Publ.* Common Ground.

There are 60 local Branches. A list of these is obtainable from the central office.

LEAGUE OF JEWISH WOMEN

24-32 Stephenson Way, London NW1 2JW.

☎ 020-7387 7688. Fax 020-7387 2110. Email office@leagueofjewishwomen. org.uk; Website www.leagueofjewishwomen.org.uk.

(Est. 1943. Reg. Charity No. 261199) Vol. service org. to unite Jewish women of every shade of opinion who are resident in the United Kingdom; to intensify in each Jewish woman her Jewish consciousness and her sense of responsibility to the Jewish community and the community generally; to stimulate her personal sense of civic duty and to encourage her to express it by increased service to the country. *President* Judith Lever; *H. Sec.* Mrs Jean Karsberg.

Groups operate in the following centres:

Greater London

Barnet; Bushey Heath; Chigwell & Hainault; Clissold; Coombe & District; Ealing; Edgware; Finchley; Hampstead Garden Suburb; Harrow & Kenton; Hendon; Ilford; Kingston & Wimbledon; Loughton; Maidenhead and Thames Valley; Muswell Hill & Highgate; New Era; Newbury Park; North and East London; North West End; Northwood; Oakwood & Winchmore Hill; Pinner; Radlett; Richmond Park; Southgate; Stanmore; Streatham; Surrey; Watford; Wembley; Young Herts & Middlesex; Sefer Tov (Book Club); Prime Time (single women).

Outside London

Bournemouth; Cardiff; Glasgow; Leicester.

North West Region (centred at Manchester)

Bowdon & Hale; Brantwood; Bury; Cheadle & Gatley; Didsbury; Fylde; Heaton Pk.,

Higher Broughton & Polefield; Kingsway; Northenden; Park & Windsor; Prestwich; Sale & Altrincham; Southport; Whitefield & Ringley.

League Associate Division (men); Prime Time.

ORT HOUSE CONFERENCE CENTRE
126 Albert Street, London NW1 1NF.
☎ 020-7446 8509. Fax 020-7446 8651. E-mail pavilion@ort.org. Website www.pavpub.com.
(Est. 1996) A Jewish conference centre with milk kitchen. Capacity 120. Suitable for business, community or social events. *Conference Centre Man.* Debbie Lodington.

THE THREE FAITHS FORUM
Star House, 105-108 Grafton Road, London NW5 4BD.
☎ 020-7485 2538. Fax 020-7485 4512. E-mail sidney@sternberg-foundation.co.uk. Website www.threefaithsforum.org.uk
(Est. 1997. Reg. Charity No. 1092465) To encourage friendship, goodwill and understanding amongst people of the 3 monotheistic and Abrahamic faiths in the UK and elsewhere. Basis of equality and exploring and enjoying those differences where appropriate. *Patrons* H.E. Cardinal Francis Arinze; Baroness Boothroyd; HRH Dom Duarte, Duke of Bragança; Professor Jonathan Magonet; Rt.Hon. M. Martin MP; Chief Rabbi M. Rene-Samuel Sirat; Sheikh Dr Muhammad Sayyid Tantawi; Rt.Hon. Lord Weatherall DL. *Co-Chairmen* Sir Sigmund Sternberg; Sheikh Dr Zaki M.A. Badawi, OBE; Rev. M. Braybrooke, MA, M.Phil.; *Coord.* Sidney L. Shipton.

WOMEN IN THE JEWISH COMMUNITY REGIONAL CO-ORDINATING COUNCIL
(Est. 1994) To continue the work of the Chief Rabbi's Review of Women in the Jewish Community (chaired by Rosalind Preston, OBE). The Council regularly monitors grassroots progress in relation to the recommendations of the Review's Report. It meets in different cities two or three times a year and in 1999 held a national conference in Liverpool attended by 200 women from 14 cities. *Chairman* Agnes Grunwald-Spier, JP, MA (Sheffield), ☎ 0114 2360984. Email agnesgrunwald-spier@ukonline.co.uk; *Sec.* Doreen Wachmann, BA (Manchester), ☎ 0161 773 1220. Email dwachmann@hotmail.com; *T.* Judith Tankel, MA, FRSA (Glasgow), ☎ 0141 423 5830. Email h.j.glastank@talk21.com. *Publ.* Facing the Future – Five Years On (1999), with 'Update 2002'.

WORKING PARTY ON JEWISH MONUMENTS IN THE UK & IRELAND
c/o Jewish Memorial Council, 25 Enford Street, London W1H 2DD.
(Est. Dec. 1991. Reg. Charity No. 206565) For the preservation and documentation of Jewish monuments of architectural and historical importance. (See listings p.208.) ☎ 020-7724 7778. Fax 020-7706 1710; *Chairman* E. Jamilly (☎ 020-7636 0776); *T.* A. Rosenzweig; *Sec.* Mrs K. B. Green. *Publ.* Alderney Road Jewish Cemetery; The Georgian Synagogue.
Project: Survey of the Jewish Built Heritage (supported by the Heritage Lottery Fund). *Project Dir.* Dr Sharman Kadish. E-mail sharman.kadish@man.ac.uk; Website www.art.man.ac.uk/reltheol/jewish/heritage; Steering Group: *Chairman* R. Hook (English Heritage); *Fieldworkers* B. Bowman, A. Petersen.

JEWISH PRESS, RADIO AND INFORMATION SERVICES

The following is a selection of the major national publications. The Representative Councils of Leeds, Manchester, Merseyside and the North East publish yearbooks. Many synagogues and communal organisations publish newsletters and magazines.

BRITISH-JEWISH PRESS

AJR Journal, 1 Hampstead Gate, 1A Frognal, London NW3 6AL. ☎ 020-7431 6161. Fax 020-7431 8454. E-mail editorial@ajr.org.uk; Website www.ajr.org.uk. Monthly. *Edr*. Richard Grunberger; *Exec. Edr.* R. Channing.

Belfast Jewish Record (Est. 1953), 42 Glandore Ave., Belfast BT15 3FD. ☎ 028-9077 9491. Quarterly. *Edr.Bd. Hon. Sec.* Mrs N. Simon.

BIMAH: The Platform of Welsh Jewry (Est. 1994), 23 Solva Avenue, Llanishen, Cardiff CF14 0NP. ☎ 02920 750990. Quarterly. *Ed.* Alan Schwartz. *Ch.* Hanuš Weisl.

Birmingham Jewish Recorder, PO Box 9276, Birmingham B13 8PB. ☎ 0121-449 7518. Email recorder@reubenuk.freeserve.co.uk. Monthly. Est. 1935. *Edr.* Liz Reuben.

Edinburgh Star, 5 Oswald Court, Edinburgh EH9 2HY. Est. 1989. 3 issues a year. *Edr.* Peter Bennett; *Ch.* John Cosgrove, 14 Gordon Terrace, Edinburgh, EH16 5QR.

Essex Jewish News, Crown House, 47 Chase Side, Southgate, London N14 5BP. ☎ 020-8920 2100. Fax 020-8447 8548. *Edr.* Manny Robinson.

European Judaism, Leo Baeck College – Centre for Jewish Education, 80 East End Rd., London N3 2SY. ☎ 020-8349 5600. Fax 020-8343 2558. Email info@lbc.ac.uk; Website www.lbc.ac.uk. Est. 1966. Two issues a year. *Edr.* Rabbi Dr A. H. Friedlander, Rabbi Professor J. Magónet.

Hamaor, Federation of Synagogues, 65 Watford Way, London NW4 3AQ. Est. 1962. Three issues a year. *Edr.*

Jewish Book News and Reviews, now incorporated in the Jewish Quarterly.

Jewish Chronicle, 25 Furnival St., London EC4A 1JT. ☎ 020-7415 1500. Fax 020-7405-9040. Est. 1841. Weekly. *Chairman* Peter M. Oppenheimer; *Edr.* Ned. Temko.

Jewish Community Pages (incorporating the Jewish Business Directory), Forum Publications Ltd., 2300 Northolt Rd., Harrow, Middx HA2 8DU. ☎ 020-8422 7086. Fax 020-8422 9175. *Edr.* B. King.

Jewish Journal of Sociology, 187 Gloucester Place, London NW1 6BU. ☎ 020-7262 8939. Fd. 1959. Published by Maurice Freedman Research Trust (Reg. Charity No. 326077). Annual. *Edr.* Judith Freedman.

Jewish Quarterly, incorporating Jewish Book News and Reviews, PO Box 35042, London NW1 7XH. ☎/Fax 020-7284 1117. Email editor@jewquart.freeserve.co.uk. Est. 1953. (Reg. Charity No. 268589.) *Edr.* Matthew Reisz.

Jewish Renaissance: Magazine of Jewish Culture, 375 Upper Richmond Road West, East Sheen, London SW14 7NX. ☎ 020-8255 9447. Email Info@jewishrenaissance.org.uk; Website www.jewishrenaissance.org.uk. Est. 2001. Four issues a year. *Edr* Janet Levin; *Chairman* L. Gordon.

Jewish Review, Mizrachi Federation, 2b Golders Green Rd., London NW11 8LH. ☎ 020-8455 2243. Fax 020-8455 2244. Email jr@mizrachi.org.uk; Website www.mizrachi.org.uk. Est. 1946. Quarterly. *Edr.* A. L. Handler.

Jewish Socialist: magazine of the Jewish Socialists' Group, BM3725, London WC1N 3XX. Email jsg@bardrose.dircon.co.uk; Website www.jewish-socialist.org. Est. 1985. Quarterly. Edr. Cttee.

Jewish Telegraph, 11 Park Hill, Bury Old Rd., Prestwich, Manchester M25 0HH. ☎ 0161-740 9321. Fax 0161-740-9325. Email mail@jewishtelegraph.com. Website www.jewishtelegraph.com. Est. 1950. Weekly. (Also in Leeds, Liverpool and Glasgow.) *Edr.* P. Harris.

Jewish Travel Guide, Vallentine Mitchell, Crown House, 47 Chase Side, Southgate, London N14 5BP. ☎ 020-8920 2100. Fax 020-8447 8548. Email jtg@vmbooks.com. (Est. 1956. Formerly published by the Jewish Chronicle.) Annual. *Edr.* M.P. Zaidner.

Jewish Tribune, 97 Stamford Hill, London N16 5DN. ☎ 020-8800 6688. Fax 020-8800 5000. Email khjt@brijnet.org. English & Yiddish. Est. 1962. Weekly. *Edr.* J. Bentov (Agudas Yisroel of Great Britain).

Jewish Year Book, Vallentine Mitchell, Crown House, 47 Chase Side, Southgate, London N14 5BP. ☎ 020-8920 2100. Fax 020-8447 8548. Email jyb@vmbooks.com. (Est. 1896. Formerly published by the Jewish Chronicle.) Annual. *Edr.* S.W. Massil.

Journal of Progressive Judaism, Two issues a year. *Edr.* Rabbi Sybil Sheridan.

Le'ela: a journal of Judaism today, London School of Jewish Studies, Albert Rd., London NW4 2SJ. ☎ 020-8203 6427, Fax 020-8203 6420. Email editor@leela.org.uk. Est. 1975. Two issues a year. *Edr.* Rachel Schenker.

Leo Baeck Institute Yearbook, 4 Devonshire Street, London W1W 5LB. Est. 1956. Ann. *Edr.* J. A. S. Grenville.

London Jewish News, 50 Colindeep Lane, Colindale, London NW9 6HB. ☎ 020-8358 6500, Fax 020-8205 9121. Email news@ljn.co.uk *Edr* Stuart Brodkin.

Manna, Sternberg Centre for Judaism, 80 East End Rd., London N3 2SY. ☎ 020-8349 5646. Fax 020-8349 5699. Email admin@reformjudaism.org.uk. Quarterly. *Edr.* Rabbi Tony Bayfield.

Mazel & Brocho, 168 Stamford Hill, 2nd Floor, N16 6QX. ☎ 020-8211-7876, Fax: 020-8211-7874. *Edr.* Sarah Schleimer.

Menorah: a magazine for Jewish members of H.M. Forces and Small Communities, 25/26 Enford St., London W1H 2DW. ☎ 020-7724 7778. Fax 020-7706 1710. Semi-Ann. *Edr.* Rev. M. Weisman, OBE.

The Scribe: Journal of Babylonian Jewry, 20 Queen's Gate Terrace, London SW7 5PF. Est. 1971. Two issues a year. *Edr.* N.E. Dangoor.

Wessex Jewish News, PO Box 2624, Poole, BH13 6ZE. ☎ 01202 762101. Fax 01202 763203. Email editor@stewgreene.clara.net.

JEWISH RADIO PROGRAMMES

BBC London 94.9: Contact: 'Jewish London', 35c Marylebone High St., W1A 4LG. Programmes at 19.00 hours, every Sunday evening on GLR 94.9FM. *Ed.* Gloria Abramoff ☎ 020-7224 2424, 020-7935 1026; *Prod.* Roma Felstein ☎ 020-7224 2424, 020-8446 0927 (home); *Res.* Osa Fowler ☎ 020-7224 2424, 020-7935 1696; *Presenter* Wendy Robbins ☎ 020-7224 2424.

Jewish Spectrum Radio, 4 Ingate Place, Battersea, London SW8 3NS. *Presenters* Michael Milston, Jon Kaye. A daily two-hour programme of news, views and discussion. Weekly features include Rabbi Shmuel Boteach, Chazanut, Israeli sports, Jewish music, live report from Israel, theatre, art and the Sedra. See Jewish press for regular programme details weekly. ☎ 020-7627 4433. Phone-In: 020-7627 8383. Fax: 020-7627 3409. Email: jewish@spectrumradio.net.

'It's Kosher': Produced by Basil Herwald. Broadcast every Thursday evening at 8.05pm–8.30pm. On G.M.R 95.1 and 104.6 FM. ☎ 0161 244-3050/3058. Write to 'It's Kosher', c/o BBC GMR, PO Box 951, New Broadcasting House, Oxford Road, Manchester M60 1SD. Email gmr.kosher@bbc.co.uk

INFORMATION SERVICES

Brijnet
11, The Lindens, Prospect Hill, Waltham Forest, London E17 3EJ.
☎ 020-8520 3531. Email info@brijnet.org.
Provider of UK Jewish communal internet services. Creates awareness of the use and benefits of the Internet in the community through training and assistance with all Internet tools. Creates and maintains a useful quality communal electronic information database. Published electronic listings including: brij-announce, daf-hashavua. Websites www.shamash.org/ejin/brijnet/; www.brijnet. org *Dir.* Rafael Salasnik.

Jewish Community Information, Board of Deputies, 6 Bloomsbury Square, London WC1A 2LP. ☎ 020-7543 5413. Fax 020-7543 0010. Email jci@bod.org.uk. *Prof. Off.* Frances Cohen. (Est. 1996.) JCI is an on-going, in-depth information service of Jewish activities and resources. It is available to communal organisations. For general enquiries: ☎ 020-7543 5421/22/23.

RELIGIOUS ORGANISATIONS

THE CHIEF RABBINATE

The Chief Rabbinate of Britain has developed from the position of the Rabbi of the Great Syn., London. From the early years of the 18th century until recently, he was acknowledged as the spiritual leader of the London Ashkenazi Com. and this recognition was also accepted in the provinces and overseas. Jonathan Sacks was inducted into office in 1991. Previous holders of the office were: Aaron Hart (1709–1756); Hart Lyon (1756–1764); David Tevele Schiff (1765–1791); Solomon Herschell (1802–1842); Nathan Marcus Adler (1845–1890); Hermann Adler (1891–1911); Joseph Herman Hertz (1913–1946); Israel Brodie (1948–1965); Immanuel Jakobovits (1967–1991).

To conform with the constitutional practice, the official designation (1845–1953) was 'Chief Rabbi of the United Hebrew Congregations of the British Commonwealth of Nations' and subsequently 'Chief Rabbi of the United Hebrew Congregations of the Commonwealth'.

Chief Rabbi Professor Jonathan Sacks, MA(Cantab), PhD. Office of the Chief Rabbi: Adler House, 735 High Road, London N12 0US. ☎ 020-8343 6301. Fax 020-8343 6310. Email info@chiefrabbi.org. Website www.chiefrabbi.org. *Exec. Dir.*: Syma Weinberg; *Dir. Communications:* Jeremy Newmark.

Chief Rabbinate Council: *Chairman* Peter Sheldon; *Publ.*: Le'ela (see p.7).

BETH DIN (COURT OF THE CHIEF RABBI)

Adler House, 735 High Road, London N12 0US. ☎ 020-8343 6270. Fax 020-8343 6257. Email info@londonbethdin.fsnet.co.uk.

Dayanim Rabbis Chanoch Ehrentreu, Menachem Gelley, Ivan Binstock, BSc., Yonason Abraham. *Registrar* D. Frei, LL.B.; *Marriage Authorisations* Rabbi J. Shindler. ☎ 020-8343 6313.

The Beth Din fulfils the following functions for the orthodox community: (i) dispute arbitration and mediation, (ii) supervision of Jewish religious divorces, adoptions and conversions, (iii) certification of religious status; (iv) supervision of shechita and kashrut.

General enquiries may be made from 9.00 a.m. to 5.00 p.m. (Monday to Thursday). Enquiries on kashrut should be made to the Kashrut Division (see below). Visitors may attend the Beth Din by appointment only. Messages left on the answerphone will be dealt with as soon as possible.

Kashrut Division. ☎ 020-8343 6255. Fax 020-8343 6257. Website www.kosher.org.uk. *Dir.* Rabbi J. Conway, B.A.; *Kashrut Admin.* N. Lauer. *Publ.:* The Really Jewish Food Guide, Snack 'n' Sweet Guide, Passover Supplement.

UNITED SYNAGOGUE

While the Act of Parliament under which it was created bears the date July 14, 1870, the United Synagogue had its origin much earlier in the history of London Jewry. Of the five Constituent Synagogues which joined to form the United Synagogue, the oldest – the Great Synagogue – had a history of more than 280 years; the Hambro dated from 1707, while the New Synagogue was founded in 1761. The Member Synagogues now number 44, and the Affiliated Synagogues 21, providing religious facilities for over 39,000 families (over 100,000 people). From the outset, the US has also taken a large share in the social and philanthropic work of the Community.

The **Community Development Department** is the interface between Head Office and the local synagogue communities. The Department provides a range of activities including US Cares, United Synagogue Volunteer Project, North West Jewish Singles and Lunch'n Learn programmes. It supports youth activities in United Synagogues and offers training for lay leaders and coordinates cross-communal events.

The **Visitation Committee** provides a caring service for all Jews who unfortunately find themselves in hospital, in prison or who are bereaved (see p.105). The Jewish Bereavement Counselling Service has a team of trained bereavement counsellors available to meet the needs of all members of the Jewish community.

Conjoint Passover Flour Committee is operated by the United Synagogue and is responsible for the distribution of Matzot and Passover provisions to the needy.

The US bears the financial responsibility for the **Beth Din** (Court of the Chief Rabbi, see above) and is the main contributor to the maintenance of the Chief Rabbinate.

The US plays a large part in the work of the **Jewish Committee for H.M. Forces**, which provides facilities for Jewish members of the Forces to maintain the practices of their faith (see below).

President Peter Sheldon; *V. Presidents* Geoffrey Hartnell, Simon Hochhauser, Stuart Taylor; *Ts.* David Cramer, Stephen Pack, Brian Wolkind; *Chief Exec.* Rabbi Saul Zneimer (Reg. Charity No. 242552).

Head Office: Adler House, 735 High Road, London N12 0US. ☎ 020-8343 8989. Fax 020-8343 6262. Website www.unitedsynagogue.org.uk. Member, Affiliated and Associated Synagogues are listed on pp.78–82.

Burial Society, *Managers, Finchley Office* Marcia Wohlman; *Ilford Office* Cilla Bloch.

INITIATION SOCIETY

President Aaron Winegarten. *Medical Off.* Dr. M. Sifman, 47 The Ridgeway, NW11 8QP. ☎ 020-8455 2008. Fax 020-8731 6276; *Sec.* A. Minn, 15 Sunny Hill Ct., Sunningfields Cres. NW4 4RB. ☎/Fax: 020-8203 1352. (Est. 1745; Reg. Charity No. 207404) To train Mohalim and to supply Mohalim in cases where required. For a list of Mohalim practising in the British Isles and registered with the Society, apply to the Secretary.

JEWISH COMMITTEE FOR H.M. FORCES

25 Enford Street, W1H 2DD.
☎ 020-7724 7778 Fax 020-7706 1710. Email jmcouncil@btinternet.com.
The Cttee. officially recognised by the Min. of Defence to appoint Jewish chaplains and to provide for the religious needs of Jewish members of H.M. Forces.

Chairman Lt.Cdr. Alan Tyler RN (Rtd); *T.* Alfred Dunitz, J.P., C.C.; *Sen. Jewish Chaplain to H.M. Forces* Rev. Malcolm Weisman, OBE, MA (Oxon.), OCF; *Sec.* Batya Mason. *Publ.* Menorah.

JEWISH MEMORIAL COUNCIL

25 Enford St., W1H 2DD.
☎ 020-7724 7778 Fax 020-7706 1710. Email jmcouncil@btinternet.com; Website www.jmcouncil.org.
(Est. 1919.) To commemorate the services rendered by Jews in the UK and British Empire in the war of 1914-18 by establishing an organisation which will carry on Jewish tradition as a permanent ennobling force in the lives of Jews in this country.
Chairman E. Astaire; *Admin.*; *President* Edmund L. de Rothschild, T.D.; *V. President* Chief Rabbi; *H. Sec.* T. M. Simon; *H. T.* A. Rosenzweig. *Sec.* Miss D. Carp.

Public Schools Committee (which provides facilities for religious education for Jewish boarders in public schools). *Chairman* E. Astaire.

Jewish Memorial Council Pensions Fund. A superannuation fund administered by the JMC, membership of which is open to all communal officials. *Chairman* A. Rosenzweig; *Admin.*

Scholarships. The following scholarships are admin. by the Council:

Alfred Louis Cohen Fund: For students of the J.F.S. Comprehensive School.

Higher Education Awards: For students of British nationality resident in the UK and studying at a UK univ. or equivalent academic institution.

Sir Robert Waley Cohen Memorial Scholarship. To provide Jewish Ministers holding appointments in any part of the British Commonwealth with Travelling Scholarships to pursue Jewish studies.

Provincial Hebrew Classes Committee. Promotes Jewish religious education by inspecting provincial classes and advising on methods and organisation. *Chairman* E. Astaire; *Educ. Adv.*

JMC Bookshop. Admin. by the JMC to provide books and educational material to the Jewish community in the UK and overseas. Mail order service available.

Small Communities Committee (Est. 1919). Admins. the funds for the Rev. Malcolm Weisman and his colleagues as visiting Mins. to the Small Communities and isolated families. The Cttee. organises regular conferences in the various regions. *Chairman* Edgar Astaire.

NATIONAL COUNCIL OF SHECHITA BOARDS

1st Floor, Elscot House, Arcadia Ave., London N3 2JU.
☎ 020-8349 9160. Fax 020-8346 2209.

To centralise information on all matters relating to the performance and administration of shechita, and to act as liaison between all the shechita boards and the various Ministries and orgs. affecting shechita and the kosher meat and poultry industry, throughout the UK and abroad.

The National Council registered a trade mark in 1955 and re-registered in 1995 a warranty of Kashrus testifying that the holder of this trade mark was a purveyor of kosher meat and/or poultry and is licensed by a recognised Shechita Board affiliated to the Council and under the supervision of a Rabbinical Authority. *President* N.C. Oster; *Jt V. Presidents* A. Schwalbe, Roy Stern; *Jt Ts.* I.R. Singer, S.D. Winegarten; *Exec. Dir.* M.T. Kester.

RABBINICAL COMMISSION FOR THE LICENSING OF SHOCHETIM

Est. under Schedule 12 of Statutory Instrument 731 of 1995 in respect of Welfare of Animals Regulations (1995), which provides for the shechita of animals and poultry by a shochet duly licensed for the purpose by the Rabbinical Com., and constitutes the Rabbinical Com. as follows: The Chief Rabbi, who shall be the permanent Chairman; one member appointed by the Spanish and Portuguese Syn. (London), who shall be a Vice-Chairman, three members appointed by the Beth Din (London); two members appointed by the Federation of Synagogues (London); one member appointed by the Union of Orthodox Hebrew Congregations (London); two members appointed by the President of the BoD to represent regional congregations. *Chairman* The Chief Rabbi. *H.Sec.* Alan Greenbat, Adler House, 735 High Rd., London N12 0US ☎ 020-8343 6301.

SINGER'S PRAYER BOOK PUBLICATION COMMITTEE

Administered by the United Syn. (☎ 020-8343 8989). *Chairman* E. D. Levy. The purpose of Singer's Prayer Book, first published in 1890, is 'to place within the reach of the Community at large a complete daily prayer Book in Hebrew and English, equally suitable for use in syns. families, and schools.' 1st edn., 1890; 26 imp., 1891-1961; 2nd revd. edn., 6 imp., 1962-1988; 3rd revd. centenary edn., 1990; enlarged centenary edn., 1992; revd. 1998.

SPANISH AND PORTUGUESE JEWS' CONGREGATION

The Community of Spanish and Portuguese Jews in London was founded by Marranos in the middle of the seventeenth century. The congregation 'Sahar Asamaim', worshipped in Creechurch Lane (where a tablet records the site) from 1657 to 1701, when the Bevis Marks Synagogue was built. It is the oldest extant syn. building in Britain except for the long-forgotten medieval syn. of Lincoln. The first branch syn. of the congregation in the West End was est. in Wigmore St. in 1853, and in 1861 removed to Bryanston Street; in 1896 the existing building in Lauderdale Road, Maida Vale was opened. In 1977 another branch of the S. & P. Jews' Cong. was opened in Wembley. The cong. is run by a Board of Elders as well as a Mahamad (five members) who act as Executive. An assessment (Finta) is levied on the Yehidim and congregational affairs are regulated by laws, termed Ascamot, the first code of which was drawn up in 1663.

The congregation maintains the Medrash of Heshaim (founded in 1664). Hebrew religious instruction is given at the Communal Centre, Ashworth Road, W9 as well as in Wembley.

A brotherhood Mikveh Israel (Lavadores), est. 1678, and a Burial Society, Hebrat Guemilut Hassadim (1665), attend to the last rites to the dead. A number of charitable and educational trusts exist for the benefit of Sephardim.

For the history of the Sephardi community in London see A. M. Hyamson: The Sephardim of England (reprinted 1991), L. D. Barnett: Bevis Marks Records Part I (1940), El Libro de los Acuerdos (1931); For genealogical records see Bevis Marks Records [Part II and III (marriages), IV (circumcisions), V (births), VI (burials)]. Available from the Synagogue offices. Other publications include: Treasures of a London Temple (1952), edr. R. D. Barnett, Laws and Charities of the Spanish and Portuguese Congregation, by Neville J. Laski, The Mitsvot of the Spanish & Portuguese Jews' Congregation, by G. H. Whitehill.

President of Elders C. Sacerdoti; *V. President of Elders* B. Mocatta; *Chief Exec.* Howard Miller; *Sec., London Sephardi Trust*. Office: 2 Ashworth Road, W9 1JY. ☎ 020-7289 2573. Fax: 020-7289 2709. Email howard@sandpsyn.demon.co.uk.

Dayan Dr P. Toledano, Ab Beth Din exercising his position as Ab Beth Din of the Congregation, Rabbi Dr. A. Levy, Communal Rabbi, exercising his position as Spiritual Head of the Congregation. (Reg. Charity No. 212517.)

Synagogues and organisations are listed on pp.87–8.

FEDERATION OF SYNAGOGUES

65 Watford Way, NW4 3AQ.
☎ 020-8202 2263. Fax 020-8203 0610.

The Federation of Synagogues, then embodying 16 small syns. in the eastern districts of London, was est. in 1887. It now comprises 13 Constituent syns. and 14 affiliated congregations situated in most parts of Greater London. The objects of the Federation include:

To provide the services of Orthodox rabbis, ministers and dayanim; the provision of a Burial Society; to assist syns. in the erection, reconstruction or redecoration of their Houses of Worship, to assist in the maintenance of Orthodox religious instruction in Talmud Torahs and Yeshivot; to obtain and maintain Kashrut; to support charitable and philanthropic works; to further the progress of Eretz Yisrael. *President* A. Finlay; *V. President* B. Mire; *Ts.* L. Newmark, P. Westbrook; *Chief Exec.* G. D. Coleman.

Associated Bodies

Emer. Rav Rashi: Dayan M. Fisher.

Beth Din of the Federation of Synagogues. Dayan Yisroel Yaakov Lichtenstein Rosh Beth Din, Dayan Berel Berkovits, LLB, Dayan M.D. Elzas; *Dayan Emer.* Dayan Z.J. Alony; *Registrar* Rabbi S.Z. Unsdorfer.

London Kashrus Board. *Kashrus Dir.* Dayan M. D. Elzas; *Chairman* A. Finlay.
Federation Burial Society. ☎ 020-8202 3903. Fax 020-8203 0610. *Admin.* M.L. Stuart; *Sexton* N. Kahler; *Ts.* H. Dony, N. Bruckheimer.
Constituent and affiliated synagogues are listed on pp.82–3.

UNION OF ORTHODOX HEBREW CONGREGATIONS

140 Stamford Hill, N16 6QT. ☎ 020-8802 6226. Fax 020-8809-7092. (Reg. Charity No. 249892) The Union of Orthodox Hebrew Congregations was est. 1926 by the late Rabbi Dr. V. Schonfeld to protect traditional Judaism. The constituents consist of bodies affiliated to the Adath Yisroel Burial Society and others desirous of co-operating in the work of protecting Orthodoxy. Membership of the Union is stated to be more than 6,000.

Rabbinate Rabbi Ephraim Padwa (Princ. Rab. Authority), Rabbi J. Dunner (Rabbi of the Union), Dayan A. D. Dunner, Dayan S. Friedman, Dayan D. Grynhaus, Rabbi E. Halpern, Rabbi P. Roberts, Rabbi H. I. Feldman (for Kashrus Ctte.), Rabbi J. Padwa; *President* D. Frand; *Registrar* J. R. Conrad.

Associated Bodies

Kashrus Committee-Kedassia, address as above. ☎ 020-8800 6833. Fax 020-8809 7092. *Chairman* E. M. Hochhauser; *Admin.* I. Feldman.
Central Mikvaoth Board, address as above. ☎ 020-8802 6226.
Adath Yisroel Burial Society, 40 Queen Elizabeth's Walk, N16 0HH. ☎ 020-8802 6262/3. Fax 020-8800 8764. *Sec.* M. Mannes. Cemeteries: Carterhatch Lane, Enfield. ☎ 020-8363 3384. Silver Street, Cheshunt Herts. ☎ 01707-874220.
Constituent and affiliated synagogues are listed on pp.83–5.

MASORTI
ASSEMBLY OF MASORTI SYNAGOGUES

1097 Finchley Road, NW11 0PU. ☎ 020-8201 8772. Fax 020-8201 8917. Email office@masorti.org.uk Website www.masorti.org.uk.
(Reg. Charity No. 801846). (Est. 1985) The Assembly of Masorti Synagogues is the umbrella body that serves all Masorti communities in Britain. It acts as a central co-ordinating body with responsibility for developing Masorti communities, providing social, cultural and educational opportunities for youth, students and young adults, and for promoting Masorti ideology. Masorti Judaism accepts the binding force for Jewish law and understands that it has developed throughout history. The Assembly of Masorti Synagogues runs leadership-training programmes, as well as the Masorti Academy, which provides adult education, Gesher Teenage Centre and Noam Youth Movement. *Vice Presidents* Jaclyn Chernett, Ivor Jacobs, Michael Rose; *Chair* Gillian Caplin, Laurence Harris; *H. T.* Leon Levy; *Dir.* M. Gluckman. Constituent synagogues in London are listed on pp.85–6. See also: Leeds, Oxford, St Albans.

REFORM SYNAGOGUES OF GREAT BRITAIN

The Sternberg Centre for Judaism, 80 East End Road, N3 2SY.
☎ 020-8349 5640. Fax 020-8349 5699. Email admin@reformjudaism.org.uk; Website www.reformjudaism.org.uk.
Founded to co-ordinate a group of synagogues, the first of which – the West London Synagogue – was est. in 1840. Objects: to promote a living Judaism, to interpret the Torah in accordance with the spirit and needs of the present generation and, through its positive, constructive, and progressive view of Jewish tradition, raise and maintain a high standard of Jewish religious life throughout the country.

President Sir Sigmund Sternberg; *Movement Chairman* Andrew Gilbert; *Movement T.* Michael Grabiner; *Immediate Past Chairman* Steven Licht; *Chair,*

Assembly of Rabbis Rabbi Sylvia Rothschild; *Chief Exec.* Rabbi Tony Bayfield; *Dir. of Operations* Nicki Landau; *Dir. of Finance* Mike Frankl; *Dir. of Synagogue Support* David Jacobs; *Living Judaism Initiative Dir.* Julian Resnick; *Dir. of Youth, Students & Young Adults* Daren Gordon; *Fundraising Dir.* Jeremy Kelly; *IT Man.* Marc Ozin. *Publ.* Manna, Reform Judaism.

Constituent Synagogues: Metropolitan: Synagogues are listed on pp.89–90.

Regions: Cambridge Beth Shalom Syn.; Blackpool Ref. Jewish Cong.; Bournemouth Ref. Syn.; Bradford Syn.; Brighton & Hove New Syn.; Cardiff New Syn.; Glasgow New Syn.; Hull Reform Syn.; Maidenhead Ref. Syn.; Manchester Ref Syn.; Menorah Syn., Cheshire; Milton Keynes Ref. Syn.; Newcastle Ref Syn.; Sinai Syn., Leeds; Sha'arei Shalom N. Manchester Reform Cong. Sheffield & Distr. Ref. Jewish Syn.; South Hampshire Ref. Jewish Com.; Southend & Distr. Reform Syn.; Southport New Syn.; Thanet & Distr. Ref. Jewish Com.

Associated Communities: Beit Klal Yisrael (North Kensington Ref. Syn); Coventry Jewish Ref. Syn; Darlington Hebrew Cong.; Swindon Jewish Com.; Totnes Jewish Com.; Cornwall Jewish Com.; Beth Shalom (Munich).

Assembly of Rabbis: *Chairman* Rabbi Sylvia Rothschild. ☎ 020-8460 5460.

Rabbinical Court: (Beit Din). ☎ 020-8349 2568. *Convenor* Rabbi Rodney Mariner.

Associated Schools: Akiva Finchley, Clore Shalom Shenley, Clore Tikva Redbridge (see p.94)

RSY-Netzer (RSGB's Youth & Students); *Shlicha* Liat Konitchki; *Mazkira* Talya Smith; *Student Activities Co-Ord.* Carla Garnelas.

Reform Foundation Trust: *Chairman* Neil W. Benson.

THE STERNBERG CENTRE FOR JUDAISM

80 East End Road, N3 2SY.
☎ 020-8349 5640. Fax 020-8349 5699.

(Est. 1982. Reg. Charity No. 283083) A major national centre for the promotion of Jewish religious, educational, intellectual and cultural matters. The Centre includes a Holocaust Memorial Garden and a Biblical garden and a mikveh; it houses the Akiva School; C. of Reform & Liberal Rabbis; Jewish Museum, Finchley; Leo Baeck College – Centre for Jewish Education; Michael Goulston Educ. Foundation; Manor House Books; Manor House Centre for Psychotherapy & Counselling; Pro-Zion; Reform and Liberal Association of Mohalim; RSGB; and the Masorti New North London Synagogue.

Chairman of Trs. Sir Sigmund Sternberg, KCSG, JP; *T.* H. Cohen; *Dir.* Rabbi Tony Bayfield, MA. *Publ.:* Manna (quarterly).

UNION OF LIBERAL AND PROGRESSIVE SYNAGOGUES

(Jewish Religious Union) 21 Maple St., London W1T 4BE. ☎ 020-7580 1663. Fax 020-7436-4184. Email montagu@ulps.org; Website www.ulps.org.

Est. 1902 for the advancement of Liberal Judaism and to establish and organise Congregations, Groups and Religion Schools on Liberal Jewish principles.

Hon. Life President Rabbi John Rayner, CBE; *Senior V. President* Rabbi Dr Sidney Brichto, MA, DD; *Chairman* David Pick; *Exec. Dir.*; *Admin. Dir.* Michael A. Burman.

Constituents: Barkingside Progressive Syn.; Birmingham Progressive Syn.; Brighton & Hove Progressive Syn.; Bristol & West Progressive Jewish Cong.; Bedfordshire Progressive Syn.; Crawley Jewish Com; Dublin Jewish Progressive Cong.; Ealing L. Syn.; East Anglia Progressive Jewish Com; Finchley Progressive Syn.; Harrow & Wembley Progressive Syn.; Hereford Jewish Com.; Hertsmere Progressive Syn.; Kent L. Jewish Community; Kingston L. Syn.; Leicester Progressive Jewish Cong.; The Liberal Jewish Syn., London; Lincoln Jewish Community; Liverpool Progressive Syn.; North London Progressive Jewish

Community; Northwood & Pinner L. Syn.; Nottingham Progressive Syn.; Peterborough Liberal Jewish Com; South Bucks (Amersham) Liberal Jewish Com.; Southgate Progressive Syn.; South London L. Syn.; Thames Valley (Reading) Progressive Jewish Com.; West Central L. Syn. (Lond.); Woodford Progressive L. Jewish Syn.

Rabbinic Conference: *Chair* Rabbi Frank Dabba Smith.

Associate Communities: Leamington & Distr. Progressive Jewish Group; Oxford; Welshpool; Or Chadash Liberal Jewish Community, Luxembourg.

ULPS Youth Dept/ULPSNYC Netzer. *Dir.*; *Admin.* Sandra Levene.

For further information see under the respective headings.

ASSOCIATION OF REFORM AND LIBERAL MOHALIM

The Sternberg Centre for Judaism, 80 East End Road, London N3 2SY. ☎ 020-8349-4731; Fax 020-8343-0901.

(Est. 1988.) A full list of practitioners may be obtained from constituent synagogues, from RSGB (020-8349 4731), ULPS (020-7580 1663) or by writing to the Association at the Sternberg Centre.

COUNCIL OF REFORM AND LIBERAL RABBIS

The Sternberg Centre, Manor House, 80 East End Road, N3 2SY. ☎ 020-8349 4731. Body est. to represent Progressive Rabbinate (RSGB & ULPS) in Britain.

WELFARE ORGANISATIONS

BRITISH ORT

The British branch of World ORT Union (Est. 1880)

126 Albert Street, London NW1 7NE.

☎ 020-7446 8520. Fax 020-7446 8654. Email british.ort@ort.org; Website www.ort.org/britort.

(Est. 1920. Reg. Charity No. 225975) Education, schooling and vocational training for Jews throughout the world. *Patron* M. Naughton; *President* The Hon. Sir David Sieff; *Co. Chairs* A. Stern, D. Woolf; *Chief Exec.* J. Benjamin.

BRITISH TAY-SACHS FOUNDATION

Now under the administration of Jewish Care (see p.15). ☎ 020-8922 2222.

CHAI-LIFELINE

Shield House, Harmony Way, off Victoria Road, London NW4 2BZ. ☎ Office: 020-8202-2211. Helpline Freephone 0808-808 4567. Fax 020-8202-2111. Email info@chai-lifeline.org.uk; Website www.chai-lifeline.org.uk.

(Reg. Charity No. 1078956). Provides emotional, spiritual and physical support to cancer patients, their families and friends. Freephone help-line, weekly support groups, educational lectures, resource library. Professional counselling available where required. Screening Clinics. Complementary; Therapy Clinics; legal and financial advice; genetic counselling. For more information or appointments contact Sue Heimann. *Co-chairmen* Susan Shipman and Frances Winegarten; *Chief Exec.*

CHILDREN'S AID COMMITTEE CHARITABLE FUND

9 Weymouth Ave., London NW7 3JD.

(Est. 2001. Reg. Charity No. 302933) *Chair* Michael Green; *Vice-Chair* Lira Winston; *T.* Ian Marcusfield; *Sec.* Beverley Hoffman.

FINNART HOUSE SCHOOL TRUST

707 High Road, London N12 0BT.

☎ 020-8445 1670. Fax: 020-8446 7370. Email: finnart@anjy.org.

(Est. 1901. Reg. Charity No. 220917). A charitable trust, the object of which is to relieve children of the Jewish faith who are delinquent, deprived, sick, neglected and in need of care or education. *Chairman of Trustees* Dr Louis Marks; *Clerk* Peter Shaw.

GET (*Religious Divorce*) *Advisory Service*, 23 Ravenshurst Ave., London NW4 4EE. ☎ 020-8203-6314. Trained negotiators to help people who have problems in obtaining a Get.

JEWISH AIDS TRUST
Head Office: Walsingham House, 1331 High Road, London N20 9HR. ☎ 020-8446 8228. Fax 020-8446 8227. Email admin@jat-uk.org; Website www.jat-uk.org.
(Est. 1988. Reg. Charity No. 327936). The Jewish AIDS Trust works across the entire Jewish community. Its aims are to raise awareness of HIV/AIDS; to provide tailor-made education programmes for youth and community groups; and emotional, social, practical and financial support for people living with HIV/AIDS. *Patrons* Professor Michael Adler, CBE, Mrs. Veronica Cohen, Clive Lawton, Rabbi Professor Jonathan Magonet, Lady Morris of Kenwood, The Hon. Miriam Rothschild, Chief Rabbi Jonathan Sacks; *Chairman of Tr.* Harry Rich; *Dir.* Rosalind Collin.

JEWISH ASSOCIATION FOR THE MENTALLY ILL – JAMI
16a North End Rd, Golders Green, London NW11 7PH.
☎ 020-8458 2223. Fax 020-8458 1117. Email ruth.jami@btopenworld.com.
(Reg. Charity No. 1003345). JAMI provides guidance, support and advice for sufferers and carers. Principal objectives are: recognition and support for the mentally ill through education and training; to ensure the provision of efficient and effective Jewish social and welfare services.

JAMI operates day-care facilities and a social club for the mentally ill at JAMI House, 131 Golders Green Road, London NW11. ☎ 020-8731 7319. A new residential home for 15 sufferers is planned to open in Golders Green in 2002.

JEWISH CARE
Stuart Young House, 221 Golders Green Road, London NW11 9DQ. For information and referrals call Jewish Care Direct on 020-8922 2222. For general enquiries call 020-8922 2000. Fax 020-8922 1998. Email info@jcare.org; Website www.jewishcare.org (Est. 1990. Reg. Charity No. 802559)

Formed in 1990 following the merger of the Jewish Blind Society (est. 1819) and the Jewish Welfare Board (est. 1859), Jewish Care incorporates the following charities: Jewish Home & Hospital at Tottenham, Food for the Jewish Poor (Soup Kitchen), British Tay-Sachs Foundation, Clore Manor (previously Waverley Manor), Friends of the London Jewish Hospital, Hyman Fine House (previously Brighton & Hove Jewish Home), Stepney Jewish (B'nai B'rith) Clubs & Settlements, and Sinclair House – Redbridge Jewish Youth & Community Centre. Jewish Care also works in partnership with Otto Schiff Housing Association (OSHA) and the Jewish Association for the Mentally Ill (JAMI).

Jewish Care is the largest provider of health and social care services for the Jewish community in the UK. Its services include care for older people and people with mental health problems, physical disabilities or visual impairments, as well as people suffering from strokes, Parkinson's disease, Alzheimer's disease and other forms of dementia. Services are also available for unemployed people, Holocaust survivors and refugees, and people who have been bereaved, separated or divorced. A carers support service helps carers of people with health or disability issues, including addictive disorders. In addition, programmes for children and younger people are run in community centres.

Its resources include: residential/nursing homes, day care centres, special day care centres, youth and community centres, hostels, sheltered accommodation, social work teams, home care services and an Employment Resource Centre. Establishments in London are listed on p.99. *President* The Lord Levy; *Chairman* Malcolm Dagul; *Chief Exec.* Jeremy Oppenheim; *Fin. Dir.* Henry Solomon.

JEWISH CHILD'S DAY
707 High Road, North Finchley, London N12 0BT
☎ 020-8446 8804. Fax: 020-8446 7370. Email: info@jewishchildsday.co.uk; Website http://www.jewish childsday.co.uk.
(Est. 1947, Reg. Charity No. 209266) Raises funds to distribute to agencies providing services to Jewish children in need of special care throughout the world. Provides equipment of all kinds and supports specific projects for children who are blind, deaf, mentally, physically or multi-handicapped, orphaned, neglected, deprived, abused, refugee or in need of medical care. *Life President* Mrs. J. Jacobs; *Chairman* Mrs. J. Moss; *T.* S. Moss, O.B.E.; *Exec. Dir.* Peter Shaw.

JEWISH LESBIAN AND GAY HELPLINE
BM Jewish Helpline, London WC1N 3XX
☎ 020-7706 3123.
(Est. 1987; Reg. Charity No. 1008035.) An information, support and confidential counselling service for Jewish lesbians, gay men, bisexuals, those unsure about their sexuality, and their family and friends. It also provides a programme of outreach, educating individuals and organisations to be more aware of the needs and experiences of Jewish lesbians, gay men and bisexuals. The phone line is open every Monday and Wednesday 7.00 p.m. to 10.00 p.m. (except festivals and Bank Holidays). *Patrons* Leo Abse; Rabbi A. M. Bayfield; Rabbi Lionel Blue; Prof. Sir Herman Bondi, K.C.B., F.R.S; Maria Charles; Dr. Wendy Greengross; Miriam Margolyes; Rabbi Julia Neuberger; Claire Rayner; *Co-ord.* Jack Gilbert; *Sec.* David Marks.

JEWISH MARRIAGE COUNCIL
23 Ravenshurst Avenue, NW4 4EE.
☎ 020-8203 6311. Fax 020-8203 8727. Email info@jmc-uk.org; Website www.jmc-uk.org.
(Est. 1946) The Council provides the following services: a counselling service for individual, marital and family problems; it assists anyone with a relationship problem whether they are single, married, divorced or separated (020-8203 6311); preventative counselling in the form of groups for engaged couples, newly-weds, adolescents as well as assertiveness and social skills courses; support groups for divorced and separated people; it provides a mediation service (Dialogue), a Get Advisory Service (020-8203 6314) (see p.15), Connect Marriage Bureau (020-8203 5207) and Miyad the Nationwide Jewish Crisis Helpline (08457-581 999). *Dir.*

JMC Manchester: Levi House, Bury Old Road, Manchester M8 6FX. ☎ 0161-795 1240. Appointments 0161-740 5764; 08457 585159.

JEWISH WOMEN'S AID (JWA)
JWA, PO Box 2670, London N12 9ZE.
☎ 020-8445 8060. Fax 020-8445 0305; Helpline 0800-591203. Email jwa@dircon.co.uk.
(Est. 1992. Reg. Charity No. 1047045) JWA aims to break the silence surrounding domestic violence through education and awareness-raising programmes. JWA operates a freephone confidential national helpline and the first Refuge in Europe for Jewish women and their children fleeing domestic violence is now open. Informal Drop-In groups meet weekly and counselling, support and befriending services are available. *H. President* Judith Usiskin; *Chair.*

THE MANOR HOUSE CENTRE FOR PSYCHOTHERAPY AND COUNSELLING
The Sternberg Centre, 80 East End Road, N3 2SY.
☎ 020-8371 0180. Fax 01923 855141. Email admin@manorhousecentre.org.uk.
(Reg. Charity No. 1054223) The Centre provides: Certificate in Counselling Skills; Diploma in psychodynamic counselling (accredited by the British Association for Counselling and Psychotherapy); short courses for continuing professional development; individually designed courses; counselling referral service.

MAZAL TOV: THE PROGRESSIVE JEWISH MARRIAGE BUREAU
c/o 28 St Johns Wood Rd, London NW8 7HA. ☎ 020-7289 8591. Email mazaltov@ulps.org.
(Est. 1995. Reg. Charity no. 236590) Non-profit making marriage bureau under aegis of the Union of Liberal and Progressive Synagogues. *Chairperson Management Team* Rita Adler; *Admin* Ruth Green.

NATHAN AND ADOLPHE HAENDLER CHARITY
c/o World Jewish Relief, 74-80 Camden Street, London NW1 0EG.
☎ 020-7691 1771. Fax: 020-7691 1780. Email wjri@wjr.org.uk.
This charity is governed by a scheme which was approved by the Royal Courts of Justice in 1928, whereby the income of the Fund is applicable by the Trustees for the purpose of assisting poor Jews who, in consequence of religious persecution or other misfortune, have come or shall come to take refuge in England. Trustees now World Jewish Relief.

NATIONAL NETWORK OF JEWISH SOCIAL HOUSING
c/o Harmony Close, Princes Park Avenue, London NW11 0JJ. ☎ 020-8381 4901. Fax 020-8458 1772.
Co-ordinates the work of Jewish housing associations, enabling them to share information and assess the housing needs in the Jewish community. *President* Fred Worms, OBE; *Chairman* Robert Manning.

NATIONAL TAY-SACHS AND BIOCHEMICAL GENETICS CENTRE
1st Floor, Ward 2, Booth Hall Children's Hospital, Charlestown Road, Blackley, Manchester, M9 7AA. ☎ 0161-795 7000 Ext. 5094. Website www.zyworld.com/taysachs.
(Reg. Charity No. 326403). Screening and counselling services for Tay-Sachs, Gauchers, Nieman-Pick etc. Community screening sessions in the north of England. Postal screening UK and Europe. Informative literature for students and families. Tay-Sachs Coordinator, any morning, or leave message on 24-hour answerphone. No fixed charge. Donations welcome. Medical enquiries to Dr. Sybil Simon (Research Centre).

OTTO SCHIFF HOUSING ASSOCIATION (OSHA)
The Bishop's Avenue, N2 0BG.
☎ 020-8209 0022. Fax 020-8201 8089.
(Reg. Charity No. 210396. Est. 1934.) Merged in 2000 with Jewish Care, OSHA has been the specialist provider of residential, nursing care and sheltered housing in the UK to Jewish refugees from Nazi persecution for over 60 years. Services include short-term respite care, daycare and specialist care for people with dementia. *Inquiries* ☎ 020-8922 2222; *Chairman* Ashley Mitchell; *H.T.* Frank Harding; *Hon. Sec.* Andrew Kaufman; Harry Kleeman, CBE, Ernie Ellis, Margot Gremson, Rosemary Lewis, Jeoff Samson; *Gp. Man.* Gaby Wills.

TAY-SACHS SCREENING CENTRE
Genetics Centre, 7th Floor, New Guy's House, Guy's Hospital, St. Thomas

Street, London SE1 9RT. ☎ 020-7955 4648. Fax 020-7955 2550.
Provides information, carrier testing and genetic counselling for Tay-Sachs disease, and a walk-in clinic. *Sec.* Mrs R. Demant; *Genetic Counsellor* Sara Levene.

WORLD JEWISH RELIEF
74–80 Camden Street, London NW1 OEG. ☎ 020-7691 1771. Fax 020-7691 1780. Email info@wjr.org.uk. Website www.tolife.info.uk.
(Est. 1933. Reg. Charity No. 290767) World Jewish Relief is the overseas (non-Israel) aid arm of the Jewish community of the United Kingdom. Currently working mainly in Eastern Europe, especially the Ukraine, the former Yugoslavia and Bulgaria, providing humanitarian aid and vital welfare services. Supports children's homes, the elderly and welfare centres, through both financial and 'Gifts-in-Kind' fundraising. *Chairman* Nigel Layton; *Exec. Dir.* Vivienne Lewis.

Jewish Refugees Committee (Est. 1933) ☎ 020-7691 1782. Email jrc@wjr.org.uk. This committee, which originally organised the 'Kindertransport' evacuation of Jews from Nazi Europe, currently provides assistance and support to Jewish refugees fleeing persecution to the UK. Work includes support for asylum-seekers and Bosnian refugees. A member of INTERCO (International Council on Jewish Social andWelfare Services), the cross-communal body co-ordinating the response to Jewish social and welfare services in the UK. *Chairman* Mrs J. Cohen, J.P.

REFUGEE ORGANISATIONS

45 AID SOCIETY HOLOCAUST SURVIVORS
46 Amery Road, Harrow, Middx HA1 3UQ.
☎ 020-8422 1512.
(Est. 1963) The Society consists mainly of survivors who came to England in 1945/6 and others who have immigrated subsequently. It maintains close links with members who have emigrated to Israel, USA, Canada and other countries. The Society is active in the community, helps members as well as others in need. It furthers Holocaust education and other charitable causes.
President Sir Martin Gilbert; *Chairman* Ben Helfgott, MBE; *V. Chairman* Harry Balsam; *T.* Krvlik Wilder; *Sec.* Mick Zwirek.

ACJR (Association of Children of Jewish Refugees)
☎ 020-8427 4091. Email info@acjr.org.uk; Website www.acjr.org.uk.
Cultural and social group for people whose parents were victims of or who fled from Nazi persecution in the 1930s and 1940s. *Publ.* Monthly newsletter. *Chair* Oliver Walter.

AJR CHARITABLE TRUST (Association of Jewish Refugees in Great Britain)
1 Hampstead Gate, 1A Frognal, London NW3 6AL.
☎ 020-7431 6161. Fax: 020-7431 8454. Email enquiries@ajr.org.uk; Website www.ajr.org.uk.
(Reg. Charity No. 211239). The Trust's aim is to assist Jewish refugees from Nazi oppression and their families, primarily from Central Europe, by providing a wide range of services. It acts as the central office for Holocaust claims. *Hd of Admin.* Carol Rossen; *Hd of Media* Ronald Channing; *Hd of Finance* Gordon Greenfield. *Publ.* AJR Journal (monthly).

ANNE FRANK TRUST UK
PO Box 11880, London N6 4LN.
☎ 020-8340 9077. Email afet@afet.org.uk; Website www.annefrank.org.uk.
The Trust helps teachers to educate against prejudice, bigotry, anti semitism and

racism. 'The Anne Frank, a History for Today exhibition' tours communities and campuses. The Trust launched a major schools project, 'Moral Courage – Who's Got It?', in 2002.

ASSOCIATION OF JEWISH EX-BERLINERS (AJEB)
45 Brockley Ave., Stanmore, Middx HA7 4LT.
☎ 020-8958 8814. Fax 020-8958 9703. Email alf-ella@ascali.co.uk.
(Est. 1990) To exchange shared experiences of the most traumatic period of Jewish European history at social gatherings as well as record them in writings, individually and collectively. *Chairman* A. Silverman; *T.* Manfred Alweiss, 22 Middleton Rd., London NW11 7NS. ☎ 020-8455 0115. *Publ.* 'So What's New?'.

ASSOCIATION OF JEWS FROM EGYPT (AJE)
4 Folly Close, Radlett, Herts WD7 8DR.
☎ 01923 856801. Email maurice.maleh@bnpparibas.com.
(Est. 2002) To preserve the cultural and social links of Jews from Egypt. *Tr/President* Maurice Maleh, 4 Folley Close, Radlett, Herts WD7 8DR; *Chairman* Esther Dee, 15 Broadlands Lodge, Broadlands Road, London N6 4AW; *Membership Sec.* Gerard de Botton, 1/6 Crescent Mews, London N22 7GG; *Hon. Sec.* Ted Nahmias, 121 Cholmeley Gardens, Fortune Green Road, London NW6 1AA.

CLUB 1943: ANGLO-GERMAN CULTURAL FORUM
51 Belsize Square, NW3 (Synagogue)
☎ 01442-54360.
The Society's aim and purpose was to preserve and develop their cultural standard attained in the country they had to leave. *Chairman* Hans Seelig, 27 Wood End Lane, Hemel Hempstead. ☎ 01442-54360; *Publ. Rel.* Julia Schwarz ☎020-8209 0318; *Sec.* Leni Ehrenberg. ☎ 020-7263 0434.

HOLOCAUST SURVIVORS' CENTRE
Corner of Parson Street/Church Road, London NW4 1QA.
☎ 020-8202 9844. Fax 020-8202 5534. Email hsc@jcare.org.
Dir. Judith Hassan; *Co-ord.* Rachelle Lazarus.
And **SHALVATA**
Parson Street/Corner of Church Road, London NW4 1QA
☎ 020-8203 9033. Fax 020-8201 5534. Email shalvata@jcare.org.
The HSC is a social centre for Holocaust survivors and refugees. The Centre is administered by Jewish Care with funding from World Jewish Relief and Jewish Care. Testimonies are recorded.

Shalvata, funded and administered by Jewish Care, is a therapy centre for Holocaust survivors, Kindertransporten and refugees, and their families. It is also known as a training and consultation service for professionals working with war trauma. In conjunction with World Jewish Relief, Shalvata is currently working with a group of Bosnian refugees.

HSC and Shalvata together provide a wide range of support services for survivors and their families.

POLISH JEWISH EX-SERVICEMEN'S ASSOCIATION
12 Antrim Grove, London NW3 4XR.
(Est. 1945.) To aid and protect Polish-Jewish ex-Servicemen in the UK, look after the interests of Polish-Jewish refugees, perpetuate the memory of Jewish martyrs of Nazi persecution. *Chairman* L. Kurzer; *V. Chairman* L. Feit; *H. Sec.* L. Kleiner. *H. T.* J. Tigner.

POLISH JEWISH REFUGEE FUND
143 Brondesbury Pk., NW2 5JL ☎ 020-8451 3425.
Chairman W. Schindler; *H. Sec.* Mrs. R. Gluckstein.

SOCIETY OF FRIENDS OF JEWISH REFUGEES
Balfour House, 741 High Road, Finchley N12 0BQ.
☎ 020-8446 1477. Fax 020-8446 1180.
(Reg. Charity No.227889.) *Chairman* D.M. Cohen; *H. Sec.* I. Connick; *H.T.* P.C. Leach; *Fin. Sec.* E.H. Kraines.

ORGANISATIONS CONCERNED WITH THE JEWS OF EASTERN EUROPE

BRITISH COUNCIL FOR JEWS IN EASTERN EUROPE
Salisbury Hall, Park Road, Hull HU3 1TD.
☎ 01482 326848 (office), 01482 353981 (private). Fax 01482 568756.
(Est. 1990.) Support for Jewish revival in Eastern Europe. *Publ.* Working for a Cause.
(Belarus office: Apt. 19, 69a Pervomayskaya Str, Mogilev 212030. ☎ +7 1222 25 39 34 (Igor Ilyin)).

THE EAST EUROPEAN JEWISH HERITAGE PROJECT
26 South Street, Oxford OX2 0BE.
☎ 01865 429360. Email eejhp@yahoo.com. Website www.eejhp.tripod.ca.
(Reg. Charity No. 1061629) The EEJHP works in East Europe, primarily the Republic of Belarus, to promote Jewish cultural and material self-sufficiency. There is currently an emphasis on medical programmes for the young and elderly, and the EEJHP also engages in heritage activities, including a long-term oral history project about pre-Holocaust life and the restoration of sites of Jewish significance. *Exec. Dir.* F. J. Swartz; *Dirs* D. Solomon, Jane Buekett.

EXODUS 2000
Sternberg Centre for Judaism, 80 East End Road, London N3 2SY.
☎ 020-8349 5651. Fax 020-8349 5699. Email linda.kann@reformjudaism.org.uk.
RSGB and ULPS Campaign for Progressive Judaism in Eastern Europe. Exodus has a national exec. and grps. in many Reform Syns. Its major areas of work are: (i) supporting the growth of Progressive Judaism in the former Soviet Union; (ii) twinning with new Eastern European Progressive Congregations; (iii) sending Rabbis and lay educators to teach. Exodus 2000 works closely with the World Union of Progressive Judaism in Israel and America. *Chairman* Rabbi David Soetendorp; *Admin* Linda Kann; *T.*

JEWISH RELIEF AND EDUCATION TRUST (JRET)
75 Abbotts Gardens, London N2.
☎ 020-8883 7006.
(Est. 1991. Reg. Charity No. 1007025.) The support of Jewish student and youth activities in the former Soviet Union. *Chairman* Adam Rose.

NATIONAL COUNCIL FOR JEWS IN THE FORMER SOVIET UNION
Contact: 6 Links Drive, Elstree, Herts WD6 3PS.
☎ 020-8953 8764.
(Est. 1975) Initiates and coordinates activities on behalf of Jews in the FSU including safeguarding and promoting their human, civic, religious and cultural rights. It acts as the umbrella org. for all bodies in Britain with similar objects. The Council is the voice of the community to Government and other bodies in the UK & internationally on FSU Jewish issues. *President* E. Tabachnik Q.C.; *Acting Chairman* Jonathan Arkush.

WOMEN'S CAMPAIGN FOR SOVIET JEWRY (The 35's)
Pannell House, 779/781 Finchley Road, NW11 8DN.
☎ 020-8458 7148/9. Fax 020-8458 9971.
An activist organisation which helps disadvantaged families after they arrive in Israel. The campaign publicises the situation in the former Soviet Union and in Israel through a regular newsletter and through contacts with the media and professional and religious associations. Support is given to ex-Refuseniks, to children in need and to the new Olim in Israel with the organisation of the annual ONE TO ONE sponsored treks in Israel and the One to One Children's Fund. *Co-Chairmen* Mrs Rita Eker, MBE, Mrs Margaret Rigal.

ZIONIST ORGANISATIONS

BRITISH ALIYAH MOVEMENT
Balfour House, 741 High Road, Finchley, London N12 0BQ.
☎ 020-8369 5220. Fax 020-8369 5221. Email bam@jazouk.org. Website www.jazouk.org.aliyah.
A support organisation providing practical information for future Olim and promoting Aliyah. Local groups around Britain meet regularly with guest speakers and Shlichim in attendance on Israel-related topics. *Co-ord* A. Schlagman.

BRITISH EMUNAH (Child Resettlement Fund)
Shield House, Harmony Way, off Victoria Rd., London NW4 2BZ.
☎ 020-8203 6066. Fax 020-8203 6668. Email british.emunah@btinternet.com. Website britishemunah.org
(Est. 1933. Reg. Charity No. 215398) A charity organisation with groups throughout the country working to support 32 projects in Israel. *H. L. President* The Lady Jakobovits; *H. President* Mrs Elaine Sacks; *Founder President* Mrs Gertie Landy; *Exec. President* Mrs Guggy Grahame; *Exec. Vice President* Mrs Vera Garbacz; *Chairman* Mrs Lilian Brodie; *Israel Liaison Chairman* Mrs D. Kaufman.

BRITISH OLIM RELATIVES ASSOCIATION (BORA)
Balfour House, 741 High Road, Finchley, N12 0BQ
☎ 020-8343 9756/446 1477. Fax 020-8446 0639.
(Est. 1984.) To maintain closer links between Brit. immigrants in Israel and their relatives in UK by providing services and concessions whenever possible, including reduced air fare, an emergency phone or fax link with Israel and monthly meetings. *President* Mrs. E. Imber-Lithman; *Chairman* J. Daniels.

BRITISH WIZO
105/107 Gloucester Place, London W1U 6BY.
☎ 020-7486 2691. Fax 020-7486 7521. Finance Fax 020-7486 0703. Email central@britishwizo.org.uk; Website www.britishwizo.org.uk.
(Est. 1918; Reg. Charity No. 296444) WIZO (FWZ) is the British Branch of World WIZO and a constituent of the Zionist Fed. of Great Brit. & Ireland and is non-party. It has some 180 affiliated groups with over 11,000 members. Its mission is to help support and strengthen families in Israel through its network of groups and independent members. *President* Sarah Glyn; *Chairman* Michele Vogel; *H. Sec.* Loraine Warren; *Ts.* Jill Show, Gill Woodbridge; *Exec. Dir.* Marcus Fielding. *Publ.* Vision Magazine (2 issues a year).

GENERAL ZIONIST ORGANISATION OF GREAT BRITAIN
c/o Balfour House, 741 High Road, N12 0BQ.
Chairman A. Stanton; *T.* J. Chart; *H. Sec.* Mrs. Y. M. Stanton.

ISRAEL EMBASSY: 2 Palace Green, Kensington, W8 4QB. ☎ 020-7957 9500. Fax 020-7957 9555. Email info-assist@london.mfa.gov.il. Website www.israel-embassy. org.uk. Opening Hours: Mon.-Thur. 09.00-17.30 and Fri. 09.00-13.30. *Defence Sec.* 2A Palace Green, Kensington, W8 4QB; ☎ 020-7957 9548. *Consular Sec.* 15A Old Court Place, Kensington, W8 4QB. ☎ 020-7957 9516; *Ambassador* H. E. Zvi Shtauber; *Min. Plenipotentiary* Zvi Rav-Ner; *Min.-Cllr.* D. Shaham (Public Aff.); M. Harari (Political Aff.); Carmela Shamir (Cultural Aff.); Shuli Davidovitch (Press); M. Langerman (Economic Aff.); M. Hacohen (Comm. Aff.); Techiya Weinstein (Consular Aff.); E. Mazor (Admin.).

JEWISH AGENCY FOR ISRAEL
London office: 741 High Road, Finchley, N12 0BQ.
☎ 020-8369 5200. Fax 020-8369 5201. Email general@jazouk.org.
The reconstituted Jewish Agency, consisting of representatives of the World Zionist Organisation and of bodies raising funds on behalf of Israel, has assumed the following responsibilities: Aliyah; Rescue and Absorption; Jewish Education; Youth Care and Training; Social Welfare services for immigrants; partnership 2000; Project Renewal. *Chairman of the Exec.* Salai Meridor; *Hd. UK Delegation* Z. Kahana.

JEWISH NATIONAL FUND (JNF)
Head Office: 58-70 Edgware Way, Edgware, Middx HA8 8GQ.
☎ 020-8421 7600 (JNF); 020-8421 7601 (KKL Wills & Bequests); 020-8421 7602 (KKL Charity Accounts); 020-8421 7603 (Education). Fax 020-8905 4299. Email info@jnf.co.uk.
President Gail Seal; *Jt. Vice-Presidents* Stanley Lovatt, Jeffrey Zinkin, F.C.A.; *H. T.* David Kibel, F.C.A.; *Chief Exec.* Simon Winters, M.IDM, M.IOD; *Admin.* Joan Lozowick.
JNF Charitable Trust: *Chairman* Gail Seal; *Company Sec.* Harvey Bratt, LL.B.
KKL Executor & Trustee Co. Ltd.: *Chairman* Jeffrey Zinkin; *Company Sec.* Harvey Bratt, LL.B. Objects: Bequests, advisory and covenant services for charity.
Education Department: *Chairman* Helen Rosen. Supplies JNF/Israel educational resources to schools, nurseries, religion classes, youth movements and others. Arranges Bar/Bat Mitzvah ceremonies in Israel. Organises events in London and Provinces.
Bloomsbury Advertising Agency Ltd.: *Company Sec.* Harvey Bratt, LL.B.

LIKUD-HERUT MOVEMENT OF GREAT BRITAIN
143-145 Brondesbury Park, NW2 5JL.
☎ 020-8451 0003. Fax 020-8459 8766.
(Est. 1970) To promote the Zionist ideology as conceived by Ze'ev Jabotinsky. Member of Likud Haolami and affiliated to National Zionist Council of Gt. Britain and a member of the Board of Deputies. *Life President* E. Graus; *Life Vice-Presidents* M. Benjamin, J. Gellert; *Chairman* R. Jacobs; *V. Chairmen* B. Gordon, LL.B., M. Kahtan; *H. T.* G. Avis; *H. Sec.* M. Malinsky; *Memb. Sec.* M. Kayne; *Exec. Dir.* D. M. Jacobs.
Affiliated Organisations: Young Likud Herut; (Brit Nashim Herut Women's League); Betar-Tagar, Brit Hashmonayim.

MERETZ FOR A DEMOCRATIC ISRAEL
Hashomer House, 37A Broadhurst Gardens, NW6 3BN.
☎ 020-7328 5451. Fax 020-7624 6748.
(Reg. Charity No. 269903) An Anglo-Jewish organisation which identifies with Meretz' world outlook and strives to vitalise Anglo-Jewry in the spirit of Jewish humanism and democracy. It seeks to promote Socialist Zionism, the unity of the Jewish people, aliya, social justice in Israel, Jewish educ., culture and peace as vital elements of Zionism, complete political, social and economic equality for all Israeli

citizens, with religion left to the conscience of each individual. Affiliated to: World Union of Meretz; Z. Fed.; BoD.

MIZRACHI FEDERATION
2b Golders Green Road, NW11 8LH.
☎ 020-8455 2243. Fax 020-8455 2244. Email office@mizrachi.org.uk; Website www.mizrachi.org.uk.
(Est. 1918) *President* A. L. Handler; *Chairman* S. Taylor; *Jt. Ts* T. Berman, N. Cohen; *Exec. Dir.* E. Ovits; *Admin.* D. Ahronee; *Steering Gp* Rabbi E. Mirvis, E. Abeles, H. Bratt, T. Fraenkel, J. Kaye, M. Weinberg, D. Whitfield. *Publ.* Jewish Review.
Constituent Orgs.: British Emunah; Bnei Akiva; Bachad Fellowship.
Affiliated Orgs.: Tehilla; Torah Mitzion; Yavne Olami; Mifal Hatorah.
Mobile Midrasha – UK Centre for the Studies of Eretz Yisrael.

POALE ZION–LABOUR ZIONIST MOVEMENT
(Affiliated to the British Labour Party.)
PO Box 695, Harrow, Middx HA3 0HF.
☎ 020-8261 4574. Fax 020-8907 2411. Email lmnerva@aol.com.
Poale Zion, the Brit. section of the World Labour Zionist Movement, is the sister party of the Israel Labour Party. It encourages aliya and demands effective internat. guarantees for the civil and political rights of Jews and other minorities. It is affiliated to the BoD, the Z. Fed. and the Jewish Council for Racial Equality. *Chair* J. Rodin; *V. Chair* L. Nerva; *H. T.* Nadia Nathan; *H. Sec.* Dr J. Bara.

PRO-ZION: PROGRESSIVE RELIGIOUS ZIONISTS
The Sternberg Centre for Judaism, 80 East End Road, N3 2SY.
☎ 020-8349 4731.
(Est. 1978) To work for full legal and rel. rights for Progressive Judaism in Israel, to affirm the centrality in Jewish life of the State of Israel. *Chairman* Estelle Gilston; *H. Sec.* M. Elliott; *H. T.* B. Noah.

UJIA (United Jewish Israel Appeal)
Balfour House, 741 High Road, Finchley N12 0BQ.
☎ 020-8369 5000. Fax 020-8369 5001. Email central@ujia.org.
(Reg. Charity No. 1060078, Reg. Company 3295115) The UJIA is the leading supporter of Israel and young Jewish people in the UK. Through a wide range of projects in Israel, the UJIA reaches out to some of the country's most needy populations – from new immigrants and underprivileged children to terror victims. The UJIA also works to ensure a Jewish future in the UK, supporting a variety of educational programmes for young people. *H. Presidents* Chief Rabbi Jonathan Sacks, The Lord Levy, The Rt. Hon. The Lord Woolf; *Hon. V. Presidents* The Lord Janner QC, Sir Jack Lyons, The Lord Mishcon QC, DL, Gerald M. Ronson, Cyril Stein, Fred S. Worms, OBE; *Presidents* Sir Trevor Chinn, CVO, Brian Kerner; *V. Presidents* Stanley Cohen, OBE, Alan Fox, Ronald Preston, Stephen Rubin, Anthony Spitz; *Bd. Chairman* David M. Cohen; *Chief Exec.* Benjamin Leon; *Fin. Dir.* Eldred Kraines, CA (SA).

UNITED ZIONISTS OF GREAT BRITAIN & IRELAND
(affiliated to the World Confederation of United Zionists)
Balfour House, 741 High Road, London N12 0BQ.
☎ 020-8455 0987. Fax 020-8455 0987.
(Est. 1899) A founder of the World Confederation of General Zionists (originally the British Zionist Federation was affiliated to the World Confederation until the 1980s). The United Zionists are the British and Irish constituents of The World

Confederation of United Zionists, the only Zionist faction within the WZO which is not affiliated to or associated with any Israeli political party. The United Zionists believe in a Zionism which takes a general approach to all issues. *Chairman* Sidney L. Shipton, LL.B MBA; *H. T.* Steven Elstein, M.Chem.; *H. Sec.* Judith Shipton.

WORLD ZIONIST ORGANISATION
741 High Road, Finchley, N12 0BQ.
☎ 020-8446 1144. Fax 020-8446 8296. Email general@jazouk.org.
The WZO was established by the first Zionist Congress, which met in Basle on August 29, 1897. The aim of the Org., as defined in the programme adopted by the Basle Congress, was to secure for the Jewish people a home in Palestine guaranteed by public law. At the Congress a constitution providing for a self-governing World Organisation, with the Zionist Congress as the supreme body, was adopted.

In 1908 the Z.O. embarked upon the work of practical settlement and development in Palestine. When the Z.O. was recognised in 1922 as the Jewish Agency under the Palestine Mandate, it was already responsible for a wide field of development and settlement activities and it commanded the support of important Jewish groups throughout the world.

The aims of Zionism, as enunciated in the 'New Jerusalem Programme' adopted by the 27th World Zionist Congress in June, 1968, are:

The unity of the Jewish People and the centrality of Israel in Jewish Life;

The ingathering of the Jewish people in its historic homeland, Eretz Israel, through Aliya from all countries;

The strengthening of the State of Israel which is based on the prophetic vision of justice and peace;

The preservation of the identity of the Jewish people through the fostering of Jewish and Hebrew education and of Jewish spiritual and cultural values.

ZIONIST FEDERATION OF GT. BRITAIN AND IRELAND
Balfour House, 741 High Road, N12 0BQ.
☎ 020-8343 9756. Fax 020-8446 0639. Email zion-fed@dircon.co.uk.
(Est. 1899) The Zionist Federation is an umbrella organisation encompassing most of the Zionist organisations and individuals in the country and, as such, represents the Zionist Movement in the United Kingdom. Its function is to support, co-ordinate and facilitate the work of all its affiliates nationwide. The Zionist Federation aims to encourage the participation of Jews in Zionist activities including education, culture, Hebrew language and Israel information, underpinned by our belief that the main goal of Zionism is Aliyah.

Executive: *President* Prof. Eric Moonman, OBE; *Hon. President* Geoffrey Gelberg; *Chairman* Ralph Stern; *V. Chairmen* Estelle Gilston, Steve Elstein; *Hon. Sec.* Adrian Korsner; *Hon. T.* Joel Rose; *Dir.* Alan Aziz; *Admin.* Barbara Simia; *PR* Rona Hart; *Marketing* Laurence Stein; *Finance* Nadia Nathan.

Committees: Constitution – *Chairman* Sidney Shipton; Finance – *Chairman* Joel Rose; Fundraising – *Chairman* Muriel Thompson; Israel Response – *Chairmen* E. Moonman, Rona Hart; Israel Conference – *Chairman* Estelle Gilston; Yom Ha'atzmaut – *Chairman* Jacques Weisser; Young Leadership Israel Connect – *Chairman* Steven Elstein.

OTHER ORGANISATIONS CONCERNED WITH ISRAEL AND ISRAELI ORGANISATIONS

ACADEMIC STUDY GROUP ON ISRAEL AND THE MIDDLE EAST
PO Box 7545, London NW2 2QZ.
☎ 020-7435 6803. Fax 020-7794 0291. Email info@foi-asg.org.
(Reg. Charity No. 801772) An academic org. which aims at forging and

expanding contacts between academics in this country and their colleagues in Israel and develop among them an interest in their corresponding fields in Israel. Organises study missions to Israel and lectures and meetings on campuses throughout Britain. *President* Sir Walter Bodmer, Hertford College, Oxon; *Chairman* Prof. J. Friend, Hull Univ.; *V. Chairman* Prof. Graham Zellick, University of London; *T.* Aviva Petrie, Eastman Dental Institute; *Dir.* J. D. A. Levy.

AKIM
(Est. 1964. Reg. Charity No. 241458) To assist with the rehabilitation of mentally handicapped children in Israel. *President* Sir S. W. Samuelson CBE. *V. Presidents* Judge B. Lightman, L. Gamsa; *Jt. Chairmen* A. Broza, D.R. Marlowe; *Jt.H.T.* W. Raychbart, V. Cohen. *Corr. to*: 22 Golf Close, Stanmore, Middx HA7 2PP. ☎ 020-8954 2772. Fax 020-8954 2999. *H. Sec.* Mrs B. Kober.

ANGLO-ISRAEL ARCHAEOLOGICAL SOCIETY
126 Albert St., London NW1 7NE.
☎ 020-7691 1467. Website www.aias.org.uk.
(Reg. Charity No. 220367) Lectures on recent archaeological discoveries in Israel, publication of annual research bulletin and award of travel grants to students to participate in excavations in Israel. *Chairman* Prof. H.G.M. Williamson, Oriental Instit., Pusey Lane, Oxford OX1 2LE; *Admin.* Mrs D. Davis.

ANGLO-ISRAEL ASSOCIATION
9 Bentinck Street, W1U 2EL.
☎ 020-7486 2300/935 9505. Fax 020-7935 4690. Email info@angloisraelassocation.com.
(Est. 1949. Registered Charity No. 313523) The purpose of the Association is to promote wider and more positive understanding of Israel in the UK; to encourage exchanges in both directions; and generally to support activities which foster goodwill between the two countries. *Founder* The late Brigadier-General Sir Wyndham Deedes, CMG, DSO; *Hon. President* The Israeli Ambassador; *Chairman of C.* The Hon. Sir David Sieff; *Chairman Exec. Cttee* Lady Sainsbury; *H.T.* G.R. Pinto; *Dir.* Geoffrey Paul, OBE.

THE BALFOUR DIAMOND JUBILEE TRUST
67 Addison Road, London W14 8JL.
Fax 020-7371 6656.
(Est. 1977. Reg. Charity No. 276353) To consolidate and strengthen cultural relations between the UK and Israel. Provides the community with a diverse programme of topical activities throughout the year – in literature and the arts. Makes financial support available to individuals and small organisations – both in the UK and Israel – whose work will make an enduring cultural contribution.

The Lord Goodman Fellowship Award, a joint venture with the British Council and the Foreign & Commonwealth Office, encourages the annual exchange of distinguished scholars between the UK and Israel by awarding scholarships for up to a full year of study or research in a field related to the Environment (see www.britcoun.org/israel/isrgoodmantm). *Exec. Sec.* Sasha Treuherz.

BANK LEUMI (UK) plc.
London Office: 20 Stratford Place, London W1C 1BG.
☎ 020-7907 8000.
One office in London; Northern branch in Manchester; subsidiary in Jersey, C.I., Bank Leumi Overseas Trust Corporation, Jersey, Ltd. Incorporated in 1959 as a subsidiary of Bank Leumi Le-Israel B.M. Originally established in London in 1902 as the financial instrument of the Zionist Movement under the name of Jewish

Colonial Tr. *Chairman* E. Roff; *Dep. Chairman* Sir Bernard Schreier; *Man. Dir. & Chief Exec.* U. Rosen; *Hd. Corp. Banking* C. Cumberland; *T.* M. Shear; *Company Sec.* M. P. Levene.

BEN GURION UNIVERSITY FOUNDATION
1st Fl., Bouverie House, 154 Fleet St., London EC4A 2JD.
☎ 020-7353 1395. Fax 020-7353 1396. Email bengurionfoundation@blplaw.com.
(Est. 1974. Reg. Charity No. 276203). To promote Ben-Gurion University of the Negev in Beer-Sheva, Israel, as an international centre for academic excellence and advanced research in medicine, science and desert agriculture – by donations, books, equipment and subscriptions. *Presidents* The Lord Weidenfeld; The Countess of Avon; *V. President* Suzanne Zlotowski; *Chairman* Harold Paisner.

BRITISH & EUROPEAN MACHAL ASSOCIATION
6 Broadlands Close, London N6 4AF.
☎/Fax 020-8348 8695.
MACHAL (Mitnadvei Chutz L'Aretz). Volunteers from abroad in the 1948 Israel War of Independence. To collect stories and memorabilia appertaining to Machal's crucial contribution for a new historical museum in Israel. To publicise Machal's endeavour and sacrifice. *Co-ordinator* Stanley Medicks. *Sec.* Sidney Lightman, FIS.

BRITISH COMMITTEE OF BNEI BRAK HOSPITAL
273 Green Lanes, N4 2EX.
☎ 020-8800 2996
European Off. 21D Devonshire Place, W1. Est. 1979 as part of communal efforts in many countries to build an Orthodox hosp. with a special cardiac dept. in Bnei Brak. Maternity and other wards are open. *Chairman* Dr. L. Freedman; *V. Chairmen* Dayan M. Fisher, V. Lucas, F.S.V.A.; *H. T.* B. Freshwater; *Med. Dir.-Gen.* Dr. M. Rothschild.

BRITISH COMMITTEE OF KEREN YALDENU
(Est. 1955.) To protect Jewish children in Israel through the opening of special centres and institutions from missionary activities and influences alien to Judaism. *Chairman* Mrs. A. Finn, 4 Cheyne Walk, NW4 3W ☎ 020-8202 9689.

BRITISH FRIENDS OF THE ART MUSEUMS OF ISRAEL
Wizo House, Suite 3, 105–107 Gloucester Place, London W1U 6BY.
☎ 020-7935 3954. Fax 020-7224 0744. Email info@bfami.fsnet.co.uk.
(Est. 1948. Reg. Charity No. 313008) BFAMI raises funds to help maintain museums in Israel, acquire works of art and antiquities for them, sponsor exhibitions and youth-art educational programmes. *Patrons* H.E. The Ambassador of Israel, Avigdor Arikha, Sir Anthony Caro, CBE, the Duke of Devonshire, Walter Griessmann, Anish Kapoor, Sir Timothy Sainsbury P.C., Dame V. Duffield, CBE.; *Chairman* Mrs J. Atkin; *Exec. Dir.* Mrs M. Hyman.

BRITISH FRIENDS OF ASSAF HAROFEH MEDICAL CENTRE
PO Box 244, Edgware, Middx HA8 8WF.
☎ 020-8905 3650. Email friendsofassaf@ukonline.co.uk.
(Est. 1980. Reg. Charity No. 281754) Committed to raise funds for Assaf Harofeh Medical Centre, Zrifin 70300, Israel, which is the third largest government hospital and is affiliated to the Sackler Faculty of Medicine, Tel-Aviv University. Assaf Harofeh Medical Centre provides comprehensive medical services for a population of over 400,000, including Arabs, new immigrants, army personnel and some of Israel's poorest communities. *President* David Elias, BEM, MWI, FINO; *Jt Chairmen* Dr Les Berger, David Pearl; *Vice-Chairman* Mayer Aron; *H.T.* David Onona; *Consult.* Y. Pre-El, MHFS, ICHT.

BRITISH FRIENDS OF HAIFA UNIVERSITY
26 Enford St., London W1H 2DD.
☎ 020-7724 3777.
(Reg. Charity No. 270733) To further the interests and development of Haifa Univ. by donations, books, equipment and subscriptions. The Brit. Frs. are represented at the Bd. of Govs. of Haifa Univ. *Chairman* Victor Conway, F.C.A.; Lord Jacobs (Chairman of Board of Govs); *Dir.* Dr Joseph Shub.

BRITISH FRIENDS OF THE ISRAEL FREE LOAN ASSOCIATION
c/o Mrs. Audrey Druce, 30 Greyhound Hill, London NW4 4JP.
☎ 020-8203 7196. Fax 020-8203 3394.
(Reg. Charity No. 1009568). Provides interest free loans to Russian and Ethiopian immigrants in Israel and other needy Israelis, including small business loans, emergency housing, medical loans, and loans to families with handicapped children.

Established in Jerusalem, 1990, and in 1992 in London.

Chairman Dr. Joshua Saper, 1 High Sheldon, Sheldon Avenue, London N6 4NJ; *H. T.* Mrs. A. Druce; *Patrons* Chief Rabbi Dr Jonathan Sacks, Lady Jakobovits.

THE BRITISH FRIENDS OF THE ISRAEL PHILHARMONIC ORCHESTRA FOUNDATION
c/o 10 Rainville Road, London W6 9HA.
☎ 020-7389 5648. Fax 020-7385 4320.
(Reg. Charity No. 291129) *Contact* Oded Gera.

BRITISH FRIENDS OF ISRAEL WAR DISABLED
8 Hatton Garden, London EC1N 8AH.
☎ 020-7242 9618. Fax 020-7404 1360. Email bfiwd@aol.com.
(Est. 1974. Reg. Charity No. 269269) BFIWD is a non-political organisation dedicated to helping disabled soldiers rebuild their lives. Aid is given in purchasing rehabilitation equipment. Working with the ZAHAL Disabled Veterans' Organisation, BFIWD brings groups of injured soldiers to the UK to stay with caring families. Seven local committees (London, Manchester, Birmingham, Bournemouth, Brighton etc.) *Chairman* D.R. Caspi; *Hon. Solicitor* B.B. Harris; *Sec.* Mrs G. Daniels; *H.T.* C. Niran.

BRITISH FRIENDS OF LANIADO HOSPITAL
2nd Floor, Pearl House, 746 Finchley Road, London NW11 7TH.
☎ 020-8455 4332. Fax 020-8455 3236. Email friends@laniado.co.uk; Website www. laniado.co.uk.
(Est. 1976. Reg. Charity No. 267133). Committed to fundraising and promoting the work of the Laniado Hospital of Netanya. *Chairman* B. Y. Bodner; *Hon. Life Ts* L. Feiner, N. Rokach; *T.* M. Stimler; *Leeds Chairman* C. Evans; *Manchester Chairman* D. Hamburger; *Exec. Dir.* D. V. Kaplan; *Northern Coord.* Mrs K. Dawson ☎ 0114 2368743.

BRITISH FRIENDS OF MERKAZ HARMONY
2nd Floor, 32 Wigmore Street, London W1V 2RP. ☎ 020-7535 5900. Fax 020-7935 6746. Email afrei@hew.co.uk.
(Est. 1989. Reg. Charity No. 801969) Supports provision of care and education for special needs children in Israel. *Chairman* Michel Reik; *H. T.* Alfred Frei.

BRITISH FRIENDS OF PEACE NOW
PO Box 16579, London NW6 3ZE.
☎ 020-7286 5614. Email info@peacenow-uk.org; Website www.peacenow.org.il/English.asp.

(Est. 1982. Reg. Charity No. 297295) Peace Now is a grassroots Israeli movement dedicated to Israeli–Palestinian and Israeli–Arab peace. Peace Now organises pro-peace activities and monitors Israel's settlement policy on the West Bank and Gaza Strip. The first and primary goal of Peace Now is to press the Israeli government to seek peace – through negotiations and mutual compromise – with Israel's Arab neighbours and the Palestinian people. Only peace will bring security to Israel and ensure the future of our peoples. British Friends of Peace Now mobilises support for the Israeli peace movement and the peace process among British Jews and the wider community. It is a membership organisation funded by annual membership fees and donations, and has a charitable arm. Membership expresses support for the many Israelis actively working for peace, security, justice and reconciliation in the Middle East.

BRITISH FRIENDS OF RAMBAM MEDICAL CENTRE
51 The Vale, London NW11 8SE.
☎ 020-8458 0024. Fax 020-8455 3797.
(Reg. Charity No. 028061) Voluntary organisation raising funds for the purchase of medical equipment for all hospital departments for sufferers from cancer and leukaemia. *Dir.* Anita Alexander-Passe.

BRITISH FRIENDS OF SARAH HERZOG MEMORIAL HOSPITAL (EZRATH NASHIM), JERUSALEM
609 Nelson House, Dolphin Square, London SW1V 3NZ.
☎/Fax 020-7798 5628.
(Reg. Charity No. 1024814) 300-bed teaching hospital affiliated with Hebrew Univ, Hadassah Med Sch, provides 210 geriatric beds and day hosp for health care and rehabilitation, plus 90 psychiatric beds. Community out-patient clinic has over 15,000 visits a year, gives comprehensive family and child counselling. In-depth research into Alzheimer's, Parkinson's diseases. *President* Lady Jakobovits; *V. President* Mrs Elaine Sacks, BA; *Chairman* J. Lehrer; *Admin.* Marion Press.

BRITISH FRIENDS OF SHALVA
c/o Joseph Kahan Associates, 923 Finchley Road, London NW11 7PE.
☎ 020-8209 0159. Fax 020 8209 0150. Email josephkahan@hotmail.com. Website www.shalva.org.
(Est 1990. Reg. Charity No.1081887) To support the Israel Association to assist mentally and physically handicapped children. *Chairman* H. Goldring, 6 Alberon Gardens, NW11 0AG; *Hon. Tr.* J. Joseph, 923 Finchley Rd, NW11 7PE.

BRITISH ISRAEL ARTS FOUNDATION
98 Belsize Lane, London NW3 5BB
☎ 020-7435 9878. Fax 020-7435 9879.
(Est. 1985) To promote all forms of bilateral culture between Britain and Israel. The Foundation organises concerts, theatre, dance and literary events and exhibitions. Arts Liaison Group est. to coordinate Israeli culture activities in UK. *President* Lilian Hochhauser; *V. President* Norman Hyams; *Chairman* S. Soffair; *Dir.* Ruth Kohn-Corman.

BRITISH-ISRAEL CHAMBER OF COMMERCE
PO Box 4268, London WIA 7WH.
☎ 020-7224 3212. Fax 020-7224 3171. Email mail@b-icc.org.uk;
Website www.b-icc.org.uk.
(Est. 1950) To promote and develop trade and economic relations between the UK and Israel. *Chairman* The Rt Hon. Lord Young of Graffham, PC, DL; *Chief Exec.* I. Levene, OBE. **North-West** *Regional Dir.* Gideon Klaus, ☎ 0161-929 8916. Fax

0161-929 6277. **North-East** *Regional Dir.* Jane Clynes, ☎/Fax 0113-393 0200.

BRITISH-ISRAEL PARLIAMENTARY GROUP
House of Commons, SW1A 0AA. ☎ 020-7222 5853.

BRITISH TECHNION SOCIETY
62 Grosvenor Street, W1K 3JF.
☎ 020-7495 6824. Fax 020-7355 1525. Email bts62@aol.com
(Est. 1951. Reg. Charity No. 1092207) To further the development of the Israel Institute of Technology (the Technion) at Haifa. *H. Presidents* Lord Mishcon Q.C, Hon. D.L., Sidney Corob CBE; *V. President* W. S. Churchill; *Co-Chairmen* Lois Peltz, M. Heller; *H.T.* M. Sorkin; *Exec. Dir.* T. Bernstein; *Sec.* Suzanne Posner. Social Cttees. in London and Regions.

CONSERVATIVE FRIENDS OF ISRAEL
45b Westbourne Terrace, W2 3UR.
☎ 020-7262 2493. Fax 020-7224 8941. Email admin@cfoi.co.uk
CFI is committed to the Conservative Party and to the welfare of the State of Israel and dedicated to establishing close links between GB and Israel. CFI distributes balanced and accurate information on events in the Middle East and through visits to Israel, gives MPs and candidates a greater understanding and insight into the Middle East. *President* Rt. Hon. Sir Timothy Sainsbury; *Chairman* Rt. Hon. Gillian Shephard, MP; *Jt. V. Chairmen* Jeremy Galbraith, Mrs Betty Geller, John Taylor, CBE; *Deputy Chairman* David Meller; *T.* R. Harrington; *H. Sec.* Jonathan Metliss. **Parliamentary Group**: *Chairman* Rt. Hon. Gillian Shepherd; *V. Chairmen* John Butterfill, James Clappison; *T.* Nick Hawkins; *H. Sec.* David Amess; *Dir.* Stuart Polak.

FEDERATION OF JEWISH RELIEF ORGANISATIONS
143 Brondesbury Pk., NW2 5JL.
☎ 020-8451 3425. Fax 020-8459 8059.
(Reg. Charity No. 250006) *President* The Chief Rabbi; *Chairman* W. Schindler; *H. Sec.* Mrs. R. Gluckstein.

FRIENDS OF ALYN
88 Ossulton Way, London N2 0LB.
☎ 020-8883 4716. Email friendsofalyn@btopenworld.com. Website www.alyn.org.
(Est. 1962. Reg. Charity No. 232689) To assist the work of the Alyn Orthopaedic Hospital for physically handicapped children in Jerusalem, and provide free medical, surgical and educational aid for needy children. *H.Sec.* Mrs Maureen Lowry.

FRIENDS OF BAR-ILAN UNIVERSITY
2B Golders Green Rd., London NW11 8LH.
☎ 020-8455 6363. Fax 020-8905 5872. Email ukbarilanfriends@aol.com.
(Est. 1957. Reg. Charity No. 314139) To assist the development of the Bar-Ilan University at Ramat Gan. *Chairman* C. Morris; *Admin.* Mrs J. Raperport.

FRIENDS OF THE BIKUR CHOLIM HOSPITAL, JERUSALEM & BRITISH AID COMMITTEE
3A Princes Parade, Golders Green Road, NW11 9PS.
☎/Fax020-8458 8649.
Bikur Cholim, Jerusalem's oldest hosp. is now the largest med. centre in the heart of the city. *President* Lady Jakobovits; *V. President* Mrs. N. Freshwater; *Chairman* J.

Cohen, BA; British Aid Committee: *Chairman* David Godfrey, MA; *V. Chairman* Morley Franks; *Jt. H. Ts.* B.S.E. Freshwater, P. Englard.

FRIENDS OF BOYS TOWN JERUSALEM
Heather House, Heather Gardens, NW11 9HS.
☎ 020-8731 9550. Fax 020-8731 9599.
(Est. 1963. Reg. Charity No. 227895) To organise support for secondary education and technical training for 1,500 residential students at Boys Town Jerusalem (Kiryat Noar, Bayit Vegan). *Chairman* E. Tabachnik, Q.C.; *T.* J. Pinnick, F.C.A.; *Exec. Dir.* J. Gastwirth.

FRIENDS OF THE HEBREW UNIVERSITY OF JERUSALEM
126 Albert St., London NW1 7NE.
☎ 020-7691 1500. Fax 020-7691 1501. Email friends@fhu.org.uk
(Est. 1926. Reg. Charity No. 209691) To promote the interests and development of the Hebrew University of Jerusalem through lectures, dinners, specialised events, student courses and Legacy Tours.

President John Sacher C.B.E.; *Chairman* Michael Gee; *Exec Dir.* Andrea Mail, MA. The Brit. & Irish Friends are represented on the Hebrew Univ. Bd. of Govs.

Groups: Legacies/Legacy Angels; Students/Alumni; Women's Group; Legal; Medical; New Leadership; The Jewish & National University Library Group; British Friends of YISSUM (commercialisation of HU research); and regional groups.

FRIENDS OF THE ISRAEL AGED (RE'UTH)
51 Woodlands, London NW11 9QS.
☎ 020-8455 1450.
(Est. 1950. Reg. Charity No. 278505) To assist the work of the Women's Social Service (Re'uth) in maintaining sheltered housing, old age homes and the Re'uth Medical Centre in Israel. *President* Arieh L. Handler; *V. President* Anthony Rau; *H. Sec.* Carmel Gradenwitz; *H. T.* David Toledano.

FRIENDS OF THE ISRAEL CANCER ASSOCIATION
2 Serjeants' Inn, Fleet Street, London, EC4Y 1LT.
☎ 020-7583 5353. Fax 020-7353 3683. Email charles.corman@dechert.eu.com.
(Est. 1955. Reg. Charity No. 260710) The Charity is the UK fund raising arm of the Israel Cancer Association. The ICA plays a prominent part in the fields of detection, research, treatment and education, supporting oncological institutes, nationwide screening, patient care and information services. *President* Mrs H. Gestetner, OBE; *V. Presidents* Dame Vivien Duffield, CBE, Lady Alliance, Stephan Wingate; *H. Ts* Charles Corman, Mrs M. Brown; *Cttee Chairman* Mrs V. Aaron.

FRIENDS OF ISRAEL EDUCATIONAL TRUST
PO Box 7545, London NW2 2QZ.
☎ 020-7435 6803. Fax 020-7794 0291. Email info@foi-asg.org.
(Reg. Charity No. 271983) To promote and advance the education of the public in the knowledge of the country of Israel and its citizens. F.O.I.E.T. undertakes an extensive UK education programme and sponsors a variety of young adult and professional scholarships in Israel. *Bd.:* Peter Levy (co-chair), Jeremy Manuel, Hon. Gerard Noel, Peter Oppenheimer, David Kaye, The Hon. Adrianne Marks (co-chair); *Dir.* J. D. A. Levy.

FRIENDS OF ISRAEL SPORT CENTRE FOR THE DISABLED
23 Bentinck Street, London W1U 2EZ.

☎ 020-7935 5541. Fax 020-7935 6638. Email fiscd@btinternet.com.
(Est. 2001. Reg. Charity No. 1086205) Supports the work of the Centre at Ramat Gan through donations. *Chairman* Brian B. Harris; *V. Chairman* Irwyn Yentis; *T.* Jeremy S. Harris; *Sec.* Jane C. Jukes.

FRIENDS OF JERUSALEM ACADEMY OF MUSIC AND DANCE
11 Radnor Mews, W2 2SA.
☎ 020-7402 3167. Fax 020-7706 3045.
To provide scholarships for talented children and to help in providing musical instruments, publications, etc. *Jt. Chairmen* Manja Leigh, Lilian Hochhauser.

FRIENDS OF THE JERUSALEM COLLEGE OF TECHNOLOGY
PO Box 9700, London NW6 1WF.
☎/Fax 020-7435 5501.
(Est. 1971. Reg. Charity No. 263003) To promote the interests of the College and to support its charitable work. To endow and contribute towards campus projects and to further the work of development and research. *Chairman* R. Sherrington; *T.* H. Kramer.

FRIENDS OF THE MIDRASHIA
79 Princes Park Avenue, London NW11 0JS.
☎ 020-8459 8877. Fax 020-8459 1177.
(Reg. Charity No. 285047) The British Commonwealth and Eire Cttee. was est. in 1952 to aid the Midrashia, the boys' boarding schools at Pardess Hana and Kfar Saba with over 1,000 pupils. *Founder* The late Dr J. Braude; *Chairman* A. J. Braude.

FRIENDS OF PROGRESSIVE JUDAISM IN ISRAEL AND EUROPE
The Sternberg Centre, 80 East End Road, London N3 2SY.
☎ 020-8349 3779. Fax 020-8343 0901. Email EuropeanRegion@directmail.org
(Reg. Charity No. 241337) *Admin.* Neil Drapkin.

FRIENDS OF YAD SARAH
(Reg. Charity No. 294801) Yad Sarah, a volunteer-operated home care organization, lends free, regular and hi-tech medical rehabilitative equipment and provides a spectrum of home care supportive services. Services available to tourists. Head offices, Jerusalem; 77 branches in Israel. *Trustee* D.S. Davis, c/o Cohen Arnold & Co., 13–17 New Burlington Place, London W1S 2HL. ☎ 020-7734 1362. Fax 020-7434 1117.

FRIENDS OF YESHIVAT DVAR YERUSHALAYIM
(Jat: The Jerusalem Academy Trust)
Office: 1007 Finchley Road, London NW11 7HB.
☎/Fax 020-8458 8563.
(Reg. Charity No. 262716) London Cttee: *Jt. Chairmen* A. Maslo, BCom; FCA, and M.A. Sprei, MA(Cantab), MSc; *V. Chairman* M.A. Toperoff; *H. Sec.* C. Cohen, BA; *Patrons* Chief Rabbi Dr Jonathan Sacks, Rabbi J. Dunner, Dayan M. Fisher; *Principal* Rabbi B. Horovitz, MA; *V. Principal* Rabbi Aryeh Carmell, BSc; *Exec. Dir.* Dov Horovitz.

HADASSAH MEDICAL RELIEF ASSOCIATION UK
26 Enford Street, London W1H 1DW.
☎ 020-7723 1144. Fax 020-7723 1222. Email hmrauk@btinternet.com
(Est. 1986. Reg. Charity No. 1040848) Committed to fund-raising and promoting the work of the Hadassah medical organisation, Hebrew Univ. Med.

Centre at Ein Kerem and the Hadassah Univ. Hosp. on Mt. Scopus in Jerusalem. *H.President* Lady Wolfson; *Chairman* Juliet Dawood; *H. Sec.* Ruth David; *H.T.* Jonathan Prevezer; *Exec. Dir.* Norman Brodie.

HOLYLAND PHILATELIC SOCIETY
(form. British Association of Palestine Israel Philatelists)
(Est. 1952.) For the study and encouragement of all branches of the philately of Palestine and the State of Israel, and of other countries connected with the postal history of the region. *H. Mem. Sec.* A. Tyler, 9 Ashcombe Avenue, Surbiton, Surrey KT6 6PX. ☎ 020-8399 1542.

ISRAEL DISCOUNT BANK LTD.
ISRAEL DISCOUNT BANK OF NEW YORK
(UK Representative Office) 65 Curzon Street, London W1Y 7PE.
☎ 020-7499 1444. Fax 020-7499 1414.
(Est. 1935) Israel Discount Bank Ltd. is one of the three largest banks in Israel. The Bank in Israel offers a complete range of domestic and international banking services. The London office is FSA regulated.

Israel Discount Bank of New York is the largest Israeli-owned bank operating overseas. *UK Rep.* Michael Fokschaner.

ISRAEL GOVERNMENT TOURIST OFFICE
UK House, 180 Oxford Street, London W1N 9DJ.
☎ 020-7299 1111. Fax 020-7299 1112. Email information@igto.co.uk; Website www.infotour.co.il
(Est. 1954) *Dir.* Oren Drori. The office provides information about Israel as a tourist destination, and assistance to the British and Irish travel trade wishing to promote Israel as a holiday destination.

ISRAEL–JUDAICA STAMP CLUB
(formerly Judaica Philatelic Society)
☎ 020-8886 9331. Fax 020-8886 5116.
A committee of the JNF and a ZF affiliate. Services collectors of the Jewish theme in philately; promotes KKL/JNF labels, Jewish education through philately, commemorative covers, and production of the Journal, the Israel-Judaica Collector, including an alphabetical listing of Jews and their achievements honoured on stamps and Judaica issues world-wide. Also illustrated lectures on this theme. *Patron* Sir Martin Gilbert; *President* M. Persoff, MA, FRSA; *Chairman* C. H. Rosen, F.C. Optom.; *V. Chairman* A. Field; *Sec.* S. Kosky; *T.* E. Pollard. *Publ.* The Israel–Judaica Collector: C. H. Rosen, E. Sugerman (jt. eds).

ISRAEL PHILATELIC AGENCY IN GREAT BRITAIN
PO Box 2, Watford, Herts. WD24 4HX.
☎ 01923 475548. Fax 01923 475556. Email enquiries@harryallen.co.uk
Official Agents of the Philatelic Service, Israel Postal Authority, Tel Aviv-Yafo, Israel, for the distribution and promotion of postage stamps and related products of Israel (in the United Kingdom). *New Issues Man.* Mrs Val Crowhurst on behalf of Harry Allen (International Philatelic Agencies).

THE JERUSALEM FOUNDATION
ORT House, 126 Albert Street, London NW1 7NE.
☎ 020-7482 6076. Fax 020-7482 6025.
(Est. 1969. Reg. Charity No. 258306) To support charitable projects in the city of Jerusalem embracing (*inter alia*) education, social welfare, the arts and preservation

of its historic heritage. *President* Alex Bernstein; *Chairman* Martin Paisner; *UK Dir.* Jane Biran.

JEWISH BLIND IN ISRAEL ASSOCIATION
c/o K. C. Keller F.C.A., Lynwood House, 373/375 Station Road, Harrow, Middx. HA1 2AW.
☎ 020-8357 2727. Fax 020-8357 2027.
(Reg. Charity No. 1006756) Provides financial support and equipment to the Jewish registered blind in Israel. *Adv:* Prof. Lutza Yanko & Prof. Eliezer D. Jaffe, Dr Ben-Zion Silverstone (Jerusalem), Joseph S. Conway, F.R.C.S. (London). *Chairman* Dr J. Saper.

LABOUR FRIENDS OF ISRAEL
BM LFI, London, WC1N 3XX.
☎ 020-7222 4323. Fax 020-7222 4324.
To present the facts of the Middle East situation; to build bridges of understanding between the British and Israeli Labour Movements; to encourage study groups and visits to Israel; to welcome Israeli Labour representatives to the UK; to forge strong links between the Jewish community and the British Labour Party. *Chairman* Stephen Twigg, MP; *Dep. Chair* Mike Gapes, MP; *V. Chairs* Ivor Caplin, MP, Ivan Lewis, MP, Jim Murphy, MP; *Dir.* Nick Cosgrove.

LIBERAL DEMOCRAT FRIENDS OF ISRAEL
c/o 318 Whitchurch Lane, Canons Park, Edgware, Middlesex. ☎ 020-8952 8987. or 31 The Vale, London NW11 8SE. ☎ 020-8455 5140.
Open to all supporters of the Liberal Democrats in UK who recognise the right of Israel to a free, independent, permanent and prosperous existence as a member state of the United Nations. The Assoc. exists to foster good relations and understanding between Britain and state of Israel. *President* Lord Jacobs; *V. Presidents* Alan Beith, MP, The Lord Carlile, QC; *Chairman* Monroe Palmer, O.B.E.; *Sec.* David Lerner.

LIFELINE FOR THE OLD
6 Charlton Lodge, Temple Fortune Lane, London NW11 7TY.
☎ 020-8455 9059.
(Reg. Charity No. 232084) To assist the work of Lifeline for the Old in Jerusalem, which aims to relieve poverty among the aged in Israel by providing training in occupational skills, and improve the welfare and quality of life of Jerusalem's elderly and disabled. *H. Sec.* Miss J. Mitzman. *Leeds Branch*: *Chairman* Mrs A. Ziff.

MAGEN DAVID ADOM UK
Pearl House, 746 Finchley Road, London NW11 7TH.
☎/Fax 020-8381 4849. Fax 020-8381 4898. Email info@ukmda.org; Website www.ukmda.org
(Reg. Charity No. 210770) To assist the work of Israel's voluntary emergency medical and national ambulance services which are responsible for supplying and maintaining first-aid posts and casualty stations, national blood services, medical wing of Israel Civil Defence, medical care of immigrants, missing persons bureaux, beach rescue stations, national responsibility for First-Aid training and all the other services usually supplied by a Red Cross Society. *Nat. Chairman* M. Barnett; *V. Chairman* A. Nedas; *H. T.* Nicholas Posnansky, F.C.A.; *Exec. Dir.* Eli Benson. Groups in many districts of London and the Regions.

MEDICAL AID COMMITTEE FOR ISRAEL
MAC-I: Reg. Charity No. 258697.
c/o 69 Hampstead Way, London NW11 7LG.

(Est. 1969.) To provide med. and lab. equipment and offer technical and prof. advice. To assist and promote health and welfare projects in Israel. Applications from the Director Inter. Relations, Israel Min. of Health, 2 Ben Tabai Street, Jerusalem 93591. Dr Lionel P. Balfour-Lynn, MA, MD (Cambs), FRCPCH, DCH.

NEW ISRAEL FUND
25-26 Enford Street, London W1H 2DD.
☎ 020-7724 2266. Fax 020-7724 2299. Email info@uknif.org.
(Est. 1992. Reg. Charity No. 1060081) The New Israel Fund works to strengthen Israel's great founding vision of a free and democratic society. NIF is at the forefront of social change in Israel, providing hundreds of Israeli non-profit organisations with financial and technical support each year. NIF projects safeguard civil and human rights, promote Jewish–Arab coexistence and foster religious understanding in Israel. NIF also supports women's groups and environmental protection programmes. *Chair* Lady Dahrendorf; *Chief Exec.* Alan Bolchover.

OPERATION WHEELCHAIRS COMMITTEE
51 The Vale, London NW11 8SE.
☎ 020-8458 0024. Fax 020-8455 3797.
(Est. 1970. Reg. Charity No. 263089) Voluntary organisation providing rehabilitation and general medical equipment to hospitals in Israel treating wounded soldiers, and equipment for Beit Halochem. *Founder* Mrs. Lily Perry; *Chairman* Mrs. Anita Alexander-Passe.

POALE AGUDAT ISRAEL
Unites Orthodox religious workers to build up Eretz Yisrael in the spirit of the Torah. **World Central Off.**: 64 Frishman Street, Tel Aviv. *President* Rabbi A. Werdiger. **European Office and Great Britain**: P.A.I. Ho., 2A Alba Gardens, NW11 9NR. ☎/Fax 020-8458 5372. *Chairman* F. Wolkenfeld; *Corr.* D. Winter. *Publ.:* PAI Views.

RSGB ISRAEL POLICY & PLANNING GROUP
Sternberg Centre for Judaism, Manor House, 80 East End Road, London N3 2SY.
☎ 020-8349 5651. Fax 020-8349 5699. Email linda.kann@reformjudaism.org.uk
(Est. 1989) Aims to create knowledge and love of Israel through theology, education and Israel action by raising Israel consciousness within the Reform Movement and by building links with IMPJ (Israel Movement Progressive Judaism) and its constituent communities. *Chairman* Ben Overlander.

SHAARE ZEDEK UK
766 Finchley Road, London NW11 7TH.
☎ 020-8201 8933. Fax 020-8201 8935. Email office@shaarezedek.org.uk; Website www.szmc.org.il
(Hospital est. Jerusalem 1902.) (Reg. Charity No. 262870) Raising funds by way of donations and legacies to support the hospital's programmes. *President* Lord Mishcon DL; *Chairman* Mrs M. Rothem; *H.T.* Alfred Frei, F.C.A.; *Exec. Dir.* Mrs R. Goodman.

STATE OF ISRAEL BONDS
Development Company for Israel (UK) Ltd.
79 Wimpole Street, London W1G 9RY.
☎ 020-7224 6220. Fax 020-7224 6334. Website www.israelukbonds.com.
(Est. 1981.) Promotes and sells State of Israel Bonds (Israel's gilt-edged securities). *Managing Dir.* D. Elkani; *Sales Dir. & Comp. Sec.* Dr H. Stellman.

TEHILLA
Balfour House, 741 High Road, North Finchley, N12 0BQ.
☎ 020-8446 1477 Ext 2273. Fax 020-8446 4419.
Tehilla is a non-political voluntary organisation dedicated to encouraging Aliyah and providing the support services needed by religious Jews coming to live in Israel. *U.K. Rep.* Mrs E. Singer.

TEL AVIV UNIVERSITY TRUST
1 Bentinck Street, W1U 2EB.
☎ 020-7487 5280. Fax 020-7224 3908.
(Reg. Charity No. 314179) The principal aim of the Trust is to raise funds to promote the work of Tel Aviv University and to encourage support for academic projects, scholarships and campus development. The Trust also advises those who may wish to study at the University. *H. Presidents* Lord and Lady Wolfson, Sir Leslie and Dame Shirley Porter; *Chairman* D. Meller.

TRADE UNION FRIENDS OF ISRAEL
BM LFI, London, WC1N 3XX.
☎ 020-7222 4323. Fax 020-7222 4324.
To create and foster fraternal links between the Histadrut and the British Trade Union Movement; to educate and promote within the British Trade Union Movement the State of Israel and the Histadrut; to encourage study groups and delegations to visit Israel; to initiate dialogue between British Trade Union Movements and their Israeli counterparts. *H. Chairman* Gavid Laird; *Dir.*; *Admin.* Suzanne Weiniger.

UK FRIENDS OF THE ASSOCIATION FOR THE WELLBEING OF ISRAEL'S SOLDIERS
(A Charity for the Welfare and Education of Israel's Soldiers)
87 Bell Lane, London NW4 2 AS. ☎ 020-8203 7135. Fax 020-8203 6918. Websites www.ukawis@hotmail.com; www.ukawis.co.uk.
(Est. 2001. Reg. Charity No. 1084272). To support the work of the Association in Israel, primarily by raising funds for university scholarships for young Israeli servicemen and women from deprived backgrounds. *Tr.* Anke Adler-Slottke, Andrew Balcombe, Julian Kemble, Peter Sussman, Zeev Remez; *Exec. Dir.* Alice Krieger.

UK SOCIETY FOR THE PROTECTION OF NATURE IN ISRAEL
PO Box 7545, London NW2 2QZ.
☎ 020-7435 6803. Fax 020-7794 0291. Email info@foi-asg.org.
(Est. 1986. Reg. Charity No. 327268) To generate interest in the beauty of Israel's natural landscapes; muster support for the conservation lobby in Israel. *Trs.* Godfrey Bradman, Edward Goldsmith, Zak Goldsmith, Arnold Kransdorff, John D. A. Levy, Bob Lewin, Bill Oddie.

UNITED MIZRAHI BANK LTD.
Finsbury House, 23 Finsbury Circus, EC2M 7UB.
☎ 020-7448 0600. Fax 020-7448 3810.
Br. of United Mizrahi Bank in Israel. *Gen. Man.* David Halperin.

WEIZMANN INSTITUTE FOUNDATION
126 Albert St, London NW1 7NE.
☎ 020-7424 6860. Fax 020-7424 6869. Email post@weizmann.org.uk; Website www. weizmann.org uk
(Est. 1956. Reg. Charity No. 232666) To stimulate financial, scientific and cultural support in the UK for the Weizmann Institute of Science in Rehovot. *Chairman of*

Exec. Cttee. Barry Townsley; *V. Chairman* Dame Vivien Duffield, DBE; *H. Sec.* J. Kropman; *Co-H.T.* J. Nedas, R. Ohrenstein; *Chief Exec. Off.* Stuart Rogers.

YOUTH ALIYAH-CHILD RESCUE
Britannia House, 960 High Road, North Finchley, London N12 9YA.
☎ 020-8446 4321. Fax 020-8343 7383. Email info@youthaliyah.com.
(Est. 1933. Reg. Charity No. 1077913) Object: to offer a secure home for underprivileged and deprived refugee, immigrant and native Israeli children. Our five Youth Villages offer an enriching environment through residential community care. *Jt. Chairman* Gerald Gaffin, Adrienne Sussman; *H. Dir. Israel* Nanette Sacki; *Exec. Dir.* Claudia Rubenstein. *Publ.* Youth Aliyah-Child Rescue.

EDUCATIONAL AND CULTURAL ORGANISATIONS

Hebrew and Religion Classes are attached to most synagogues listed.
For University Centres and Institutions see pp.43–7.

AGENCY FOR JEWISH EDUCATION
Beit Meir, 44a Albert Road, NW4 2SJ.
☎ 020-8457 9700. Fax 020-8457 9707. Email info@aje.org.uk; Website www.aje.org.uk
Training, resourcing, curriculum and servicing schools, nurseries and part-time education organisations of the Jewish community in Britain. *Chief Exec.* Simon Goulden; *Dir. Education.* Jeffrey Leader.

ASSOCIATION OF JEWISH TEACHERS
c/o Agency for Jewish Education, 44 Albert Road, London NW4 2SJ.
☎ 020-8906 0816. Fax 020-8457 9707.
(Est. 1986) To promote, enhance and support the welfare and professional development of Jewish teachers in schools. *Chairman* R. Marks; *V. Chairman* P. Resnick.

BETH SHALOM HOLOCAUST MEMORIAL CENTRE
Laxton, Newark, Notts NG22 0PA.
☎ 01623-836627. Fax 01623-836647. Email office@bethshalom.com; Website www.bethshalom.com.
(Est. 1978 (as Beth Shalom Ltd.) Reg. Charity No. 509022) Holocaust education and commemoration. *Dir.* Dr Stephen D. Smith, Dr James M. Smith, Mrs Marina H. Smith.

DAVAR, The Jewish Institute in Bristol and the South West
1-3 Percival Road, Clifton, Bristol, BS8 3LF.
☎/Fax 0117-970 6594. Email office@davar/freeserve.co.uk; Website www.davar.freeserve.co.uk
DAVAR provides a wide programme of cultural, educational and social activities for the Jewish community in Bristol and the South-West. A regular newsletter is available, and Jewish groups in the area advertise their own events via the DAVAR mailing list. *Acting Chairman* Martin Weitz; *Admin.* Vena Bunker.

DVAR YERUSHALAYIM (London Jewish Academy)
24 Templars Avenue, NW11 0NS.
☎/Fax 020-8455 8631.
(Est. 1978. Reg. Charity No. 284740) To provide full- and part-time courses in adult education to enable men and women of limited Jewish knowledge and background to further their understanding of Jewish thought and practice. *Princ.* Rabbi J. Freilich, Ph.C.

ENCOUNTER (Jewish Outreach Network)
PO Box 24046, London NW4 2ZP
☎ 020 8201 5070
(Est. 1996; Reg. Charity no. 1064674) The Jewish Outreach Network (J.O.I.N.), organised by Encounter, provides a showcase for Orthodox Judaism. The executive comprises representatives from Ohr Somayach, Aish, Project SEED and the United Synagogue Rabbinate. The Jewish Outreach Network/Encounter is the impetus behind an annual winter Encounter Conference, a day of inspiration and learning, and the Crash Courses in Judaism and Living Judaism, five-week lecture series which are offered periodically throughout the year. Encounter co-ordinates weekly explanatory services and High Holyday explanatory services throughout England, Speaker Tours and Shabbatonim. *Exec. Dir.*

HOLOCAUST EDUCATIONAL TRUST
BCM Box 7892, London WC1N 3XX.
☎ 020-7222 6822/5853. Fax 020-7233 0161. Email info@het.org.uk. Website www.het.org.uk
(Est. 1988. Reg. Charity No. 327640) To promote Holocaust education and research, not only formally but also to the wider public. The Trust works in schools and higher education, providing teacher-training workshops and lectures, as well as supplying teaching aids and resource material. New academic research on Holocaust-related issues are also produced by the Trust. *Patrons* His Grace the Duke of Norfolk, KG GCVO CB CBE MC DL, Lord Mackay of Clashfern, Prof. Elie Wiesel; *President* R. Stephen Rubin; *V. Presidents* Rt Hon. Lord Merlyn-Rees PC, Rt Hon. Lord Hunt of Wirral; *Chairman* Lord Janner of Braunstone QC; *Sec.* Sir Ivan Lawrence QC; *T.* Paul Philips; *Trustees* Lord Levy, Ivan Lewis MP, Jon Mendelsohn, Martin Paisner LLM, David Sumberg MEP; *Bd of Man.* David Gryn, Kitty Hart, Ben Helfgott, Nigel Ross, Sir Antony Sher, Alberta Strage; *Dir.* Karen Pollock; *Head of Ed.* Rosie Boston; *Ed. Off.* Tito Newell; *Press & Inf. Off.* Tamar Burman; *Holocaust Memorial Day Off.* Vicki Nash; *Fundraising & Events Off.* Amanda Laws.

ISRAEL FOLK DANCE INSTITUTE
Balfour House, 741 High Road, London N12 0JL.
Daytime ☎/fax 020-8446 6427. Evening ☎/fax 020-8445 6765. Email info@ifdiuk.org; Website www.ifdiuk.org
(Reg Charity No. 279801) The Institute is an educational charity whose main work is promoting Jewish and Israeli cultural heritage through the medium of dance and song. The Institute publishes unique educational programmes for schools, religion schools and youth groups, organises an annual London Children and Youth Dance Festival, runs training seminar for worldwide Israeli dance teachers in the UK and in the former Soviet Union, and holds weekly dance classes for all ages. *Chairman and Hon. Dir.* Maurice Stone.

ISRAEL ZANGWILL MEMORIAL FUND
c/o Manor House Tr., Sternberg Centre For Judaism, 80 East End Road, N3 2SY.
☎ 020-8349 5645. Email admin@reformjudaism.org.uk
(Est. 1929) To assist poor Jews engaged in literary, artistic, dramatic and scientific work.

JEWISH BOOK COUNCIL
PO Box 38247, London NW3 5YQ.
Fax 020-7487 4211. Email jewishbookcouncil@btopenworld.com; Website www.jewishbookweek.com. *Admin.* Pam Lewis ☎ 020-8343 4675.
(Est. 1947. Reg. Charity No. 293800) To stimulate and encourage the reading of books on Judaism and on every aspect of Jewish thought, life, history and

literature; organises annual Jewish Book Week, now Europe's largest Jewish book fair, and associated events. Administers a triennial prize for Hebrew translation. *President* Mrs M. R. Lehrer, MA(Oxon); *Chairman* Anne Webber, M.Phil.; *H. T.* P. Harris; *H. Sec.* R. Tager, QC.

JEWISH CHRONICLE
25 Furnival Street, London EC4A 1JT.
☎ 020-7415 1500. Fax 020-7405 9040. Website www.jchron.co.uk
(Est. 1841.) The world's oldest independent Jewish weekly newspaper. *Chairman* Lionel Gordon; *Edr.* Mr Ned Temko.

JEWISH COMMUNITY DAY SCHOOL ADVISORY BOARD
c/o Leo Baeck College – Centre for Jewish Education, Sternberg Centre, 80 East End Road, London N3 2SY.
☎ 020-8349 5620. Fax 020-8349 5639. Email admin@cje.org.uk
(Est. 1998) Jewish promotion and development of cross-community primary day schools throughout the UK. *Chairman* Peter L. Levy; *Educ. Consult.* Susan Moss.

JEWISH COMMUNITY THEATRE
157 Denmark Hill, London SE5 8EH.
☎/Fax 020-7737 4361.
(Est. 1990. Reg. Charity No. 1000187) To advance, develop and maintain public education and awareness of the history of British Jews by the presentation at theatres and other suitable venues of plays reflecting the cultural identity of Anglo-Jewry. *Chair* Ruth Franklin; *T.* David Franklin.

JEWISH EDUCATION AID SOCIETY
(Est. 1896.) To investigate and advise on cases of highly talented students and in certain circumstances to provide interest-free loans to enable them to train for professions or the pursuit of art. Now under the administration of Anglo-Jewish Association (see p.3).

JEWISH FILM FOUNDATION
c/o 46a Minster Road, London NW2 3RD.
The Jewish Film Foundation is an educational charity whose aim is to promote the exhibition, distribution, production and study of Jewish cinema, television and video programmes. It initiates and co-ordinates education and cultural activities involving film and video and advises those who make and use programmes on Jewish themes. Organises an annual Jewish Film Festival in London. *Bd. of Dir.* Michael Green, Dorothy Berwin, Jonathan Davis, Dominique Green, Jeremy Isaacs, Verity Lambert, Michael May, Louis Marks, Alan Yentob; *Prog. Dir.* Sam Maser.

JEWISH GENEALOGICAL SOCIETY OF GREAT BRITAIN
PO. Box 13288, London N3 3WD. Website www.jgsgb.org.uk.
Membership: 20 Camperdown, Maidenhead, Berks SL6 8DU.
Genealogical enquiries: 14 St Helens Road, Alverstoke, Gosport, Hants, PO12 2RN.
(Est. 1992. Reg. Charity No. 1022738) To promote and encourage the study of Jewish genealogy on a secular basis. The Society organises lectures, seminars and family history workshops (including those at The London Museum of Jewish Life, Sternberg Centre); publishes *Shemot*, and guides to study of Jewish genealogy; promotes research; and operates a library. *President* Dr Anthony Joseph; *V. Presidents* David Jacobs, Graham Jaffe; *Chairman* Antony Winner; *Membership Sec.* Marion Kaye; *T.* D. Glazer; *Sec.* Norman King; *Groups:* South Manchester (Janina Hochland), North Manchester (Lorna Kay), South West (Alan Tobias),

South Coast (Jacqueline Gill and Richard Cooper), Oxford (Michelle Anderson), South East London, South West London (Ena Black), East London/Essex (Shirley Collier).

JEWISH HISTORICAL SOCIETY OF ENGLAND
33 Seymour Place, W1H 5AP.
☎/Fax 020-7723 5852. Email jhse@dircon.co.uk
(Est. 1893. Reg. Charity No. 217331) *President* Prof. Bill Rubinstein (Aberystwyth); *H. T.* Raphael Langham; *H. Sec.* Dr G. Black; *Admin.* Mrs G. Black. **Branches: Birmingham**: *Chairman* Dr Anthony Joseph, 25 Westbourne Road, Edgbaston, Birmingham B15 3TX; **Essex:** *Contact* Mrs S. Lassman ☎ 020-8554 9921; **Leeds**: *Contact* Murray Winer, 21 Primley Park Ave., Leeds LS17 7HX ☎ 0113 294 0789; **Liverpool**: *Chairman* Arnold Lewis, 61 Menlove Ave., L18 2EH; **Manchester**: *Chairman* Frank Baigel, 25 Ravensway, Bury Old Rd., Prestwich M25 0EU.

JEWISH LITERARY TRUST
PO Box 335042, London NW1 7XH.
☎ 020-7284 1117. Website www.jewishquarterly.org.
(Est. 1984. Reg. Charity No. 268589). Established on the death of Jacob Sonntag, founding editor of the Jewish Quarterly, to ensure the continuity of the Jewish Quarterly. *Patrons* Elizabeth and Sidney Corob, Sue Hammerson, Peter Held, Sir Sidney Kalms, Diana and Michael Lazarus, Colette Littman, Clive Marks, Ronald Wingate, Delia and Fred Worms; *Chairman* Jeffrey Greenwood; *Exec. Cttee* Richard Bolchover, Marion Cohen, Michael Daniels, Andrew Franklin, Emmanuel Grodzinski, Michael Joseph, Stephen Massil; *Admin.* G. Don; *Ed.* Matthew Reisz. *Publ.* Jewish Quarterly (see page 6).

JEWISH MUSIC INSTITUTE
PO Box 232, Harrow, Middx, HA1 2NN.
☎ 020-8909 2445. Fax 020-8909 1030. Email jewishmusic@jmi.org.uk; Website www.jmi.org.uk
(Reg. Charity No. 328228) The Jewish Music Heritage Institute promotes study and performance of Jewish music to preserve this great heritage and teach it to successive generations. *Dir.* Mrs Geraldine Auerbach, MBE.
Activities include:
London International Jewish Music Festival: a biennial, month-long festival featuring concerts, recitals, workshops, masterclasses, lectures, Yiddish theatre and comedy; in major concert halls in London and around the country.
Commissioning of new Jewish Music.
Jewish Music Library – SOAS (see p.56).
Joe Loss Lectureship in Jewish Music at School of Oriental and African Studies, University of London (see p.45).
Jewish Music Distribution: Specialists in Jewish music, CDs, etc. and printed music from around the world.
Gregori Schechter's Klezmer Festival Band: Founding and promotion of band for concerts and functions.
Klezmer Classes: Teaching sessions for youth and adults.

KESHER – THE LEARNING CONNECTION
50 Colindeep Lane, London NW9 6HB.
☎ 020-8905 9115. Fax 020-8905 9114. Email rsimon@kesher.org.uk
(Est. 1997. Reg Charity no. 1061689). Jewish Education and Outreach to singles and young couples. Reconnecting Jews of all backgrounds with their heritage. *Dir.* Rabbi Rashi Simon, MA.

LEO BAECK COLLEGE – CENTRE FOR JEWISH EDUCATION (LBC – CJE)
The Sternberg Centre for Judaism, 80 East End Road, London N3 2SY. Email info@lbc.ac.uk; Website www.lbc.ac.uk.
(Est. 1956. Reg. Charity No. 209777). Established for the study of Judaism and the training of rabbis and teachers. Under the joint auspices of the Reform Synagogues of Great Britain and the Union of Liberal and Progressive Synagogues. *Principal* Rabbi Professor Jonathan Magonet; *Vice-Principal* Rabbi Dr Michael J. Shire; *Chair of Board of Governors* Gerald Rothman; *Dir. of Finance & Admin.* Stephen Ross; *Hd of Academic & Student Services* Irit Burkeman; *Hd of Admin.* Rhona Lesner.
The Department of Rabbinic Studies offers a five-year programme leading to Rabbinic Ordination.
The Department of Higher Jewish Studies offers full-time and part-time degrees; BA (Hons) in Hebrew and Jewish Studies, an MA, as well as Open Univ. MPhil and DPhil degrees.
The Department of Jewish Lifelong Learning caters for those wishing to further their Jewish knowledge. The Adult Learning Programme consists of six modules taken over two years.
The Department of Education and Professional Development (formerly CJE) ☎ 020-8349 5620. Fax 020-8349 5639. Email admin@cje.org.uk; Website www.knowledge.co.uk/cje. (Est. 1987) Formerly the Centre for Jewish Education and now merged to become the Leo Baeck College – Centre for Jewish Education, this department serves the Progressive Movements, providing services to part-time religion schools and primary schools; offering teacher training, community/family education, Hebrew programming, outreach projects, a purchasing service for text-books for schools, and three Resource Centres. This department also runs an MA in Jewish Education and an Advanced Diploma in Professional Development: Jewish Education. Consultants are available to visit communities and offer programmes around the country. *Dir.* Dr Helena Miller. Branches: Sternberg Centre Resource Centre and Book Service, 80 East End Road, Finchley N3 2SY. ☎ 020-8349 5620. Fax 020-8349 5639; Peggy Lang Resource Centre, Montague Centre, 21 Maple Street, W1T 4BE. ☎ 020-7580 0214. Fax 020-7436 4184; Sandra Vigon Resource & Learning Centre, Jackson's Row, Manchester M2 5WD. ☎ 0161-831 7092. Fax 0161-839 4865.

LIMMUD
1 Dennington Park Road, London NW6 1AX.
☎ 020-7431 9444. Fax 020-7431 9555. Email office@limmud.org; Website www.limmud.org
(Reg. Charity No. 327111) Limmud is a cross-communal, adult educational organisation. The main event Limmud organises is its annual five-day residential conference in December. In addition, Limmud organises Family Limmud in August, themed education events and regional Limmud days throughout the year. *Chair* Claire Straus; *Exec. Dir.* Clive A. Lawton; *Admin.* Helen Lyons.

LITTMAN LIBRARY OF JEWISH CIVILIZATION
PO Box 645, Oxford OX2 0UJ. ☎/Fax 01865 514688. Email enquiries@littman.co.uk; Website www.littman.co.uk.
(Est. 1965. Reg. Charity No. 1000784) Established for the purpose of publishing scholarly works aimed at disseminating an understanding of the Jewish heritage and Jewish history and making Jewish religious thought and literary creativity accessible to the English-speaking world. *Dirs.* Mrs C. C. Littman, R. J. Littman; *Contact* Connie Webber (Editorial); *Chief Exec. Off.* Ludo Craddock.

LONDON ACADEMY OF JEWISH STUDIES
2–4 Highfield Avenue, NW11 9ET.
☎ 020-8455 5938; 020-8458 1264.
(Est. in 1975) To assist post-Yeshiva students to further their Jewish educ. and engage in advanced Talmudic research. Graduates are expected to take up rabbinical and teaching posts in the com. The Kolel also serves as a Torah-study centre for laymen. Its specialised library is open to the gen. public throughout the year incl. Shabbat and Yom Tov. *H. Princ.* Rabbi G. Hager.

LONDON JEWISH CULTURAL CENTRE (incorporating the work of the Spiro Institute)
The Old House, c/o King's College, Kidderpore Avenue, London NW3 7SX.
☎ 020-7431 0345. Fax 020-7431 0361. Email admin@ljcc.org.uk; Website www.ljcc.org.uk
(Reg. Charity No. 1081014) The London Jewish Cultural Centre was launched in June 2000 and is built on the bedrock of the Spiro Institute which has successfully taught Jewish history, culture and Modern Hebrew for over 20 years. The LJCC offers tours of Jewish interest and is extending its programme in the areas of art, music, film and literature. In addition, it will continue to teach Modern Hebrew at all levels and to provide Holocaust Education in schools. The LJCC works in close co-operation with other Jewish organisations. For full details of the academic programme please apply for the prospectus or look at the website. *Exec. Dir. Adult Education* Trudy Gold, LLB; *Exec. Dir. Admin.* Diana Mocatta. *Dir. Educ.* J. Newman; *Hd. Hebrew* H. Inbar-Littas.

MASORTI ACADEMY
1097 Finchley Rd., NW11 0PU.
☎ 020-8201 8772. Fax 020-8201 8917. Email office@masorti.org.uk
Provides adult education in a number of different formats, offering seminars, evening classes, distance learning courses, residential study events and lectures, all within the Masorti context of open-minded enquiry within a spirit of authentic traditional Judaism. *Dir.* Michael Gluckman.

MICHAEL GOULSTON EDUCATIONAL FOUNDATION
Sternberg Centre for Judaism, Manor House, 80 East End Road, N3 2SY.
☎ 020-8349 5620. Fax 020-8349 5639.
Established 1972 in memory of Rabbi Michael Goulston to pub. Jewish educ. materials, including books, audio visuals and study programmes. *Dir.* Rabbi Dr Michael J. Shire.

POLACK'S HOUSE, CLIFTON COLLEGE
1 Percival Road, Bristol BS8 3LF.
☎ 0117 3157370. Email jgreenbury@clifton-college.avon.sch.uk.
(Reg. Charity No. 1040218) Polack's House at Clifton College has provided boarding facilities and Jewish education since 1878. Now reconstituted as the Polack's House Educational Trust it houses Jewish boys aged 13–18 within the House, and provides Jewish education and kosher meals for Jewish boys and girls aged 8–18, fully integrated into Clifton College. *Housemaster* Jonathan Greenbury; *Dir.* David Prashker.

REFORM YOUNG ADULTS
The Sternberg Centre, 80 East End Road, London N3 2SY.
☎ 020 8349 5682 Fax 020 8349 5696 Email jessica.brummer@reform judaism.org.uk
(Est. 2000. Registered Charity no. 250060). Design and implementation of programmes for the 18–40 age range within the framework of the Reform

Movement. Programmes in the areas of worship, Jewish learning, social action and cultural/social events.

SCOPUS JEWISH EDUCATIONAL TRUST (formerly ZFET)
52 Queen Anne St., London W1G 8HL.
☎ 020-7935 0100. Fax 020-7935 7787.
(Est. 1953. Reg. Charity No. 313154) To raise funds by way of endowment, legacy, bequest, gift or donation in order to provide a first-class education in Jewish Studies and Hebrew throughout its national network of day schools, all of which have a Zionist ethos and emphasize the centrality of Israel in Jewish life. *H. President* Stanley S. Cohen, OBE; *Chairman* Peter Ohrenstein; *H.T.* Jonathan M. Kramer; *H. Sec.* Brenda Hyman. Schools: **London**: Harry & Abe Sherman Rosh Pinah School, Sebba Rosh Pinah Nursery, Mathilda Marks-Kennedy School, Ella & Ernst Frankel Kindergarten, Simon Marks School, Simon Marks Sherman Nursery; **Leeds**: Brodetsky Primary and Nursery School; Deborah Taylor Playgroup; **Manchester**: North Cheshire Primary School.

Seed
Middlesex House, 29-45 High Street, Edgware, Middx HA8 7UU.
☎ 020-8381 1555. Fax 020-8381 1666. Email info@seed.uk.net; Website www.seed.uk.net
London contact for One to One and Kehillas Netzach Ysroel, Rabbi D. Roberts; *Educational programmes contact* Rabbi M. Herman; *Seminars* Y. Silkin; *Regions* Rabbi A. Hassan.
(Est. 1980. Reg. Charity No. 281307 Project Seed) To provide Jewish adult education through courses, weekend seminars and One to One study throughout the year. *Dir.* Rabbi J. Grunfeld.

Weekly study sessions in Greater London, men and women, in the following areas: Barnet, Borehamwood/Elstree, Edgware, Finchley/HGS, Golders Green, Hendon, Ilford, Kenton, Maida Vale, Marble Arch, Mill Hill, Pinner, Southgate, Stanmore, Stoke Newington, Westcliffe; men only: Belmont, Chigwell, Kingsbury, Wembley; ladies only: Bushey.

Weekly study sessions in the Regions, men and women, in the following areas: Bury, Fallowfield, Gatley, Prestwich, Sale Whitefield, Glasgow, Leeds, Liverpool, Newcastle; men only: Sunderland.

THE SEPHARDI CENTRE
2 Ashworth Road, Maida Vale, London W9 1JY.
☎ 020-7266 3682. Fax 020-7289 5957. Email sephardicentre@onetel.net.uk.
(Est. 1994. Reg. Charity No. 1039937) The Centre's aim is to promote Sephardi culture. Courses, open to all, focus on Religion, History, Music, Art and Cuisine. A library and reading room specialising in Sephardi literature is open to the public (see p.60). *Dir.* Rabbi S. Djanogly.

SOCIETY FOR JEWISH STUDY
(Est. 1946. Reg. Charity No. 283732) *Sec.* Rosemary Goldstein, 1A Church Mount, London N2 0RW. The Society's objectives are the furtherance of learning and research through regular public lectures.

THE SPIRO ARK
Springwood Crescent (off Broadfields Avenue), Edgware, Middx HA8 8FT.
☎ 020-8958 6272. Fax 020-8905 4367. Email spiroark@aol.com; Website www. spiroark.org
(Reg. Charity No.1070926) The Spiro Ark has been established to meet the urgent problems facing the Jewish people in the twenty-first century and uses

innovative teaching methods in order to encourage a learning community: 'My People are destroyed through lack of knowledge' (*Hosea, IV, 6*). Hebrew and Yiddish are taught at all levels, together with Jewish history, biblical studies and other related subjects; outstanding cultural events and tours. Courses and activities throughout London all week. *Founders* Nitza and Robin Spiro.

SPRINGBOARD EDUCATION TRUST
32 Foscote Road, London NW4 3SD.
☎ 020-8202 7147. Fax 020-8203 8293. Email aumie@shap32.fsworld.co.uk
(Est. 1979. Reg. Charity No. 277946) Whilst specialising in reminiscence and stimulation programmes for senior citizens, Springboard has extended its range of audio-visual and video productions to cover Jewish and Zionist history, synagogue and home traditions, inter-faith projects.

Springboard also produces low-cost audio-visual/video programmes for other orgs. and provides seminars for teachers and welfare workers in the use of its programmes with substantial back-up materials.

Dirs. Aumie and Michael Shapiro.

YAKAR
2 Egerton Gardens, London NW4 4BA.
☎ 020-8202 5551. Fax 020-8202 9653. Email yakar@yakar.org.uk; Website www.yakar.org.uk.
(Est. 1978. Reg. Charity No. 277818) Founded by Rabbi Dr Michael Rosen, YAKAR is an independent study centre devoted to exploring Jewish religious, philosophical and spiritual issues. YAKAR is open and non-prescriptive and welcomes students from any position or background. YAKAR offers lectures, classes and tutorials for men and women throughout the week and religious services on Sabbaths and Festivals. The YAKAR community is informal, experimental and welcoming. *Dir.* Jeremy Rosen; *Admin.* Rosemary Genn.

UNIVERSITY CENTRES AND ORGANISATIONS

(See also Organisations concerned with Jewish students on pp.52–4, and Libraries on pp.54–60).

BRITISH ASSOCIATION FOR JEWISH STUDIES
Website www.BAJSBulletin.org.
(Est. 1975.) Membership is open to scholars concerned with the academic pursuit of Jewish studies in the British Isles. The Assoc. promotes and defends the scholarly study of Jewish culture in all its aspects and organizes an annual conference. *President (2003)* Prof. C.T.R. Hayward, Dept. of Theology, University of Durham, Abbey House, Palace Green, Durham DH1 3RS; *Sec.* Dr D. Langton, University of Manchester, The Centre for Jewish Studies, Dept. of Religions and Theology, Oxford Road, Manchester M13 9PL; *T.* Dr J. Aitken, Dept. of Classics, University of Reading, Whiteknights, Reading RG6 6AA.

CENTRE FOR GERMAN-JEWISH STUDIES
University of Sussex, Falmer, Brighton BN1 9QN. ☎ 01273-678495.
Dir. Professor Edward Timms; *Admin. Liaison Off.* Diana Franklin. ☎ 020-8381 4721. Email dianafranklin@waitrose.com

CENTRE FOR JEWISH–CHRISTIAN RELATIONS
Wesley House, Jesus Lane, Cambridge CB5 8BJ.
☎ 01223 741048. Email enquiries@cjcr.cam.ac.uk.
(Est. 1997. Reg. Charity No. 1059772) The Centre for Jewish–Christian Relations is an independent institution dedicated to the study and teaching of all aspects of

the Jewish–Christian encounter throughout the ages. It offers an educational programme including the first MA in Jewish–Christian Relations in the UK. Courses are available on a full- or part-time basis and delivered both on-site and by distance-learning. *Exec. Dir.* Dr Edward Kessler; *Dev. Dir.* Deborah Patterson Jones; *Acad. Dir.* Dr Melanie Wright; *Distance Learning Man.* Lucia Faltin.

CENTRE FOR JEWISH STUDIES (University of Leeds)
Leeds LS2 9JT.
☎ 0113-233 5197. Fax 0113-245 1977. Email e.frojmovic@leeds.ac.uk
(Est. 1995) Teaching of Jewish Studies: undergraduate minor in Jewish Studies, BA in Jewish Civilisation and a range of Joint-Honours; taught MA in Modern Jewish Studies and supervision of research degrees. *Dir.* Dr Eva Frojmović.

CENTRE FOR JEWISH STUDIES (University of London)
School of Oriental and African Studies, Thornhaugh Street, Russell Square, London WC1H 0XG. ☎ 020-7898 4350. Email cjs@soas.ac.uk; Website www.soas.ac.uk/centres/jewish studies. *Dir.* Dr T. Parfitt; *Chairman* Dr Colin Shindler; *Co-ord.* Dalia Manor.

CENTRE FOR JEWISH STUDIES (University of Manchester)
Arts Building, University of Manchester, Oxford Road, Manchester M13 9PL.
☎ 0161-275 3614. Fax 0161-275 3613. Email cjs@man.ac.uk; Website www.mucjs.org.
(Est. 1997) The Centre seeks to maximise the teaching, undergraduate and postgraduate, of Jewish Studies in the University of Manchester, through support of courses and student bursaries; to foster collaborative research between staff of the University of Manchester and others in the region through research seminars and research projects (including local Jewish history); to bring the results of academic work in Jewish Studies to the wider community through public lectures (including the Sherman Lectures) and conferences; and to disseminate the results of these activities on the internet. The website also features an internet exhibition and a new electronic journal, Melilah. *Co-Dirs* Prof. Philip S. Alexander, Prof. Bernard S. Jackson; *Co-ord.* Dr Daniel Langton.

CENTRE FOR MODERN HEBREW STUDIES
Faculty of Oriental Studies, Sidgwick Avenue, Cambridge CB3 9DA.
☎ 01223-335117. Fax 01223-335110.
A centre established within the University of Cambridge for study, research and the promotion of modern Hebrew language, literature and culture. *H. Dir.* Dr R. Domb.

INSTITUTE OF JEWISH STUDIES
University College London, Gower Street, WC1E 6BT.
☎ 020-7679 3520. Fax 020-7209 1026. Email uclhvtm@ucl.ac.uk; Website www.ucl.ac.uk/hebrew-jewish/ijs.
(Est. 1953. Reg. Charity No. 213114) Founded by the late Prof. Alexander Altmann, IJS is now located within the Dept. of Hebrew and Jewish Studies at Univ. College, London, while retaining its autonomous status. Funded by the private sector. Programme of activities dedicated to the academic study of all branches of Jewish history and civilisation, including series of public lectures, seminars, symposia, major internat. conferences, research projects and publs., especially of its conference proceedings. It brings together scholars, students, academic instits. from all sections inside and outside the Univ. of London and the scholarly scene in and outside the UK, worldwide. It equally reaches the community at large and acts as a unifying force between the Jewish and non-Jewish academic and lay public. The 2002 conference was

on 'Jewish Theatre'. The 2003 conference will be on 'Science among the Jews'. List of publications and programme mailings available on request.
Patrons The Lord Mishcon, The Lord Moser, The Rt. Hon. The Lord Woolf; Bd. of Govs: *Chairman* Philip L. Morgenstern, BA; *H. Ts.* Daniel Peltz, BA, David J. Lewis, BSc, FRICS, Edward M.Lee, BSc (Econ), Philipp, MA, FRCS, FRCOG, Nick Ritblat, MA, J. Caplan, FCA (also *H. Sec.*); *Dir.* Prof. Mark J. Geller. The Trustees of the Institute of Jewish Studies, a non-profit making company limited by guarantee, registered in England No. 2598783.

JOE LOSS LECTURESHIP IN JEWISH MUSIC
Music Department, School of Oriental and African Studies, University of London, Thornhaugh St., Russell Sq., WC1H 0XG.
☎ 020-7898 4688. Fax 020-7898 4699. Email ak42@soas.ac.uk.
(Est. 1991) Incorporates Jewish Music Resource Centre, and the Harry Rosencweig Collection of Jewish Music (see p.56). Sponsored by the Jewish Music Institute (see p.39). Research, lecturing, teaching, consultancy. Studies cover the liturgical, semi-religious, folk, popular and art music of Ashkenazi, Sephardi and Oriental ethnic groups, in the context of Jewish culture, society, history, geography, language, psychology, religion and tradition (within wider Christian and Islamic environments). Specialized resources comprise extensive collections of books and audio-visual materials. *Lect.* Alexander Knapp.

LEO BAECK INSTITUTE
4 Devonshire Street, W1W 5LB.
☎ 020-7580 3493. Fax 020-7436 8634. Email ap@lbilon.demon.co.uk. Website www.leobaeck.co.uk.
(Est. 1955. Reg. Charity No. 235163) Research and publications on history of Central European German-speaking Jewry. *Chairman* Prof. Peter Pulzer; *Dir.* Dr R. Gross; *T.* Dr A. Paucker. *Publ.:* Year Book (*Edr.* Prof. J. A. S. Grenville), symposia, monographs, etc.

LONDON SCHOOL OF JEWISH STUDIES (formerly Jews' College)
Schaller House, Albert Road, Hendon NW4 2SJ.
☎ 020-8203 6427. Fax 020-8203 6420. Email enquiries@lsjs.ac.uk; Website www.lsjs.ac.uk
(Est. 1855) Provides BA, MA and PhD courses in Hebrew and Jewish Studies, and its rabbinical ordination and training programmes. It also houses one of the most extensive Judaica libraries in Europe.
Governing Body: *President* The Chief Rabbi Professor Jonathan Sacks, MA (Cantab); *Deputy President* Rabbi Abraham Levy, BA, PhD; *Chairman* Alan Grant, BA, Clive Marks, FCA, ATII, Hon FLCM; *Ts.* Bernard Waiman, MA; *Hon. Sec.* Rabbi E. Mirvis, BA.
Principal; *Dir.* Dr Ian Rabinowitz, MSc, MBA, MA, PhD; *Hd of Acad. Dept* Rabbi Dr Sacha Stern, MA, D Phil (Oxon); *Faculty* Dr Tamra Wright, MA, PhD, Dr Daniel Rynhold, MA, PhD, Clive Lawton, MA, MEd, MSc, Fiona Blumfield, MA, Rabbi Michael Newman, MPhil, Clive Fierstone, MA, MPhil; *Hd Librarian* Esra Kahn; *Admin.* Esther Miller; *Publ.* Le'ela (twice yearly).

OXFORD CENTRE FOR HEBREW AND JEWISH STUDIES
Yarnton Manor, Yarnton, Oxford, OX5 1PY.
☎ 01865 377946. Fax 01865 375079. Email ochjs@herald.ox.ac.uk; Website www.associnst.ox.ac.uk/ochjs.
Teaching Unit: Oriental Institute. ☎ 01865 278200. Fax 01865 278190
(Est. 1972) The Centre is one of Europe's leading teaching and research institutions in the area of Hebrew and Jewish studies. Its work includes Jewish

history and literature, ancient, medieval and modern; Talmudic studies; Jewish/Islamic and Jewish/Christian relationships at all periods; Hebrew and Yiddish language; anthropology; sociology; law; and theology. It provides instruction in Jewish studies towards the Oxford University BA, M.St., M.Phil, M.Litt and D.Phil degrees. The Centre initiated and runs the one-year Master of Studies (M.St.) in Jewish Studies in Oxford.

Publications: Journal of Jewish Studies (half-yearly); the Jewish Law Annual; and numerous books and articles by Fellows past and present. The Programme of Activities and the Annual Report of the Centre are available on request. *President* Peter Oppenheimer; *Chairman Bd. Gov.* Sir Richard Greenbury. (The Centre also houses the Leopold Muller Memorial Library, see p.58).

PARKES INSTITUTE FOR THE STUDY OF JEWISH/NON-JEWISH RELATIONS

Department of History, University of Southampton, Southampton SO17 1BJ.
☎ 023 80592261. Fax 023 80593458.

The Parkes Institute promotes teaching, research, publications and outreach work in the area of Jewish/non-Jewish relations, developing the approach of its founder Rev. Dr James Parkes, and is based on the extensive Parkes Library and related Jewish archives. It offers undergraduate and MA degrees in Jewish History and Culture. Publications linked to the Institute include three journals (Patterns of Prejudice, Jewish History and Culture, and The Journal of Holocaust Education) and the Parkes–Wiener Jewish studies book series. *Hd of Institute* Prof. Tony Kushner.

SCHOOL OF ORIENTAL AND AFRICAN STUDIES (SOAS)

Dept. of the Languages and Cultures of the Near and Middle East, Thornhaugh Street, Russell Square, London WC1H OXG.
☎ 020-7898 4320. Fax 020-7898 4359. Website www.soas.ac.uk

SOAS is one of the world's greatest concentrations of expertise on Africa and Asia. The Near & Middle East Department offers a B.A. in Hebrew & Israeli Studies and degrees combining Hebrew with Law, Economics, Management, Arabic and with many other subjects – all affording a year's study at the Hebrew University of Jerusalem. The one-year Diploma in Jewish Studies caters for postgraduates from around the world seeking an entrée into the field. These programmes have the benefit of one of the largest open-stack Jewish Studies libraries in Europe. Also based at SOAS is the Centre for Jewish Studies, which hosts lecture series and symposia on a wide range of issues (see p.44).

STANLEY BURTON CENTRE FOR HOLOCAUST STUDIES

Dept. of History, University of Leicester, Leicester LE1 7RH.
☎ 0116-2522800 Fax 0116-2523986

To promote the study of and research into the Holocaust. *Dir.* Steve G. Paulsson; *H. Assoc. Dir.* Aubrey Newman; *H. Res. Fellow* Dr J. Scott.

UNIVERSITY COLLEGE LONDON

Department of Hebrew and Jewish Studies, Gower Street, WC1E 6BT.
☎ 020-7679 7171. Fax 020-7209 1026. Email jewishstudies@ucl.ac.uk; Website www.ucl.ac.uk/hebrew-jewish/.

The largest univ. dept. in the UK and Europe for obtaining honours degrees (BA in Hebrew or Jewish History; MA in Hebrew and Jewish Studies or Holocaust Studies or Modern Israeli Studies; MPhil and PhD). Fields of teaching and research include: the Ancient Near East; Biblical Languages and Literature; Jews in the Classical World; Medieval and Modern Jewish History and Culture; Jews in Central and Eastern Europe; Modern Hebrew and Yiddish Language and

Literature; Jews in Islamic Societies; Modern Israeli Politics; Jewish Mysticism and Spirituality, esp. Hasidism; Women in the Jewish Tradition; the Holocaust in Historical Perspective. Undergraduate students spend a year of the course at the Hebrew University of Jerusalem. The dept. hosts visiting staff from the Hebrew University on an annual basis. The dept. comprises nine full-time and seven part-time members of staff. There are over 50 undergraduate and 40 graduate students. The dept. hosts the Institute of Jewish Studies (see p. 44) *Head* Dr Ada Rapoport-Albert.

Centre for Israeli Studies
(Est. 2000) *Dir.* Dr Neill Lochery; *President, International Adv. Bd.* Sir Martin Gilbert.

ORGANISATIONS CONCERNED WITH JEWISH YOUTH

B'NAI B'RITH YOUTH ORGANISATION

1–2 Endsleigh Street, WC1H 0DS.
☎ 020-7387 3115. Fax 020-7387 8014. Email bbyo@anjy.org
BBYO is a unique, peer-led Zionist youth organisation. It promotes Zionism, Judaism, leadership, welfare and social awareness in a pluralist, open and totally youth-led environment. There are weekly meetings in 12 chapters, national events, Israel summer tour, 'Atid' Leadership tour and a one-year programme in Israel. *Youth Dir.* Daniele Pearlman; *Movement Worker* Nicki Davies.

JEWISH GUIDE ADVISORY COUNCIL

JGAC furthers the Guide movement in the Jewish Com. *Nat. Chairman* Mrs Ruth Tunkel, 44 West Hill Way, Totteridge, London N20 8QS. ☎ 020-8446 3871; *T.* Mrs Judy Woolf, 14 Audley Close, Borehamwood, WD6 1UF. ☎ 020-8207 1102.

JEWISH LADS' AND GIRLS' BRIGADE

HQ: Camperdown, 3 Beechcroft Road, South Woodford, E18 1LA.
☎ 020-8989 8990. Fax 020-8518 8832.
(Est. 1895. Reg. Charity No. 286950) The JLGB is the longest-established Jewish youth movement in the UK. There are groups throughout the country. Members are encouraged to develop an awareness of the needs of others, through voluntary service projects, and through its 'Hand in Hand' Project partnerships have been established with Ravenswood/Unity and Jewish Care to set up volunteer groups around the UK.

It is the only Jewish Operating Authority for the Duke of Edinburgh's Award. The JLGB also offers its own Challenge Award for Jewish Youth, which includes sections on Jewish Heritage and Israel and the annual Sir Peter E. Lazarus Debating Competition.

Patron Edmund L. de Rothschild, CBE, TD; *President* Dame Simone Prendergast, DBE, JP, DL; *Commandant* Mrs Jill Attfield; *Chairman* C.S. Kay, MBE; *Chaplain* Rev Stanley Cohen; *Brigade Sec.* R.S. Weber.

JEWISH LEARNING EXCHANGE

Lincoln Gate, 152–154 Golders Green Road, London NW11 8HE.
☎ 020-8458 4588. Fax 020-8458 4587. Email jle@jle.org.uk; Website www.jle.org.uk.
A service of Ohr Somayach Institutions. Organises social and educational events for young adults including trips abroad and study programmes in Israel. *Dir.* Rabbi D. Kirsch, 29 The Drive, London NW11 9SX. ☎ 020-8458 4391. Fax 020-8458 5694.

JEWISH SCOUT ADVISORY COUNCIL

Furthers scouting in the Jewish com. *H. Sec.* R. Simmons, 103 Kenton Lane, Kenton, Harrow, Middx HA3 8UJ. ☎ 020-8907 3446. Fax 020-8907 6297.

JEWISH YOUTH FUND
707 High Road, North Finchley, London N12 0BT.
☎ 020-8445 1670. Fax 020-8446 7370. Email jyf@anjy.org.
(Est. 1937. Reg. Charity No. 251902) Provides funds to promote the social education of Jewish young people through the provision of leisure time facilities to clubs, movements and other Jewish youth organisations in the United Kingdom. *Chairman of Adv. Cttee* Jonathan Gestetner; *T.* Miss Wendy Pollecoff; *Tr.* Jonathan Gestetner, Lady Morris of Kenwood, R. McGratty, Miss Wendy Pollecoff; *Sec.* Peter Shaw.

JEWISH YOUTH ORCHESTRA OF GREAT BRITAIN
Rehearsals: Hillel House, 1-2 Endsleigh Street, WC1H 0DS.
(Est. 1970. Reg. Charity No. 294994) For young musicians (aged 13–20, Grade V and above) to give regular concerts in London and other cities. Occasional summer courses. Rehearsals Sunday mornings during term-time. *Co-founder and conductor* Sydney Fixman; *Chairman* Dr J. W. Frank, PO Box 24006, London NW4 4ZF, ☎ 0958 434999; *T.* S. Admoni.

JNF YOUTH & EDUCATION DEPT.
58-70 Edgware Way, Edgware, Middx HA8 8GQ.
☎ 020-8421 7603. Fax 020-8905 4299. Email education@jnf.co.uk.
Provides educational resources and speakers for nurseries, schools, religion classes, youth movements, youth clubs and university campuses, in the areas of Israel partnership, land reclamation and ecological issues. Assists in co-ordinating and arranging Bar/Bat Mitzvahs in Israel. *Educ. Co-ord.* D. Fraser.

JYSG – Jewish Youth Study Groups
Beit Meir, 44a Albert Rd., London NW4 2SJ.
☎ 020-8457 9709. Fax 020-8457 9707. Email jysg@aje.org.uk; Website www.jysg.org.uk.
Holds weekly Sunday meetings for 13–18 age group on a variety of Jewish and secular topics in 13 areas around London and in the Regions as well as annual summer and winter schools, a post-GCSE Israel Tour and a pre-university 6-month programme in Israel. *Contact* Melanie Shutz.

MACCABI GB
Shield House, Harmony Way, Hendon, London NW4 2BZ.
☎ 020-8457 2333. Fax 020-8203 3237. Email enquiries@maccabigb.org; Website www.maccabigb.org.
To promote the active participation in sports and education of Jewish men, women and children, in order to enhance their Jewish identity, values and commitment to the community. *Chairman* Richard Feldman; *Vice-Chair.* Sandy Kattan; *Chief Exec.* Martin Berliner; *H. Sec.* Diane Minkoff; *Hon. Sports Dir.* Elaine Levy.

Twenty-three affiliated clubs, eight affiliated sports leagues, and 14 affiliated schools and universities both in London and in the Regions.

MAKOR-AJY Centre for Informal Jewish Education
Balfour House, 741 High Road, London N12 0BQ.
☎ 020-8369 5270. Fax 020-8369 5271. Email info@makor.org.uk
Makor-AJY works with professionals and volunteers involved in informal Jewish education throughout the community, and provides them with the following five key services: education programmes and seminars; leadership training; advice and guidance; resources; innovations and analysis. Makor-AJY is a project of the UJIA and the Jewish Agency. *Dir.* Roy Graham, LLB, MA; *Deputy Dir.* Eric Finestone, MA.

NOAM (NOAR MASORTI)
1097 Finchley Road, London NW11 0PU.
☎ 020-8201 8773. Fax 020-8201 8917. Email noam@masorti.org.uk.
(Est. 1985. Reg. Charity No. 801846) NOAM is the Masorti Zionist youth movement. We run a wide variety of educational and social activities including clubs, weekends, summer camps and Israel tours for 8–16 year olds. NOAM also runs the MELTAM leadership course for Year 11s. Other activities include: Noam Israel Tour (post-GCSE); Drachim – year-in-Israel including Machon, kibbutz, volunteer work and Jewish learning; summer camps in Britain and Spain; weekly clubs; weekends away; social action and charity projects; and contact with Masorti youth in Israel, Europe and America. *Mazkira* Rachel Sklan; *Education* Claudia Waller; *Activities* Nic Schlagman; *Shlicha* Avigail ben Aryeh. *Publ.* Hadashot Noam (termly newsletter); Norm (bi-annual magazine).

RSY-NETZER/RSGB YOUTH, STUDENTS AND YOUNG ADULTS
Manor House, 80 East End Road, N3 2SY.
☎ 020-8349 5680. Email admin@rsy-netzer.org.uk; admin@reformstudents.org.uk
Northern Office Sandra Vigon Resource & Learning Centre, Jacksons Row, Albert Square, Manchester M2 5WD.
To educate young people towards a love of Reform Judaism and Reform Zionism and to offer them Jewish life options within an equal opportunity perspective.

The Department offers youth work development and training to RSGB communities as well as developing innovative models of youth work practice and provides programmes, activities and support for Reform Jewish students.

SIR MAX BONN MEMORIAL JEWISH YOUTH CENTRE
Leigh House, 63 Ethelbert Road, Cliftonville, Kent.
(Est. 1947) To provide a holiday centre for young people and adolescents, conferences and discussion groups among clubs and institutions. *Contact* Mrs Doris Cohen, 2 Priory Court, Sparrows Herne, Bushey, Herts WD2 1EF. ☎ 020-8950 5141.

ULPSNYC–NETZER (*The youth movement of Liberal Judaism*)
The Montagu Centre, 21 Maple Street, W1T 4BE.
☎ 020-7631 0584. Fax 020-7436 4184. Email office@ulpsnyc.org; Website www.ulpsnyc.org.
To help young Jewish people towards a strong identity within a Liberal Jewish and Progressive Zionist framework, through training in youth leadership and informal education. *Admin.* Sandra Levene; *Shaliach* Eran Shafir; *Fieldworker* Asher Jacobsberg.

YOUNG JEWISH CARE
Jewish Care's young fundraising arm offers events and committees for 11–30+ year olds. YJC is in the forefront of young Jewish fundraising. *Contact* yjc@jcare.org or www.jewishcare.org for further information.

ZEST
Bet Meir, 44a Albert Road, London NW4 2SJ.
☎ 020-8457 9709. Fax 020-8457 9707. Email info@zest-uk.org; Website www.zest-uk.org.
Provides social, educational events and leadership training for students and young adults aged 18–30 years. Hosts an annual weekend abroad to places of secular and Jewish interest. *Contact* Melanie Shutz.

The following groups are associated with the Zionist Movement.

BACHAD FELLOWSHIP
Friends of Bnei Akiva, Alexander Margulies Youth Centre, 2 Halleswelle Road, London NW11 0DJ.
☎ 020-8458 9370. Fax 020-8209 0107.
(Est. 1942. Reg. Charity No. 227509) To promote Jewish religious education and provide agricultural and vocational training for Jewish youth. Establishes and maintains Youth Centres in London, Leeds, Manchester, Glasgow and Dublin. *Hon. Presidents* Chief Rabbi Dr. Jonathan Sacks, Rabbi Cyril Harris, Chief Rabbi of South Africa; *Chairman* Arieh L. Handler; *V. Chairman* Jack Lass; *H. Ts.* Harry T. Klahr, Frank Weinberg; *H. Sec* Mrs. Susan Sperber; *Admin.* Mrs Tania Fraenkel. Bnei Akiva Scholarship Institute (BASI) arranges for senior members to spend one or two years in Israel working and studying to prepare for ultimate settlement in the country after returning here to act as youth leaders for a period.

BETAR-TAGAR
143–145 Brondesbury Park, London NW2 5JL.
☎ 020-8451 0002. Fax 020-8459 8766. Email betar@betar.co.uk
(Reg. Charity No. 290571) Betar-Tagar Zionist youth and students' movement educates Jewish students and youth towards Zionism by stressing Aliya, the value of Jewish tradition and concern for Jewish people everywhere, self-defence and Jewish identity. *Shaliah* S. Shamila.

BNEI AKIVA
2 Halleswelle Road, London NW11 0DJ.
☎ 020-8209 1319. Fax 020-8209 0107. Email office@bauk.org; Website www.bauk.org.
(Est. 1939) Bnei Akiva is the largest religious Zionist youth movement in the world. Supports Aliya to the State of Israel as the movement objective. Aims to educate young people, aged between 7 and 25 years, in ideals of Religious Zionism and Torah Ve-Avodah. Bnei Akiva runs a year scheme in Israel known as Hachshara which has two tracks – a yeshiva-based programme, and a scheme centred around volunteering and learning. *Mazkir* Jonathan Lipczer; *Admin.* Rosemary Davidson. *Publ.* Monthly education booklets, Yediot (termly movement magazine), weekly Sidrah sheet, annual educational journal. **Regional centres:** 72 Singleton Road, Salford M7 4LU. ☎ 0161-740 1621. Fax 0161-740 8018. Email office@bneiakiva.org

EZRA YOUTH MOVEMENT
British and European Off.: 2a Alba Gardens, London, NW11 9NR.
☎/Fax 020-8458 5372.
Associated with Poale Agudat Israel.
Orthodox Jewish movement based in London with a branch in Manchester and branches in Israel and other parts of the world.

FEDERATION OF ZIONIST YOUTH
45 The Burroughs, Hendon, London NW4 4AX (Head Office).
☎ 020-8201 6661 (Head Office). ☎ 0161-721 4782 (Northern Office). Email office@fzy.org.uk; Website www.fzy.org.uk.
FZY is a Zionist youth movement with chavurot throughout Britain. It is a pluralist movement and educates its members around Jewish and Zionist themes with the aim of fulfilling the four aims of FZY: Aliya, Tarbut (Jewish culture), Tzedaka and Magen (defence of Jewish rights). It offers a dynamic and creative environment for Jewish youth to express their heritage, culture and identity. Its courses allow FZYniks

to explore and understand Israel and themselves, and encourages them to return as leaders in the community. *President* Paul Lenga; *Hon. President* Abba Eban; *Mazkir* Russell Wolkind; *Oved Chinuch* Aron Lazarus; *Camps Organiser* Matt Bick; *Northern Fieldworker* Ilana Simons; *Rekaz Shnat* Toby Greene; *Org. Sec.* Louise Jacobs; *Year Course Admin.* Vivienne Stone. *Publ.* The Young Zionist and FrenZY.

HABONIM–DROR
523 Finchley Road, London NW3 7BD.
☎ 020-7435 9033/4. Fax 020-7431 4503.
(Est. 1929) Habonim was founded in the East End of London, and became the leading international socialist Zionist Jewish youth movement, merging with Dror in 1979. Habonim Dror's ideology is centred around meaningful, cultural Judaism, socialism and Zionism, educating members, aged 9–23, towards strong, Jewish identities, striving for a more equal and compassionate Israeli society. Weekly activities around the UK focus on informal education. Habonim Dror's Shnat Hachshara involves living together as a community in Jerusalem and engaging in social activism projects, intensive educational and leadership-training seminars, and tours of Israel. *President* Ruth Lady Morris of Kenwood; *Admin.* David Arram; *Nat. Sec.* Louise Dobrin. *Publ.* Koleinu, Ma hadash, Ma Koreh.

Youth Centres

London: North West London and Central Office, 523 Finchley Rd, London NW3 7BD, ☎ 020-7435 9033. Fax 020-7431 4503. Email mail@habodror.org.uk; Belsize Square, c/o Central Office; Hackney, c/o Central Office; Radlett, c/o Central Office.

Manchester: South, Southsdie, 34 Ashley Rd, Altrincham. ☎ 0161 929 6670; North, Central Northern Office, 11 Upper Park Rd, Salford. ☎ 0161 795 9447. Email manchester@habodror.org.uk

Leeds: Etz Chaim Synagogue, 411 Harrogate Rd, c/o Central Northern Office.

Birmingham: c/o Central Office.

Bristol: Clifton College, c/o Central Office.

Glasgow: 59 Barrhead Rd, Glasgow, c/o Central Northern Office.

HANOAR HATZIONI
The Youth Centre, 31 Tetherdown, Muswell Hill, London N10 1ND.
☎ 020-88831022/3. Fax 020-8365 2272. Email email@hanoar.co.uk; Website www. hanoar.co.uk
(Reg. Charity No. 296973) Hanoar Hatzioni are a non-political Zionist Youth Movement catering for people between the ages of 7 and 23. Groups are run all over the country. Annual events include Summer and Winter Camps, Israel Tours for 16 year olds, outings, educational and social programmes. Hanoar Hatzioni also run the Shnat Sherut Year Scheme and the Gesher 6 months Scheme in Israel. *Mazkir* Greg Krieger; *Rosh Chinuch* Adam Ross.

HASHOMER HATZAIR
Hashomer House, 37A Broadhurst Gardens, NW6 3BN.
☎ 020-7328 5451.
(Est. 1940) The British constituent of a world movement to educate its members in Socialist Zionist ideals as a basis for life in Israel especially kibbutz.

JNF FUTURE
58-70 Edgware Way, Edgware, Middx HA8 8GQ.
☎ 020-8421 7603. Fax 020-8905 4299. Email info@jnf.co.uk.
(Est. 1998) To support the work of the JNF in Israel in afforestation, land reclamation, environmental and ecological issues by fund-raising events organised for and by young people (18–30) nationwide. *Co-Ord.* Elisa Ziff.

KIBBUTZ REPRESENTATIVES
1A Accommodation Road, London NW11 8ED.
☎ 020-8458 9235. Fax 020-8455 7930. Email enquiries@kibbutz.org.uk.
(Reg. Charity No. 294564) Representing all the Kibbutz movements in Israel. The organisation arranges Working Visits on Kibbutz for persons aged 18–32; Kibbutz Ulpan for persons aged 18–35, including the 'Oren' enrichment programme; and a 2-month short Summer Ulpan, for persons aged 18–26. Religious Kibbutz options are available.

KIDMAH
c/o Hashomer House, 37a Broadhurst Gdns, London NW6 3BN.
☎ 020-7328 5451.
Left-Zionist student organisation promoting Jewish-Arab recognisation, religious pluralism, anti-racism. Educational, social, political activities; provides lecturers to Jewish and non-Jewish groups. *Fieldworker* Daniel Marcus.

YOUNG MAPAM
Hashomer House, 37A Broadhurst Gardens, London NW6 3BN.
☎ 020-7328 5451.
Anglo-Jewish youth and student group, ages 18–35, with a Socialist-Zionist outlook. Social, cultural, educ. and political programme stressing humanistic values of Judaism and progressive Zionist elements. Aliya of members encouraged. *Chairman* Marc Bernstein.

The following organisations are concerned with Jewish students

AJ6 (ASSOCIATION OF JEWISH SIXTH FORMERS)
1–2 Endsleigh Street, London WC1H 0DS.
☎ 020-7387 3384. Fax 020-7387 3392. Email office@aj6.org; Website www.aj6.org.
(Est. 1977. Reg. Charity No. 1076442) Jewish youth organisation for fifth and sixth formers (membership 600, service outreach 2000). AJ6's vision is of an educated and tolerant Community, responsibility for each other, excited and enriched by their Judaism, and inspired by their Youth. Its mission is to educate and develop Jewish fifth and sixthformers. Events include tours to Israel and Europe, conferences, national weekends, and regional meetings in nine centres around the country. Services include the AJ6 Guide to Jewish Student Life. *Nat. Dir.* Natalie Saunderson; *Educ. Dev. Worker* Charlotte Benjamin; *Schools Worker* Ruth Cohen.

B'NAI B'RITH HILLEL FOUNDATION
Hillel House, 1–2 Endsleigh Street, London WC1H 0DS.
☎ 020-7388 0801. Fax 020-7916 3973. Email info@hillel.co.uk. Website www.hillel.co.uk.
(Reg. Charity No. 313503) Jewish Student Centre, devoted to social and educational activities among Jewish students at colleges and universities. Facilities include meeting rooms, common room, Kosher Restaurant. Closed Shabbat and Festivals, other than by arrangement. *President* Fred S. Worms, OBE; *Chairman* Sir Victor Blank; *Deputy Chairman* Dr Alan Webber; *H.T.* G. Weinberg; *Exec. Dir.* Gerry Lucas.

Residential and social facilities available at **Hillel Houses** in the following locations (contact person named for further details):

London: *Endsleigh Street (non-residential),* Gerry Lucas, ☎ 020 7388 0801; *London Hillels: Contact* Herman Greenbourne, ☎ 020 8998 7865; **Birmingham:** Patricia Harris, ☎ 01564 778710; **Bournemouth:** Marilyn Dexter, ☎ 01202 780 030; **Brighton:** Corinne Blass, ☎ 01273 555089; **Bristol:** Sheila Tobias, ☎ 01454 412

831; **Cardiff:** Lisa Gerson, ☎ 029-2075 9982; **Edinburgh:** Myrna Kaplan, ☎ 0131 339 8201; **Glasgow:** Linda Lovat, ☎ 0141 639 7741; Adele Conn, ☎ 0141 638 1154; **Hull:** Ian Dysch, ☎ 01482 354 947; **Leeds:** Sheila Sive, ☎ 0113 266 6346; **Leicester:** Melissa Morrison, ☎ 0116 270 5771; **Liverpool:** Gareth Jones, ☎ 0151 280 0551; **Manchester:** Dr Sydney Baigel, ☎ 0161 740 2521; **Newcastle:** Susan Olsburgh, ☎ 0191 213 0665; Melanie Mark, ☎ 0191 284 1903; **Nottingham:** Susan Litman, ☎ 0115 963 5451; **Reading:** Janette Sassoon, ☎ 0118 961 3367; **Sheffield:** Elaine Jacob, ☎ 0114 230 8688; Prof. Martin Black, ☎ 0114 262 0337; **Southampton:** ☎ 02380 340898; **York:** Phil Prosser, ☎ 01904 432165.

MASORTI GESHER TEENAGE CENTRE

1097 Finchley Road, London NW11 0PU
☎ 020-8201 8772. Fax 020-8201 8917. Email office@masorti.org.uk
Gesher provides formal Jewish education for young people of secondary-school age. It offers an environment where friendships and identity develop together with the skills and knowledge to keep young people connected to Judaism throughout their teenage years. Gesher is a project of the Assembly of Masorti Synagogues. *Dir.* Cheryl Sklan.

NATIONAL JEWISH CHAPLAINCY BOARD

21 Gloucester Gardens, London NW11 9AB
☎ 020-8731 7471. Fax 020-8209 0927. Email njcb@brijnet.org.
(Reg. Charity no. 261324) Appointment of full-time chaplains to serve all Jewish students at universities in the United Kingdom, in conjunction with local boards. For local contacts, apply to administrator. Chaplains available for personal counselling, practical support, as an educational resource and for spiritual guidance. *President:* The Chief Rabbi; *Hon. V. President* Michael Weinstein; *T.* Robert Gershon; *Dir.* Ruth Marriott.
Chaplains: Scotland/Northern Region, Rabbi Dovid Cohen ☎ 0141-577 8246; Birmingham/Midland Region, Rabbi Fishel Cohen ☎ 0121-440 1359; Leeds/North East Region, Rabbi Dovid Hodges ☎ 0113-268 3526; Cambridge/East Anglia Region, Rabbi Julian Sinclair ☎ 01223-366388; Bristol/Western Region, Enq. Andrea Hutter ☎ 0117-962 1076; London Region, Rabbi Gavin Broder ☎ 020-7380 0207; Assoc. Chaplain Central Manchester, Rabbi Y.Y. Rubinstein ☎ 0161-721 4066.

REFORM STUDENTS

The Sternberg Centre for Judaism, 80 East End Road, Finchley, London N3 2SY.
☎ 020-8349 5667. Fax 020-8349 5696. Email admin@reformstudents.org.uk; Website www.reformstudents.org.uk.
Aims to inspire and educate Reform students to become skilled and motivated Reform leaders of the Jewish community. Represents Reform Judaism at all UJS events. Contact: *Student Co-ord.* Carla Garnelas.

UNION OF JEWISH STUDENTS

of the United Kingdom and Ireland
(formerly: Inter-University Jewish Federation of Gt. Britain and Ireland).
Hillel House, 1/2 Endsleigh Street, WC1H 0DS.
☎ 020-7387 4644. Fax 020-7383 0390. Email ujs@ujs.org.uk; Website www.ujs.org.uk.
(Est 1919) Co-ordinates the activities of the Jewish societies in the universities and colleges of the UK and Ireland. It stimulates an interest among Jewish students in Judaism, Zionism, Jewish history and education, and in Jewish thought. It encourages members to play their part in the religious and social life of the community. (Est. 1919.) Jewish student societies are attached to many universities and colleges. See under separate towns. *Chair* Alan Senitt.

WINGATE YOUTH TRUST
(Est. 1975. Reg. Charity No. 269678) To provide facilities for youth, for recreation and leisure. *Chairman* B. Myers; *T.* M. Rebak, 58 Southwood Park, Southwood Lawn Road, N6 5SQ. ☎ 020-8340 1287; *Sec.* Malcolm Davis.

LIBRARIES, MUSEUMS AND EXHIBITIONS

Anglo-Jewish Archives. An independent Registered Charity under the auspices of the Jewish Historical Society of England. The genealogical collections have been deposited at the Society of Genealogists and the main archive collection has been deposited with the Hartley Library, University of Southampton (see p.55). *H. Sec.* Dr Gerry Black, (JHSE), 33 Seymour Place, London W1H 5AP. ☎/Fax 020-7723 5852.

Hebraica Libraries Group, c/o Huguenot Library, University College, Gower Street, London WC1E 6BT. Websites www.bodley.ox.ac.uk/users/gae/NCOLR/NCOLRWEB.htm; www.lib.cam/ac.uk/~jb127/ (Est. 1979) The Group brings together representatives of all the major Judaica and Hebraica collections in Great Britain and Ireland (as listed below) together with other academic libraries with an interest in the field. It holds an annual meeting and is affiliated to both the British Association of Jewish Studies and the European Association of Jewish Studies, and to the National Council on Orientalist Library Resources (NCOLR). It offers expertise in all aspects of Hebraica collections, preservation, security, conservation, cataloguing, computer systems and collection development. *Convenor* S.W. Massil.

AJEX Military Museum, AJEX House, East Bank, Stamford Hill, London N16 5RT. ☎ 020-8800 2844. Fax 020-8880 1117. Email ajexuk@talk21.com; Website www.ajex.org.uk. A display of books, photographs and memorabilia from the reign of George III to the present. *Archivist* H. Morris.

Ben Uri Gallery, The London Jewish Museum of Art, 108 Boundary Road, London NW8 0RH. ☎ 020-7604 3991. Fax 020-7604 3992. Email info@benuri.org.uk; Website (for opening times and programmes) www.benuri.com.
(Est. 1915. Reg. Charity No. 280389) The objectives of the gallery are to promote education, entertainment and outreach by celebrating the artistic achievement of Jewish artists as part of the Jewish cultural heritage. A full programme of exhibitions and interesting activities is provided for 'Friends' including lectures, visits to other galleries and the Annual Picture Fair. *Chairman* David Glasser; *V. Chairman*, David Stern; *H. Sec.* Gordon Hausmann; *H. T.* John Wosner; *Chairman of Exhibitions Cttee* David Stern; *Chairman of Permanent Collection Cttee* Peter Gross; *V. President* Anne Fealdman.

Biesenthal Collection, Special Libraries and Archives, King's College, Old Aberdeen. ☎ 001224 272598. Consists of some 2,000 volumes and one of Britain's finest Rabbinical collections acquired in 1872. The Special Libraries and Archives also feature the collections and papers of Malcolm Hay of Seaton which include material on Zionism and correspondence in Hebrew.

Bodleian Library, Broad Street, Oxford OX1 3BG. ☎ 01865 277000. *Bodley's Librarian* R. Carr. The Hebrew and Yiddish collections comprise 3,000 manuscript volumes and 60,000 printed books, including many incunabula, fragments from the Cairo Genizah and the Oppenheimer library, the finest collection of Hebrew books and manuscripts ever assembled. Intending readers should always contact the Admissions Office in advance. Open to holders of a reader's ticket Mon. to Fri. 9-7, Sat. 9-1. *Hebrew Specialist Libr.* R. C. Judd, M.A., M.Phil. Email rcj@bodley.ox.ac.uk.

The British Library, Asia, Pacific and Africa Collections – Hebrew Section, 96 Euston Road, London NW1 2DB. ☎ 020-7412/7646. Fax 020-7412 7641. Email oioc-enquiries@ bl.uk. The Hebrew collection comprises over 3,000 manuscript volumes and 10,000 fragments (incl. Moses Gaster's collection and many fragments from the Cairo Genizah); Hebrew printed books, about 70,000 titles, incl. some 100 incunabula, rabbinic and modern Hebrew literature; Yiddish, Ladino, Judeo-Arabic and Judeo-Persian books; some 1,000 Hebrew and Yiddish periodicals and newspapers. Oriental Reading Room open to holders of readers' passes. (Hours of opening may be subject to revision at any time. Normal opening: Mon. 10.00–5.00; Tues.-Sat. 9.30–5.00). Some Hebrew manuscripts are on permanent display in the British Library Exhibition Galleries, open (free of charge): Mon., Wed. to Fri. 9.30–6.00, Tues. 9.30–8.00, Sat. 9.30–5.00, Sun. 11.00–5.00. The Golden Haggadah is included in the electronic 'Turning the Pages' programme. *Hebrew Specialist* Ilana Tahan, M.Phil. Email ilana.tahan@bl.uk.

Brotherton Library, University of Leeds, Leeds LS2 9JT. ☎ 0113 3435518. Fax 0113 3435561. Email special-collections@library.leeds.ac.uk; Website www.leeds.ac.uk/library. *Librarian* Jan Wilkinson. Holdings include substantial materials for Hebrew and Jewish studies and the Travers Herford Collection on Judaism and Talmudic studies. The primary Judaica collection is the Roth Collection comprising the manuscripts and printed books from the library of Cecil Roth, including 350 mss., 900 printed books (pre-1850) 6,000 modern books and other archival material. Available to bona fide scholars who should write to the Librarian in the first instance enclosing an appropriate recommendation. *Asst. Libr.* M. C. Davis. *Publ.* Selig Brodetsky lecture series.

Cambridge University Library, West Rd, Cambridge CB3 9DR. ☎ 01223 333000. Fax 01223 333160. Email library@ula.cam.ac.uk; Website www.lib.cam.ac.uk *Dir.* Mr P. K. Fox. The Hebraica and Judaica collections comprise c. 140,000 Cairo Genizah fragments (being catalogued in the Genizah Series, CUP); 1,000 complete Hebrew codices (see S.C. Reif, Hebrew Manuscripts at Cambridge University Library, CUP, 1997); approximately 40,000 printed books. Available to members of the University and bona fide scholars by application, preferably in writing in advance, to the Admissions Officer. Reading rooms open 9.30–6.45; Admissions Office: 9.30–12.30, 2.00–4.15. *Dir. Genizah Res. Unit and Oriental Div.* Professor S. C. Reif; *Hebraica Libr.* M. Muehlhaeusler.

Czech Memorial Scrolls Centre (Memorial Scrolls Trust), Kent House, Rutland Gardens, London SW7 1BX. ☎ 020-7584 3741. Fax 020-7581 8012. (Reg. Charity No. 278900) This permanent exhibition tells the unique story of the rescue from Prague, in 1964, of 1,564 Torah Scrolls and of their restoration and distribution on permanent loan to communities throughout the world. The exhibits include some of the scrolls, a remarkable display of Torah binders, some dating from the 18th century, and other moving reminders of the vanished communities of Bohemia and Moravia. The centre is open on Tuesdays and Thursdays from 10am to 4pm and other times by arrangement.

Harry Rosencweig Collection of Jewish Music, School of Oriental & African Studies, University of London. Printed sheet music includes 17th–20th century European, American and Israeli liturgical and art music, and various anthologies of folk music. Text books on Jewish music and dance. A few LPs. Many rare items.

The Hartley Library, University of Southampton, Highfield, Southampton SO17 1BJ. Holdings of the Special Collections Division include (i) the **Parkes Library**, founded by the late Revd Dr James Parkes in 1935 to promote the study of relations between the Jewish and the non-Jewish worlds, now containing 18,000 books and periodicals; (ii) extensive collections of manuscripts relating to Anglo-Jewry (containing many of the collections of **Anglo-Jewish Archives**) and encompassing the papers of the Council of Christians and Jews, the Anglo-Jewish Association, the papers of Rabbi Solomon Schonfeld and the Chief Rabbi's Religious Emergency Fund, archives of the Union of Jewish Women, private papers of Chief Rabbi Hertz, early records of the Board of Shechita, archives of the Federation of Jewish Relief Organisations, Zangwill family papers, the papers of the Jewish Board of Guardians and of the Jewish Blind Society, and more than 500 other collections, comprising in excess of 2 million items. A catalogue of the archives was published by the library in 1992 and a supplement published in 2000. Visits by appointment. *Contact* ☎ 023-80593335 (Parkes), 023-80592721 (MSS). Fax 023-80593007. Email library@soton.ac.uk (for Parkes); archives@soton.ac.uk (for MSS); Website www. archives.lib.soton.ac.uk. *Archivist* Dr C. M. Woolgar.

The Hidden Legacy Foundation, Kent House, Rutland Gardens, London SW7 1BX. ☎ 020-7584 2754. Fax 020-7584 6896. (Est. 1988. Reg. Charity no. 326032) Devoted to promoting the awareness of provincial (English) and rural (German) Jewish history as seen through buildings and artefacts, and has become particularly identified with German Genizot. It organises exhibitions: Genizah (1992), Mappot (1997), The Jews of Devon and Cornwall (2000), and, having been active in Germany, is now working in England cataloguing Judaica. Library, slide and photo archives on rural German Jewry. *Exec. Dir.* Evelyn Friedlander. *Publ.* Newsletter.

Imperial War Museum Holocaust Exhibition, Lambeth Road, London SE1 6HZ. *Project Office* ☎ 020-7416 5204/5285. Fax 020-7416 5278. Website www. iwm.org.uk. *Project Dir.* Suzanne Bardgett; *Founding Patrons* Lord Bramall, Sir Martin Gilbert, Ben Helfgott, Lord Moser, Lord Rothschild, Lord Weidenfeld, Lord Wolfson of Marylebone, Stephen Rubin; *Advisory Gp.* Professor D. Cesarani, Sir Martin Gilbert, Ben Helfgott, Antony Lerman, Martin Smith.

Institute of Contemporary History and Wiener Library, Ltd., 4 Devonshire Street, London W1W 5BH. ☎ 020-7636 7247. Fax 020-7436 6428. Email info@wienerlibrary.co.uk; Website www.wienerlibrary.co.uk (Reg. Charity No. 313015) Founded by Dr A. Wiener in Amsterdam, 1933, and since 1939 in London. Research Library and Institute on contemporary European and Jewish history, especially the rise and fall of the Third Reich; survival and revival of Nazi and fascist movements; antisemitism; racism; the Middle East; post-war Germany. Holds Britain's largest collection of documents, testimonies, books and videos on the Holocaust. Active educ. programme of lectures, seminars and conferences. *Chairman of Exec. Cttee.* Ernst Fraenkel; *Dir.* B. Barkow.

Jewish Community Exhibition Centre, c/o David Turner, 1 Village Close, Belsize Lane, London NW3. ☎ 020-7794 1542. (Est. 1985) To provide exhibition material on subjects of Jewish interest. The central exhibition under the responsibility of the Education Dept. of the BoD is 'The Jewish Way of Life' which has travelled to many venues in the UK. Other exhibitions include 'The Anschluss', 'Sir Moses Montefiore', 'Shalosh Regalim', the three Foot Festivals and 'The Anglo Jewish Experience 1066-1990', the history of the Jews in England. *Co-Chairmen* David Turner and Mrs. Ruth Winston Fox, MBE, JP.

The Jewish Museum – London's Museum of Jewish Life
Website www.jewishmuseum.org.
(Est. 1932. Reg. Charity No. 10098819) The Jewish Museum aims to recover, preserve and exhibit material relating to the roots and heritage of Jewish people

in Britain, and to illustrate and explain Jewish religious practice with objects of rarity and beauty. It seeks to increase knowledge and understanding about Jewish life and history through its programme of education and exhibitions, and also has a programme of holocaust education. The Friends of the Jewish Museum has been established to suport the work of the museum. *Publ.* include: Research Papers, Education Resources, Map of the Jewish East End, *Living up West – Jewish Life in London's West End, What about the Children? – 200 Years of Norwood Child Care, The Portuguese Jewish Community in London (1656–1830); Immigrant Furniture Workers in London, 1881–1939 (and Supplement), Yiddish Theatre in London, The Last Goodbye – An Education Resource on the Kindertransport, Israel Zangwill and the Wanderers of Kilburn, Simeon Solomon – Pre-Raphaelite Artist. Dir.* Rickie Burman, MA, MPhil; *Chairman* Kenneth Rubens, OBE, FRSA; *Dep. Chairman* Robert Craig, LLM; *Friends Admin.* Sidney Berg and Sidney Budd.

The Jewish Museum – Camden Town
The museum has been awarded Designated status by the Museums and Galleries Commission in recognition of its outstanding collections. History and Ceremonial Art Galleries, audio-visual programmes and a Temporary Exhibitions Gallery with changing exhibitions. Educational programmes available. Open: Mon–Thurs, 10 am–4 pm; Sundays 10am–5pm. Closed Jewish Festivals and Public Holidays. Address: Raymond Burton House, 129–131 Albert Street, NW1 7NB. ☎ 020-7284 1997. Fax 020-7267 9008. Email admin@jmus.org.uk

The Jewish Museum – Finchley
Displays relating to the history of Jewish immigration and settlement in London, including reconstructions of East End tailoring and furniture workshops. Holocaust Education Gallery with a moving exhibition on London-born Holocaust survivor, Leon Greenman. Travelling Exhibitions, Educational Programmes and Resources and Walking Tours of Jewish London. Open: Sun. 10.30 am–4.30 pm, Mon–Thurs, 10.30 am–5 pm. Closed Jewish Festivals, Public Holidays, on Sundays in August and Bank Holiday weekends. Address: 80 East End Road, N3 2SY. ☎ 020-8349 1143. Fax 020-8343 2162. Email enquiries@jewishmuseum.org.uk.

Jewish Studies Library (Incorporating the Library of the Jewish Historical Society of England), University College London, Gower Street, WC1E 6BT. ☎ 020-7679 2598. Fax 020-7679 7373. Email library@ucl.ac.uk; Website www.ucl.ac.uk/library
All collections are housed together in the Arnold Mishcon Reading Room. These are the Mocatta Library, the Brodie Library, the Altmann Library, the Abramsky Library, the William Margulies Yiddish Library, in addition to books and periodicals acquired for the support of teaching and research by the College's Department of Hebrew and Jewish Studies. The Jewish Studies Library serves the academic community of UCL and affiliates and is open for reference purposes to the general public engaged in research. The Arnold Mishcon Reading Room is part of the Main Library. Contact the library to obtain current opening hours and admissions procedure. Genealogical enquiries are referred to a professional genealogist unless specifically related to collections in the Library. *Libr.* Dr P. Ayris.

John Rylands University Library of Manchester, Oxford Road, Manchester M13 9PP. The Special Collections Repository, 150 Deansgate, Manchester M3 3EH. ☎ 0161-834 5343. Fax 0161-834 5574. Email spcdl72@fs1.liman.ac.uk; Website www.rylibweb.man.ac.uk. The Hebraica and Judaica comprise over 10,500 fragments from the Cairo Genizah; manuscripts and codices from the Crawford and Gaster collections; Samaritan manuscripts from the Gaster collection; 6,600 items of printed Hebraica and Talmudic literature in the Marmorstein collection; 1,000 volumes of the Haskalah collection; the Moses Gaster collection; and some 5,000 volumes in the Near Eastern collection in the main library dealing with Hebrew language and literature. Although primarily serving the staff and students of the University, other readers may obtain reference only access to the library on application (letter of introduction and evidence of identity required). A fee is charged to external readers requiring regular access to the main library. *Head of Special Collections* Dr Stella Butler.

Keren Hatorah Library, 97 Stamford Hill, London N16 5DN. ☎ 020-8800 6688. A comprehensive collection of Torah literature for the whole family. Operates as a lending library. Open Sun., Tues., Thurs., 10.30am–12.30pm, Mon. 3.30-5.00pm. *Libr.* Mrs N. Grossnass.

Keren Hatorah Tape Library, 97 Stamford Hill, London N16. ☎ 020-8802 6388. Over ten thousand cassette recordings including the complete Talmud in English and Yiddish and a range of other Torah and Jewish topics. Open Sun 11.30–1.00, Mon to Thurs 11.00–4.30. *Man.* A. Lauer.

Leo Baeck College – Centre for Jewish Education Library, 80 East End Road, N3 2SY. ☎ 020-8349 5610/1. Fax 020-8343 2558. Email Library@lbc.ac.uk. Est. 1956 to provide a library for Jewish Studies and research. Holdings: 45,000 vols; 85 current periodicals; 5,000 pamphlets with a special collection on Zionism; 15,000 sound records (shiurim and public lectures); 170 rabbinic and MA theses. Range: Bible, rabbinic literature, codes, liturgy, education, literature, history, holocaust and post-holocaust studies, Israel and Zionism. Open to members and occasional readers from Mon.–Thurs. 9.00–5.00, Fri. 9.00–1.00. Closed on Jewish Festivals, bank holidays and during the last week of December. During July and August, visits can be made only by appointment with the librarian. For regular access to the library a yearly contribution of £15 is to be made. For borrowing rights a further £10 will be charged. *Hd. Libr.* César Merchán Hamann, PhD; *Asst. Libr.* Philippa Claiden, Marian Smelik.

Leopold Muller Memorial Library, Oxford Centre for Hebrew & Jewish Studies, Yarnton Manor, Yarnton, Oxford OX5 1PY. ☎ 01865-377946 (library office: ext. 117; librarian: ext. 119). Fax 01865-375079. Email muller.library@ochjs.ac.uk. (Reg. Charity No. 309720) The Leopold Muller Memorial Library is an open access lending library of about 45,000 volumes and 70 current periodicals, covering the full range of Hebrew and Jewish studies, with special focus on Hebrew literature of the 19th and 20th centuries, Haskalah, modern Jewish history, Zionism, Israeli and Hebrew bibliography. Special collections: an extensive microfilm collection of Hebrew manuscripts and early Hebrew prints, the largest collection of *Yizkor* books in Europe, and an archive of 400,000 newspaper cuttings on 12,000 Jewish personalities and on the early Yishuv in Palestine, as well as representative samples of the Hebrew and Yiddish press. For opening times, access and borrowing rights see website associnst.ox.ac.uk/ochjs. *Libr.* Dr P. W. van Boxel.

London Metropolitan Archives, 40 Northampton Road, London EC1R 0HB. ☎ 020-7332 3820. Fax 020 7833 9136. Email ask.lma@corpoflondon.gov.uk; Website wwwl.cityoflondon.gov.uk/lma. LMA is the regional archive for Greater London. The collections within it of Jewish interest include: Board of Deputies of

British Jews, Office of the Chief Rabbi, United Synagogue, London Beth Din, Jews Free School, Jews Temporary Shelter, London School of Jewish Studies and World Jewish Relief. Many collections are available to researchers only with the prior permission of the depositor, so please contact LMA in advance for relevant addresses (as in this volume). **Opening Hours:** Monday, Wednesday, Friday 0930-1645; Tuesday, Thursday 0930-1930. Open selected Saturdays 0930-1645 (call for open dates or see website).

The London School of Jewish Studies (formerly Jews' College) **Library,** Schaller House, Albert Road, London NW4 2SJ. ☎ 020-8203 6427. Fax 020-8203 6420. Email kroberg@lsjs.ac.uk (Est. 1855. Reg. Charity No. 310023) One of the most extensive Judaica libraries in Europe, the library contains 80,000 volumes, 20,000 pamphlets and 150 manuscripts. Call for opening times. *Hd. Libr.* Esra Kahn.

Lubavitch Lending Library, 107–115 Stamford Hill, N16 5RP. ☎ 020-8800 5823. Established in 1972 to help the Jewish public study traditional Jewish culture and aid scholarship. The library contains 15,000 volumes in Hebrew, English and Yiddish. Services include a reference libr., a children's libr. and postal lending. Lectures and displays org. anywhere. Open Sun., 10am–12.30pm, 4pm–8pm; Mon.–Fri., 10am–4pm. Some weekday evgs. Other times available by appointment. *Libr.* Z. Rabin, ALA.

National Life Story Collection, at the British Library National Sound Archive, 96 Euston Road, London, NW1 2DB. ☎ 020-7412 7404. Fax 020-7412 7441. Email nsa-nlsc@bl.uk; Website www.bl.uk. (Est. 1987. Reg. Charity No. 327571) To 'record first-hand experiences of as wide a cross-section of present-day society as possible'. As an independent charitable trust within the Oral History Section of the British Library's National Sound Archive, NLSC's key focus and expertise has been oral history fieldwork.

Living Memory of the Jewish Community (C410) is a major collection with a primary focus on pre-Second World War Jewish refugees to Britain, those fleeing from Nazi persecution during the Second World War and Holocaust survivors. The collection has recently expanded to include interviews with children of survivors. The collection complements other National Sound Archive material on Jewish life, notably the Holocaust Survivors' Centre interviews (C830), Central British Fund Kindertransport interviews (C526), Testimony: Video Interviews with British Holocaust Survivors (C533) and London Museum of Jewish Life oral history interviews (C525).

Porton Collection, Central Library, Municipal Buildings, Leeds LS1 3AB. ☎ 0113 2478282. Fax 0113 2478426. Comprises 3,700 items covering all aspects of the religion and culture of the Jewish people in English, Hebrew and Yiddish. Available for reference use only.

School of Oriental and African Studies (Univ. of London), Thornhaugh Street, Russell Square, London WC1H 0XG. ☎ 020-7898 4154. Fax 020-7898 4159. Email ps4@soas.ac.uk; Website www.soas.ac.uk/library. Ancient Near East, Semitics and Judaica Section of SOAS Library. *Section Head* P. S. Salinger. The Semitics and Judaica collections comprise about 15,000 Hebrew items covering the fields of modern Hebrew language and literature (one of the finest collections in Europe), biblical and intertestamental studies, Judaism, the Jewish people, and the land of Israel. There are also a considerable number of books in Western languages covering the above mentioned fields. In addition, largely owing to the acquisition of the Stencl and Leftwich collections in 1983 and some books from the Whitechapel collection in 1984, there are about 3000 books on Yiddish language and literature. Periodicals, of which the Library holds about 200 Hebrew titles, are shelved separately. The transfer of the Joe Loss Lectureship in Jewish Music from the City University to SOAS has also brought the Harry Rosencweig Collection of Jewish Music to the library (see p.55). For details of services, please refer to the Library's web pages.

Spanish & Portuguese Jews' Congregation, 2 Ashworth Road, W9 1JY. ☎ 020-7289 2573. Fax: 020-7289 2709. **Archives** The archives of the Spanish & Portuguese Jews' Congregation, London, and its institutions, which date from the mid-17th century, include Minute and Account Books, Registers of Births, Circumcisions, Marriages and Burials. Most of the Registers have now been published and copies may be purchased from the Congregation's offices. The archives are not open to the public. Queries and requests by bona fide researchers should be submitted in writing to the Hon. Archivist. Advice and help will be given to general enquirers wherever possible. A search fee may be charged. *Hon. Archivist* Miriam Rodrigues-Pereira. **Shasha Library** (Est 1936.) Designed to contain books on Jewish history, religion, literature and kindred interest from the Sephardi standpoint. The Library is intended for the use of members of the congregation. It contains over 1,200 books. These collections have been brought into the new Sephardi Centre opened at the end of 1994 (see p.42). *Libr.* Rebecca Cohen.

PROFESSIONAL ORGANISATIONS

AGUDAS HARABBONIM (ASSOCIATION OF RABBIS OF GREAT BRITAIN)

(in association with the Agudas Israel World Rabbinical Council) 273 Green Lanes, London N4 2EX. ☎ 020-8802 1544. (Est. 1929) *Chairman Princ.* Rabbi E. Padwa, Av Beth Din, U.O.H.C.; *H. Dir.* Rabbi Ben Zion Blau; *H. Gen. Sec.* vacant.

AGUDATH HASHOCHTIM V'HASHOMRIM OF GREAT BRITAIN

Cattle Section: *H. Sec.* S. B. Spitzer, 33 Elm Park Avenue, N15 6AR.
Poultry Section: *H. Sec.* S. Leaman, 25 Rostrevor Road, N.15.

ASSOCIATION OF MINISTERS (CHAZANIM) OF GREAT BRITAIN

Chairman Rev. S. I. Brickman, 9 Marlborough Mansions, Cannon Hill, London NW6 1JP. ☎ 020-7431 0575; *V. Chairman* Rev. A. Levin, ☎ 020-8554 0499; *Sec.* Rabbi D. A. Katanka; *T.* Rev. M. Haschel. ☎ 020-7483 1017.

ASSOCIATION OF ORTHODOX JEWISH PROFESSIONALS OF GREAT BRITAIN

53 Wentworth Road, NW11 0RT.
(Est. 1962) To promote research in matters of common interest, and the general acceptance of Torah and Halacha as relevant and decisive in all aspects of modern life and thought. *President* Prof C. Domb; *Chairman* H. J. Adler.

GUILD OF JEWISH JOURNALISTS

Affiliated to the World Federation of Jewish Journalists. *L. President* The Lord Janner; *V. President* D. Jacobs; *Chairman*; *H.T.* Susan Kosky, 51 Century Court, Grove End Road, London NW8 9LD. ☎ 020-7286 2791. Fax 020-7286 8958. Email ssperber@tiscali.co.uk.

JEWISH NURSES & MIDWIVES ASSOCIATION

89 Highmount, Station Rd., London NW4 3ST.
☎ 07932-730 944. Email sara@smbarnett.com
(Est. 1993) A social, educational and support group for all Jewish nurses, midwives and members of allied professions. *Chair* Sara Barnett.

RABBINIC CONFERENCE OF THE UNION OF LIBERAL & PROGRESSIVE SYNAGOGUES

The Montagu Centre, 21 Maple Street, W1T 4BE.
☎ 020-7580 1663. Fax 020-7436 4184. Email montagu@ulps.org
Rabbinic Chairman: Rabbi Frank Dabba Smith; *Admin Dir* Michael A. Burman.

RABBINICAL COUNCIL OF EAST LONDON AND WEST ESSEX

8 The Lindens, Prospect Hill, Waltham Forest, E17 3EJ.
☎ 020-85201759.
(Est. 1981) To co-ordinate and enhance Jewish com. and educ. facilities within the East London and West Essex area. *Patron* The Chief Rabbi; *Chairman* Rabbi E. Salasnik; *V. Chairman* Rev. S. Black; *Sec.* Rev. S. Kreiman.

RABBINICAL COUNCIL OF THE PROVINCES

c/o 71 Upper Park Road, Salford M7.
☎ 0161-773 1978. Fax 0161-773 7015.
President Chief Rabbi Dr Jonathan Sacks; *Chairman* Rabbi Mordechai S. Ginsbury; *V. Chairman* Rabbi Ian Goodhardt; *H. T.* Rabbi Yoinosson Golomb; *H. Sec.* Rabbi Adam S. Hill, 163 Bristol Road, Birmingham B5 7UA. Email srni@heharim.sofnet. co.uk

RABBINICAL COUNCIL OF THE UNITED SYNAGOGUE

Adler House, 735 High Road, London N12 0US.
☎ 020-8343 6313. Fax 020-8343 6310.
Chairman Rabbi M. Salasnik, BA (Hons), FJC; *V. Chairmen* Rabbi Emanuel Levy, BA (Hons), Rabbi M. Ginsbury; *Exec. Dir.* Rabbi Dr J. Shindler, MSc; *H.T.* Rabbi S. Coten, BSc Econ (Hons), MA, PGCE; *H. Sec.* Rabbi M. Van Den Bergh, BEd.

UNITED SYNAGOGUE ADMINISTRATORS' ASSOCIATION

☎ 020-7286 3838.
Chair Mrs L. Young, St John's Wood Synagogue, Grove End Road, London NW8 1AP.

MISCELLANEOUS ORGANISATIONS

ADVISORY COMMITTEE FOR THE ADMISSION OF JEWISH ECCLESIASTICAL OFFICERS

1-2 Endsleigh Street, WC1H 0DS. ☎/Fax 020-7387 7447.
(Est. 1932) To advise the Home Office in connection with applications for the admission of eccl. officers, including rabbis, ministers, readers, Talmudical students, etc. The Cttee. comprises nominees from the major synagogal and religious orgs. in the UK. Its work is conducted from the Jews' Temporary Shelter Offices. *H. Sec.*

ASSOCIATION OF JEWISH EX-SERVICEMEN AND WOMEN (AJEX)

Ajex House, East Bank, Stamford Hill, N16 5RT.
☎ 020-8800 2844. Fax 020-8880 1117. Email ajexuk@talk21.com; Website www.ajex.org.uk
(Est. 1923) *Nat. Chairman* Arthur Lawson; *Gen. Sec.* J. Weisser; *H. Chaplain* Rev. Malcolm Weisman, OBE. A list of London and Regional Branches can be obtained from the Secretary. For the Military Museum contact H. Morris, *Archivist*.

ASSOCIATION OF JEWISH GOLF CLUBS & SOCIETIES

Officers: *President* Martin S. Caller, 2 Sergeants Lane, Whitefield, Manchester M45 7TS; *Sec.* Martin Prevezer, 42 Springfield Road, London NW8 0QN; *Tournament Sec.* Mervyn Berg; *Assist. Tournament Secs.* Stanley Fingret, Michael Bartle.

ASSOCIATION OF JEWISH HUMANISTS
12 Woodland Court, Woodlands, NW11 9QQ.
☎ 020-8455 2393.
(Est. 1983) Humanistic Jews believe each Jew has the right to create a meaningful Jewish lifestyle free from supernatural authority and imposed tradition.

Humanistic Jews believe the goal of life is personal dignity and self-esteem. Humanist Jews believe the secular roots of Jewish life are as important as the religious ones, and the survival of the Jewish people needs a reconciliation between science, personal autonomy and Jewish loyalty.

The Association of Jewish Humanists is a constituent member of the International Institute for Secular Humanistic Judaism (Jerusalem); an Associate of the Society for Humanistic Judaism, Farmington Hills, MI, USA; an Affiliate of the British Humanist Association, London WC1R 4RH.

H. Jt. Chairmen M. Miller, 12 Woodland Court, Woodlands, NW11 9QQ, D. Wilkes, 7 Ashley Close, Hendon, NW4; *H. Sec.* M. Miller, 12 Woodland Court, Woodlands, NW11 9QQ; *H. T.* J. Hulman, 60 Morley Crescent East, Stanmore, Middlesex.

THE BURNING BUSH
19 Patshull Road, London NW5 2JX.
☎ 020-7458 3957. Fax 020-7267 2957. Email lucieskeaping@hotmail.com; Website www.theburningbush.co.uk.
(Est. 1990) A musical ensemble specialising in the music and song of the old Jewish worlds. *Dir.* Lucie Skeaping; *Admin.* Patricia Finch.

CAMPAIGN FOR THE PROTECTION OF SHECHITA
66 Townshend Court, Townshend Road, Regents Park, London NW8 6LE.
☎ 020-7722 8523.
(Est. 1985) To protect the freedom of Jews to perform Shechita; to make representations to Government on proposed legislation or other measures which may affect the proper performance of Shechita. *Nat. Co-ord. and Hon. Solicitors* Neville Kesselman; *Reg. Coord.* Chanoch Kesselman, London; *Rabbinical Adv.* Rabbi Benjamin Vorst and Rabbi Dr David Miller, MA, MSc, DPhil (Oxon).

CELEBRITIES GUILD OF GREAT BRITAIN
Knight House, 29-31 East Barnet Road, New Barnet, Herts EN4 8RN.
☎ 020-8449 1234, 020-8449 1515, weekdays 10.00–4.00. Fax 020-8449 4994.
(Est. 1977. Reg. Charity No. 282298) A social and fund-raising Guild of prominent people in British Jewry who organise events to raise funds to provide equipment for disabled and handicapped people. *H. Exec. Guilder* Mrs Ella Glazer, MBE; *H. Life President* Stanley Black, OBE; *Master Guilders* Ronnie Wolfe and Leonard Fenton.

CENTRE FOR PSYCHOTHERAPY IN HEBREW
☎ 020-8632 1764.
(Est. 2001) A psychotherapy service for Hebrew speakers in England. *Contact* T. Schonfield.

CONNECT – THE JEWISH MARRIAGE BUREAU
23 Ravenshurst Avenue, NW4 4EE.
☎ 020-8203 5207.
See Jewish Marriage Council, p.16.

HIGH SEAS SAILING CLUB

6 Fairhazel Gardens, London NW6 3SG.
☎ 020-7328 5169. Website www.contect.to/wavelength
(Est. 1989.) The UK's only sailing club for people with a 'Jewish affinity or friendship'. Dinghy and motorboat sections also. Membership of 200 from throughout UK and overseas. The club holds coastal sailing meets throughout the summer months. During the winter there is an active programme of lectures, sail training and social activities in the NW London area. Crewing Register maintained. Monthly newsletters. *Publ.* Wavelength (annual). *Club Commodore* Dr B. Sheinman; *V. Commodore* Victor Stone; *Rear Commodore* N. Reese; *T.* L. Factor; *Sec.* E. de Mesquita.

INSTITUTE OF COMMUNITY RELATIONS

101 Dunsmure Road, London N16 5HT.
☎ 020-8800 8612.
(Est. 1975) Objects: To promote racial equality and good community relations in particular between Orthodox Jews and other ethnic groups. It seeks to promote marriage and the family, human rights and moral values, and to foster Franco-British friendship. Activities: Running a number of projects including campaigns for racial equality in education and television, a campaign for single sex health services, a campaign to support marriage and the family, an information project and a project to relieve poverty. *Dir.* Rabbi Henri Brand; *H.T.* Rabbi C. Pinter; *H. Sec.* I. Kraus.

JEWISH ASSOCIATION FOR BUSINESS ETHICS

PO Box 3840, The Hyde, Colindale, NW9 6LG
☎ 020-8200 8007 Fax 020-8200 8061. Email info@jabe.org
(Reg. Charity No. 1038453) To encourage the highest standards of integrity in business and professional conduct by promoting the Jewish ethical approach to business. *Chairman:* Stephen Rubin; *Exec. Dir.* Lorraine Spector.

JEWISH ASSOCIATION OF SPIRITUAL HEALERS

24 Greenacres, Hendon Lane, Finchley, London N3 3SF.
☎ 020-8349 1544.
(Est. 1966. Reg. Charity No. 275081) Aims: (1) To attempt to relieve sickness and suffering; (2) To demonstrate that Spiritual Healing is in keeping with the teachings of Judaism. *Chairman* Steve Sharpe, 22 Boldmere Road, Pinner HA5 1PS; *Sec.* Audrey Cane, 24 Greenacres, Hendon Lane, Finchley, London N3 3SF; *Healing Centre* Ruth Green, West London Synagogue, 33 Seymour Place, London W1.

THE JEWISH COUNCIL FOR RACIAL EQUALITY

33 Seymour Place, London W1H 6AU.
☎ 020-8455 0896. Fax 020-8458 4700. Email jcore@btinternet.com
(Est. 1976. Reg. Charity No. 281236) To improve race relations in Britain, encourage awareness in the Jewish community of responsibilities of a multi-racial society and join other organisations to combat racism. *Chairman* Dr. R. Stone; *V. Chairs* Mrs June Jacobs, Melanie Levy; *H. Sec.* Nicola Cobbold; *H.T.* Valerie Lipman; *Dir.* Dr Edie Friedman.

Projects: Developing Jewish anti-racist educational materials for schools, cheders and youth clubs; training for teachers and youth leaders on the use of anti-racist materials; campaigning on refugee and immigration issues, working with refugee doctors, collecting and distributing food and clothing to refugees; fostering Black-Jewish dialogue; development of Black-Jewish History project; organising seminars with Jewish organisations and working with other minority groups to combat racism.

JEWISH FEMINIST GROUP
Box 39, Sisterwrite, 190 Upper Street, London N1.
(Est. 1979) To raise consciousness among Jewish women about their position in society, both as Jews and as women, and strive to improve both and combat antisemitism. *Publ.* Quarterly newsletter.

JEWISH FRIENDLY SOCIETIES
Grand Order of Israel and Shield of David. *Grand Sec.* R. Salasnik
11 The Lindens, Prospect Hill, Waltham Forest, London E17 3EJ.
☎ 020-8520 3531. Email info@goisd.org.uk; Website www.goisd.org.uk
(Est. 1896) The membership is contained in four Lodges in the Metropolitan area and one in Birmingham.

JEWISH GAY AND LESBIAN GROUP
BM-JGLG, London WC1N 3XX
☎ 020-8922 5214. Email info@jglg.org.uk
(Est. 1972) Social group for Jewish gay men, lesbians and bisexuals of all ages. *President* Sonia Lawrence.

JEWISH SOCIALISTS' GROUP
BM 3725, London WC1N 3XX.
Email jsg@bardrose.dircon.co.uk
(Est. 1974) Political, cultural and campaigning organisation committed to socialism, diasporism and secularism, aiming to unite the Jewish community with other oppressed/persecuted minorities. Active on local, national and international issues. National Committee (collective leadership).

JEWS FOR JUSTICE FOR PALESTINIANS
PO Box 34702, London N3 2XG.
Email justicefp@yahoo.co.uk; Website www.jfjfp.org.
(Est. 2002) A network of Jews in Britain who oppose Israeli policies that undermine the livelihoods and the human, civil and political rights of Palestinians. *Contact* Ines Newman.

THE MAIMONIDES FOUNDATION
38 Great Smith Street, London SW1P 3BU.
☎ 020-7222 1992. Fax 020-7233 0161. Email info@maimonides.org.uk
(Est. 1995. Reg. Charity No. 1044028) The foundation works at all levels of the Jewish and Muslim communities, in the UK and internationally, to promote contact and understanding through dialogue, education, sport and research and advocacy, among others. *President* Lord Janner of Braunstone QC; *Chairman* Professor N. David Khalili; *V. Chairman* Dr Richard Stone; *T.* Ivor Levene; *Exec. Cttee* Sydney S. Assor, Denise Cattan, Robin Fisher, Laura Janner-Klausner, Rabbi Dr Abraham Levy, Rabbi Professor Jonathan Magonet, Mehri Niknam, Freddy Salem, Eitan Wertheimer, Robert Yentob; *Exec. Dir.* Steven Fine; *Admin. Dir.* Karen Wellings.

MONTAGU JEWISH COMMUNITY TRUST
c/o Flat 27, 40 Eastcote Road, Pinner, Middx HA5 1DH.
☎ 020-8869 9298.
(Est. 1893 as West Central Club and Settlement.) A Trust concerned with the allocation of grants for community activities principally in the field of training and education.

NE'IMAH SINGERS
c/o 21 Holders Hill Drive, London NW4 1NL.

☎ 020-8202 2924. Fax 020-8922 0779. Email neimah@freeserve.co.uk.
(Est. 1993) Choir performing Synagogue music. *Fd and Conductor* Marc Temerlies; *Co-Fd* Jonathan Weissbart; *Ass. Chazan* Moshe Haschel.

NOAH PROJECT
PO Box 1828, London W10 5RT.
☎ 020-8747 9518. Email info@noahproject.org.uk; Website www.noah project.org.uk
(Est. 1997) Through 'Jewish Education, Celebration and Action for the Earth', the Noah Project promotes awareness of environmental issues throughout the community, and demonstrates how Jewish teachings provide guidance for greener living. It provides a Jewish voice to secular and multi-faith environmental movements. *Admin.* Vicky Joseph; *Educ. Co-ord.* Vivienne Cato. *Publ.* Newsletter, *Edr.* John Schlackman. Groups in Birmingham and Manchester.

OPERATION JUDAISM
95 Willows Road, Birmingham B12 9QF.
☎ 0121-440 6673 (24 hrs ansaphone). Fax 0121-446-4199.
(Est. 1986) Operation Judaism is the community's defence against missionary attack. It operates nationally an information and counselling service. Information and support for those involved with cults. Man. Cttee. consists of representatives from: Office of the C. Rabbi, Board of Deputies and Lubavitch Foundation.

ROYAL BRITISH LEGION (MONASH BRANCH)
(Est. 1936. Reg. Charity No. 219279) *Chairman* G. J. Kaufman; *H. Sec.* A. Lawson, 21 Woronzow Road, London NW8 6BA. ☎ 020-7722 5405. Fax 020-7483 2592.

SHATNEZ CENTRE TRUST
22 Bell Lane, Hendon, London NW4 2AD
☎ 020-8202 4005.
(Est. 1990. Reg. Charity No. 1013840) To provide Shatnez checking at the Shatnez Centre and promote Shatnez observance in the community. *Ts.* A. E. Bude, David Rabson.

SUPPORT GROUP FOR PARENTS OF JEWISH GAYS AND LESBIANS
BM JGLG, London WC1N 3XX.
☎ 020-8958 4827. Fax 020-8905 3479. Email kenmowbray@aol.com
(Est. 1996) To give support and help to parents of Jewish gays and lesbians. *H. Sec.* Kenneth Morris.

TJSPN
PO Box 33317, London NW11 9FR.
☎ 020-8632 0216. Fax 020-8458 3261. Email jr6287@yahoo.co.uk
The Jewish Single Parent Network aims to assist single parents with a range of services focusing on the practical difficulties of single parenting. *Patron* The Lady Jakobovits; enq. to R. Zrihen.

TZEDEK
(Jewish Action for a Just World)
Steven Derby, Development Officer, 25 Kings Close, London NW4 2JU.
☎ 020-8202 4744. Email tzedekuk@aol.com; Website www.tzedek.org.uk
(Est. 1990. Reg. Charity No. 1016767.) To provide direct support to the

developing world working towards the relief and elimination of poverty regardless of race or religion; to educate people, particularly in the Jewish community, as to the causes and effects of poverty and the Jewish obligation to respond.

Programmes: support for development projects through a grant-making programme targeted at self-help, sustainable developments in Africa, Asia and South America; providing educational workshops on the themes of aid, development and Jewish values to schools, youth clubs and adult groups; Overseas Volunteer Programme – in which Jewish volunteers have the opportunity to work during the summer at development projects in the developing world; fundraising activities.

UNITED KINGDOM ASSOCIATION OF JEWISH LAWYERS & JURISTS
27 Hazel Gardens, Edgware, Middx. HA8 8PD.
☎ 020-8958 6110. Fax 020-8905 4406. Email admin@ukajlj.fsnet.co.uk
(Est. 1990) The objectives of the Association are: to contribute, alone or in co-operation with other international or national organisations, towards the establishment of an international legal order based on the Rule of Law in relations between all nations and states; to promote human rights and the principles of equality of men and the right of all states and peoples to live in peace; to act against racism and anti-semitism, whether openly expressed or covertly exercised, *inter alia,* where necessary, by legal proceedings; to promote the study of legal problems affecting the world's Jewish communities in the context of national and international law; to promote, in consultation with the legal profession within the State of Israel and its agencies, the study of legal problems of particular concern to the State of Israel; to promote the study of Jewish law in comparison with other laws and facilitate the exchange of any information resulting from research thereto among member groups; to collect and disseminate information concerning the *de facto* and *de jure* status of the Jewish communities and other minority ethnic and religious groups throughout the world and where the occasion arises, to give help and support pursuant to human rights treaties; to promote and support co-operation and communication between the Association's member groups; to concern itself with any other matter of legal interest considered of relevance by any of the member groups.

President The Rt. Hon. The Lord Woolf; *V. Presidents* The Rt. Hon. The Lord Millett, The Rt. Hon. The Lord Justice Rix, His Honour Israel Finestein QC; *Chairman*; *V. Chairman* Jonathan M. Lewis; *Sec.* Mrs Deanna Levine; *T.* Barry Abrahamson; *Admin.* Mrs Shirley March.

VIKTOR ULLMAN FOUNDATION UK
7 Roma Road Close, London SW15 4AZ.
☎ 020-8785 4772. Email viktorfoundation@aol.com; Website www.viktorullmannfoundation.org.uk
(Est. 2002) To remember and celebrate the genius of Viktor Ullmann, 1898–1944, and to promote his music in association with the Terezin Music Memorial Foundation, the Jewish Music Institute and other bodies. *Exec. Cttee* Anita Lask Wallfisch, Martin Anderson, Alexander Knapp, Gloria Tessler; *Exec. Dir.* Jacqueline Cole.

INTERNATIONAL ORGANISATIONS

JEWISH ORGANISATIONS HAVING CONSULTATIVE STATUS WITH THE ECONOMIC AND SOCIAL COUNCIL OF THE UNITED NATIONS

Agudas Israel World Org.; Coordinating Bd. of Jewish Orgs. (comprising the British BoD, the South African BoD, and the B'nai B'rith); Consultative Council of Jewish Orgs. (comprising the Anglo-Jewish Assn., the Alliance Israélite Universelle, and the Canadian Friends of the Alliance); W.J.C. Internat. Council on Jewish Social and Welfare Services (comprising American Joint Distribution Committee, World Jewish Relief, Jewish Colonization Assn., European Council of Jewish Community Services, United Hias Service, World ORT Union); Internat. Council of Jewish Women.

AGUDAS ISRAEL WORLD ORGANISATIONS

The organisation was founded in Kattowitz in 1912. Its programme was defined as being 'the solution – in the spirit of the Torah – of problems which periodically confront the Jewish people in Eretz Yisroel and the Diaspora'. This object was to be fulfilled 'by coordination of Orthodox Jewish effort throughout the world ... by the representation and protection of the interests of Torah-true Jewish communities'. The programme was formulated by our ancestors for the unconditional acceptance by all Jewish generations of the Biblical injunction 'And ye shall be unto Me a kingdom of priests and a holy nation'. The organisation seeks to implement this injunction by its endeavours. It opposes assimilation and different interpretations of Jewish nationhood. Consult. status with United Nations, New York and Geneva, and Unesco in Paris.

Agudas Israel of Gt. Britain. *Presidium* Rabbi J. H. Dunner, Rabbi Y. M. Rosenbaum, Rabbi B. Rakow, 95-99 Stamford Hill, N16 5DN. ☎ 020-8800 6688. Fax 020-8800-5000. *Publ.* Jewish Tribune (weekly).

Zeire Agudas Israel (Reg. Charity No. 253513.), 95 Stamford Hill, N16; 35a Northumberland Street, Salford, 7. *Chairman* J. Schleider.

Agudas Israel Community Services, (Reg. Charity No. 287367), 97 Stamford Hill, N16 5DN. ☎ 020-8800 6688/8802 6627. Est. 1980 to help find suitable employment for observant Jews, including immigrants and Yiddish speakers, and other social services. *Dirs.* J. Davis, M.M. Posen.

Jewish Rescue and Relief Cttee. (Reg. Charity No. X99706ES), 215 Golders Green Rd., NW11 9BY. ☎ 020-8458 1710. *Chairman* A. Strom.

Keren Hatorah Cttee. (Reg. Charity No. 281384). (For the relief of religious, educational and social institutions, a division of Agudas Yisroel in Great Britain), 97 Stamford Hill, N16 5DN. ☎ 020-8800 6688, 020-8800 5000. *Exec. Dir.* Rabbi C. Y. Davis.

Russian Immigrant Aid Fund, for the material and spiritual rehabilitation of Russian immigrants in Israel; 97 Stamford Hill, N16 5DN. ☎ 020-8800 6688. *Chairman* I. M. Cymerman.

Society of Friends of the Torah (Reg. Charity No. 238230), 97 Stamford Hill, N16 5DN, and, 215 Golders Green Rd., NW11 9BY. ☎ 020-8800 6687, 020-8458 9988. Fax 020-8800 5000. *Dir.* Rabbi C.Y. Davis.

ALLIANCE ISRAELITE UNIVERSELLE
45 rue La Bruyère, F 75425 Paris Cedex 09.
☎ (01)53 328855. Fax (01) 48 745133. Email info@aiu.org
(Est. 1860.) This educative and cultural-oriented organisation essentially works through a network of schools which affects today more than 20,000 pupils and its century-old defence of human rights before governmental and international institutions all over the world. Has two publs: Les Cahiers de L'Alliance Israélite Universelle and Les Cahiers du Judaïsme and a centre for pedagogical publs: Créer-Didactique, and NADIR publishing house. Its library with more than 120,000 books in the field of Hebraica-Judaica and its College des Etudes juives make it one of the most important Jewish centres in Europe. Today the Alliance operates in Belgium, Canada, France, Israel, Morocco, Spain, U.S.A. *President* Prof. A. Steg; *Dir.* Jean-Jacques Wahl.

AUSTRALIA/ISRAEL AND JEWISH AFFAIRS COUNCIL (AIJAC)
Level 2, 578 St Kilda Road, Melbourne, Victoria 3004.
☎ 3-9529 5022. Fax 3-9529-8571. Email aijac@aijac.org.au
The Assn. is the regional rep. org. for the Jewish coms. in Australia, Fiji, Hawaii, Hong Kong, India, Japan, Korea, New Caledonia, New Zealand, Papua New Guinea, Philippines, Singapore, Sri Lanka, Tahiti, Taiwan and Thailand. *Exec. Dir.* Dr Colin Rubenstein; *Contact* Charla Smith.

B'NAI B'RITH
(Est. 1843) B'nai B'rith is the world's largest Jewish human rights, philanthropic and community action group, active in 58 countries around the world, with its head office in Washington DC, NGO status at the United Nations in New York, an office at the European Union in Brussels, and a World Centre in Jerusalem. It brings Jews together to work in harmony for the common good, to help the poor and oppressed, and to become active in cultural and humanitarian projects. B'nai B'rith United Kingdom is a Major National Structure within B'nai B'rith Europe, which consists of 27 countries covering eastern, western and central Europe. In 2003, B'nai B'rith celebrates its 160th anniversary

The Core Objectives of B'nai B'rith in the United Kingdom are:

- to foster friendship through social, cultural and recreational programmes;
- to support the State of Israel and World Jewry;
- to work for charitable endeavours;
- to initiate and develop community projects;
- to strengthen B'nai B'rith links across Europe.

B'nai B'rith has been instrumental in setting up and supporting:

- the B'nai B'rith Hillel Foundation (p.52);
- the B'nai B'rith Housing Association (p.98);
- the B'nai B'rith Jewish Music Festival (p.39);
- BBYO (p.47);
- Jewish Community Information (p.8).

The London Bureau of International Afairs is an associate office of the Centre for Public Policy of B'nai B'rith International in Washington DC, and of B'nai B'rith Europe in Brussels. The London Bureau of International Affairs provides information and acts as a resource centre, serving as a major activity and lobbying facility where Jewish intrests worldwide are concerned.
International HQ, 1640 Rhode Island Avenue NW, Washington DC 20036, USA. ☎ 202 857 6600. Fax 202 857 1099. Website www.bnaibrith.org

B'nai B'rith Europe, 36 rue Dautzenberg/Bte 3, B-1050 Brussels, Belgium, ☎ 00 32 2 646 8949. Fax 00 32 02 646 8949. Email bb_europe@compuserve.com; Website www.bnaibrith-europe.org. *President* Seymour G. Saideman; *Admin. Dir.* Aline Brandon.

B'nai B'rith United Kingdom, B'nai B'rith Hillel House, 1-2 Endsleigh Street, London WC1H 0DS. ☎ 020-8387 5278, Fax 020-8387 8014. Email office@bbuk.org; Website www.bbuk.org (Reg Charity No. 1061661) *Nat. President* Dr Michael Bliss; *V. President* Antoinette Port; *Nat. Sec.* Jack Finkler; *T.* Harvey Josephs; *Exec. Admin.* Hayley Symons.

London Bureau of International Affairs, B'nai B'rith Hillel House, 1-2 Endsleigh Street, London WC1H 0DS. ☎ 020-7383 0442. Fax 020-7387 8014. Email bb@lbia.org.uk. *Chairman* Martin Kudlick; *V. Chairman* Mark Marcus; *Bureau Chief* Yaffa Wagner.

Lodges

Abraham Lewin (Enfield) Unity; BB4T Yovel (Stanmore) Unity; Bournemouth Unity; Cheshire Unity; Edgware Women; Finchley Joint; First Lodge of England; First Unity; Ilford (Golda Meir) Unity; Jerusalem (Wembley & District); Leeds Unity; Leo Baeck Bogrim; Leo Baeck Men's; Leo Baeck Women's; Manchester; North Manchester; Pegasus Unity; Raoul Wallenberg Unity; Shlomo Argov Unity; Southgate (Ben Gurion) Joint; Thames; West Riding Shalom (Bradford); Yad B'Yad Unity; Yitzchak Rabin; Young International.

CENTRAL REGISTRY OF INFORMATION ON LOOTED CULTURAL PROPERTY 1933–1945

76 Gloucester Place, London W1U 6HJ.
☎ 020-7487 3401. Fax 020-7487 4211. Email info@lootedart.com; Website www.lootedart.com
(Est. 2001. Reg. Charity No. 309720. IRS No. for the American Friends 13-2943469) A charitable body under the auspices of the Oxford Centre for Hebrew and Jewish Studies. Provides a central database of all information and research internationally on cultural property looted between 1933 and 1945 – paintings, drawings, books, manuscripts, Judaica, archives, etc. *Dir.* Anne Webber; *Content Dir.* Shauna Isaac.

COMMISSION FOR LOOTED ART IN EUROPE

76 Gloucester Place, London W1U 6HJ.
☎ 020-7487 3401. Fax 020-7487 4211. Email info@lootedartcommission.com; Website www.lootedartcommission.com
(Est. 1999) Assists individuals, communities and institutions worldwide to identify looted cultural property, and supports, pursues and negotiates restitution claims and procedures in all countries. *Co-chairs* David Lewis, Anne Webber.

COMMITTEE FOR THE PRESERVATION OF JEWISH CEMETERIES IN EUROPE

81A Fairholt Rd., London N16 5EW.
☎ 020-8802 3917. Fax 020-8802 3756. Email cpjce@ic24.net
(Est 1991. Reg. Charity No. 1073225) Preservation of Jewish burial sites in Europe to ensure that they are maintained according to Jewish law and tradition. *President* Rabbi E. Schlesinger; *Hon. Sec.* Y. Marmorstein; *H.T.* A. Goldman. *Exec. Dir.* A. Ginsberg.

COMMONWEALTH JEWISH COUNCIL AND TRUST

BCM Box 6871, London WC1N 3XX.
☎ 020-7222 2120. Fax 020-7222 1781. Email jo-silverman@yahoo.com; Website: www.cjc.org.uk.
(Est. 1982.) To provide links between Commonwealth Jewish communities; to provide a central representative voice for Commonwealth Jewish communities and to help preserve their religious and cultural heritage; to seek ways to

strengthen Commonwealth Jewish communities in accordance with their individual needs and wishes and provide mutual help and cooperation. *President* The Lord Janner, QC; *Vice Presidents* Jonathan Metliss, Paul Secher, Jeff Durkin; *Sec.* J. Galaun, FCA; *H. T.* H.B. Lipsith; *Dir.* Maureen Gold; *Contact* Jo Silverman.

There are 38 members including those in Antigua, Australia, Bahamas, Barbados, Belize, Bermuda, Botswana, Canada, Cayman Is., Cyprus, Fiji, Gibraltar, Guernsey, India, Isle of Man, Jamaica, Jersey, Kenya, Mauritius, Namibia, New Zealand, Singapore, Sri Lanka, Trinidad & Tobago, Turks & Caicos Is., United Kingdom, Zambia and Zimbabwe.

Commonwealth Jewish Trust (Reg. Charity No. 287564). *Trs.* Edward Bronfman, Harvey Lipsith, Dorothy Reitman, Jack Galaun, Sir Jack Zunz. The Trust undertakes charitable projects in Jewish communities throughout the Commonwealth, with special emphasis on smaller communities.

CONFERENCE OF EUROPEAN RABBIS

19 Rue St Georges, Paris 75009, France.
☎ 020-8343 8989.
President Chief Rabbi J. Sitruk, Chief Rabbi of France; *Assoc. President* Chief Rabbi J. Sacks; *Chairman Standing Cittee* Chief Rabbi P. Goldschmidt; *Dir.* Rabbi M. Rose, POB 5324, Jerusalem, Israel. ☎ 02 5812859; *Sec. Gen.* Cllr A.M. Dunner, 87 Hodford Road, London NW11 8NH. ☎ 020-8455 9960. Fax 020-8455 4968.

Est. 1957, to provide a medium for co-operation on matters of common concern to rabbis of European communities.

CONFERENCE ON JEWISH MATERIAL CLAIMS AGAINST GERMANY, Inc.

15 East 26th Street, New York, N.Y. 10010.
☎ 212-696 4944. Fax 212-679 2126. Email info@claimscon.org; Website www.claimscon.org
(Est. 1951) Represents world Jewry in negotiating for compensation and restitution for victims of Nazi persecution and their heirs. More than 500,000 Holocaust survivors in 67 countries have received payments from Germany and Austria due to the work of the Claims Conference. Administers compensation funds, recovers unclaimed Jewish property and allocates funds to institutions that provide social welfare services to Holocaust survivors and preserve the memory and lessons of the Shoah. *President* Dr I. Singer; *Chairman* Julius Berman; *Exec. V. President* Gideon Taylor.

CONSULTATIVE COUNCIL OF JEWISH ORGANISATIONS

420 Lexington Avenue, New York City, N.Y. 10170.
☎ (212) 808-5437. Fax (212) 983-0094.
Est. 1946 for the purpose of cooperating with the U.N. and other intergovernmental orgs. and agencies in the advancement of human rights and the safeguarding of Jewish interests. Constituent Orgs.: Alliance Israelite Universelle, AJA, Canadian Frs. A.I.U. *Chairmen* Prof. Ady Steg, Clemens Nathan, Gary Waxman; *Sec. Gen.* Warren Green.

EUROPEAN ASSOCIATION FOR JEWISH CULTURE

London office: 79 Wimpole Street, London W1G 9RY. ☎ 020-7935 8266. Fax 020-7935 3252. Email london@jewishcultureineurope.org; Website www.jewishcultureineurope.org
Paris office: 45 rue la Bruyère, 75009 Paris. ☎ +33(0) 1 53 32 88 55. Fax +33(0) 1 48 74 51 33. Email paris@jewishcultureineurope.org; Website www.jewishcultureineurope.org

(Est. 2001) An independent grant-making body, which fosters and supports artistic creativity and encourages access to Jewish culture in Europe. *President* Prof. Ady Steg; *V. President* Peter L. Levy OBE; *T.* Prof Barry Kosmin; *Sec.* Jean-Jacques Wahl; *Dir.* Lena Stanley-Clamp.

EUROPEAN ASSOCIATION FOR JEWISH STUDIES
Secretariat: Oxford Centre for Hebrew and Jewish Studies, Yarnton Manor, Yarnton, Oxon OX5 1PY. ☎ 01865 377946 (x111). Email eajs@herald.ox.ac.uk. *Admin.* Karina Stern. *Publ.* Newsletter; Directory of Jewish Studies in Europe.

EUROPEAN COUNCIL OF JEWISH COMMUNITIES (ECJC)
PO Box 282, CH – 8027 Zurich, Switzerland.
☎ (+41)1 201 70 10. Fax (+41)1 201 70 28. Email ecjc@ecjc.org; Website www.ecjc.org.
(Est. 1968) Originally founded as the European Council of Jewish Community Services (ECJCS), the organisation realigned itself because of the dramatic changes after 1989, becoming the European Council of Jewish Communities (ECJC). It has 70 members from all European countries. In addition to its traditional mission in education, social welfare and culture, the ECJC has strongly pursued the field of communal development, adding to its previous objectives the dimensions of leadership training, regional programmes, Jewish heritage and restitution – partly in co-operation with the JDC. In order to promote networking among the Jewish leadership, ECJC is setting up platforms and forums at which European Jewish leaders can meet each other – as well as Israeli, US and other Jewish leaders world wide – such as the bi-annual General Assembly of European Jewry (the last, in Madrid in 2001, had over 700 participants) and the bi-annual Conference of the Presidents. *President* Cobi J. Benatoff (Milan); *V. Presidents* Gabrielle Rosenstein (Zurich), Michael Goldmeier (London), Gregory Krupnikov (Riga), Boris Khait (Moscow), Jonathan Joseph (London); *Exec. Dir.* Gabriel Taus (Zurich). UK enquiries to Jonathan Joseph (Email jonathan@bellhousejoseph.com).

EUROPEAN ISRAELI FORUM
c/o 30 Bentley Way, Stanmore, Middx HA7 3RP.
☎ 020-8954 7440. Fax 020-8385 7221. Website www.carmel.cz/eif/
(Est. 1989) Development of individual personal links between European Jewish community and Israel. *Chairman* Claude Benoliel (France); *V. Chairs* Muriel Cardozo (Netherlands), Andrej Ernyei (Czech Rep.); *Sec.* Thelma Epstein (G.B.).

EUROPEAN JEWISH CONGRESS
78 Avenue des Champs-Elysées, 75008 Paris.
☎ (33)1 43 59 94 63. Fax (33)1 42 25 45 28. Email jewcong@imaginet.fr
(Est. 1986, previously the European Branch of the World Jewish Congress) Federates and co-ordinates the initiatives of 37 communities in Europe and acts as their spokesman. Has consultative status with the Council of Europe, European Commission and Parliament. Current concerns are the democratic development of Eastern Europe and the problems of racism and antisemitism throughout Europe. *President* Michael Friedman; *Sec. Gen.* Serge Cwajgenbaum.

EUROPEAN JEWISH PUBLICATION SOCIETY
P.O. Box 19948, London N3 3ZL.
☎ 020-8346 1668. Fax 020-8346 1776. Email cs@ejps.org.uk; Website www.ejps.org.uk.
(Est. 1994. Reg. Charity No. 3002158) A registered charity which makes grants to

assist in the publication, translation and distribution of books relating to Jewish literature, history, religion, philosophy, politics, poetry and culture. *Chairman* Frederick Worms; *Ed. Dir.* Dr Colin Shindler.

EUROPEAN UNION OF JEWISH STUDENTS
89 Chaussée de Vleurgat, B-1050, Brussels, Belgium.
☎ 010-32-2-647 72 79. Fax 010-32-2-6482431. Email 106211.2511@compuserve.com; Website www-students.unisg.ch/eujs/
Est. 1978 for co-ordination purposes between nat. unions in 32 countries. It represents more than 170,000 European Jewish students in international Jewish and non-Jewish forums dealing with cultural and political matters and opposes all forms of racism and fascism. The EUJS is also a 'service org.' for students. It helps with courses abroad, supplies material on different subjects for univ. students and organises visits and seminars. *H. Presidents* Mrs Simone Veil, Maram Stern; *H. Mems.* The Lord Janner, QC, David Susskind (Belgium), Suzy Jurysta (B.), Laslov Kadelburg (Yu.); *President* Ariane Platt.

Member unions in: Austria, Belgium, Belorus, Britain, Bulgaria, Czech, Croatia, Denmark, Estonia, Finland, France, Germany, Gibraltar, Greece, Holland, Hungary, Ireland, Italy, Latvia, Lithuania, Luxembourg, Norway, Poland, Portugal, Russia, Serbia, Slovakia, Spain, Sweden, Switzerland, Turkey, Ukraine.

FRIENDSHIP WITH ISRAEL (European Parliament)
51 Tavistock Court, Tavistock Square, WC1H 9HG.
☎ 020-7387 4925.
(Est. 1979) All-Party Group in European Parl. with more than 120 MEPs. Aims at promoting friendship and co-operation between the European Com. and Israel. Provides up-to-date inf. on Israeli matters and a balanced view of Middle East events. Holds regular meetings in Strasbourg at Palais de l'Europe when the Euro-Parl. sits. Recognised as an official 'Inter-Parl. Group'. *H. Patron* Mrs. Simone Veil MEP, past President, Euro-Parl.; *Chairman* Tom Normanton, MEP (UK); *V. Chairmen* Erik Blumenfeld, MEP, Hans-Joachim Seeler, MEP (West Germany), Hans Nord, MEP (Holland), John Tomlinson, MEP (UK); *H. Sec.* John Marshall, MEP (UK); *Dir.* Mrs Sylvia Sheff, JP, BA.

HEBREWARE® USER GROUP
46 Norfolk Avenue, N15 6JX.
☎ 020-8802 6143. Fax 020-8802 1130. Email info@hebreware.org.uk; Website www.hebreware.org.uk
The leading User Group for Hebrew computer software users in Europe. *Contact* Mr Menasche Scharf. Branches: USA, Belgium, Israel.

HEIMLER INTERNATIONAL
(formerly The Heimler Foundation)
Peter Hudson, 47 Rosebery Road, SW2 4DQ
☎ 020-8674 6999.
(Est. 1972.) Heimler International was set up to facilitate the work and ideas of Prof. Eugene Heimler. Its aims are: (1) to provide counselling and therapy for individuals and groups, using the Heimler approach; (2) to provide basic and advanced training in the Heimler Method; (3) to recognise advanced practitioners and lecturers in the Heimler Method; (4) to sanction and collect bona fide research, act as a focal point, publish books/tapes describing the Heimler Method. There are Branches in several different countries in Europe, Canada, USA.

HIAS
333 7th Avenue, New York, NY 1001, USA. ☎ 212 967-4100

(Est. 1954, through merger of the Hebrew Sheltering and Immigrant Aid Society (HIAS), United Service for New Americans (USNA) and the migration service of the American Joint Distribution Committee (AJDC).)

HIAS, the Hebrew Immigrant Aid Society, has been the international migration agency of the organised American Jewish community since its founding in 1881. It assists Jewish migrants and refugees to countries of freedom and security, arranges reception on arrival, helps newcomers become integrated in their new coms. Works with govt. agencies and other orgs. to promote increased immigration opportunities. *President* Leonard Glickman; *Chairman* N. Greenbaum.

INSTITUTE FOR JEWISH POLICY RESEARCH (JPR)

79 Wimpole Street, W1G 9RY.

☎ 020-7935 8266. Fax 020-7935 3252. Email jpr@jpr.org.uk. Website www.jpr.org.uk

JPR is an independent think-tank which informs and influences policy, opinion and decision-making on issues affecting Jewish life worldwide by conducting and commissioning research, developing and disseminating policy proposals and promoting public debate. JPR's public activities include lectures, policy seminars and conferences. *Hon. President* The Lord Rothschild; *President* Lord Haskel; *V. Presidents* William Frankel CBE, The Lord Weidenfeld; *Chairman* Peter L. Levy OBE; *Jt. T.* Larry Levine, Milton Z. Levine; *Exec. Dir.* Prof. Barry Kosmin; *Res. Dir.* Prof. Stanley Waterman; *Dir. Pub. Activities* Lena Stanley-Clamp. *Publ.* Antisemitism and Xenophobia Today (on-line axt.org.uk); Patterns of Prejudice (quarterly); JPR Reports and Policy Papers; JPR News.

INTERNATIONAL COUNCIL OF CHRISTIANS AND JEWS

Martin Buber Haus, Werlestrasse 2, Postfach 1129, D-64629, Heppenheim, Germany.

☎ 6252 93120. Fax 6252-68331. Email iccj-buberhouse@t-online.de; Website www.iccj.org

President Fr. Prof. Dr John T. Pawlikowski; *Gen. Sec.* Rev. Friedhelm Pieper; *Patron* Sir Sigmund Sternberg; *Consultant* Ruth Weyl, Northwood, Middx HA6 3NG. Est. 1974 to strengthen Jewish–Christian understanding on an international basis and to co-ordinate and initiate programmes and activities for this purpose.

INTERNATIONAL COUNCIL OF JEWISH WOMEN

PO Box 12130 Local 4, Montevideo 11300, Uruguay.

☎/Fax +598 (0)2 628 5874. Email icjw@montevideo.com.uy; Website www.icjw.org.uk

ICJW is made up of 43 Jewish women's organisations in 40 countries, covering between them almost the whole spectrum of the Jewish world. The core purpose of ICJW is to bring together Jewish women from all walks of life in order to create a driving force for social justice for all races and creeds. ICJW has consultative status with ECOSOC at the United Nations and is represented on many international organisations. Headquarters currently in Uruguay. *President* Sara Winkowski.

INTERNATIONAL COUNCIL ON JEWISH SOCIAL AND WELFARE SERVICES

The Forum, 74-80 Camden Street, London NW1 0EG. ☎ 020-7691 1771. Fax 020-7691 1780. Email info@wjr.org.uk

(Est. 1961) Member Organisations: Amer. Jt. Distribution Cttee.; WJR.; European Council of Jewish Com. Services; HIAS; World ORT Union. *Exec. Dir.* V. Lewis.

INTERNATIONAL JEWISH GENEALOGICAL RESOURCES (IJGR(UK))

25 Westbourne Road, Edgbaston, Birmingham B15 3TX.

☎ 0121-454 0408. Fax 0121-454 9758. Website www.jewishgen.org/london2001
(Est. 1988) Provides guidance on Jewish genealogy; has a library including material on Anglo-Jewry/Anglo-Australasian Jewry; microfilm of Jewish Chronicle, etc. Research undertaken. *Org.* Dr Anthony P. Joseph and Mrs Judith Joseph.

INTERNATIONAL JEWISH VEGETARIAN SOCIETY
Bet Teva, 853/855 Finchley Road, NW11 8LX.
☎ 020-8455 0692. Fax 020-8455 1465. Email ijvs@yahoo.com
(Est. 1965. Reg. Charity No. 258581.) Affiliated to the International Vegetarian Union. Branches: N. and S. America, S. Africa, Israel, Australia. *H. Sec.* S. Labelda.

IRANIAN JEWISH CENTRE
Sceptre House, 169/173 Regent Street, London W1B 4JH
☎ 020-7292 2662. Fax 020-7292 2601. Website www.ijc.org.uk
(Est. 1981. Reg. Charity No. 287256) Fundraising to support Iranian Jewish communities in Britain, Iran and the USA. Promotion of Iranian/Jewish heritage and culture. *Chairman* Victor Hagani.

JCA CHARITABLE FOUNDATION
Victoria Palace Theatre, Victoria St., SW1E 5EA.
☎ 020-7828 0600. Fax 020-7828 6882.
(Reg. Charity No. 207031) Charitable company est. in 1891 by Baron Maurice de Hirsch to assist poor and needy Jews. The JCA was instrumental in promoting the emigration from Russia of thousands of Jews who were settled in farm 'colonies' in North and South America, Palestine/Israël and elsewhere. Today JCA's main efforts are in Israel in rural areas where it supports schs., instits. of higher learning, agricultural research and helps to promote the subsistence of needy Jews. *President* Sir Stephen Waley-Cohen, Bt.; *Man.* Y. Lothan.

JEWISH AFFILIATES OF THE UNITED NATIONS ASSOCIATION
6 Bloomsbury Square, London WC1A 2LP.
☎ 020-7543 5400.
(Est. 1971) A co-ordinating group of Jewish organisations and individuals affiliated to the United Nations Association. Members of the group represent their organisations at the UNA where they have two functions. Firstly to promote the interests of Israel and the Jewish People, and secondly to present the Jewish view on general international and humanitarian issues. *Chairman* David M. Jacobs.

JEWISH RECONSTRUCTIONIST FEDERATION (JRF, formerly FRCH)
7804 Montgomery Ave., St. #9, Elkins Park, PA 19027, USA.
☎ (215) 782-8500. Fax (215) 782-8805. Email info@jrf.org; Website www.jrf.org
(Est. 1955) JRF is the congregational arm of the Reconstructionist movement, representing 103 affiliates in North America. Dedicated to the concept of Judaism as an evolving religious civilisation, JRF provides outreach, consulting, programmatic and educational support to its congregations and havurot. JRF is the publisher of a new Haggadah and a variety of books, magazines and the *Kol Haneshamah* prayerbook series.

MACCABI WORLD UNION
Kfar Maccabiah, Ramat Gan 52105, Israel.
(Est. 1921) The union is a co-ordinating body for the promotion and advancement of sports, educational and cultural activities among Jewish communities

worldwide. *President* R. Bakalarz; *Chairman* Oudi Recanati; *Chairman, European Maccabi Confederation* Leo Dan-Bensky; *Exec. Dir.* E. Tiberger. See Maccabi Assns., p.48.

MEMORIAL FOUNDATION FOR JEWISH CULTURE
1703, 15 East 26th Street, New York, NY 10010. ☎ 212 679-4074. Fax 212-889-9080. Website www.mfjc.org
(Est. 1964) Supports Jewish cultural and educational programmes all over the world in co-operation with educational research and scholarly organisationss, and provides scholarship and fellowship grants. *President Exec. Cttee* Anita Shapira; *Exec. V. President* Dr J. Hochbaum.

SIMON WIESENTHAL CENTRE
European office: 64 Avenue Marceau, 75008 Paris, France. ☎ (331) 4723-7637. Fax (331) 4720-8401.
London office: Simon Wiesenthal Centre UK, 27 Old Gloucester Street, WC1N 3XX (Reg. Charity No. 1030966). *Chairman* Graham Morris. ☎ 020-7419 5014. Fax 020-7831 9489. Email csweurope@compuserve.com.
(Est. Los Angeles, 1979) To study the contemporary Jewish and general social condition in Europe by drawing lessons from the Holocaust experience. To monitor, combat and educate against anti-semitism, racism and prejudice. *Int. Dir.* Rabbi Marvin Hier; *Chairman, Board of Trustees* Samuel Belzberg; *Dir. for Int. Affairs* Dr Shimon Samuels. 400,000 members. Headquarters: Los Angeles. Offices in: New York, Chicago, Washington DC, Miami, Toronto, Jerusalem, Paris, Buenos Aires.

UK JEWISH AID & INTERNATIONAL DEVELOPMENT (UKJAID)
44a New Cavendish Street, London W1G 8TR.
☎ 020-7224 3788. Fax 020-7224 0788. Email ukjaid@talk21.com
(Est. 1989. Reg. Charity No. 328488) UKJAID is a Jewish humanitarian organisation which leads the UK Jewish community in response to international disasters and mobilises Jewish resources for international development projects. It has projects ongoing in the former Yugoslavia, in Kosovo, Macedonia, Mozambique, Zambia, Nicaragua, India (earthquake response), India (Tibet Jewish Youth Exchange) and is preparing projects in Nepal and Madagascar.

Since the January 2001 earthquake in Gujarat, UKJAID has worked with the Hindu community and with Jewish organisations worldwide to aid in the rehabilitation of the lives of victims.

In 2001 the Target 2015 campaign was launched within the Jewish community. Its aim is to halve world poverty by 2015. This involves publications, lectures and seminars, some of which are sponsored by the UK government's Department for International Development (DFID).

UKJAID plays a role as an educator in the Jewish community as to the ethical significance and positive benefit of the Jewish contribution to emergency aid and development.

Patrons The Chief Rabbi, the Communal Rabbi of the Spanish & Portugese Jews' Cong., the Chairman of the Council of Reform and Liberal Rabbis, the President of the Board of Deputies of British Jews, the President of the Masorti Rabbinic Liaison Committee, The Lord Janner of Braunstone, The Lord Mishcon QC, DL, Dame Simone Prendergast DBE, JP, Professor Sir Hans Singer; *Chairman* Tony Leifer; *Hon. Consult.* Dr T. Scarlett Epstein; *Chief Exec.* Daniel Casson.

WORLD COUNCIL OF CONSERVATIVE/MASORTI SYNAGOGUES
155 Fifth Avenue, New York, N.Y. 10010.
☎ 212-533 7800 (Ext. 2014). Fax 212-353 9439. Email worldcouncil@com puserve.com.

2 Agron St., PO Box 7456, Jerusalem 91073.
☎ 02-256 386.
(Est. 1957) To foster the growth of Conservative Judaism in more than 30 countries in which it operates and to co-ordinate the activities of its autonomous orgs. and regions. Its constituents include the Utd. Syn. of Conservative Judaism, Rabbinical Assembly, Women's League for Conservative Judaism, Nat. Fed. of Jewish Men's Clubs, Jewish Educators Assembly, Israeli Masorti Movement, British Masorti Assembly of Synagogues, Utd. Syn. of India, and the Seminario Rabinico Latinamericano, Buenos Aires. *President* Rabbi Alan Silverstein; *Rabbi* Dr Benjamin Z. Kreitman; *Chairman of Bd.* Mark Sternfeld; *Chairman of Steering Cttee.* Rabbi Jack Topal.

WORLD JEWISH CONGRESS

(a) To co-ordinate the efforts of its affliated orgs., in respect of the political, economic, social, religious and cultural problems of the Jewish people; (b) to secure the rights, status and interests of Jews and Jewish communities and to defend them wherever they are denied, violated or imperilled; (c) to encourage and assist the creative development of Jewish social, religious and cultural life throughout the world; (d) to represent and act on behalf of its affiliated orgs. before governmental, intergovernmental and other international authorities in respect of matters which concern the Jewish people as a whole. *Fdr President* Late Dr N. Goldmann; *President* Edgar M. Bronfman; *Chairman, Exec.* Mendel Kaplan; *Chairman, Gov. Bd.* Israel Singer; *Sec. Gen.* Dr Avi Beker; *Chairmen of Regions:* **North America**: Evelyn Sommer, Keith Landy; **Latin America**: Jack Terpins, José Hercman; **Europe**: Jo Wagerman, Michel Friedman, Roger Cukierman; **Israel**: Matityahu Droblas, Yehiel Leket; **Euro-Asia**: Alexander Machkevich, Michael Chlenov.

Principal Offices: New York, 501 Madison Avenue, 17th Fl., NY 10022. ☎ 755 5770; Geneva, 1 rue de Varembe. ☎ 734-13-25; Paris, 78 Av. des Champs Elysées. ☎ 4359 9463, Fax 4225 4528; Buenos Aires, Casilla 20, Suc. 53. ☎ 5411-4962-5028; Jerusalem, P.O.B. 4293, Jerusalem 91042. ☎ (02) 563-5261/4.

Publ.: Dateline World Jewry (monthly), WJC Report (quarterly), Boletin de Información OJI (Spanish, monthly), Gesher (Hebrew, quarterly), Batfutzot (Hebrew).

WORLD ORT

1 Rue de Varembé, 1211 Geneva 20, Switzerland.
☎ (022) 919 4234. Fax (022) 919 4232. Email ortsuisse@vtx.ch
(Est. 1880.) Organisation for educational Resources and Technological training. Over three and a half million students have been trained since 1880, and currently 330,000 students are being trained in 60 countries in different parts of the world.

Operational Headquarters in UK: World ORT Trust, 126 Albert St., London NW1 7NE. ☎ 020-7446 8500. Website www.ort.org

WORLD UNION FOR PROGRESSIVE JUDAISM

13 King David Street, 94101 Jerusalem. ☎ 972 26203 447. Fax 262 203 446
(Est. 1926.) To foster the international growth and practice of Progressive Judaism, and to co-ordinate the activities of its autonomous constituent organisations. *President* Austin Beutel; *Exec. Dir.* Rabbi D. Marmur.

European Region: The Sternberg Centre, 80 East End Rd., London N3 2SY. ☎ 020-8349 3779. Fax 020-8349 5699. Email administrator@europeanregion.org *Chairman* Dr L. Hepner; *Sec.* Paul Zatz.

WORLD UNION OF JEWISH STUDENTS

P.O. Box 7914, Jerusalem 91077, Israel.

☎ 025610133. Fax 025610741.
Est. 1924 to fight antisemitism and to act as an umbrella organisation for national Jewish students' bodies; organises educational programmes, leadership training seminars, Am Echad project, Project Areivim, Kol Isha – women's seminar, JADE which is a service programme for Diaspora communities; divided into six regions; Congress every two years; members: 51 national unions representing over 700,000 students; NGO member of UNESCO; youth affiliate of the World Jewish Congress; member organisation of the World Zionist Organisation. *First President* Prof. Albert Einstein; *Chairperson* Ilanit Sasson Melchior. *Publs.* Heritage & History, WUJS Reports, WUJS Leads, the Jewish student activist handbook, supplement to the Pesach Haggada, MASUA – monthly educational material, etc.

ZIONIST COUNCIL OF EUROPE
741 High Road, London N2 0BQ
☎ 020-8343 9756. Fax 020-8446 0639. Email zion-fed@dircon.co.uk
(Est. 1980) An umbrella organisation, consisting of the Zionist Federations from around Europe, with the aim of co-ordinating Zionist activities and developing young leadership on the continent. *Chairman* Howard Schaverien; *Dir.* Alan Aziz.

LONDON (196,000)

SYNAGOGUES

(D) where shown indicates regular daily services are held.

Ashkenazi

United Synagogue

Constituent and Affiliated Synagogues of the United Synagogue, Adler House, 735 High Road, North Finchley, N12 0US. (Reg. Charity no. 242552) *Chief Exec.* Rabbi S. Zneimer. ☎ 020-8343 8989. Fax 020-8343 6262. Website www.united synagogue.org.uk.

MEMBER SYNAGOGUES

Belmont Synagogue, 101 Vernon Dr, Stanmore, Middx HA7 2BW. *M.* Rabbi D. Roselaar; *Admin.* Mrs C. Fletcher. ☎ 020-8426 0104. Fax 020-8427 2046. Email office@belmontshul.fsnet.co.uk; Website www.brijnet.org/belmont. (D)

Borehamwood & Elstree Synagogue, P.O. Box 47, Croxdale Road, Borehamwood, Herts WD6 4QF. ☎ 020-8386 5227. Fax 020-8386 3303. Email admin@bwoodshul.demon.co.uk; Website www.bwoodshul.demon.co.uk (Est. 1955.) *M.* Rabbi A. Plancey; *Admin.* B. Winterman. (D)

Bushey & District Synagogue, 177/189 Sparrows Herne, Bushey, Herts WD23 1AJ. ☎ 020-8950 7340. Fax 020-8421 8267. Email adminstrator@busheyus. org. *M.* Rabbi Z. M. Salasnik, BA, FJC; *Admin.* Mrs M. Chambers; *Youth Dir.* Rabbi Shalom Bloom ☎ 020 8950 0876. (D)

Central Synagogue, (Great Portland St.), 36-40 Hallam St., W1W 6NW. ☎ 020-7580 1355. Fax 020-7636 3831. Website www.brijnet.org/centralsyn. (Consecrated 1870, destroyed by enemy action May 1941, rebuilt 1958.) *Admin. Office* 36 Hallam Street, W1W 6NW; *M.* Rabbi B. Marcus; *R.* J. Murgraff; *Admin.* Mrs C. Jowell.

Chigwell and Hainault Synagogue, Limes Ave., Chigwell, Essex IG7 5NT. ☎ 020-8500 2451. Email chshul@breahemail.net; Website www.chigshul.net. *M.* Rabbi B. Davis; *Admin.* W. Land; *Youth Dir.* Rabbi D. Lewis. ☎ 020-8500 4604. (D)

Clayhall Synagogue, Sinclair Hse., Woodford Bridge Rd., Ilford, Essex IG4 5LN. ☎ 020-8551 6533. Fax 020-8551 9803. Email clayhallsynagogue@hotmail.com; Website www.clayhallsynagogue.org.uk. *M.* Rabbi J. Kleiman; *Admin.* Mrs M. Mervish.

Cockfosters & N. Southgate Synagogue, Old Farm Av., Southgate, N14 5QR. ☎ 020-8886 8225. Fax 020-8886 8234. Email cns-syn@brijnet.org. (Est. 1948. Consecrated Dec. 1954.) *M.* Rabbi Y. Fine, BA; *R.* ; *Admin.* Mrs L. Brandon.

Cricklewood Synagogue, 131 Walm Lane, NW2 3AU. ☎/Fax 020-8452 1739. (Consecrated 1931.) *M.*; *Admin.* Mrs Grayson. (D)

Dollis Hill Synagogue, Parkside, Dollis Hill Lane, NW2 6RJ. ☎ 020-8958 6777. *M.* Rev. M. Fine; *Admin.* W. Land.

Ealing Synagogue, 15 Grange Road, Ealing, W5 5QN. ☎ 020-8579 4894. *M.* Rabbi H. Vogel, MA; *Admin.* Mrs M. Gilford.

Edgware Synagogue, Parnell Close, Edgware Way, Edgware, Middx HA8 8YE. ☎ 020-8958 7508. Fax 020-8905 4449. Email edgewareunited@talk21.com; Website www.edgewaresynagogue.org. *M.* Rabbi B. Rabinowitz, BA, MPhil; *R.* S. Craimer; *Com. Dev.* Rabbi J. Bruce, BA; *Admin.* L. J. Ford. (D)

Finchley Synagogue, Kinloss Gdns., N3 3DU. ☎ 020-8346 8551. Fax 020-8349 1579. Email admin@kinloss.freeserve.co.uk. (Consecrated 1935.) *M.* Rabbi E. Mirvis; *Admin.* Mrs B. Fireman. (D)

Finsbury Park Synagogue, 220 Green Lanes, N4 2NT. ☎ 020-8800 3526. *M.* Rabbi A. Cohn; *R.* Rev. E. Krausher; *Admin.* H. Mather.

Golders Green Synagogue, 41 Dunstan Road, NW11 8AE. ☎ 020-8455 2460. Fax 020-8731 9296. (Consecrated 1922.) *M.; Admin.* Mrs N. Hill; *Youth Dir.* M. Sunlovitch ☎ 020-8203 3183. (D)

Hackney & East London Synagogue, Brenthouse Road, Mare Street, E9 6QG. ☎ 020-8985 4600. Fax 020-8986 9507. (Consecrated 1897; enlarged and reconsecrated 1936, amalgamated 1993.) *M.* Rev. N. Tiefenbrun; *Admin.* Mrs B. Heumann.

Hampstead Garden Suburb Synagogue, Norrice Lea, N2 0RE. ☎ 020-8455 8126. Fax 020-8201 9247. Email office@hgss.org.uk; Website www.hgss.org.uk. (Consecrated 1934). *M.* Rabbi R. Livingstone; *R.* Chazan A. Freilich; *Admin.* Mrs M. S. Wolff; *Youth Dir.* Rabbi S. Gaffin ☎ 020-8209 1941. (D)

Hampstead Synagogue, Dennington Park Road, West Hampstead, NW6 1AX. ☎ 020-7435 1518. Fax 020-7431 8369. (Consecrated 1892.) *M.* Rabbi Dr M.J. Harris; *R.* Rev. S. Brickman; *Admin.* I. Nadel; *Youth Dir.* Zaki Cooper ☎ 07939 224695. (D)

Hendon Synagogue, 18 Raleigh Close, Wykeham Road, NW4 2TA. ☎ 020-8202 6924. Fax 020-8202 1720. Email benson118@aol.com. (Consecrated 1935.) *M.* Rabbi M.S. Ginsbury; *Emer. M.* Rev. L. Hardman, MA; *R.* Rabbi S. Neuman; *Exec. Sec.* J. Benson. (D)

Highgate Synagogue (Est. 1929.), Grimshaw Close, 57 North Road, Highgate, N6 4BJ. *M.* Rabbi I.H. Sufrin, ☎ 020-8882-6464; *Admin.* Charles Loeb. ☎/Fax 020-8340 7655. Email highgateshul@ic24.net.

Ilford Synagogue, 22 Beehive Lane, Ilford, Essex IG1 3RT. ☎ 020-8554 5969. Fax 020-8554 4543. Email office@ilfordsynagogue.co.uk; Website www.ilfordsynagogue.co.uk. (Est. 1936.) *M.* Rabbi C. Rapoport; *R.* Rev. A. Levin; *Admin.* Ms H.R. Michaels. (D)

Kenton Synagogue, Shaftesbury Avenue, Kenton, Middx HA3 0RD. ☎ 020-8907 5959. Fax 020-8909 2677. Email synagogue@kenton613.freeserve.co.uk; Website www.brijnet.org/kenton. *M.* Rabbi Ch. Kanterovitz; *Admin.* Mrs A. Primhak.

Kingsbury Synagogue, Kingsbury Green, NW9 8XR. ☎ 020-8204 8089. Email kingsburysynagogue@hotmail.com. *M.* Rabbi M. Hool; *R.* ; *Admin.* Mrs C. DiConsiglio. (D)

Mill Hill Synagogue, Brockenhurst Gdns., NW7 2JY. ☎ 020-8959 1137. Fax 020-8959 6484. Email shulmail@aol.com; Website www.shul.co.uk. *M.* Rabbi Y.Y. Schochet; *Admin.* Mrs M. Vogel; *Sec.* Mrs R. Newman. (D)

Muswell Hill Synagogue, 31 Tetherdown, N10 1ND. ☎/Fax 020-8883 5925. Email muswellhillsynagogue@tesco.net. (Est. 1908.) *M.* Rabbi D. Lister; *Sec.* C. Loeb.

New Synagogue, Victoria Community Centre, Egerton Rd., Stamford Hill, N16 6UB. (Est. in Leadenhall St., 1761.) ☎ 020-8880 2731. Fax 020-8809 0550. *Admin.* (D)

New West End Synagogue, St Petersburgh Place, Bayswater Road, W2 4JT. ☎ 020-7229 2631. Fax 020-7229 2355. Email nwes@newwestend.org.uk; Website www.newwestend.org.uk. (Consec. 1879.) *M.* Rabbi G. Shisler; *Admin.* Mrs S. Hayman.

Newbury Park Synagogue, 23 Wessex Close, off Suffolk Road, Newbury Pk., Ilford, Essex IG3 8JU. ☎/Fax 020-8597 2919. *M.* Rev. G. Newman; *Admin.* Mrs E. M. Benjamin. (D)

Northwood Synagogue, 21-23 Murray Road, Middx HA6 2YP. ☎ 01923 820004. Fax 01923-820020. Email nusbo@hotmail.com; Website www.northwoodunitedsynagogue.org. *M.* Rabbi N.Y. Brawer; *Admin.* Mrs E. Granger; *Youth Dir.* Donna Solomon ☎ 020-8868 7938.

Palmers Green and Southgate Synagogue, Brownlow Road, N11 2BN. ☎ 020-8881 0037. Fax 020-8441 8832. Email palmgrnsyn@yahoo.co.uk. *M.* Rabbi E. Levy, BA; *R.* B. Segal; *Admin.* M. Lewis. (D)

Pinner Synagogue, 1 Cecil Park, Pinner, Middx HA5 5HJ. ☎ 020-8868 7204. Fax 020-8868 7011. Website www.pinnersynagogue.com. *M.* Rabbi J. Grunewald, BA;

Admin. Mrs A. Freeman; *Youth Off. Donna Solomon.* ☎ 020-8868 7938. (D)

Radlett Synagogue, 22 Watling St., P.O. Box 28, Radlett, Herts WD7 7PN. ☎ 01923-856878. Fax 01923-856698. *M.* Rabbi G. D. Sylvester. *Admin.* Mrs J. Bower.

Richmond Synagogue, Lichfield Gardens, Richmond-on-Thames, Surrey TW9 1AP. ☎ 020-8940 3526. (Est. 1916.) *M.* Rabbi D. Rose; *Admin.* Mrs Fellows.

St John's Wood Synagogue, 37/41 Grove End Road, St John's Wood, NW8 9NG. ☎ 020-7286 3838. Fax 020-7266 2123. Email office@shulinthewood.com; Website www.stjohnswoodsynagogue.com. (Est. in Abbey Road 1882; present building consecrated 1964.) *M.* Dayan I. Binstock, B.Sc.; *R.* Rev. M. Haschel; *Admin.* Mrs Loraine Young; *Youth Dir.* Rev. S. Odze ☎ 020 7286 8336; *Community Dir.* (Elderly Care) Mrs Yaffa Amit. (D)

Shenley Synagogue, c/o W. Susman. ☎ 01923 857786.

South Hampstead Synagogue, 21 Eton Villas, Eton Road, NW3 4SP. ☎ 020-7722 1807. Fax 020-7586 3459. Email muriel@southhampstead.org; Website www.southhampstead.org. *M.* Rabbi S. Levin; *Admin.* Mrs M. Spector; *Youth Dir.* Mark & Dalia Mays ☎ 020-7483 2734.

South London Synagogue, 45 Leigham Ct. Road, SW16 2NF. ☎ 020-8677 0234. Fax 020-8677 5107. *M.* Rabbi P. N. Ginsbury, M.A.; *Admin.* D. Saul.

South Tottenham Synagogue, 111 Crowland Road, N15 6UR. (Sun 10.30-1pm; Wed. 7.00-7.45pm): ☎ 020-8880 2731. Fax 020-8809 0550. (Est. 1938.) *M.* Rabbi C. M. Biberfeld; *R.* Rev. A. Greenberg; *Admin.* L. Newmark.

Stanmore and Canons Park Synagogue, London Road, Stanmore Middx HA7 4NS. ☎ 020-8954 2210. Fax 020-8954 4369. Email mail@stanmoresynagogue.org. *M.* Rabbi Dr J. M. Cohen, BA, M.Phil., AJC, PhD; *R.* H. Black; *Asst. M.* Rabbi Andrew Shaw ☎ 020-8385 7263; *Admin.* Mrs B. S. Dresner. (D)

Watford Synagogue, 16 Nascot Road, Watford, Herts WD17 3RE. ☎ 01923-222755. Email info@wat.syn.fsnet.co.uk. (Est. 1946.) *M.* Rabbi B. Lerer; *Admin.* Mrs C. Silverman.

Wembley Synagogue, Forty Avenue, Wembley, Middx HA9 8JW. ☎ 020-8904 6565. Fax 020-8908 2740. E.mail office@wembleysyn.org. *M.* Rabbi M. van den Bergh, BEd, MA; *R.* Rev. A. Wolfson, BEd (Hons), MA, NPQH; *Admin.* Mrs R. Koten. (D)

West Ham and Upton Park Synagogue, 95 Earlham Grove, Forest Gate, E7 9AN. ☎ 020-8522 1917. *M.* Rabbi E. Levine; *Admin.* Mrs E. Benjamin.

Willesden and Brondesbury Synagogue, 143 Brondesbury Park, NW2 5JL. ☎ 020-8459 1083. (Est. 1934.) *R.* ; *Admin.* Mrs J. Questle. (D)

Woodside Park Synagogue, Woodside Park Road, N12 8RZ. ☎ 020-8445 4236. Fax 020-8446 5515. Email admin@woodsidepark.org.uk. *M.* Rabbi H. Rader; *R.* Rev. S. Robins; *Chairman* Mr D. Gilbert; *Admin.* Mrs D. Bruce; *Youth Dir.* A. Davis ☎ 020-8445 5010. (D)

ASSOCIATE SYNAGOGUE

Western Marble Arch, 32 Great Cumberland Place, London, W1H 7TN. ☎ 020-7723 9333. Fax 020-7224 8065. *M.* ; *President* H. Knobil; *Exec. Sec.* S. Garcia.

AFFILIATED SYNAGOGUES

These are syns. belonging to U.S. by means of a scheme for small and newly est. congregations.

Barking and Becontree (Affiliated) Synagogue, 200 Becontree Avenue, Dagenham, Essex RM8 2TR. ☎ 020-8590 2737. *R.*; *Chairman* M. Leigh; *Hon. Sec.* Mrs B. Berman.

Barnet and District Affiliated Synagogue, Eversleigh Road, New Barnet, Herts EN5 1NE. ☎ 020-8449 0145. Email administrator@barnetsynagogue.org.uk; Website www.barnetsynagogue.org.uk. *M.* Rabbi S. Robinson; *H. Admin.* Mrs S. Shaw

☎ 020-8441 1059; *Youth Dir.* D. Hanstater ☎ 020-8458 8574.

Catford & Bromley Affiliated Synagogue (est. 1937), 6 Crantock Road, SE6 2QS. ☎ 020-8698 9496. *M.* Rev. Z.A. Amit. Enq. P.O. Box 4724, London SE6 2YA. *Admin.* Mrs E. Govendir ☎ 01322-527239.

Chelsea Affiliated Synagogue, Smith Terrace, Smith Street, Chelsea, SW3 4DL. (Reg. Charity No. 242552) ☎ 020-7352 6046. *M.* Rabbi M. Atkins ☎ 020-7351 6292; *Admin.* Mrs E. Atkins.

Enfield & Winchmore Hill Synagogue, 53 Wellington Road, Bush Hill Park, Middx EN1 2PG ☎ 020-8363 2697. Email enfieldsynagogue@aol.com. Website www.myshul.co.uk. (Est. 1950.) *M.* Rabbi L. Brackman; *Hon. Sec.* S. Marco ☎ 020-8360 8524.

Harold Hill and District Affiliated Synagogue, Trowbridge Road, Harold Hill, Essex RM3 8YW. (Est. 1953.) *T.* D. Jacobs ☎ 020-8928 8686; *H. Sec.* Miss D. Meid, 4 Portmadoc House, Broseley Road, Harold Hill, Essex RM3 9BT. ☎ 01708-348904.

Hemel Hempstead and District Affiliated Synagogue, c/o 1 Devreaux Drive, Watford, WD1 3DD. *Admin.* H. Nathan. ☎ 01923 232007.

High Wycombe Affiliated Synagogue. *H. Sec.* Mrs R. Weiss, 33 Hampden Road, High Wycombe, Bucks. HP13 6SZ. ☎ 01494 529821.

Highams Park and Chingford Affiliated Synagogue, 81a Marlborough Road, Chingford, E4 9AJ. ☎ 020-8527 0937. *M.* Rev. M. Lester; *Chairman* S. Dunstan, 105 Oak Hill, Woodford Green, Essex IG8 9PF. ☎ 020-8527 9327. *Admin.* Mrs S.R. Benjamin, 77 Royston Avenue, Chingford, E4 9DE. ☎ 020-8527 4750.

Hounslow, Heathrow and District Affiliated Synagogue, 100 Staines Road, Hounslow, Middx TW3 3LF. (Est. 1944.) ☎ 020-8572 2100. *H. Admin.* L. Gilbert, 9 Park Ave., Hounslow, Middx. TW3 2NA. ☎ 020-8894 4020.

Kingston, Surbiton and District Affiliated Synagogue, 33-35 Uxbridge Road, Kingston on Thames, Surrey KT1 2LL. (Est. 1947) ☎ 020-8546 9370. *M.* Rabbi S. Coten. ☎/Fax 020-8399 8689. Email stanley@coten.freeserve.co.uk. *H. Admin.* Mrs C. Abrahams, 15 Albany Reach, Queens Road, Thames Ditton, KTY 0QH. ☎ 020-8224 2073. Email gcabrahams@cwcom.net.

Peterborough Affiliated Synagogue, 142 Cobden Avenue, Peterborough, PEI 2NU. *Admin.* C. Salamon ☎ 01733 264151.

Potters Bar and Brookmans Park District Affiliated Synagogue, Meadowcroft, Great North Road, Bell Bar (nr. Potters Bar), Hatfield, Herts AL9 6DB. ☎/Fax 01707 656202. Email office@pottersbarshul.org.uk; Website www.pottersbarshul.org.uk. *M.* Rabbi Z. Solomons.

Romford and District Affiliated Synagogue (Reg. Charity No. 242552), 25 Eastern Road, Romford, Essex RM1 3NH. ☎ 01708-741690. (Est. 1929.) *Admin.* J. Rose. ☎ 01708-748199.

Ruislip and District Affiliated Synagogue, 9 Shenley Avenue, Ruislip Manor, Middx HA4 6BP. ☎ 01895 622059. Fax 01895 622059. (Est. 1946.) *M.* Rev D. Wolfson; *Sec.* Mrs S. Green.

St Albans Affiliated Synagogue, Oswald Road, St Albans, Herts AL1 3AQ. ☎ 01727 854872.

Staines and District Affiliated Synagogue, Westbrook Road, South Street, Staines, Middx TW18 4PR. ☎ 01784-462557. Email staines.synagogue@btinternet.com. *M.* Rev. M. Binstock; *H. Sec.* Mrs P.D. Fellman. ☎ 01784 254604.

Sutton & District Synagogue, 14 Cedar Road, Sutton, Surrey SM2 5DA. ☎ 020-8642 5419. *M.* Rabbi A. Groner; *Admin.* Mrs L. Field.

Wanstead and Woodford Affiliated Synagogue, 20 Churchfields, South Woodford, E18 2QZ. ☎ 020-8504 1990. Email wwsyn@aol.com. *M.* Rabbi A. Lewis; *Admin.* Mrs S. Braude. (D)

Welwyn Garden City Affiliated Synagogue, Barn Close, Handside Lane, Welwyn

Garden City, Herts AL8 6ST. ☎ 01438-715686. *M.* Rabbi G. Hyman. *H. Sec.* Mrs D. Prag.

BURIAL SOCIETY

Finchley Office: *Man.* Mrs M. Wohlman, Finchley Synagogue, P.O. Box 9537, Kinloss Gardens, N3 3DU. ☎ 020-8343 3456. Fax 020-8346 3402 (Bushey and Willesden). Ilford Office, Schaller House, Ilford Synagogue, 22 Beehive Lane, Ilford, Essex IG1 3RT. ☎ 020-8518 2868. Fax 020-8518 2926 (Waltham Abbey, East Ham, West Ham and Plashet). *Man.* Mrs C. Block.

CEMETERIES

Willesden, Beaconsfield Road, NW10 2JE. Opened 1873. ☎ 020-8459 0394. Fax 020-8451 0478; East Ham, Marlow Road, High St. South, E6 3QG. Opened 1919. ☎ 020-8472 0554. Fax 020-8471 2822; Bushey, Little Bushey Lane, Bushey, Herts, WD2 3TP. Opened 1947. ☎ 020-8950 6299. Fax 020-8420 4973; Waltham Abbey, Skillet Hill (Honey Lane), Waltham Abbey, Essex. Opened 1960. ☎ 01992 714492. Fax 01992-650 735. Plashet, High Street North, E12 6PQ. Opened 1896. West Ham, Buckingham Road, Forest Lane, E15 1SP. Opened 1857. ☎ 020-8472 0554. Alderney Road, E1. Opened for Great Syn. in 1696 (disused). Brady street, E1. Opened for the New Syn, in 1761; subsequently used also by Great Syn. (disused); Hackney, Lauriston Road, E9. Opened for Hambro' Syn. in 1788 (disused).

Federation of Synagogues

Constituent and Affiliated Synagogues of the Federation of Synagogues, 65 Watford Way, NW4 3AQ. ☎ 020-8202 2263. Fax 020-8203 0610.

CONSTITUENT SYNAGOGUES

Clapton Federation Synagogue (Sha'are Shomayim), 47 Lea Bridge Road, E5 9QB. ☎ 020-8806 4369.(Est. 1919.) *M.* Rev. H. Daviest; *Sec.* W. Jacobs ☎ 020-8989 5211.

Croydon & District Synagogue, The Almonds, Shirley Oaks, CRO 8YX. *M.* Rev. M. Daniels; *H. Secs.* Mrs B. Harris, Mrs V. Harris. ☎ 01883-348939.

East London Central Synagogue, 30/40 Nelson Street, E1 2DE. ☎ 020-7790 9809. *Sec.* L. Gayer. ☎ 020-8554 5267.

Elstree Beis Hamedrash, Allum Commmunity Centre, Allum Lane, Elstree, Herts WD6 3PJ. *M.* Rabbi D. Tugendhaft ☎ 020-8953 8385. *Sec.* M. Slyper ☎ 020-8953 8444. Email ebh@kinetic.clara.net

Finchley Central Synagogue, Redbourne Avenue, N3 2BS. ☎ 020-8346 1892. *Rab.* Rabbi Z. H. Telsner; *Sec.* M. Moller.

Hendon Beis Hamedrash, 65 Watford Way NW4 3AQ. *M.* Dayan Y.Y Lichtenstein; *H. Sec.* J. Craimer ☎ 020-8202 3138.

Ilford Federation Synagogue, 14 Coventry Road, Ilford, Essex IG1 4QR. ☎/Fax 020-8554 7003. Email ilfordfeds@lineone.net. (Est. 1927). *M.* Rabbi H. Belovski; *Sec.* Mrs E. Conway. (D)

Machzike Hadath Synagogue, 1-4 Highfield Road, NW11 9LU. ☎ 020-8455 9816 *M.* Rabbi C. Z. Pearlman; *H. Sec.* R. Shaw ☎ 020-8204 1887.

Ohel Jacob Beth Hamedrash: (1st Floor) 478 Cranbrook Road, Ilford, Essex IG2 2LE. ☎ 020-8518 3792. *M.* Rav R. Godlewsky ☎ 020-8554 8587; *H. Sec.* Mrs R. Pressman. ☎ 020-8550 4596.

Shomrei Hadath Synagogue, 64 Burrard Road, NW6 1DD. *M.* Rabbi M. Fachler; *Sec.* Mrs P. Schotten ☎ 020-7435 6906.

Sinai Synagogue, 54 Woodstock Avenue, NW11 9RJ. (Est. 1935.) *Rab.* Rabbi B. Knopfler; *Sec.* E. Cohen ☎ 020-8458 8201. (D)

Yeshurun Synagogue, Fernhurst Gdns., Stonegrove, Edgware, Middx HA8 7PH.

☎ 020-8952 5167. (Est. 1946.) *Rab.* Dayan G. Lopian; *Sec.* D. H. Cohen. Fax 020-8905 7439. Email admin@yeshurun.org; Website www.yeshurun.org.

AFFILIATED SYNAGOGUES

Congregation of Jacob, 351/353 Commercial Road, E1 2PS. (Est. 1904.) Contact D. Brandes and D. Behr.

Fieldgate Street Great Synagogue, 41 Fieldgate Street, E1. ☎ 020-7247 2644. *M.*; *Sec.* Mrs D. Jacobson. (D)

Finchley Road Synagogue, 4 Helenslea Avenue, NW11. (Est. 1941.) *Rab.* Rabbi S. Rubin. ☎ 020-8458 6813.

Leytonstone & Wanstead Synagogue, 2 Fillebrook Road, E11 4AT. (Est. 1932.) *H. Sec.* Cllr. Laurie Braham, 322 Grove Green Road, Leytonstone, E11 4EA. ☎ 020-8539 0088. Fax 020-8518 7977. Email cllr.l.braham@lbwf.gov.uk.

Loughton Synagogue, Borders La., Loughton, Essex IG10 1TE. *M.* Rev. J. Lorraine. ☎ 020-8508 0270. *Admin.* Mrs M. Lewis. ☎ 020-8508 0303. Email loughtonsynagogue@lineone.net.

Netzach Israel Synagogue, 281 Golders Green Rd., NW11 9JJ. ☎ 020-8455 0087. *M.* Rabbi A. Doron; *Sec.* C. David.

Springfield Synagogue, 202 Upper Clapton Road, E5 9DH. (Est. 1929.) *Rab.* Dayan I. Gukovitski; *President/Hon. Sec.* L. Blackman, 45 Midhurst Avenue, Westcliff on Sea, Essex SS0 0NP. ☎ 01702 340 762.

Stamford Hill Beth Hamedrash, 50 Clapton Common, E5 9AL. *M.* Dayan Grynhaus; *Sec.* M. Chontow. ☎ 020-8800 5465.

Tottenham Hebrew Congregation, 366A High Road, N17 9HT. (Est. 1904.) *M.* Rabbi S. Lewis. ☎ 020-8800 2772; *Sec.* Dr S. S. Cohen. ☎ 020-8482-3428.

Waltham Forest Hebrew Congregation, 140 Boundary Road, E17 8LA. *Rab.* Rabbi A. Abel; *Sec.* A. Wolpert. ☎ 020-8509 0775.

West End Great Synagogue, 32 Great Cumberland Place, W1H 7TN. ☎ 020-7724 8121. Fax 020-7723 4413. *M.* Ari Cohen; *Sec.* S. B. Levy.

West Hackney Synagogue & Montague Rd Beth Hamedrash, 233 Amhurst Road, E8 2BS (Est. 1903.) *Chairman* I. Leigh. ☎ 020-8550 9543. *Sec.* Mrs R. Glaser. ☎ 020-7254 8078.

BURIAL SOCIETY

Office: 65 Watford Way, Hendon NW4 3AQ. ☎ 020-8202 3903; Fax 020-8203 0610. *Admin.* M. L. Stuart; *Sexton* N. Kahler; *Ts.* H. Dony, N. Bruckheimer.

CEMETERIES

Montague Rd., Angel Road, Lower Edmonton, N18. ☎ 020-8807 2268.

Upminster Road North, Rainham, Essex. Supt. E. Brown. ☎ 01708-552825.

Union of Orthodox Hebrew Congregations

140 Stamford Hill, N16 6QT.
☎ 020-8802 6226 Fax 020-8809 7092.

CONSTITUENTS

Adath Yisroel (Parent) Synagogue, 40 Queen Elizabeth's Walk, N16 0HH. *Rab.* Rabbi J. Dunner; *Sec.* M. Mannes. ☎ 020-8802 6262/3. (D)

Adath Yisroel Tottenham Beth Hamedrash, 55/57 Ravensdale Road, N16. *Rab.* Dayan A. D. Dunner. ☎ 020-8800 3978. (D)

Ahavat Israel Synagogue, D'Chasidey Viznitz, 89 Stamford Hill, N16. ☎ 020-8800 9359. *Rab.* Rabbi A. Weiss. (D)

Beit Knesset Chida, Egerton Road, N16.

Beth Abraham Synagogue, 46 The Ridgeway, NW11. *Rab.* Rabbi C. Schmahl. ☎ 020-8455 2848.

Beth Chodosh Synagogue, 51 Queen Elizabeth's Walk, N16. *Rab.* Rabbi E. Friedman ☎ 020-8800 6754.

Beth Hamedrash Beis Nadvorna, 45 Darenth Road, N16 6ES. ☎ 020-8806 3903. *Rab.* Rabbi M. Leifer. (D)

Beth Hamedrash Cheishev Sofer d' Pressburg, 103 Clapton Common, E5. *Rab.* S. Ludmir. (D)

Beth Hamedrash Chelkas Yehoshua (Biala), 110 Castlewood Road, London N15. *Rab.* Rabbi L Rabbinowitz.

Beth Hamedrash D'Chasidey Belz, 99 Bethune Road, N16. *R.* Rabbi E. Friedman ☎ 020-8802 8233. (D)

Beth Hamedrash D'Chasidey Belz, 96 Clapton Common, E5. *R.* Dayan J.D. Babad. (D)

Beth Hamedrash D'Chasidey Gur, 2 Lampard Grove, N16. ☎ 020-8806 4333, 122 Cazenove Rd., N16, and 98 Bridge Lane, NW11. ☎ 020-8458 6243. (D)

Beth Hamedrash D'Chasidey Ryzin, 33 Paget Road, N16. ☎ 020-8800 7979. (D)

Beth Hamedrash D'Chasidey Sanz Klausenburg, 124 Stamford Hill, N16 6DJ. (D)

Beth Hamedrash D'Chassidey Square, 47 East Bank, N16. ☎ 020-8800 8448.

Beth Hamedrash Divrei Chaim, 71 Bridge La., NW11. ☎ 020-8458 1161. *Rab.* Rabbi Chaim A. Z. Halpern. (D)

Beth Hamedrash Hendon, 3 The Approach, NW4 2HU. *Rab.* Rabbi D. Halpern (D)

Beth Hamedrash Imrey Chaim D'Chasidey Vishnitz-Monsey, 121 Clapton Common, E5. ☎ 020-8800 3741. *Rab.* Rabbi D. Hager (D)

Beth Hamedrash Kehillas Yacov, 35 Highfield Av., NW11 ☎ 020-8455 3066. (D)

Beth Hamedrash Ohel Moshe, 202B Upper Clapton Road, E5. (D)

Beth Hamedrash Ohel Naphtoli (Bobov), 87 Egerton Road, N16. ☎ 020-8802 3979. *Rab.* Dayan B. Blum (D)

Beth Hamedrash of the Agudah Youth Movement, 69 Lordship Road, N.16. Also 95 Stamford Hill, N16. ☎ 020-8800 8873. *Rab.* Rabbi M. J. Kamionka. (D)

Beth Hamedrash Or Yisroel (Sadigur), 269 Golders Green Road, NW11. *Rab.* Y.M. Friedman. (D)

Beth Hamedrash Spinke, 36 Bergholt Cres., N16 5SE. ☎ 020-8809 6903. *Rab.* Rabbi M. Kahana.

Beth Hamedrash Torah Etz Chayim, 69 Lordship Road, N16. ☎ 020-8800 7726. *Rab.* Rabbi Z. Feldman. (D)

Beth Hamedrash Torah Chaim Liege, 145 Upper Clapton Road, E5. *Rab.* Rabbi M. Meisels. (D)

Beth Hamedrash Toras Chaim, 37 Craven Walk, N16 6BS. ☎ 020-8800 3868. *Rab.* Rabbi J. Meisels. (D)

Beth Hamedrash Vayoel Moshe, 67 Heathland Road, N16.

Beth Hamedrash Yetiv Lev, D'Satmar, 86 Cazenove Road, N16. ☎ 020-8800 2633. (D) Also 26 Clapton Common, E5, and 42 Craven Walk, N16 1DJ. ☎ 020-8806 7439. *Rab.* Rabbi C. Wosner. (D)

Beth Shmuel Synagogue, 171 Golders Green Road, NW11. ☎ 020-8458 7511. *Rab.* Rabbi E. Halpern. (D)

Beth Sholom Synagogue, 42 St. Kilda's Road, N16. ☎ 020-8809 6224. *Rab.* Rabbi S. Deutsch. (D)

Beth Talmud Centre, 78 Cazenove Road, N16.

Beth Yisochor Dov Beth Hamedrash, 2-4 Highfield Avenue, NW11. *Rab.* Rabbi G. Hager. (D)

Birkath Yehuda (Halaser) Beth Hamedrash, 47 Moundfield Road, N16 6DT. *Rab.* Rabbi M. Lebovits. ☎ 020-8806 4962. (D)

Bridge Lane Beth Hamedrash, 44 Bridge Lane, NW11 0EG. *Rab.* Rabbi S. Winegarten. (D)

Etz Chaim Yeshiva, 83/85 Bridge Lane, NW11. *Rab.* Z. Rabi. (D)

Finchley Road Synagogue, 4 Helenslea Avenue, NW11. ☎ 020-8455 4305 *Rab.* Rabbi S. Rubin. (D)

Heichal Hatorah, 27 St. Kildas Road, N16. ☎ 020-8809 4331. *R.* L. Rakow.

Hendon Adath Yisroel Synagogue, 11 Brent Street, NW4 2EU. ☎ 020-8202 9183. *Rab.* Rabbi P. Roberts; *Sec.* N. Hammond. (D)

Kehal Chasidim D'Munkatch Synagogue, 85 Cazenove Road, N16. *Rab.* Rabbi S. Gluck.

Kingsley Way Beth Hamedrash (Lubavitch), 3-5 Kingsley Way, London N2. ☎ 020-8458 2312. *Rab.* Rabbi Y. Hertz.

Knightland Road Synagogue of the Law of Truth Talmudical College, 50 Knightland Road, E5 9HS. Corr: 27 Warwick Grove, E5 9HX. ☎ 020-8806 2963. *Rab.* Rabbi M. Halpern.

Kol Yaakov, 47 Mowbray Rd., Edgware HA8 8JH. ☎ 020-8959 6131. *M.* Rabbi A. Friedman. (D)

Lubavitch of Edgware, 230 Hall Lane, HA6 9AZ. ☎ 020-8905 4141. *M.* Rabbi L.Y. Sudak.

Lubavitch Synagogue, 107-115 Stamford Hill, N16. ☎ 020-8800 0022. *Rab.* Rabbi N. Sudak. (D)

Machzikei Hadass Edgware Beth Hamedrash, 269 Hale Lane, Edgware HA8. *R.* Rabbi E. Schneelbag. ☎ 020-8958 1030. (D)

Mesifta Synagogue, 82-84 Cazenove Road, N16. (D)

North Hendon Adath Yisroel Synagogue, Holders Hill Road, NW4 1NA. *Rab.* Rabbi D. Kohn, Emer. Rabbi D. Cooper; *Sec.* A. H. Ehreich. ☎ 020-8203 0797; corr.: 31 Holders Hill Crescent, NW4 1NE. (D)

Ohel Israel (Skoler) Synagogue, 11 Brent Street, NW4. (D)

Shaare Zion, 10 Woodberry Down, N4.

Stanislowa Beth Hamedrash, 93 Lordship Park, N16. ☎ 020-8800 2040. *Rab.* Rabbi E. Aschkenasi. (D)

Yeshiva Horomoh Beth Hamedrash, 100 Fairholt Road, N16 5HH. ☎ 020-8809 3904; 020-8800 4522 (students). *Rab.* Rabbi E. Schlesinger. ☎ 020-8800 2194. (D)

Yeshuath Chaim Synagogue, 45 Heathland Road, N16. ☎ 020-8800 2332. *Rab.* Rabbi C. Pinter; *H. Sec.* I. Kohn. (D)

Yesodey Hatorah Synagogue, 2/4 Amhurst Pk., N16.

Zichron Shlomo Beth Hamedrash, 11 Elm Park Av., N15. ☎ 020-8809 7850. *R.* Rabbi S. Meisels.

The Assembly of Masorti Synagogues

1097 Finchley Road, NW11 0PU.

☎ 020-8201 8772, Fax 020-8201 8917. Email office@masorti.org.uk; Website www.masorti.org.uk.

(Est. 1985. Reg. Charity No. 801846). *Dir.* M. Gluckman; *Chairmen* G. Caplin, C. Harris; *Admin.* Mrs J. Garfinkel.

New London Synagogue, 33 Abbey Road, NW8 0AT. ☎ 020-7328 1026. Fax 020-7372 3142. Email nls@masorti.org.uk. (Est. 1964) *M.* Rabbi Chaim Weiner; *Chairman* Anne Cowen; *Exec. Dir.* Ronnie Cohen; *Sec.* S. Sanders.

New North London Synagogue, The Manor House, 80 East End Road, N3 2SY. ☎ 020-8346 8560. Fax 020-8346 9710. (Est. 1974.) An independent traditional com. following the philosophy of Rabbi Dr L. Jacobs. *M.* Rabbi J. Wittenberg;. *Co-Chairpersons* B. Berelovitz, Emily Cass; *T.* S. Coleman; *Sec.* Veronica Kennard; *Off.* Mrs Barbara Anders; *Community Co-ord.* Mrs Bette Rabie.

Edgware Masorti Synagogue. Synagogue Office/Post/Weekly entrance: Pearl Community Centre, Stream Lane, Edgware, Middx. HA8 7YA. (Reg. Charity No. 291010.) Shabbat entrance: Bakery Path (off Station Road), Edgware,

Middx. HA8 7YE. ☎ 020-8905 4096. Fax 020-8905 4333. Email admin@edgwaremasorti.org.uk. *M.* Rabbi Jeremy Collick; *Co-Chairpersons* H. Cronin, M. Sobell; *T.* S. Maisel; *Admin.* L. Lassman.

Hatch End Masorti, *Co-Chairpersons* M. Reindorp ☎ 020-8866 5484.

Kol Nefesh Masorti Synagogue, PO Box 204, Edgware, Middx HA8 7FQ. (Reg. Charity No. 1081444). Enq. ☎ 0776 980 7356. Email kolnefesh.masorti@virgin.net. Website www.kolnefeshmasorti.org.uk. *M.* Rabbi Joel Levy.

New Essex Masorti Congregation, Services: Roding Valley Hall, Station Way, Buckhurst Hill, Essex IG9 6LN. Enqs. ☎/Fax 020-8524 3564. Email nemasorti@hotmail.com; Website www.way.to/shul. *Chairman* Darren Silverne; *Admin.* Anne Luder.

New Whetstone Synagogue, Enquiries: 020-8368 3936. *Chairman* E. Slater.

St Albans Masorti Synagogue, P.O. Box 23, St Albans, Herts AL1 4PH. *M.* Rabbi Paul Glantz; *Co-Chair.* P. Hoffbrand, L. Oppedwyk; *T.* P. Hart; *Sec.* Mrs K. Phillips. ☎ 01727 860642.

Independent Congregations

Belsize Square Synagogue, 51 Belsize Square, London NW3 4HX. ☎ 020-7794 3949. Fax 020-7431 4559. Email office@synagogue.org.uk; Website www.synagogue. org.uk. (Est. 1939. Reg. Charity No. 233742.) An Independent Synagogue combining traditional forms of worship with progressive ideals. *M.* Rabbi Rodney J. Mariner; *Cantor* Rev. Lawrence Fine; *Sec.* Ms. J. Berman; *Chairman* Steven M. Bruck; *H. T.* David Rothenberg; *H. Sec.* Thomas Tausz.

Commercial Road Talmud Torah Synagogue (formerly 9-11 Christian Street, E1), 153 Stamford Hill, London N16 5LG. ☎ 020-8800 1618. (Est. 1898.) *Sec.* A. Becker. Burial Society. Cemeteries: Carterhatch Lane, Enfield. ☎ 020-8363 3384. Silver Street, Cheshunt, Herts. ☎ 01707 874220.

Edgware Adath Yisroel Synagogue, 261 Hale Lane, Edgware HA8 8NX. ☎ 020-8931 7917. Fax 020-8931 7916. Email sec@eayc.org. *Rab.* Rabbi Zvi Lieberman. (Affiliated to Adath Yisroel Burial Soc.) (D)

Golders Green Beth Hamedrash Congregation, The Riding, Golders Green Road, NW11 8HL. ☎ 020-8455 2974. (Est. 1934.) *Rab.* Rabbi H. I. Feldman; *R.* Rev. N. Gluck.

Ner Yisrael, The Crest (off Brent St.), Hendon, NW4. ☎ 020-8202 6687. Fax 020-8203 5158. *M.* Rabbi A.A. Kimche. ☎ 020-8455 7347. *Admin.* Mrs L. Brayam, Email secretary@neryisrael.co.uk.

Porat Yosef (Est. 1988.), Moroccan Hebrew Congregation. 9 Burroughs Gardens, Hendon, NW4 4AU. ☎ 020-8203 9989. Email neryisrael@londonweb.net. *President* Jacques Onona; *R.* Rabbi M. Bitton; *Sec.* B. Benarroch.

Saatchi Synagogue (Est. 1998. Reg. Charity No. 289066), 21 Andover Place, NW6 5ED. ☎ 020-7625 2266. Fax 020-7625 2277. Website www.coolshul.org. *Admin.* Ruth Aarons; *Rab.* Rabbi Pini Dunner.

Sandy's Row Synagogue (est. 1854), Sandy's Row, Middlesex Street, E1 7HW. *M. Sec.* E. Wilder. ☎ 020-7253 8311; 020-7377 5854. (D)

Sarah Klausner Synagogue, 10A Canfield Gardens NW6 ☎ 020-7722 6146.

Synagogue Française de Londres (La), 101 Dunsmure Road, N16 5HT. Le Grand Rabbin Henri Brand, 54 Bethune Road, N16 5BD. ☎ 020-8800 8612. *H. T.* Rabbi C. Pinter; *H. Sec.* I. Kraus.

Walford Road Synagogue, 99 Walford Road, Stoke Newington, N16 8EF. *M.* Rabbi H. Gluck; *Sec.* S. Raymond.

Waltham Forest Hebrew Congregation, 140 Boundary Road, E17 8LA. Email waltham.forestsyn@aol.com. (Est. 1902.) ☎ Off.: 020-8509 0775. Fax 020-8518 8200. *M.* Rabbi Michael Davis; *President* R. Jacobs; *Admin.* A. Wolpert. (D)

West End Great Synagogue, 32 Great Cumberland Place, W1H 7TN. ☎ 020-7724 8121. Fax 020-7723 4413 (Est. 1880.) *M.* Ari Cohen; *Sec.* S. B. Levy.

Chesed V'Emeth. Cemeteries: Rowan Road, Greyhound Lane, SW16. ☎ 020-8764 1566; Cheshunt Cemetery (Western), Bullscross Ride, Cheshunt, Herts. ☎ 01992 717820.

Affiliated Synagogues: retaining burial rights: *Commercial Road Great Syn., Teesdale Street Syn., *Great Garden Street Syn., *Cong. of Jacob, *Ezras Chaim Syn., *Nelson Street Sephardish Syn., Sandy's Row Syn., *Fieldgate St. Syn.

The synagogues marked * still have a section of members affiliated for burial rights under the Federation of Synagogues.

Western Marble Arch Synagogue, successor to the Western Synagogue (est. 1761) and the Marble Arch Synagogue, 32 Great Cumberland Place, W1H 7TN. ☎ 020-7723 9333. Fax 020-7224 8065. Email office@wma-synagogue.org. *M.* ; *President* P. Faiman; *Exec. Sec.* Stephen Garcia. Affiliated for burial rights with Western Charitable Foundation in the following Cemeteries: Edmonton, Montague Road, N18, Bullscross Ride, Cheshunt, Herts; *Supt.* R. Ezekiel, Bullscross Ride, Cheshunt, Herts. ☎ 01992 717820.

Affiliated Orgs.: Western Charitable Foundation. *Chairman* S. Jacque, J.P.; *Tr.* W. Ward.

Westminster Synagogue (Est. 1957), Rutland Gdns., Knightsbridge, SW7 1BX. ☎ 020-7584 3953. Fax 020-7581 8012. *M. Emer.* Rabbi A. H. Friedlander, OBE, PhD, Rabbi T. Salamon; *President* Mrs C. Landes; *Chairman* H.D. Leigh.

Yakar Synagogue, 2 Egerton Gardens, London NW4 4BA. *M.* Rabbi Jeremy Rosen; *Chair* Adele Lustig. ☎ 020-8202 5551.

Sephardi

Spanish and Portuguese Jews' Congregation (Reg. Charity No. 212517)
2 Ashworth Rd, Maida Vale, W9 1JY. ☎ 020-7289 2573. Fax 020-7289 2709. *Admin.* H. Miller.

SYNAGOGUES

Bevis Marks (1701), EC3A 5DQ. ☎ 020-7626 1274. Fax 020-7283 8825. Rabbi Dr A. Levy B.A. *M.* Rev. H. Benarroch, B.A.

Lauderdale Road Syn. (1896), Maida Vale, W9 1JY.☎ 020-7289 2573. *Rabbi & M.* Rabbi Dr A. Levy, B.A., Rabbi I. Elia.

Wembley Synagogue, 46 Forty Ave., Wembley, Middx HA9 8LQ. ☎ 020-8904 9912. *Rabbi & M.* Dayan Dr P. Toledano, B.A.

Sir Moses Montefiore Synagogue, Honeysuckle Road, Ramsgate, Kent.

OTHER INSTITUTIONS

Burial Society, 2 Ashworth Road, W9 1JY. ☎ 020-7289 2573.

Welfare Board, 2 Ashworth Road, W9 1JY. ☎ 020-7289 2573. (Est. 1837.)

Sephardi Kashrut Authority, 2 Ashworth Road, W9 1JY. ☎ 020-7289 2573. *Chairman* E. Cohen; *Dir.* D. Steinhof.

Communal Centre, Montefiore Hall, 2 Ashworth Road, W9 1JY. ☎ 020-7289 2573.

Beth Hamedrash Heshaim (Instituted 1664), 2 Ashworth Road, W9 1JY. ☎ 020-7289 2573. *T.* C. Sacerdoti.

Montefiore Endowment at Ramsgate (incorporating the **Judith Lady Montefiore College Trust**), 2 Ashworth Road, W9 1JY. (☎ 020-7289 2573.) Est. by Sir Moses Montefiore 1866. New scheme est. by the Charity Commission in 1989 'for the maintenance of the Synagogue, the Mausoleum and the Jewish Cemetery in Ramsgate', also 'for the promotion of the advanced study of the Holy Law as revealed on Sinai and expounded by the revered sages of the Mishna and Talmud' by making grants to charitable institutions for the training of Orthodox Jewish Teachers, Ministers and Rabbis and by awarding scholarships to such trainees.

The Mausoleum with the remains of Sir Moses and Lady Montefiore is situated next to the Synagogue in Ramsgate (see above). Sir Moses's seats in Bevis Marks and Ramsgate Syns. are still preserved.

Edinburgh House (Beth Holim), 36/44 Forty Avenue, Wembley. (Est. 1747.) Home for the Aged. *Hd. of Home* C. Gilmour. ☎ 020-8908 4151.

CEMETERIES

253 Mile End Rd., E1. (Disused.) Opened in 1657, the oldest Jewish burial ground in the United Kingdom. 329 Mile End Road, E1. (Opened 1725. Disused.) Hoop Lane, Golders Green, NW11. *Keeper* B. H. Calo. ☎ 020-8455 2569. Edgwarebury Lane, Edgware. ☎ 020-8958 3388. *Keeper* B. H. Calo. Dytchleys, Coxtie Green, Brentwood. (Disused.)

Independent Sephardi Synagogues

Aden Jews' Congregation, 117 Clapton Common, E5. *H. Sec.* M. A. Solomon. ☎ 020-8806 1320.

David Ishag Synagogue, Neveh Shalom Community, 352-4 Preston Road, Harrow, Middx., HA3 0QJ. *H. Secs.* F. Lichaa, M. Sullam. ☎ 020-8904 3009.

Eastern Jewry Community (Est. 1955.) Newbury Park Station, Newbury Park. *M.* Rabbi C. Tangy; *H. Sec.* D. Elias. ☎ 020-8809 4387.

Ilford Congregation (Ohel David), Newbury Park Station, Ilford. *H. Sec.* ☎ 020-8809 4387. Fax 020-8809 4441; 020-8458 1468.

Jacob Benjamin Elias Synagogue (Reg. Charity No. 291531), 140 Stamford Hill, N16 6QT. *M.* Rabbi C. Tangy; *H. Sec.* D. Elias. ☎ 020-8809 4387, 020-8458 8693. Fax 020-8809 4441; 020-8458 1468.

Od Yosef Hai Synagogue, 48 Finchley Lane, NW4 1DJ. *M.* Rabbi A. David ☎ 020-8202 8374; 020-8203 5701.

Ohel David Eastern Synagogue, Lincoln Institute, Broadwalk Lane, Golders Green Road, NW11. (Reg. Charity No. 243901) *M.* Rabbi Abraham Gubbay; ☎ 020-8455 8125. *H. Sec.* C. Silas. ☎ 020-8455 4830.

Persian Hebrew Congregation, 5a East Bank, Stamford Hill, N16. ☎ 020-8800 9261.

Shivtei Israel Hekhal Leah (UHC), 62 Brent Street, NW4 2ES. ☎ 020-8922 3721. *M.* Rabbi M. Cohen. (D)

Spanish & Portuguese Synagogue, Holland Park (Est. 1928 under Deed of Association with Spanish and Portuguese Jews' Congregation. Reg. Charity No. 248945), 8 St James's Gdns., W11 4RB. ☎ 020-7603 7961/3232. Fax 020-7603 9471. *Sec.* Mrs R. Lynton.

Reform

(Constituents of the Reform Synagogues of Great Britain), The Sternberg Centre for Judaism, 80 East End Road, N3 2SY. *Chief Executive* Rabbi Tony Bayfield. ☎ 020-8349 5640. Fax 020-8349 5699. Email admin@reformjudaism.org.uk.

West London Synagogue of British Jews (Reg. Charity No. 212143), 34 Upper Berkeley Street, W1. Office, 33 Seymour Place, W1H 5AU. ☎ 020-7723 4404. Fax 020-7224 8258.

The congregation was organised April 15, 1840, to establish a synagogue 'where a revised service may be performed at hours more suited to our habits and in a manner more calculated to inspire feelings of devotion, where religious instruction may be afforded by competent persons, and where, to effect these purposes, Jews generally may form a united congregation under the denomination of British Jews.'

Senior M. Rabbi Mark Winer, PhD, DD; *M.* Rabbi Helen Freeman, Rabbi M. Farbman; *President* Prof G. Zellick; *Chairman* S. Ross; *Exec. Dir.* M. Ross.

Funerals: ☎ 020-7723 4404. Fax 020-7224 8258.

Cemeteries: Golders Green, Hoop Lane, NW11; Edgwarebury, Edgwarebury Lane, Middx. *Supt.* B. H. Calo. ☎ 020-8958 3388.

Beit Klal Yisrael (North Kensington Reform Syn.) (Reg. Charity No.1034282), P.O. Box 1828, W10 5RT. Services in Notting Hill Gate. *M.* Rabbi Sheila Shulman. *Chairman* S. Sutcliffe. ☎ 020-8969 5080. Email beit-klal-yisrael@bigfoot. com.

Bromley Reform Synagogue (Est. 1964. Reg. Charity No. 1059190). 28 Highland Road, Bromley, Kent BR1 4AD. ☎/Fax 020-8460 5460. *M.* Rabbi Sylvia Rothschild; *H. Sec.* Ms B. Kurtz. Email bromleyshul@fsmail.net.

Edgware and District Reform Synagogue, (Reg. Charity No. 1038116). 118 Stonegrove, Edgware, HA8 8AB. (Est. 1934.) ☎ 020-8958 9782. Fax 020-8905 4710. Email admin@edrs.org.uk; Website www.edrs.org.uk. *M.* Rabbi A.D. Smith, MA; *Assoc. M.* Rabbi N. S. Kraft, MA; *Admin.* Mrs K. B. Senitt.

Finchley Reform Synagogue, Fallow Court Avenue, Finchley, N12 0BE. ☎ 020-8446 3244. Fax 020-8446 5980. *Ms.* Rabbi Emer. J. Newman, Rabbi C. Eimer, Rabbi S. Shulman, Rabbi L. Wax; *Admin.* R. Gerber. Email admin@frs.demon. co.uk.

Harlow Jewish Community, Harberts Road, Hare Street, Harlow, Essex CM19 4DT. ☎ 01279-432503; 01992-447814. *Ms.* Rabbi emer. J. Newman, Rabbi M. Pertz; *Sec.* Mrs H. Reeves. Email hjc@ianj.claranet.com

Hendon Reform Synagogue, Danescroft Avenue, NW4 2NA (Est. 1949.) ☎ 020-8203 4168. Fax 020-8203 9385. *M.* Rabbi S. Katz; *Sec.* Mrs R. Bloom. Email office@hendonreform.org.uk. Cemetery: New Southgate Cemetery, Brunswick Park Road, N11. ☎ 020-8203 4168.

Kol Chai-Hatch End Jewish Community (Reg. Charity No. 299063), 434 Uxbridge Road, Hatch End, Middx HA5 4RG. ☎ 020-8866 5390. Email admin@ kolchai.sagehost.co.uk. *M.* Rabbi M. Hilton; *Sec.* Mrs V. Collins.

Middlesex New Synagogue, 39 Bessborough Road, Harrow, HA1 3BS. ☎ 020-8864 0133. Fax 020-8864 5323. (Est. 1959.) *M.* Rabbi S.J. Franses; *Sec.* Mrs A. Simon. Email admin@mns.org.uk.

North West Surrey Synagogue (Est. 1956. Reg Charity no. 256232), Horvath Close, Rosslyn Pk., Oatlands Dr, Weybridge, Surrey KT13 9QZ. ☎/Fax 01932 855400 Email admin@nwss.freeserve.co.uk; Website www.nwss.org.uk. *M.* Rabbi Jacqueline Tabick; *H. Sec.* D.Hallé.

North Western Reform Synagogue, Alyth Gdns., Finchley Road, NW11 7EN. ☎ 020-8455 6763/4. Fax 020-8458 2469. Email mail@alyth.org. (Est. 1933; Reg. Charity No. 247081.) *M.* Rabbi C. Emanuel; *Comm. Dir.* Lynette Chazen-Hart. (D)

Radlett & Bushey Reform Synagogue, 118 Watling Street, Radlett, Herts WD7 7AA. ☎ 01923 85 6110. Fax 01923-858444. Email shofar@blaston.net. *M.* Rabbi Alexandra Wright. *Admin.* Mrs S. Denby, BA.

Shir Hayim (Hampstead Reform Jewish Community), 37a, Broadhurst Gdns., NW6 3BN. Email mail@shirhayim.org.uk. *M.* Rabbi L. Tabick; *Contact* M. Teper. ☎ 020-7794 8488. Email wober@clara.co.uk.

South West Essex and Settlement Reform Synagogue (Est. 1956. Reg. Charity No. 236663), Oaks Lane, Newbury Park, Essex IG2 7PL. ☎ 020-8599 0936. Fax 020-8597 9164. Email admin@swesrs.fsnet.co.uk. *M.* Rabbi M. Michaels, Rabbi L. Rigal; *Office* Mrs C. Gardiner.

Southgate and District Reform Synagogue (Reg. Charity No. 145765), 120 Oakleigh Road North, Whetstone N20 9EZ. ☎ 020-8445 3400. Fax 020-8445 3737. *M.* Rabbi C. Eimer; *Admin.* Mrs R. Minsky. Email info@our-shul.com.

Sukkat Shalom (Reg. Charity No. 283615). Hermon Hill, London E11. ☎ 020-8530 3345. *M.* Rabbi David Hulbert; *Admin.* Mrs M. Joseph. Email enquiries@sukkatshalom.co.uk.

Wimbledon and District Synagogue, 1 Queensmere Rd., Wimbledon Parkside, SW19 5QD. ☎ 020-8946 4836 Fax 020-8944 7790. Email office@wimshul.org. Website www.wimshul.org. (Est. 1949. Reg. Charity No. 1040712) *M.* Rabbi Sylvia Rothschild, Rabbi Sybil Sheridan; *Admin.* Ms A. Wilson.

Jewish Joint Burial Society (serving Reform & Masorti communities), North Western Reform Synagogue, Alyth Gdns, off Finchley Road NW11 7EN. (Est. 1968; Reg. Charity no. 257345) *Sexton* G.P.D Conway ☎ 020-8455 8579/020-8209 0018. Fax 020-8731 9980. Email funerals@jjbs.freeserve.co.uk.

Liberal and Progressive

(Constituents of the Union of Liberal and Progressive Synagogues), The Montagu Centre, 21 Maple St., London W1T 4BE. *Senior V. President* Rabbi Dr Sidney Brichto, MA, DD; *Dir.* ; *Admin. Dir.* Michael A. Burman. ☎ 020-7580 1663. Fax 020-7436 4184. Email montagu@ulps.org.

Barkingside Progressive Synagogue (Reg. Charity No. 283547), 129 Perrymans Farm Road, Barkingside, Ilford, Essex IG2 7LX. *Sec.* P. Ordever. ☎ 020-8554 9682. Email bps.synagogue@virgin.net; Website www.freespace.virgin.net/bps.synagogue. *M.* Rabbi D. Hulbert.

Bedfordshire Progressive Synagogue Rodef Shalom, c/o The ULPS, The Montagu Centre, 21 Maple St., W1T 4BE. ☎ 01582 873414.

Ealing Liberal Synagogue, Lynton Av., Drayton Green, Ealing, W13 0EB. ☎/Fax: 020-8997 0528. (Est. 1943. Reg. Charity No. 1037099) *M.* Rabbi Melinda Michelson-Carr, MA; *Admin.* A. Aarons.

Finchley Progressive Synagogue (Reg. Charity no. 1071040), 54 Hutton Gro., N12 8DR (Est. 1953.) ☎ 020-8446 4063. Fax 020-8446 9599. Email roz@thefps.free-online.co.uk. Website www.thesynagogue.freeserve.co.uk. *M.* Rabbi Mark Goldsmith; *Admin.* Mrs R. Lester.

Harrow & Wembley Progressive Synagogue, 326 Preston Road, Harrow, HA3 0QH. (Reg. Charity No. 251172) ☎ 020-8904 8581. Fax 020-8904 6540. Email hwps@ulps.org; Website www.hwps.org (Est. 1947.) *M.* Rabbi Frank Dabba Smith; *Admin.* Mrs S. Rose.

Hertsmere Progressive Synagogue, High Street, Elstree, Herts. WD6 3EY. ☎ 020-8953 8889. *M.* Leo Baeck College Rabbi; *H. Sec.* M. Beral ☎ 01923 855367. Email honsec@hpselstree.org.uk.

Kingston Liberal Synagogue, Rushett Road, Long Ditton, Surrey, KT7 0UX., Reg. Charity No. 270792. ☎ 020-8398 7400. Fax 020-8873 2405. Email kls@kingstonls.freeserve.co.uk. *M.* Rabbi Danny Rich. ☎/Fax 020-8398 4252; *Chair* L. Siteman; *Admin.*

The Liberal Jewish Synagogue (Reg. Charity No. 235668), 28 St. John's Wood Road, London, NW8 7HA. ☎ 020-7286 5181. Fax 020-7266 3591. Email ljs@lsjs.org. Est. 1910 by the Jewish Religious Union, the LJS, as it is known, was the first Liberal synagogue in the UK. Syn. rebuilt 1991. *Chairman* Trevor Moross. *Ms.* Rabbi Emeritus Dr J. D. Rayner, CBE; *Senior Rabbi* Rabbi D. J. Goldberg; *Asst. M.* Rabbi M. L. Solomon, Rabbi Kathleen de Magtige-Middleton.

North London Progressive Jewish Community (Est. 1921), PO Box 42702, N19 5WR. ☎ 020-8800 8931. Email nlpjc@yahoo.co.uk.

Northwood and Pinner Liberal Synagogue, Oaklands Gate, Green La., Northwood HA6 3AA. (Est. 1964. Reg. Charity No. 243618) *M.* Rabbi Dr A. Goldstein Rabbi Rachel Benjamin; *H. Sec.* Mrs T. Price. ☎ 01923 822592. Fax 01923-824454. Email admin@npls.org.uk.

South London Liberal Synagogue, (Reg. Charity No. 2367711), P.O.Box 14475, Prentis Rd., Streatham, SW16 1QB. (Est. 1929.) ☎ 020-8769 4787. Fax 020-8664 6439. Email slls@ulps.org. *M.* Rabbi James Baaden; *Sec./Admin.* Mrs R.

Edwards; *President* J. Rich.

Southgate Progressive Synagogue, 75 Chase Road, N14 4QY. (Reg. Charity No. 239096). ☎/Fax 020-8886 0977. Email sps@ulps.org. Website www.sps.uk.com. (Est. 1943.) *M.* Rabbi S. Howard; *Sec.* Mrs B. Martin.

West Central Liberal Synagogue, The Montagu Centre, 21, Maple St., W1T 4BE. ☎ 020-7636 7627. Fax 020-7436 4184. Email wcls@ulps.org. Website www.wcls.org.uk. (Cong. est. 1928; present syn. opened 1954.) *M.* Rabbi Janet Burden; *Cantor* Rev. A. Harman ALCM; *Chairman*: Dr L. Hepner; *H. Sec.* H. Berman.

Woodford Progressive Synagogue, Marlborough Road, South Woodford, E18 1AR. (Est. 1960. Reg. Charity No. 232980). *M.* Rabbi Rebecca Qassim Birk; *Chair* Mrs Joseph; *H.T.* Mrs Nathanson; *Admin.* Mrs Goodman. ☎ 020-8989 7619. Email wps@ulps.org; Website www.synagogue.demon.co.uk.

CEMETERIES

Funeral-Dir. Martin Broad and Son. ☎ 020-8455 2797. Fax 020-8343 9463.

Edgwarebury Lane, Edgware, Middx. ☎ 020-8958 3388. *Supt.* Mr B. Calo.

Liberal Jewish Cemetery, Pound Lane, Willesden, NW10. *Supt.* A. O'Brian. ☎ 020-8459 1635.

Western Cemetery, Bulls Cross Ride, Cheshunt, Herts. EN7 5HT. ☎ 01992 717820. *Supt.* R. Ezekiel.

Religious Organisations

Association of United Synagogue Women. (Est. 1968.) The Association promotes the interests and involvement of women as an integral part of the United Synagogue. It aims to promote and facilitate Jewish cultural and educational schemes that strengthen Orthodox traditional Jewish values. It represents women in Synagogue and communal affairs and also acts in an advisory capacity to Ladies Guilds. *President* Mrs E. Sacks; *Admin. Off.* Mrs S. Mann, c/o United Synagogue, Adler House, 735 High Rd., N12 0US. ☎ 020-8343 8989. Fax 020-8343 6262. *Chair* Mrs R. Ross; *Jt. H. Secs.* Mrs S. Mann, Mrs A. Churnin.

London Board for Shechita (Reg. Charity No. 233467), 1st Floor, Elscot House, Arcadia Ave, N3 2JU. ☎ 020-8349 9160. Fax 020-8346 2209. Email shechita@tiscali.co.uk. (Est. 1804.) To administer the affairs of Shechita in London. *President* A. Magnus; *V. Presidents* A. J. Kennard, S.D. Winegarten; *H. T.* A. Stuart; *Exec. Dir.* M. T. Kester. ☎ 020-8349 9160. Fax 020-8346 2209.

Sabbath Observance Employment Bureau (Est. 1909. Reg. Charity No. 209451), Unit 2, 107 Gloucester Place, W1U 6BY. ☎ 020-7224 3433. To obtain employment for those desirous of observing the Sabbath and Holy-days. *Trs* I.M. Katz, S.D. Winegarten; *Man.* Mrs E. Statham; *Chairman.* D. Winter, FCA.

Ritual Baths (Mikvaot)

Central Mikvaot Board, 140 Stamford Hill, N16 6QT. ☎ 020-8802 6226/7.

Edgware & District Communal Mikvah, Edgware United Synagogue, Edgware Way, Edgware, Middlesex. (Reg. Charity No. 281586). ☎ 020-8958 3233. Fax 020-8958 4004. Email mikveh@estrin.co.uk. Gen. enquiries: Mrs Mandy Estrin ☎ 020-8958 4488, 020-8621 4488, 0780 1332508.

Ilford Mikvah, 463 Cranbrook Road, Ilford. ☎ 020-8554 8532.

Kingsbury Mikvah, see below. United Synagogue Mikvah.

Lordship Park Mikvah, 55 Lordship Park, N16 (entrance in Queen Elizabeth's Walk). ☎ 020-8800 9621 (day) 020-8800 5801 (evening).

New Central London Mikveh, 21 Andover Place, NW6 5ED. Appointments ☎ 020-7372 7237, 07870 696 570.

North London Mikvah, adjoining 40 Queen Elizabeth's Walk, N16 (entrance, Grazebrook Road). ☎ 020-8802 2554. Fax 020-8800 8764. *H. Sec.* M. Mannes.
Northwest London Communal Mikvah, 10a Shirehall Lane, Hendon, NW4. ☎ 020-8202 1427 (day), 020-8202 8517/5706 (evening).
Mikveh of the Reform Synagogues of Great Britain, Sternberg Centre, 80 East End Rd., N3 2SY. Appointments ☎ 020-8349 4731.
Satmar Mikvah, 62 Filey Avenue, N16. ☎ 020-8806 3961.
South London Mikvah, 42 St. George's Rd., Wimbledon SW19 4ED. (Reg. Charity No. 1009208) ☎ 020-8944 7149. Fax 020-8944 7563. *Hon. Sec.* L. Cohen. *Contact:* Mrs S. Dubov.
Stamford Hill Mikvah, 26 Lampard Grove, N16 (entrance in Margaret Road). ☎ 020-8806 3880.
United Synagogue Mikvah, Kingsbury United Synagogue, Kingsbury Green, NW9 8XR. ☎ 020-8204 6390. (See also Friends Group, p.98.)

Memorials

Holocaust Memorial and Garden, Hyde Park, near Hyde Park Corner. Opened in July 1983, on a site given to the Board of Deputies by the British Government.
Holocaust Memorial, Waltham Abbey Cemetery, Skillet Hill, Honey La., Waltham Abbey, Essex. Consecrated 1985 under U.S. auspices.
Holocaust Memorial, Rainham Cemetery, Upminster Road North, Rainham, Essex.
Holocaust Memorial, Sternberg Centre, 80 East End Road, Finchley N3.
Kindertransport, plaque at the House of Commons.
Memorial in Willesden Jewish Cemetery, Beaconsfield Road, NW10, to Jewish Servicemen and Women in the British Armed Forces who died in the two World Wars and have no known graves. Annual service organised by Ajex.
Prisoners' Memorial, Gladstone Park, Dollis Hill Lane, NW2, to those who died in prisoner-of-war camps and concentration camps during the Second World War. Annual service jointly org. by Ajex and the Royal Brit. Legion.
RAF Church, crypt of St Clements Danes, Strand. Memorial plaque with 12 tribes emblems to British and Israeli RAF personnel in the Second World War.
Raoul Wallenberg statue in Great Cumberland Place.
Royal Fusiliers, City of London Regiment Memorial, High Holborn, by City boundary. The names of the 38th, 39th and 40th Battalions are inscribed on the monument, together with all other battalions which served in the First World War. Ajex is represented at the annual service.

Cemeteries

US = United Synagogue. F = Federation of Synagogues. UO = Union of Orthodox Hebrew Congregations. SP = Spanish and Portuguese Synagogue. W = Western Marble Arch Synagogue. WG = West End Great Synagogue. R = Reform. L = Liberal.
Alderney Road Cemetery (disused), E1. ☎ 020-8790 1445. (US).
Brady Street Cemetery, E1. (US).
Bullscross Ride Cemetery, Cheshunt, Herts. ☎ 01992 717820 (W, L and WG)
Bushey Cemetery, Little Bushey Lane, Bushey, Herts. ☎ 020-8950 6299. (US).
East Ham Cemetery, Marlow Road, High St. South, E6. (US). ☎ 020-8472 0554.
Edgwarebury Cemetery, Edgwarebury Lane, Edgware, Middx. ☎ 020-8958 3388. (SP, R and L.).
Edmonton Federation Cemetery, Montagu Road, Angel Road, Lower Edmonton, N18. ☎ 020-8807 2268. (F).
Enfield Cemetery, Carterhatch Lane, Enfield, Middx. ☎ 020-8363 3384. (UO).

Hackney Cemetery (disused), Lauriston Road, E9. ☎ 020-8985 1527. (US).
Hoop Lane Cemetery, Golders Green, NW11. ☎ 020-8455 2569. (SP and R).
Kingsbury Road Cemetery, Balls Pond Road, N1. (R).
Liberal Jewish Cemetery, Pound Lane and Harlesden Road, NW10. (L).
Mile End Road (disused), E1. (SP).
Plashet Cemetery, High St. North E12. ☎ 020-8472 0554. (US). [Closed except prior to New Year].
Queen's Elm Parade Cemetery (disused), Fulham Road, SW3. (W).
Rainham Cemetery, Upminster Road North, Rainham, Essex. ☎ 017085-52825. (F).
Rowan Road Cemetery, Greyhound Lane, SW16. ☎ 020-8764 1566. (WG).
Silver Street Cemetery, Cheshunt, Herts. ☎ 020-8802 6262. (UO).
Waltham Abbey Cemetery, Skillet Hill (Honey Lane), Waltham Abbey, Essex. ☎ 01992 714492. (US).
West Ham Cemetery, Buckingham Road, Forest Lane, E15. ☎ 020-8472 0554. (US).
Western Synagogue Cemetery, Montagu Road, N18. ☎ 020-8971 7820. (W).
Willesden Cemetery, Beaconsfield Road, NW10. ☎ 020-8459 0394. (US).

EDUCATIONAL ORGANISATIONS

Withdrawal on Friday Afternoons:
When the Sabbath begins at 5 p.m. or earlier, parents of Jewish children attending either State or State-aided schools can request that their children be withdrawn at such time as to reach their homes before the commencement of the Sabbath. Such requests should be submitted to the Head Teacher in writing. Hebrew and Religion Classes are attached to nearly all the syns. listed.

GENERAL

Agency for Jewish Education. (See p.36).

Binoh: The Jewish Special Educational Needs Service. (Reg. Charity No. 291978). Email binoh@norwood.org. Binoh is part of Norwood and is a multi-disciplinary Special Education Service for Jewish children. A range of services is provided for children with special educational needs from birth to the end of their school years. Our educational psychologists, therapists, support teachers and other staff aim to help children with special needs to remain within the ordinary school system and to access the best opportunities for developing their potential. *Hd. of Educ. Services* Kathryn Finlay.

Training courses and workshops for parents and teachers, Parent Advisory Service and multi-disciplinary services including teaching and therapeutic services. **Kennedy Leigh Centre**, Edgworth Close, Hendon NW4 4HJ. ☎ 020-8457 4745, Fax 020-8203 8233; **Somers Hackney Family and Community Centre**, 85a, Lordship Road, N16 0QY. ☎ 020-8802 2777.

Interlink Foundation, Lower Ground Offices, 124 Stamford Hill, N16 6QT. ☎ 020-8802 2496. Fax 020-8800 5153. Email director@interlink-foundation.org.uk. (Est. 1993. Reg. Charity No. 1079311) Umbrella development agency for the Orthodox Jewish voluntary sector. Services include: capacity-building (including training) with groups, information/quarterly newsletter plus regular mailings, policy and regeneration work. *Dir.* Mrs E. Sterngold.

Jewish Resource Centre (JRC at CRREDE), Centre for Research in Religious Education and Development, Roehampton University of Surrey, Digby Stuart College, Roehampton Lane, SW15 5PH. ☎/Fax 020-8392 3349. Email JRC@roehampton.co.uk. JRC at CRREDE was set up in 1996 – to serve as a resource for all sections of the Jewish community in South London, as well as for the non-Jewish teaching community. The Centre houses a large stock of books and religious articles for purchase, loan and consultation, and provides a base for educational and cultural activities. Staff are available to visit synagogues, religion schools/chadarim and teachers' centres in the area to run book sales and other events. Wednesday afternoons during term-time from 2.00 to 5.00 p.m., and at other times by appointment. *Dir.* Anne Clark, BA (Hons), MA, Dip. Couns., UJIA Ashdown Fellow.

Schools' J-Link, Unit 23, Dollis Hill Estate, 105 Brook Rd., NW2 7BZ. ☎ 020-8208 2333. Fax 020-8208 0506. Email info@jlink.org.uk. (Est. 1993; Reg. Charity No. 1062551). Schools' J–Link aims to raise the sense of identity and commitment of Jewish pupils in non-Jewish secondary schools. It runs school assemblies and classes, less formal Jewish society meetings and lunch and learn sessions, and totally informal parties at Succot, Purim and other occasions, offering a broad Jewish input by co-opting rabbis, youth workers, representatives of Jewish organisations and visiting speakers from abroad. It also runs training programmes for non-Jewish teachers who are teaching Judaism. Schools' J-Link operates in 60 schools in the London area and several provincial towns, and communicates with upwards of 6,000 Jewish youngsters each year. *Dir.* Rabbi Arye Forta, BA; *Dir. of Dev.* Rabbi Dr S. Gaffin; *Admin.* Mrs R. Stemmer.

SCHOOLS

Akiva School, Levy House, The Sternberg Centre, 80 East End Road, N3 2SY. ☎ 020-8349 4980. Fax 020-8349 4959. Email akiva@akiva.demon.co.uk (Est. 1981.) Primary educ. for pupils, aged 4-11 years, under Reform & Liberal Synagogue auspices. *Head Teacher* Mrs S. de Botton, LGSM Cert. Ed.; *Admin.* Mrs V. Chapman.

Avigdor Hirsch Torah Temimah Primary School, Parkside, Dollis Hill, NW2 6RJ. ☎ 020-8450 4377. Fax 020-8830 6202. Email admin@torahtemimah.brent.sch.uk. Voluntary-aided (London Borough of Brent) Orthodox Jewish primary school and nursery for boys aged 3-11. (Est. 1989. Reg. Charity No. 1000146). *Princ.* Rabbi E. Klyne, MA (Ed); *Hd* A. Wolfson, BEd (Hons), MA, NPQH; *Chairman of Govs.* Allan Becker.

Avigdor Primary School, 63-67 Lordship Road, N.16. Voluntary-aided school for boys and girls, 3-11. *H.M.* Mrs S. Isaacs; *Sec.* Mrs Y. Ricketts. ☎ 020-8800 8339.

Beth Jacob Seminary of London, 196–198 Lordship Road, N16 5ES. Teacher Training College and finishing school for Hebrew Studies and vocational qualifications. *Fnd. Princ.* Rabbi J. H. Dunner; *Princ.* Rabbi B. Dunner. ☎ 020-8800 4719. Fax 020-8800 6067. (Reg. Charity No. 312913).

Clore Shalom School, Hugo Gryn Way, Shenley, Herts WD7 9BL. ☎ 01923 855631; Fax 01923 853722; Email admin.cloreshalom@thegrid.org.uk. (Est. 1999) Community, state-aided primary school (3-11), under Liberal, Masorti and Reform auspices. *H.T.* Irene Kay; *Admin.* Angela Peters.

Clore Tikva School Redbridge, 115 Fullwell Ave., Ilford, Essex IG6 2JN. ☎ 020-8551 1097; Fax 020-8551 2070. Email cloretikva@btopenworld.com. (Est. 1999). Community, state-aided primary school (4-11), under Reform, Masorti and Liberal auspices. *Hd.* Mrs L. Rosenberg; *Admin.* Mrs Valerie Garnelas.

Gan Aviv Kindergarten, Bushey & District Synagogue, 177–189, Sparrows Herne, Bushey, Herts., WD23 1AJ. ☎ 020-8386 1616. Fax 020-8421 8267. (For children 2½-5). *H. Princ.* Rabbi Z. M. Salasnik BA; *H. M.* Mrs E. Levine, Cert. Ed.

Hasmonean High School:

Boys, 11/18, Holders Hill Road, NW4 1 NA. ☎ 020-8203 1411. Fax 020-8202 4526.

Girls, 2/4, Page Street, NW7 2EU. ☎ 020-8203 4294. Fax 020-8202 4527.

Recognised by Dept. of Education. Voluntary Aided, London Borough of Barnet. *H. T.* Rabbi D. Radomsky, MA, NPQH; *Dep. Hd.* Rabbi C. Baddiel, BA, Mrs B. Perin, BA, NPQH, Rabbi D. Meyer, BA, MBA; *Admin.* J. Curzon, BA, FCMA.

Hasmonean Kindergarten, 8-10 Shirehall Lane, NW4 2PD. ☎ 020-8201 6252. Fax

020-8202 1605 (children 2-4). *Hd.* Mrs M. Knepler.

Hasmonean Primary School, 8-10 Shirehall Lane, NW4 2PD. ☎ 020-8202 7704. Fax 020-8202 1605. (Boys and Girls 4-11.) *Hd.* Mrs J. Rodin, M.Sc. (Ed.Mang.), Cert Ed. Premier Degré (Paris). Rabbi M. Beaton, Rav of the School. Email admin@hasmonean-pri.barnet.sch.uk.

Hertsmere Jewish Primary School, Watling Street, Radlett, Herts WD7 7LQ. ☎ 01923 855857. Fax 01923 853399. Email admin.hertsmerejewish-pri@thegrid.org.uk. *H.T.* Mrs Michèle Bazak; *Admin.* Mrs R. Temerlies. Voluntary-aided primary school for ages 3-11.

Ilford Jewish Primary School, Carlton Dr, Ilford, Essex IG6 1LZ. ☎ 020-8551 4294. Fax 020-8551 4295. Website www.ilfordjewish.redbridge.sch.uk. *H. T.* Mrs L. Hagon.

Immanuel College (The Charles Kalms, Henry Ronson Immanuel College), 87/91 Elstree Road, Bushey, Herts., WD23 4BE. ☎ 020-8950 0604. Fax: 020-8950 8687. Email immanuel@herts.sch.uk; Website www.immanuel.college.co.uk. (Reg Charity No. 803179) Independent mixed selective school. *H.* Philip Skelker, MA, PGCE; *Dep. H.* Richard Felsenstein BA(Hons), Cert Ed.

Independent Jewish Day School, 46 Green Lane, NW4 2AH. ☎ 020-8203 2299. Email info@independentjewishday.barnet.sch.uk. Orthodox Primary Sch. & Kindergarten (est. 1979). *Chairman* J. Kornbluth; *Princ.* A.A. Kimche, BA; *H. T.* Mrs H. Cohen, BA (Hons), PGCE.

Jewish Secondary Schools Movement, Holders Hill Road, NW4. ☎ 020-8203 1411. Fax 020-8202 4526. (Est. 1929.) *Principal.*

J.F.S. (moved to Kenton in September 2002), The Mall, Kenton HA3 9UA. ☎ 020-8206 3100. (Est. 1958.) *H. T.* Miss R. Robins, BA, TTHD; *Clerk to Govs.* Dr A. Fox, Goldbloom (Hebrew Studies) Dept.

Kerem House, 18 Kingsley Way, N2 0ER. ☎ 020-8455 7524. (Boys and Girls 2½-5.) *H. T.* Mrs D. Rose, MA, Cert. Ed.

Kerem School, Norrice Lea, N2 0RE. ☎ 020-8455 0909. (Boys and Girls 4-11.) *H. Princ.* Rabbi R. Livingstone; *H. T.* Mrs R. Goulden, M. Ed.

King Solomon High School, Forest Road, Barkingside, Ilford Essex IG6 3HB. ☎ 020-8501 2083. Fax 020-8559 9445. *H.M.* A. Falk MA (Cantab), M Ed; *Chairman of Govs.* Mrs P. Stanton; *Denominational Body:* United Synagogue; *Auth.* London Borough of Redbridge.

Kisharon, Head Office, 1011 Finchley Road, NW11 7HB. ☎ 020-8731 7009. Fax 020-8731 7005. Email info@Kisharon.org.uk. (Reg. Charity No. 271519). *Exec. Dir.* David Goodman; *Chairman of Tr.* Walter Bentley; *Chairman of Govs.* Stephen Greenman.

Tuffkid Nursery, 3 Western Avenue, London NW11. ☎ 020-8731 7009. An integrated nursery for children between the ages of two and five years, providing pre-school education to mainstream and special needs children.

Kisharon Day School, 1011 Finchley Road, NW11 7HB. ☎ 020-8455 7483. Fax 020-8731 7005. Email geraldlebrett@lineone.net. Education for children of 5-16 years with learning disabilities.

Kisharon College, 54 Parson Street, London, NW4 1TP. ☎ 020-8457 2525. Fax 020-8457 2535. Email kisharonhls@aol.com. Further education and vocational training for adults of 16 years and above with learning disabilities. The Centre also houses our Autistic Unit.

Hanna Schwalbe Home, 48 Leeside Crescent, London, NW11 0LA. ☎ 020-8458 3810. Fax 020-8922 7454. Provides residential and respite care for eight young adults with learning difficulties.

Supported Living, 1011 Finchley Road, London, NW11 7HB. ☎ 020-8201 9817. Fax 020-8731 7005. Email gill@kisharon.org.uk. Provides independent support for service users living in rented accommodation in the community.

Law of Truth Talmudical College (Reg. Charity No.: T31648Z/1), 50 Knightland

Road, E5 9HS. *Corr.* 27 Warwick Grove, E5 9HX. ☎ 020-8806 2963. Fax 020-8806 9318. Students: 020-8806 6642. (Est. by Rabbi M. Szneider in Memel, 1911, Frankfurt 1918, London 1938.) *Princ.* Rabbi S. A. Halpern.

Lubavitch Foundation, 107-115 Stamford Hill, N16 5RP. ☎ 020-8800 0022. Fax 020-8809 7324. (Est. 1959.) To further Jewish religious education, identity and commitment. Separate depts. for adult education, summer and day camps, youth clubs and training, univ. counsellors, publications, welfare, and orgs. concerned with Israel. *Princ.* Rabbi N. Sudak, OBE; *Dir.* Rabbi S. F. Vogel; *Admin.* Rabbi I. H. Sufrin. Lubavitch House School–Boys' Senior, 133 Clapton Common, E5. ☎ 020-8809 7476. Girls' Senior, 107 Stamford Hill, N16. ☎ 020-8800 0022. *H. M.* Rabbi S. Lew. Boys' Primary, 135 Clapton Common E5. ☎ 020-8800 1044. *H. M.* Rabbi D. Karnowsky. Girls' Primary, 113-115 Stamford Hill, N16 5RP. ☎ 020-8800 0022. Fax 020-8809 7324; *Admin.* Mrs S. Sudak. Kindergarten, 107 Stamford Hill, N16. ☎ 020-8800 0022. *H. T.* Mrs F. Sudak. *Librarian* Zvi Rabin, ALA. ☎ 020-8800 5823. Vista Vocational Training, 107 Stamford Hill, N16 5RP. ☎ 020-8802 8772. *Man.* Mrs H. Lew. Women's Centre, 19 Northfield Rd, N16 5RL. ☎ 020-8809 6508. *Admin.* Mrs R. Bernstein. *Publ.* Lubavitch Direct.

Menorah Foundation School, Abbotts Road, Edgware, Middx. HA8 0QS. ☎ 020-8906 9992. Fax 020-8906 9993. *H. T.* Mrs C. Neuberger, BSc, PGCE, NFQH; *Principal* Rabbi H.I. Feldman; *Chairman* Alan Perrin.

Menorah Primary School (and Menorah Nursery), Woodstock Avenue, NW11. ☎ 020-8458 1276. Vol. Aided (Lond. Borough of Barnet) for Boys & Girls 3-11. (Est. 1944.) *Princ.* Rabbi H.I. Feldman; *Hd.* Mrs J. Menczer.

Michael Sobell Sinai School, Shakespeare Dr, Kenton, Harrow, Middx HA3 9UD. ☎ 020-8204 1550. (Est. 1981.) Vol. aided primary sch. for boys & girls, aged 3-11. *Chairman Govs.* C. Goodman; *H. T.* Mrs V. Orloff; *Denominational body* Bd. of Rel. Educ.; *Auth.* Lond. Borough of Brent.

MST College (formerly Massoret), 240-242 Hendon Way, NW4 3NL. ☎ 020-8202 2212. ☎/Fax 020-8203 2212. Orthodox women's college providing tertiary education and professional training. Operates within four faculties – Education (Teacher Training); Health and Community Care; Art, Design and Technology; I.T. (Computing) and Business Studies. Full-time and part-time courses combined with essential Torah and Hebrew studies. *Dean* Mrs J. Nemeth; *Exec. Dir.* Mrs O. Joseph.

Naima Jewish Preparatory School (Reg. Charity no. 289066), 21 Andover Place, NW6 5ED. ☎ 020-7328 2802 Fax 020-7624 0161. School for children aged 3-11 years offering a broad secular curriculum together with rich programme of Orthodox Jewish studies. Catering for children of all abilities through flexible learning programme. *H. Princ.* Rabbi Dr A. Levy; *Hd. T.* Mrs K. Peters.

North-West London Jewish Day School, 180 Willesden Lane, NW6 7PP. ☎ 020-8459 3378. Fax 020-8451 7298. Website www.nwljds.org.uk. Email admin @nwljds.org.uk. Voluntary Aided. Orthodox Primary sch. and nursery for boys and girls, 3-11 (Est. 1945). *Principal* Dayan I. Binstock; *H. M.* D. Collins, B.Sc., Dip. Ed. Admin., A.C.P.

Pardes House Primary School, Hendon Lane, N3 1SA. ☎ 020-8343 3568. *H. Princ.* Rabbi E. Halpern. *Hd.* C. Ryan; *Menahel* Rabbi D. Rosenberg. Kindergarten: Hendon Lane, N3 1SA. ☎ 020-8371 8292. *Hd.* Rabbi D. Rosenberg.

Pardes House Grammar School, Hendon Lane, N3 1SA. ☎ 020-8343 3568. *H. Princ.* Rabbi E. Halpern; *Head M.* Rabbi D. Dunner.

Scopus Jewish Educational Trust Schools: (see p.42).

Harry & Abe Sherman Rosh Pinah Jewish Primary School Glengall Road, Edgware, HA8 8TE. ☎ 020-8958 8599. (Est. 1956.) *H. Princ.* Rabbi Y. Schochet; *Act. H. T.* Mrs Anthea Goodman.

Sebba Rosh Pinah Nursery School and Play Group, Mowbray Road, Edgware, Middx., HA8 8JL. ☎ 020-8958 1597. For children aged 2½-5. *H. T.* Mrs B.

Mailer, Dip. Ed. (SA).

Mathilda Marks-Kennedy School and Ella and Ernst Frankel Pre-School, 68 Hale Lane, NW7 3RT. ☎ 020-8959 6089. (Est. 1959.) For children between 2½-11. *H. Princ.* Rabbi G. Sylvester; *H. T.* Mrs S. Kushner, BA, PGCE, MEd.

Simon Marks Jewish Primary School & Nursery, 75 Cazenove Road, N16 6PD. ☎ 020-8806 6048. Fax 020-8442 4722. *H.T.* L. Rosenberg, BEd, CAES, ACP, FRSA; *H. Princ.* Rev. R. Turner.

Sharon Kindergarten, Finchley Synagogue, Kinloss Gdns., N3 3DU. ☎ 020-8346 2039. (For children 2½-5.) *H. T.* Mrs E. Elek.

Side by Side Kids Ltd, 10 Egerton Road, N16 6UA. ☎ 020-8880 1488. Fax 020-8880 2898. Email sidebyside@btopenworld.com. Website www.sidebyside.org.uk. Side by Side is an integrated nursery and special needs school providing therapy and education for children and a support network for their families. *Dir.* Mrs R. Rumpler.

Torah Centre Trust, 84 Leadale Road, N15 6BH. ☎ 020-8802 3586. (Est. 1975.) To provide full or part-time facilities for children, in particular those from 'uncommitted' families, to enable them to further their secular and Hebrew educ. *Chairman* Rabbi J. Dunner; *Educ. Dir.* Rabbi M. Bernstein, B.Ed.

Wolfson Hillel Primary School, 154 Chase Road, Southgate, N14 4LG. ☎ 020-8882 6487. Fax 020-8882 7965. (Est. 1992) Email schooloffice@wolfsonhillel.enfield.sch.uk. Website www.wolfsonhillel.enfield.sch.uk. Vol. aided primary school for boys & girls aged 3-11. *Chairman Govs.* H. Rosen; *H. T.* Mrs S. Margolis. (*Auth.* London Borough of Enfield.)

Yeshiva Gedola, 3/5 Kingsley Way, N2. ☎ 020-8455 3262. *Rosh Yeshiva* Rabbi I. M. Hertz.

Yeshivah Ohel Moshe Etz Chaim, 85 Bridge Lane, NW11.(Reg. Charity No. 312232) ☎ 020-8458 5149. *Princ.* Rabbi Z. Rabi.

Yesodey Hatorah Schools, 2 and 4 Amhurst Park, N16 5AE. ☎ 020-8800 8612. (Est. 1943.) *Princ.* Rabbi A. Pinter; *V. President* Rabbi C. Pinter.

Yesodey Hatorah Nursery, 2 Amhurst Pk., N16 SAE. ☎ 020-8800 9221. *Hd.*

Yesodey Hatorah Kindergarten, 2 Amhurst Pk., N16 5AE. ☎ 020-8800 8612. *Matron* Mrs B. Gottlieb.

Yesodey Hatorah Primary School (Boys), 2 Amhurst Pk., N16 5AE. ☎ 020-8800 8612. *Princ* Rabbi A. Pinter; *Menahel* Rabbi C. Tomlin.

Yesodey Hatorah Senior School (Boys), 4 Amhurst Pk., N16 5AE. ☎ 020-8800 8612. *Princ.* Rabbi A. Pinter; *Menahel* Rabbi D. Mapper.

Yesodey Hatorah Primary School (Girls), 153 Stamford Hill, N16 5LG. ☎ 020-8800 8612. *Princ.* Rabbi A. Pinter; *H. M.* Mrs D. Luria.

Yesodey Hatorah Senior School (Girls), 153 Stamford Hill, N16 5LG. ☎ 020-8800 8612. *Princ.* Rabbi A. Pinter; *H. M.* Mrs R. Pinter

WELFARE ORGANISATIONS

Abbeyfield Camden (Jewish) Society, 178 Walm Lane, London NW2 3AX. ☎ 020-8452 7375. The Society runs three small residential homes for the able-bodied elderly, with facilities for short-stay visitors. *Hon. Sec.* Mrs J. Kessler ☎ 020-8886 9279. Fax 020-8886 8479. Email joannakess@kesslers.fsnet.uk.com. Branches: Peggy Lang House, 178 Walm Lane, London NW2 3AX; Lily Montagu House, 36–38 Orchard Drive, Stanmore, Middx. HA8 7SD; Belmont Lodge, 59 Belmont Road, Bushey, Herts. WD23 2JR.

Agudas Israel Housing Association Ltd, 206 Lordship Rd., N16 5ES. ☎ 020-8802 3819. Fax 020-8809 6206. Email info@aihaltd.co.uk. (Reg. Charity No. 23535). *Chief Exec.* Mrs Ita Symons, MBE.

Schonfeld Square Foundation, 1 Schonfeld Square, Lordship Road, N16 0QQ. ☎ 020-8802 3819. Fax 020-8809 6206. Email info@aihaltd.co.uk. (Reg. Charity No. 1049179). *Co.ord.* Sholom Salzman.

Includes ownership of: **Beenstock Home** (Home for the Frail and Elderly), 19–21 Northumberland Street, Salford, M7 4RP. ☎ 0161-792 1515. Fax 0161-792 1616. *Care Man.* Mrs Pat Yates.

Beis Brucha (Mother and Baby Home), 208 Lordship Road, N16 5ES. ☎/Fax 020-8211 8081. *Man.* L. Hirschler.

Beis Pinchos (Residential Home for the Frail and Elderly), and **Fradel Lodge** (Sheltered Accommodation for the Frail and Elderly), Schonfeld Square, Lordship Road, N16 0QQ. ☎ 020-8802 7477. Fax 020-8809 7000. Email info@aihaltd.co.uk. *Care Man.* Mrs Freda Lipszyc.

Beis Rochel (Supported Housing for Vulnerable Women), 52 Lordship Park, N16 5UD. ☎ (Office) 020-8802 2160, (Residents) 020-8802 2909. Email info@aihaltd.co.uk. *Man.* Sholom Salzman.

30 Dunsmure Road (Supported Housing for Vulnerable Men), N16 5PW. ☎ (Office) 020-8800 2860, (Residents) 020-8802 0073. Email info@aihaltd.co.uk. *Man.* Sholom Salzman.

Ajex Housing Association Ltd. ☎/Fax 020-8802 3348 Warden. Email ajexuk@talk21.com. Website www.ajex.org.uk (I.R. Charity Ref. 914/A5110; Friendly Society Reg. 17760DR; Housing Corporation: Registered Housing Association L0669). Provides flatlets for elderly and disabled ex-servicemen and women and/or their dependants. *Chairman* H. Newman; *H. Sec.* G. J. Kaufman; *Admin.* Ajex House, East Bank, N16 5RT.

Arbib Lucas Trust (Reg. Charity No. 208666). Provides financial assistance to women in reduced circumstances. *H. Sec.* Mrs Anita Kafton, 16 Sunny Hill, NW4 4LL.

Bnai Brith JBG Housing Association, Harmony Close, Princes Park Ave. NW11 0JJ. ☎ 020-8381 4901. Fax 020-8458 1772. *Chairman* E. Shapiro; *T.* ; *Chief Exec.* S. Clarke. The Association owns and/or manages sheltered housing in London, Hertfordshire and Kent. Supported housing for people with special needs is managed on the Association's behalf by Jewish Care and Norwood Ravenswood. Short-term accommodation for young people is located in Golders Green.

Camp Simcha, 19 Ambrose Ave., London NW11 9AP. ☎ 020-8731 6788. Fax 020-8207 0568. Email info@campsimcha.org.uk. (Est. 1994. Reg. Charity No. 1044685) London-based charity to help improve the quality of life for children with cancer. Kosher summer camp in the USA and a full year activity programme. *Chief Exec.* Meir Plancey.

Drugsline Chabad (Reg. Charity No. 1067573), 395 Eastern Avenue, Gants Hill, Ilford, Essex IG2 6LR. Crisis Helpline: Freephone 0800 731 0713 or 020-8518 6470. Office: 020-8554 3220. Fax: 020-8518 2126. Drop in service for those people with drug-related problems, their families and friends. Drug and alcohol education services offered to schools, youth clubs and other organisations. *Dir.* Rabbi Aryeh Sufrin.

Finchley Kosher Lunch Service, (Meals-on-Wheels for the housebound and disabled), Covers Edgware, Finchley, Golders Green, Hampstead Garden Suburb, Hendon, Mill Hill. *H. T.* Mrs Ruth Freed, ☎ 020-8202 8129. Admin. by the League of Jewish Women. (See p.4)

Food for the Jewish Poor, To provide (a) food throughout the year; (b) grocery during Passover; (c) special relief for approved emergency cases. (See Jewish Care).

Friends of the Kingsbury Mikveh – Educational and Support Group (Reg. Charity No. 1041629), Kingsbury United Synagogue, Kingsbury Green, NW9 8XR. ☎ 020-8204 6390. *H.T.* Janet Rabson, 16 Broadfields Ave., Edgware, HA8 8PG. ☎ 020-8958 9035.

Friends of the Sick (Chevrat Bikkur Cholim), (Reg. Charity No. 91468A), 463a Finchley Road, NW3 6HN. ☎ 020-7435 0836. (Est. 1947.) To nurse sick and aged needy persons in their own homes. *President* Peter Gillis; *H. T.* M. Wechsler; *Gen. Sec.* Mrs E. Weitzman.

Hagadolim Charitable Organisation (Est. 1950) To provide financial assistance to Homes and charities in England and Israel, and to visit and provide comforts in private homes in the Home Counties. *Chairman* L. Dunitz; *Jt. Ts.* B. Wallach, Mrs R. J. Dunitz; *Sec.* Mrs S. Levy, 4 Edgwarebury Ct., Edgwarebury La., Edgware, Middx. HA8 8LP. ☎ 020-8958 8558.

Haven Foundation (Regd. Charity No. 264029), Alfred House, 1 Holly Park, Crouch Hill, N4 4BN. ☎ 020-7272 1345 (Admin. by Ravenswood Foundation). Est. 1971. To provide permanent residential care and development training for Jewish mildly mentally handicapped adults in its hostel, group homes and soc. development unit. *L. President* Eve Alfred; *Chairman* N. Freeder; *Jt. V. Chairman* R. Rosenberg, ACA.

Hospital Kosher Meals Service (Reg. Charity No.: 1025601), Lanmor House, 370/386 High Road, Wembley, Middx. HA9 6AX. ☎ 020-8795 2058. Fax 020-8900 2462. Email hkms@compuserve.com. Provides supervised kosher meals to patients in hospitals throughout Greater London. *Chairman* M.G. Freedman, MBA, FCA; *V. Chairman* H. Glyn, BSc, FRICS; *Sec.* G. Calvert; *Admin.* Mrs E. Stone.

Jewish Aged Needy Pension Society (Reg. Charity no. 206262; Est. 1829.) Provides pensions for members of the Jewish community aged 60 or over, who have known better times and who, in their old age, find themselves in reduced circumstances. Also supplements income provided from statutory sources. Services to the middle-class of society who find themselves in greater financial need and who do not seem to fall within the purview of any other charitable organisations. *President* M.E.G. Prince; *Ts.* A.H.E. Prince; *H. Sec.* Mrs G. B. Rigal; *Sec./Admin.* Mrs Sheila A. Taylor, 34 Dalkeith Grove, Stanmore, Middx HA5 4EG. ☎ 020-8958 5390 Fax 020-8958 8046.

Jewish Bereavement Counselling Service (Est. 1980. Reg. Charity No. 1047473), P.O. Box 6748, N3 3BX. ☎/Fax 020-8349 0839 (24 hour answerphone). Email jbcs@jvisit.org.uk. Offers bereavement counselling provided by trained voluntary counsellors under supervision and support to members of the Jewish community who have been bereaved. Covers North and NW London and Hertfordshire. *Chairman* Joy Conway, *Co-ord.* Rae Adler, *Consults.* Roni Goldberg, Jacqueline Toff.

Jewish Blind & Disabled (JBD), the working name of the Jewish Blind & Physically Handicapped Society (Reg. Charity No. 259480). Care & Campaign Office: 164 East End Road, N2 0RR. ☎ 020-8883 1000. Fax 020-8444 6729. Email info@jbd.org; Website www.jbd.org. Founded in 1969 by the late Cecil Rosen, Jewish Blind & Disabled (JBD) provides sheltered housing with communal and welfare services for visually and physically disabled people, to improve the quality of life, maximise freedom of choice, respect dignity at all times and help achieve independent living. JBD currently has six modern sheltered projects providing 234 purpose-built apartments able to accommodate up to 360 residents. *Chairman* John Joseph; *Hon. Chief Exec.* Malcolm J. Ozin; *Exec. Dir.* Jason J. Ozin.

JBD Projects: *Sheltered housing schemes*: Fairacres, 164 East End Road, Finchley, N2; Cherry Tree Court, Roe Green, Kingsbury, NW9; Cecil Rosen Court, East Lane, North Wembley, Middx; Milne Court, Churchfields, South Woodford, E18; Hilary Dennis Court, Sylvan Road, Wanstead, E11; Aztec House, Redbridge.

Day Centres: Aztec House Day Centre, daily; Monday Club, Fairacres; Monday Club, Milne Court; Milne Court Clubbers; Tuesday Club, Hilary Dennis Court; Wednesday Club, Cherry Tree Court, Kingsbury; Luncheon Club, Tuesday, Cherry Tree Court, Thursday Cecil Rosen Court and Fairacres.

Jewish Blind Society (incorporating Jewish Assn. for the Physically Handicapped). See below: Jewish Care.

Jewish Care, Stuart Young House, 221 Golders Green Road, NW11 9DQ. ☎ 020-8922 2000. Help Desk, Information and Referrals 020-8922 2222. Fax 020-8922

1998. Email info@jcare.org; Website www.jewishcare.org. (Reg. Charity No. 802559. Est. 1990).

Institutions administered by Jewish Care:

Residential Homes –

Braemar Royal, Bournemouth; Carlton Dene (holiday home), Bournemouth; Charles Clore, N10; Brighton & Hove Jewish Home; Ella & Ridley Jacobs, NW4; Kay Court, NW3; Lady Sarah Cohen House, N11; Morton House, Hemel Hempstead; Princess Alexandra Home, Stanmore; Raymond House, Southend-on-Sea; Rela Goldhill Lodge (specialist for younger people with a physical disability), NW11; Rubens, N3; Sarah Tankel, N5; Vi & John Rubens, Redbridge; Clore Manor, NW4; Wolfson House, N4.

Day Centres –

Michael Sobell Community Centre, NW11; Stamford Hill Community Centre, N16; Redbridge Jewish Day Centre (in conjunction with Redbridge Jewish Youth & Community Centre); Stepney Jewish Day Centre (in conjunction with B'nai B'rith), E1; Southend & Westcliff Jewish Day Centre.

Special Day Care Units –

The Dennis Centre, Ilford; Sam Beckman Special Day Care Centre, NW4; Stanmore & Edgware Special Day Care Centre; Stepney Special Day Care Unit, E1; Wolfson House Special Day Care Centre, N4.

Specialist units: Employment Resource Centre, N3; Holocaust Survivors Centre, NW4; Carers' Centre, NW11.

Flatlet Schemes (sheltered housing) –

Shine House (in conjunction with JBG Housing Ltd), N3; Maitland House (in conjuction with JBG Housing Ltd), Hemel Hempstead; Rosetta House (in conjuction with JBG Housing Ltd), Hemel Hempstead; Rabbi Pinchas Shebson Lodge, Southend-on-Sea; Sir John & Lady Cohen Court (Joel Emanuel Almshouse Trust), N16; Posnansky Court (in conjunction with JBG Housing Ltd), N4.

Mental Health Provision –

Mitkadem, Ilford; The Sholom Centre, NW11; 7A Mapesbury Road (therapeutic hostel), NW2.

Social Work Teams – c/o Help desk ☎ 020-8922 2222.

Organisations concerned with Jewish youth, Sinclair House – Redbridge Jewish Youth and Community Centre; Young Jewish Care.

Jewish Children's Holidays Fund (formerly the Jewish Branch of the Children's Country Holidays Fund). (Reg. Charity No.: 295361). (Est. 1888.) *President* Mrs Joyce Kemble, JP; *Chairman* Ian Donoff; *Sec.* Mrs F. Warshawsky, 60 Oundle Ave., Bushey, Herts WD23 4QQ. ☎ 020-8950 3383.

Jewish Crisis Help Line, Miyad. ☎ 0345 581999. Confidential listening service for those experiencing stress in their lives. Sponsored by the Jewish Marriage Council.

Jewish Deaf Association, Julius Newman House, Woodside Park Rd., London N12 8RP. ☎ 020-8446 0502 (voice), 020-8446 4037 (text). Fax 020-8445 7451; Email jda@dircon.co.uk. (Reg. Charity No. 209892) Provides a welfare and social environment for the profoundly deaf and hearing-impaired. Maintains a Day Centre for deaf people. Runs an Advisory and Resource Room exhibiting aids to daily living for deaf and hard of hearing people of all ages. ☎ 020-8446 0214. *President* G.M. Gee, JP; *Chairman* Mrs E. Gee; *Exec. Dir.* Susan Cipin.

Jewish Society for the Mentally Handicapped, now merged with Norwood Ravenswood (see below).

Jewish Welfare Board (incorporating the Jewish Bread, Meat and Coal Society, est. 1779), see Jewish Care, (p.15).

Jews' Temporary Shelter (Reg. Charity no. 212071), 1-2 Endsleigh St., WC1H 0DS. ☎/Fax 020-7387 7447. *Admin.* Mrs R. Lewis.

Lewis Hammerson Memorial Home, Hammerson House, 50A, The Bishop's

Avenue, N2 OBE. ☎ 020-8458 4523. Fax 020-8458 2537. Email hammersonhouse@aol.com. (Est. 1962, Reg. Charity No. 286002.) *President* Mrs S. Hammerson, OBE; *Chairman* Julian Anderson. Applications for admission: 020-8458 4523.

MIYAD: Jewish Telephone Crisis Line, ☎ 020-8203 6211, 0345 581999. Sponsored by the Jewish Marriage Council. Confidential telephone line offered to the Jewish community for people needing help in crisis situations.

Necessitous Ladies' Fund, incorporating Delissa Joseph Memorial Fund (both funds founded by Union of Jewish Women). For the relief of Jewish women who are in need, hardship or distress (Reg. Charity No. 266921 A3L1). *Chairman* Mrs J. Nathan; *H. Sec.* Mrs D. Curzon, 14 Blessington Close, SE13 5ED.

Nightingale House, 105 Nightingale Lane, SW12 8NB. ☎ 020-8673 3495. Fax 020-8675 2258 (Est. 1840, Reg. Charity No. 207316) *Patrons* Lord Rayne, Dame Vivien Duffield, DBE; *President* G. Lipton, MBE; *Chairman* Mrs R. Preston, OBE; *Jt Ts.* M. Lawson; L. Green, FCA; K. Goodman, FCA; *Exec. Dir.* Leon Smith. Aid Societies: N.W. London; S.W. London; Nightingale Ladies' Cttee; Literary Lunch Cttee; The Kentongales. Also manages Rayne House sheltered housing flats.

Norwood Ravenswood, Broadway House, 80/82, The Broadway, Stanmore, HA7 4HB. ☎ 020-8954 4555. Fax 020-8420 6800. Email norwoodravenswood@nwrw.org; Website www.nwrw.org. Locally based social service teams are in Hackney (020-8880 2244), North West London (020-8203-3386), Redbridge (020-8559 6200). (Reg. Charity No.1059050.) Norwood Ravenswood is a leading National Child and Family Services charity. Every year, the charity helps thousands of children and their families by providing a range of over 60 specialist support services such as social work, counselling, family and community centres, special educational needs services, and residential and day care opportunties for vulnerable children, adolescents and people of all ages with physical and learning disabilities. Norwood Ravenswood also runs the only Jewish Adoption Agency in the United Kingdom and runs the Adoption Register for England and Wales on behalf of the Department of Health and the National Assembly for Wales. This is a stand-alone project, entirely funded by the government which will be run by a specially appointed team of professionals. *Patron* HM The Queen; *President* Sir Trevor Chinn, CVO; *Chairman* John Libson; *Exec. Dir.* Norma Brier, MSc.

Raphael Centre (a Jewish Counselling Service) (Reg. Charity No. 278522), PO Box 172, Stanmore HA7 3WB. ☎ 020-8203 9881 (24 hour). Aims: To provide short- or long-term counselling by professional counsellors and psychotherapists for Jewish people with emotional or psychological problems, such as depression, stress, anxiety, loss or bereavement, relationship or family problems. Counselling supports, and helps with personal growth and the development of personal resources. A contribution is requested within every client's means.

Rishon Multiple Sclerosis Aid Group, Flat 6, 40 Eastcote Rd., Pinner, Middx. HA5 1DH. ☎ 020-8868 1557. (Est. 1966. Reg. Charity No. 252359) Affiliated to the Multiple Sclerosis Society of Great Britain. Provides social and cultural activities, help and welfare, for Multiple Sclerosis sufferers and raises funds for this and the encouragement of research into the causes and cure of the disease. *H. Sec.* B. Gold.

Stamford Hill Community Centre, 91-93 Stamford Hill, N16 5TP. ☎ 020-8800 5672. Fax 020-8800 1678 (Reg. Charity No. 802559). Administered by Jewish Care. Community Centre for the elderly and visually handicapped and others with special needs. *Centre Man.* R. Jacobs.

Sunridge Housing Association Ltd., 76 The Ridgeway, NW11 8PT. ☎ 020-8458 3389; *Chairman* Brian Levy; *H. Sec.* Robin Michaelson. *Man.* Mrs M. Lewis.

Westlon and Westmount, 850 Finchley Road, NW11 6BB. ☎ 020-8201 8484. Fax 020-8731 8847. Two separate organisations share this address:

Westlon Housing Association. *H. L. President* His Hon. Alan King-Hamilton,

QC; *President* H. Steel; *Chairman* Cllr Mrs Joan Ansell; *Admin.* J.W. Silverman. **Annette White Lodge**, 287/289 High Road, N2 8HB. **Deborah Rayne House**, 33b Sunningfields Road, NW4 4QX. **The Woodville**, Woodville Road, W5 2SE. Applications to 020-8201 8484.

Westmount Charitable Trust (Est. 1978) and **Westmount Housing Association.** *Chairman* Mrs E. Corob; *T.* S. Corob; *Sec.* Mrs S. Berg; *Admin.* J.W. Silverman. Accommodation and amenities for the elderly. **Westmount**, 126 Fortune Green Road, NW6 1DN. Residence for 40 elderly persons. Applications to 020-8201 8484.

Yad Voezer, 80 Queen Elizabeth's Walk, N16 5UQ. ☎/Fax 020-8809 4303. Email yadvo@btopenworld.com. (Est. 1975, Reg. Charity No. 277771) Care and support for people with learning disabilities. Services include residential/respite care, Sunday and Holiday Clubs, day care, employment schemes, advice, counselling and family support. Services are managed and run within the N16 area. *Chairman* Rabbi E. Landau; *Exec. Dir.* Mrs Z. Landau.

Clubs and Cultural Societies

See also under Synagogues (pp.78–87); Organisations concerned with Jewish Youth (pp.47–52).

London Jewish News (incorporating New Moon), 28 St Albans Lane, NW11 7QE. ☎ 020-8731 8031. Fax 020-8381 4033.

Aisha HaTorah, UK, 379 Hendon Way, NW4 3LP. ☎ 020-8457 4444. Fax 020-8457 4445. Email info@aish.org.uk. (Est 1992; Reg. Charity no. 1069048.) Adult Education. *Dir.* Rabbi S. Rosenblatt, Rabbi N. Schiff; *Chairman* J. Faith.

Alyth Choral Society, North Western Reform Synagogue, Alyth Gdns., NW11 7EN. ☎ 020-8455 6763 (Est. 1983.) *Musical Dir.* Vivienne Bellos; *Chairman* M. Cohen; *Sec.* Ms L. Perez.

Association of Jewish Friendship Clubs, 26 Enford St., W1H 2DD. ☎ 020-7724 8100. Fax 020-7724 8203 (Head Office). An umbrella organisation for men and women in the 60-plus age group, providing companionship throughout 70 clubs in London and the Provinces. A network of social clubs joining together for activities on a national basis, e.g. group holidays and central London based functions. *Jt Hon. Life Presidents* Lady Jakobovits and Rabbanit Elaine Sacks; *National Chairman* Mrs L. Bromley; *Hon. Chaplain* Rev. G. Glausiusz.

Besht Tellers, 33 Abbey Road, NW8 0AT. ☎ 020-8340 4421. Email info@beshttellers.org. (Reg. Charity No. 1075867) Professional Jewish Theatre company producing international, national and community performances of original Jewish Theatre. Touring productions, including performances for children and young people, educational programmes and individual workshops. *Dir.* Rebecca Wolman; *Educ.* Gabrielle Moss; *Producer* Suzanna Rosenthal.

Brady-Maccabi, Youth and Community Centre, 4 Manor Pk. Cresc., Edgware, Middx. HA8 7NL. ☎ 020-8952 2948. Fax 020-8952 2393. Email office@bradymaccabi.com; Website www.bradymaccabi.com. (Est. 1979.) Open Sun. to Thurs. Snr. Citizens clubs meet Tues. and Thurs. pm. *President* John Cutner J.P., F.C.A.; *Chairman* J. Lane; *Admin.* Mrs T. Cutner, JP.

Chabad Lubavitch Centre (Reg. Charity No. 227638), 395 Eastern Avenue, Ilford, Essex IG2 6LR. ☎ 020-8554 1624. Fax 020-8518 2126. (Est. 1986). *Dir.* Rabbi A.M. Sufrin; *Programme Co-ord.* Rabbi M. Muller.

Friends of Jewish Youth, formerly Old Boys' Association. Martin Shaw, c/o A. J. Y., 128 East Lane, Wembley, Middx. ☎ 020-8908 4747. Fax 020-8904 4323.

Friends of Yiddish *Contact* Chaim Neslen, 232 Cranbrook Road, Ilford, Essex IG1 4UT. ☎ 020-8554 6112. We meet every Saturday afternoon at Toynbee Hall, nr Aldgate East Tube Station. The programme is entirely in Yiddish, and includes readings, live music and some discussion. Special events are advertised in the

Jewish press.

Institute for Jewish Music Studies and Performance, 33 Seymour Pl., W1H 6AT. ☎ 020-7723 4404. (Est. 1982) To further the study and knowledge of Jewish music, both liturgical and secular, at the highest academic and performing level. *Dir.* S. Fixman.

Jewish Appreciation Group Tours, 32 Anworth Close, Woodford Green, Essex IG8 0DR ☎ 020-8504 9159. (Est. 1960.) Full history tours of the Jewish East End and the Jews in England from 1066. Historic walks and tours throughout the year. *Tours Org.* Adam Joseph.

Jewish Association of Cultural Societies (J.A.C.S.), Edgware Synagogue, Edgware Way, Edgware Middx. HA8 9YE. ☎ 020-8954 1353. (Est. 1978.) Twenty-eight clubs have been opened throughout the Greater London com., with two in Surrey, one in Bournemouth, one in Brighton, one in Westcliff-on-Sea and one in Cardiff, providing weekly meetings for the 50+, embracing cultural and social programmes. *H. President* Rev. Saul Amias, M.B.E.; *Nat. Chairman* Mrs Annette Pearlman; *H. Sec.* Mrs Lonnie Levey.

Jewish Research Group, c/o 43 Churchill Ct., Ainsley Close, Edmonton, N9 9XJ. ☎ 020-8364 3518. Email jcbmrchess@aol.com. The Jewish Research Group is an autonomous part of the Edmonton Hundred Historical Society and was established in 1978 when the Committee of the 1st Jewish Way of Life Exhibition, held to mark the 50th Anniversary of the Palmers Green and Southgate Synagogue, decided not to disband. The main aim of the J.R.G. is to research Jewish history in the 'Edmonton Hundred', which corresponds approximately to the boundaries of the London Boroughs of Enfield and Haringey, and to publish its findings.

Current membership: 100. Monthly meetings are held at which prominent speakers are invited to address the Group on Jewish historical subjects. Five publications have been printed under the title of 'Heritage'. *President* Mrs Marjorie Glick, BA; *V. President* R.E. Landau, BSc; *Chairman* P. Venit, BA; *V. Chairman* Anita Shapiro; *H. Sec.* Jeffrey Baum; *H. T.* Harold Temerlies.

Kadimah/Victoria Youth Club (Reg. Charity No.: 299323), 127/129 Clapton Common, E5 9AB. ☎ 020-8809 3618. Catering for the traditional and non-traditional Ashkenazi and Sephardi communities. Membership for 5-14 yrs. *Senior Youth Workers* G. Nissim, C. Jackson; *Chairman* Yoel Salem.

L'Chaim Society, Cricklewood Business Centre (Ground Floor), Cricklewood Lane, Cricklewood, NW2 1ET. ☎ 020-88830 5533. Fax 020-8830 5530.

London Jewish Male Choir. *H. Sec.* Bernard Jackson, 62 Rotherwick Rd., NW11 7DB. ☎ 020-8458 6803. Fax 020-8455 5435. Email bees@dircon.co.uk. (Inland Revenue Number: X 91533). Rehearsals Thurs. evgs., Hendon Synagogue.

Lubavitch of South London (Reg. Charity No. 227638), 42 St. George's Road, Wimbledon, SW19 4ED. ☎ 020-8944 1581. Fax 020-8944 7563. Email lubwdon@aol.com (Est. 1988) Adult Jewish educ., library, food and bookshop, mailings, assemblies, tuition, Mitzva campaigns, youth activities. *Dir.* Rabbi Nissan Dubov.

The Maccabaeans (Est. 1891). Consisting primarily of those engaged in professional pursuits, its aims being to provide 'social intercourse and co-operation among its members with a view to the promotion of the interests of Jews, including the support of any professional or learned bodies and charities'. *President* Sir Ian Gainsford; *H. T.* A. Gainsford; *H. Sec.* L. Slowe, 4 Corringway, NW11 7ED.

Oxford & St. George's (Reg. Charity No. 207191), 120 Oakleigh Road North, N20 9EZ. ☎ 020-8446 3101. Communal provision and youth clubs.

Redbridge Jewish Community Resource Centre, Sinclair House, Woodford Bridge Road, Ilford, Essex, IG5 4LN. ☎ 020-8551 0017. Fax 020-8551 9027. The Resource Centre is a creative dynamic centre for informal Jewish and Zionist education. The Centre has operated in the community for 12 years as a resource for educators who require support and advice in this field. The Resource Centre is a focus for leadership training in the community. The Redbridge Jewish Community Resource Centre is a Sinclair House project in association with JPMP. *Resource Centre Worker* Gia Midda.

Redbridge Jewish Youth and Community Centre (Reg. Charity No.: 3013185), Sinclair House, Woodford Bridge Road, Ilford, Essex, IG4 5LN. ☎ 020-8551 0017. Fax 020-8551 9027. *Chairman Man. Cttee.* Bernard Sinclair; *Dir.* Myra Whiskar. Sinclair House, home of the Redbridge Jewish Youth and Community Centre, meets the social, educational and welfare needs of all sections of the Redbridge and District Jewish Community. More than 3,500 people make use of the centre's facilities each week. The Redbridge Jewish Day Centre provides a high level of essential care for over 450 elderly and disabled people. There are programmes and services for young people, including those with special needs, and social, educational, welfare and active sports programmes for young and adults alike. The Centre is also the base for the Community Shlicha, Clayhall Synagogue, Redbridge Jewish Community Resource Centre (JPMP), the Redbridge Jewish Youth Council and many communal events and activities.
The Redbridge Jewish Youth and Community Centre is part of Jewish Care.

Spec Jewish Youth and Community Centre (Reg. Charity No. 302921), 87 Brookside South, East Barnet, Herts EN4 8LL. ☎ 020-8368 5117. Fax 020-8368 0891. Email speconline@yahoo.com. Est. 1962 to enable Jewish young people to meet in a secure environment and offer opportunities for personal growth. Activities include youth clubs for 5½-16 age grps. *Chairman* J. Masters; *Tr.* J. Hartstone; *H. Sec.* Jeffrey Leifer; *Sec.* Linda Rich; *Contact* M. Lent.

Spitalfields Centre and Synagogue, 19 Princelet Street, E1 6QH. ☎ 020-7247 5352. Fax 020-7375 1490. Email info@19princeletstreet.org.uk; Website www.19princelet street.org.uk

Stepney Jewish Community Centre, 2-8 Beaumont Grove, E1 4NQ. ☎ 020-7790 6441. Fax 020-7265 8342. (Reg. Charity No. 802559) Administered by **Jewish Care.** Community Centre for the Elderly; Special Care Centre for Physically and Mentally Frail; Kosher Meals on Wheels; and Friendship Clubs. *Centre Man.* Philippa Paine.

Western Charitable Foundation, 32 Gt. Cumberland Place, W1H 7TN. ☎ 020-7723 7246. *Chairman* Sidney Jaque, JP; *V. Chairman* Harold Pasha; *Tr.* A. Yadgaroff.

Zemel Choir (Reg. Charity No. 252572/ACL), Britain's leading mixed Jewish Choir performing a varied repertoire, with an emphasis on Hebrew, Yiddish, Israeli and liturgical music, and contemporary compositions of Jewish interest. Overseas tours, prestige concerts in London and provinces, recordings, social events. Zemel welcomes enthusiastic and committed singers who read music fairly fluently. Rehearsals most Mondays 8-10.30 p.m. North West London. *Musical Dir.* Vivienne Bellos. *Contact:* Michael Morris, 4 Mandeville Rd, N14 7NH. ☎ 020-8368 6289. Email syl.mike@virgin.net.

Miscellaneous Organisations

ALL ABOARD SHOPS LIMITED

All Aboard operate Charity Shops for the benefit of UK-based Jewish Charities only via their ever-expanding chain of Charity Shops in London and the Provinces. All Aboard welcome donations of clothing, bric-a-brac, etc, and welcome volunteers to assist in the shops and at Head Office. *Exec. Bd.* Stella Lucas, Monique Landau, Jeffrey Pinnick; *Exec. Dir.* Carol Marks. ☎ 020-8381 1717. Fax 020-8381 1718. Website www.allaboardshops.com; Email info@allaboardshops.com.

Shops are located at: **Camden Town**, 59 Camden High Street, NW1 7JL; **East**

Finchley, 124 High Rd., N2 9ED; **Edgware**, 3 Boot Parade, 92 High St., HA8 7HE; **Finchley Road**, 150 Finchley Rd., NW3 5HS; **Golders Green**, 616 Finchley Rd., NW11, 7RR; **Golders Green**, 125 Golders Green Road, NW11 8HR; **Temple Fortune**, 1111 Finchley Road, NW11 0QB; **Hendon** 98 Brent Street, NW4 2HH; **Ilford**, 107 Cranbrook Road, Ilford, Essex IG1 4PU; **Manchester: Cheetham Hill**, 3 St Margaret's Buildings, Bury Old Road, M8 5EJ, **Prestwich**, Unit 10, Longfield Centre, Prestwich, Manchester M25 5AY, **Urmston**, 4 Station Bridge, Urmston, Manchester M41 9JN; **Paddington**, 12 Spring Street, W2 3RA; **Porchester Road**, 3 Porchester Road, W2 5DP; **Stamford Hill**, 2a Regent Parade, Amhurst Park, N16 5LP; **Streatham**, 83 Streatham High Road, SW16 1PH; **West Hampstead**, 224 West End Lane, NW6 1UU; **Westcliff-on-Sea**, 157 Hamlet Court Road, Westcliff-on-Sea, SS0 7EL.

JEWISH POLICE ASSOCIATION

Golders Green Police Station, 1069 Finchley Road, London NW11 0QE.
☎ 020-8733 5558 (45558 Metline). Fax 020-8733 5557 (4557 Metline). Email info@jewishpoliceassociation.org.uk. Website www.jewishpoliceassociation.org.uk.
(Est. 2001) Provides a network for support and advice of Jewish staff within the Metropolitan Police Service; to promote understanding of the Jewish faith within the Police Service; and to act as a resource reference for Police Services regarding religious and cultural issues, in particular those that affect front-line policing. *Chair* Jo Poole; *Deputy Chair* John Moran; *T.* Peter Russell, MBE; *Sec.* D. Phillips; *Exec.* Andrew Gee; *Hon. Chaplain* Rabbi Alan Plancey.

LONDON JEWISH MEDICAL SOCIETY

The Medical Society of London, PO Box 382, Wembley, Middx. HA9 9FA. ☎ 020-8933 0361.
(Est. 1928.) A learned society for doctors, senior medical students and members of allied professions. 2002-2003: *President* Dr Adrian Naftalin; *H. Sec.* Dr J. Stern.

LONDON SOCIETY OF JEWS AND CHRISTIANS

28 St John's Wood Road, NW8 7HA.
☎ 020-7286 5181. Fax 020-7266 3591.
(Est. 1927). The oldest interfaith organisation of its kind in the UK, established to give an opportunity to Jews and Christians to confer together on the basis of their common ideals and with mutual respect for differences of religion. *President* The Rev. Professor Geoffrey Parrinder; *Jt. Chairmen* Rabbi Dr David J. Goldberg, Dr Anthony Harvey; *Memb. Sec.* Margaret Rigal.

VISITATION COMMITTEE

The Visitation Committee, while under the administration of the United Synagogue, includes Hospital Visiting, Prison Visiting and Bereavement Counselling and services to all those who claim to be Jewish, irrespective of any synagogue affiliation. The Committee is recognised by the National Health Service as the provider of hospital chaplaincy for Jewish patients, servicing over 300 hospitals in London and the South East. Visits by chaplains and lay visitors are made in those hospitals where there is a regular intake of Jewish patients, and information is given to other hospitals for emergency requirement and occasional visits. The Prison section, officially recognised by HM Prison Service, provides chaplaincy for approximately 70 prisons in the southern part of England and advises Jewish chaplains in other parts of the country. *Admin.* Josephine Wayne, United Synagogue, 8–10 Forty Avenue, Wembley, Middx. HA9 8JW. ☎ 020-8385 1855. Fax 020-8385 1856. Email jo.wayne@visit.org.uk.
Bereavement Counselling Service (see p.99).

THE REGIONS

Figures in brackets after place names indicate estimated Jewish population (see pp.199–200).

There are Zionist societies in almost every Jewish regional centre, and Women's Zionist societies in most of them.
Details of current burial arrangements have been listed where forthcoming.

Disused cemeteries are maintained by the Board of Deputies of British Jews at a number of towns in the British Isles. General enquiries about these and other locations should be addressed to the Board's Community Issues Division. **Bath:** Bradford Road, cnr of Greendown Place, abt. 2 miles from town centre. Keys held by City of Bath Probation Office. **Canterbury:** Entrance at end of passageway between 26 and 28 Whitstable Road **Douglas:** Jewish enclosure in municipal cemetery. **Dover:** (maintained by the US) On Old Charlton Road, overlooking the harbour at Copt Hill. **Falmouth:** On main Penryn Road, Ponsharden. Keys from Vospers Garage (adjacent) ☎ 01326-372011. **Ipswich:** In Star Lane, premises of BOCM Pauls Ltd., and Jewish section of municipal cemetery. **King's Lynn:** In Millfleet (pedestrian precinct). Keys from Mr. C.J. Hilton, West Norfolk District Council, Hardwick Narrows Estate, King's Lynn. **Penzance:** Historic walled Georgian Cemetery; approx. 50 headstones. Passage between 19 and 20 Leskinnick Ter., right at end of arch, cemetery on left. (Access road unsuitable for cars.) Key from Keith Pearce, ☎ 01736-368778. **Sheerness:** Jewish enclosure in municipal cemetery. Another site is behind shops at cnr. Hope St./High St. **Yarmouth:** On Blackfriars Road, Alma Road, on perimeter of old city walls. Key from Dept. of Technical Services, Gt. Yarmouth Town Hall.
(See also **Listed Synagogues and Other Jewish Monuments in the UK**, pp.208–11).

Mikvaoth are maintained in the following centres: Birmingham, Bournemouth, Brighton, Gateshead, Leeds, Leicester, Liverpool, Manchester, Newcastle, Sheffield, Southend, Southport, Sunderland and Glasgow.

Memorials: Large stone/slate memorial in Aberdovey Town Centre Park, West Wales, to No.3 Jewish Troop, No.10 Commando – plaque opposite on sea wall explains the Jewish refugee make-up of the troop; Clifford's Tower, York; Lincoln Cathedral.

Menorah: a magazine for Jewish members of H.M. Forces and Small Jewish Communities is published by the Jewish Committee for H.M. Forces. *Corr*. Rev. Malcolm Weisman, OBE, 25/26 Enford Street, London W1H 2DW. Email jmcouncil@btinternet.com. Website www.jmcouncil.org.

AMERSHAM (70)
South Bucks. Jewish Community (ULPS).
PO Box 391, Chesham, Bucks. HP5 1WB. ☎ 01494 431885. Email info@sbjc.org.uk. Website www.sbjc.org.uk. **Cemetery:** See Edgwarebury Cemetery (p.92).

BASILDON (Essex) (10)
Services are held in members' homes. *Chairman*
Burials arranged through Southend & Westcliff Hebrew Congregation at their cemetery in Southend.

BATH
The last synagogue closed in 1910. Services are currently being revived under the auspices of the Bristol and West Progressive Jewish Congregation (see p.111) at The Friends' Meeting House, York St.

BEDFORD (45)
In medieval times Bedford was one of the centres of English Jewry. A number of congregations existed at various times from 1803 onwards. The present com. originated during the 1939–45 war.

Hebrew Congregation. *Sec.* R. Berman. ☎ 01234 364723.

See also under Luton for Bedfordshire Progressive Synagogue for Saturday morning services.

BIRMINGHAM (3,000)
This Jewish community is one of the oldest in the provinces, dating from 1730, if not earlier. Birmingham manufacturing attracted early Jewish settlers. In the Anglo-Jewish economy Birmingham's position was similar to a port, a centre from which Jewish pedlars covered the surrounding country week by week, returning to their homes for the Sabbath. The first synagogue of which there is any record was in The Froggery in 1780. But there was a Jewish cemetery in the same neighbourhood in 1730, and Moses Aaron is said to have been born in Birmingham in 1718. The history of the Birmingham community has been investigated by the Birmingham Jewish History Research Group under the leadership of the late Zoë Josephs.

Representative Council of Birmingham and Midland Jewry. (Est. 1937.) *Chairman* Prof. S. Abudarham; *H. Sec.* L. Jacobs. ☎ 0121-236 1801; *Admin.* Mrs R. Jacobs, Singers Hill, Blucher St., B1 1HL. ☎/Fax 0121-643 2688. Email bjrepco@dircon.co.uk; Website www.brijnet.org//birmingham

Board of Shechita, c/o Hebrew Cong., Singers Hill, Ellis Street, B1 1HL; *Sec.* B. Gingold.

SYNAGOGUES

Hebrew Congregation, Singers Hill, Ellis Street, B1 1HL. ☎ 0121-643 0884. The present syn. was consecrated on September 24, 1856. *M.* Rabbi L. L. Tann; *Admin.* B. Gingold.

Central Synagogue, 133 Pershore Road, B5 7PA. ☎/Fax 0121-440 4044. *M.* Rabbi A. S. Hill; *Sec.* S.Cohen.

Progressive Synagogue (ULPS), 4 Sheepcote Street, B16 8AA. ☎ 0121-643 5640 (9.30 a.m.-1.00 p.m. w/d). *H. Sec.* Mrs A. Grant, ☎ 0121-458 6257. Website www. bps-pro-syn.co.uk; *M.* Rabbi Dr Margaret Jacobi.

OTHER INSTITUTIONS

Birmingham Community Jewish Care, 1 Rake Way, B15 1EG. ☎ 0121-643 2835. Fax 0121-643 5291. *President* Dr B. Roseman; *Dir.* I. Myers.

Birmingham Jewish Youth Trust, 1 Rake Way, Tennant St., B15 1EG. ☎ 0121-687 1223. Email bjyt@bjyt.fsnet.co.uk. *Youth Worker* C. Jennings.

Birmingham Rabbinic Board. *Chairman* Rabbi L. Tann ☎ 0121-440 8375.

Birmingham Union of Jewish Students, c/o Hillel House, 26 Somerset Road, Edgbaston, B15 2QD. ☎ 0121-454 5684.

Hillel House, 26 Somerset Road, Edgbaston, B15 2QD. ☎ 0121-454 5684. Website www. hillel-bhm.fsnet.co.uk. Applications for admission to Mrs P. Harris, 4 High Trees Rd., Knowle, Solihull, B93 9PR. ☎ 01564-778710. Email pat@hillelbhm.fsnet.co.uk.

B'nai Brith Joint Lodge. *Jt. Secs.* F. & H. Linden, 7 Westbourne Gardens, Edgbaston, B15 3TJ. ☎ 0121-454 5042.

Home for Aged, Andrew Cohen House, Riverbrook Drive, Stirchley, B30 2SH. ☎ 0121-458 5000.

Jewish Graduates Association. *Sec.* Prof. A. Travis ☎ 0121-454 1215. Email tony@e-w-tourism.demon.co.uk.

King David School, 244 Alcester Road, B13 8EY. ☎ 0121-499 3364. *H.T.* Mrs E. Lesser.

Lubavitch Centre & Bookshop, 95 Willows Road, B12 9QF. ☎ 0121-440 6673. Fax 0121-446 4299. *M.* Rabbi S. Arkush. Also at this address: Operation Judaism (see p.64).

Mikva at Central Synagogue, For appointments ☎ 0121-440 5853.

Israel Information Centre, Bookshop and Reference Library, Singers Hill, Ellis St., B1 1HL. *Dir.* Mrs R. Jacobs ☎ 0121-643 2688. Email rjacobs@iicmids.u-net.com.

Jewish Education Board. *Chairman* A. Gremson, c/o Hebrew Congregation. ☎ 0121-643 0884.

CEMETERIES

Brandwood End Cemetery, Kings Heath 14. Enqs. to Hebrew Congregation (☎ 0121-643 0884).

Witton Cemetery, The Ridgeway, College Road, Erdington 23. ☎ 0121-356 4615.

BLACKPOOL (1,500)

United Hebrew Congregation, Leamington Road. (Consecrated 1916.) Services were first held in the 1890s in a private house. Later a syn. was built in Springfield Road. *M.* Rev. D. Braunold. ☎ 01253 392382; *President* F. H. Freeman. ☎ 01253 393767.

Reform Synagogue, 40 Raikes Parade, FY1 4EX. (A constituent of R.S.G.B.) ☎ 01253 23687. *M.* Rabbi N. Zalud; *H. T.* Mrs E. R. Ballan, 177 Hornby Road, Blackpool, FY2 4JA. ☎ 01253 25839.

Blackpool Council of Christians and Jews. Rev D. Braunold, 31 Marlborough Road, Blackpool North. ☎ 01253 392382. *H. Sec.* Mrs G. Kay.

Blackpool and Fylde Ajex. *H. Sec.* F. Tomlinson. ☎ 01253 728659.

Blackpool and Fylde Jewish Welfare Society. *President*: Mrs G. Kay; *H. T.* D. Lewis ☎ 01253 295608.

Fylde League of Jewish Women. *H. Sec.* Mrs A. Lewis, 17 Poulton Ave, Lytham St Annes, FY8 3JR. ☎ 01253 723970.

BOGNOR REGIS (30)

Hebrew Congregation. *H. Sec.* J. S. Jacobs, Elm Lodge, Sylvan Way. ☎ 01243 823006. Fax 01243 866859.

BOURNEMOUTH (3,000)

The Bournemouth Hebrew Cong. was est. in 1905 and met in the Assembly Rooms, where the Bournemouth Pavilion now stands. A syn., built in Wootton Gdns. in 1911, was rebuilt in 1961 to seat some 950 congregants. The Menorah suite was added in 1974, and a mikva in 1976.

Bournemouth Reform Synagogue was started by a small band of enthusiasts in 1947. Ten years later the congregation was large enough to build the present synagogue building at 53 Christchurch Road. It was extended in 1980 and now has a membership of over 700 persons, with a voluntary mixed choir, active Cheder, and many social activities, and is host to the Jewish Day Centre every Monday.

Bournemouth is the religious and social centre for the fast growing community in Dorset, West Hampshire and Wiltshire.

Bournemouth District Jewish Representative Council (incorp. Southampton). *Co-chairs* Linda Ford-Horne, Gillian Walker; *H. Sec.* Mrs A. Sklan, 3 De Lisle Road, BH3 7NF. ☎ 01202-520671.

Wessex Jewish News (community newsletter), P.O. Box 2287, BH3 7ZD.

Hebrew Congregation, Wootton Gdns. BH1 1PW. ☎ 01202 557433. *President* I. Weintroub; *M.* Rabbi G. Shisler.
Mikva, Gertrude Preston Hall, Wootton Gdns. ☎ 01202 557433.
Yavneh Kindergarten, Gertrude Preston Hall, Wootton Gdns. BH1 3PW. ☎ 01202 295414. *Princ.* Mrs R. Nash.
Bournemouth Jewish Day School, Synagogue Chambers, Wootton Gardens, BH1 1PW. ☎ 01202-553373. *H.T.*
Reform Syngagogue, 53 Christchurch Road, P.O. Box 8, BH1 3PN. (Est. 1947.) (A Constituent of the R.S.G.B.) ☎ 01202-557736. *M.* Rabbi D. Soetendorp; *Chairman* J. Gee; *H. Sec.* Mrs B. Watkin.
Day Centre, *Co-ordinator* Mrs R. Lesser, 40A East Avenue, BH3 7DA. ☎ 01202 766039.
Bournemouth Sephardi Association, 69 Orchard Avenue, Poole, Dorset BH14 8AH. ☎ 01202-745168 after 8p.m. *Chairman* Simon Tammam; *Sec.* Jack Valencia; *T.* David Kalfon
Bournemouth University Jewish Society, Wallisdown Road, Poole. ☎ 01202 524111.
Home for Aged: Hannah Levy House, 15 Poole Road, Bournemouth. ☎ 01202 765361.
Lubavitch Centre, Chabad House, 8 Gordon Road, Boscombe, Bournemouth. ☎ 01202 396615.
Cemeteries: Kinson Cemetery (used by both Hebrew Cong. and Reform Syn.); Boscombe Cemetery (used by old established mems. Hebrew Cong.); Throop Cemetery (Hebrew Cong.)

BRADFORD (170)

Jews of German birth, who began settling in Bradford in the first half of the nineteenth century, were in a large measure responsible for the development of its wool yarns and fabrics exports to all parts of the world. Jewish services, first held in the 1830s in private houses, were held in 1873, on Reform lines, in a public hall. About the same period saw the beginnings of the Orthodox community.
Hebrew Congregation (Orthodox), Springhurst Road, Shipley, West Yorks. BD18 3DN. (Cong. est. 1886, Syn. erected 1970.) *President* A. A. Waxman; *H. Sec.* Mrs A.E. Dye, Brookfield, Hebden Hall Park, Hebden, Grassington, BD23 5DX. ☎ 01756-752012.
Synagogue, Bowland Street, Bradford, BD1 3BW. (Est. 1880.) (A constituent of R.S.G.B.) *Chairmen* R. Stroud, R. Leavor, 76 Heaton Park Drive, BD9 5QE. s☎ 01274 544198; *H. Sec.* Mrs C. Chapman, 9 Woodvale Way, BD7 2SJ ☎ 01274 575993.
Jewish Benevolent Society. *President* A.A. Waxman; *H. T.* M. Levi.
Cemetery (both Orthodox and Reform), Scholemoor, Necropolis Road, Cemetery Road, Bradford.

BRIGHTON & HOVE (8,000)

There were Jews resident in Brighton in the second half of the eighteenth century, and by the beginning of the nineteenth century there was an organised community. (The earliest syn. was founded in Jew Street in 1792.)
Brighton and Hove Jewish Representative Council. Meetings at Ralli Hall, Denmark Villas, Hove. P.O. Box 2001, Hove, BN3 4HY. ☎ 01273 747722.
Joint Kashrut Board. ☎ 01273 739670.
Sussex Jewish News, P.O. Box 2178, Hove BN1 5NX. ☎ 01273 330550. Fax 01273 504455. Email doris@sussexjewishnews.freeserve.co.uk.
Brighton & Hove Hebrew Congregation (Reg. Charity No. 233221).
Synagogues: 31 New Church Road, Hove BN3 4AD and 66 Middle Street, BN1 1AL. *M.* Rabbi P. Efune; *Hon. Sexton* B. Goldberg. ☎ 01273 601088; *Admin.* Rachel Cohen. ☎ 01273 888855. Fax 01273 888810. Email bhhc@breathemail.net.

Mikva, Prince Regent Swimming Complex. ☎ 01273 685692.

Hove Hebrew Congregation, 79 Holland Road, Hove. *M.* Rabbi V. Silverman. ☎ 01273 732035.

Brighton & Hove New Synagogue (Reform, Est. 1955, Constituent of RSGB), Palmeira Avenue, Hove, BN3 3GE. ☎ 01273 735343. *Chairman* A. Lewis; *M.* Rabbi D. Meyer.

J.A.C.S. meet every Wednesday at 2pm at the Ajex Hall of the New Synagogue. ☎ 01273 774037.

Brighton & Hove Progressive Synagogue (ULPS), (Est. 1935). 6 Lansdowne Road, Hove, BN3 1FF. ☎ 01273 737223. *M.*; *H. Sec.* Mandy Randell-Gavin.

Brighton and Hove Jewish Housing Association. ☎ 01273 207328.

Brighton & Hove Jewish Centre (Reg. Charity No. 269474) (incorporating Brighton and Hove Maccabi, B.B.Y.O.; Ralli Hall Amateur Theatrical Society; New Ralli Bridge Club and Jewish Community Art Society), Ralli Hall, 81 Denmark Villas, Hove BN3 3TH. ☎ 01273 202254. *Admin.* Norina Duke; *Chairman* Roger Abrahams. Meeting centre for various senior citizens clubs and youth clubs. Facilities include snooker room, work-out gym, library/reading room, cafeteria, etc. Kosher kitchen (lunch available on Thursdays).

Ajex. *Contact* Aubrey Cole. ☎ 01273 737417.

Ben Gurion University Foundation. *Contact* Godfrey Gould. ☎ 01273 419412.

B&H Arts Society. *Contact* Audrey Davis, 396 Whittingham Gdns, BN1 6PU.

JIA Ladies Committee. Mrs S. Carlton. ☎ 01273 5522821.

Jewish Welfare Board. ☎ 01273 722523. Est. 1846. *H. T.* G.E. Burkeman.

Lubavitch Foundation. ☎ 01273 321919.

Magen David Adom. Mrs E. Hagard, 53a New Church Rd., Hove.

Torah Academy. Mrs S. Granville, 31 New Church Road ☎ 01273 328675.

Hyman Fine Jewish Home, 20 Burlington Street, BN2 1AU. ☎ 01273 688226. (Jewish Care).

Hillel House, 18 Harrington Road, Brighton BN1 6RE. *Admin.* Mrs A. Lee. ☎ 01273 503450.

Sussex Jewish Continuity (Reg. Charity No. 1069737). *Contact* Doris Levinson. ☎ 01273 747722.

Sussex ORT. *Contact* Estelle Josephs. ☎ 01903 232932.

Sussex Jewish Golfing Society. *Contact* Ivor Richards. ☎ 01273 720366.

Sussex Tikvah (Home for Jewish adults with severe learning difficulties) ☎ 01273 564021. *Chairman* Peter Senker; *Head of House* Mrs C. Nicholls; *Bursar* Mrs M. Bomzer. ☎ 01273 506665.

Youth Aliyah. *Contact* Mrs E. Posner. ☎ 01273 776671.

Centre for German-Jewish Studies at Sussex University, see p.43.

Cemetery: ☎ 01273 606961.

BRISTOL (375)

Bristol was one of the principal Jewish centres of medieval England. Even after the Expulsion from England in 1290 there were occasional Jewish residents or visitors. A community of Marranos lived here during the Tudor period. There had been a Jewish community in the City before 1754 and the original Synagogue opened in 1786. The present building dates from 1871 and was renovated in 1981-83. Polack's House (Clifton College) was founded in 1878. The Progressive Synagogue was founded in 1961 and their present building was consecrated in 1971.

Bristol Jewish Representative Council, *Chairman* M. Romain, 7 College Fields, BS8 3HP. ☎ 0117-973 9312. Email romain@netgates.co.uk. *Sec.* Mrs K. Balint-Kurti, P.O. Box 327, BS9 91NX. ☎ 0117-973 1150.

Synagogues:

Bristol Hebrew Congregation, 9 Park Row BS1 5LP, Rabbi Hillel Simon.

☎ 0117-925 5160. Enq. to Mrs E. Levin. ☎ 0117-9624888. Email evelevin@hotmail.com.

Bristol & West Progressive Jewish Cong (ULPS). (Reg. Charity No. 73879), 43-45 Bannerman Road, Easton BS5 0RR. *M.* Rabbi Hadassah Davis. ☎ 0118-954 3768. Enq. to Mrs R. Baker. ☎ 01179 738744. Email ruth.baker@scl.org;

Bristol University Jewish & Israel Soc., c/o Hillel House.

Hillel House, 45 Oakfield Road, Clifton, BS8 2BA. ☎ 0117-946 6589. Accommodation enquiries: Mrs S. Tobias, ☎ 01454 412831.

Davar, The Jewish Institute in Bristol, cultural and educational organisation aims to encourage Jewish identity with the widest possible spectrum. ☎ 0117-970 6594. 1-3, Percival Rd., Clifton BS8 3LF. *Admin.* Vena Bunker.

Polack's House, Clifton College, Housemaster, Mr Jo Greenbury. ☎ 0117-315370. Email jgreenbury@cliftoncollege.avon.sch.uk.

Cemetery: Oakdene Avenue, Fishponds, Bristol BS5 6QQ.

CAMBRIDGE (resident Jewish pop. approx 500, students 500)

The present congregation was founded in 1888 but an organised community was present from 1774. The synagogue in Thompson's Lane was opened in 1937. Services held there are traditionally orthodox; the building serves also as a student centre.

Cambridge Traditional Jewish Congregation (Est. 1937. Reg. Charity No. 282849), 3 Thompson's Lane, CB5 8AQ. ☎ 01223-501916. *Chairman* Dr Simon Goldhill, 21 Guest Rd., CB3. ☎ 01223 365680. Email sdg1001@hermes.cam.ac.uk.

Mikvah Committee (Reg. Charity No. 1067075). Enquiries to Mrs C. Klein, c/o The Synagogue.

Beth Shalom Reform Synagogue (RSGB), services and cheder and adult education programme. *Chairman* Ellis Weinberger. P.O. Box 756, Cambridge CB5 9WB. Email info@beth-shalom.org.uk; Website www.beth-shalom.org.uk.

Cambridge Jewish Residents' Association (Est. 1940). ☎ 01223-352963. Provides religious, cultural, educational and welfare facilities for its members.

Cambridge University Jewish Society (Est. 1937). ☎ 01223-701646. Email soc-cujs@lists.com.ac.uk. Website www.cam.ac.uk/societies/cujs/. Organises orthodox services at the synagogue during term time. Kosher meals available. *Student Chaplain* Rabbi Julian Sinclair.

CANTERBURY & DISTRICT (100)

The history of the Canterbury community, 'The Jews of Canterbury, 1760–1931' by Dan Cohn-Sherbok, was published in 1984.

Jewish Community includes members in the whole of East Kent. Regular monthly programme. *Chairman* V. Simmons, 51 Yew Tree Gardens, Birchington, CT7 9AL; *H. Sec.* Miss P. Brown. There are a number of Jewish students at Kent University.

CHATHAM (ca. 50)

There was an organised Jewish community in Chatham from the first half of the eighteenth century. The present syn., erected in 1869 in memory of Captain Lazarus Simon Magnus, by his father, Simon Magnus, is on the site of its predecessor, erected about 1740. A Centenary Hall and Mid-Kent Jewish Youth Centre was consecrated in 1972. The old cemetery, dating back to about 1790, is behind the syn.

Chatham Memorial Synagogue, 366 High Street, Rochester. Inquiries: Dr C. Harris, Sutton Place, Sutton Road Maidstone, Kent ME15 9DU. ☎ 01622 753040.

CHELMSFORD (145)

Jewish Community (Reg. Charity No. 281498), Graphic Impressions, Merlin

House, 23 Parker Road, CM2 0ES. ☎ 01245-475444. Email info@jewishcommunitychelmsford.co.uk; Website www.jewishcommunitychelmsford.co.uk. The community, est. in 1974, holds regular services, religion classes and social activities. It has burial arrangements through the Joint Jewish Burial Society.

CHELTENHAM (90)

The congregation was est. in 1824 and the present syn. in St. James's Sq. opened in 1839, furnished with fittings from the New Synagogue, Leadenhall Street (1761), which relocated to Great St Helen's in 1837, thus endowing the Cheltenham community with the oldest extant Ashkenazi furniture in the country. 'The History of the Hebrew Community of Cheltenham, Gloucester and Stroud', by Brian Torode, was reprinted in 1999. After two generations, the cong. dwindled and the syn. closed in 1903. Refugees from Central Europe and evacuated children and others from Jewish centres in England, however, formed a new community and a cong. was re-formed in 1939 and the old syn. reopened. The cemetery, dating from 1824, is in Elm St.

Hebrew Congregation, St. James's Sq. (Reg. Charity No. 261470-R). *H. Sec.* A. Silverston, 7 Loweswater Rd., GL51 5AZ. ☎ 01242-242724.

CHESTER (35)

Hebrew Congregation, Ian and Lesley Daniels, Porthouse, 6 South Crescent Rd, Queens Park, CH4 7AU. ☎ 01244 677776.

COLCHESTER (100)

Colchester and District Jewish Community (Reg. Charity No. 237240), Synagogue, Fennings Chase, Priory St., CO1 2QG. The community has close links with the University of Essex at Colchester. For information about services, Cheder and social events please contact the Hon. Secretary, Mrs N. B. Stevenson, ☎ 01206 545992.

COVENTRY (140)

There were Jews settled in Coventry in 1775, if not earlier, and by the beginning of the nineteenth century there was a relatively large community.

Synagogue, Barras Lane. (Cons. 1870) ☎ (02476) 220168. *H. Sec.* L. R. Benjamin, 25 Hathaway Drive, Warwick CV34 5RD. ☎ 01926 747691. Email laurence.benjamin@ntlworld.com.

Reform Community, *Chairman* Dr M. Been, 24 Nightingale Lane, Canley Gardens, CV6 6AY. ☎ 024 7662027.

CRAWLEY (ca. 50)

Progressive Jewish Community (ULPS). (Est. 1959.) *H. Sec.* Mrs L. Bloom, c/o Tanyard Farmhouse, Lansholt, Horley, Surrey RH6 9LN.

DARLINGTON (40)

Hebrew Congregation (RSGB), Bloomfield Road (Est. 1904.) *Sec.* M. Craster, 25 Mayfield, Uplands Road, DL3 7TU; *Chairman* P. Freitag, 237 Parkside, DL1 5TG. ☎ 01325-468812.

Cemetery: Contained in a consecrated section of: The West Cemetery, Carmel Road, Darlington.

EAST GRINSTEAD AND DISTRICT (35)

Jewish Community (Reg. Charity No. 288189). (Est. 1978). *H. M.* Rev. M. Weisman, M.A.; *Warden* E. Godfrey, 7 Jefferies Way, Crowborough, Sussex TN6 2UH. ☎ 01892 653949. Corr: Mrs M. Beevor, 6 Court Close, East Grinstead, West Sussex RH19 3YQ. ☎ 01342 312148.

EASTBOURNE (63)

Hebrew Congregation, 22 Susans Road, BN21 3TJ; *H. Sec.* ☎ 01323 640441.

Cemetery: Eastbourne Borough Cemetery has a part set aside for the comm. in conjunction with the Brighton Chevra Kedusha.

EXETER (150)

Before the expulsion, Exeter was an important Jewish centre. The syn. off Mary Arches St. was built in 1763, and the cemetery in Magdalen Road dates from 1757, but Jews are known to have lived in Exeter 30 years earlier and the com. is said to have been founded as early as 1728. The community greatly decreased during the 19th century, but has revived in recent years. Ring for dates of monthly Shabbat services. Synagogue ☎ 01392 251529.

Hebrew Congregation (Reg. Charity No.20929). Synagogue, Synagogue Place, Mary Arches St., EX4 3BA. ☎ 01392 251529. Email exeshul@eclipse.co.uk; Website www.eclipse.co.uk/exeshul. *President* Frank Gent. ☎ 01392 251529.

GATESHEAD (1,400)

Synagogue, 180 Bewick Road, NE8. ☎ 0191 4770111 (Mikva. ☎ 0191-477 3552). *Rab.* Rabbi B. Rakow, 138 Whitehall Road, NE8. ☎ 0191-477 3012; *Senior Warden.*

Kolel Synagogue, 22 Claremont Place, NE8 1TL. (Constituent of the Union of Orthodox Hebrew Congregations.) *Sec.* S. Ehrentreu. ☎ 0191-477 2189.

Beis Hatalmud, 1 Ashgrove Tce., NE8. *Princ.* Rabbi S. Steinhouse. ☎ 0191-478 4352.

Beth Midrash Lemoroth, 50 Bewick Road, NE8. (Teachers Training College for Girls.) ☎ 0191-477 2620. *Princ.* Rabbi M. Miller. *H. T.* M. Pearlman.

Institute for Higher Rabbinical Studies (Kolel Harabbonim), 22 Claremont Place, NE8 ITL. ☎ 0191-477 2189. *Sec.* S. Ehrentreu.

Sunderland Talmudical College and Yeshiva, Prince Consort Road, NE3 4DS. ☎ 0191-490 0195 (Off.); 0191-490 0193 (Students). *Princ.* Rabbi J. Ehrentreu.

Sunderland Kolel – Institute for Higher Rabbinical Studies, 139 Prince Consort Rd., NE8 1LR. ☎ 0191-477 5690. *Princ.*

Yeshiva, 88 Windermere Street, 8. ☎ 0191-478 5210 and 477 2616. Students, 179 Bewick Road ☎ 0191-477 1646. *Sec.* S. Esofsky

Yeshive Lezeirim, 36 Gladstone Tce., NE8 1RP. (Reg. Charity No. 514963). *Princ.* Rabbi E. Jaffe. ☎ 0191-477 0744. Email yltuk@yahoo.co.uk.

Gateshead Girls High School, 6 Gladstone Tce., NE8 4DU. ☎ 0191-477 3471. *Princ.* Rabbi D. Bowden; *Sec.* Mrs R. Dunner.

Jewish Boarding School (Boys, aged 10-16), 36-38 Gladstone Terr. (Union of Orthodox Hebrew Congregations.) *Princ.* Rabbi N. Lieberman; *Sec.* J. Salomon. ☎ 0191-477 1431 & 477 2066 (Students).

Jewish Primary School, 18 Gladstone Terr., NE8 4EA. (Reg. Charity No. 527372). ☎ 0191-477 2154. Fax 0191-478 7554. *Princ.*; *H. Sec.* Mrs C. Rabinowitz.

Ohel Rivka Kindergarten, Alexandra Road, NE8. ☎ 0191-478 3723; *H. Sec.* Mrs Esofsky, 13 Grasmere St. ☎ 0191-477 4102.

GRIMSBY (40)

There are records of Jews living here prior to 1290 and a community of sorts existed in the early 1800s. Mass immigration from eastern Europe, when Grimsby, like so many east coast ports, was the first landfall for these 'escapees' from persecution, saw many passing through *en route* for the larger northern cities and even further onward to Canada and the United States but a fair number remained, and a proper community was created. The synagogue and cemetery were consecrated in 1885. The community reached its numerical peak in the 1930s, when it numbered between 450/500, but its gradual decline began in the immediate post-war years. The history of the community has been published: D. and L. Gerlis, 'The Story of the Grimsby Jewish Community', 1986. Regular services are held every Friday evening at 7.00pm, and also on all the major festivals and holidays.

Sir Moses Montefiore Synagogue, Holme Hill, Heneage Road, DN32 9DZ. *President* L. Solomon; *T.* H. S. Kalson; *H. Sec.* B. Greenberg, 21 Abbey Park Road, DN32 0HJ. ☎ 01472 351404.

Cemetery: (Chevra Kadisha) First Avenue, Nunsthorpe, Grimsby. *Sec.* B. Greenberg; *T.* H. Kalson, 12A Welholme Avenue, DN32 0HP.

GUILDFORD (100)

Synagogue (1979), York Road, GU1 4DR. The community has grown up since the Second World War. Regular services; Cheder and social activities. *Chairman* Dr S. Cornbleet. ☎ 01483 575787; *Sec.* Mrs B. Gould. ☎ 01483 576470.

University of Surrey Jewish Society, c/o Professor R. Spier. ☎ 01483 259265.
Cemetery: Consecrated section of municipal cemetery.

HARLOW (190)

Jewish Community, Harberts Road, Hare St, CM19 4DT. ☎ 01279-432503. (A Constituent of R.S.G.B.) *President* E. Clayman; *Vice-President* C. Jackson; *Chairman* Mrs C. Peter ☎ 01992-465482; *M.* Rabbi M. Pertz; *Sec.* Mrs H. Reeves.

HARROGATE (150)

'The History of the Harrogate Jewish Community' by Rosalyn Livshin was published in 1995.

Hebrew Congregation, St. Mary's Walk, HG2 0LW. (Est. 1918.) *President* Leslie Fox ☎ 01423 523439. Email miznerfox@ntlworld.com; *Sec.* P.E. Morris. ☎ 01423 871713. Email philip.morris@ukgateway.net.

Zionist Group. *Chairman* Anita Royston. ☎ 01423 561188.

HASTINGS (33)

Hastings and District Jewish Society (Reg. Charity No. 273806). Regular meetings of the Society including a short service are held on the first Friday of the month in Bexhill, at 7 p.m. *H. Sec.* A. Ross, P.O. Box 74, Bexhill-on-Sea, East Sussex TN39 4ZZ. ☎ 01424-848344.

HEMEL HEMPSTEAD (270)

Hebrew Congregation (affiliated to U.S.) Est. 1956. Synagogue, Lady Sarah Cohen Community Centre, Midland Road, Hemel Hempstead, Herts. HD1 1RP. *H. Sec.* H. Nathan. ☎ 01923 32007.

Morton House, Midland Road, HP2 5BH (Jewish Care residential home).

HEREFORD

Hereford Jewish Community (Associate Community of ULPS). Enquiries to Josephine Woolfson. ☎ 01432 271678.

HIGH WYCOMBE (35)

Hebrew Congregation (affiliated to the U.S.). *H. Sec.* Mrs R. Weiss, 33 Hampden Road, High Wycombe, Bucks. HP13 6SZ. ☎ 01494 529821.

HOVE (see Brighton & Hove)

HITCHIN

Yeshivas Toras Chessed, Wellbury House, Great Offley, Hitchin, Herts. *Rab.* A. S. Stern. ☎ 01462 768698.

HULL (650)

In Hull, as in other English ports, a Jewish community was formed earlier than in the neighbouring inland towns. The exact date is unknown, but as a Catholic chapel, damaged in the riots of 1780, was acquired as a syn., the formal constitution of a community was probably about that date. In 1810 a cemetery had been in existence some years. Hull was then the principal port of entry from Northern Europe and most of the Jewish immigrants came through it. In 1851 the Jewish community numbered about 200. Both the old syn. in Osborne St. and the Central Syn., in Cogan St. were destroyed in air raids during the Second World War.

Jewish Representative Council. *President* Prof. J. Friend, 9 Allanhall Way, Kirkella, HU10 7QU. ☎ 01482 658930; *H. Sec.* Mrs A. Segelman, 251 Beverley Road, Kirkella, HU10 7AG. ☎ 01482 650288.

SYNAGOGUES

Hull Hebrew Congregation, 30 Pryme Street, Anlaby HU10 6SH. *H. Sec.* S. Pearlman. ☎ 01482 653242.

Reform Synagogue (Constituent of R.S.G.B.), Great Gutter Lane, Willerby HU10 7JT. *H. Sec.* Mrs G. Barker, The Cherries, Temple Close, Welton, Brough, East Yorks HU15 1NX. ☎ 01482 665375.

OTHER INSTITUTIONS

Hull Jewish Community Care. (Est. 1880.) *H. Sec.* V. Appleson, 1 Tranby Ride, Anlaby, HU10 7ED. ☎ 01482 653018.

Hillel House, 18 Auckland Avenue HU6 7SG. ☎ 01482 48196. Enquiries to: *H. Sec.* I. Dysch, 1000 Anlaby High Road, HU4 6AT. ☎ 01482 354947.

Talmud Torah, 30 Pryme St., Anlaby, HU10 6SH. *H. Sec.* Mrs. D. Levine, 104 Beverley Rd., Kirkella HU10 7HA. ☎ 01482-657188.

University Jewish Students' Society, c/o Hillel House. ☎ 01482 48196.

Board of Shechita, *H. Sec.* Dr C. Rosen, c/o Hebrew Congregation.

LEAMINGTON & DISTRICT (132)

Progressive Jewish Group. (A branch of the Progressive Synagogue Birmingham, ULPS.) Inq. ☎ 01926 421300.

LEEDS (9,000)

Leeds has the third largest Jewish community in Britain. Jews have lived in Leeds at least from the middle of the eighteenth century, but it was only in 1840 that a Jewish cemetery was acquired. The first so-called synagogue was a converted room in Bridge Street, where services were held up to 1846. Thereafter the place of worship was transferred to the Back Rockingham Street Synagogue, which was replaced by the Belgrave Street Synagogue built in 1860. Another syn. was built in 1877, but this closed in 1983.

The Leeds Jewish community is mainly the product of the persecution of Russian Jewry in the latter half of the nineteenth century. The bulk of immigration settled in Leeds between 1881 and 1905, enhancing the growth of the clothing industry which developed from the woollen and worsted manufacturing in the West Riding of Yorkshire. This industry was made world famous by John Barran, a non-Jew, and his Jewish associate Herman Friend, who was responsible for introducing division of labour into the clothing industry. While the sweating system existed in Leeds, both wages and working conditions were better than in London or Manchester. Trade unionism was successful and the first recorded strike by Jewish industrial workers took place spontaneously in Leeds in 1885.

During the early decades of this century the old Leylands ghetto, where most of the immigrants lived, began to break up. The main move of the Jewish people was to northern districts of Leeds, first to Chapeltown, which flourished in the 1940s, and then to the Moortown and Alwoodley suburbs. The Leeds Rep. C. republished in 1985 the late Louis Saipe's 'A History of the Jews of Leeds'.

Today this well-organised strong community of approx. 9,000 provides for Leeds Jews with over 100 organisations which are affiliated to the Leeds Jewish Representative Council, the official spokesman of the Leeds Jewish community.

GENERAL ORGANISATIONS

Jewish Representative Council, Shadwell La. Synagogue, 151 Shadwell La., LS17 8DW. ☎ 0113 2697520. Fax 0113 2370851. Nearly every synagogue, charitable organisation, social and cultural instititution and Zionist Soc. is affiliated to this council and on its exec. cttee. serve ex-officio all local Jewish magistrates, public reps. and BoD members. *President* Mr Ian J. Goldman; *V. Presidents* Hillary Miller, JP, Sue Baker, JP; *T.* Sue Dorsey; *Hon. Sec.* Robert Bartfield; *Exec. Off.* Michele Jackson.

A.J.E.X. *Chairman* Stanley Graham; *H. Sec.* Leonard Cohen, 76 The Avenue, LS17 7NZ.

Beth Din, Etz Chaim Synagogue, 411 Harrogate Rd., LS17 7TT. ☎/Fax 0113 2370893. *M.* Dayan Y. Refson; Rev. A. Gilbert, B.A.

Community Shaliach, 411 Harrogate Rd., LS17 7TT. ☎ 0113 2680899. Fax 0113 2668419.

JNF and Zionist Council, 411 Harrogate Rd., LS17 7BY. ☎ 0113 2371951. Fax 0113 2370568. *District org.* S. Cohen.

Kashrut Authority, 151 Shadwell Lane, LS17 8DW. ☎ 0113 2697520. Fax 0113 2370851.

Leeds Emunah Council. *Co-ordinator* Mrs M. Gray, 4 Belvedere Court, LS17 8NF. ☎ 0113 266 1902.

Mikvah, 411 Harrogate Road, LS17 7BY. ☎ 0113 2371096 (answer machine).

UJIA Office, Balfour House, 299 Street La., LS17 6HQ. ☎ 0113 2693136. Fax 0113 2693961.

Women's Zionist Council (Wizo), 411 Harrogate Rd., LS17 7BY. ☎ 0113 2684773. *Chairman* Mrs L. Jacoby.

Yorkshire Israel Office, 411 Harrogate Rd., LS17 7TT. ☎ 0113 2680899. Fax 0113 2688419.

SYNAGOGUES

Beth Hamedrash Hagadol Synagogue, 399 Street Lane, LS17 6HQ. (Est. 1874.) *M.* Rabbi D. Sedley; *R.* D. Apfel; *Exec. Off.* Mrs J. Schlesinger. ☎ 0113 2692181.

Chassidishe Synagogue (Est. 1897), c/o Donisthorpe Hall, Shadwell Lane, LS17 6AW. All enq. to J. Lewis, 4 Well House Rd., LS8 4BS.

Etz Chaim Synagogue, 411 Harrogate Road, LS17 7TT. *Rab.* Rabbi Y. Angyalfi; *R.* Rev. A. Gilbert; *Sec.* Sandhill Pde., 584 Harrogate Road, LS17 7DP ☎ 0113 2662214. Fax 0113 2371183.

Masorti, *Contact* M. Berwin ☎ 0113 2685605.

Queenshill Synagogue, 26 Queenshill Avenue, LS17 6AX.

Shomrei Hadass Congregation, 368 Harrogate Road, LS17 6QB. ☎ 0113 2681461. *M.* Dayan Y. Refson.

Sinai Synagogue, Roman Avenue, Street Lane, LS8 2AN. ☎ 0113 2665256. (A Constituent of R.S.G.B.) (Est. 1944.) *M.* Rabbi I. Morris; *H. Sec.* Mrs P. Mason. Mon-Fri 9.30am-2pm.

United Hebrew Congregation (Reg. Charity No. 515316) 151 Shadwell La., LS17 8DW. ☎ 0113-269 6141. Fax 0113-237 0851. *M.* Rabbi D. Levy. ☎ 0113-237 0852; *R.* Rev. H. Miller; *Admin.* Mrs C. Tolkin.

Cemeteries: For information refer to the Representative Council as above.

CULTURAL AND EDUCATIONAL ORGANISATIONS

B'nai B'rith Lodge of Leeds. *President* D. Levy. ☎ 0113 2686247.

Brodetsky Jewish Primary School, Primley Park Rd., LS17 7HR. *H. M.* Mrs R. Raphael, BEd. Primary School ☎ 0113 2930578; Nursery School and Play Group, George Lyttleton Centre, LS17 7HR. ☎ 0113 2930579

Jewish Education Board (Talmud Torah), 2 Sandhill La., LS17 6AQ. (Est. 1879.) Houses the Talmud Torah classes. Administers Jewish Assemblies for pupils attending State schools. ☎ 0113 2172533. *H. T.* Mrs Sharon Saffer.

Jewish Education Bureau, 8 Westcombe Avenue, LS8. ☎ 0113 663613. Provides information and materials on all aspects of Judaism to non-Jewish educationalists and clergy. *Dir.* Rabbi D. S. Charing. ☎ 0870-8008 JEB (532). Fax 0870-800 8533. 'Ask the Rabbi' 0906-690 3042 (premium line). Email jewishedbreau @easicom.com.

Jewish Day Schools' Administrative Office, George Lyttleton Centre, Wentworth Avenue, LS17 7TN. *Admin.* Mrs A. Grant. ☎ 0113 2693176.

Jewish Historical Society (Branch). *President* His Honour Judge John Altman; *H. Sec.* Mrs A. Buxbaum, 17 Pepper Hills, Harrogate Rd., LS17 8EJ. ☎ 0113 2665641.

Jewish Students' Association, Hillel House, 2 Springfield Mount, LS2 9NE. ☎ 0113 2433211. (Est. 1912.) *Sec.*, c/o Leeds University Union, LS2.

Leeds Council of Christians and Jews (Reg. Charity No. 238005), *Chairman* A.M. Conway, ☎ 0113 2680444; *H. Secs* Rabbi Morris, Mrs S. Crowther ☎ 0113 2561407.

Leeds Jewish Dental Society. *Sec.* Paul H. Leslie, 16 High Ash Ave., LS17 8RG. ☎ 0113-2694510.

Leeds Jewish Youth Service, 2 Sand Hill Lane, LS17 6AQ. ☎ 0113 2172531.

Leeds University Library, Judaica collections (see p.55).

Limelight Drama Group. *Chairman* Harry Venet. ☎ 0113 2250651.

Maccabi Sports and Social Centre, 393 Street Lane, LS17 6HQ. ☎ 0113 2693381. *Manager* R.A. Ross.

Makor–Jewish Resource Centre and Israel Information Centre (JPMP), 411 Harrogate Rd., LS17 7TT. ☎ 0113 2680899. *Sec.*

Menorah School, 2 Sandhill Lane, Leeds LS17 6AQW.

Porton Collection, Central Library, LS1 3AB (see p.59). ☎ 0113 2462016

Reform Hebrew Classes, Sinai Synagogue, 22 Roman Avenue, LS8 2AN. ☎ 0113 2665256.

S.E.E.D. Project. Contact: Rabbi Y. Angyalfi, ☎ 0113 2663311.

WELFARE ORGANISATIONS

Chaplaincy Board–Yorkshire & Humberside, 17 Queens Road, LS6 1NY. ☎ 0113 2789597. *Hon. Chairman* M. Sender. ☎ 0113-2680048.

Chevra Kadisha. Leeds Joint: *Chairmen* L. Burton, Mrs S. Myerson; *Org.* I. Baum. ☎ 0113 2955748; *Corr.* Susan Cohen, 7 Sandhill Grove, LS17. ☎ 0113 2693815.

Chevra Kadisha: Reform. Convenors Rabbi Morris, Maxine Brown ☎ 0113 2683526

Jewish Day Centre, 26 Queenshill Avenue, LS17 6AX. ☎ 0113 2692018. *Chairman* Angela Frieze; *Man.* Naomi Chaplin. ☎ 0113 2692018.

Jewish Welfare Board, 311 Stonegate Road, LS17 6AZ. ☎ 0113 2684211. Fax 0113 2664754. *President* R. Manning; *Chief Exec.* Ms. S. Saunders.

Miyad Helpline. ☎ 08457 581999.

Residential Nursing Home for the Jewish Elderly, Donisthorpe Hall, Shadwell Lane, LS17 6AW. (Est. 1923.) ☎ 0113 2684248. *Gen. Man.* Carol Whitehead.

Chessed, hospital meals and visitation. *Co-ord.* Helene Clarke ☎ 0113 2370269.

LEICESTER (670)

There have been Jewish communities in Leicester since the Middle Ages, but the first record of a Jews' Synagogue appears in the 1861 Leicester Directory and the first marriages were consecrated in 1875. The present syn. dates from 1897.

Synagogue, Highfield St. *M.* Rabbi S. Pink. ☎ 0116 2706622. *H. Sec.* G. D. Kramer. ☎ 01858 440022.

Mikva, Synagogue building, Highfield St.

Communal Centre, Highfield St. ☎ 0116 2540477.

Shalom Club for Sr. Citizens. ☎ 0116 2540477.

Jewish Library, Communal Centre, Highfield St.

Ladies' Guild. *Chairman* Mrs H. Reggel, 22 Sackville Gardens, ☎ 0116 270 9687.

Jewish Students' Society, c/o The Union, Leicester University.

Maccabi Association, Communal Centre, Highfield St. ☎ 0116 2540477.

Leicester Progressive Jewish Synagogue (ULPS). (Est. 1950) 24 Avenue Rd. *M.* Rabbi E. Sarah; *H. Sec.* J. Kaufman, ☎ 01162-715584. Fax 01162-717571.

Cemeteries: Leicester Hebrew Cong. uses a section of the Gilroes Cemetery, Groby Road. The Progressive congregation uses a section of the Loughborough Municipal C.

LINCOLN

Lincolnshire Jewish Community (Associate Community of ULPS). Enquiries to the Secretary, Dr Karen Genard ☎ 01469 588951.

LIVERPOOL (3,000)

Liverpool, for centuries an important port, first for Ireland, later also for America, had a natural attraction for Jews looking for a place in which to start their new lives. There is evidence of an organised community before 1750. It appears to have had a burial ground attached. Little is known of this early community. It declined but about 1770 was reinforced by a new wave of settlers chiefly from Europe, who worshipped in a house in Frederick Street, near the river front, with a Mikva and a cemetery. In 1807 a synagogue of some size was built in Seel Street, the parent of the present syn. in Princes Road, one of the handsomest in the country. At this time Liverpool was already one of the four leading regional coms. The site for the Seel St. Synagogue was a gift of the Liverpool Corporation.

Merseyside Jewish Representative Council (Reg. Charity No. 1039809). *President* Mrs E. Morron; *Chair of Council* Mrs N.S. Kingston; *H. Sec.* Shifrin House, 433 Smithdown Road, L15 3JL. ☎ 0151-733 2292. Fax 0151-734 0212. Email mjrcshifrin@hotmail.com. *Communal Archivist* J.Wolfman, MA.

Liverpool Kashrut Commission, c/o 433 Smithdown Road, L15 3JL. ☎ 0151-733 2292. Fax 0151-734 0212. *Rab.* Rabbi L. Cofnas.

Mikva. Childwall Synagogue. *Chairman* Rabbi L. Cofnas. ☎ 0151-722 2079.

SYNAGOGUES

Old Hebrew Congregation, Princes Road, L8. ☎ 0151-709 3431 (Congregation founded c. 1740; Synagogue consecrated 1874.) *M.* Rabbi A. Abel; *Sec.* Mrs P. Nevitt.

Allerton Hebrew Congregation, Mather Avenue, L18. ☎ 0151-427 6848. *Emer. Rabbi* M. Malits, MA, MBE; *M.* Rabbi D. Golomb; *Admin.* P. Fisher.

Childwall Synagogue, Dunbabin Road, L15. ☎ 0151-722 2079. (Est. 1935; consecrated 1938.) Rabbi L. Cofnas; *Admin.* Mrs A. Reuben.

Greenbank Drive Synagogue. (Incorporating Hope Pl. and Sefton Park Hebrew Congregations.) (Est. 1836. Syn. consecrated 1937.) ☎ 0151-733 1417. *M.* Rabbi A. Balkany; *Sec.*

Progressive Synagogue (ULPS), 28 Church Road North, L15 6TF. ☎ 0151-733 5871. (Est. 1929. Affiliated to U.L.P.S.) *M.* Rabbi N. Zalud; *H. Sec.* Ruth Stephenson-Tobin. ☎ 0151-733 5871.

Cemeteries: Liverpool Jewish Cemeteries: Springwood; Lowerhouse Lane; Broad Green; Long Lane.

CULTURAL AND EDUCATIONAL ORGANISATIONS

Adult Jewish Education Committee. Mr. E. Rosen. ☎ 0151-475 5671.

Community Centre (Harold House), Dunbabin Road, L15 6XL. ☎ 0151-475 5825.

Crosby Jewish Literary Society. *H. Secs.* Mrs C. Hoddes, Mrs Y. Mendick. ☎ 0151 924 1795.

Hillel House, 12 Greenbank Dr, L17 1AW. ☎ 0151-735 0793. Applications to: ☎ 0151-280 0551; *Chaplain* Rabbi Y.Y. Rubinstein. ☎ 0161-721 4066.

Jewish Bookshop, *Chairman* M. Turner. Open at Youth and Community Centre, Sundays 11-1.

Jewish Historical Society (Branch). *Chairman* A. Lewis, 61 Menlove Ave., L18 2EH.

Jewish Youth Centre, Dunbabin Road, L15 6XL. ☎ 0151-475 5671.

King David Foundation, 433 Smithdown Road, L15 3JL. ☎ 0151-733 2292. Fax 0151-734 0212. *President* G. Abrams; *Clerk* Mrs N. Sneeden.

King David High School, Childwall Road, L15 6UZ. ☎ 0151-722 7496. Clerk to Govs. 433 Smithdown Road, L15 3JL. ☎ 0151-733 2292. Fax 0151-734 0212. *H. T.* J. Smartt, B.Ed., Cert Ed.

King David Kindergarten, Community Centre, Dunbabin Road, L15 6XL. *Teachers-in-charge*. ☎ 0151-475 5661.

King David Primary School, Beauclair Drive, L15 6XH. ☎ 0151-722 3372. Clerk to Govs. 433 Smithdown Road, L15 3JL. ☎ 0151-733 2292. Fax 0151-734 0212; *H. T.* Mrs E. Spencer, Cert.Ed.

Liverpool Jewish Resource Centre, Harold House, Dunbabin Road L15 6XL. ☎ 0151-722 3514. Fax 0151-475 2212. Sundays 11-1, Mon.-Thurs. 1-5pm. *Admin.* Mrs A. Lewis.

Liverpool Yeshivah, Childwall Synagogue, Dunbabin Road, L15. *Rosh Yeshiva* Rabbi M. L. Cofnas.

Merseyside Amalgamated Talmud Torah, King David Primary School. *Chairman* Mrs J. Bennett.

Midrasha for Girls, c/o Childwall Synagogue, Dunbabin Road, L15.

University Jewish Students' Society, c/o Students' Union, Bedford Street, 7.

WELFARE ORGANISATIONS

Jewish Community Care. (Est. 1875.) *Chief Exec.* Mrs L. Dolan, 433 Smithdown Road, L15 3JL. ☎ 0151-733 2292. Fax 0151-734 0212.

Jewish Women's Aid Society. *H. Sec.* Mrs S. Gore, 433 Smithdown Road, L15 3JL.

Stapely Residential Home for Aged Jews, North Mossley Hill Road, L18. Admin. ☎ 0151-724 3260 (Adm.), 0151-724 4548 (Hosp. wing).

LUTON & DUNSTABLE & DISTRICT (550)

Luton Hebrew Congregation Synagogue, Postal address: P.O. Box No. 215, LU1 1HW. ☎ 01582 725032.

Bedfordshire Progressive Synagogue (ULPS), c/o David Corfan, 39 Broadacres, Bushmead LU2 7FY. ☎ 01234-218387. Email bedsps@onebox.com; Website www.bedfordshire-ps.org.uk. *Sec.* Hilary Fox.

MAIDENHEAD (1,480)

Synagogue, Grenfell Lodge, Ray Park Rd., SL6 8QX. ☎ 01628 673012. (A Constituent of R.S.G.B.). *M.* Rabbi Dr J. A. Romain. ☎ 01628 671058.

Cemetery: Braywick Cemetery, Maidenhead.

MAIDSTONE

Kent Liberal Jewish Community. Enquiries to Dinah Binstead ☎ 01732 461994.

MANCHESTER (30,000)

The Manchester community of nearly 30,000 Jews is the second largest in the U.K. and, in contrast to other communities outside London, is still growing. In 1865 there were 4,500. The rapid and great increase came between 1883 and 1905, a consequence of the intensified persecution of the Jews in Russia.

Newcomers to England in the eighteenth century were encouraged by their co-religionists in London to go farther afield. This they did, generally financed by their longer-settled fellow-Jews in London, as pedlars along the countryside. As these newcomers prospered they settled in the ports, on their part sending out a wave of later arrivals similarly supplied with small stocks to peddle them in the inland towns and villages. This new wave also ultimately settled down, but for the most part in the interior of the country. Thus was laid the foundation of the Jewish community of Manchester.

The middle of the 1780s saw the first signs of an organized community, when two pedlar brothers, Jacob and Lemon Nathan, opened small shops in the centre of Manchester. In 1794 a plot for Jewish burials was rented just outside the city, and in 1796 a large warehouse was hired for public worship. This period coincided with Manchester's development as a major centre of industry and commerce, and Manchester Jewry steadily increased in number, attracting many enterprising settlers, including merchants and men of substance from the European mainland. Among these was Nathan Mayer Rothschild, the first of that family to settle in England.

A later influx was from North Africa and the Levant, lands closely connected with the cotton industry of which Manchester was then the centre. This was the origin of the Sephardi community still prominent in Manchester. The last two decades of the nineteenth century saw the mass immigration to Manchester of eastern European Jews, fleeing from poverty and persecution. By the end of the century Manchester had the largest Jewish population in the provinces, reaching a peak of 35,000 just before the First World War. (Acknowledgement to Bill Williams, 'The Making of Manchester Jewry, 1740–1875' (1976).)

GENERAL ORGANISATIONS

Jewish Representative Council of Greater Manchester and Region. The representative body for the Jewish community of Manchester, Salford and the surrounding region including Stoke, Blackpool and St Annes. Constituted of reps from all syns and other orgs, local Jewish MPs and MEPs, local members of the Board of Deputies, magistrates and town councillors. **Offices:** Jewish Cultural Centre, Bury Old Road, M7 4QY. ☎/Fax 0161-720 8721. Email jewishmanchester@anjy.org. *President* D. Arnold. ☎ 0161-773 6222; *V. Presidents* E. Bolchover, L. Rapaport; *H. T.* Dr S. Baigel; *H. Sec.* B. D. Goldstone, L. Jacobs. *Publ.* Year Book; twice-yearly newsletter (RepPresents).

Joseph Mamlock House, 142 Bury Old Road, M8 4HE. ☎ 0161-740 1825. Organisations at this address include:

Zionist Central Council of Greater Manchester. *President* Mrs J. Wolfe. ☎ 0161-740 8835

Jewish Agency Aliyah Dept. ☎ 0161-740 2864.

Jewish National Fund. *Campaign Exec.* Lorraine Palastrand. ☎ 0161-795 7565.

UJIA. *Reg. Dir.* Itzik Shtrosberg. ☎ 0161-740 1825.

WIZO. *Chairman* Beryl Steinberg, Elaine Hamburger. ☎ 0161-740 3367.

Council of Synagogues (Orthodox). *Chairman* S. Lopian; *Sec.* M. Green, c/o Central-North Manch. Syn., Leicester Road, Salford M7 4GP. ☎ 0161-740 4830.

Beth Din, Jewish Cultural Centre. ☎ 0161-740 9711. Fax 0161-721 4249. Dayan I. Berger; Dayan G. Krausz; Dayan O.Y. Westheim; Dayan Y.O. Steiner. *Registrar* Rabbi Y. Brodie, BA (Hons).

Kashrus Authority, Jewish Cultural Centre. ☎ 0161-740 9711. Fax 0161-721 4249. *President* D. Pine; *Admin.* Rabbi Y. Brodie.

Communal Mikva (under Beth Din authority), Broom Holme, Tetlow La., Salford, M7 0BU. ☎ 0161-792 3970.

(Naomi Greenberg) South Manchester Mikva (under Beth Din Authority), Shay Lane, Hale Barns, Altrincham, Cheshire. ☎ 0161-904 8296.

Whitefield Mikveh, Telephone for appointments 0161-796 1054.

Manchester Trades Advisory Council, Jewish Cultural Centre, Bury Old Road, M7 4QY. ☎/Fax 0161-720 8721.

SYNAGOGUES

Adass Yeshurun Synagogue, Cheltenham Cres., Salford, M7 4FE. ☎ 0161-792 0795. *M.* Rabbi J. Wreschner; *H. Sec.* M.R. Goldman. ☎/Fax 0161-740 3935.

Adath Israel Synagogue, Up. Park Road, Salford M7 0HL. (Form. Kahal Chassidim Syn., present building opened in 1957). Inq.: 105 Leicester Road, Salford 7. *Sec.* Rev. S. Simon. ☎ 0161-740 3905.

Bury Hebrew Congregation. Sunnybank Road, Bury, BL9 8ET. ☎ 0161-796 5062. *M.* Rabbi B. Singer; *Admin.* Mrs M. Wilson.

Central-North Manchester Synagogue (merged 1978), Leicester Road, Salford M7 4GP. *M.* Rabbi J. Rubinstein. ☎ 0161-740 7762; *Sec.* M. Green. ☎ 0161-740 4830. (Central Syn. est. 1871; N. Manch. Syn. est. 1899).

Cheetham Hebrew Congregation, 453 Cheetham Hill Road, M8 9PA. ☎ 0161-740 7788. *President* B. M. Stone. *M.* Rabbi Y. Abenson.

Cheshire Reform Congregation, (Reg. Charity No. 234762), Menorah Synagogue, 198 Altrincham Road, M22 4RZ. ☎ 0161-428 7746. (Est. 1964.) (A Constituent of R.S.G.B.). *M.* Rabbi B. Fox, AM, DD; *H. Sec.* D. Rabin.

Damesek Eliezer Synagogue, Prestwich Beth Hamedrash, 74 Kings Road, Prestwich. *M.* Rabbi S. Goldberg. ☎ 0161-798 9298.

Hale and District Hebrew Congregation, Shay Lane, Hale Barns, Cheshire WA15 8PA. ☎ 0161-980 8846. (Est. 1976.) *M.* Rabbi J. Portnoy; *H. Sec.* S. Ferster.

Heaton Park Hebrew Congregation, Ashdown, Middleton Road M8 4JX. *M.* Rev. L. Olsberg, ☎ 0161-740 2767; *Sec.* K.D. Radivan. ☎ 0161-740 4766.

Higher Crumpsall and Higher Broughton Hebrew Congregation, Bury Old Road, Salford, M7 4PX. ☎ 0161-740 1210. *M.* Rabbi A. Saunders, Rev. A. Hillman. ☎ 0161-740 4179; *Admin.* Mrs E. Somers. ☎ 0161-740 8155.

Higher Prestwich Hebrew Congregation, 445 Bury Old Road, Prestwich M25 1QP. ☎ 0161-773 4800. *M.* Rabbi A. Z. Herman; *Sec.* Mrs B. Task.

Hillock Hebrew Congregation, Beverley Close, Ribble Drive, Whitefield, M45. *H. Sec.* R. Walker, 13 Mersey Close, Whitefield, M45 8LB. ☎ 0161-959 5663.

Holy Law South Broughton Congregation, Bury Old Road, Prestwich M25 0EX. ☎ 0161-740 1634. Fax 0161-720 6623. Email office@holylaw.org.uk. (Est. 1865, present building opened 1935, merged with South Broughton Syn., 1978). *M.* Rabbi Y. Chazan. ☎ 0161-792 6349 (Study 0161-721 4705); *Chief Exec.* B. S. Levey; *Burial Bd.* ☎ 0161-740 1634. (D)

Hulme Hebrew Congregation, Hillel House, Greenheys La., M15 6LR.

Kahal Chassidim Synagogue (Lubavitch), 62 Singleton Road, Salford M7 4LU. ☎ 0161-740 3632. *M.* Rabbi A. Jaffe; *Sec.* D. Lipsidge ☎ 0161-740 1629

Lubavitch Foundation (Reg. Charity No. X98704), 62 Singleton Road, Salford M7 4LU. ☎/Fax 0161-720 9514. *M.* Rabbi L. Wineberg.

Machzikei Hadass Communities, 17 Northumberland Street, Salford M7 0FE. ☎ 0161-792 1313. *Rav.* Rav. M. Schneebalg. ☎ 0161-792 3063. *Sec.* A. Vogel. ☎ 0161-792 1313.

Constituent Syn.: Machzikei Hadass. **Mikva:** Sedgley Park Road, Prestwich. ☎ 0161-773 1537/0161-721 4341.

Manchester Great and New Synagogue (and Community Centre) (Est. 1740), 'Stenecourt', Singleton Road, Holden Road, Salford, M7 4LN. *M.* Rev. G. Brodie, 43 Stanley Road, Salford M7 0FR. ☎ 0161-740 2506. Fax 0161-792 1991; *H. Sec.* J. Dover. ☎ 0161-792 8399 (Sun.-Fri, 9.00am-12.00pm). Email orenstein@cwctv.net.

Manchester Reform Synagogue, Jackson's Row, M2 5NH. ☎ 0161-834 0415. (Est. 1856). (A Constituent of R.S.G.B.). The former syn. in Park Pl. was destroyed by enemy action in 1941; present premises occupied since 1953. *M.* Rabbi Dr. R. Silverman; *Sec.* Mrs F. Morris. ☎ 0161-834 0415. Fax 0161-834 0415.

North Salford Synagogue, 2 Vine St., Kersal, Salford M7 0NX. *M.* Rabbi L. W. Rabinowitz. ☎ 0161-740 7958.

Ohel Torah Congregation, 132 Leicester Road, Salford M7 0ES. (Constituent of the Union of Orthodox Hebrew Congregations.) *M.*; *Sec.* D. Spielman. ☎ 0161-740 2568.

Prestwich Hebrew Congregation, Bury New Road, Prestwich M25 9WN. ☎ 0161-773 1978. *M.* Rabbi Y. Landes; *Admin.* A. Frankel.

Sale and District Hebrew Congregation, Hesketh Road, Sale, Cheshire M33 5AA. ☎ 0161-973 3013. *Sec.* C. Michaels ☎ 0161-969 5371.

Sedgley Park Synagogue (Shomrei Hadass), Parkview Road, Prestwich M25 SFA. *Jt.H. Secs.* D. Gordon, S. Baddiel. ☎ 0161-740 0677.

Sephardi Congregation of South Manchester, Shaare Hayim (Reg. Charity No. 1067759), 8 Queenston Road, West Didsbury M20 2WZ. ☎ 0161-445 1943. Fax 0161-438 0571. Email shaarehayim@ukgateway.net. *M.* Rabbi S. Ellituv. ☎ 0161-434 6903. Amalgamated with the former Sha'are Sedek Synagogue.

Sha'arei Shalom, North Manchester Reform Congregation, (Reg. Charity No. 506117), Elms Street, Whitefield, M45 8GQ. (Est. 1977). (A Constituent of RSGB). ☎ 0161-796 6736. Website www.shaarei-shalom.org.uk. *M.* Rabbi N. Zalud. *H. Sec.*

South Manchester Synagogue, (Reg. Charity No. 231976), Wilbraham Road, M14 6JS. (Est. 1872.) ☎ 0161-224 1366. Fax 0161-225 8033. *M.* Rabbi Y. Rubin; *Admin.* Mrs T. Hyams.

Spanish & Portuguese Synagogue, (Est. 1873), 18 Moor La., Salford M7 4WX. ☎ 0161-792 7406. Fax 0161-792 7406. Website www.18moorlane.freeserve.co.uk. *H. Sec.* A. Hodari.

Talmud Torah Chinuch N'orim Synagogue, 11 Wellington Street, East, Salford M7 9AU. ☎ 0161-792 4522. (Constituent of the Union of Orthodox Hebrew Congregations.) *Ms.* Rev. N. Friedman, Rev. P. Koppenheim; *H. Sec.* S. Kornbluh.

United Synagogue, Meade Hill Road, M8 6LS. ☎ 0161-740 9586. *President* Sidney Huller; *Sec.* Reuben Wilner. ☎ 0161-740 9586.

Whitefield Hebrew Congregation, Park Lane, M45 7PB. ☎ 0161-766 3732. Fax 0161-767 9453. (Est. 1959). *M.* Rabbi J. Guttentag, (B.A. Hons.); *Admin.* Mrs P. M. Deach.

Yeshurun Hebrew Congregation, Coniston Road, Gatley, Cheshire SK8 4AP (Reg. Charity No. XN10469A). ☎ 0161-428 8242. Fax 0161-491 5265. Email yeshurun@btinternet.com. *M.* Rev. Dr A. Unterman, ☎ 0161-490 6050; *R.* ; *Admin.* L. Kaufmann.

Zerei Agudas Israel Synagogue, 35 Northumberland Street, Salford M7 0DQ. *M.* Dayan O. Westheim.

Zichron Yitzchak (Sephardi Congregation), 2 New Hall Road, Salford 7. *Emer. R.* Rabbi S. Amor; *Sec.* A. J. Tesciuba. ☎ 0161-795 0822.

CULTURAL ORGANISATIONS

Institute of Contemporary Jewish Studies, ICJS Conference Facility, Abramovitch

Wing, Machon Levi Yitschok, Bury Old Road, Manchester. *Youth & Outreach Dir.* Rabbi Peretz Chein. *Contact* ☎ 0161-795 4000. *Admin.* ☎ 0161-720 9908. Fax 0161-720 9998.

Israel Information Centre, 142 Bury Old Road, M8 6HD. ☎ 0161-721 4344. Fax 0161-795 3387. Email iicmcr@dircon.co.uk. Information and presentation of Israel's culture. *Dir.* Doreen Gerson. (Est. 1984.)

Jewish Historical Society of England (Branch), *Chairman* F. Baigel, 25 Ravensway, Bury Old Road, Prestwich, M25 0EU. ☎ 0161-740 6403. Email frankbaigel@iname.com.

Jewish Library, Central Library. ☎ 0161-236 9422. Stock now absorbed into main Social Sciences Library collection.

Jewish Museum, 190 Cheetham Hill Road, M8 8LW. ☎ 0161-834 9879 and 0161-832 7353. Fax 0161-834 9801. Email info@manchesterjewishmuseum.com. Website www.manchesterjewishmuseum.com. Mon.-Thurs., 10.30 a.m. to 4 p.m. Sun., 10.30 a.m. to 5 p.m. (Reg. Charity No. 508278). Admission charge. Exhibitions, heritage trails, demonstrations and talks. Educational visits for schools and adult groups must be booked in advance with the Administrator. *Contact* Don Rainger.

Jewish Male Voice Choir. *Cond.* A. Isaacs. ☎ 0161-740 1210.

EDUCATIONAL ORGANISATIONS

Academy for Rabbinical Research (Kolel), (Reg. Charity No. 526665), 134 Leicester Road, Salford M7 4GB. ☎ 0161-740 1960. *Princ.* Rabbi W. Kaufman; *Sec.* Rev. J. Freedman.

Bnos Yisroel School, Leicester Road, Salford, M7 0AH. ☎ 0161-792 3896.

Broughton Jewish Cassel Fox Primary School, Legh Road, Salford M7 4RT. ☎ 0161-792 7773 (school), ☎ 0161-792 2588 (nursery), 792 7738 (kindergarten). Fax 0161-792 7768. *Hd.* Rabbi James Kennard.

Bury & Whitefield Jewish Primary School, Parr La., Bury, Lancs. BL9 8JT. ☎/Fax 0161-766 2888. *H. T.* Miss C. Potter; *Chairman of Govs.* Rabbi A.J. Jaffe. Nursery School, Parr La., Bury, Lancs. ☎ 0161-767 9390. (Children 2 yrs. plus).

Delamere Forest School, Blakemere Lane, Norley, Nr. Frodsham, Cheshire WA6 6NP. ☎ 01928 788263. Fax 01928 788263. Email admin@dfschool.u-net.com. (Reg Charity No. 525913). For Jewish children with special needs. *Chairman of Gov.* D. Clayton; *H.T.* H. Burman.

Hillel House, Greenheys La., M15 6LR. ☎ 0161-226 10161.

Hubert Jewish High School for Girls, 10 Radford Street, Salford, M7 4NT. ☎ 0161-792 2118. Fax 0161-792 1733. *Princ.* Rabbi Y. Goldblat, MA (Oxon), PGCE.

Jerusalem Academy Study Groups. *Chairman* Rev. G. Brodie, 43 Stanley Road, Salford M7 4FR. ☎ 0161-740 2506.

Jewish Senior Boys School - Kesser Torah, Hubert House, 4 New Hall Road, Salford M7 4EL. ☎ 0161-708 9175.

Jewish Education Bureau Resources Centre, Sacred Trinity Centre, Chapel Street, Salford M3 7AJ. ☎ 0161-832 3709. *Dir.* Rabbi D. S. Charing; *Org. Sec.* Mrs G. Abrahams.

Jewish Programme Materials Project (JPMP), 34 Ashley Road, Altrincham, Cheshire WA14 2DW. ☎ 0161-929 5008. Email s.manchester.jyt@ort.org. *Contact* Adam Kaye, B.Soc.Sc. ☎ 0161-941 4358.

King David Schools. (Est. 1838. Reg. Charity No. 526631)

King David High School, Eaton Road, M8 5DY. ☎ 0161-740 7248. Fax 0161-740 0790. *H.T.* B. N. Levy, BEd; *H. of Sixth Form* Mrs J. Bentley, B. Comm, STCSE; *H. Yavneh* Rabbi Y. Peles.

King David Junior School, Wilton Polygon, M8 5DJ. ☎ 0161-740 3343. *H.T.* P.L. Parker, BEd (Hons), ALAM.

King David Infant School, Wilton Polygon, M8 6DJ. ☎ 0161-740 4110. *H.T.* Mrs J. Rich, BA.

King David Nursery & Crèche, Eaton Road, M8 5DY. ☎ 0161-740 3481. *Nursery Man.* Mrs S. Isaacs; *Crèche Man.* Mrs L. Marks.

Governors' Admin. Michael D. Epstein. ☎ 0161-740 3181. Fax 0161-740 3182.

Lubavitch Yeshiva, Lubavitch House, 62 Singleton Road, Salford M7 4LU. ☎ 0161-792 7649. *Dean* Rabbi A. Cohen. *Admin.* S. Weiss, ☎ 01161-740 4243.

Manchester Central Board for Hebrew Education and Talmud Torah (Reg. Charity No. 526164), 24A Bury New road, Prestwich, M25 0LD. ☎/Fax 0161-798 5577. *Chairman* J. M. Nathan; *Admin.* Mrs Y. E. Klein.

Centres: Polygon Hebrew Classes at Yavneh Campus, *Hd.* Mrs Liesbeth Harris; Shaarei Deoh Cheder (special needs) at the Jewish Cultural Centre, *Hd.* Mrs Mina Gold; GCSE Class, *Hd.* Mrs R. Levenson, *Assembly Co-ord.* Daniel Epstein.

Manchester Jewish Grammar School (Reg. Charity No. 526607), Beechwood, Charlton Avenue, Prestwich M25 0PH ☎ 0161-773 1789. Fax 0161-773 6117. *Princ.* Rabbi D. Kestenbaum; *H. M.* P. Pink, BSc(Econ), DipEd.

Mechinah Leyshiva, 13 Up. Park Road, Salford M7 0HY. ☎ 0161-795 9275.

Moriah Institute for Further Education, Y. Y. Rubinstein, 97 Singleton Road, Salford M7.

North Cheshire Jewish Primary School, St. Anns Road North, Heald Green, Cheadle, Cheshire SK8 4RZ. ☎ 0161-282 4500. Fax 0161-282 4501. *H. M.* Mrs N. Massel, BEd (Hons).

North Manchester Jewish Youth Project (Reg. Charity No. 1050928), 27 Bury Old Road, Prestwich, M26 0EY. ☎ 0161-720 9199. Fax 0161-740 6169. Email the-project@anjy.org. (Est. 1994). The Project aims to provide an overall youth service for 13-18 year olds. *Chair* P. Broude; *V. Chair* J. Wineberg; *Sec.* Helena Broude.

North Manchester Jewish Teenage Centre (Reg. Charity No. 1009785), at the Bnei Akiva Bayit, 72 Singleton Road, Salford M7 4LU. Open Sunday morning only. Under the auspices of the Manchester Centre Hebrew Board, 57 Leicester Road, Salford M7 4DA. ☎/Fax 0161-798 5577. *Corres.* D. Finkelstein.

Project seed, (Reg. Charity No. 281307), 47 Stanley Rd., Salford M7 4FR. ☎ 0161-740 0906. Website www.project.seed.org.uk. Rabbi A. Hassan.

Reshet Torah Education Network, Rabbi S.M. Kupetz, 4 Hanover Gdns., Salford M7 4FQ. ☎ 0161-740 5735.

South Manchester Jewish Youth Trust, (Reg. Charity No. 1040648), c/o North Cheshire Jewish Primary School, St Anne's Road North, Heald Green, Cheshire SK8 4RZ. ☎ 0161-428 3623. Fax 0161-491 0140. Email: s.manchester.jyt@ort.org. *Community Youth Worker* Andy Sollofe; *Chair* David Zucker. Working with young people in the South Manchester community.

Talmud Torah Chinuch N'orim, 11 Wellington Street, East, Salford M7 9AU. ☎ 0161-792 4522. *Chairman, Bd. of Govs.* B. Waldman.

Whitefield Community Kollel, c/o Whitefield Hebrew Congregation, Park Lane, Whitefield, M45 7PB. *Hon. Admin.* P. Struel. ☎ 0161-766 2150.

Academy of Higher Jewish Learning & Rabbinical Training College. *One to One Learning. Contact* Rabbi Malcolm Herman. ☎ 0161-766 6715/8138.

The Kollel also runs informal educational programmes.

J.A.M. (Judaism and Me) Post-Barmitzvah groups through to students, with an associated girls group and discussion groups for teenagers.

C.A.F.E. (Community & Family Education) Lectures and discussions for adults.

Missing Link Adult Education lecture series, particularly refresher courses in Judaism and a Shabbas morning Explanatory Service.

Whitefield Jewish Youth Centre. *Co-ord.* Mrs B. Howard. ☎ 0161-796 8564.

Yeshiva (Talmudical College), Saul Rosenberg House, Seymour Road, Higher

Crumpsall, M8 5BQ. (Est. 1911). ☎ 0161-740 0214. *Princ.* Rabbi Y. Ehrentreu; *Sec.* Rev. G. Brodie.

Yesoiday HaTorah School, Sedgley Park Rd., off Bury New Rd., Prestwich M25 0JW. ☎ 0161-798 9725. Fax 0161-773 3914. *Princ.* Rabbi Y. Yodaiken; *Clerk* Mrs V. Fagleman.

Yocheved Segal Kindergarten, Sedgley Pk. Road, Prestwich M25 0JW. ☎ 0161-773 8413.

WELFARE ORGANISATIONS

Manchester Jewish Federation (Reg. Charity No. 1082313). 12 Holland Road, M8 4NP. ☎ 0161-795 0024. Branch office: Southside, 34 Ashley Road, Altrincham, WA14 2DW. ☎ 0161-928 7799. *Chief Exec.* K. Phillips.

Aguda Community Services, 35 Northumberland Street, Salford M7 4DQ. (Reg. Charity No. 287367). ☎ 0161-792 6265. Fax 0161-708 9177. Seeks to provide employment for Jewish people wishing to observe the Sabbath and Holy-days. *Sec.*

Brookvale, Caring for People with Special Needs (Reg. Charity No. 526086), Simister Lane, Prestwich, M25 2SF. ☎ 0161-653 1767. Fax 0161-655 3635. *Exec. Dir.* Mrs L. Richmond; *Fin. Dir.* M. Walters.

Heathlands Village (Reg. Charity No. 221890), Heathlands Dr., Prestwich, M25 9SB. ☎ 0161-772 4800. Fax 0161-772 4934. (Care Home with nursing input). *President* H. E. Hamburger. *Gen. Man.* R.B. Farrar.

Jewish Marriage Council, Manchester Branch, 85 Middleton Road, M8 4JY. Appointments: ☎ 0161-740 5764. Offers: Confidential family and marriage counselling, assisting couples and individuals with relationship problems whether they are single, married, widowed, divorced or separated.

Jewish Soup Kitchen (Meals-on-Wheels Service), (Reg. Charity No. 226424), Rita Glickman House, Ravensway, Prestwich M25 0EX. ☎ 0161-795 4930. *H. Sec.* Mrs D. Phillips, B.E.M. ☎ 0161-740 1287.

Manchester Jewish Community Care (formerly Manchester Jewish Blind Society), (Reg. Charity No. 257238), Nicky Alliance Day Centre, 85 Middleton Road M8 4JY. ☎ 0161-740 0111. Fax 0161-721 4273. Email mail@mjcc.fsnet.co.uk. Day Centre and social work support for the visually and physically disabled, the elderly and those suffering from dementia. *Dir. Services* Rebecca Weinberg; *Chairman* H. Krebs.

Manchester Jewish Visitation Board. (Est. 1903.) *Convenor* Y. Brodie; *Chairman* Rev. L. Olsberg. ☎ 0161-740 9711.

Morris Feinmann Home (Care Home for older people), 178 Palatine Road, Didsbury, M20 2YW. ☎ 0161-445 3533. Fax 0161-448 1755. Website www.morrisfeinmannhome.com. *Gen. Man.* Mrs T. L. Paine.

Outreach Community & Residential Services (Reg. Charity No. 509119), 1 Delaunays Road, Crumpsall, M8 4QS ☎ 0161-740 3456. Fax 0161-740 5678. Email outreach@dial.pipex.com; Website outreach.co.uk. *Chief Exec.* Mrs S. Bitaye; *Dir. of Care* P. Williamson.

MARGATE (200)

Margate Hebrew Congregation. Synagogue, Albion Road, Cliftonville, CT9 2HP. (Est. 1904; new syn. consecrated 1929; Reg. Charity No. 273506) *President* Dr N. Jacobs. ☎ 01843 831587. Enquiries to *Hon. Admin.* D.A. Coberman ☎ 01843 228550.

Thanet and District Reform Synagogue, 293A Margate Road, Ramsgate, Kent CT12 6TE. ☎ 01843 851164.

Cemetery: For Margate Hebrew Congregation & Thanet Reform at Manston Road, Margate.

MIDDLESBROUGH (65)
(Incorporating Stockton and Hartlepool.) Synagogue reported closed during 1999.
Synagogue, Park Road South. (Est. 1873.) *H. Sec.* L. Simons. ☎ 01642 819034 (for details of services and Chevra Kaddisha). J. Bloom. ☎ 01609 8832272.
Cemetery: Ayresome Green Lane, Middlesbrough.

MILTON KEYNES & DISTRICT (182)
Reform Synagogue (Est. 1978. Reg. Charity No. 1058193). (Affiliated to RSGB) Hainault Ave., Giffard Park, MK14 5PQ. Website www.mkdrs.org.uk. Inq: Sarah Friedman ☎ 01908 560134.

NEWARK
Beth Shalom Holocaust Memorial Centre, Laxton, Newark NG22 0PA. ☎ 01623 836627. Fax 01623 836647. Email office@bethshalom.com; Website www. bethshalom.com. *Dirs* Dr S.D. Smith, Dr J.M. Smith, Mrs M.H. Smith.

NEWCASTLE UPON TYNE (1,110)
The community was est. in the 1820s, when services were held and a Shochet employed. A cemetery was acquired in 1831. Jews, however, had been resident in Newcastle since before 1775. In the Middle Ages Jews are known to have been est. in Newcastle in 1176. The population figure quoted is that of the community's recent census.

Representative Council of North-East Jewry. (Reg. Charity No. 1071515). *President* Joe Gellert, 34 Edgehill, Darras Hall, Ponteland, NE20 9RW, ☎ 01661-871755 (H), 0191 266 6900 (W); Fax 0191 266 6040 (W); *V. Presidents* Gillian Pearlman, Jackie Slesenger; *Hon. Sec.* Henry Ross, 56 Southwood Gardens, NE3 3BX, ☎ 0191 285 403 (H), 0191 215 6253 (W), Fax 0191 215 6080 (W); *H. T.* Theo Benjamin; *Press and Public Rel.* Clive Van der Velde.
North East Jewish Recorder (communal journal published by the Representative Council).
United Hebrew Congregation (Est. 1973). The Synagogue, Graham Park Road, Gosforth NE3 4BH. ☎ 0191-284 0959. *President* H.Ross; *M.* Rabbi Y. Black; *Sec.* Mrs P. Ashton. Mikva on premises. **Burial Cttee:** *Chairman* B. Lewis ☎ 0191-285 5505.
Reform Synagogue, The Croft, off Kenton Road, Gosforth, NE3 4RF. ☎ 0191-284 8621. (Est. 1965.) (A Constituent of RSGB) *Chairman* A. Cowan; *M.* Rabbi R. Ash; **Burial Cttee** ☎ 0191-284 8621. **Cheder** B. Ross ☎ 0191-285 8400.

OTHER ORGANISATIONS
North East Jewish Community Services. *Chairman* V. Gallant, ☎ 0191-285 7533; *Community Care. Off.* Bernard Shaffer, Lionel Jacobson House, Graham Park Road, Gosforth NE3 4BH. ☎ 0191-284 1968. **Community Transport** ☎ 0191-284 1968.
AJEX, *Chairman* C. Topaz. ☎ 01661 824819.
Education and Youth Cttee., c/o United Hebrew Cong. *Chairman* Vivienne Erdos.
Jewish Students' Society and Hillel House, 29-31 Hawthorn Road, Gosforth, NE3 4DE. ☎ 0191-284 1407. *Contact* Susan Olsburgh ☎ 0191 213 0919. Email susan.olsburgh@unn.ac.uk
Jewish Welfare Society, Lionel Jacobson House, Graham Park Road, Gosforth NE3 4BH. *Sec.* Mrs P. Ashton. ☎ 0191-284 0959.
UJIA. *H. Sec.* J. Mark. ☎ 0191-284 1903.
Kashrus Cttee., c/o United Hebrew Cong. *Contact* Rabbi Y. Black ☎ 0191-284 6048.
Kol Hashirim Choir. *Contact* Agi Gilbert ☎ 0191-285 7001.
Jewish Literary Society. *Contact* Freddie Ingram ☎ 0191-284 8118.

Junior Maccabi. For children aged 7-14 years. *Contact* Adrienne Ross ☎ 0191-285 4043 or Vivienne Erdos ☎ 0191-213 0706.

Newcastle Jewish Housing Association Ltd., *Chairman* S. Doberman, c/o Lionel Jacobson House. ☎ 0191-284 0959.

Newcastle Jewish Players. *Co-Chairmen* Caroline Boobis ☎ 0191-284 1214, Louise Karter ☎ 0191-284 6619.

North East Jewish Golfing Society. *Contact* Anthony Josephs. ☎ 0191 285 7173. The Swingers (Ladies' Section of Golfing Society). *Contact* Faga Speker. ☎ 0191 285 3110.

Philip Cussins House (Residential Care for Jewish Aged in the North East), 33/35 Linden Road, NE3 4EY. ☎ 0191 213 5353. Fax 0191 213 5354. Residents 0191 213 5355.

WIZO:

Sharon Group, *Chairmen* Phyllis Leigh, ☎ 0191-285 6227; Audrey Veeder, ☎ 0191-285 8013.

Rosa Wollstein Group, *Chairman* Anne Jacobson, ☎ 0191-285 0650; Faga Speker ☎ 0191-285 3110.

Zelda's (Kosher meats and delicatessen), Unit 7, Kenton Park Shopping Centre, NE3 4RU. ☎ 0191-213 0013.

Cemeteries: Hazelrigg and Heaton (UHC); North Shields (Reform).

NORTHAMPTON (185)

The community marked its centenary in 1988. For a history of the medieval and modern settlement in the town see 'A Short History of the Jews of Northampton, 1159–1996' (1996), by M. Jolles.

Hebrew Congregation, Overstone Road, Northampton, NN1 3JW. ☎ 01604 33345. *M.*; *Sec.* A. Moss, ☎ 01604-633345.

Cemetery: Towcester Road.

NORWICH (170)

The present community was founded in 1813, Jews having been resident in Norwich during the Middle Ages, and connected with the woollen and worsted trade, for which the city was at that time famous. A resettlement of Jews is believed to have been completed by the middle of the eighteenth century. A synagogue was built in 1848 and destroyed in an air raid in 1942. A temporary synagogue opened in 1948 and the present building was consecrated by the Chief Rabbi in 1969. The congregation serves a large area, having members in Ipswich, Gt. Yarmouth, Lowestoft and Cromer.

Norwich Hebrew Congregation Synagogue, 3a Earlham Road, NR2 3RA. ☎ 01603 623948. *M.* A. Bennett ☎ 01263 710726; *President* V. Bishop; *H. Sec.* P. Prinsley, FRCS. ☎ 01603 506482. Fax 01603 508131.

Chevra Kadisha, 3a Earlham Road, Norwich. *President* B. C. Leveton. ☎ 01603 749706.

Progressive Jewish Community of East Anglia (Norwich). A new community based in Norwich. Affiliated to the ULPS. Regular services at The Old Meeting House, Colegate, Norwich. *Chairman* Dr E. Crasnow; *M.* Rabbi Melinda Carr; Enquiries to: *H. Sec.* Dr J. Lawrence, ☎ 01603 259271. *Publ.* PJCEA Newsletter.

Jewish Ladies' Society, 3a Earlham Road. *President* Mrs P. Young; *H. Sec.* Mrs E. Griffiths.

Norfolk and Norwich Branch of the Council of Christians and Jews (Est. 1991). *Sec.* G. Willson.

Norwich Israel Social Society (NISS), *Chairman* B. Leveton. ☎ 01603 749706.

NOTTINGHAM (1,050)

A small community has lived in Nottingham since the early 19th century, and in 1890, with a com. increased by immigrants to some 100 families, the Hebrew Congregation built its first synagogue in Chaucer St. During the Second World War, there was a sharp growth in the community, and the congregation acquired its present synagogue in 1954. With the closure of the Derby syn. in 1986, many of its members joined the Nottingham Hebrew Cong. The Progressive Jewish Cong. was est. in 1959.

Nottingham Representative Council, 265 Wollaton Vale, Wollaton NG8 2PX. ☎ 0115 928 1613. Fax 0115 916 2960. Email lynnechapman@innotts.co.uk. *Chairman* D. Lipman. ☎ 0115 966 4690. *Sec.* L. Chapman.

Hebrew Congregation, Shakespeare Villas, NG1 4FQ. ☎ 0115 472004. Email OfficeNHC@aol.com. *President* Alan Hyman.

Progressive Jewish Congregation (ULPS), Lloyd Street, NG5 4BP. ☎ 0115 9624761. *Chairman* P. Scott ☎ 0115 924 5660. Email npjc@ulps.org. *M.; H. Sec.* Mrs N. Bogod. ☎ 0115 945 2170.

Federation of Women Zionists. *H.T.* Mrs S. Cresswell.

Jewish Welfare Board. *Chairman* Dr M. Caplan. ☎ 0115 260245. *Hon. Sec.* P. Seymour, 115 Selby Rd., West Bridgford, NG2 7BB. ☎ 0115 452895.

Miriam Kaplowitch House, Jewish rest home, 470 Mansfield Road, NG5 2DR ☎ 0115 624274 (Residents) and 0115 9622038 (Matron & Admin.) (Est. 1986).

University of Nottingham Jewish and Israel Society, c/o The University of Nottingham, NG7 2RD.

Women's Benevolent Society. *Chairman* Mrs S. Besbrode. ☎ 0115 9373620.

OXFORD (Resident Jewish pop. 700 approx.)

An important centre in the medieval period. The modern community was est. in 1842. In 1974 the Oxford Synagogue and Jewish Centre was built on the site of the earlier synagogue. It serves the resident community and a fluctuating number of university students, and is available for all forms of Jewish worship.

Jewish Congregation, The Synagogue, 21 Richmond Road, OX1 2JL. ☎ 01865 53042. *President* S. Dwek.

Oxford Masorti (services held the last Shabbat each month). *Contact* Mrs W. Fidler. ☎ 01565 726959. Email: wendyfidler@compuserve.com.

The Progressive Jewish Group of Oxford. Inq: Katherine Shock, ☎/Fax 01865 515584, or Ruth Cohen ☎ 01865 765197.

Oxford University L'Chaim Society, Albion House, Albion Place, Little Gate, OX1 1QZ. ☎ 01865 794462.

University Jewish Society. (Est. 1903). *Senior Member* Mike Woodin, Balliol College, ☎ 01865 248073; *Sec.*; *Chaplain* Rev. M. Weisman, M.A. (Oxon.). ☎ 020-8451 3484.

PETERBOROUGH (105)

Hebrew Congregation, 142 Cobden Avenue, PE1 2NU. ☎ 01733 571282. (Congregation est. 1940. Syn. opened 1954. Affiliated to the U.S.) *Admin.* C. Conn. ☎ 01733 571282. Services Kabbalat Shabbat 8pm. Liberal Jewish Community. *Admin*. N. Gordon ☎ 01733 22813; Juliet Vart ☎ 01733 53269. Services first and third Shabbat at 10.30am.

Liberal Jewish Community (ULPS). Enquiries to Elisabeth Walker. ☎ 01733 266188.

PLYMOUTH (100)

The Plymouth community was founded in 1745, when a cemetery was opened. Jews lived in the city even earlier. The syn., built in 1762, is the oldest Ashkenazi house of worship still standing in the English-speaking world. Its 225th anniver-

sary in 1987 was marked by a service attended by representatives of the United Synagogue, the Board of Deputies and the Civic Authorities. In the early 19th century, Plymouth was one of the four most important provincial centres of Anglo-Jewry. The history of the community, 'The Plymouth Synagogue 1761–1961' by Doris Black, was published in 1961.
Hebrew Congregation (Reg. Charity 220010), Catherine Street, PL1 2AD. ☎ 01752 301955. (Est. 1761.) *H. Sec.* A. V. H. Aggiss. ☎ 01822 617 340. Email info@plymouthsynagogue.co.uk. Website www.plymouthsynagogue.co.uk.

PORTSMOUTH (150)
The com. was est. in 1746 and opened a syn. in Oyster Row, later to move to a building in White's Row, off Queen St. which was occupied for over 150 years. The present syn. was built in 1936. The cemetery was acquired in 1749 and is the oldest in the Regions still in use. It is situated in Fawcett Road, which has been known for more than 200 years as Jews' Lane. By 1815 Portsmouth was one of the four main Jewish centres outside London, the others being Plymouth, Liverpool and Birmingham. Portsmouth's prosperity declined after the Napoleonic Wars.
For South Hampshire Reform Jewish Community see under Southampton.
Portsmouth & Southsea Hebrew Congregation. Synagogue, The Thicket, Elm Grove, Southsea PO5 2AA. ☎ 023-92821494. (Reg. Charity No.: X50585) *M.* Rev. H. Caplan; *H. Sec.* Mrs P. Jurd.
Board of Guardians, The Thicket (Est. 1804)
Chevra Kadisha, The Thicket.
Jewish Ladies' Benevolent Society (Est. 1770.), The Thicket.
Cemeteries: Fawcett Road, Kingston, New Road; Catherington.

POTTERS BAR (250)
Est. in the 1940s, the com. met at members homes until 1983 when the current synagogue was purchased.
Synagogue (affiliated to the United Synagogue), Meadowcroft, Great North Road, Bell Bar (nr Potters Bar), Hatfield, Herts AL9 6DB. ☎/Fax 01707 656202. Email office@pottersbarshul.org.uk. *M.* Rabbi Z. Solomons.

PRESTON (25)
Synagogue, est. 1882, now closed. *H. Sec.* Dr C. E. Nelson, 31 Avondale Road, Southport PR9 0NH. ☎ 01704 538276.

RADLETT (750)
Synagogues:
Radlett (U.S.), 22 Watling St., P.O. Box 28, Herts. WD7 7PN. *M.* Rabbi G. Sylvester ☎ 01923-856878; *Admin.* Mrs J. Bower.
Radlett & Bushey Reform Synagogue (RSBG), 118 Watling St., Herts. WD7 7AA. ☎ 01923 856110. Fax 01923 858444. Email office@r-brs.freeserve.co.uk. *M.* Rabbi Alexandra Wright. *Admin.* Sandra Denby.
Hertsmere Progressive Synagogue (ULPS), High St., Elstree, Herts. WD6 3EY. *M.* Rabbi J. Black. *H. Sec.* M. Beral. ☎ 020-8953 8889. Email honsec@hpselstree.org.uk. Website www.hpselstree.org.uk.

READING (500)
The community began in 1886 with the settlement of a number of tailors from London. They attracted the help of such personages as Samuel Montagu, Claude Montefiore, Sir Hermann Gollancz and Lady Lucas to build and support a synagogue in 1900, and the syn. has been in continuous use ever since. This flourishes today as the centre of the Reading Hebrew Cong., and is the only Orthodox cong. in Berkshire. The Sir Hermann Gollancz Hall next to the syn. is

the venue of many social groups. The Progressive Community was founded in 1979 and attracts membership from across the Thames Valley.

Berkshire Jewish Representative Council (Est. 1998.). *Chairman* J. Foreman, 2b Tilehurst Rd., RG1 7TN. ☎ 0118-957 1167. Fax 0118-951 0740. *Contact*

Reading Hebrew Congregation. Synagogue (Reg. Charity No. 220098), Goldsmid Road, RG1 7YB. ☎ 0118 9573954. Website www.rhc.org.uk; Email secretary @rhc.datanet.co.uk. *M.* Rabbi Alex Chapper.

WIZO & Judaica Shop. Mrs Pamela Kay ☎ 0118 9573680.

Food Shop. Kosher meat and provisions. Mrs Carol Kay ☎ 0118 575069.

Thames Valley Progressive Jewish Community (Est. 1979. Constituent of ULPS), 6 Church Street, Reading. For details of services, religious and social events, contact: *Chairman* Faye Cohen ☎ 01276 32235; *M.* Rabbi Sybil Sheridan ☎ 01628 71058.

University Jewish Society, c/o Reading Hillette, 82 Basingstoke Road, Reading. ☎ 0118 9873282.

REIGATE AND REDHILL (45)

Jewish Community. (Est. 1968.) *Chairman* M. J. Kemper, 59 Gatton Road, Reigate, Surrey. ☎ 017372 42076.

ST. ALBANS (200)

Synagogue (Affiliated to the U.S.), Oswald Road, AL1 3AQ. ☎ 01727 854872. *H. Sec.* Mrs R. Wenzerul.

St. Albans Masorti Synagogue, P.O. Box 23, AL1 4PH. *Co-Chair* P. Hoffbrand, Mrs L. Oppedijk; *T.* P. Hart; *M.* Rabbi Paul Glantz; *Sec.* Mrs K. Phillips. ☎ 01727 860642.

ST. ANNE'S ON SEA (500)

Hebrew Congregation, Orchard Road, FY8 1PJ. (Reg. Charity no. 66492) ☎ 01253 721831. *President* P. Davidson. ☎ 01253 723920. *H. Secs.* A. Brown; L. Jackson. *M.* Rabbi I. Broder. ☎ 01253-781815.

Ladies Guild, *Chairman* J. Kendall ☎ 01253 723088.

Cemetery: Consecrated section of municipal cemetery at Regents Avenue, Lytham.

SHEFFIELD (ca. 500)

The earliest records of an organised Jewish community in Sheffield date from 1850, but the congregation had already been in existence for some time and Jews are known to have been living in the city from the eighteenth century. At its peak in the 1960s, the community numbered over 2,000. A study of the community, 'Sheffield Jewry' by Armin Krausz, was published in 1980. In 2000, the Orthodox congregation moved from the large Wilson Road synagogue (built 1929) into a new and smaller synagogue within the grounds of the Jewish Centre which was consecrated by the Chief Rabbi in 2000. The Reform congregation was founded in 1989 and was admitted as a full constituent member of the RSGB in 2000. Though now a smaller community, Sheffield has an exceptional range of societies and groups, covering all varieties of Jewish interests.

Representative Council of Sheffield & District Jews. ☎ 0114 2360984. Fax 0114 2353045. *President* B. Rosenberg; *H. Sec.* M.J. Rose, Kingfield Synagogue, Brincliffe Crescent, S11 8UX.

Sheffield Jewish Congregation and Centre (Orthodox). (Reg. Charity No. 250281). Kingfield Synagogue, Brincliffe Crescent, S11 8UX. ☎ 0114 281 7459 (home), or 0114 258 8855 (office). Email rabbigolomb@aol.com. *M.* Rabbi Y. Golomb; *President* D. Grunweg. Mikvah on premises.

Sheffield Jewish Welfare Organisation in association with SJCC (Inland Reg. Charity No. X75608). *Chairman* A. Kaddish ☎ 0114 2236 7958.

Sheffield & District Reform Jewish Congregation. *Chair* B.C. Rosenberg, TD. For information contact PO Box 675, S11 8SP or Website www.shef-ref.co.uk.

SOLIHULL (450)

The community began in 1962. The synagogue was built in 1977. Its close proximity to Birmingham means that many of the facilities of the Birmingham community are shared by Solihull.

Solihull & District Hebrew Congregation, 3 Monastery Drive, Solihull, West Midlands, B91 1DW. ☎/Fax 0121 706 8736. Website www.solihullshul.org; Email rabbi@solihullshul.org. *M.* Rabbi Y. Pink ☎ 0121-706 8736; *Admin.* Mrs H. Woolf, 49 Charles Rd., B91 1TT. ☎ 0121-603 5170.

Solihull Jewish Social & Cultural Society. *Chairman* H. Kay ☎ 0121-705 3870; *H.Sec.* Mrs M. Leveson, 19 Bishopton Close, B90 4AH. ☎ 0121-744 8391.

Solihull & District Cheder. *H.T.* Rabbi Y. Pink ☎ 0121-706 8736. Email cheder@solihullshul.org.

Stanley Middleburgh Library, 3 Monastery Drive, B91 1DW. Email library@solihullshul.org. Open Sunday 9.30am–1.00pm or by appointment.

Hakol – Community Magazine, 3 Monastery Drive, B91 1DW. Email hakol@solihullshul.org.

SOUTH SHIELDS (9)

Hebrew Congregation, Contact: Mr H. Tavroges. ☎ 0191-285 4834. The synagogue is now closed.

Cemetery: Consecrated section of the municipal cemetery.

SOUTHAMPTON (105)

The orthodox congregation dates from 1833 when the first synagogue in East Street was founded. The synagogue built in 1864 in Albion Place was demolished in 1963, when the present one was consecrated. There were Jewish residents in Southampton in 1786. Since 1838, when Abraham Abraham was elected to the Town Council, they have shared in civic affairs. The South Hampshire Reform Jewish Community was formed in 1983.

Orthodox Synagogue, Mordaunt Road, Inner Ave. ☎ 023-80220129. *President* M. Rose. *H. Sec.* C.D. Freeman, 23 Roslin Hall, 6 Manor Rd., Bournemouth BH1 3ES.

South Hampshire Reform Jewish Community (Est. 1983; Reg. Charity no. 1040109), for Hampshire and the Isle of Wight. *Chair* Deborah Wright; *Sec.* Frances Dowty, 61 Newfield Road, Liss Forest, GU33 7BW. ☎ 01730 892155. Email fran@lissonline.co.uk.

Hartley Library, University of Southampton, Highfield, houses the Anglo-Jewish Archives and Parkes Library (see p.55).

Hillel House, 5 Brookvale Road. ☎ 023-80557742.

Cemetery: Consecrated section at the municipal Hollybrook cemetery.

SOUTHEND, WESTCLIFF & LEIGH-ON-SEA (4,500)

Jewish families settled in the Southend area in the late nineteenth century, mainly from London's East End. In 1906 the first temporary synagogue was built in wood in Station Road, Westcliff. In 1912 a synagogue was built in Alexandra Road, which served the community until February 2001 when it was sold. A second synagogue was built in Ceylon Road, Westcliff, in 1928, but when a new synagogue was built in Finchley Road, the Ceylon Road premises were converted into a youth centre. The Ceylon Road premises have now been sold and a new youth centre has been opened at the Talmud Torah premises.

Southend-on-Sea & District Jewish Representative Council. *Chairman* Derek Baum, MBE. ☎ 01702 343789; *Sec.* Jeffrey Barcan. ☎ 01702-343192.

Southend and Westcliff Hebrew Congregation, Finchley Rd., Westcliff-on-Sea,

Essex SS0 8AD. *President* David Gold ☎ 01702 344900. *M.* Rabbi M. Lew. ☎ 01702 344900. Fax 01702 391131. Email swhc@btclick.com. Website www.swhc.org.uk; *Fin. Sec.* Mrs A. Marx ☎ 01702 344900; *Secs.* Mrs Janice Steele, Mrs Pamela Freedman. Synagogues at: Finchley Road, Westcliff; 99 Alexandra Road, Southend.

Southend and District Reform Synagogue, 851 London Road, Westcliff-on-Sea. ☎ 01702 475809. Email southend_district_reform@listmail.com. *Chairman* F. Potter. ☎ 01702 473303; *Sec.* Mrs D. Miller ☎ 01702 464919.

Mikva, 44 Genesta Road, Westcliff-on-Sea. ☎ 01702 344900. *Supt.* Rivki Lew.

Orthodox Jewish Cemetery, Sutton Road, Southend. (Entr. Stock Road). ☎ 01702 344900.

Reform Jewish Cemetery, Sutton Road, Southend. (Entr. Stock Road).

Myers Communal Hall, Finchley Road, Westcliff. ☎ 01702 344900.

Kashrut Commission, *Chairman* Mrs J. Sheldon. ☎ 01702 344900.

Ladies' Guild (Orthodox). *Chairman* Mrs G. Jay ☎ 01702 715015.

Ladies' Guild (Reform). *Sec.* Mrs D. Phillips. ☎ 01702 432477.

EDUCATIONAL AND YOUTH ORGANISATIONS

Coleman & Lilian Levene Talmud Torah (Orthodox), Finchley Road, Westcliff. ☎ 01702 344900. *H.T.* Mrs R. Lew.

Hebrew Education Board. *Chairman* N. Rosehill. ☎ 01702 344900.

Herzlia Day School, Finchley Road, Westcliff. ☎ 01702 340986. *H. T.* Mrs R. Rattner.

Jewish Lads' & Girls' Brigade. *Chairman* Mrs J. Jacks. ☎ 01702 315966; *Sec.* Mr R. Rams.

Lecture Board. Mrs S. Greenstein. ☎ 01702 477617.

Talmud Torah (Reform), 851 London Road, Westcliff. *Princ.* Mrs B. Barber. ☎ 01702 297238.

Youth Centre (Orthodox), 38 Ceylon Road, Westcliff. ☎ 01702 346545. *Chairman* A. Witzenfeld. ☎ 01702 435354.

SOCIAL, CULTURAL & WELFARE ORGANISATIONS

AJEX Social Club, Communal Hall, Finchley Road Synagogue, Westcliff. *Chairperson* Rene Plaskow. ☎ 01702 340995.

Council of Christians and Jews. *Chairperson* Mrs Joan Carlisle; *Hon. Sec.* Derek Baum, MBE. ☎ 01702 343789.

Emunah Ladies Society. *Chairperson* Mrs Fay Sober. ☎ 01702 330440. *Sec.* Mrs M. Simons.

Friendship Club. *Chairperson* Mrs Minn Rose ☎ 01702 390230.

Hospital Kosher Meals Service. Rabbi Mendel Lew. ☎ 01702 344900.

JNF Impact. *Chairman* A. Larholt; *Sec.* Mrs Laraine Barnes.

Kosher Meals-on-Wheels Service. *Chairperson.* Anthony Rubin. ☎ 01702 345568.

Raymond House for Aged, 5 Clifton Terrace, SS1 1DT (a Jewish Care residential home). *Man.* Ross Farmer ☎ 01702 352956; Residents ☎ 01702 340054; Matron 01702 341687.

Southend Friends of Ravenswood. Jules Freedman. ☎ 01702 343677.

Southend Aid Society. *Sec.* H. Kanutin. ☎ 01702 582996.

Southend & District AJEX. *President* Derek Baum, MBE; *Chairman* A. Stuart; *H. Sec.* J. Barcan. ☎ 01702 343192.

Southend District Social Committee (Reform). *Chairman* Mrs S. Kaye ☎ 01702 475809.

Southend & Westcliff Community Centre, 1 Cobham Road, Westcliff-on-Sea, SSO 8EG (a Jewish Care day centre). ☎ 01702 334655.

Tuesday Nighters. *Chairman* Lewis Herlitz. ☎ 01702 715676.

UJIA. *Chairman* S. Salt ☎ 01702 476349.

Women's Zionist Society. *Chairperson* Mrs Jackie Kalms; *H. Sec.* Mrs Jane Barnett. ☎ 01702 340731.

SOUTHPORT (650)

The first Synagogue was consecrated in 1893 and the congregation moved to Arnside Road, in 1924. The New Synagogue (Reform) was est. in 1948. The community grew between and during the First and Second World Wars, but is now decreasing.

Jewish Representative Council. *President* Mrs Sonia Abrahamson, 65 Beach Priory Gardens, PR8 2SA. ☎ 01704 540704; *H. Sec.* Lawrence Abelson.

Synagogue, Arnside Road, PR9 0QX. ☎ 01704 532964. *M.* ; *Senior Warden* Dr Cyril Nelson; *Sec.* Mrs Maureen Cohen.

Mikveh, Arnside Road. ☎ 01704 532964.

New Synagogue, Portland St. PR8 1LR. ☎ 01704 535950. *M.* ; *Emer. Rabbi* Rabbi S. Kay; *Sec.* Mrs E. Lippa.

Jewish Convalescent and Aged Home, 81 Albert Road. ☎ 01704 531975 (office); 01704 530207 (visitors.)

Beth Hasepher, Arnside Road. ☎ 01704 532964.

Manchester House, 83 Albert Road. ☎ 01704 534920 (office); 01704 530436 (visitors).

STAINES & DISTRICT (390)

(Incorporating Slough & Windsor)

Synagogue (affiliated to the U.S.), Westbrook Road, South Street, Middx. TW18 4PR. *H. Sec.* Mrs P. D. Fellman. ☎ 01784 254604.

STOKE-ON-TRENT AND NORTH STAFFORDSHIRE (30)

Hebrew Congregation, Birch Terr., Hanley. (Est. 1873. Reg. Charity No. 232104) *President* H. S. Morris, 27 The Avenue, Basford, Newcastle, Staffs. ST5 0ND. ☎ 01782 616417; *Jt. T.* H.S. Morris, R. Elias ☎ 01782 318110.

SUNDERLAND (45)

The first Jewish settlement was in 1755. The first congregation was est. about 1768; and was the first regional community to be represented at the BoD. A syn. was erected in Moor St. in 1862; rebuilt in 1900; and in 1928 the cong. moved to Ryhope Road, The Beth Hamedrash, which was est. in Villiers St. in 1899, and moved to Mowbray Road in 1938, closed in December 1984. Arnold Levy published a 'History of the Sunderland Jewish Community' in 1956.

Hebrew Congregation, incorporating Sunderland Beth Hamedrash, Ryhope Road, SR2 7EQ. ☎ 0191-5658093. (Reg. Charity No. 1078345). *Contact* Ivor Saville, ☎ 0191-522 9710.

Chevra Kadisha. *President* Dr H. Davis. *Contact* Ivor Saville.

Hebrew Board of Guardians. (Est. 1869). *Contact* Ivor Saville.

Talmudical College and Yeshiva. ☎ 0191 490 1606. (See Gateshead p. 113). *Princ.*

Cemetery: Bishopwearmouth Cemetery, Hylton Road, Sunderland.

SWINDON (72)

The community formed by Second World War evacuees has dispersed, but a community was re-formed in 1983.

Jewish Community. (Associated Community of R.S.G.B. Reg. Charity No. 296761). *Enq.* Martin Vandervelde, ☎ 01793-521910; Carol Ennis, ☎ 01793-831335.

TORQUAY (TORBAY) (20)

Synagogue, Old Town Hall, Abbey Road. The synagogue was closed at the end of 2000 and the congregation dissolved. Inq.: E. Freed, 'Son Bou', 7 Broadstone

Park Road, Livermead, Torquay TQ2 6TY. ☎ 01803 607197.
Chevra Kadisha: Cemetery, Colley End Road, Paignton, Torbay. *Chairman* E. Freed.

TOTNES

Totnes Jewish Community (Assoc. RSGB). *Contact* 1 Maudlin Cottages, Maudlin Road, Devon TQ9 5TG. ☎ 01803 867461.

TRURO

Kehillat Kernow Jewish Community (Assoc. RSGB). *Contact* Owl Cottage, 11 Mill Road, Penponds, Cornwall TR14 0QH. ☎ 01209 719672.

WALLASEY (50)

Hebrew Congregation, c/o H. Sec. (Est. 1911.) *President* D. Daniels; *T.* D. J. Waldman; *H. Sec.* L. S. Goldman, 28 Grant Road, Wirral, Merseyside, L46 2RY. ☎ 0151-638 6945.

WELWYN GARDEN CITY (290)

Synagogue (Affiliated to U.S.), Handside Lane, Barn Close, Herts AL8 6ST. ☎ 01438-715686. *H. Sec.* Mrs D. Prag.

WOLVERHAMPTON (15)

Synagogue, Fryer St. (Est. 1850.) Closure of the synagogue was reported in 1999. Contact Mrs J. Kronheim, 94 Wergs Road, Tettenhall WV6 8TH. ☎ 01902 752474.
Cemetery: Consecrated section at Jeffcock Road Corporation Cemetery, Wolverhampton.

YORK (25)

A memorial stone was consecrated at Clifford's Tower, York Castle, in 1978 in memory of the York Jewish community massacred there in 1190. A small community resettled and continued to live in York until the 1290 expulsion. There is now a small com. in the city and a Jewish Soc. at York Univ.
York Hebrew Congregation. *Contact* A. S. Burton ☎ 01423 330537.

WALES

CARDIFF (1,200)

Jews settled in Cardiff about the year 1787. The present community was founded in 1840.
Jewish Representative Council. *Chairman* Prof. P.D.J. Weitzman; *H. Sec.* Mrs R. Levene. ☎ 029-2075 2277. Email ruthlevene@hotmail.com.
Israel Information Centre Wales & the West of England, P.O.B. 98, CF2 6XN. ☎/Fax 02920-461780. *Dir.* Jean A. Evans.
Orthodox Synagogue, Brandreth Road, Penylan, CF23 5LB. ☎ 029-2047 3728. Email rabbi@cardiffunited.org.uk. *Sec.*
New Synagogue, Moira Terrace, CF2 1EJ. (opp. Howard Gardens.). (A Constituent of R.S.G.B.) ☎ 029-2049 1689. Email info@cardiffnewsyn.org. *Chairman* S. Masters; *Sec.* Mrs C. Salmon.
Hillel House, 89 Crwys Rd. ☎ 029-2023 1114. Applications for admission: Mrs L. Gerson. ☎ 029-2075 9982. Email lisa@gersonfamily.freeserve.co.uk.
Cardiff Jewish Helpline (formerly Cardiff Jewish Board of Guardians). *Chairman* Mr A. Schwartz ☎ 029-2075 0990.
Kashrus Commission. Rabbi Ives at Penylan Synagogue Office. ☎ 029-2047 3728.
South Wales Jewish Retirement and Nursing Home, Penylan House, Penylan Road. (Est. 1945.) ☎ 029-2048 5327. *President* Mrs J. Cotsen; *Matron/Man.* Geraldine Bassett.

Union of Jewish Students, c/o Hillel House. ☎ 029-2023 1114.
Bimah. South Wales Jewish Communual magazine. *Edr.* A. Schwartz. Email editor@bimah.org.uk.
Cemeteries: Old Cemetery – High Fields Road, Roath Park; New Cemetery – Greenfarm Road, Ely; Reform: at Cowbridge Road Entrance, Ely Cemetery.

LLANDUDNO AND COLWYN BAY (45)
Hebrew Congregation, 28 Church Walks, Llandudno LL30 2HL. (Est. 1905). *Sec.* B. Hyman, 9 Glyn Isaf, Llandudno Junction, Gwynedd LL31 9HT. ☎ 01492 572549. Llandudno serves as the centre for the dwindling coms. of North Wales, including Bangor, Rhyl, Colwyn Bay and Caernarvon.

MERTHYR TYDFIL
Synagogue now closed. The com. was est. before 1850. The cemetery is still being maintained. Apply to the Cardiff Jewish Rep. C. (see above).

NEWPORT (Gwent) (10)
Synagogue (opened 1871), 45 St Marks Crescent, Risca Road, NP20 5HE. ☎ 01633 262308. *Chairman* I. Rocker.
Burial Society, c/o Cardiff United Synagogue, Penylan, Cardiff.
Cemetery: Risca Road, Newport.

SWANSEA (65)
The Jewish community dates at the latest from 1768, when the Corporation granted a plot of land for use as a cemetery. In 1780 a syn. was built. Probably its history is even older, for Jews are known to have been living in the town from about 1730. The syn. in Goat St. was destroyed in an air raid in Feb. 1941, but another was erected in the Ffynone district. The former Llanelli cong. is now part of the Swansea com.
Hebrew Congregation. (Est. 1780.) Synagogue, Ffynone. *Chairman* H. M. Sherman, 17 Mayals Green, Mayals, Swansea SA3 5JR. ☎ 01792 401205.
Chevra Kadisha. *Chairman* D. Sandler. ☎ 01792 206285.
Cemeteries at Oystermouth and Townhill.

WELSHPOOL
Welshpool Jewish Group, Elmhurst, Severn Rd., Welshpool, Powys, SY21 7AR. Inq.: Dr A. L. Solomon. ☎ 01938 552744. Email anthony.solomon@lineone.net.

SCOTLAND
Scottish Council of Jewish Communities, Jewish Community Centre, 222 Fenwick Rd., Giffnock, Glasgow G46 6UE. ☎ 0141-577 8208. Fax 0141-577 8202. Email j-scot@j-scot.org. (Est. 1987 as Standing Committee of Scottish Jewry.) Democratic umbrella body representing the Jewish Community of Scotland. *Chairman* Dr K. Collins (Glasgow); *V. Chair* Dr I. Leifer (Edinburgh); *H. Sec.* Ephraim Borowski; *Public Affairs Off.* B. Jackson
The Scottish Jewish Archives Centre. Garnethill Synagogue, 129 Hill Street, Glasgow G3 6UB. ☎/Fax 0141 332 4911. Email archives@sjac.fsbusiness.co.uk; Website www.sjac.org.uk. (Est. 1987) To collect, catalogue, preserve and exhibit records of communal interest. To stimulate study in the history of the Jews of Scotland. To heighten awareness in the Jewish communities of Scotland of their cultural and religious heritages. *H. Life President* Dr Jack E. Miller, OBE, JP; *Chairman* Dr Kenneth Collins, PhD; *H. T.* Joe Sacharin; *Dir.* Harvey L. Kaplan, MA.

ABERDEEN (30)
Refurbished synagogue and community centre opened 1983.

Hebrew Congregation, 74 Dee Street, AB11 6DS. ☎ 01224 582135. (Est. 1893. Reg. Charity No. SC002901) *H. Sec.* Esther Shoshan. ☎ 01224 642749.

DUNDEE (22)

Hebrew Congregation, 9 St. Mary Place. (Est. 1874. New synagogue opened 1978.) *Chairman*

Dundee Univ. Jewish Society is centred at the synagogue.

DUNOON

Argyll and Bute Jewish Community. *Contact* Barry Kaye, Edgemont, 34 Argyll Road, Dunoon, PA23 8ES. ☎/Fax 01369-705 118.

EDINBURGH (500)

The Edinburgh Town Council and Burgess Roll, Minutes of 1691 and 1717, record applications by Jews for permission to reside and trade in Edinburgh. Local directories of the eighteenth century contain Jewish names. There is some reason to believe that there was an organised Jewish community in 1780 but no cemetery, and in 1817 it removed to Richmond Ct. where there was also for a time a rival congregation. In 1795, the Town Council sold a plot of ground on the Calton Hill to Herman Lyon, a Jewish dentist, to provide a burying place for himself and members of his family. In 1816, when a syn. was opened a cemetery was also acquired. The present syn. in Salisbury Road was consecrated in 1932 and renovated in 1980.

Hebrew Congregation, 4 Salisbury Road. ☎ 0131-667 3144. (Est. 1816, New Synagogue built 1932.) *M.* ; *H. Sec.* J. Danzig.

Board of Guardians. *H. Sec.* I. Shein (as above).

Chevra Kadisha. *H. Sec.* R. I. Brodie, 60 Telford Road, Edinburgh EH4 2LY. ☎ 0131-332 4386.

Friendship Club. *President* W. Caplan, 25 Watertoun Road, Edinburgh EH9. ☎ 0131-667 7984.

Jewish Literary Society. *President* Ms E. Samuel, c/o Hebrew Congregation ☎ 0131-229 5541.

Jewish Old Age Home for Scotland (Edinburgh Cttee). *President* J. S. Caplan; *H. Sec.* Miss A. Lurie, 26 South Lauder Road, 9. ☎ 0131-667 5500.

Ladies' Guild. *President* Mrs H. Rifkind, 37 Cluny Drive, Edinburgh EH10 6DU. ☎ 0131-447 7386.

The Edinburgh Star. Community Journal. Published 3 times a year. Editor, 9 Warrington Crescent, EH3 5LA. ☎ 0131-556 7774.

University Jewish Society. *President* P. Albert, c/o Societies' Centre, Room 6, 21 Hill Place.

GLASGOW (6,700)

The Glasgow Jewish community was founded in 1823 although there are records of Jewish activity in the city for many years prior to that. The first Jewish cemetery was opened in the prestigious Glasgow Necropolis in 1831 and the community was housed in a variety of synagogues in the city centre for many years. The community grew in the 1870s and the Garnethill Synagogue, the oldest Jewish building in Scotland and home of the Scottish Jewish Archives Centre, was opened in 1879. At the same time Jews began settling in the Gorbals district just south of the River Clyde where there was a substantial Jewish community with many synagogues and Jewish shops and communal institutions until the 1950s. None of these now remains. In more recent years the community has been centred in the southern suburbs such as Giffnock and Newton Mearns where most Jewish institutions are now situated.

Details of Jewish history in Glasgow in the early days (1790–1919) can be found in 'Second City Jewry' and 'Scotland's Jews' by Dr Kenneth Collins, available from the Glasgow Jewish Representative Council.

Jewish Representative Council, 222 Fenwick Rd., Giffnock, G46 6UE. ☎ 0141-577 8200. Email glasgow@j-scot.org. Website www.j-scot.org/glasgow. (Est. 1914. Reg. Charity No. SCO16626.) *President* S. I. Kliner; *Hon. Sec.* E. Isaacs; *Admin.* Mrs B. Taylor. Information Desk ☎ 0141-577 8228. Fax 0141-577 8202.

West Scotland Kashrut Commission, *Chairman* M. Livingstone; *M.* Rabbi A. Weiss ☎ 0796-8221083; *H. Sec.* H. Tankel. ☎ 0141-423 5830.

Hebrew Burial Society (as Rep. Council), ☎ 0141-577 8226. *Chairman* S. Shenkin. *Enquiries* J. Arthur.

Mikvah, Giffnock & Newlands Syn., Maryville Avenue, Giffnock. *Enquiries* Mrs Borowski ☎ 07831 104110.

United Synagogue Council, Queen's Park Syn., Falloch Road. ☎ 0141-632 1743.

SYNAGOGUES

Garnethill Synagogue, 125/7 Hill Street, G3. ☎ 0141-332 4151. (Est. 1875.) *M.* A. Soudry; *Chairman* G. Levin; *H. Sec.* Mrs R. Livingston.

Queen's Park Synagogue, Falloch Road, G42. ☎ 0141-632 2139. *M. Sec.* Mrs G. Fox. *Chairman* D. Jackson.

Giffnock and Newlands Synagogue, Maryville Avenue, Giffnock G46. ☎ 0141-577 8250. *M.* Rabbi A.M. Rubin; *R.*; *Chairman* E. Borowski; *Sec.* Mrs G. Gardner.

Glasgow New Synagogue, 147 Ayr Road, Newton Mearns G77 5ND. *Chairman* D. Goodman; *M.* Rabbi P. Tobias; *Sec.* P. Kraven. ☎ 0141-639 1838.

Langside Hebrew Congregation, 125 Niddrie Road, G42. ☎ 0141-423 4062. *M. Chairman* J. Levingstone; *H. Sec.* N. Barnes.

Netherlee and Clarkston Hebrew Congregation, Clarkston Road, Clarkston. *M.* Rabbi A. Jesner; *Co-Chairman* Mrs P. Livingstone, A. Shroot. ☎ 0141-637 8206.

Newton Mearns Synagogue, 14 Larchfield Court, G77 5BH. ☎ 0141-639 4000. *M.* Rev. Philip Copperman; *Chairman* D. Links; *Hon. Sec.* H. Hyman. ☎ 0141-639 3399.

EDUCATIONAL AND COMMUNAL ORGANISATIONS

Board of Jewish Education, 28 Calderwood Road, G43 2RU. ☎ 0141-637 7409. *Chairman* M. Clerck; *H. Sec.* N. Allon.

Calderwood Lodge Jewish Primary School, 28 Calderwood Road, G43 2RU. ☎ 0141-637 5654. H.M. Mrs R. Levey.

Chaim Bermant Library, 222 Fenwick Rd., Giffnock G46 6UE. ☎ 0141-577 8230. *Admin.* Mrs D. Zolkwer.

Glasgow Israel Committee, 222 Fenwick Rd., Giffnock G46 6UE. ☎ 0141-620 2194. *Chairman* K. Davidson.

Glasgow Kollel. *Dir.* Rabbi M. Bamberger. ☎ 0141-638 6664/0141-577 8260.

Glasgow Maccabi, May Terrace, Giffnock, G46 6DL. ☎ 0141-638 7655. *Chairman* B. Cohen; *Sec.* Mrs A. Lovatt.

Israel Scottish Information Service, Jewish Community Centre. ☎ 0141-577 8240.

Jewish Choral Society. *Co-Chairmen* Mrs J. Tankel, Mrs D. Mandelstam; *H. Sec.* Mrs A. Sakol. ☎ 0141-639 1756.

Jewish Community Centre. ☎ 0141-577 8222.

Jewish Male Voice Choir. *Chairman* S. Smullen; *Sec.* G. Kitchener. ☎ 0141-638 2982.

Jewish Students' Society. *Contact* Abbie Lynn ☎ 07779-298992, Y. Silverman ☎ 0141-337 3220.

Jewish Youth Forum. ☎ 0141-577 8230.

Lubavitch Foundation, 8 Orchard Dr, Giffnock. ☎ 0141-638 6116. *Dir.* Rabbi Chaim Jacobs.

Maccabi Youth Centre, May Terrace, Giffnock G46. *Chairman* B. Cohen. ☎ 0141-638 7655; *H. Sec.* Mrs D. Minster.

Northern Region Chaplaincy. *Chairman* D. Kaplan; *H. Sec.* S. Marks. ☎ 0141-639 4497; *Chaplain* Rabbi D. Cohen.

Teenage Centre (Atid), at Jewish Community Centre. *Contact* Rosamund Steinberg ☎ 0141-577 8220.

UJIA (incorporating Glasgow Jewish Continuity), Jewish Community Centre, 222 Fenwick Rd., Giffnock, G46 6UE. ☎ 0141-577 8210. Renewal ☎ 0141-577 8220. Fax 0141-577 8212. *Dir.* Alex Steen; *Renewal Dir.* Mrs S. Simpson.

Yeshivah, Giffnock Syn., Maryville Avenue. *Chairman* Dr K. Collins. ☎ 0141-577 8260. *H. M.* Rabbi A.M. Rubin.

WELFARE ORGANISATIONS

Cosgrove Care, May Terrace, Giffnock, G46 6LD. *Chairman* Mr J. Dover; *Dir.* Mrs L. Goldberg; *H. Sec.* Mrs M. Goldman. ☎ 0141-620 2500. Fax 0141-620 2501.

Jewish Housing Association, Barrland Court, Barrland Drive, Giffnock, G46 7QD. *Dir.* Mrs Joan Leifer. ☎ 0141-620 1890. Fax 0141-620 3044.

Jewish Blind Society Centre (Reg. Charity No. SCO11789), Walton Community Care Centre, May Terrace, Giffnock, G46 6DL. ☎ 0141-620 3339. Fax 0141-620 2409. *Chairman* D. Strang; *Sec.* Mrs C. Blake.

Jewish Care Scotland (founded 1868), May Terrace Giffnock, G46 6DL. ☎ 0141-620 1800. Fax 0141-620 1088. *Chairman* A. Tankel. *Dir.* Mrs E. Woldman.

Jewish Hospital and Sick Visiting Association. ☎ 0141-638 6048. *Chairman* H. Cowen.

Newark Care, 43 Newark Drive. ☎ 0141-423 8941. *Chairman* A. Jacobson; *Dir.* M. Maddox.

Senior Citizens Club, *Chairman* B. Mann, *Sec.* Mrs V. Mann. ☎ 0141-644 3611.

NORTHERN IRELAND

BELFAST (550)

There was a Jewish community in Belfast about the year 1771, but the present community was founded in 1865.

Hebrew Congregation, 49 Somerton Rd. (Est. 1872; Syn. erected at Carlisle Circus, 1904, present building consecrated, 1964.) *President* Mr. R. Appleton; *Chairman* I. Selig; *H. Sec.* Mrs Norma Simon, 42 Glandore Ave., BT15 3FD. ☎ 028-9077 9491.

Jewish Community Centre, 49 Somerton Rd. ☎ 028-9077 7974.

Wizo. *Chairperson* Mrs H. Black; *H. Secs.* Mrs N. Simon, Mrs N. Hurwitz.

Belfast Jewish Record. *H. Sec.* Mrs N. Simon, 42 Glandore Ave., BT15 3FD.

ISLE OF MAN (ca. 35)

Hebrew Congregation. *Contact* Carol Jempson, 8 Mountain View, Douglas IM2 5HU; *Visiting M.* Rev. M. Weisman, OBE, M.A. (Oxon.).

Cemetery: Consecrated section of the Douglas Cemetery, Glencrutchery Rd.

CHANNEL ISLANDS

JERSEY (120)

A syn. existed in St. Helier, the capital of the island, from 1843 until about 1870. The present com. was founded in 1962.

Jersey Jewish Congregation, La Petite Route des Mielles, St Brelade, JE3 8FY. ☎ 01534 44946. *President* S.J. Regal; *H. Sec.* M. Morton, 16 La Rocquaise, La Route des Genets, St Brelade, JE3 8HY. ☎ 01534 742819; *H.T.* M. Kalman; *Visiting M.* Rev. M. Weisman, OBE, MA. Seven families of the Jersey cong. live in Guernsey.

REPUBLIC OF IRELAND (1,300)

Jews lived in Ireland in the Middle Ages, and a Sephardi community was established in Dublin in 1660, four years after the Resettlement in England. In the eighteenth century there was a community also at Cork. The Dublin congregation declined in the reign of George III, and was dissolved in 1791, but was revived in 1822. The community received its largest influx of members around 1900, the immigrants coming from Eastern Europe, Lithuania in particular. There are now some 1,300 Jews in the country. (See Hyman: The Jews of Ireland, 1972, repr. 1996.)

Chief Rabbi: Rabbi Dr Y. Perlman. Office: Herzog House, Zion Rd., Dublin, 6. ☎ 01-492-3751. *Sec.* N. Caine.

Jewish Community Office, Herzog House, Zion Rd., Dublin, 6. ☎ 492-3751. Fax 492-4680. *Gen. Sec.* N. Caine.

Jewish Representative Council of Ireland, Herzog House, Dublin, 6. *Chairman* A. Benson.

General Board of Shechita & Kashrut Commission. (Est. 1915.) Herzog House, Zion Rd., Dublin, 6.

Irish Jewish Genealological Society (Est. 1998), c/o Jewish Museum.

Irish-Jewish Museum. (Est. 1984.) 3-4 Walworth Rd., off Victoria St., Portobello, Dublin 8. ☎ 453-1797, *Curator* R. Siev. Times: May to September: 11am to 3.30pm on Sundays, Tuesdays and Thursdays; October to April: 10.30am to 2.30pm on Sundays only. The Museum was opened by Irish-born Chaim Herzog, late former President of Israel, on 20th June, 1985 and contains memorabilia of the Irish Jewish Community and a former synagogue is on view.

Jewish Board of Guardians. (Est. 1889.) *H. Sec.* D. Stein, 14 Wasdale Grove, Dublin 6. ☎ 490 5139.

Jewish Home of Ireland, Denmark Hill, Leicester Rd., W6. *Admin.* ☎ 497-2004.

Joint Israel Appeal, Herzog House, Zion Rd., Dublin, 6. ☎ 492-2318. *H. Sec.* L. Bloomfield.

Jewish National Fund, Herzog House, Zion Rd., Dublin, 6. ☎ 492-2318. *H. Sec.* A. Schwartzman.

CORK (30)

Hebrew Congregation, 10 South Terrace. (Est. 1880). *Chairman of Trustees.* F. Rosehill, 7 Beverly, Ovens, Co. Cork. ☎ 021-4870413. Fax 021-4876537. Email rosehill@iol.ie

DUBLIN (1,300)

Chief Rabbi: Rabbi Yaacov Perlman.

SYNAGOGUES

Dublin Hebrew Congregation, 37 Adelaide Rd. (Est. 1836. Syn. opened 1892; enlarged 1925.) Closed in 1999. Holding services at Terenure. *President* Martin Simmons; *Vice President/H.T.* Don Buchalter; *H. Sec.* Dr Seton Menton, ☎ 2694044.

Terenure Hebrew Congregation, Rathfarnham Rd., Terenure, 6. ☎ 490-8037. *H. Sec.* W. Stein.

Synagogue Machzikei Hadass, 77 Terenure Rd. North, 6. (Est. ca. 1890.) ☎ 493-8991. *H. Sec.* D. Ross.

Jewish Progressive Congregation, 7 Leicester Ave., Rathgar, 6. *Corr*: PO Box 3059, Rathgar, 6. Email finkeljj@indigo.ie (Est. 1945.) *H. Sec.* Mrs J. Finkel. ☎ 490-7605.

Talmud Torah, Stratford Schools, Zion Rd., Rathgar 6. ☎ 492-2315. Fax 492-4680. *H. Sec.* Mrs M. Adler.

Cemeteries: Aughavannagh Rd., Dolphin's Barn, 8. ☎ 454-0806. Inq. to caretaker. The old Jewish cemetery at Ballybough (☎ Ballybough 836-9756) may be visited on application to the caretaker. There is a Progressive cemetery at Woodtown, Co. Dublin.

OTHER COUNTRIES

*Denotes the organisation(s) from which further information about the Jewish community in that country can be obtained. For more detailed information about Jewish communities overseas consult **The Jewish Travel Guide** (Vallentine Mitchell). Population figures taken from 'The Jewish communities handbook 1991' (IJPR and WJC).

AFGHANISTAN

Jews have lived in Afghanistan since antiquity. Just over 100 years ago they reportedly numbered 40,000. Since 1948 there has been a mass emigration to Israel, and only a few families remain in Kabul and Herat.

ALBANIA

After the recent emigration to Israel very few Albanian Jews remain in the country.

ALGERIA (150)

It is believed that there were Jews in Algeria as early as the fourth century, BCE. The fortunes of the community varied under the Turkish regime, which began in 1519. After the French conquered Algeria the community was reorganised and in 1870 most Jews were granted French citizenship. However, there have been anti-Jewish excesses even in the present century. After Algeria's bitter fight for independence, the Jews, like other French nationals, lost their possessions when they left the country. About 120,000 at independence in 1962, they remain less than 150 today: almost all fled to France.

Communal Centre and Synagogue: 6 Rue Hassena Ahmed, Algiers. ☎ (213-2) 62 85 72.

American Joint Distribution Committee, 11 Ali Boumdemdjel, Algiers. ☎ (213-2) 63 29 49.

ANTIGUA (West Indies)

A few Jewish residents live permanently on the island. Corr.: B. Rabinowitz, Cedar Valley P.O.B. 399. ☎ 461 4150.

ARGENTINA (240,000)

The early Jewish settlers in Argentina were Marranos, who were gradually absorbed in the general population. The present community grew through immigration (beginning in 1862) from Germany, the Balkans, and North Africa. From Eastern Europe immigrants began to arrive in 1889, many of them going to the agricultural settlements est. by the Jewish Colonization Assn. (see p.72). The com. is est. to number 300,000, incl. 60,000 Sephardim, who have their own separate institutions, according to D.A.I.A., the representative org. of Argentine Jews. The Jewish pop. of Greater Buenos Aires is estimated at 220,000. A survey conducted by the Hebrew Univ. of Jerusalem estimates the Jewish pop. at 240,000, of whom 210,000 are Ashkenazim and 30,000 are Sephardim. This source estimates 180,000 Jews live in Gtr. Buenos Aires.

There are nine other major coms. in Parana, Rosario, Cordoba, Bahia Blanca, Posadas, Resistencia, Tucuman, Mendoza and La Plata. There is a small but very active community in Mar del Plata, south of Buenos Aires. Very few Jewish families remain on the former J.C.A. settlements. There are about 100 syns. (80 Orthodox, one Reform, the rest Conservative or Liberal), and a well-organised network of communal and educ. instits. There are communal offices in **Cordoba** at Alvear 254, and in **Rosario** at Paraguay 1152.

BUENOS AIRES
Congreso Judio Latinoamericano, Larrea 744, 1030. ☎ 961-44532. Fax 963-7056.
Representative Organisation of Argentine Jews: DAIA, Pasteur 633, 5th floor.
Amia Central Ashkenazi Community, Pasteur 633.
Central Sephardi Community: ECSA, Larrea 674.
Latin American Rabbinical Seminary (Conservative), Jose Hernandez 1750.
Argentine Zionist Organisation & Jewish Agency (Sochnut), Cangallo 2471.

ARMENIA (500)

Jews have lived in Armenia for many hundreds of years and the various communities were spread around different parts of the country. There was a synagogue in Yerevan, but in the 1930s it was destroyed. Nowadays, nearly all the Armenian Jews live in Yerevan, with only a few families living in Vanadzor (Kirovakan) and Gjumri (Leninakan), while others are scattered in other small towns and villages. When 'perestroyka' was introduced in 1989, the Jewish community organised itself and in 1991 was registered as a non-formal organisation. Perestroyka opened the doors, so that a large number of the population emigrated to Israel. In 1991 a Jewish Sunday school was opened both for children and adults. In 1992 the Israeli embassy in Moscow financed the school. Over 60 per cent of the population is over 60 years of age and there are about 40 children below the age of 16 years.

President: Mr Willi Weiner, ☎ (7-8852) 525882; *Dir. of Education:* Dr George Fajvush, ☎ (7-8852) 735852; *Rabbi:* Gersh Bourstein, ☎ (7-8852) 271115.

ARUBA (50)

Beth Israel Synagogue. Dedicated in 1962, this syn. serves the needs of the com. in this island in the Antilles in the Caribbean, of some 35 Jewish families. Jews from Curaçao settled in Aruba early in the nineteenth century, but did not stay there long, and the present com. dates from 1924.

AUSTRALIA (106,000)

The earliest org. of Jews in Australia was in 1817 when 20 Jews in New South Wales formed a burial society. In 1828 a congregation was formed in Sydney and the first specially erected syn. was opened in 1844. The first Jewish service was held in Melbourne in 1839, four years after the beginning of the colonisation on the banks of the River Yarra, and a syn. was opened in 1847. Congregations were est. at Ballarat (1853) and Geelong (1854). In South Australia, a permanent congregation was formed in Adelaide in 1848. A congregation in Brisbane was est. in 1865. In Western Australia the first congregation (now ended) was formed at Fremantle in 1887, and the present Perth congregation est. in 1892, with Kalgoorlie in 1895. In Tasmania a syn. was opened in Hobart in 1845 and another at Launceston in 1846. Organised Jewish coms. were est. in other States a few years later.

In Australia's public life Jews have played a distinguished part, many having risen to high office in the Federal and State Parliaments or on the Judicial bench. Two Governors-General of Australia have been Jews, Sir Zelman Cowen and the late Sir Isaac Isaacs. Sir John Monash, the Commander of the Australian Expeditionary Forces in the First World War, was a Jew. The Executive Council of Australian Jewry represents the central Jewish organisations in each State.

The Australian census has an optional question on religious affiliation. In 1981, 62,127 people declared themselves Jews by religion. If a proportionate number of 'no religion/religion not stated' replies are regarded as Jewish, the number of Jews rises to 79,345. Recent demographic res. indicated that there are probably about 92,000 people in Australia who are religiously or ethnically Jewish. The main Jewish coms. are in Melbourne (50,000); Sydney (40,000); Perth (4,870); Brisbane (1,500); Adelaide (1,250); The Gold Coast, Queensland (1,000); Canberra (500); Hobart (100).

MAIN JEWISH ORGANISATIONS

Executive Council of Australian Jewry, 146 Darlinghurst Rd, Darlinghurst, NSW 2010. ☎ (02) 9360 5415. Fax (02) 9360 5416. *President* Jeremy Jones.

***N.S.W. Jewish Board of Deputies,** 146 Darlinghurst Rd., Darlinghurst, NSW, 2010. ☎ 2-9360-1600. Fax 2-9331-4712. *Exec. Dir.* Mrs S. Faktor.

Jewish Community Council of Victoria, 306 Hawthorn Rd., South Caulfield, Victoria 3162. *President* G. Leonard; *Exec. Off.* Mrs H. McMahon. ☎ 3-92725566.

Australia/Israel and Jewish Affairs Council (AIJAC), Level 2, 578 St Kilda Road, Melbourne, Victoria 3004. ☎ 3-9529-5022. Fax 3-9529-8571. Email aijac@aijac.org.au. *Exec. Dir.* Dr Colin Rubenstein (see p.67).

Jewish National Fund of Australia, 306 Hawthorn Road, Caulfield, Victoria 3162. ☎ 3-92725566. Fax 3-92725573. *President* M. Naphtali.

Jewish Museum of Australia, 26 Alma Rd., St. Kilda, Victoria 3182. ☎ (03) 9534 0083.

Kadimah – Jewish Cultural Centre and Jewish National Library (Est. 1911), 7 Selwyn Street, Elsternwick, Victoria 3185. ☎ 03 9523 9817. Fax 03 9523 6161. Email jlibrary@vicnet.net.au.

Zionist Federation of Australia, 306 Hawthorn Road, Caulfield, Victoria 3162. ☎ 3-9272-5644. Fax 3-9272-5640. *President* Dr R. Weiser.

Australian, Asian & New Zealand Union for Progressive Judaism, POBox 128, St Kilda, Victoria 3182. ☎ (03) 9533 8587. Fax (03) 952 1229. Email anzup@bigpond.com.

Australian Federation of Sephardim, 40-42 Fletcher St., Bondi Junction, NSW, 2022. ☎ 2-9389-3355. Fax 2-9369-2143. *President*: A. Gubbay.

Victoria Union for Progressive Judaism, 78-82 Alma Rd., St Kilda, Victoria 3182. ☎ 3-9510-1488. Fax 3-9521-1229.

Federation of Australian Jewish Welfare Societies, P.O.Box 500, St Kilda, Victoria 3182. ☎ (3) 9525 4000. Fax (03) 9525 3737.

National Council of Jewish Women of Australia, 133 Hawthorn Road, Caulfield, Victoria 3161. ☎ (03) 9523 0535. Fax (03) 9523 0156. *President* Dr G. Solomon, OAM.

Australian Federation of WIZO, 53 Edgecliff Road, Woollahra, NSW 2025. ☎ (02) 9386 4444. Fax (02) 9387 5373.

B'nai B'rith Australia/New Zealand, 99 Hotham Street, St Kilda East, 3183. ☎ (03) 9527 8249. Fax (03) 9527 8259. *President* Dr Peter Schiff.

Australasian Union of Jewish Students, 306 Hawthorn Road, Caulfield, Victoria 3162. ☎ (03) 9272 5622. Fax (03) 9272 5620.

MAIN SYNAGOGUES AND COMMUNAL CENTRES

SYDNEY

New South Wales Jewish Board of Deputies, 146 Darlinghurst Rd, Darlinghurst, NSW 2010. ☎ 2-9360 1600. Fax 2-9331 4712.

The Great Synagogue (Ashk. Orth.), Elizabeth St. (Office: 166 Castlereagh St.), NSW 2000. ☎ 2-9267 2477. Fax 2-9264 8871.

Central Synagogue (Orth.), 15 Bon Accord Ave, Bondi Junction, NSW 2022. ☎ 2-9389 5622. Fax 2-9389 5418.

North Shore Synagogue (Orth.), 15 Treatts Rd, Lindfield, NSW 2070. ☎ 2-9416 3710. Fax 2-9416 7659.

North Shore Temple Emanuel (Lib.), 28 Chatswood Ave., Chatswood, NSW 2067. ☎ 2-9419 7011. Fax 2-9413 1474. Email nste@nste.or.au.

Sephardi Synagogue (Orth.), 40-42 Fletcher St, Bondi Junction, NSW 2025. ☎ 2-9389 3355. Fax 2-9365 3856.

Temple Emanuel (Lib.), 7 Ocean St, Woollahra, NSW 2025. ☎ 2-9328 7833. Fax 2-9327 8715. Email emanuel@ozmail.com.au.

Yeshiva Synagogue (Orth.), 36 Flood St, Bondi NSW 2026. ☎ 2-9387 3822. Fax 2-9389 7652.

MELBOURNE

Melbourne Hebrew Congregation (Orth.), One Toorak Rd., South Yarra, Victoria 3141. ☎ 3-9866-2255.

St. Kilda Hebrew Congregation, 12 Charnwood Gr., St. Kilda, Victoria 3182. ☎ 3-9537-1433.

Temple Beth Israel (Lib.), 76 Alma Rd., St. Kilda, Victoria 3182. ☎ 3-9510-1488. Fax 3-9521-1229. Email tempbeth@starnet.com.au.

Beth Weizmann Community Centre, 306 Hawthorn Rd., Caulfield South, Victoria 3162. ☎ 3-9272-5555.

Caulfield Hebrew Congregation, 572 Inkerman Rd., Caulfield, Victoria 3161. ☎ 3-9525-9492.

PERTH

Perth Hebrew Congregation, Cnr. Plantation St. and Freedman Rd., Menora, WA 6050. ☎ 9-271-0539. Email phc@theperthshule.asu.au.

Temple David Congregation (Lib.), 34 Clifton Crescent, Mt. Lawley, 6050. ☎ 9-271-1458. Fax 9-272-2827. Email temdavid@iinet.net.au.

Beit Midrash of WA (Inc) – Daniella Shule (Orth.), 68 Woodrow Ave., Yorkine, WA 6060. *President* Marcel Goodman; *Sec.* Peter Katz; *M.* Rabbi Marcus Solomon. ☎ 9375 8985/1276/1664. Website www.bigfoot.com/~bmwa.

Chabad of Western Australia (Inc.) (Orth.), 395 Alexander Drive, Noranda, WA 6062. *M.* Rabbi Mordi Gutnick; *Contact* Max Green ☎ 9375 1078.

Northern Suburbs Hebrew Congregation (Orth.), Garson Court, Noranda, WA 6062. *M.* Rabbi Moshe Rothchild ☎ 9275 3500. Fax 9275 3424. Email shul@iinet.net.au. Website http://shul.iinet.net.au.

Jewish Centre, 61 Woodrow Ave., Mt. Yokine, WA 6060. ☎ 9-276-8572.

ADELAIDE

See B.K. Hyams, 'Surviving: A History of The Institutions and Organisations of the Adelaide Jewish Community' (1998).

Hebrew Congregation, Synagogue Pl., 13 Flemington St., PO Box 338, Glenside, SA 5065. ☎ 8-338-2922. Fax 8-379-0142.

Beit Shalom Synagogue, 41 Hackney Rd., SA 5069. ☎ 8-362-8281. Fax 8-362-4406. Email bshalom@senet.com.au.

Jewish Community Council, 13 Flemington St. *President* Norman Schueler. ☎ 8-240-0066. Fax 8-447-6668.

BRISBANE

Brisbane Hebrew Congregation (Orth.), 98 Margaret St., Brisbane, Qld. 4000. ☎ 7-3229-3412. Fax 7-3366-8311. Email pgt_levy@world.net.

Temple Shalom (Lib.), 15 Koolatah St., Camp Hill, Qld. 4152. ☎ 7-398-8843.

CANBERRA

National Jewish Memorial Centre (A.C.T. Jewish Community Centre), Canberra Ave. and National Circuit, Forrest, P.O. Box 3105, Manuka, ACT 2603. ☎ (02) 6295 1052. Website www.actjewish.org.uk.

TASMANIA

Hobart Synagogue, PO Box 128, 7001. ☎ 3-6234-4720. The synagogue is the oldest in Australia, having been consecrated in July 1845. See H. Fixel, Hobart Hebrew Congregation: 150 Years of Survival Against All Odds (1999).

Jewish Centre, Chabad House, 93 Lord Street, Sandy Bay, 7005. ☎/Fax 3-6223-7116.
Hobart Hebrew Congregation (Progressive), 59 Argyle Street, 7000. ☎ 3-6234-4720. Email shule@hobart.org.
Launceston Synagogue, PO Box 66, St John Street, 7250. ☎ 3-6343-1143. This is the second oldest synagogue in Australia, founded in 1846.

AUSTRIA (12,000)

The story of Austrian Jewry is punctuated by accounts of expulsion and re-immigration, of persecution on false accusations of ritual murder and other pretexts and recovery. After the 1848 Revolution the Jews gained equality, and their economic and cultural importance grew. But antisemitism had not ended; it culminated in the violence of the years preceding the Second World War. Austria's Jewish population in 1934 was 191,481 (with 176,034 in Vienna), the number today is about 12,000, almost all of them in Vienna. Other coms. are in Graz, Innsbruck, Linz and Salzburg.
***Jewish Community Centre**, Israelitische Kulturgemeinde, Seitenstettengasse 4, 1010 Vienna. ☎ 53 1040. Fax 531-04108. *President* Dr A. Muzicant; *Dir.* Dr A. Hodik.
Main Syns. Stadttempel, Seitenstettengasse 4 (Trad.); Machsike Hadass, Grosse Mohrengasse 19, 1020 (Orth.); Khal Israel, Tempelgasse 3, 1020 (Orth.); Ohel Moshe, Lilienbrunngasse 19, 1020 (Orth.); Misrachi, Judenplatz 8, 1010; Khal Chassidim, Gr. Schiffgasse 8, 1020 (Orth.); Or Chaddasch Cong. (Prog.), Heidgasse 1, 1020.
Chief Rabbi: Rabbi Paul Chaim Eisenberg. ☎ 53 104-111.
Jewish Welcome Service, A-1010 Vienna, Stephansplatz 10. ☎ 533 88 91. Fax 533 4098. *Dir.* Dr L. Zelman.

BAHAMAS (200)

Freeport Hebrew Congregation. 20 families.
Luis de Torres Synagogue, East Sunrise Highway, P.O. Box F-42515, Freeport. ☎ (242) 373 2008. *President* Geoff Hurst. ☎ (242) 373-4025. Fax (242) 373-2130. Email hurst100@yahoo.com; *V.President* Tony Gee. ☎ (242) 373-8994; *Sec.* Don Nyveen, ☎ (242) 373-7652. Email don@wertend.coralwave.com. Please contact for times of service. Geoff Hurst is happy to make arrangements for tourists, and is the Bahamian Marriage Officer.

BARBADOS (55)

A Jewish com. was formed in Barbados by refugees from Brazil after its reconquest by the Portuguese about the year 1650. In 1802 by Local Govt. Act, all political disabilities of the Jews were removed, but were not confirmed by Westminster until 1820. Barbados was the first British possession to grant full political emancipation to its Jews; Gt. Britain herself doing so more than 50 years later. With the economic decline of the West Indies the fortunes of their Jewish inhabitants also declined. In 1929, only one practising Jew remained, but in 1932 a gp. of Jews settled on the island from Europe. In December, 1987, the Old Synagogue in Bridgetown, one of the two oldest houses of worship in the Western Hemisphere (the other is in Curaçao), reopened for services for the first time in nearly 60 years, following restoration with the island community's support. An appeal fund was launched with Sir Hugh Springer, the Governor-General, as patron. There is a Jewish cemetery by the syn. In 1985, the Barbadian Govt. vested the syn. in the Barbadian Nat. Trust.

***Jewish Community Council**, P.O.B. 256, Bridgetown. ☎ 426 4764. Fax 426 4768. *Contact* Benny Gilbert.

BELARUS (28,000)

GOMMEL

Syn.: 13 Sennaya St.
Jewish Cultural Society, 1A Krasnoarmeyska St., 24600. *Chairman* V. F. Iofedov.

GRODNO

Menorah Jewish Community, Blk 43, Flat 37, 230009. Email sh10@grsu.grodno.by. *Chairpersons* Misha and Ira Kemerov.

MINSK

Syn.: 22 Kropotkin St. ☎ (017-2) 55-82-70.

ORSHA

Syn.: Nogrin St.

RECHITSA

Syn.: 120 Lunacharsky St.
There are also Jewish communities in Bobruisk, Mozyr, Pinsk, Brest, Grodno, Vitebsk and Borisov.

BELGIUM (30,000)

Jews have lived in Belgium since Roman times. After the fall of Napoleon the Belgian provinces were annexed by Holland. In 1816 a decree by the Dutch King ordered the erection of two syns. in Maastricht and Brussels. But Belgian Jews had to wait until 1830, when Belgium became independent, to see their status formally recognised. The Constitution accorded freedom of religion in 1831. Before the Second World War the Jewish population was 80,000. Today there are flourishing communities in Antwerp, Brussels, Ostend, Liège, Charleroi and Waterloo totalling (together with the smaller communities) about 30,000 Jews.

ANTWERP

Synagogues and rel. orgs.: Shomre Hadass (Israelitische Gemeente), Terlistr 35, 2018. ☎ 226.05.54. Rabbi D. Lieberman. Syns.: Bouwmeesterstr., Romi Goldmuntz, Van den Nestlei.
Machsike Hadass (Orth.) Jacob Jacobstr. 22. *Rab.* Main syn.: Oostenstr. 42-44.
Sephardi Syn.: Hovenierstr. 31.
Central Jewish Welfare Organisation, Jacob Jacobsstr. 2. ☎ 232 3890.
Home for the Aged and Nursing Home, Marialei 6-8.
Residentie Apfelbaum-Laub., Marialei 2-4. ☎ 218.9399.
Holiday camp, Villa Altol, Coxyde-on-Sea, Damesweg 10. ☎ 058 512661.
Other orgs.: Zionist Fed., Pelikaanstr. 108; Mizrachi, Isabellalei 65; Romi Goldmuntz Centre, Nervierstr. 12; B'nai B'rith–Nervierstr 12AAT 14.

BRUSSELS

*__Comité de Coordination des Organisations Juives de Belgique__ (C.C.O.J.B.). Av. Ducpétiaux 68, 1060 Brussels. ☎ 537 1691. Fax 539 2295. Email ccojb@yucom.be.
Consistoire Central Israélite de Belgique, 2 rue Joseph Dupont, 1000 Brussels. ☎ 02 512 21 90.
Cercle Ben-Gurion, 89 Chausée de Vleurgat, 1050 Brussels.
Centre Communautaire Laic Juif, 52 Rue Hotel des Monnaies, 1060 Brussels.
Zionist Offices, 66-68 Avenue Ducpétiaux, 1060 Brussels.
Synagogues: 32 rue de la Régence; 67a rue de la Clinique; 73 rue de Thy; 126 rue Rogier; 11 Ave. Messidor; 47 rue Pavillon (Sephardi); Beth Hillel (Lib.) 96 Ave. de Kersbeek; Brussels airport, Zaventem.

MONS

SHAPE International Jewish Community, c/o SHAPE Chaplains' Office, B-7010 SHAPE, Belgium. ☎/Fax (32) 6572 8769. (Est. 1967) To meet the spiritual, social and educational needs of Jewish military and civilian personnel and their families serving at or temporarily assigned to SHAPE, Mons, Belgium. *Lay Leader* Wing Commander Stephen Griffiths, MBE, RAF.

BERMUDA (125)

The small community drawn from a dozen countries has never had a synagogue or communal building. A lay leader conducts a Friday service each month at the Chamber of Commerce, Albouys Point, Hamilton; a visiting Rabbi conducts High Holy day services and children's classes are held regularly.

Jewish Community of Bermuda, P.O. Box HM 1793, Hamilton, HMHX Bermuda. ☎ 441-291 1785. Website www.jcb.bm.

BOLIVIA (640)

Although there have been Jews in Latin America for many centuries, they are comparative newcomers to Bolivia, which received its first Jewish immigrants only in 1905. They remained a mere handful until the 1920s, when some Russian Jews made their way to the country. After 1935, German Jewish refugees, began to arrived in Bolivia. Also from Rumania and mostly from Poland. Today some 640 Jews live there, mostly in the capital of La Paz (about 430), Cochambamba (120) and Santa Cruz (85), Tarija and other cities (5).

COCHABAMBA

Syn.: Calle Junin y Calle Colombia, Casilla 349.

Asociación Israelita de Cochabamba, P.O.B. 349, Calle Valdivieso. *President* German Grumbaum.

LA PAZ

Syns.: Circulo Israelita de Bolivia, Casilla 1545, Calle Landaeta 346, P.O.B. 1545. Services Sat. morn. only. *President* Ricardo Udler.

Comunidad Israelita Synagogue, Calle Canada Stronguest 1846, P.O.B. 2198. ☎ 313602, is affiliated to the Circulo. Fri. evening services are held. There is a Jewish sch. at this address. Circulo Israelita, P.O.B. 1545 is the representative body of Bolivian Jewry. All La Paz organisations are affiliated to it.

Two Homes for Aged: Calle Rosendo Gutierrez 307, and Calle Diaz Romero 1765.

Israel Tourist Information Office: Centro Shalom, Calle Canada Stronguest 1846, La Paz Country Club, Quinta J.K.G. Obrajes. Calle 1, esquina calle Hector Ormachea Casilla 1545, La Paz.

SANTA CRUZ

Centro Cruceño P.O.B. 469, WIZO, Casilla 3409. *President* Sra Guicha Schwartz.

BOSNIA HERCEGOVINA (1,100)

Sarajevo Jewish Community, Hamdije Kreševlijakovica 59. ☎ 38733 663 973. Email la_bene@open.net.ba.

BRAZIL (250,000)

The early history of Brazilian Jewry was affected by the struggles for power between the Portuguese and Dutch. The Inquisition, revived in Brazil, increased the number of Marrano Jews. The Dutch, after their victory in 1624, granted full religious freedom to the Jews, but 30 years afterwards the Portuguese reconquered the land and reintroduced the Inquisition. In 1822 Brazil declared its independence and liberty of worship was proclaimed. It is believed that about 250,000 Jews are living in Brazil, distributed as follows: Sao Paulo State, 90,000; Rio de Janeiro State, 80,000; Rio Grande do Sul (Porto Alegre) 25,000; Parana State (Curitiba) 2,408; Minas Gerais State (Bel Horizonte) 1,656; Pernambuco State (Recife) 1,276.

RIO DE JANEIRO

*__Federacão Israelita__, R. Buenos Aires 68, AN15.

Fundo Communitario, R. Buenos Aires 68, AN15.

Orthodox Rabbinate, R. Pompeu Loureiro No.40. ☎/Fax 2360249.

Chevre Kedishe, Rua Barao de Iguatemi 306 (Orthodox).

Congrecão Beth El, Rua Barata Ribeiro 489 (Sephardi).

Associacão Religiosa Israelita, Rua Gen. Severiano 170 (Liberal). ☎ 295 6599. Fax 542 6499.

Synagogues: Agudat Israel, Rua Nascimento Silva, 109, Beth Aron, Rua Gado Coutinho, 63, Kehilat Yaacov Copacabana, Rua Capelao Alvares da Silva 15; Templo Uniao Israel, Rua Jose Higino, 375-381.

Associacão Feminina Israelita, Av. Almte. Barroso, 6/14°.

Organizacão Sionista Unificada, Rua Decio Vilares, 258.

Museu Judaico, Rua Mexico, 90/1° andar-Castelo.

SÃO PAULO

Federacao Israelita do Estado de São Paulo, Av. Paulista 726, 2nd floor. ☎ 288 6411.

Syngogues and religious centres: Centro Judaico Religioso de Sao Paulo (Orthodox). ☎ 220 5642; Beit Chabad, Rua Chabad 56/60; Communidade Israelita Sefaradi, Rua da Abolicao 457; Congregacão Israelita Paulista, "Einheitsgemeinde" (Liberal), Rua Antonico Carlos 653.

Zionist Offices, Rua Correa Mello 75.

BULGARIA (6,500)

Bulgarian Jewry dates from the second century C.E. Before the Second World War there were 50,000 Jews in Bulgaria. From 1948-49 to about 1954/55, 45,000 emigrated to Israel. Today the number is about 6,500 of whom about 3,000 live in Sofia.

Central Jewish Religious Council and Synagogue, 16 Exarch Joseph St., Sofia 1000. ☎ 359-2/831-273. *President* Joseph Levy.

Organization of the Jews in Bulgaria "Shalom", 50 Al. Stambolijski St., Sofia 130. ☎/Fax 359-2/870-163. *President* Emile Callo. Publishes newspaper "Evrejski Vesti" and research compendium "Annual". Jewish museum in the Synagogue: Sofia, 16 Exarch Joseph St. Joseph Caro permanent exhibition in the city Museum and a memorial stone in the town of Nikopol. Publishing house "Shalom", Jewish Sunday School, Jewish Resource Centre, Memorial stone dedicated to the Salvation of the Bulgarian Jews near the Parliament. B'nai Brith, Maccabi and other Jewish organizations.

BURMA (Myanmar)

About 25 Burmese Jews live in Rangoon (Yangon), the capital.

Musmeah Yeshua Synagogue (est. 1896), 85 26th St., P.O. Box 45, Rangoon. Man. Tr. J. Samuels. ☎ 951-75062.

Israel Embassy, 49 Pyay Rd. ☎ 951 22290/01. Fax 951-22463.

CANADA (356,300)

Jews were prohibited by law from living in Canada so long as it remained a French possession. Nevertheless, Jews from Bordeaux – David Gradis, a wealthy merchant and shipowner, and his son Abraham Gradis, in particular – had a large share in the commercial development of the colony.

Jews played some part in the British occupation of Canada. Half a dozen Jewish officers, including Aaron Hart, whose descendants played important roles in Jewish and Canadian life for several generations, were suppliers to the expeditionary force which occupied Quebec.

A number of Jews settled at an early date in Montreal, where the Spanish and Portuguese Synagogue, Shearith Israel (still flourishing), was established in the 1770s and a cong. of 'German, Polish and English' Jews was granted a charter in 1846. A burial society was formed in Toronto in 1849. Montreal Jews were also among the fur traders in the Indian territories. In the 19th century, Jewish immigrants arrived in Canada in some numbers, and in 1832 – a quarter of a century earlier than in Britain – the Lower Canada Jews received full civil rights.

A fresh era in the history of Canadian Jewry opened at the close of the century, when emigration on a large scale from Eastern Europe began. Montreal, Toronto, and, to a lesser degree, Winnipeg became the seats of Jewish coms. of some importance.

On the history of the Jews in Canada generally, see A. D. Hart, *The Jew in Canada*, 1926; L. Rosenberg, *Canada's Jews*, 1939; B. G. Sack, *The History of the Jews in Canada*, 1945; and I.M. Abella, *A Coat of Many Colours: Two Centuries of Jewish Life in Canada*, 1990. The early colonial period in North America is covered in Sheldon and Judith Godfrey, *Search Out the Land*, 1995.

NATIONAL INSTITUTIONS

Canadian Jewish Congress. (Est. 1919, reorganised 1934.)

National Office: 100 Sparks Street, Suite 650, Ottawa, Ontario K1P 5B7. ☎ (613) 233-8703. Fax (613) 233-8748. Email canadianjewishcongress@cjc.ca; Website www.cjc.ca. *Nat. President* Keith M. Landy; *Exec. V. President* and *Gen. Counsel* Jack Silverstone.

Administrative Head Office: 1590 Docteur Penfield Avenue, Montreal, Quebec H3G 1C5. ☎ (514) 931-7531. Fax (514) 931-0548.

Atlantic Region: 5670 Spring Garden Road, Suite 508, Halifax, NS B3J 1H6. ☎ (902) 422-7491. Fax (902) 425-3722. *Exec. Dir.* Jon M. Goldberg.

Quebec Region: 1 Cummings Square, Montreal, Quebec H3W 1M6. ☎ (514) 345-6411. Fax (514) 345-6412. *Exec. Dir.* David Birnbaum.

Ontario Region: 4600 Bathurst St., Willowdale, M2R 3V2. ☎ (416) 635 2883. Fax 635-1408. *Exec. Dir.* Bernie Farber.

National Capital District: 21 Nadolny Sachs Private, Ottawa, Ontario K2A 1R9. ☎ (613) 798-4696. Fax (613) 798-4695. *Exec. Dir.* Mitchell Bellman.

Manitoba Region: 123 Doncaster Street #C300, Winnipeg, Manitoba R3N 2B2. ☎ (204) 477-7400. Fax (204) 477-7405. *Exec. Dir.* Robert Freedman.

Alberta Region (Calgary): Calgary Jewish Community Council, 1607, 90th Ave. S.W., Calgary, T2V 4V7. ☎ (403) 253-8600. Fax 253-7915. *Exec. Dir.* Myrna Linder.

Alberta Region (Edmonton): Jewish Federation of Edmonton, 7200, 156th Street, Edmonton, T5R 1X3. ☎ (780) 487 5120. Fax 481-1854. *Exec. Dir.* Gayle Tallman.

Saskatchewan Region (Regina): c/o 4715 McTavish St., Regina, S4S 6H2. ☎ (306) 569-8166. Fax (306) 569-8166. *Comm. Dev. Off.* Helene Kesten.

Saskatchewan Region (Saskatoon), c/o 715 McKinnon Ave, S7H 2G2. ☎ (306) 343-7023. Fax (306) 343-1244. *Officer* June Avivi.

Pacific Region: 950 West 41st Ave., Vancouver V5Z 2N7. ☎ (604) 257-5101. Fax 257-5131. *Exec. Dir.* Erwin Nest.

Canada-Israel Committee, 130 Slater St., Suite 630, Ottawa K1P 6E2. *Exec. Dir.* Shimon Fogel. ☎ (613) 234 8271. Ontario Office: 2221 Yonge St. #502, Toronto M4S 2B4. ☎ (416) 489 8889.

Canadian Association for Labour Israel. (Est. 1939) 7005 Kildare Rd., #14 Côte

St. Luc, Quebec H4W 1C1.

Canadian Jewish Historical Society, 7489 Briar Rd., Côte St. Luc, Quebec, H4W 1K9. ☎ (514) 848 2066. *President.* Dr I. Robinson.

Canadian ORT, 3101 Bathurst St #604, Toronto, Ontario M6A 2A6.

Emunah Women of Canada. Nat. *President* R. Schneidman, 7005 Kildare Rd, #18 Montreal H3W 3C3. ☎ (514) 485 2397.

Hadassah-Wizo of Canada, 1310 Greene Av. #650, Montreal H3Z 2B8. (Est. 1917.) *Exec. V. President* Mrs L. Frank. Chapters: 220, in most Jewish centres. Toronto office: 638A Sheppard Ave W, #209, M3H 2S1. ☎(416) 630 8373.

Jewish Immigrant Aid Services of Canada. (Est. 1919.) 4600 Bathurst St., Willowdale, Ont., M2R 3V3. *Exec. Dir.* ☎ (416) 630 9051.

Jewish National Fund. 1980 Sherbrooke St. W., Montreal, H3H 1E8. ☎ (514) 934 0313.

Labour Zionist Movement (Est. 1939), 272 Codsell Ave., Downsview, Ont. M3H 3X2.

Mizrachi Organization of Canada. *Nat. Exec. Dir.* Rabbi M. Gopin, 159 Almore Ave., Downsview, Ont. M3H 2H9. ☎ (416) 630 7575.

National Council of Jewish Women of Canada, 1588 Main St., #118, Winnipeg, Manitoba R2V 1Y3. ☎ (204) 339 9700.

Canadian Zionist Federation (Est. 1967), 5250 Decarie Blvd., #550, Montreal, H3X 2H9. ☎ (514) 486 9526.

United Israel Appeal Federations Canada. *Exec. V. President* Ms M. Finkelstein, 4600 Bathurst St., Willowdale, Ont. M2R 3V3. ☎ (416) 636 7655. Fax (416) 635-5806.

CAYMAN ISLANDS (50)

There are approx. 50 Jewish residents in the 3 Cayman Islands, nearly all living on Grand Cayman. They are joined by about 40 others who are regular visitors. Services in private homes. *Contact:* Harvey De Souza, P.O. Box 72, Grand Cayman, Cayman Islands, British West Indies.

CHILE (25,000)

The number of Jews in Chile is about 25,000. The great majority live in the Santiago area. Communities also in Arica, Chillan, Chuquicamata, Concepción, Iquique, La Serena, Puerto Montt, Punta Arenas, Rancagua, San Fernando, Santa Cruz, Temuco, Valdivia, Vina del Mar/Valparaiso.

SANTIAGO

***Comité Representativo de las Entidades Judias de Chile (CREJ),** Miguel Claro 196. ☎ 235 8669. Fax 235 0754.

Comunidad Israelita de Santiago, Tarapaca 870. (Ashkenazi). ☎ 633 1436. Fax 638 2076.

Comunidad Israelita de Santiago Congregacion Jafetz Jayim (Orthodox) Miguel Claro 196. ☎ 274 5389.

Comunidad Israelita Sefaradi de Chile, R. Lyon 812. ☎ 209 8086. Fax 204 7382.

Sociedad Cultural, Bne Jisroel, Mar Jónico 8860, Vitacura. ☎/Fax 201 1623 (German).

MAZsE, (Hungarian) Pedro Bannen 0166. ☎ 2742536.

B'nai Brith, Ricardo Lyon 1933. ☎274 2006. Fax 225 2039.

Zionist Federation Offices, Rafael Cañas 246. ☎251 8821. Fax 251 0961.

Estadio Israelita Maccabi, Club, Las Condes 8361. ☎ 235 9096. Fax 251 0105.

Wizo Chile, M. Montt 207. ☎ 235 9096. Fax 251 105.

CHINA (3,100)

In recent years, Jewish tourists from a number of countries, including Britain and the U.S., have visited the ancient city of Kaifeng, 300 miles south of Peking, and met people who claim descent from a sizeable com. which lived there for centuries and dispersed in the 19th century. Some experts believe the Kaifeng Jews to have originated from Persia or Yemen. Few are left of the coms. formed by other immigrants from Asia at the end of the 19th century and by the Russian and German refugees of the First and Second World Wars.

A comprehensive bibliography on the Jews of China was published in 1998: Jews and Judaism in Traditional China: A Comprehensive Bibliography, Donald Daniel Leslie (Sankt Petersburg: Steyler Verlag, 1998) (Monumenta serica, XLIV).

HONG KONG (3,000)

The Hong Kong com. dates from about 1857. The Ohel Leah synagogue, built in 1901, has recently been restored. The history of the community is published in A Social History of the Jews of Hong Kong: A Resource Guide by Dr Caroline B. Pluss.

The Jewish Community Centre, One Robinson Place, 70 Robinson Road, Mid-levels. ☎ (852) 2868-0828. *Information* ☎ (852) 2801-5440. Fax 2877-0917. Website www.jcc.org.hk. *Gen. Man.* Michael Sheppard.

Synagogues:

Ohel Leah Syn., One Robinson Place, 70 Robinson Rd. ☎ (852) 2589-2621. Fax 852 2548 2000. Email pauline@ohelleah.org. Website www.ohelleah.org. *M.* Rabbi Y. Kermaier.

Mikvah *Contact* Revital Ben Yishai. ☎ (852) 2140 6475.

Chabad-Lubavitch in the Far East. The Chabad Shul is located in the Furama Hotel, Suite 601, in Central District. Rabbi Mordechai Avtzon. ☎ (852) 2523-9770. Fax (852) 2845-2772. Email chabadhk@netvigator.com. Website www.chabadhk.org.

The United Jewish Congregation of Hong Kong (Liberal/Reform) (Est. 1991). One Robinson Place, 70 Robinson Road, Mid-levels. Rabbi Jordan Cohen. ☎ (852) 2523-2985. Fax (852) 2523-3961. Email michael@ujc.org.hk. Website www.ujc.org.hk.

Kehilat Zion (Orth), Synagogue of Kowloon, 4/F, 21 Chatham Road, Tsim Sha Tsui, Kowloon. Rabbi Netanel Meoded. ☎/Fax (852) 2366-6364.

Shuva Israel Beit Medrash and Community Centre and **Shuva Israel Synagogue** (Seph), 2/F, Fortune House, 61 Connaught Road Central. ☎ (852) 2851-6218/6300. Fax (952) 2851-7482.

Israel Consulate-General, Admiralty Centre, Tower II, Room 701, 18 Harcourt Road. ☎ (852) 2529-6091. Fax 2865-0220.

The Jewish Historical Society. Publishes monographs on subjects of Sino-Judaic interest. Information from Mrs J. Green. ☎ (852) 2807-9400. Fax (852) 2887-5235.

The **Jewish cemetery** is situated at 13 Shan Kwong Road, Happy Valley. ☎ (852) 2589-2621. Fax (852) 2548-4200.

The Jewish Women's Assn. is affiliated to WIZO and ICJW. *Chair* Mrs A. Milstein. ☎ (852) 2891-9634. Fax (852) 2891-3694.

United Israel Appeal is affiliated to Keren Hayesod. *Information* Dr J. Diestel. ☎ (852) 2522-2099. Fax (852) 2868-5336.

SHANGHAI

Notice has been received of a new community established in Shanghai in 1998.

Bnai Yisrael, 1277 Beijing Rd, 19th Floor, Shanghai. *President* Albert Sassoon. ☎ 86-21-6289-9903. Fax 86-21-6289-9957.

COLOMBIA (7,000)

The Jewish population is about 7,000 with the majority living in Bogota. There are also coms. in Barranquilla, Cali and Medellin.

*__Centro Comunitario Israelita de Bogotá,__ Carrera 29 126-31, Apartado 12372 Bogotá. ☎ 274 9069.

COMMONWEALTH OF INDEPENDENT STATES (former USSR)

Before World War I, Russian Jewry was the largest Jewish community in the world. For centuries, until the Revolution of 1917, the Jews were cruelly persecuted under the antisemitic policy of the Tsars. The subsequent Soviet regime virtually destroyed the former religious life and organisation of the Jewish communities. According to the official Soviet 1989 census the Jewish population was 1,449,000 but recent mass emigration will have reduced that total. The break up of the Soviet Union following August 1991 is reflected in the new entries under the separate republics, e.g. Belarus, Latvia, Moldova, Ukraine, etc. Population figures are difficult to estimate but some 400,000 Jews have left the country since 1989.

RUSSIA (440,000) (Russian Federation)

MOSCOW

Synagogues: Central ul. Archipova 8; Marina Roshcha, 2nd Vysheslavtsev per.5-A.

ST. PETERSBURG

Synagogue: 2 Lermontovsky Prospekt. ☎ 216-11-53.

Jewish Association 'LEA', Ryleeva 29-31, 191123. ☎ 812-2756104. Fax 812-2756103.

Jewish Tourist and Research Center HA-IR), Stachek 212-46, 198262. ☎ (812) 184 12 48. Fax (812) 310 61 48.

Other centres of Jewish population include those of Astrakhan, Berdichev, Beregovo, Birobidjan, Irkutsk, Krasnoyarsk, Kuybyshev, Kursk, Malakhavka, Nalchik, Novosibirsk, Ordzhonikidze, Penza, Perm, Rostov Saratov, Sverdlovsk, Tula.

COSTA RICA (2,500)

Most of the Jewish population of 2,500 live in San José, the capital, where there are a synagogue, mikveh and a Jewish primary and secondary school. There is also a country club.

*__Centro Israelita Sionista de Costa Rica__, Calle 22 y 24. P.O.B. 1473, 1000 San José, Costa Rica. ☎ 233-9222. Fax 233-9321. *President* G. Prifer; *Sec.* A. Kierszenson. *Chief Rabbi* Rabbi Gershon Miletski. *Community Dir.* Frida Lang. Email cisd-cr@sol.racsa.co.cr

CROATIA (2,500)

(Former constituent republic of Yugoslavia)

There are nine Jewish coms. in Croatia with a total Jewish population of 2,500 affiliated members.

ZAGREB

Jewish Com. and Synagogue. *President* Prof. Dr Ognjen Kraus; *Sec. Gen.* Deon Friedrich; Palmotićeva St. 16., P.O.B. 986; ☎ 434 619; 425 517. Fax 434 638.

The Com. Centre was rebuilt in 1992 after being seriously damaged in an explosion. Services are held on Friday eves and holy days. It houses a Jewish kindergarten, Judaica and Hebraica Library, art gallery, auditorium with daily progammes and other facilities. Here are the headquarters of the Fed. of Jewish Coms. in Croatia, Maccabi Sports Club, Jewish Ladies Assn., the Cultural Society and Union of Jewish Students in Croatia.

The com. publishes an occasional newspaper ha-Kol.

There is an impressive monument to Jewish victims of Holocaust in the Jewish cemetery of Mirogoj and a monument to Jewish soliders fallen in the First World War.

There is a plaque in Praška St. 7 on the site of the pre-war Central Syn. of Zagreb.

Before 1941 the com. numbered over 12,000 Jews. Today there are 1,500 members.

Lavoslav Shwartz Old People's Home. *President* Dr Branko Breyer; *Man.* Paula Novak, Bukovacka c. 55; ☎ 210 026; 219 922.

DUBROVNIK

Jewish Com. and Syn., Zudioska St. 3 (Jewish Street).

This is the second oldest syn. in Europe, dating back to the 14th century damaged in the 1991-2 war. There are 47 Jews in the city and services are held on Jewish holidays.

OSIJEK

Jewish Com. and Syn. *President* Ing. Darko Fisher; Braće Radića St. 13; ☎ 24 926. There are 150 Jews in the city and the com. is quite active. It suffered some damage during the 1991-92 war.

RIJEKA

Jewish Com. and Syn.: *President* Josip Engel; *V. Presidents* Dr Josip Musafia; Ivana Filipovića St. 9; P.O.B. 65. ☎ 425 156.

There are 80 Jews in Rijeka. Services are held on Jewish holidays.

SPLIT

Jewish Com. and Syn.: *President* Eduard Tauber, Zidovski prolaz 1 (Jewish Passage). ☎ 45 672.

There are 200 Jews in Split and the com. is very active, with daily meetings. The syn. is over 350 years old and services are held on Jewish holidays. There is an impressive cemetery dating back to the 16th century.

There are smaller Jewish coms. in Čakovec, Virovitica, Slavonski Brod and Daruvar. In many towns in north Croatia there are old Jewish cemeteries and former syn. buildings.

CUBA (1,500)

Marranos from Spain settled in Cuba in the sixteenth century, but a real immigration of Jews did not start until the end of the nineteenth century. The majority of the 1,000 Jews live in Havana.

***Comission Coordinadora de las Sociedades Hebreas de Cuba,** Calle Bel Vedado, Havana. ☎ 32-8953.

CURAÇAO (350)

A Sephardi Jewish settlement was est. in 1651, making it the oldest community in the New World. The Mikve Israel-Emanuel Syn. building, which dates from 1732, is the oldest in continuous use in the western Hemisphere; there is a small Jewish museum in the synagogue compound. About 350 Jews live in Curaçao. The cemetery (Bet Hayim) at Blenheim (est. 1659) is the oldest in the Americas.

Synagogues: Sephardi-Mikve Israel-Emanuel, Hanchi di Snoa 29, P.O. Box 322. ☎ 4611067. Fax 4654141. *M.*

Ashkenazi: Shaarei Tsedek, Leliweg 1A, P.O. Box 498. ☎ 7375738. *M.*

Israel Consulate: Dr P. Ackerman, Blauwduifweg 5. ☎ 7365068. Fax 7370707.

CYPRUS (50)

At the beginning of the present era and earlier, Cyprus was an important and large Jewish centre. An unsuccessful revolt against the Romans in 117, however, was followed by a ruthless suppression and the end of the great period of Jewish history in Cyprus. A new period of prosperity and immigration started in the 12th century but came to an end with the coming of the Genoese and later the Venetians as the island's rulers. By 1560 only 25 families remained in Famagusta, mostly physicians. Attempts at agricultural settlement in the 19th century were unsuccessful.

The Jewish population now numbers about 50. The cemetery is at Larnaca.

Jewish Committee has offices in Nicosia c/o S. Ammar, P.O. Box 3807 Nicosia. ☎ 441085.

CZECH REPUBLIC (10,000)

Records show that Jews were settled in Bohemia in the 11th century and in Moravia as early as the 9th cent. There were flourishing Jewish coms. in the Middle Ages. The Jewish pop. of Czechoslovakia in 1930 was 356,830. The coms. were decimated in the Holocaust.

Today the Jewish population of the Czech Republic is est. at 10,000. Of these 3,000 are registered as members of the Jewish com., with some 1,500 in Prague. There are today 10 Jewish coms. in Bohemia and Moravia in the regional cities of Prague, Plzen, Decin, Usti nad Labem, Karlovy Vary, Liberec, Teplice, Brno, Ostrava, Olomouc. There are regular Shabbat and holiday services held in all these places. There is a kosher kitchen and restaurant in Prague with rabbinical supervision of the chief rabbi of Prague and Bohemia and Moravia (Rav. K. Sidon).

Federation of Jewish Communities in the Czech Republic. Maiselova 18, 11001, Prague. ☎ 2481-1090. Fax 2481-0912. Email sekretariat@kehilaprag.cz. *President* Jan Munk; *Exec. Dir.* Dr Thomas Kraus.

PRAGUE

Jewish Community of Prague, Maiselova 18, 11001. Tel/Fax 2318-664. *Chairman* T. Jelinek.

B'nai B'rith Lodge, Maiselova 18, 11001.

Old-New Synagogue (Altneu), Cervena ul. 1, Praha 1 - Stare Mesto.

Jubilee Synagogue, Jeruzalemska 7, Praha 1 - Nove Mesto.

DENMARK (7,000)

The history of the Jews in Denmark goes back to the early years of the seventeenth century. Nearly all of Denmark's 9,000 Jews today live in Copenhagen. Jews have had full civic equality since 1814.

COPENHAGEN

Chief Rabbi: Rabbi Bent Lexner, Bomhusvej, 18, DK 2100. ☎ 39 299520. Fax 39 292517. Email bent_lexner@hotmail.com. Private: Oestbanegade 9, DK 2100. ☎ 3526 3540.

***Det Mosaiske Troessamfund i Kobenhavn (Jewish Congregation of Copenhagen)**, Ny Kongensgade 6, DK 1472. ☎ (33)-128-868. Fax (33) 123-357. Email mt@mosaiske.dk. Website www.mosaiske.dk.

Synagogues: Krystalgade 12, DK 1172.

Community Centre, Ny Kongensgade 6, DK 1472.

DOMINICAN REPUBLIC

The Jewish community which settled in Santo Domingo in the sixteenth century has completely disappeared. The present Jewish community, formed shortly before the Second World War, numbers about 150 in Santo Domingo and Sosua.

SANTO DOMINGO

Synagogue, Avenida Ciudad de Sarasota, 5. ☎ 533-1675.

ECUADOR (1,000)

The Jewish population in Ecuador is about 1,000, mainly resident in Quito and Guayaquil.

Comunidad Judia del Ecuador, Calle Roberto Andrade OE3-580 y Jaime Roldos, Urbanizacion Einstein (Carcelen), POBox 17-03-800. ☎ 483-800/927 – 486-

749/750/751/752. Fax 593 2 486-755. Email aiq@uio.satnet.net.
*Comunidad de Culto Israelita, Cnr. Calle Paradiso and El Bosque, Guayaquil.

EGYPT (240)

The history of the Jewish community in Egypt goes back to Biblical times. Following the establishment of the State of Israel in 1948 and the subsequent wars, only about 200 Jews remain, about 150 in Cairo and 50 in Alexandria. Services are conducted in Shaar Hashamayim Synagogue during the High Holy Days.

CAIRO

***Jewish Community Headquarters**, 13 rue Sebil el Khazendar, Midan el Gueish, Abbasiya. ☎ 0202-4824613. Email bassatine@yahoo.com. *President* Mrs Esther Weinstein. ☎ 0202-3935896.

Great Synagogue Shaar Hashamayim, 17 Adly Pasha St. ☎ 0202-3929025.

Ben-Ezra Synagogue, 6 Haret il-Sitt Barbara, Old Cairo.

Heliopolis Synagogue "Vitali Madjar", 5 rue Misalla, Korba, Heliopolis.

Maadi Synagogue Meir Enaim, 55 rue 13, Maadi.

Rav Moshe Maimonides Synagogue, Haret el Yehoud; **Rav Haim Capucci Synagogue,** Haret el Yehoud; **Pashad Ishak Synagogue,** Daher; **Etz Haim Synagogue,** Daher.

ALEXANDRIA

Great Synagogue Eliahu HaNabi, 69 rue Nebi Daniel, Ramla Station. *President* Dr Max Salama.

ESTONIA (3,000)

TALLINN

Jewish Community of Estonia. Karu Str. 16. *Contact* Cilja Laud, POB 3576 Tallinn 10507. ☎/Fax 662 3034. Email ciljal@icom.ee

Syn., 16 Karu St. ☎ 662 3050.

Jewish Cultural Centre. *EDr* Eugenia Gurin-Loov, POB 3576.

WIZO Estonia. *Contact* Revekka Blumberg, POB 3576, EE0090. ☎ 43-646 1777. Fax 43-8566.

There are Jewish communities in Kohtla-Järve, Narva, Tartu and Pärnu.

ETHIOPIA

The indigenous Jews of Ethiopia, known as Falashas, have probably lived in the country for about 2,000 years. Their origin is obscure but they are believed to be the descendants of members of the Agau tribe who accepted pre-Talmudic Judaism brought into Ethiopia (Abyssinia) from Jewish settlements in Egypt, such as that at Elephantine (Aswan). They were estimated to number half-a-million in the 17th century but by the 1970s the population had shrunk to less than 30,000. In 1975 the Israel Govt. recognised their right to enter under the Law of Return. Towards the end of 1984 the Israel Govt. undertook Operation Moses which entailed transporting about 8,000 Ethiopian Jews from refugee camps in Sudan to Israel. It is estimated that approximately 3,000 died from famine and disease before they could reach Israel. A further dramatic mass emigration to Israel was completed in 1991 and very few remain. A useful book on the subject is David Kessler's The Falashas, the Forgotten Jews of Ethiopia (3rd ed., London 1996), obtainable from Frank Cass Publishers.

Jewish Community, POB 50 Addis Ababa.

FIJI

Many Jews, mostly from Britain and some from Australia, settled in the islands in the

19th and early 20th centuries. About 12 Jewish families now live in Suva. *Corr.* K.R. Fleischman, GPO Box 905, Suva or Cherry Schneider, POB 882, Suva.

FINLAND (1,500)

The settlement of Jews in Finland dates from about 1850. The number living there today is about 1,500, with 1,200 in Helsinki, the rest in Turku and other parts of the country.

*__Synagogue and Communal Centre__: Malminkatu 26, 00100 Helsinki 10. ☎ (09) 5860310. Fax 6948916. Email srk@jchelsinki.fi.

Synagogue and Communal Centre: Brahenkatu 17, Turku. ☎ (02) 2312557.

FRANCE (650,000)

The first Jewish settlers in France arrived with the Greek founders of Marseilles some 500 years B.C.E. After the destruction of the Second Temple, Jewish exiles established new communities, or reinforced old ones. Rashi and Rabenu Tam are the best known of hundreds of brilliant medieval French rabbis and scholars. In 1791 the emancipation of French Jewry was the signal for the ghetto walls to crumble throughout Europe. During the Second World War, under the German occupation, 120,000 Jews were deported or massacred; but the post-war influx from Central and Eastern Europe and particularly from North Africa has increased the numbers of French Jewry to about 600,000 (the fourth largest in the world), of whom 380,000 are in Paris and Greater Paris. There are Jewish coms. in about 150 other towns.

PARIS

*__Consistoire Central:__ The principal Jewish religious org. in France. It administers the **Union des Communautés Juives de France**, 19 rue St. Georges, 75009. *President* Jean Kahn; *Dir. Gen.* F. Attali. ☎ 49708800. Fax.: 42810366.

Association Consistoriale Israélite de Paris, 17 rue St. Georges, 75009. The principal Jewish religious org. for the Paris area. *President* and *Gen. Sec.* Moché Cohen. ☎ 40 82 26 26.

Alliance Israélite Universelle, 45 rue La Bruyère, 75009. This org. works through its network of schools in France, but also in 7 countries, especially in North Africa, Asia and North America. It houses the 'College des Etudes juives' and a library, which includes more than 120,000 books in the field of Hebraica-Judaica and the Nayir Publishing House. *President* Prof. A. Steg; *Dir.* Jean-Jacques Wahl. ☎ 0153328855. Fax 0148745133. Email info@aiu.org. www.aiu.org.

American Jewish Joint Distribution Committee, 5 Ave. de Matignon, 75008. ☎ 01.56.59.79.79. Fax 01.56.59.79.89. *Dir.* Alberto Senderey.

Appel Unifié Juif de France (A.U.J.F.), Espace Rachi, 39 Rue Broca, 75005. ☎ 01.42.17.11.40. Fax 01.42.17.11.45. *President* David de Rothschild.

Association Culturelle Israélite Agudas Hakehilos, 10 rue Pavée, 75004. ☎ 488721 54.

B'nai B'rith France, 5 Bis, rue de Rochechouart, 75009. ☎ 01.55.07.85.45. Fax 01.42.82.70.63. Email BBFRANCE@wanadoo.Fr; Website http/www-bnaibrith-France.org. *Dir.* Mrs Yaël Simon.

Bureau du Chabbath, 8 Rue Maillard, 75011. ☎ 01.44.64.64.64. Fax 01.44.64.64.60. *Dir.* Mrs Noémie Konopnicki. This service helps unemployed people to find work.

CASIP-COJADOR Fondation, 8 Rue de Pali-kao, 75020. ☎ 01.44.62.13.13. Fax 01.44.62.13.14. The CASIP helps people with social and private problems and gives them money and assistance. The COJASOR takes care of old people and assists them in their everyday lives.

Centre de Documentation Juive Contemporaine, 17 Rue Geoffroy l'Asnier, 75004. (Est. 1943.) This org. has gathered and organised data of Jewish life under the Hitler regime in Europe. *Founder* The late Isaac Schneersohn; *President* Baron Eric de Rothschild; *Dir.* Jacky Fredj.

Communauté Israélite de la Stricte Observance, 10 rue Cadet, 75009. ☎ 42 46 36 47.

***Conseil Représentatif des Institutions Juives de France (CRIF),** Espace Rachi, 39 Rue Broca, 75005. ☎ 01.42.17.11.11. Fax 01.42.17.11.13. *President* Henri Hajdenberg; *Dir.* Haïm Musicant. This organisation represents French Judaïsm at a political level.

Conseil Représentatif du Judaisme Traditionaliste, c/o Eric Schieber, 6 rue Albert Camus, le Montigny 75010 Paris. 16i. Rep. org. of Orthodox Jewry. ☎ 45 04 94 00. *President* I. Frankforter; *Sec. Gen.* E. Schieber.

Fédération des Organisations Sionistes de France (FOSF), 10 Rue Richer, 75009. ☎ 01.48.24.04.23.

Fédération des Sociétés Juives de France (FSJF), 70 Rue de Turbigo, 75003. ☎ 01.44.61.29.15. Fax 01.44.61.29.16.

Fonds Social Juif Unifié (F.S.J.U.), Espace Rachi, 39 Rue Broca, 75005. ☎ 01.42.17.10.10. Fax 01.42.17.10.45.

Jeunesse Loubavitch, 8 Rue Lamartine, 75009. ☎ 01.45.26.87.60. Fax 01.45.26.24.37.

Keren Kayemeth Leisrael, 11 Rue du 4 Septembre, 75002. ☎ 42.86.88.88. Fax 01.42.60.18.13.

Mouvement Juif Libéral de France (MJLF), 11 Rue Gaston de Caillavet, 75015. ☎ 01.44.37.48.48. Fax 01.44.37.48.50. (Affil. to World Union of Progressive Judaism.) *President* Félix Mosbacher; *Rabbis* Daniel and Gabriel Farhi.

Mouvement Loubavitch, 8 rue Lamartine 9°. ☎ 45 26 87 60.

Musée d'Art et d'Histoire du Judaisme, Hôtel de St Aignan, 71 rue du Temple, 75003 ☎ 01.53.01.86.60. Fax 01.42.72.97.47. Email info@mahj.org

ORT, 10 Villa D'Eylau, 75016. ☎ 01.45.00.74.22.

Renouveau Juif, 18 passage du Chantier 12°. ☎ 43 40 40 55. Est. 1979 by Henri Hajdenberg. Advocates stronger pro-Israel stand.

Siona, 52 rue Richer 9°. ☎ 42 46 01 91. Sephardi Z. movement est. by Roger Pinto.

Union des Juifs pour la Résistance et l'Entr'aide, 14 rue de Paradis, 10°. Social, cultural and political org. of extreme Left-wing political views, founded as an armed Resistance group in 1943 under German occupation. *President* Charles Lederman. ☎ 47 70 62 16.

Union Libérale Israélite, 24 rue Copernic, 75116. Org. of Liberal Judaism. *President* C Bloch. ☎ 47 04 37 27. Fax 47 27 81 02.

Union des Sociétés Mutalistes Juives de France, 58 rue du Chateau d'Eau 10°. ☎ 42 06 62 88. East European background.

Wizo, 54 rue de Paradis, 10°. French women Zionists' centre. ☎ 48 01 97 70. *President* Nora Gailland-Hofman.

Chief Rabbi of France: Rabbi Joseph Sitruk, Consistoire Central, 19 rue Saint-Georges, 75009. ☎ 49 70 88 00. Fax 40 16 06 11.

SYNAGOGUES

Synagogues of the Consistoire de Paris, 44 rue de la Victoire, 9°; 15 rue Notre-Dame-de-Nazareth, 3°; 21 bis rue des Tournelles, 4°; 28 rue Buffault, 9°Ñ Sephardi; 14 rue Chasseloup-Laubat, 15°; 18 rue Sainte-Isaure, 18°; 75 rue Julien Lacroix, 20°; 9 rue Vauquelin, 5°; 70 Avenue Secretan, 19°; 13 rue Fondary, 15°; 6 bis rue Michel Ange, 16°; 14 Place des Vosges, 4°; 84 rue de la Roquette; 120 Boulevard de Belleville 20°; 120 rue des Saule, 18°; 19 Blvd. Poissonniére; 18 rue St. Lazare, 9° (Algerian).

Orthodox Synagogues: 10 rue Cadet, 9°; 31 rue de Montévidéo, 16°; 10 rue Pavee, 4°; 6 rue Ambroise Thomas, 9°; 3 rue Saulnier, 9°; 32 rue Basfroi, H°; 25 rue des Rosiers, 4°; 17 rue des Rosiers, 4°; 24 rue de Bourg Tibourg, 4°; 80 rue

Doudeauville, 18°; 5 rue Duc, 18°; 18 rue des Ecouffes, 4°.

Conservative Syn., Adath Shalom, 22 bis, rue des Belles Feuilles, 75116 Paris. ☎ 45 53 84 09.

Liberal Synagogues, 24 rue Copernic, 16°; 11 rue Gaston de Caillavet 15°.

There are also many syns. in the Paris suburbs and in the Provinces.

GERMANY (100,000)

A large Jewish community has existed continuously in Germany since Roman times. Despite recurring periods of persecution, the Jewish communities contributed much of lasting value to culture and civilisation. Hitler and the Nazi regime destroyed the community, which numbered more than half a million before 1933, 160,000 of whom lived in Berlin. Today there are about 100,000 (incl. 12,000 in Berlin, 6,600 in Frankfurt and 7,200 in Munich). There are 80 other coms. in Germany. See Hidden Legacy Foundation, p.55.

***Zentralrat der Jüden in Deutschland** (Central Council of Jews in Germany), Tucholskystr. 9, 10117 Berlin. ☎ 030 284 4560. Fax 030 284 5613. Email info@zentralratdjuden.de. Website www.zentralratdjuden.

Central Welfare Org. of Jews in Germany, Hebelstr. 6, 60318 Frankfurt. ☎ 069-944371-0. Fax 069-494817.

Conference of German Rabbis, Landesrabbiner Joel Berger, Hospitalstr. 36, 70174 Stuttgart 1. ☎/Fax 0711-22836.

The Union of Progressive Jews in Germany, Austria & Switzerland, Herman-Hummel-Str. 18, 82166 Grafelfing. ☎ 8980 9373. Fax 8980 9374. Email v.u.j.muehlstein@tonline.de.

B'nai B'rith Lodges, Berlin, Cologne, Dusseldorf, Frankfurt, Hamburg, Munich and Saarbrucken.

***Bundesverband Jüd. Studenten**, Joachimstaler Str. 13, 10719 Berlin, and at Jewish Student Organisations at Aachen, Cologne, Frankfurt, Stuttgart, Hanover, Hamburg, Heidelberg and Munich.

Hochschule Für Jüdische Studien (University for Jewish Studies), Friedrichstr. 9, 69117 Heidelberg. ☎ 06221-22576. Fax 06221-167696.

Jewish Agency for Israel, Hebelstr. 6, 60318 Frankfurt. ☎ 069-7140225. Fax 069-94333420.

Jewish National Fund, Liebigstr.2, 60323 Frankfurt. ☎ 069-9714020. Fax 069-97140225.

Jewish Women's League (Frauenbund), c/o ZWST, Hebelstr. 6, 60318 Frankfurt.

Jewish Restitution Successor Organisation, Sophienstr. 26, 60481, Frankfurt.

Jüdische Liberale Gemeinde, Köln, Stammheimer Str. 22, 50735 Köln. ☎/Fax 221 287 0424. Email jlg.köln@gmx.de.

Keren Hayessod, Vereinigte Israel Aktion e.v., Gartenstr. 6, 60594 Frankfurt a.M. ☎ 069-6109380.

Makkabi, Gailenbergstr. 13, 87541 Hindelang. ☎ 08324-8386. Fax 08324-2421.

ORT, Hebelstr. 6, 60318 Frankfurt. ☎ 069-9449081.

Wizo, Joachimstalerstr. 13, 10719 Berlin.

Youth Aliyah, Hebelstr. 6, 60318 Frankfurt.

Zentralarchiv zur Erforschung der Geschichte der Juden in Deutschland, Bienenstr. 5, 69117 Heidelberg. ☎ 06221-164141. Fax 06221-181049.

Zionist Organisation in Germany, Hebelstr. 6, 60318 Frankfurt. ☎ 069-498-0251. Fax 069-490473.

Zionist Youth, Falkensteiner St. 1, 60322 Frankfurt. ☎ 069-556963.

GIBRALTAR (600)

In 1473 there was a suggestion that the promontory should be reserved for Marranos (see D. Lamelas, 'The Sale of Gibraltar in 1474', 1992). The present Jewish community was formed of immigrants from North Africa shortly after the

British annexation in 1704, but Jews had no legal right to settle in the city until 1749, by which year however, the Jewish residents numbered about 600, a third of the total number of residents, and possessed two syns.

During the siege of 1779 to 1783 the size of the Jewish population was reduced, a large proportion removing to England. After the siege the numbers rose again, being at their highest in the middle of the nineteenth century, when they rose above two thousand. (For the history of the Jews of Gibraltar, see A. B. M. Serrfaty, 'The Jews of Gibraltar under British Rule,' 1933.)

***Managing Board of the Jewish Community**, 10 Bomb House Lane. ☎ 72606. *President* H.J.M. Levy. Fax 40487. *Admin.* Mrs E. Benady.

Synagogue Shaar Hashamayim, Engineer Lane. ☎ 78069. Fax 74029. (Est. before 1749; rebuilt 1768.) *H. Sec.* J. de M. Benyunes, P.O. Box 174.

Synagogue Nefusot Yehudah, Line Wall Rd. (Est. 1781.) *H. Sec.* I. Beniso. ☎ 74791. Fax 40907.

Synagogue Es Hayim, Irish Town. (Est. 1759.) *H. M. & Sec.* S. Benaim. ☎ 75563.

Synagogue, Abudarham, Parliament Lane. (Est. 1820.) *H. Sec.* D. J. Abudarham. ☎ 78506. Fax 73249.

Mikveh, Mrs G. Hassan. ☎ 74929; Mrs R. Serfaty ☎ 73090.

Joint Israel Appeal. *H. Sec.* E. Benamor. ☎ 77680. Fax 40493.

GREECE (4,800)

There have been Jewish communities in Greece since the days of antiquity. Before 1939, 77,200 Jews lived in Greece (56,000 in Salonika, now known as Thessaloniki.). Today there are fewer than 5,000, all Sephardim, of these about 2,800 live in Athens; some 1,100 in Thessaloniki; and the rest in some 12 provincial towns.

ATHENS

***Central Board of Jewish Communities**, 36 Voulis St., GR 105 57. *President* Moissis Constantinis. ☎ (010) 3244315. Fax 3313852. Email hhkis@hellasnet.gr. Website www.kis.gr.

American Joint Distribution Committee, 4 Nikis St., 105 63. ☎/Fax (010) 32-31-034.

B'nai B'rith, 15 Paparigopoulou St., 105 61. ☎ (010) 3230405.

Jewish Community Office, 8 Melidoni St., 105 53. ☎ (010) 3252823. Fax 3220-761.

Synagogue, Beth Shalom, 5 Melidoni St., 105 53. *M.* Rabbi Jakob Arar. ☎ (010) 325 2773.

Jewish Museum of Greece, 39 Nikis St., 105 57. ☎ (010) 32 25 582. Fax 32 31 577.

Communal Centre, 9 Vissarionos St., 106 72. ☎ (010) 36 37 092. Fax 360 8896.

THESSALONIKI

Jewish Community Office, 24 Tsimiski St., 54624. ☎ 031 27 5701. Fax 031-22 9063.

Monastirioton Synagogue, 35 Sigrou St., 54630. ☎ 524968.

Synagogue Yad Le Zicaron, 24 Vasileos Irakliou St., 54624. ☎ 223231.

Museum, 13 Agiou Mina Str., 54624 ☎ 031 250406/250407.

Other communities:

Corfu Jewish Community, 5 Riz. Voulefton St., 49100. *President* Raphael Soussis. ☎ 0661 30591. Fax 0661-31898.

Halkis Jewish Community, *President* M. Maissis. 5 Papingi Str., 34100. ☎ 0221 60111. Fax 0221 83781.

Ioannina Jewish Community, 18 Joseph Eliyia Str. GR 452 21. ☎ 0651 25195. *President* M. Elisaf.

Larissa Jewish Community, Platia Evreon Martiron, GR 412 22. ☎ 041 532965. *President* A. Albelansis.

Rodos Jewish Community, 5 Polidorou Str. GR 85100. ☎ 0241 22364. Fax 0241 73039. *President*.

Trikala Jewish Community, *President* I. Venouziou, Kondili-Philippou, 42100. ☎ 0431 25-834.

Volos Jewish Community, 21B Vassani Str., GR 383 33. *President* R. Frezis. ☎ 4210-25640, 23079. Fax 4210-31917. Email jcvol@otenet.gr. Website www.atlantis.gr/kis/volos.html.

GUATEMALA (1,500)

Jews have been resident in Guatemala since 1898. The present population is about 1,500, made up of some 300 families all living in the capital.

GUATEMALA CITY

*__Comunidad Judia Guatemalteca__, 7a. Av. 13-51 Zona 9, Guatemala City, C.A. ☎ (502) 3601509. Email Comjugua@guate.net. *President* Jaime Camhi.

Centro Hebreo (East European Jews) 7a. Av. 13-51 Zona 9. ☎ 3311975. *President* Ricardo Rich.

Maguen David (Sephardi), 7a. Avenida 3-80 Zona 2. ☎ 2320932. Fax 360 1589. *President* Saúl Mishaan

Consejo Central Sionista de la Comunidad Judia de Guatemala, Apto. Postal 502, Guatemala, C.A. *President* Mano Permuth.

HAITI (150)

There has been a Jewish community in Haiti for the past 80 years, and it now numbers about 150 people.

HOLLAND (25,000)

From the sixteenth century onwards the Jews of Holland had a distinguished historical record. Since 1792 they have had the same constitutional and civil rights as all other citizens. In 1940 there were approximately 140,000 Jews in the country, but as the result of the Nazi occupation only some 25,000 remain, of whom about half are in Amsterdam. Other small coms. are in Amersfoort, Arnhem, Bussum, Eindhoven, Groningen, Haarlem, The Hague, Rotterdam, Utrecht and Zwolle.

Rabbinate Ashkenazic Community: Rabbi F. J. Lewis, Rabbi I. Vorst (both in Amsterdam); Rabbi J. S. Jacobs (Amersfoort).

Rabbinate Sephardic Community: Rabbi B. Drukarch.

Rabbinate Liberal Jewish Congregations: Rabbi D. Lilienthal (Amsterdam); Rabbi A. Soetendorp (The Hague); Rabbi Dr E. van Voolen (Arnhem).

AMSTERDAM

*__Ashkenazi Community Centre and Offices__: Van der Boechorststraat 26, 1081 BT. ☎ 646 00 46. Fax 646-4357.

*__Sephardi Communal Centre__: Mr Visserplein, 3, 1011 RD. ☎ 624 53 51. Fax 625-4680.

Ashkenazi Synagogues: Jacob Obrechtplein; Lekstr 61; Gerard Doustr. 238; Van der Boechorststraat, 26; Straat van Messina 10, Amstelveen.

East European Jew' Synagogue: G. van der Veenstr. 26-28.

Portuguese Synagogue, Mr Visserplein 3.

Liberal Community Centre and Synagogue. J. Soetendorpstraat, 8, 1079. ☎ 6423562. Fax 642-8135. Amsterdam and Dutch Liberal Rabbinate. ☎ 644-2619. Fax 642-8135. Email ljg@x$4all.nl.

Zionist Offices: Joh. Vermeerstr. 24. Netzer-Kadima at the Liberal Community Centre.

Jewish Historical Museum: Synagogue Bldg., J. D. Meyerplein.
Anne Frank House, Prinsengracht 263. Judith Drake Library at the Liberal Community Centre.

HONDURAS (150)

There has been a Jewish community in Honduras for the past 50 years.
Tegucigalpa Community. *Sec.* H. Seidel.
Israel Embassy S. Cohen, Ambassador; H. Schiftan, Consul. ☎ 32-4232/32-5176. Telex: 1606 Memistra.
San Pedro Sula, Syn. and Com. Centre. *Sec.* M. Weizenblut. ☎ 552 8136. Fax 557 5244.

HUNGARY (100,000)

Jews have lived in this part of Europe since Roman times. Tombstones with Hebrew inscription have been found originating from the 3rd century. Before World War II, Hungary's Jewish population was about 800,000, of whom some 250,000 lived in Budapest. Some 600,000 perished in the Holocaust. The estimated Jewish population now is 100,000 and some 80,000 live in Budapest and the remainder in the provincial Jewish communities, all affiliated to the Central Board of the Federation of the Jewish Communities in Hungary.

BUDAPEST

***Federation of the Jewish Communities in Hungary (Magyarországi Zsidó Hitközségek Szövetsége) and the Budapest Jewish Community**, 1075 Budapest VII Sip utca 12. ☎ 1-3226-475. Fax 342-1790. *Man. Dir.* Gusztav Zoltai; *Dir. Foreign Rel.* Ernö Lazarovits.
Main Synagogue, Budapest VII Dohany utca 2 (Conservative). Chief Rabbi Robert Frölich.
Central Rabbinate, Budapest VII Sip utca 12. *Dir.* Robert Deutsch, Chief Rabbi.
Orthodox Synagogue, Budapest VII Kazinczy utca 27. *President* Herman Fixler.
Rabbinical Seminary and Jewish University, Budapest VIII, József körut 27. *Dir.* Chief Rabbi Dr Jozsef Schweitzer, Chief Rabbi of Hungary; *Rector* Dr A. Schöner.
There are 20 other syns. and prayer houses in Budapest.

MAZSOK The Jewish Heritage of Hungary Public Endowment, 1062 Budapest, Lendvay u.17–19. *Dir.* Gabor Sebes; *Fin.* Gyorgy Sessler.
The main provincial coms. are at Debrecen, Miskolc, Szeged, Pécs, Györ.

INDIA (5,600)

The settlement of Jews in India goes back at least to the early centuries of the Christian era. The Indian Jews of today may be divided into four groups: (i) those who arrived in this and the last century mainly from Baghdad, Iran, Afghanistan, etc., known as "Yehudim," forming communities in Bombay, Pune and Calcutta; (ii) Bene Israel, who believe that their ancestors arrived in India after the destruction of the First Temple, and who maintained a distinct religious identity while using local language and dress over the centuries; their main centre is the Bombay area; (iii) the Cochin Jews, in Cochin and the neighbouring centres of the Malabar Coast, in Kerala State in South India, who have records dating back to the fourth century, but who believe that there was a Jewish settlement in Craganore as early as 78 C.E.; (iv) European Jews who came within the last 50 years or so. Since 1948 there has been steady emigration to Israel. According to the 1971 census the Jewish pop. was 6,134. Today, it is estimated at 5,618.

The largest com. is in Maharastra State (4,354), mainly in the Bombay area. Smaller coms. are in Calcutta, Madras, New Delhi and Pune Ahmedabad. In Manipur there are 464 and in Gujarat 217.

*__Council of Indian Jewry__, c/o The Jewish Club, Jeroo Bldg., Second Fl., 137 Mahatma Gandhi Rd., Bombay, 400023. ☎ 271628. *President* N. Talkar. ☎ 8515195, 861941; *V. Presidents* A. Talegawkar, A. Samson; *Sec.* Mrs J. Bhattacharya. ☎ 6320589.

INDONESIA

Of the 16 Jews living in Indonesia, 15, made up of five families, live in Surabaya where there is provision for prayers. One lives in Jakarta.

IRAN (27,000)

Jews have lived in the country at least since the time of the Persian King Cyrus in the sixth century BCE. Many of the tombs of Jewish prophets, such as Daniel, Habakuk, Esther and Mordechai, are located in the cities of Iran. These holy places are respected by both Jews and Muslims. From the beginning of the twentieth century, the Iranian Jewish population has been under 70,000. Today it is in the region of 27,000. there are some legal differences between the majority and minority religions in Iran, and in some areas Jewish rights are under threat. Nevertheless, Jews in Iran have been free to maintain their religious affairs and ceremonies, and the cultural training of Jewish students since the Islamic Revolution of 1979. There has been a Jewish representative in every Islamic parliament in the modern period. Iranian Jews live in Tehran, Shiraz, Isfahan, Kerman, Kermanshah and Yazd.

TEHRAN

Comité Central de la Communauté Juive de Tehran, 385 Sheikh-Hadi St., 11397-3-3317. ☎ 6702556/6707612. Fax 6716429.

Synagogues: Yousefabad, 15th Street, Seyed Jamaleddin Assadabadi Ave.; Abrishami, 4th Street, North Felestin Ave. *Chief Rabbi* Hakham Yosef Haim Hamedani Cohen.

IRAQ (75)

The Jewish community in Iraq (anciently known as Babylonia) is the oldest in the Diaspora. Strong hostility exists towards the Jewish remnant of about 200, mainly elderly, that is now left. They mostly live in Baghdad and a few in Basra.

ISRAEL (4,847,000)

Palestine was administered until May 14, 1948, by Gt. Britain under a Mandate approved by the Council of the League of Nations, the preamble to which incorporated the Balfour Declaration. On November 20, 1947, the Assembly of the United Nations recommended that Palestine should be reorganised as two States, one Jewish, the other Arab, together with an internationalised Jerusalem and district combined in an economic union. On the surrender of the Mandate by Britain on May 14, 1948, the Jewish territory, with a Jewish pop. of 655,000, took the name of Israel and set up a Provisional Govt., with Dr Chaim Weizmann as President and David Ben-Gurion as Prime Minister. On July 5, 1950, the 'Law of Return' was proclaimed, conferring on every Jew the right to live in Israel.

The signing of a declaration of a set of principles by Israel and the PLO under the leadership of Yasser Arafat on September 13, 1993, concluded an era of forty-five years of strife between Israel and her Arab neighbours and recognised the aspirations of Palestinian Arabs for territory proposed for them by the UN in 1947. A peace treaty with Jordan was agreed in 1994. Prime Minister Rabin was assassinated in November 1995.

Key events in this history include:

The invasion of the Jewish state by the Arab armies in 1948 concluded by a series of armistices in 1949 and the recognition of Israel by the UN on May 11, 1949; the annexation of Arab Palestine by Jordan in 1950; the absorption by Israel of

Jews from Arab lands and the establishment of Palestinian refugee camps in the Arab states; seizure by Egypt of the Suez Canal Zone and the (Franco-British and Israeli) Sinai-Suez campaign of 1956; Egypt's closure of the Straits of Tiran in May 1967 which provoked the Six-Day War of June 1967 and saw the Israeli capture of Jerusalem and occupation of Gaza, Sinai, the Golan and the West Bank and the first National Unity Coalition (1967–70); the Yom Kippur War of October 1973 and the ensuing negotiations leading to partial Israeli withdrawals in Sinai and the Golan; the Likud election victory of 1977 and the visit to Israel by Egyptian President Anwar Sadat in November 1977 which led to the Camp David Agreement of March 26, 1979, the establishment of diplomatic relations between Egypt and Israel, and the Israeli withdrawal from the whole of Sinai in April 1982; Israel's 'Operation peace for Galilee' in Lebanon in June 1982 and withdrawal in 1985, a war which caused great divisions in Israel; the Intifada of the Palestinians in Gaza and the West Bank starting in 1988; the US-inspired five-point peace plan of 1989 and its failure in 1990; the Gulf War (January 1991) following the Iraqi invasion of Kuwait when the PLO supported Iraq and Israel sustained scud missile attacks without retaliation; the launching of negotiations for a comprehensive Middle East 'peace settlement' between Israel, the Arabs, and representatives of the Palestinians at a meeting in Madrid in October 1991.

It is these negotiations, conducted in public at a series of venues in Europe and the United States, and in secret in Norway since the Labour victory in the elections of June 1992, that came to fruition on the eve of the New Year 5754. Since then, a peace treaty with Jordan has also been signed. Further agreements for the transfer of controls in parts of the West Bank were signed in September 1995. In the interim, the continuing 'peace process' has repeatedly been put under threat by the actions of terrorists intent on destabilising the new situation. Anticipated stages of the process have yet to be achieved and it remains to be seen whether the principles of 'land for peace' on the Israeli side and 'recognition of Israel and peace' on the Palestinian can prevail as the basis for long-term accord between Israel and Palestine, and peace in the Middle East.

The assassination of the Prime Minister in November 1995, however, suggests that hostility to the peace process remains the greatest of all dangers to the Israeli polity. The continuing Hamas 'suicide attacks', devastating to Israeli citizens alongside the dispute over Israeli settlements within the occupied territories, and the military conflict in southern Lebanon, resurgent early in 1996 and again in late 1997, interrupted the Peace negotiations. The new *Intifada* that broke out in September 2000 continues unabated and Israel's predicament, exacerbated by the impact and aftermath of the terror of September 2001 and the war against the Taliban of Afghanistan, remains fraught in the extreme. The peace process has given way to war in everything but name.

Government

The Provisional Government of Israel was replaced by a permanent one after the election of the First **Knesset** (Parliament) in January, 1949.

Israel's Basic Law provides that elections must be 'universal, nationwide, equal, secret and proportional'. A general election must be held at least every four years. The Knesset is elected by a form of proportional representation in which members are selected in strict proportion to the votes cast for each party. Any candidate who obtains one per cent of the total votes cast is assured of a Knesset seat.

Mainly as a result of the voting system, no single party has so far been able to form a government on the basis of its own Knesset majority. Until the election in 1977, the dominant political force was a coalition of the Left, which formed governments with the help of various smaller parties, usually those with a religious programme. In the elections of 1977 and 1981 an alliance of the Right was able to form an administration with the help of religious parties. One feature of the political situation has been that the religious parties, in particular, have been able to exercise an influence out of proportion to their members.

Within recent years, however, there has been a marked polarisation of attitudes among sections of Israeli society and this was reflected by the proliferation of small parties which contested the 1984 election. The 1984 election produced an inconclusive result, with only three seats separating the two big party blocs. The two big parties formed Israel's second National Unity Government to cope with the urgent economic and other problems. The office of Prime Minister was held in rotation, first by Mr Shimon Peres, the Labour Alignment leader, and then by Mr Yitzhak Shamir, the Likud leader. The 1988 election was also inconclusive and was followed by another Coalition Government, with Mr Shamir continuing as Prime Minister and Mr Peres as Vice-Premier.The national unity government broke up in March 1990 when the Likud declined to go along with a U.S. plan to promote peace talks. Mr Shamir constructed a centre-right religious government supported by 66% of the 120 members of the Knesset. The elections of 1992 produced a Labour coalition led by Yitzhak Rabin. Demographic changes brought about by the influx of settlers from Eastern Europe and political and economic pressures contributed in large part to this outcome. The elections of 1996 were the first at which there was direct voting for the position of Prime Minister. In 1999 Ehud Barak of the Labour-led One Israel party defeated incumbent Binyamin Netanyahu. While political power rests constitutionally in the Knesset, the President of Israel, essentially a symbolic and representational figure, can in certain circumstances exercise a degree of de facto power based on his prestige. In particular, he can emerge as the voice of the Nation's conscience. The President is elected for a five-year period, renewable only once. Ezer Weizman, who was re-elected in 1998, retired in 2000 and was succeeded by Moshe Katzav.

Elections to the 15th Knesset were held in May 1999. Party votes were as follows:

One Israel (Labour, Gesher and Meimad)	26	(1996:34)	Centre Party	6	(-)
Likud	19	(32)	United Torah Judaism	5	(4)
Shas	17	(10)	Third Way		(4)
Meretz	10	(9)	United Arabs	5	(4)
National Religious	5	(9)	Moledet		(2)
Yisrael ba'Aliyah	6	(7)	Yisrael Beitenu	4	(-)
Shinui	6	(-)	National Union (Haichud Haleumi)	4	(-)
			Hadash	3	(-)

Following the resignation of Mr Barak early in 2001, Mr Sharon won a personal mandate to form a Likud-based government in the midst of the *Intifada* that broke out in September 2000.

The Presidents of Israel: Chaim Weizmann 1949–52; Yitzhak Ben Zvi 1952–63; Zalman Shazar 1963–73; Prof. Ephraim Katzir 1973–78; Yitzhak Navon 1978–83; Chaim Herzog 1983–93; Ezer Weizman 1993–2000; **Moshe Katzav** 2000–.

The Prime Ministers of Israel: David Ben-Gurion 1948–53 and Nov. 1955–63; Moshe Sharett Dec. 1953–55; Levi Eshkol 1963–69; Golda Meir 1969–74; Yitzhak Rabin 1974–77 and 1992–95; Menachem Begin 1977–83, Yitzhak Shamir Oct. 1983–Sept. 1984, Oct. 1986–June 1992; Shimon Peres Sept. 1984–Oct. 1986, Nov. 1995–May 1996; Benjamin Netanyahu, May 1996–99; Ehud Barak, May 1999–Feb. 2001; **Ariel Sharon**, Feb. 2001–.

Judiciary: The *President* appoints judges on the recommendation of an independent committee.

Defence Forces: Unified command of Army, Navy and Air Force. Small regular force; compulsory military service for persons aged between 18 and 29 followed by annual service in the Reserve.
Area: Following 1949 armistice agreements – approx. 20,750 sq. km. Following withdrawal from Sinai in April 1982, approx. 28,161 sq. km. (including Golan Heights, West Bank and Gaza Strip).
Neighbouring countries: Egypt, Jordan, Syria, Lebanon.
Population: Sept. 1998: 4,850,000. These figures include 17,000 Druse on the Golan Heights but not the other territories occupied in the Six-Day War (est. at 1,381,000).
Main Towns: Jerusalem (the capital), Tel Aviv, Haifa, Ramat Gan, Petach Tikvah, Netanya, Holon, Bnei Brak, Rehovot, Hadera, Nazareth, Rishon le-Zion, Beersheba, Ashkelon, Ashdod, Bat Yam, Tiberias, Eilat.
Industry: Main products: Cement, fertilisers, metal products, polished diamonds, ceramics, tyres and tubes, plywood, textiles, clothing and footwear, citrus by-products, electrical and electronic applicances, micro-electronics, chemicals, canned fruit, military equipment.
Agricultural Products: Citrus, fruit, vegetables, eggs, milk, wheat, barley, tobacco, groundnuts, cotton, sugarbeet, beef, fish, flowers, wine.
Minerals: Potash and bromine, magnesium, phosphate, petroleum, salt, glass, sand, clay, gypsum, granite, copper, iron, oil, natural gas.

With the exception of Jerusalem and Haifa, the country's largest port, the main centres of population are concentrated in the flat and fertile western coastal plain. Tel Aviv, the centre of Israel's largest metropolitan area, is the chief commercial and industrial centre. Fast-growing Beersheba is the capital of the arid northern Negev, while Eilat, the country's southernmost port, has been transformed from an isolated military outpost into a bustling Red Sea township linked to the northern centres by a modern highway and giving access now to Jordan as well. In the north lie the largely Arab centre of Nazareth, the popular health resort of Tiberias, overlooking the Lake, and Safad. Round Tel Aviv are clustered a number of towns, including Ramat Gan, Holon and Bnei Brak.

President of State Moshe Katzav; *Knesset Speaker* A. Burg.

ISRAELI EMBASSIES AND LEGATIONS

Israel now enjoys diplomatic relations with 160 countries and many of these ties have come into being or have been renewed following the peace agreements of 1993.

Permanent Delegation to U.N. 800 2nd Ave., New York, N.Y. 10017. ☎ (212) 449-5400. Fax (212) 490 9186. Ambassador Gad Yaacobi; *Dep.* Ambassador David Peleg. European H.Q. of U.N. Geneva, 9 Chemin de Bonvent, Geneva; Ambassador N.Y. Lamdan. ☎ 7980500; Vienna, 20 Anton Frankgasse, 1180 Vienna. ☎ 470-4742. Ambassador Dan Gillerman.
Embassy to European Communities. 40 Ave. de L'Observatoire, Brussels 1180. ☎ 373-55500. Ambassador Harry Kney-Tal.
Permanent Delegation to Council of Europe, 3 Rue Rabelais, 75008 Paris. ☎ 4076-5500. Ambassador A. Gabai.
Albania (see Italy).
Andorra (see Spain).
Angola. Emb. Rua Rainha Ngina 34, Luanda. ☎ 395295. Ambassador Tamar Golan.
Antigua and Barbuda (see Dominican Republic).
Argentina. Emb.: 701 Mayo Ave., Buenos Aires. ☎ 4338-2500. Ambassador Itzhak Aviran.
Armenia (see Georgia).

Australia. Emb.: 6 Turrana St., Yarralumla, Canberra, 2600. ☎ 6273- 1309. Ambassador Shmuel Moyal.
Austria. Emb.: Anton Frankgasse, 20, Vienna 1180. ☎ 4764-6500. Ambassador Yoel Sher. ☎ 4764-6510.
Azberbaijan. Emb: Stroiteley Prospect 1, Baku. ☎ 385282. Ambassador Eleizer Yotvath.
Bahamas. Consulate, PO Box 7776, Nassau NP. ☎ 3264421. Hon. Consul. Raphael Seligman.
Barbados. Consulate, PO Box 256, Bridgetown. Hon. Consul Bernard Gilbert.
Belarus. Emb.: Partizanski Prospekt 6A, Minsk 220002. ☎ 304444. Ambassador Eliahu Valk.
Belgium. Emb.: 40 Ave. de l'Observatoire, Brussels 1180. ☎ 373-5500. Ambassador Shaul Amor.
Belize (see San Salvador).
Benin (see Côte d'Ivoire).
Bolivia. Emb.: Edificio 'Esperanza', Ave., Mariscal, Santa Cruz; Edificio 'Esperanza', 10 Pizo, Calle 1309, La Paz. ☎ 391126. Ambassador Yair Rekanati.
Botswana (see Zimbabwe).
Brazil. Emb.: Avenida das Nacoes, Lote 38, Brasilia. ☎ 244-7675. Ambassador Yaacov Keinan.
Bulgaria. 1 Bulgaria Sq., NDK Building, 7th Floor. ☎ 5432-01. Ambassador David Cohen.
Burkina Faso (see Côte d'Ivoire).
Burundi (see Zaire).
Kingdom of **Cambodia** (see Thailand).
Cameroon. Emb.: P.O. Box 5934, Yaounde. ☎ 201644. Ambassador.
Canada. Emb.: 50 O'Connor St., Ottawa K1P 672. ☎ 5676450. Ambassador David Sultan.
Cape Verde (see Senegal).
Central African Republic (see Cameroon).
Chile. Emb.: Av. Bosque, Las Condes San Sebastian 2812, Santiago De Chile. ☎ 750-0500. Ambassador Pinchas Avivi.
China. Emb.: West Wing Offices, 1 Jianguo Menwai Da Ji, Beijing 100004. ☎ 6505-2970. Ambassador Ora Namir.
Colombia. Emb.: Edificio Caxdac Calle 35, No. 7-25, Bogota. ☎ 287 7840. Ambassador Avraham Hadad.
Congo (see Zaire).
Costa Rica. Emb.: Edificio Centro, Colon, Paseo Colon, Calle 38. ☎ 221-6444. Ambassador Shlomo Tal.
Republic of Côte D'Ivoire. O.1. B.P. 1877, Abidjan 01. ☎ 21 31 78. Ambassador Yaakov Revah.
Cyprus. Emb.: 4 Gripari St., P.O.B. 25159, W. Nicosia. ☎ 664195. Ambassador Shemi Tzur.
Czech Republic. 2 Badeniho St., Prague 7. ☎ 3332-5109. Ambassador Rephael Gvir.
Denmark. Emb.: Lundevangsvej 4, Hellerup, Copenhagen. ☎ 396 26288. Ambassador Carmi Gillon.
Dominica (see Dominican Republic).
Dominican Republic. Emb.: Pedro Henriques Unena 80. ☎ 5418974. Ambassador Pinchas Lavie.
Ecuador. Emb.: 12 De Octubrey Salazar, Edf. Plaza 2000, Quito. ☎ 238055. Ambassador Yaacov Paran.
Egypt. Emb.: 6 Shariah Ibn-el Maleck, Giza, Cairo. ☎ 3610 528. Ambassador David Sultan.
El Salvador. Emb.: 85 Av. Norte 619, Colonia Escalon, Centro de Gobierno, PO Box 1776, San Salvador. ☎ 2113434. Ambassador Yosef Livne.

Eritrea. Emb.: Ogaden St. 32, Asmara. ☎ 185626. Ambassador Ariel Kerem.
Estonia (see Latvia).
Ethiopia. PO Box 1266, Addis Ababa. ☎ 610 999. Ambassador Avi Abraham Granot.
Fiji (see Australia).
Finland. Emb.: 5a Vironkatu, Helsinki. ☎ 1356177. Ambassador Miryam Shomrat.
France. Emb.: 3 Rue Rabelais, Paris 75008. ☎ 40765500. Ambassador Elie Barnavi.
Gabon (see Cameroon).
Gambia (see Senegal).
Georgia. Emb.: Agmashenebeli Ave. 61, Tbilisi 380002. ☎ 951 709. Ambassador Lili Hahamy.
Germany. Emb.: Schinkelstrasse 10, Berlin 14193. ☎ 8904-5500. Ambassador Shimon Stein.
Ghana (see Côte d'Ivoire).
Gibraltar. Con.: 3 City Mill Lane. ☎ 59555956. Hon. Con. M. E. Benaim.
Grenada. Emb.: (see Jamaica).
Greece. Emb.: Marathonodromu No. 1. Paleo Psychico, Athens. ☎ 6719-530. Ambassador Ran Coriel.
Guatemala. Emb.: 13 Ave 14-07, Zona 10, Guatemala City. ☎ 363-5665. Ambassador Shlomo Cohen.
Guinea Bissau (see Senegal).
Guyana (see Venezuela).
Equatorial Guinea (see Cameroon).
Haiti (see Panama).
Honduras (see Guatamala).
Hong Kong. Cons.: Admiralty 701, Tower 2, 18 Harcourt Rd., Central. ☎ 25296091. Con.-Gen. Zohar Raz.
Hungary. Fulank, Utca 8, Budapest. ☎ 2000781. Ambassador Yehudit Várnai-Shorer.
Iceland. Emb.: (see Norway.) H. Con.-Gen. Pall Arnor Palsson.
India. Emb: 3 Aurangzeb Rd., New Delhi 10011. ☎ 3013238. Ambassador Yehoyada Haim. Cons.: Bombay 400 026, Kailas 50, G. Deshmukh Maro Cumballa Hill. ☎ 386 2793. Consul Walid Mansour.
Ireland. Emb.: Carrisbrook House, 122 Pembroke Rd, Ballsbridge, Dublin 4. ☎ 6680303. Ambassador.
Italy. Emb.: Via Michele Mercati 12, Rome. ☎ 36198500. Ambassador Yehuda Milo.
Jamaica. Con.: 7-9 Harbour St., Kingston. ☎ 922-5990. Hon. Consul Joseph Mayer-Matalon.
Japan. Emb.: 3 Niban-Cho, Chiyoda-ku, Tokyo. ☎ 3264-0911. Ambassador Moshe Ben Yaakov.
Jordan. Emb.: 47 Maysaloun St., Rabiya, Amman 111195. ☎ 552-4680. Ambassador Shimon Shamir.
Kazakhstan. Emb: Dgeltoxan St. 87, Almaty. ☎ 507215. Ambassador Israel Mey-Ami.
Kenya. Emb.: Bishop Rd., Fair View Hotel, P.O. Box 30354, Nairobi. ☎ 722182. Ambassador Menashe Zipori.
Kirghizstan (see Kazakhstan).
Kiribati (Republic of) (see Australia).
Korea (South). Emb.: 823-21 Daekong Building, Yoksam-Dong Kangnam-Ku. ☎ 5643448. Ambassador Arie Arazi.
Laos (see Vietnam).
Latvia. Emb.: 2 Elizabetes St., LV 1340 Riga. ☎ 732-0739. Ambassador Oded Ben-Hur.
Lesotho (see Swaziland).
Liberia. Emb.: Gardiner Avenue, Sinkor, POB 2057, Monrovia. ☎ 262073/

262861. Fax (977) 4415.
Liechtenstein. Con-Gen. G. Yarden (see Switzerland.)
Lithuania (see Latvia)
Luxembourg (see Belgium). **Macao** (see Hong Kong). **Macedonia** (see Greece). **Madagascar** (see Kenya). **Malawi** (see Zimbabwe). **Malta** (see Italy). **Marshall Islands** (see Australia).
Mauritania. Emb. Ilot-A-516, Tevraghi-Zenia, Nouakchott ☎ 254610
Mauritius (see Kenya).
Mexico. Emb.: Sierra Madre 215, Mexico City 10 D.F. ☎ 2011500. Ambassador Moshe Melamed.
Micronesia (see Australia). **Moldova** (see Ukraine).
Monaco (see France). Con.-Gen. Joseph Amihoud.
Mongolia (see China).
Morocco. Bureau de Liaison, Souissi, 52 Boulevard Mehdi Ben-Barka, Rabat. ☎ 657680. Head of Liaison Office, David Dadonn.
Mozambique (see Zimbabwe).
The Union of Mayanmar. Emb.: 49 Pyay Rd., Yangon. ☎ 222290. Fax 22463. Ambassador Gad Natan.
Namibia (see Zimbabwe).
Nauro (see Australia).
Nepal. Emb.: Bishramalaya Hse., Lazimpat, Katmandu. ☎ 413419. Ambassador Esther Efrat Smilg.
Netherlands. Emb.: Buitenhof 47, The Hague, 2513 AH. ☎ 3760500. Ambassador Yossi Gal.
Netherlands Antilles. Curaçao Consulate, Blauwduiffweg 5, Willemstad, Curaçao. ☎ 373533. Hon. Consul Paul Ackerman.
New Zealand. Emb.: PO Box 2171, DB Tower, 111 the Terrace, Wellington. ☎ 4722362. Ambassador Ruth Kahanoff.
Nicaragua (see Guatamala).
Nigeria. Emb.: 636 Adeyemo Elakija St., Victoria Island, Lagos. ☎ 260121. Ambassador Gadi Golan.
Norway. Emb.: Radisson SAS Scandinavia Hotel, Holbergsgata 30, Oslo 0166. ☎ 2236-4741. Ambassador Michael Shiloh.
Oman. Israel Trade Representation Office, PO Box 194, Aladhiba, P.C. 130 Muscat. ☎ 604857. Hd. of Mission Oded Ben Haim.
Republic of Palau (see Australia).
Panama. Emb.: Edificio Grobman, Calle Manuel Icaza, Quinto Piso, Panama City 5. ☎ 2648022. Ambassador Yaakov Brakha.
Papua, New Guinea (see Australia).
Paraguay. Emb.: Piso 8, Edificion San Rafael, Calle Yergos No. 437 C/25 De Mayo. ☎ 495097. Ambassador Yoav Bar-On.
Peru. Emb.: Sanches 125, 6 Piso, Santa Beatriz, Lima. ☎ 4334431. Ambassador Mario Joel Salpak.
Philippines. Emb.: Trafalgar Plaza 23 Floor, Emb.: Trafalgar Plaza 23 Floor, Makati, Manila. ☎ 892-5330. Fax 819-0561. Ambassador A. Shetibel.
Poland. Interests Office: Ul. L. Krzywickiego 24, Warsaw. ☎ 825-2897. Ambassador Shevach Weiss.
Portugal. Emb.: Rua Antonio Enes 16-4°, Lisbon. ☎ 355-3640. Ambassador Shmuel Tevet.
Qatar. Israel Trade Representation Office, 15 Al Buhturi St, Dohu. ☎ 689077. Hd. of Mission Shmuel Ravel.
Romania. Emb.: 5 Rue Burghelea, Bucharest. ☎ 31122299. Ambassador A. Millo.
Russia. Emb.: 56 Bolshaya Ordinka, Moscow. ☎ 2306777. Ambassador Aliza Shenhar.
Rwanda (see Zaire).

St. Christopher, St. Kitts and St. Nevis (see Dominican Republic).
St. Lucia (see Jamaica).
St. Vincent and the Grenadines (see Jamaica).
San Marino. Con.-Gen. (see Italy).
Sao Tome and Principe (see Cameroon).
Senegal. Emb.: B.P. 2096, Dakar. ☎ 8233561. Ambassador Arieh Avidor.
Seychelles (see Kenya).
Singapore. Emb.: 58 Dalvey Rd., Singapore 1025. ☎ 834 9200. Ambassador D. Megiddo.
Slovakia (see Austria).
Slovenia (see Austria).
Solomon Islands (see Australia).
South Africa. Emb.: 339 Hilda St., Hatfield, Pretoria. ☎ 3422-693. Ambassador Elazar Granot.
Spain. Emb.: Calle Velazques 150, Madrid 28002. ☎ 4111357. Ambassador Ehud Gol.
Surinam (see Venezuela).
Swaziland. Emb.: Mbabane Hse., Warner St., P.O.B. 146, Mbabane. ☎ 42626. Ambassador.
Sweden. Emb.: Torstenssonsgatan 4, Stockholm. ☎ 6630435. Ambassador Gideon Ben-Ami.
Switzerland. Emb.: Alpenstrasse 32, Berne. ☎ 3511-042. Ambassador Gavriel Padon.
Tajikistan (see Uzbekistan).
Tanzania (see Kenya).
Thailand. Emb.: 75 Sukumvit Soi 19, Ocean Tower II 25th Floor, Bangkok 10110. ☎ 2049255. Ambassador Mordechai Lewi.
Togo (see Côte d'Ivoire).
Tonga (see Australia).
Trinidad and Tobago (see Venezuela).
Tunisia. Interests Office. ☎ 795-695. Hd. Shalom Cohen.
Turkey. Emb.: Mahatma Gandhi Sok 85, Gaziosmanpasa, Ankara. ☎ 4463605. Ambassador David Sultan.
Turkmenistan. Emb.: Ambassador Shmuel Meirom (resident in Jerusalem).
Tuvalu (see Australia).
Uganda (see Kenya).
Ukraine. Emb.: GPE - S, Lesi Ukrainki 34, 252195, Kiev, Ukraine. ☎ 296-1731. Ambassador Zvi Magen.
United Kingdom. Emb.: 2 Palace Green, Kensington, W8 4QB. ☎ 0171-957 9500. Opening Hours: Mon.-Thur. 09.00-18.00 and Fri. 09.00-14.00. Ambassador **Zvi Shtauber** (see also p.20).
United States of America. Emb.: 3514 International Dr, Washington, D.C., 20008. ☎ 364 5500. Ambassador D. Ayalon.
Uruguay. Emb.: Bulevar Artigas 1585/89, Montevideo. ☎ 4004164. Ambassador Yair Ben Shalom.
Uzbekistan. Emb.: Lachuti Street, No. 16a, Tashkent. ☎ 152-5911. Ambassador.
Vanuata (see Australia).
Vatican, Via Michle Mercati 12, Rome 00197. ☎ 3619-8690. Ambassador Samuel Hadas.
Venezuela. Emb.: Avenida Franciso de Miranda, Centro Empresarial, Miranda 4 Piso Oficina 4-D, Los Ruices, Caracas. ☎ 2394-921. Ambassador Yosef Hasseen.
Vietnam. Emb.: PO Box 003, Thai Hoc, 68 Hguyen, Hanoi. ☎ 8433140. Ambassador Uri Halfon.
Western Samoa (see Australia).
Yugoslavia. Emb. 47 Bulevar Mira, Dedinje Belgrade. ☎ 367-2400.

Zaire. Emb.: P.O.B. 8343-Kin1, Gombe, Kinshasa. ☎ 45252. Ambassador S. Avital.
Zambia (see Zimbabwe).
Zimbabwe. Emb.: Three Anchor House, 6th floor, 54 Jason Moyo Ave, PO Box CY3191, Causeway. ☎ 756808. Ambassador Gershon Gan.

Main Political Parties

ISRAEL LABOUR PARTY
Est. 1968 by the merger of Mapai, Achdut Avoda and Rafi. Its programme: 'To attain national, social and pioneering aims, in the spirit of the heritage of the Jewish People, the vision of socialist Zionism and the values of the Labour movement'. *Chairman* Beniamin Ben Eliezer. Ad.: 110 Hayarkon St., Tel Aviv. ☎ 6899444.

LIKUD PARTY
Conservative Political Party. Dedicated to the principles of a free-market economy and the attainment of peace with security while preserving Israel's national interests. *Chairman* Ariel Sharon. Ad.: Metsudat Ze'ev, 38 King George St., Tel Aviv. ☎ (03) 621 0666. Email webmaster@likud.org.il

MERETZ
Mapam was founded in 1948. Mapam merged with Ratz and members of Shinui into one single party: Meretz Unification Congress 1997. *Chair* Yossi Sarid; *International Sec.* Monica Pollack. Meretz is a member party of the Socialist International and of the Party of European Socialists. Ad.: 2 Homa U'Migdal St., Tel Aviv 61201. ☎ 972-3-6360111. Fax 972-3-5375107. Email hasbara@meretz.israel.net

NATIONAL RELIGIOUS PARTY
Created through the merger of Mizrachi and Hapoel Hamizrachi in 1956. Its motto 'The People of Israel in the Land of Israel, according to the Torah of Israel'. Ad.: Sarei Yisrael 12, Jerusalem. ☎ 02-537727. *Sec.* General Zevulun Orlev.

AGUDAT ISRAEL
Founded in 1912 in Katowice, Poland. Its principle is that only the Torah unites the Jewish people. *Political Sec.* M. Porush. Central Off.: Haherut Sq., Jerusalem. (☎ 384357), and 5 Bardechefsky St., Tel Aviv. (☎ 5617844).

HISTADRUT – GENERAL FEDERATION OF LABOUR IN ISRAEL
93 Arlozoroff St., Tel-Aviv. 62098
☎ 972 3 6921513. Fax 972 3 6921512. Email histint@netvision.net.il.
Chairman Amir Peretz, MK.
Histadrut, the largest labour organisation in Israel, is a democratic organisation which strives to ensure the welfare, social security and rights of working people, to protect them and act for their professional advancement, while endeavouring to reduce the gaps in society to achieve a more just society. The executive body of Histadrut is separate from the elected body and the legislative body. The legislative and regulatory body, the Histadrut Assembly, represents the relative strengths of the different political groups of Israel.

Membership is voluntary and individual, and open to all men and women of 18 years of age and above who live on the earnings of their own labour without exploiting the work of others. Membership totals over 600,000, including workers from all spheres, housewives, the self-employed and professionals as well as the unemployed, students and pensioners. Workers' interests are protected through a number of occupational and professional unions affiliated to the Histadrut. The Histadrut operates courses for trade unionists and new immigrants and apprenticeship classes. It maintains an Institute for Social and Economic Issues and the International Institute, one of the largest centres of leadership training in Israel for students from Africa, Asia, Latin America and Eastern Europe, which includes the Levinson Centre for Adult Education and the Jewish–Arab Institute for Regional Cooperation. Attached to the Histadrut is a women's organisation, 'Na'amat', which promotes changes in legislation, operates a network of legal service bureaux and vocational training courses, and runs counselling centres for the treatment and prevention of domestic violence, etc.

Selected Educational and Research Institutions

HEBREW UNIVERSITY OF JERUSALEM
Founded in 1918 and opened in 1925 on Mount Scopus. When, contrary to the provisions of the Armistice Agreement after the War of Independence in 1949, access to Mount Scopus was denied by Jordan, the University functioned in scattered temporary quarters until a new campus was built on Givat Ram, and a medical campus in Ein Kerem, both in Jerusalem. After the Six-Day War of June 1967, the Mount Scopus campus was rebuilt and expanded. Today the University serves some 24,000 students in its seven Faculties: Humanities, Social Sciences, Science, Law, Medicine, Dental Medicine and Agricultural and Environmental Quality Sciences (the latter located in Rehovot). There are 12 Schools: Education, Business Administration, Applied Science, Nutritional Sciences, Nursing, Occupational Therapy, Pharmacy, Public Health, Social Work, Veterinary Medicine, Library, Archive and Information Studies, and School for Overseas Students. The Jewish National and University Library is on the Givat Ram campus and there are about 100 research centres. The Magnes Press/Hebrew University publishes scientific and academic works. *Ch. Bd. of Govs.* Y. Arnon; *President* Prof. Menachem Magidor; *Rector* Prof. Haim Rabinowitch. Ad.: Mount Scopus, Jerusalem, 91905. ☎ (02)5 882917. Fax (02) 5883021. Website: www.huji.ac.il

TECHNION-ISRAEL INSTITUTE OF TECHNOLOGY
Established in 1924 as a small technical institute, it now has more than 11,800 students, making it the largest full-service university wholly dedicated to science and technology in Israel. The institute has 19 faculties and departments including: Aerospace, Biomedical, Chemical, Civil, Electrical and Industrial Engineering, and Architecture, Chemistry, Computer Science and Management, Medicine and Physics. The Technion is located on Mount Carmel. The main buildings include the Winston Churchill Auditorium and the Shine Student Union. It also has a graduate school, a school for continuing education and a Research & Development Foundation. *President* Amos Lapidot. Ad.: Technion City, Mount Carmel, Haifa 32000. ☎ (04) 829 2578. Fax (04) 823 5195.

WEIZMANN INSTITUTE OF SCIENCE
The Institute at Rehovot engages in research in Mathematical Sciences, Chemistry, Physics, Biology, Biochemistry and Science Teaching. *President* Prof. Ilan Chet; *V. President* Prof. S. Safran. Ad.: POB 26, Rehovot 76100. ☎ 972-8-9343111. Fax 972-8-934107.

BAR-ILAN UNIVERSITY
Since its founding in 1955, Bar-Ilan has grown to become Israel's second-largest university, comprising a modern 70-acre campus in Ramat Gan, outside Tel Aviv, with five regional colleges across Israel. Over 6,000 courses are taught in the faculties of exact, life and social sciences, humanities, Jewish studies and law, by 1,300 academic faculty to 25,000 students. Today, Israel's largest schools of education and social work and the premier Jewish studies faculty, operate at Bar-Ilan.

Additionally, the university is home to world-class scientific research institutes in physics, medicinal chemistry, mathematics, brain reseach, economics, strategic studies, developmental psychology, musicology, archaeology, bible, Jewish law and philosophy, and more. Some 40 prominent universities around the world maintain academic cooperation agreements with Bar-Ilan. Every day, Israelis of widely varying backgrounds and religious beliefs work and study together in harmony at Bar Ilan. *Chancellor* Rabbi Prof. Emanuel Rackman; *President* Prof. Moshe Kaveh; *Rector* Prof. Hanoch Lavee. *Cor.* BIU, Ramat Gan, Israel 52900. ☎ 972-3-531-8111. *Student information:* 972-3-531-8274; Fax 972-3-535-1522. Website www.biu.ac.il.

BEN GURION UNIVERSITY OF THE NEGEV, BEERSHEVA
Founded 1969, the university comprises the following faculties: Humanities and Social Sciences, Natural Sciences, Engineering Sciences, Health Sciences, School of Management, the Kreitman School of Advanced Graduate Studies and the Jacob Blaustein Institute for Desert Research. *President* Prof. Avishay Braverman. Ad.: P.O. Box 653, BeerSheva, 84105. ☎ 08-6461279.

CENTER FOR JEWISH ART
Hebrew University of Jerusalem, Mount Scopus, Humanities Building, Jerusalem 91905. ☎ 972-2-5882281, Fax 972-2-5400105, Email cja@vms.huji.ac.il. Website www.hum.huji.ac.il/cja. *Dir.* Dr Aliza Cohen-Mushlin; *Acad. Chairman* Prof. Bezalel Narkiss.

UNIVERSITY OF HAIFA
Established in 1963, Haifa is one of the seven accredited research universities in Israel. Academic instruction is conducted in the framework of the six Faculties (Humanities, Social Science, Law, Social Welfare and Health, Education, Sciences). Most of the 45 departments and schools offer bachelor, master and Ph.D. degrees. Research activity is carried out in the framework of research institutes and centres. The Research Authority encourages and coordinates research at the University. The total student body in the academic year 1999/2000 numbered 13,000. *President* Prof. Y. Hayuth; *Rector* Prof. A. Ben-Ze'ev. Ad.: Mount Carmel, Haifa 31905. Email mtmnh17@uvm.haifa.ac.il; Internet http://www.haifa.ac.il. ☎ 972-4-8240111. Fax 972-4-8342101.

ISRAEL OCEANOGRAPHIC AND LIMNOLOGICAL RESEARCH
(Est. 1967) To develop knowledge and technology for sustainable use of marine and fresh water resources. *Dir.-Gen.* Dr Yuval Cohen. Ad.: Tel Shikmona, POB 8030, Haifa 31080. ☎ 04-8515202. Fax 04-8511911. Email yuval@ocean.org.il. Website www.ocean.org.il.

JERUSALEM ACADEMY OF JEWISH STUDIES (Yeshivat Dvar Yerushalayim)
53 Katzenellenbogen St., Har Nof, POB 5454, Jerusalem 91053. ☎ 6522817. Fax 652287. Email dvar@dvar.org.il; Website www.dvar.org.il. *Dean* Rabbi B. Horovitz, MA; UK office (Reg. Charity No. 262716), 1007, Finchley Rd., London NW11 7HB. ☎/Fax 020-8458 8563. (See p.36)

JERUSALEM COLLEGE OF TECHNOLOGY
Est. in 1969 to train engineers and applied scientists within a religious framework. The College has depts. in Electro-Optics and Applied Physics, Electronic Engineering, Computer Sciences, Management Accounting, Technology Management and Marketing, Industrial Engineering Applied Mathematics and Teacher Training. The complex includes a Bet Midrash for Jewish studies; one-year yeshiva academic programme for English-speaking students. The College awards a Bachelor's

degree in Technology and Applied Science, Managerial Accounting & Information Systems. *President* Prof. Y. Bodenheimer; *Rector* Prof. Y. Friedman. Ad.: 21 Havaad Haleumi St., Jerusalem. ☎ 9722-6751111. Fax 9722-6422075. Email pr@mail.jct.ac.il

THE LOUIS GUTTMAN ISRAEL INSTITUTE OF APPLIED SOCIAL RESEARCH
Founded in 1946 to advise governmental, public and private bodies on research in social psychology, sociology, psychology and related disciplines. *Scientific Dir.* Prof. S. Kugelmass. Ad.: 19 Washington St., Jerusalem, 91070. ☎ 231421.

MIKVEH ISRAEL AGRICULTURAL SCHOOL
The first agricultural school in Israel, it was founded by Charles Netter of the Alliance Isralite Universelle in 1870. The curriculum, in addition to training in agriculture, comprises instruction in the humanities, Jewish subjects, science, etc. Ad.: Mikveh Israel, Doar Holon. ☎ 03-842050. Zip code 58910.

ORT ISRAEL NETWORK
Est. 1948, ORT Israel manages Scientific and Technological Colleges and schools for around 80,000 young and adult students yearly. *Dir. Gen.*: I. Goralnik. Head office: 39, King David Blvd., Tel-Aviv 61160. Tel: 03-5203222.

TEL AVIV UNIVERSITY
The university sponsors studies and research in all the arts and sciences and includes among its faculties a department of space and planetary sciences, its observatory, at Mitzpe Ramon in the Negev, being the first in Israel. A science based industry utilising the university's manpower and equipment has been established. Its Graduate School of Business Administration was the first established in the country. There is a one year course which prepares new immigrants for entry into Israeli universities. *President* Prof. Itamar Rabinowitch; *Rector* Prof. Nili Cohen. Ad.: Ramat Aviv, Tel Aviv. ☎ 5450111.

WEITZ CENTER FOR DEVELOPMENT STUDIES
Founded in Rehovot in 1961, its main object is interdisciplinary research & training activities related to regional development in Israel and the developing world. Ad.: P.O.B. 2355 Rehovot, Israel 76122. ☎ 08-9474111. Fax 08-9475884. Email training@netvision.net.il.

THE ZINMAN COLLEGE OF PHYSICAL EDUCATION AND SPORTS SCIENCES AT THE WINGATE INSTITUTE
(Est. 1944) Teachers College for Physical Educators. Offers four-year Bachelor of Education course, including Teachers' Diploma. Specializations in early childhood, special education, sports for the disabled, posture cultivation, cardiac rehabilitation, physical activity for the elderly, public health, behaviour analysis, dance and movement, leisure and recreation education, nautical education, scouting education, sports media. Joint M.A. programme with Haifa University.
Faculty of 200, student body of 900 full-time students, 1,500 in part-time in-service courses. Ad.: P.E. College at Wingate Institute, Netanya, Israel 42902. ☎ 972-9-863922. Fax 972-9-8650960. Email zinman@wincol.macam98.ac.il. Internet: http://www.zin.macam98.ac.il.

Selected Commercial Organisations

BANK OF ISRAEL
Set up by the Knesset in 1954. Its functions include those usually discharged by central banks. It issues the currency and acts as Government banker, and manages

the official gold and foreign reserves. The governor is chief economic adviser to the Government. *Gov.* Ad.: Rechov Eliezer Kaplan, Kiryat Ben-Gurion, Jerusalem, 91007. ☎ (2) 6552211. Fax (2) 6528805. Email webmaster@bankisrael.gov.il

ENGLISH SPEAKING LAWYERS CENTER
PO Box 2828, Jerusalem. ☎ (02)-5820126. Fax (02)-5322094. Email wolfilaw@netvision.net.il. Provides free legal advice and consultations in all legal fields.

ISRAEL-AMERICA CHAMBER OF COMMERCE AND INDUSTRY
Exec. Dir. Nina Admoni. Ad.: 35 Shaul Hamelech Blvd., Tel Aviv. ☎ (03) 6952341. Fax (03) 6951272. Email amcham@amcham.co.il Website http://amcham.co.il

ISRAEL-BRITISH CHAMBER OF COMMERCE
(Est. 1951.) 29 Hamered St., PO Box 50321, Tel Aviv 61502. ☎ (03) 5109424. Fax (03) 5109540. Email isrbrit@netvision.net.il. Website www.ibcc.co.il. *Exec. Dir.* F. Kipper.

MANUFACTURERS' ASSOCIATION OF ISRAEL
Jerusalem: ☎ (02) 252449. Haifa: ☎ (04) 524202. Tel Aviv: ☎ (03) 5198787. *President* D. Propper.

Other Selected Organisations

ASSOCIATION OF JEWISH RELIGIOUS PROFESSIONALS FROM THE SOVIET UNION AND EASTERN EUROPE (SHAMIR)
6 David Yellin St., POB 5749, Jerusalem. ☎ 02-5385384. Fax 02-5385118. Email shamirbooks@bezeqint.net. Website www.shamirbooks.org.il. *Sec.* Martelle Urivetsky.

ASSOCIATION FOR THE WELLBEING OF ISRAEL'S SOLDIERS
(Ha'aguda Lemaan Hechayal. Charity No. 580004307) The Association for the Wellbeing of Israel's Soldiers was founded in 1942, during the Second World War, at a time when the young men of pre-state Israel were being drafted into the allied armies and the Jewish Brigade. The slogan back then was "The Heart of the People is with its Soldiers", and this sentiment continues to guide the Association's activity today. *Head Off.:* P.O. Box 21707, Tel Aviv 61217. *Overseas Dept*: 60 Weizman St., Tel Aviv 62155. ☎ 03 5465135. Fax (03) 5465145. Email awis@awis.co.il

BETH HATEFUTSOTH
The Nahum Goldmann Museum of the Jewish Diaspora, which opened in Tel-Aviv in 1978, tells the story of the Jewish people from the time of their expulsion from the Land of Israel 2,500 years ago to the present. History, tradition and the heritage of Jewish life in all parts of the world are brought to life in murals, reconstructions, dioramas, audio-visual displays, documentary films and interactive multi-media presentation. Ad: Tel-Aviv University Campus, Ramat-Aviv, P.O.B. 39359. Tel-Aviv 61392. ☎ 03-6462020. Fax 03-6462134. Email bhmuseum@post.tau.ac.il. Website: http://www.bh.org.il

CHIEF RABBINATE
The Chief Rabbinate consists of two joint Chief Rabbis and a Chief Rabbinical Council of 17. *Chief Rabbis* Rabbi Israel Meir Lau (Ashkenazi) and Rabbi Eliyahu Bakshi Doron (Rishon Lezion, Sephardi). Ad.: Beit Yahav, 80 Yirmiyahu St., POB 7525, Jerusalem. ☎ (02) 531 3192. Fax (02) 259-641. There are District Rabbinical Courts (Batei Din) in Jerusalem, Tel Aviv, Haifa, Petach Tikvah, Rehovot, Tiberias-Safad, Beersheba and Ashkelon.

ISRAEL MOVEMENT FOR PROGRESSIVE JUDAISM
13 King David Street, Jerusalem 94101. ☎ 022-6203 448. Email iri@impj.org.il. Website www.reform.org.il.

THE ISRAEL MUSEUM
HaKirya, Jerusalem, POBox 71117, Jerusalem 91710. ☎ 02-670-8811. Fax 02-563-1833. Email oritar@imj.org.il. Website www.imj.org.il. Israel's leading cultural institution and a museum of world-class status, its 20-acre campus houses an encyclopaedic collection of art and archaeology, with special emphasis on the culture of the Land of Israel and the Jewish people. The Museum has the world's most extensive collections of the archaeology of the Holy Land, Judaica and the ethnography of Diaspora Jewish Communities, as well as significant and extensive holdings in the Fine Arts, ranging from Old Masters to Contemporary Art, and including separate departments for Asian Art, the Arts of Africa and Oceania, Prints and Drawings, Photography, and Architecture and Design. The campus also includes the Shrine of the Book, which houses the Dead Sea Scrolls, the Billy Rose Art Garden and a Youth Wing. *Dir.* James Snyder.

ISRAEL NATURE AND NATIONAL PARKS PROTECTION AUTHORITY
The Authority is the result of a merger in 1998 of two bodies, one of which was in charge of the Israeli nature reserves and the other of national parks and heritage sites in Israel. Ad.: 78 Yirmeyahu St., Jerusalem. ☎ (02) 500 5444. Fax (02) 500 5444; 35 Jabotinsky St., Ramat-Gan 52511. ☎ (03) 576 6888. Fax (03) 751 1858.

JEWISH AGENCY FOR ISRAEL
Founded 1929; Reconstituted 1971. Constitutents are the World Zionist Organisation, United Israel Appeal, Inc. (USA), and Keren Hayesod. By reasons of its record and world-wide org. the Jewish Agency has come to be widely regarded as the representative org. of Jews the world over particularly in regard to the development of Israel and immigration to it. The governing bodies of the Jewish Agency are: the Assembly, which lays down basic policy, the Bd. of Governors, which manages its affairs between annual Assembly meetings, and the Executive, responsible for day-to-day operations. Jewish Agency, P.O. Box 92, Jerusalem. ☎ 972 2 6202450. Fax 972 26202303. Email ilanr@jazo.org.il *Ch. Exec.* Sallai Meridor; *Ch. Bd.* Alex Grass; *Dir.-Gen.* Aaron Abramovich; *Sec.-Gen.* Ilan Rubin.

KEREN KAYEMETH LEISRAEL (Jewish National Fund)
P.O. Box 283, Jerusalem 91002. *World Chairman* Yehiel Leket. *Head of Fund Raising* Avinoam Binder. The work of the JNF is to improve the quality of life for Israeli citizens by means of afforestation, ecology, water conservation and site preparation, and development for upbuilding the land to ensure its future.

WOMEN'S INTERNATIONAL ZIONIST ORGANISATION (Wizo)
(Reg. Charity No.: 580057321). 250,000 women, 100,000 of them in Israel, are members of this org. which maintains 800 institutions and services in Israel. World *President* Mrs M. Modai; *Chairman Exec.* Mrs H. Glaser. Ad.: 38 David Hamelech Blvd., Tel Aviv. 64237. ☎ 03-6923717. Fax 972-3-6958-267.

WORLD ZIONIST ORGANISATION
Founded by Theodor Herzl at the First Zionist Congress in Basle in 1897, it was the moving spirit in the events leading up to the establishment of the State of Israel in 1948. The 'Jerusalem Programme', adopted by the 27th Zionist Congress in Jerusalem in 1968, reformulated the aims of the Zionist Movement as: the unity of the Jewish people and the centrality of the State of Israel in its life, the ingathering of the exiles in the historic Jewish homeland by aliya; the strengthening of the State

of Israel, which is founded on the prophetic ideals of justice and peace; preserving the uniqueness of the Jewish people by promoting Jewish and Hebr. educ. and upholding Jewish spiritual and cultural values; defending the rights of Jews wherever they live. The supreme body of the WZO is the Zionist Congress, to which delegates are elected by members of Z. Federations abroad and by the Z. parties in Israel. The two governing bodies elected by the Congress are: the Executive, and the Zionist General Council to which the Executive is responsible and which decides Z. policy between Congresses. *Ch. of Executive* S. Meridor. P.O. Box 92, Jerusalem 91000. ☎ (02) 602 2080. Fax (02) 625 2352. Email sallaim@jazo.org.il.

YAD VASHEM

Har Hazikaron (Mount of Remembrance), Jerusalem, ☎ (02) 6443400. Fax (02) 6443443. POB 3477, Jerusalem 91034. Email general.information@yadvashem.org.il; Website www.yad-vashem.org.il.
Archives, Library, International School for Holocaust Studies, International Institute for Holocaust Research, Historical Museum, Art Museum, Hall of Remembrance, Hall of Names, Children's Memorial, Memorial to the Deportees, Avenue and Garden of the Righteous Among the Nations, Valley of the Communities.

British Settlements

The following are some of the settlements populated by large groups of immigrants from the United Kingdom and Ireland associated with the UJIA Israel (see below), which represents the Israeli Office of the Zionist Federation of Great Britain and Ireland. In some cases groups from Britain themselves established these settlements; in others, they joined existing settlements as 'reinforcement' groups. Entries were updated in 1998 and were last published in full in the Year Book for 2002:

Beit Chever (Kfar Daniel), Kfar Blum, Kfar Hanassi, Kfar Mordechai, Kibbutz Amiad, Kibbutz Bet Rimon, Kibbutz Beit Ha'emek, Kibbutz Kadarim, Kibbutz Lavi, Kibbutz Yassu'r, Kibbutz Zikim, Massuoth Yitzhak, Moshav Habonim (Kfar Lamm), Kibbutz Mevo Hama, Kibbutz Mishmar David, Kibbutz Machanayim, Kibbutz Alumim, Kibbutz Adamit, Moshav Sde Nitzan, Kibbutz Tuval.

UJIA Israel (incorporating the British Olim Society). Head Office: 76 Ibn Gvirol St., POB 16266, Tel Aviv 61162. ☎ 03-6965244. Fax 03-6968696. Email israel@ujia.org.il. *Man. Dir.* Shifra Levitsky. There are branches in Jerusalem and Karmiel. UJIA Israel is the official representative of the United Jewish Israel Appeal of Great Britain & Northern Ireland. Formerly known as the British Olim Society (est. 1949 in order to assist and support new immigrants from the UK settling in Israel), the merger of BOS and JIA-Israel took place in 1996 under the newly formed UJIA umbrella.

UJIA Israel represents UJIA UK on all campaign and renewal-related activities and aims at strengthening the ties between British Jewry and Israel, through projects, guests, missions and Israel Experience youth programmes.

UJIA Israel provides comprehensive absorption services to immigrants from the UK, Australia and Scandinavia and promotes absorption needs of various new immigrants in Israel.

During 1990, the BOS Charitable Trust was established as a funding conduit for new immigrant activities and programmes in Israel, essentially aimed at helping the disadvantaged and less fortunate.

English Speaking Residents Association (ESRA). P.O.B 3132, Herzliya 46104. ☎ 972-9-9508371. Fax 972-9-9543781. Email esra@trendline. co.il Website www.esra.org.il (non-profit organisation no. 550037451.) A voluntary organisation assisting absorption of English-speaking immigrants, by means of social, cultural, educational and volunteering projects, practical help in finding employment, support, and advice on emotional, social and legal problems. The ESRA Community Fund initiates and supports welfare, educational and professional projects for disadvantaged Israelis, immigrants from distressed countries, the handicapped and victimised women. Tax exemptions on donations in United States, United Kingdom, Canada and Israel. Publ. ESRA Magazine and the ESRA Directory.

Israel, Britain and the Commonwealth Association (IBCA), Industry House, 29 Hamored St., 68125, Tel Aviv. Fax (03) 5104646. Branches in Haifa and Jerusalem. The main aims of the Association are to encourage, develop, and extend social, cultural and economic relations between Israel and the British Commonwealth. *Chairman* L. Harris; *Vice-Chairman* Dr A. Lerner; *Hon. Sec.* Madelaine Mordecai; *Contact* Freida Peled.

ITALY (34,500)

The Jewish community of Italy, whose history goes back to very early times, increased considerably at the time of the Dispersion in C.E. 70. During the Middle Ages and the Renaissance there were newcomers from Spain and Germany. Rich syns. as well as rabbinical schools, yeshivot, and printing houses were set up and became known in many countries. During the first years of fascism Italian Jews did not suffer; only after 1938 (under Nazi pressure) were racial laws introduced and, during the German occupation from 1943 to 1945 nearly 12,000, especially from Rome, were murdered or banished. The number of persons registered as Jews now is around 35,000. The most important communities are those of Rome (15,000), Milan (10,000), and Turin (1,630), followed by Florence, Trieste, Livorno and Venice and other centres.

ROME

*__Central organisation__: Unione delle Comunità Ebraiche Italiane, 00153 Roma, Lungotevere Sanzio 9. ☎ 5803670. Fax 5899569. *President* A. Luzzatto.

Community: Lungotevere Cenci, 00186. ☎ 6840061. Fax 68400684. Rabbinical office. Fax 68400655.

Chief Rabbi, Dr Elio Toaff. ☎ 6875051/2/3.

Jewish Agency, Corso Vittorio Emanuele 173, 00185. ☎ 68805290. Fax 6789511.

Synagogues, Lungotevere Cenci; Via Catalana; Via Balbo 33.

Syn. of Libyan refugees-Via Padova 92. ☎ 44233334.

MILAN

Community, Via Sally Mayer, 2, 20146. ☎ (02) 48302806. Fax 02/48304660.

Synagogue, Via Guastalla, 19, 10122. ☎ (02) 5512029. Fax (02) 5512101.

JAMAICA (350)

The Jewish settlement here, first composed of fugitives from the Inquisition, goes back before the period of the British occupation in 1655. During the eighteenth century there was an Ashkenazi influx from England. Jewish disabilities were abolished in 1831. There were formerly congregations at Port Royal, Spanish Town (two syns.) and at Montego Bay (1845-1900). The Ashkenazi and Sephardi communities in Kingston merged into one in 1921, the last of eight which once flourished.

*__United Congregation of Israelites, Synagogue Shaare Shalom__, Duke St. (Syn. built 1885, rebuilt 1911.) *Acting Spiritual Leader* Stephen C. Henriques. ☎ 876-924-2451.

Hillel Academy (Est. 1969).

Home for the Aged (Est. 1864). Managed by the Jewish Ladies Organisation. *Chairman* Mrs Sandra Phillipps.

JAPAN (2,000)

The first Jewish community in Japan (at Yokohama) dates back to 1860 and old Jewish cemeteries exist in Yokohama, Kobe and Nagasaki. Jews were among the early foreign settlers. In 1940, 5,000 Jewish refugees from Germany and Poland arrived in Kobe, subsequently leaving for the USA and Shanghai. There are now about 2,000 Jews in Japan. About 1,000 live in the Tokyo area. There is a cong. of about 40 families in Kobe.

*__Jewish Community of Japan__, 8-8 Hiroo 3-chome, Shibuya-Ku, Tokyo 150-0012. ☎ 3400-2559. Fax 03-3400-1827. Email jccjapan@gol.com. *M.* Rabbi Eliot Marmon; *Man.* T. A. Pe'er. Kosher meals available on Shabbat and during the week. Advance notification requested.

KENYA (150 families)

Jewish settlement in East Africa dates from 1903, when the British Government offered the Zionist Organisation a territory in the present Kenya for an autonomous Jewish settlement. The offer was refused but not unanimously and shortly afterwards a few Jews settled in the colony. Later, a number of Central European Jewish refugees settled here. The Jewish population in today's independent Kenya is about 150 families, most of whom are Israelis. See 'Jews of Nairobi 1903-1962', by Julius Carlebach.

*__Nairobi Hebrew Congregation__, PO Box 40990, 219703. ☎ 222770. Email info@nhc.co.ke; azfactor@africaonline.co.ke. (Est. 1904.) *Chairman* Dr Vera Somen; *H. T.* M. Abbema; *H. Sec.* Ms A. Zola.

LATVIA (10,800)

The current Jewish population is 10,800, with 8,250 Jews living in Riga. Most Jews in Riga speak Russian, although some speak Latvian and a few speak Yiddish. Rezekne, Kraslava, Jurmal, Jelgava, Jekabpils, Ventspils, Liepaja (450), Ludza and Daugavpils (Dvinsk, 550) support smaller Jewish populations. About 25 towns still have Jewish cemeteries (see 'A Guide to Jewish Genealogy in Latvia and Estonia' by Arlene Beare).

RIGA

Jewish Community of Latvia, 141 Lacplesas St, LV-1003. Email latvia@fjc.ru. Community leaders: Arkadi Suharenko (secular), Dovid Kogan (religious). Chief Rabbi of Latvia Rabbi Barkan; deputy Rabbi Arie Beccer.

Synagogue, 6/8 Peitavas St. ☎ (013-2) 22-45-49

Chabad Lubavitch school and community, 141 Lacplesas St. Rabbi Mordehai Glazman; Rabbi Shneur Kot.

Jewish Community Centre, Museum and Library (LOEK), 6 Skolas St. 226050. ☎ (013-2) 28-95-80.

Old Jewish Cemetery, 2/4 Liksnas St is now a park. New Jewish Cemetery, 4 Lizuma St, Shmerli.

REZHITSA

Syn.: Kaleyu St.

LEBANON (100)

In the civil war which broke out in 1975 most of the 2,000 Jews left the country. About 100 remain in Beirut.

LIBYA (50)

About the time that Libya became an independent State in 1951 there was a mass emigration of most of its 37,000 Jews to Israel, and only very few remain in Tripoli.

LITHUANIA (11,000)

Jewish Community of Lithuania, 4 Pylimo, Vilnius 2001. ☎ 2-613-003. Fax 3705 212 7915. Email jewishcom@post.5ci.lt

KAUNAS

Syn.: 13, Ozheskienes St.
Jewish Community Offices, 26B Gedimino St. ☎ 203-717. Fax 370 7203717.

VILNIUS

Syn.: 39 Pylimo St. ☎ (2) 61-25-23.
Vilna Gaon Jewish State Museum, Pamelkalnio Str. 12, Vilnius. ☎ 620730.
There are also communities in Druskininkai, Klaipeda, Panevezys and Shiauliai.

LUXEMBOURG (1,000)

There are today about 1,000 Jews in Luxembourg, the majority in Luxembourg City. Since the French Revolution they have enjoyed the same rights as other citizens. Before 1933 there were 1,800 Jews in the country; by 1940 the influx of German and other refugees had brought the Jewish population to about 5,000. The main syn. was destroyed by the Nazis.
Synagogue: 45 Avenue Monterey, Luxembourg City 2163.
Chief Rabbi, Joseph Sayagh, 34 rue Alphonse Munchen, 2172. *Chairman* Aach Guy, 45 Av. Monterey.
Or Chadash Liberal Jewish Community (affiliated to ULPS). *Corr.* 29 rue Leandre Lacoix, 1-1913. Email D1Jaffe@aol.com. *Chair.* Erica Peresman
Esch/Alzette: Synagogue, 52 Rue du Canal. *Chairman* R. Wolf, 19 rue du Nord 4260 Esch/Alzette.

MALTA (50)

There have been Jews in Malta since pre-Roman times and, just before the Spanish-directed expulsion in 1492, one-third of the population of the then capital city, Mdina, was Jewish. After the coming of the Knights of St John, the only Jews in Malta became their captives and slaves, held for ransom. This situation persisted until Napoleon overthrew the Knights and released all their prisoners. Following the defeat of the French by the British, a small Jewish community was established early in the nineteenth century which has survived until the present day. There were never more than about 20 families with a normal total of under 100 people, and it was financially unable to build a synagogue. However, following a successful appeal, launched in 1998, local and international donations enabled the acquisition and conversion of premises into a Jewish Centre and Synagogue. The Malta Jewish Community now, once again, owns its own property, after a gap of over 500 years.
Jewish Community of Malta, 1 Florida Mansions, Enrico Mizzi Str., Ta'xbiex, Malta. Email jewsofmalta@dijigate.net; Website www.maltesejewish community.org. *President* Abraham C. Ohayon ☎ 21237309; *Sec.* S. L. Davis, OBE ☎ 21445924. Enq. to Mr Davis or to Mrs S. Tayar ☎ 21386266.

MAURITIUS

There is no permanent Jewish community. The Jewish cemetery contains the graves of 125 refugees from Europe. They were part of a group of 1,700 Jews denied entry to Palestine and interned on the island during 1940-1945. *Corr.* P.M. Birger. P.O. Box 209, Port Louis, Mauritius. ☎ 2020200. Fax 2083391.

MEXICO (48,000)

The Jewish presence in Mexico dates back to the Spanish Conquest, although it was not until the final years of the nineteenth century and the beginning of the twentieth that a mass immigration of Jews from Syria, the Balkanic countries and eastern Europe, fleeing from persecution and poverty, laid the foundations of the modern Jewish Mexican community. Today's Jewish population is about 40,000, the majority in Mexico City. The city has twelve Jewish day-schools and several Yeshivot attended by up to 90 per cent of Mexican Jewish children. There are communities in Guadalajara, Monterrey and Tijuana.

MEXICO CITY

*__Central Committee of the Jewish Community in Mexico__, Cofre de Perote 115, Col. Lomas Barrilaco, 11010 Mexico DF. ☎ 5540-7376, 5520-9393. Fax 5540-3050. *Exec. Dir.* Mauricio Lulka.

Tribuna Israelita (analysis and opinion office of the Jewish Community in Mexico), Cofre de Perote 115, Col. Lomas Barrilaco, 11010 Mexico DF. ☎ 5540-7376, 5520-9393. Fax 5540-3050. Email mailto:tribuna@ort.mx. Website tribuna.ort.org.mx. *Dir.* Renee Dayan-Shabot.

Synagogues: Askenazi, Acapulco 70, Col. Roma, ☎ 5211-0575; Bet El (Conservative) Horacio 1722, Polanco. ☎ 5281-2592; Beth Israel (Conservtive, English speaking), Virreyes 1140, Lomas. ☎ 5540-2642; Sephardic, Av. de los Bosques 292A, Tecamachalco. ☎ 5251-0880; Monte Sinaì (Damascan), Fuente de la Huerta 22, Tecamachalco. ☎ 5596-9966; Maguén David (Aleppo), Bernard Shaw 10, Polanco. ☎ 203-9964.

Jewish Sport Center, Avila Camacho 620, Lomas de Sotelo. ☎ 557-3000.

MOLDOVA (40,000)

Federation of the Jewish Communities of Moldova, ☎ (3732) 541023. Fax (3732) 541020. Email sbf@hotmail.co.il; info@jewishmoldova.org. Website www.moldova.org.

CHISINAU

Syn.: 8 Habad-Lubavici Str., 2012. ☎ (3732) 541 023/052. Fax (3732) 541 020. Website www.kishinev.org.

Towns with Jewish populations include: Tiraspol, Baltsy, Bendery, Soroky, Ribnitsa, Rezina and Orxey.

MOROCCO (7,000)

The Jews of Morocco have a history dating back to the times before it became a Roman province. Under Moslem rule they experienced alternate toleration and persecution. The expulsion from Spain and Portugal brought many newcomers to Morocco. In the nineteenth century many of the oppressed Jews sought the protection of Britain and France. The former French Protectorate removed legal disabilities, but the economic position of most Jews remained very precarious. During the Vichy period of the second World War Sultan Mohamed V protected the community. Before the est. of the independent kingdom of Morocco in 1956 many emigrated to Israel, France, Spain and Canada, and the present Jewish pop. is est. at 7,000 under the protection of King Mohammed VI.

CASABLANCA

*__Community Offices__, 12 rue Abou Abdallah Al Mahassibi. ☎ 222861.Fax 266953.

Synagogues: Temple Beth El, 61 rue Jaber Ben Hayane. ☎ 267192; Em Habanim, 14, rue Ibn Rochd; Hazan, rue Roger Farache; Tehilla Le David, Blvd. du 11 Janvier; and Benisty rue Ferhat Hachad.

International Organisations: American Joint Distribution Committee, 3 rue Rouget de Lisle. ☎ 274717. Fax 264089; Ittihad-Maroc, 13 rue Addamir Al Kabir. ☎ 2003-72. Fax 2003-09; Ose, 151 bis, blvd. Ziraoui. ☎ 267891. Fax 278924; Lubavitch-Maroc, 174 blvd. Ziraoui. ☎ 269037; Ozar Hatorah (Religious School Organisation), 31 rue Jaber Ben Hayane. ☎ 270920.

There are also coms. in Fez, Kenitra, Marrakech, Meknès, Rabat, Tangier, Tetuan, El Jadida and Agadir.

MOZAMBIQUE

Jewish Community of Mozambique, c/o Natalie Tenzer-Silva, P.O. Box 232, Maputo. ☎ 494413.

NEW ZEALAND (6,000)

The settlement of Jews in New Zealand dates from the establishment of British sovereignty in 1840. In the first emigrant ships were a number of Jews from England. But still earlier a few Jewish wayfarers had settled in the northern part of New Zealand, including John Israel Montefiore, a cousin of Sir Moses Montefiore, who settled at the Bay of Islands in 1831, Joel Samuel Polack, one of the earliest writers on the country, in which he travelled in 1831-37, and David Nathan, who laid the foundations of the Jewish community in Auckland in the early 1840s.

The Wellington Jewish com. was founded by Abraham Hort, under the authority of the Chief Rabbi, on January 7, 1843, when the first Jewish service was held. Communities were later est. in Christchurch and Dunedin and other parts of the South Island. From the earliest times Jewish settlers have helped to lay the foundation of the commercial and industrial prosperity of the country.

The number of Jews in New Zealand at the census of 2001 was over 6,000. Most live in Auckland and Wellington. During the last 15 years approximately 400 Soviet Jews have settled in New Zealand, mainly in Wellington and Auckland, but many have since emigrated to Australia. In addition, there has been recent settlement from South Africa and Israel.

Jews have occupied most important positions in New Zealand including that of Administrator, Prime Minister and Chief Justice. There have been six Jewish mayors of Auckland and two of Wellington. See: History of the Jews in New Zealand by L. M. Goldmann (1959), A Standard for the People: The 150th Anniversary of the Wellington Hebrew Congregation, edited by S. Levine (1994) and Auckland Jewry Past and Present, edited by A. and L. Gluckman (1993).

*__United Synagogues of N.Z.__ *President* S. Goldsmith, 11 Rotherglen Ave., Christchurch.

*__New Zealand Jewish Council.__ *President* Mr D. Zwartz. P.O. Box 4315 Auckland. ☎ 309-9444. Fax 373 2283.

N.Z. Council of Christians & Jews, PO Box 68-224, Newton, Auckland. ☎ (09) 638-7710.

Council of Jewish Women of N.Z., PO Box 27-156, Wellington. *President*: Mrs S. Payes. ☎ (04) 567-1679.

*__Zionist Federation of N.Z.__ S. Payes, 80 Webb St., Wellington.

Wizo Federation. *President*: Mrs Clements, 80 Webb St., Wellington.

New Zealand Jewish Chronicle (monthly), PO Box 27-211, Wellington. ☎ (04) 385-0720. Fax (04) 384-6542. *Edr.* Anna Veritt.

WELLINGTON (1,000)

Hebrew Congregration. *President* D. Lewis. 80 Webb St. ☎ 4845 081.

Beth-El Synagogue, opened 1870 rebuilt 1929, resited in Jewish Community Centre and opened 1977.

Jewish Community Centre, 80 Webb St., P.O. Box 11-173. Moriah Kindergarten open daily.

Moriah College. (Primary Day Sch.) (Est. 1987.) P.O. Box 27233. ☎ 4842401.

Liberal Jewish Congregation (Temple Sinai). *President* V. Josephs, P.O. Box 27 301. ☎ 4850 720.

Zionist Society. *President* M. Lawrence, 80 Webb Street.

AUCKLAND (1,600)
Hebrew Congregation. *President* D. Nathan. PO Box 68 224. ☎ 372 908.
Beth Israel Synagogue, 108 Greys Ave. PO Box 68 224. ☎ 373-2908 (Est. 1841).
Beth Shalom, The Auckland Congregation for Progressive Judaism, 180 Manukau Rd., Epsom. *President* D. Robinson. PO Box 26052 Epsom. ☎ 524-4139. Fax 524-7075. Email bshalom@ihug.co.nz. Website www.bethshalom.org.nz.
Kadimah College and Kindergarten, Greys Ave.
Zionist Society, (Est. 1904). PO Box 4315.
There are smaller coms. in Christchurch (640), Hamilton (50) and Dunedin (60).

NORTH YEMEN

Since 1948 the vast majority of Yemeni Jews (who then numbered about 50,000) have emigrated to Israel. It is est. about 1,200 remain in Sa'ana.

NORWAY (2,000)

The Jewish population of Norway is estimated to be about 2,000. There are two organised communities, Det Mosaiske Trossamfund Oslo (about 1,000 members) and Det Mosaiske Trossamfund Trondheim (about 130 members).

The community in Oslo is very active, with regular synagogue services (Friday night and Saturday as well as all holidays), a kindergarten, afternoon classes for children of school-going age, regular meetings and seminars for members of different age-groups, a home for the elderly as well as a shop which supplies kosher food.

*__Det Mosaiske Trossamfund__ (Jewish Community): *President* R. Kirschner, Bergstien 13 0172 Oslo ☎ 22696570. Fax 22466604. Email kontor@dmt.oslo.no. Website www.dmt.oslo.no.
Synagogue and Community Centre, Bergstien 13, Oslo 0172. Postbooks 2722, St Hanshaugen, 0131. ☎ 22696570.
Synagogue and Community Centre, Ark. Cristiesgt. 1, Trondheim. ☎ 7352 6568. *President* Julius Paltiel.

PAKISTAN

Two Jewish families remain in Pakistan's port of Karachi. The Magen Shalom Syn. built in 1893, at Jamila St. and Nishta Rd. junction, was reported closed in 1987.

PANAMA (9,250)

The community has been in existence for nearly 150 years and numbers nearly 9,250, with 8,420 in Panama City.
*__Consejo Central Comunitario Hebreo de Panama,__ Apartado 55-0882-Paitilla, Panama, Panama City. ☎ (507) 263-8411. Fax (507) 264-7936. Email sion@plazareg.com *Contact* Sion Harari (*President*).
Beth El, (Cons), Apartado 3087, Panama 3, Panama City.
Congregation Shevet Ahim, (Orth.), Apartado 6222, Panama 2, Panama City.
Kol Shearith Israel, (Reform), Apartado 4120, Panama City. ☎ 225-4100. Fax 225-6512.
There are smaller coms. in Colon (100) and David (100).

PARAGUAY (900)

The community, which has been in existence since 1912, numbers about 900.
Consejo Representativo Israelita del Paraguay (CRIP), General Diaz 657. Asuncion, POB 756. ☎ 41744.

PERU (5,000)

Marranos were prominent in the early development of Peru. Many Jews suffered martyrdom during the centuries that the Inquisition prevailed. The present Jewish population is about 5,000 nearly all living in Lima. There are an Ashkenazi community and a Sephardi community.

***Synagogue and Communal Centre**, Húsares de Junin 163 (Jesus Maria), Lima. ☎ 241-412, 31-2410.

Sociedad de Beneficencia (Sefaradim), Enrique Villar 581, Lima.

Sociedad de Beneficencia Israelita de 1870, Esq Jose Gálvez 282 Miraflores.

PHILIPPINES (250)

Jewish Association of the Philippines, 110 H.V. de la Costa, crn. Tordesillas West, Salcedo Village, Makati, Metro Manila 1227. ☎ 2815 0265; (Rabbi) 2815 0263. Fax 2840-2566. Email jap.manila@usa.net. *President* P. Rosenberg.

POLAND (6,000)

Jews first settled in Poland in the twelfth century. Casimir the Great, the last Polish King of the Piast dynasty (1303–70), was a staunch protector of the Jews. Periods of Jewish freedom and prosperity have alternated with periods of persecution and, sometimes, expulsion. Jewish learning flourished in the land from the sixteenth century onwards. Mystic Chasidism, based on study of the Cabala, had its wonder rabbis. Famous Talmudic scholars, codifiers of the ritual and other eminent men of learning were produced by Polish Jewry. Of the 3,500,000 Jews in Poland in 1939 about three million were exterminated by Hitler. Many put up an heroic fight, like those of the Warsaw Ghetto in 1943. Under half a million fled to the West and the Soviet Union. Until 1968 the Jewish population was estimated at 50,000. Large-scale emigration followed the anti-Jewish policy pursued from then on under the guise of 'anti-Zionism'. Today's Jewish pop. is estimated at between 6,000 and 8,000.

WARSAW

Synagogue and Religious Organisation: Zwiazek Religijny Wyznania Mojzeszowego (Religious Union of Mosaic Faith),Warsaw 00-105. ul. Twarda 6. ☎ 20-43-24. 20-06-76.

Secular Organisation: Towarzystwo Spoleczno-Kulturalne Zydów w Polsce (Social and Cultural Association of Jews in Poland), Zarzad Glowny (Central Board), Warsaw, 00-104, Plac., Grzybowski 12/16, ☎ 20-05-57, 20-05-54.

CRACOW

Religious Organisation: Zwiazek Religijny Wyznania Mojzeszowego, Kongregacja (Religious Union of Mosaic Faith, Congregation) Cracow, 31-066, ☎ 56-23-49. ul. Skawinska 2.

Secular Organisation: Towarzystwo Spoleczno-Kulturalne Zydów w Polsce (Social and Cultural Association of Jews in Poland), (Cracow Section), Krakow, 31-014, ☎ 22-98-41.ul. Stawkowska 30.

Jewish organisations also exist in the following 16 towns: Bielsko-Biala, Bytom, Chrzanów, Dzierzoniów, Gliwice, Katowice, Legnica, Lódz, Lublin, Piotrkow, Swindnice, Szczecin Wałbrzych, Wrocław, and Zary.

PORTUGAL (500)

Until the 15th century Jews lived in tranquillity, and were prominent in court circles. In 1496 King Manoel signed an order expelling the Jews from Portugal. But instead of being allowed to leave they were forcibly baptised. Despite the Inquisition Marranos survived in the provinces. A new community was established in Lisbon by British Jews from Gibraltar and others from Morocco during the Napoleonic era. In 1910, after the Revolution, Jews were again granted freedom of worship. The present Jewish population is about 500 centred in Lisbon. There is a synagogue in Oporto built in Moorish style. The Kadoorie family of Hong Kong has been associated with it.

LISBON

*__Communal Offices__, Rua Alexandre Herculano, 59, Lisbon 1250. ☎ 385 86 04. Fax 388 4304.

Jewish Centre, Rua Rosa Araujo 10. ☎ 357 20 41.

Synagogues: 59 Rua Alexandre Herculano (Sephardi). ☎ 388 15 92. Avenida Elias Garcia 110-1º Lisbon 1050 (Ashkenazi).

PUERTO RICO (1,500)

Some 1,500 Jews live in Puerto Rico, which is an associated Commonwealth of the USA. A syn. is maintained as well as a pre-school, an afternoon school, adult educ. classes and other organisations.

*__Shaare Zedeck Synagogue__ (Con.) and **Community Centre**, 903 Ponce de León Ave. Santurce, P.R. 00907-3390. ☎ (809)724 4157. Fax (809)722 4157.

Temple Beth Shalom (Reform), 101 San Jorge & Loiza St., Santurce, P.R. 00911. ☎ 721 6333.

ROMANIA (12,500)

Jews have been resident in the territory that now forms Romania since Roman times. Today they number 12,500, of whom some 5,500 live in Bucharest, and the rest in 68 communities. There are 57 syns., four of them in Bucharest, 12 Talmud Torahs and 9 kosher restaurants. A newspaper in Hebrew, Romanian and English, with a circulation of 4,200, is published fortnightly. There is a Yiddish theatre in Bucharest, the publishing house Hasefer, a Museum of Jewish History and a Holocaust Exhibit.

BUCHAREST

Chief Rabbi:

*__Federation of Jewish Communities__, Mamulari Str., 4, Etaj 1, Apt. 1, Sectorul 3, 4. ☎/Fax 01-336105. *Dir.* Eugen Preda.

SINGAPORE (240)

The Jewish community of Singapore dates from about the year 1840. The street in which Jewish divine service was first held in a house is now known as Synagogue Street. The first building to be erected as a syn. was the Maghain Aboth, opened in 1878. This was rebuilt and enlarged in 1925. A second syn., Chesed El, was built in 1905. The Jewish community consists mainly of Sephardim (of Baghdad origin) but with some Ashkenazim. The affairs of the community are managed by the Jewish Welfare Board, which is elected annually.

*__Jewish Welfare Board__, 24/26 Waterloo Street, 187950. ☎ 337 2189. Fax 336 2127. *President* Jacob Ballas. *H. Sec.* Mrs M. Whelan.

Synagogue Maghain Aboth, 24 Waterloo Street, 187950. ☎ 337 2189. Fax 336 2127. Email jewishwb@singnet.com.sg. Open daily except Monday mornings. Mikvah available. *Community Rabbi* Mordechai Abergel. ☎ 737-9112. Email mordehai@singnet.com.sg.

Synagogue Chesed El, 2 Oxley Rise, 238693. Open Mon. only.

United Hebrew Congregation (Reform), 65 Chulia St., OCBC Centre #31-00 East Lobby, 049513. *Pres.* K. Lewis. ☎ 536-8300.

SLOVAKIA (6,000)

Written evidence of Jewish settlement in Slovakia goes back to the 13th c. but there may have been Jews in the area as far back as Roman times.

BRATISLAVA

Central Union of Jewish Religious Coms. (UZZNO), *H. Chairman* Prof Pavel Traubner, PhD.; *Exec. Chairman* Fero Alexander. Ad.: Kozia 21/II, 81447

Bratislava. ☎ +421-2-54412167. Fax 421-2-54411106. Email uzzno@netax.sk.
Synagogue, Heydukova 11-13, Services: Monday, Thursday, Friday, Saturday.
Bratislava Jewish Com., Kozia 18, 81103 Bratislava. ☎ 421-2-54416949.
Bnai Brith "Tolerance" in Bratislava. *President* Eng. Peter Werner, PhD.
Pension Chez David (Kosher), Accommodation and Restaurant, Mikvah. Fax +42-2-54412642. ☎ +421-2-54413824, 54416943. Mausoleum of Chatham Sopher, Orthodox and Neological Jewish cemeteries.

KOSICE

Jewish Religious Community, Zvonárska 5, 04001 Kosice. Kosher restaurant, Mitvah. *President* Dr P. Sitar. ☎/Fax +421-55-6221272.
Synagogue: Puskinova St.
There are Jewish coms. in Galanta, Dunajska Streda, Presov, Banska Bystrica, Nove Zamky, Komarno, Zilina, Michalovce, Lucenec.

SLOVENIA (78)

Jewish Community of Slovenia, Tržaška 2, 1000 Ljubljana; PO Box 37, Ljubljana 1101. ☎ 1-2521836. Fax 1-2521836. Email jss@siol.net. Website www.jewishcommunity.si.

LJUBLJANA

Syn.: ☎ 315-884.

SOUTH AFRICA (90,000)

The Jewish Community began as an organised body at Cape Town on the eve of the Day of Atonement, Friday, September 26, 1841. Its first title was 'The Society of the Jewish Community of the Cape of Good Hope', but there had been Jewish residents at the Cape long before the foundation of the Hebrew Congregation. In fact, Jews have been connected with the Cape of Good Hope from the earliest days of South African history.

Jewish pilots accompanied the Portuguese navigators. During the 17th and 18th centuries when the Dutch East India Co. ruled the Cape, there were no professing Jews but it is probable that some individuals were of Jewish origin. After the British occupation in 1806, freedom of religion was extended to all Cape inhabitants and Jews eventually held official positions in the administration.

For further particulars see the 'History of the Jews in South Africa', by Louis Herrman (Victor Gollancz, 1930), The Jews in South Africa: A History, ed. by G. Saron and L. Hotz (Oxford Univ. Press, 1956), The Vision Amazing, by Marcia Gitlin (Johannesburg 1950), South African Jewry, 1976-77, ed. by Leon Feldberg (Alex White, 1977), Jews and Zionism: The South African Experience (Gideon Shimoni, 1980), South African Jewry, ed. by Marcus Arkin (Oxford Univ. Press 1984), Jewish Roots in the S.A. Economy, by Mendel Kaplan (Struik 1986), Chapters from S.A. History, Jewish and General, by Nathan Berger (Kayor, Vol. 1, 1982; Vol. 2, 1986), Jewry and Cape Society, by Milton Shain (Historical Publication Society, 1983), Tiger Tapestry, by Rudy Frankel (Struik, 1988), The Jews of S.A. - What Future? by Hoffman and Fischer (Southern, 1988), Founders and Followers Johannesburg Jewry 1887-1915, Mendel Kaplan (Vlaeberg 1991), The Roots of Antisemitism in South Africa, by M. Shain (Wits U.P. 1994); The Jewish population in South Africa, by A. Dubb (Kaplan Centre, 1994).

The Jews being scattered throughout the territory of the Republic, the organisation of Jewish religious life varies with the density of the Jewish population, which is about 90,000. Over recent years several thousand members of the community have emigrated, especially to Israel, Canada, Australia, the UK and the US, but the com. has been strengthened by the arrival of some Jews from Zimbabwe and Israel. In all, there are about 50 organised Jewish coms.

The largest coms. are in Johannesburg (58,000), Cape Town (19,000), Durban (3,000) and Pretoria (1,500).

The South African Jewish Board of Deputies is the representative institution of South African Jewry. The B.o.D. for the Transvaal and Natal was founded in 1903, and a similar organisation at the Cape in 1904. The two were united in 1912. The headquarters of the Board is in Johannesburg, and there are provincial committees in Cape Town, Pretoria, Durban, Bloemfontein and Port Elizabeth.

COMMUNAL INSTITUTIONS

***S.A. Jewish Board of Deputies,** 2 Elray Street, Raedene, 2192, PO Box 87557, Houghton 2041. ☎ 645-2523. Fax 645-2559. Email sajbod@africa.com. Website www.jewish.org.sa. *National Dir.* Y. Kay.

S.A. Zionist Federation, PO Box 29203, Sandringham 2131. ☎ 485-1020. Fax 640-6758. *Dir. General* Mrs I. Brito-Feldman.

S.A. Board of Jewish Education, PO Box 46204, Orange Grove 2119. ☎ 480-4700. *Gen. Dir.* A. Zulberg.

S.A. Jewish Ex-Service League. ☎ 786-5408.

Union of Orthodox Synagogues of South Africa, 58 Oaklands Rd, Orchards 2192, Johannesburg. ☎ 485-4865. Fax 640-7528. Rabbi C.K. Harris, BA, MPhil, Chief Rabbi of S. Africa. **S.A. Rabbinical Association.**

S.A. Union for Progressive Judaism, POB 1190, Houghton 2041. ☎ 636-7903. Fax 646 7904. Email saupj@worldonline.co.za.

Bnai B'rith, PO Box 8425 Johannesburg, 2000. ☎ 648-3804.

Jewish Family and Community Council, Private Bag X7, Sandringham 2131. ☎ 640-9116.

Kollel Yad Shaul, 5 Water Lane, Orchards 2198. ☎ 728-1308.

Lubavitch Foundation of S.A., 55 Oaklands Rd., Orchards 2192 Johannesburg. ☎ 640-7561.

ORT SA, PO Box 95090, Grant Park, 2051. ☎ 728-7154.

Union of Jewish Women of S.A., 1 Oak St., Houghton, Johannesburg, 2198. ☎ 648-1053.

Mizrachi Organisation of S.A., PO Box 29189, Sandringham 2192. ☎ 640 4420.

Zionist Revisionist Organisation of S.A., 2 Elray St., Raedene, 2192. ☎ 640-5114. Telegrams: Nezorg.

JOHANNESBURG

United Hebrew Congregation (est. 1915).

Beth Din. ☎ 485-4865.

Main synagogues. Glenhazel Hebrew Cong., Long Ave., Glenhazel, 2192. Tel: 640-5016 (Orth). Sydenham/Highlands North Heb Cong., 24 Main St., Rouxville, 2192 (Orth) ☎ 640-5021. Temple Emanuel, 38 Oxford Road, Parktown, 2193 (Reform). ☎ 646-6170; Great Park, Glenhovse Rd., Houghton. ☎ 728-8531.

CAPE TOWN

Western Province Zionist Council, 87 Hatfield St., Cape Town, 8001. PO Box 4176, Cape Town 8000. ☎ 021-461-5821. Fax 021-461-5805. Email wpzc@ctjc.co.za. *Dir. Gen.* Rachel Shapiro.

The Jacob Gitlin Library, Albow Centre, 88 Hatfield St., Cape Town, 8001 ☎ 021-462-5088. Fax 021-465-8671. Email gitlib@netactive.co.za.

Union of Orthodox Synagogues of S.A., and Beth Din, 191, Buitenkant St. ☎ 461-6310. Fax 461-8320. *Exec. Dir.* M. Glass.

Main synagogues. Great Syn. Government Ave. (Orth.), Temple Israel, Upper Portswood Rd., Green Point (Reform).

SOUTH KOREA

About 25 Jewish families live in Seoul, the capital. Religious services are held on Friday evenings at the 8th U.S. Army Religious Retreat Centre. ☎ 7904-4113.

SPAIN (25,000)

Jews were settled in Spain in Roman times. They made an outstanding contribution to culture and civilisation in medieval times. Persecution by the Church culminated in the Inquisition and the Expulsion in 1492. Today there are about 25,000 Jews in Spain, of whom 8,000 live in Barcelona, 9,000 in Madrid 2,000 in Malaga, and the rest in Valencia, Seville, Alicante, Majorca and the Canary Islands. The Jewish com. in Melilla has 1,500 members and that in Ceuta 1,000. Ancient syns. of pre-Inquisition times (now put to other uses) exist in Cordoba, Seville and Toledo. The first synagogue and community centre in Spain since the Inquisition opened in Barcelona in 1954. The Madrid com. was legally recognised in 1965 and the city's first syn. was consecrated in 1968. Synagogues and Community Centres:

Madrid, 28010-Calle Balmes, No. 3. ☎ 915913131. Fax 915941517.

Barcelona, Communitat Jueva ATID de Catalunya, Catanyer 27, 08022 Barcelona. ☎/Fax 93 417 37 04. Email atid@arquired.es; Website www.atid.freeservers.com; Syn., Calle Avenir, No. 24, 08021. ☎ 2008513. Fax 2006148.

Alicante, Federación de Comunidades Israelitas de Espana. *Contact* Carlos Schorr.

Ceuta, Calle Sargento, Coriat, No. 8.

Majorca. The first synagogue in 600 years was opened in 1987. *Contact* Ap. de Correos, 389, Palma 07014. ☎ 971-283799. ☎ *President* J. Segal. ☎ 700243.

Malaga, 29001 Alameda Principal, 47, 2ºB. *President* Mr Benzaquen.

Marbella. Sr Amselem, Calle Camicentro, Ave, Mercado s/n.

Melilla, 29804-Calle General Mola, No.19.

Seville, 41003-Bustos Tavera, 8. ☎ 427-5517.

Valencia. 46006 Calle Ingenicero Joaquín Belloch.

Tenerife 38001-Jewish Community, P. Abecasis, Ap. de Correos 939, Villalba Hervas, Santa Cruz de Tenerife.

Torremolinos, 29620 Calle Skal. *President* Alberto Amselem.

Las Palmas de Gran Canaria, *President* Mr Bendahan, Ap. Correos 2142, Las Palmas 35080.

SRI LANKA

Corr. Mrs A. Ranasinghe, 82 Rosmead Place, Colombo 7. ☎ 941-695642. Fax 947-4715306.

SURINAM (300)

Surinam is one of the oldest permanent Jewish settlements in the Western Hemisphere. The Sephardi Cong. was est. about 1661, but earlier settlements in 1632, 1639 and 1652 have been reported. Some 225 Jews are members of the two synagogues, where Sephardi services are conducted.

Neve Salom Synagogue, Keizerstr. 82, Paramaribo.

Sedek Ve Salom Synagogue, Herenstr. 20, Paramaribo. The synagogue has been restored but is no longer used for services. *President* René Fernandes, Commewijnestraat 21, Paramaribo. ☎ 400236; PO Box 1834, Paramaribo. ☎ 597-411998; Fax 597-471154; 597-402380 (home).

SWEDEN (18,000)

In 1774, the first Jew was granted the right to live in Sweden. In 1782 Jews were admitted to three Swedish towns, Stockholm, Gothenburg and Norrköping, and the Karlskrona com. was founded soon afterwards. After the emancipation of the Jews in Sweden in 1870, coms. were founded in Malmö and several other towns. Today there are some 18,000 Jews in Sweden, 9–10,000 of them in Stockholm. Others are in Gothenburg, Malmö, Borås and Västerås.

STOCKHOLM

*Judiska Församlingen (Jewish community), Wahrendorffsgatan 3, Box 7427 103 91 Stockholm. ☎ 08-587-85800. Fax 08-587-85858. Email kansli@jf-stockolm.org.

Jewish Centre, Nybrogatan 19. ☎ 08-587-85860.

Synagogues: Wahrendorffsgatan 3 (Great Synagogue, Masorti); Adas Jeshurun, Riddargatan 5 (Orthodox); Adas Jisroel, St. Paulsgatan 13 (Orth).

SWITZERLAND (17,600)

The Jews were expelled from Switzerland in the fifteenth century, and it was not until early in the seventeenth century that they received permission to settle in the Lengnau and Endingen coms. In 1856 immigration increased, most of the immigrants coming from Southern Germany, Alsace and Eastern Europe. The Jewish pop. is now about 17,600 The largest coms. are in Zurich (6,252), Basle (2,005) and Geneva (3,901). The Swiss Federation of Jewish Communites comprised in 1998 19 coms. with a total membership of 14,000.

Federation of Jewish Communities, PO Box 564, 8027 Zurich. ☎ (01) 201.55.83. Fax (01) 202.16.72. Email info@swissjews.org. Website www.swissjews.org.

American Joint Distribution Committee, European Headquarters, 75 rue de Lyon, 1211 Geneva 13. ☎ (022) 344.90.00.

OSE, rue du Mont-Blanc 11, 1201 Geneva. ☎ (022) 732.33.01.

World Jewish Congress, rue de Varembé 1, 1211 Geneva. ☎ (022) 734.13.25.

B'nai B'rith, chemin Rieu 10, 1208 Geneva. ☎ (022) 731.69.80.

Basle Communal Centre, Leimenstrasse 24. ☎ (061) 279.98.50. Email igb@igb.ch. Website www.igb.ch; Synagogues: (Orth. Ashk.) Leimenstrasse 24, Rabbi Dr Israel Meir Levinger, Leimenstrasse 45. ☎ (061) 271.60.24; (Orth. Ashk.) Ahornstrasse 14, Rabbi Benzion Snyders, Rudolfstrasse 28. ☎ (061) 302.53.91.

Berne Communal Centre and Synagogue, Kapellenstrasse 2. ☎ (031) 381.49.92, Email info@jgb.ch. Website www.jgb.ch. *M.* Rabbi Dr M. Leipziger.

Fribourg Synagogue, 9 rue Joseph-Philler. ☎ (026) 322.16.70.

Geneva Communal Centre, Rue St Léger 10. ☎ (022) 317.89.00. Email secretgen@comista.ch. Synagogues: (Orth. Ashk.) Grande Synagogue Beit Yaakov, Place de la Synagogue; (Orth. Ashk.) Machsike Hadass, 2 Place des Eaux Vives. Rabbi Abraham Schlesinger. ☎ (022) 735.22.98; (Seph.) Hekhal Haness, 54ter, route de Malagnou. ☎ (022) 736.96.32; (Ref.) Liberal Syn., 12 Quai du Seujet. ☎ (022) 732.32.45. Rabbi François Garaï. ☎ (022) 738.19.11.

Lausanne Communal Centre, 3 ave. Georgette. ☎ (021) 341.72.40. Email citl@urbanet.ch. Website www.cistl.ch. Synagogue: 1 Ave. Juste-Oliver (corner Ave. Florimont). Chief Rabbi Hervé Krief. ☎ (021) 311.10.60.

Zürich Communal Centre, Lavaterstrasse 33, 8002. ☎ (01) 283.22.22. Email info@icz.org, Website www.icz.org; Synagogues: (Modern Orth. Ashk.) Nüschelerstrasse 36, 8001. ☎ (01) 283.22.99. Rabbi Dr Zalman Kossowsky. ☎ (01) 283.22.44; (Orth. Ashk.) Freigutstrasse 37. ☎ (01) 241.80.57, Email irg@bluewin.ch. Rabbi Daniel Levy. ☎ (01) 202.48.19; (Orth. Ashk.) Erikastrasse 8. ☎ (01) 463.80.33. Rabbi Schoul Breisch. ☎ (01) 461.30.40; Beth Chabad, Rüdigerstrasse 10. ☎ (01) 289.70.50; Minyan Sikna, Sallenbachstrasse 40. ☎ (01) 455.75.75; Minyan Wollishofen, Etzelstrasse 6. ☎ (01) 482.87.51; (Ref.) Dr Chadasch, Hallwylstrass 78. ☎ 043 322 0114. Email info@jlg.ch. Website www.jlg.ch; Rabbi Tovia Ben Chorin. ☎ (01) 342.40.23.

SYRIA (1,500)

The remnants of this historic Jewish community resident in Damascus, Aleppo and Kamishli, have been estimated at 1,500 following recent aliyah.

DAMASCUS

President of Rabbinical Court Rabbi Ibrahim Hamura, Ecole Ben-Maymoun, Kattatib. Al-Ittihad Al-Ahlieh School (Alliance Israélite), rue El Amine.

TAIWAN (180)

More than 30 Jewish families live on the Island, most of them in Taipei, the capital. **Taiwan Jewish Community Centre.** Information: F. Chitayat. ☎ 2861-6303. Mailing address: Donald Shapiro, Trade Winds Company, P.O.Box 7-179, Taipei 10602, Taiwan. ☎ 886-2-23960159. Fax 886-2-23964022. Email dshapiro@ topz.ficnet. Services are held at Landis Hotel, 41 Min Chuan East Road, Sec. 2, Taipei. For details contact Rabbi Dr E. Einhorn at (886) 2597-1234. Fax (886) 2596-9223. Email mailto:einhorn@ttn.net.

THAILAND (250)

The community consists of approx. 250 persons, including citizens of the country and expatriates.

Jewish Association of Thailand, Beth Elisheva Synagogue, Mikveh, Jewish Centre, 121 Soi Sai Nam Thip 2, Sukhumvit 22, Bangkok. ☎ 258-2195. Fax 663-0245. Email ykantor@ksc15.th.com

Even-Chen Synagogue, The Bossotel Inn, weekly classes & activities. 55/12-14 Soi Charoengkrung, 42/1 New Road, Bangkok. ☎ 630 6120. Fax 237 3225.

Ohr Menachem-Chabad, 108/1 Ram Buttri Rd., Kaosarn Rd., Banglampoo. Daily services. *M.* Rabbi Y. Kantor. ☎ 282-6388. Fax 629 1153.

TRINIDAD AND TOBAGO

Jewish links go back to 1658 when Portuguese Jews from Livorno and Amsterdam settled there. Most of them left by the end of the 17th century. Portuguese Jews from Venezuela and Curaçao settled in Trinidad in the 19th century. The names of many Catholic families are traceable to 'conversos' of the earlier period. In the mid-1930s some 800 Jews sought temporary refuge in Trinidad and Tobago from Nazi persecution in Germany and Austria and later from other parts of Nazi-occupied Europe. Those with German and Austrian passports were subject to internment between 1940 and 1943. Numbers have dropped since with only a few Jews living there now. *Corr.* Hans Stecher, c/o West Mall, Westmoorings, Port of Spain, Trinidad, W.I. (Caribbean). ☎/Fax (868) 637-3870.

TUNISIA (3,000)

The history of the community goes back to antiquity. After Tunisia became a French protectorate in 1881 Jews obtained equal rights with the Moslems, and the continuance of these rights was promised by the authorities of the independent State established in 1957. The Jewish population fell from nearly 100,000 in 1950 to 25,000 in June 1967, and to some 3,000 today. There are coms. in Tunis, Sfax, Sousse and Jerba island, where the ancient El Ghriba synagogue in Hara Sghire village is a listed building.

TUNIS

Grand Rabbinat de Tunisie, 26 Rue Palestine. Communal Offices, 15 Rue du Cap Vert.

Synagogues: 43 Ave. de la Liberté: 3 Rue Eve Nöelle.

American Joint Distribution Committee, 101 Ave. de la Liberté.

TURKEY (25,000)

During the Spanish Inquisition, the Ottoman Empire was one of the principal lands of refuge. With the proclamation of the Turkish Republic, the Jews were granted full citizenship rights. Today their number is estimated at about 25,000 of whom about 23,000 live in Istanbul, 2,000 in Izmir, and 100 each in Ankara, Adana, Bursa, Edirne and Kirklareli.

ISTANBUL

Chief Rabbinate: Yemenici Sok. No. 23 Tünel, Beyoğlu. ☎ (212) 2938794-95. Fax (212) 244-1980. *Sec. General.*

Communal Centre, Büyük Hendek Sokak No. 61, Galata. ☎ (212) 2441576. Fax (212) 292 0385.

Synagogues: Neve Shalom, 61 Büyük Hendek Sokak, Galata. ☎ (212) 293-7566; Beth Israel, Efe Sok. 4, Şişli, ☎ (212) 2406599; Etz Ahayim, Muallim Naci Sok. 40/1. ☎ (212) 2601896; (Ashkenazi), 37 Yüksekkaldirim sok, Galata. ☎ 243-6909; (Italian), 29, Şair Ziya Paşa Yokusu, Galata. ☎ (212) 2937784; Hemdat Israel, Izzettin Sok 65 Kadiköy ☎ (216) 336 5293; Heset Leavraam, Pancur Sok, 15, Büyükada ☎ (216) 382-5788 (summer); Caddebostan, Taş Mektep Sokak Göztepe. ☎ (216) 356-5922.

There are ten charitable and social institutions, six youth clubs, a high school and an elementary school in Istanbul. Synagogues also in Izmir, Ankara, Bursa and Adane.

UKRAINE (300,000)

KIEV

Syn.: 29 Shchekovichnaya St., 252071. ☎ (044) 463 7085. Fax 463 7088.

Assoc. of Jewish Organisations, Kurskaya ul. 6, ☎ (044) 276-7431.

Jewish Historical Society, Iskrovskaya Str., 3, Apt. 6, 252087. ☎ (044) 242-7944.

Makor Centre for Jewish Youth Activities, 10/1 Gorodeskogo St., Apt. 10, 252001. ☎ 044-229-6141. Fax 044-229-8069.

Association of Progressive Jewish Congregations in Ukraine, 01023 Kiev-23, POB 517, 'Hatikva' Congregation, *M.* Rabbi A. Dukhovny. ☎ 0038-044-234-2215, ☎/Fax 0038-044-234-8482. Email ravdukh@alfacom.net.

Other towns with Jewish centres include Bershad, Chernigor, Chernovtsy, Kharkov, Kremenchug, Lviv, Odessa, Simferopol, Uzhgorod and Zhitomir.

UNITED STATES OF AMERICA (5,800,000)

Though there had been individual Jewish settlers before 1654 in the territory which is now the United States, it was not until that year that Jewish immigrants arrived in a group at New Amsterdam (renamed New York in 1664) 23 of them, who came from Brazil by way of Cuba and Jamaica. The story of the growth of Jewry in the U.S.A. is the story of successive waves of immigration resulting from persecution in Russia, Poland, Romania, Germany and other countries. Today the Jewish population is est. at 5,950,000, of whom 1,720,000 live in the New York Metropolitan Area.

For general information about the American Jewish Community write to: ***UJA - Federation Resource Line,*** *130 E 59th St., New York City, 10022. Email resource-line@ujafedny.org; Website www.ujafedny.org.*

REPRESENTATIVE ORGANISATIONS

American Jewish Committee, 165 E. 56th St., New York City, 10022.

American Jewish Congress, Stephen Wise Hse., 15 E. 84th St., New York City, 10028.

Anti-Defamation League of B'nai B'rith, 823 United Nations Plaza, New York City, 10017.

B'nai B'rith International, 1640 Rhode Island Av., N.W. Washington, D.C., 20036.

Conference of Presidents of Major Jewish Organizations, 110 E 59th St., NYC 10022.

Consultative Council of Jewish Organizations, 420 Lexington Av., Suite 1733, NYC 10170. ☎ 212-808-5437.

Co-ordinating Board of Jewish Organizations, 1640 Rhode Island Ave., N.W.

Washington, D.C., 20036.
Jewish Labour Committee, Atran Centre, 25 E. 21st St., New York City, 10010.
Jewish War Veterans of the United States of America, 1811 R St., N.W. Washington, D.C. 20009.
National Jewish Community Relations Advisory Council, 443 Park Ave. S., I Ith floor, New York City, 10016.
National Council of Jewish Women, 15 E. 26th St., New York City, 10010.
National Conference on Soviet Jewry, 10 E. 40th St., Suite 907, New York City, 10016.
National Council of Young Israel, 3 W. 16th St., New York City, 10011.
North American Jewish Students Network, 501 Madison Ave., 17th Fl., New York City, 10022.
United Jewish Appeal, 99 Park Ave. New York City, 10016.
World Confederation of Jewish Community Centers, 15 E. 26th St. New York City, 10010.
World Jewish Congress, 501 Madison Ave., 17th Fl., New York City, 10022. ☎ 755 5770.

RELIGIOUS ORGANISATIONS
Agudath Israel of America, 84 William St., New York City, 10038.
Agudath Israel World Organization, 84 William St., New York City, 10038.
Association of Orthodox Jewish Scientists, 1373 Coney Island Ave., Brooklyn, New York, 11219.
Central Conference of American Rabbis, 355 Lexington Ave., New York City, 10017-6603. ☎ 212-972 3636 (Reform).
Jewish Reconstructionist Federation, 7804 Montgomery Ave., St. No.9, Elkins Park, PA 19027. ☎ 215-782 8500. Fax 215-782 8805. Email info@jrf.org.
Lubavitcher Headquarters, 770 Eastem Parkway, Brooklyn, N.Y. 11213. New York Board of Rabbis, 10 E. 73rd St., New York City, 10021.
Rabbinical Alliance of America, 3 W. 16th St., 4th Fl., New York City, 10011. (Orthodox.)
Rabbinical Assembly (Cons.), 3080 Broadway, New York City, 10027.
Rabbinical Council of America, 275 7th Ave., New York City, 10001. (Modern Orthodox).
Reconstructionist Rabbinical Association, 7804 Montgomery Ave., St. No.9, Elkins Park, PA 19027. ☎ 215-782 8500. Fax 215-782 8805. Email info@jrf.org
Synagogue Council of America, 327 Lexington Ave., New York City 10016.
Union of American Hebrew Congregations, 633 Third Ave, New York City 10017. ☎ 212-650 4000. Email uahc@uahc.org.
Union of Orthodox Jewish Congregations, 333 Seventh Ave., New York City, 1000
Union of Orthodox Rabbis, 235 E. Broadway, New York City, 10002.
Union of Sephardic Congregations, 8 W 70th St., New York City, 10023.
United Synagogue of America, 155 Fifth Ave., New York City, 100 10. (Conservative.)
World Union for Progressive Judaism, 838 Fifth Ave., New York City, 10021.

WELFARE AND REFUGEE ORGANISATIONS
American Association for Ethiopian Jews, 2028 P. St., N.W. Washington DC., 20036.
American Federation of Jews from Central Europe, 570 7th Ave., New York City, 10018.
American Jewish Joint Distribution Committee (I.D.C.), 711 Third Ave . New York City, 10017.
American ORT Federation, 817 Broadway, New York City, 10003.
Council of Jewish Federations, 730 Broadway, New York City, 10003.
HIAS, 333 7th Ave., New York City, 1000.

Jewish Conciliation Board, 235 Park Ave. S., New York City, 10003.
JWB, 15 East 26th St., New York City, 10010.
U.J.A. Federation of New York, 130 E. 59th St., New York City, 10022.

ZIONIST ORGANISATIONS and others concerned with Israel

American Associates of Ben-Gurion University of Negev, 342 Madison Ave., Suite 1924, New York City, 10173.
American Committee for Weizmann Institute, 515 Park Ave., New York City, 10022.
American Friends of the Hebrew University, 11 E. 69th St., New York City, 10021.
American Friends of Tel Aviv University, 360 Lexington Ave., New York City, 10017.
American Friends of Haifa University, 41 E. 42nd St., 828, New York City, 10017.
American-Israel Cultural Foundation, 485 Madison Ave., New York City, 10022.
American-Israel Public Affairs Committee, 500 N. Capitol St., N.W. Washington, D.C. 20001.
American Jewish League for Israel, 30 E. 60th St., New York City, 10022.
American Red Magen David for Israel, 888 7th Ave., New York City, 10106.
American Technion Society, 271 Madison Ave., New York City, 10016.
American Zionist Federation, 515 Park Ave., New York City, 10022 from whom information on Zionist organisations and activities can be obtained.
American Zionist Youth Foundation, 515 Park Ave., New York City, 10022.
Americans for Progressive Israel, 150 Fifth Ave., Suite 911, New York City, 10011.
ARZA–Assn. of Reform Zionists of America, 838 5th Ave., New York City, 10021.
Bar-Ilan University in Israel, 853 Seventh Ave., New York City, 10019.
Bnei Akiva of North America, 25 W. 26th St., New York City, 10010.
Betar Zionist Youth Movement, 9 E. 38th St., New York City, 10016.
Dror-Young Kibbutz Movement-Habonim, 27 W. 20th St., New York City, 10011.
Emunah Women of America, 370 7th Ave., New York City, 10001.
Hadassah, Women's Zionist Organization of America, 50 W. 58th St., New York City, 10019.
Hashomer Hatzair, 150 Fifth Ave. Suite 911, New York City, 10011.
Herut–U.S.A., 9 E. 38th St., New York City, 10016.
Theodor Herzl Foundation, 515 Park Ave., New York City, 10022.
Jewish National Fund, 42 E. 69th St., New York City, 10021.
Labor Zionist Alliance (formerly Poale Zion United Labour Org. of America), 275 Seventh Ave., New York City, 10001.
Mercaz, Conservative Zionists, 155 Fifth Ave., New York City, 10010.
Mizrachi-Hapoel Hamizrachi (Religious Zionists of America), 25 W. 26th St., New York City, 10010.
National Committee for Labor Israel–Histadrut, 33 E. 67th St., New York City, 10021.
PEC Israel Economic Corporation, 511 Fifth Ave., New York City, 10017.
Pioneer Women Na'armat, The Women's Labour Zionist Organisation of America, 200 Madison Ave., New York City, 10016.
State of Israel Bonds, 730 Broadway, New York City, 10003
Women's League for Israel, 515 Park Ave., New York City, 10022.
World Confederation of United Zionists, 30 E. 60th St., New York City 10022.
World Zionist Organization, American Section, 515 Park Ave., New York City, 10022.

EDUCATIONAL AND CULTURAL ORGANISATIONS

American Friends of the Alliance Israélite Universelle, 135 William St., New York City, 10038.
Annenberg Research Institute, formerly Dropsie College, 250 N. Highland Ave., Merion. Pa., 19066.

Leo Baeck Institute, 129 E. 73rd St., New York City, 10021. Brandeis University, Waltham Mass., 02254.
Centre for Holocaust Studies, Documentation & Research, 1610 Ave. J., Brooklyn, New York 11230.
Centre for Jewish History, 15 West 16th St., New York City, 10011. ☎ (212) 294-6160.
Central Yiddish Culture Organization, 25 E. 21st St., New York Clty, 10010.
Gratz College, 10th St., & Tabor Rd., Phila., Pa., 19141.
Theodor Herzl Institute and Foundation, 515 Park Ave., New York City, 10022.
Hebrew Arts School, 129 W. 67th St., New York City, 10023.
Hebrew College, 43 Hawes St., Brookline, Mass., 02146.
Hebrew Union College-Jewish Institute of Religion, 3101 Clifton Ave., Cincinnati, Ohio, 45220; 1 W. 4th St., New York City, 10012, 3077 University Mall, Los Angeles, Calif. 90007; 13 King David St., Jerusalem Israel 94101.
Herzliah Jewish Teachers' Seminary, Touro College, Jewish Peoples, University of the Air, 30 W. 44th St., New York City, 10036.
Histadruth Ivrith of America, 1841 Broadway, New York City, 10023.
JWB Jewish Book Council, 15 E. 26th St., New York City, 10010.
Jewish Education Service of North America, 730 Broadway, New York
Jewish Publication Society, 1930 Chestnut St., Philadelphia, Pa., 19103.
Jewish Museum, 1109 Fifth Ave., New York City, 10028.
Jewish Theological Seminary of America, 3080 Broadway, New York City, 10027.
Memorial Foundation for Jewish Culture, 15 E. 26th St., New York City 10010.
Mesivta Yeshiva Rabbi Chaim Berlin Rabbinical Academy, 1593 Coney Island Ave., Brooklyn, N.Y.
National Foundation for Jewish Culture, 330 7th Ave., 21st. Fl., New York City, 10001.
National Yiddish Book Center, Weinberg Building, Amherst, MH. 01002-3375. ☎ (800) 535-3595; Fax (413) 256-4700.
Reconstructionist Rabbinical College, Church Road and Greenwood Ave., Wyncote, PA, 19095.
Shomrei AdamahÑA Jewish Resource Center for the Environment, Church Road and Greenwood Ave., Wyncote, PA, 19095.
Simon Wiesenthal Centre, 9760 W. Pico Blvd., Los Angeles, Ca., 90035.
Torah Umesorah–National Society for Hebrew Day Schools, 160 Broadway, New York City, 10038.
United Lubavitcher Yeshivoth, 841 Ocean Parkway, Brooklyn, N.Y., 11230.
Yeshiva University, 500 W. 185th St., New York City, 10033; 9760 W. Pico Blvd., Los Angeles, Ca., 90035.
Yivo Institute for Jewish Research, 555 West 57th St., 11th Floor, New York City 10019 (Temporary removal) ☎ (212) 535-6700.

URUGUAY (25,000)

Jewish immigration to Uruguay began in the early 20th century, with a large influx in the 1920s. Some 10,000 European Jews fled to Uruguay with Hitler's rise to power and large numbers came after the Second World War. In the 1940s, 50,000 Jews were est. to be living in the country. At present there are about 35,000, mostly in Montevideo, the capital. Some 12,000 emigrated to Israel before the State was established, during the War of Independence and since.

MONTEVIDEO

*__Central and representative org.__: Comite Central Israelita del Uruguay, Rio Negro 1308 Piso 5 Esc. 9. ☎ 90 06562. Fax 91 6057.
Communities: Comunidad Israelita del Uruguay, Canelones 1084 Piso 1°; Comunidad Israelita Sefaradi, 21 de Setiembre 3111 (office), Buenos Aires 234 (syn.); Nueva Congregacion Israelita, Wilson Ferreira Aldunate 1168;

Comunidad Israelita Hungara, Durazno 972. Each com. maintains its own syns. There are 3 Jewish schs. and an ORT training centre.

Zionist Organisation of Uruguay, H. Gutierrez Ruiz 1278 Piso 4°.

International Council of Jewish Women, PO Box 12130 Local 4, Montevideo 11300, Uruguay. ☎/Fax +598 (0)2 628 5874. Email icjw@montevideo.com.uy. Website www.icjw.org.uk. *President* Sara Winkowski.

There are also communities at Maldonado and Paysandu.

VENEZUELA (20,000)

The first community was established in the coastal town of Coro by Sephardi Jews early in the 19th century. Today the Jews in Venezuela number some 21,000, most of whom live in Caracas and the rest mainly in Maracaibo.

CARACAS

*__Confederación de Asociaciones Israelitas de Venezuela__ (CAIV), Representative organisation of Venezuelan Jewry, Av. Marqués del Toro No. 9, San Bernardino. ☎ (58-2) 551.03.68; 550.24.54. Fax (58-2) 551.03.77; 550.17.21.

Ashkenazi Synagogue and Centre: **Unión Israelita de Caracas,** Av. Marqués del Toro, San Bernardino. ☎ (58-2) 551.52.53. Fax (58-2) 552.79.56. *M.* Rabbi Pynchas Brener.

Sephardic Synagogue and Centre: **Asociación Israelita de Venezuela,** Tiferet Yisrael, Av. Maripérez, Frente al Paseo Colón, Los Caobos. ☎ (58-2) 574.49.75; 574.82.97. Fax 577.02.59. *M.* Rabbi Isaac Cohén.

B'nai B'rith, 9ª. Transversal entre 7ª. Y Av. Avila, Altarmira. ☎ 261.74.97, 261.40.83. Fax (58-2) 261.40.83.

Zionist Federation **(Federación Sionista de Venezuela)**, Edif. Bet Am, Av. Washington, San Bernardino. ☎ (58-2) 551.25.62; 551.48.52. Fax (58-2) 551.30.89.

VIRGIN ISLANDS (500)

Jews have lived in the Virgin Islands since the seventeenth century and played an important part under Danish rule. Since 1917 the Virgin Islands have been USA territory. The congregation was established in 1796. There are some 80 families in the community and the number of affiliated and non-affiliated Jews is about 350. The 150th anniversary of the rebuilding of the synagogue, situated in Crystal Gade, St. Thomas, was celebrated in 1983, and the synagogue was restored in 2000.

Jewish Community, Crystal Gade, Charlotte Amalie. *M.* Rabbi S. T. Relkin.

Hebrew Congretation of St Thomas (Reform), POB 266, St Thomas, 00904. ☎ 1340-774 4312. Fax 1340-774 3249. Email hebrewcong@islands.vi. Website www.onepaper.com/synagogue.

YUGOSLAVIA (3,500)

(Federal Republic, Serbia and Montenegro)

Jews have lived in this territory since Roman times. In 1941 there were about 34,000 Jews in the territory of present Yugoslavia and some 29,000 perished in the Holocaust.

BELGRADE (BEOGRAD)

*__Federation of Jewish Communities of Yugoslavia,__ Ulica Kralja Petra 7la, 111000 Belgrade. POB 512 Belgrade. ☎ 624-359/621-837. Fax 626 674. *President* Aca Singer; *Sec.* D. Shalom.

Jewish Community of Belgrade, Ulica Kralja Petra 71a/II. ☎/Fax 624 289; 622 449. *President* Mirko Levi.

Synagogue, Marsala Birjuzova 19.

Jewish Historical Museum, Ulica Kralja Petra 71a/II. ☎ 622 634.

Communities also in Kikinda, Novi Sad, Niš, Pančevo, Priština, Sombor, Subotica, Zemun and Zrenjanin.

ZAIRE (Republic of the Congo) (65)

Before the Congo obtained independence from Belgian rule in 1960, there were about 2,500 Jews, with eight communities affiliated with the central community in Elisabethville. Now these are about 52 in Kinshasa (formerly Leopoldville), 2 in Lubumbashi (formerly Elisabethville), and six others in Likasi, Kannga and Kisangani. There are also some temporary Israeli residents.

Chief Rabbi of Zaire: Rabbi Moishe Levy. 50, W. Churchill Ave., Box 15, 1180 Brussels, Belgium.

ZAMBIA (35)

*__The Council for Zambia Jewry Ltd.__, PO Box 30020, Lusaka 10101. *Chairman* M. C. Galaun. ☎ 229190. Fax 221428. Email galaun@zamnet.zm.

Lusaka Hebrew Congregation, PO Box 30020. (Est. 1941.) *Chairman* M. C. Galaun.

ZIMBABWE (700)

Jews came to Rhodesia (Zimbabwe) even before the British South Africa Company received its charter in 1889. Daniel Montague Kisch arrived in the territory in 1869, becoming chief adviser to King Lobengula.

In the 1880s the number of Jewish pioneers, most of them of East European origin, gradually increased. Among those who took a leading part in the development and admin. of the country was Sir Roy Welensky, Prime Minister of the former Central African Federation (1956-1963).

Most of the Jewish settlers came from Russia or Lithuania but others settled from the Aegean Island of Rhodes. Many came up from the South, some through the east coast Portuguese territory of Beira. Joe van Praagh, who became Mayor of Salisbury, walked from Beira. During the 1930s, a small influx of German refugees settled mainly in Salisbury (now Harare) and Bulawayo. Post World War II, others joined them mostly from the United Kingdom and South Africa.

Today, most of Zimbabwe's Jews live in Harare and Bulawayo with a very few residing in the smaller districts around the country about 400 in Harare, 250 in Bulawayo and 10 in other centres. There are two synagogues in Harare and one in Bulawayo and each city has its own Jewish primary day school.

Zimbabwe Jewish Board of Deputies (Head Office), 54 Josiah Chinamano Ave., PO Box 1954, Harare. ☎ 04-702507. Fax 04-702506. Email cazo@zol.co.zw. *President* P. Sternberg; *Sec.* Mrs E. Alhadeff.

Zimbabwe Jewish Board of Deputies (Bulawayo Office), PO Box AC 783, Ascot, Bulawayo. ☎ 09-250443. Email cazobyo@gatorzw.com.

Central African Zionist Organisation (Head Office), 54 Josiah Chinamano Ave., PO Box 1954, Harare. *Sec.* Mrs L. Mizan. ☎ 04-702507. Fax 04-702506. Email cazo@zol.co.zw. *Co-Presidents* A. Leon, I. Menashe (Northern Region).

Central African Zionist Organisation (Bulawayo Office), PO Box AC 783, Ascot, Bulawayo. ☎ 09-250443. Email cazobyo@gatorzw.com. *President* Mrs C. Bernstein (Southern Region).

Women's Zionist Council of Central Africa, PO Box AC 783, Ascot, Bulawayo. ☎ 09-250443. *President* Mrs Rhebe Tatz.

*__Synagogues.__ *Harare*: Harare Hebrew Congregation, Lezard Ave., PO Box 342. (Est. 1895.) ☎ 04-727576. Email hhc@zol.co.zw; Sephardi Hebrew Congregation, 54 Josiah Chinamano Ave., PO Box 1051. (Est. 1932.) ☎ 04-722899. *M.* Rev. L. Mayo. *Bulawayo*: Bulawayo Hebrew Congregation, Jason Moyo St, PO Box 337. ☎ 09-250443.

There are branches of the Union of Jewish Women in both Bulawayo and Harare.

JEWISH STATISTICS

In view of the large movements of population in recent years and the difficulty of obtaining exact figures, the compilation of Jewish population statistics can only be based on estimates received from a variety of sources. Data from censuses of 2001 in various coutries have yet to be digested.

The exodus of Russian Jewry of the 1980s and 1990s has compounded the problem of maintaining reliable figures but for the time being we can only repeat previous figures pending formal revisions from our informants, most notably the IJPR who have furnished the principle figures on Table I (1991), the World Jewish Congress (1998), and the American Jewish Year Book (2000).

Estimates of the present world Jewish population give a total of about 13,000,000. Some 1,600,000 are in Europe, about 6,483,900 in North and South America, some 4,932,900 in Asia, including 4,847,000 in Israel, about 89,800 in Africa and about 101,900 in Oceania. Based on the 1996 census in Australia, W. D. Rubinstein has provided new figures for the state centres. Figures for the USA have been revised in the light of Kosman & Scheckner (AJYB 1993). The number of Jews in Moslem countries is about 71,600.

The number of Jews in the world before the outbreak of war in 1939 was estimated at a figure slightly under 17,000,000, of whom about 10,000,000 lived in Europe, 5,375,000 in North and South America (which seems to have been an overestimate), 830,000 in Asia, 600,000 in Africa, and less than 33,000 in Oceania. The difference between the pre-war and post-war figures is accounted for principally by the enormous losses suffered by the Jewish people between 1939 and 1945. Although estimates of Jews murdered by the Nazis and their collaborators vary, the number is commonly accepted to be 6,000,000.

From the seizure of power by Hitler until the outbreak of war in 1939, 80,000 refugees from Central Europe were admitted to Britain. During the six years of war, a further 70,000 were admitted and since the end of the war about 70,000 displaced persons as well as refugees from a number of other countries. Probably some 80 per cent of these were Jews. Many of these were, however, only temporary residents.

Table III has been revised in the light of new figures made available in 1998 by the Community Research Unit of the Board of Deputies and the IJPR survey of the community for 1995. Figures from the census of 2001, which will include religious indicators, have not yet been published.

Table I
POPULATION OF THE PRINCIPAL COUNTRIES

Country	Population
Afghanistan	50
Albania	50
Algeria	150
Argentina	240,000
Armenia	500
Aruba & Curacao	500
Australia	97,000
Austria	12,000
Azerbaijan	6,000
Bahamas	300
Barbados	55
Belarus	28,000
Belgium	30,000
Bermuda	125
Bolivia	640
Bosnia Hercegovina	1,100
Brazil	250,000
Bulgaria	6,500
Canada	362,000
Chile	25,000
China	3,100
Colombia	3,800
Costa Rica	2,500
Croatia	1,300
Cuba	1,500
Czech Republic	10,000
Denmark	9,000
Dominican Rep.	150
Ecuador	1,000
Egypt	240

(Table I continued)

Country	Population
El Salvador	100
Estonia	2,000
Ethiopia	100
Fiji	40
Finland	1,500
France	650,000
Germany	91,000
Gibraltar	600
* Great Britain and N. Ireland	285,000
Greece	4,800
Guatemala	1,500
Haiti	150
Holland	25,000
Honduras	150
Hungary	100,000
India	5,600
Iran	27,000
Iraq	75
Ireland	1,300
¶ Israel	4,847,000
Italy	35,000
Jamaica	350
Japan	2,000
Kazakhstan	7,000
Kenya	330
Latvia	10,800
Lebanon	100
Libya	50
Lithuania	11,000
Luxembourg	1,000
Malta	50
Mexico	48,000
Moldova	40,000
Morocco	5,800
New Zealand	6,600
New Caledonia	120
Norway	1,200
Panama	5,000
Paraguay	900
Peru	5,000
Poland	3,500
Portugal	500
Puerto Rico	1,500
Romania	12,500
Russia	440,000
Singapore	300
Slovakia	6,000
South Africa	90,000
Spain	25,000
Surinam	300
Sweden	18,000
Switzerland	17,600
Syria	1,500
Tahiti	130
Taiwan	180
Thailand	250
Trinidad	10
Tunisia	1,500
Turkey	25,000
U.S.A.	5,800,000
Uruguay	25,000
Ukraine	300,000
Uzbekistan	35,000
Venezuela	20,000
Virgin Islands	500
Yemen, North	1,000
Yugoslavia (Serbia)	1,800
Zaire	100
Zambia	35
Zimbabwe	700

¶ Israel Statistical Abstract 1999. Including Eastern Jerusalem and West Bank Settlements. Total Israeli population is 6,145,000.

* According to a report by the Board of Deputies' demographic unit in 1998.

Table II
MAJOR CENTRES OF JEWISH POPULATION

EUROPE

Amsterdam	15,000
Antwerp	15,000
Athens	2,800
Barcelona	3,000
Basle	2,000
Belgrade	1,627
Berlin	10,000
Bordeaux	6,000
Brussels	23,000
Bucharest	11,000
Budapest	40,000
Cisinau	50,000
Cologne	1,260
Copenhagen	8,500
Dublin	1,300
Dusseldorf	1,710
Florence	1,290
Frankfurt	5,000
Geneva	3,900
Gothenburg	2,500
Grenoble	5,000
Hamburg	1,415
Helsinki	1,200
Istanbul	23,000
Izmir	1,000
Kaunas	5,500
Kazan	10,000
Kharkov	80,000
Kiev	50,000
Lille	3,000
Lisbon	300
Lodz	1,500
Lvov	25,000
Lyons	30,000
Madrid	3,500
Malaga	1,500
Malmo	1,950
Marseilles	70,000
Metz	2,500
Milan	10,000
Minsk	45,000
Moscow	200,000
Munich	4,000
Nancy	2,000
Nice	25,000
Odessa	20,000
Oslo	900
Paris, Greater	350,000
Prague	1,400
Riga	15,000
Rome	15,000
Rotterdam	1,500
St. Petersburg	100,000
Salonika	1,100
Sarajevo	1,090
Sofia	3,200
Stockholm	9,500
Strasbourg	18,000
Sverdlovsk	20,000
The Hague	2,500
Toulouse	25,000
Turin	1,630
Vienna	1,000
Vilnius	4,500
Warsaw	2,000
Wrocław	1,500
Zagreb	1,500
Zhitomir	20,000
Zurich	6,252

ASIA

Ankara	100
Bombay	4,354
Damascus	1,000
Hong Kong	3,000
Sa'ana	1,000
Shiraz	3,000
Tashkent	50,000
Teheran	20,000
Tokyo	750

(Table II continued)

ISRAEL

City	Population	City	Population
Acco	28,900	Kiryat Gat	27,400
Afula	24,200	Kiryat Motzkin	29,300
Ashdod	72,900	Kiryat Ono	22,000
Askelon	55,700	Kiryat Yam	31,700
Bat Yam	132,800	Lod	33,200
Beersheba	114,600	Nahariya	29,400
Bnei Brak	107,400	Netanya	114,400
Dimona	25,400	Or Yehuda	19,900
Eilat	24,200	Petach Tikva	132,100
Givatayim	45,900	Ramat Gan	115,600
Hadera	43,200	Ramat Hasharon	35,800
Haifa	203,400	Ramle	36,800
Herzlia	70,200	Ra'anana	48,000
Hod Hasharon	23,700	Rehovot	71,900
Holon	143,600	Rishon le Zion	120,100
Jerusalem	346,100	Tel Aviv-Jaffa	308,700
Kfar Saba	52,800	Tiberias	30,800
Kiryat Atta	35,100	Upper Nazareth	21,900
Kiryat Bialik	32,400	West Bank Settlements	140,000

AMERICAS

City	Population	City	Population
Alameda (Ca.)	30,000	Miami	535,000
Atlanta	50,000	Middlesex Co. (N.J.)	40,000
Baltimore	94,000	Milwaukee (Wisc.)	29,000
Bergen County (N.J.)	83,700	Minneapolis (Min.)	22,000
Boca Raton-Delray (Florida)	50,000	Montgomery & Prince Georges	105,000
Boston	210,000	Montreal (Que.)	100,000
Buenos Aires	180,000	New Haven (Con.)	26,000
Calgary (Alberta)	5,500	New York (Greater)	1,750,000
Camden (New Jersey)	28,000	Newark & Essex County (N.J.)	79,000
Caracas	18,000	Orange County (Ca.)	75,000
Chicago	248,000	Ottawa (Ont.)	9,000
Cincinnati	22,000	Palm Beach County (Florida)	209,000
Cleveland	70,000	Philadelphia	254,000
Dallas	24,000	Phoenix	50,000
Denver	45,000	Pittsburgh (Pa.)	45,000
Detroit	94,000	Rio de Janeiro	80,000
Edmonton (Alberta)	3,700	Rockland County (N.Y.)	57,000
Elizabeth & Union County (N.J.)	30,000	St. Louis (Mis.)	53,500
Englewood & Bergen Co. (N.J.)	100,000	San Diego	36,400
Fort Lauderdale (Florida)	284,000	San Jose (Ca)	32,000
Halifax (N.S.)	1,500	San Francisco	210,000
Hamilton (Ont.)	4,600	Santiago	21,000
Hartford (Con.)	27,500	Sao Paulo	90,000
Hollywood (Florida)	60,000	Seattle	19,500
Houston	40,000	Toronto (Ont.)	175,000
Kansas City	22,000	Vancouver (B.C.)	18,000
Lima	5,000	Washington (D.C.)	165,000
London (Ont.)	1,900	Windsor (Ont.)	2,500
Los Angeles	490,000	Winnipeg (Man.)	16,000
Mexico City	50,000		

(Table II continued)

AFRICA		OCEANIA	
Alexandria	100	Adelaide	1,250
Bulawayo	350	Auckland	3,100
Cape Town	28,600	Brisbane	1,500
Durban	6,420	Canberra	500
Fez	1,500	Christchurch	650
Harare	625	Dunedin	100
Johannesburg	63,620	Hamilton	50
Kinshasa	300	Hobart	100
Port Elizabeth	2,740	Melbourne	50,000
Pretoria	3,750	Noumea (New Caledonia)	100
Rabat	1,500	Perth	4,800
Tangier	1,000	Sydney	40,000
Tunis	2,200	Wellington	1,200

Table III
JEWS IN BRITAIN AND NORTHERN IRELAND

Aberdeen	30	Hemel Hempstead	270
Amersham	70	High Wycombe	35
Basildon	10	Hull	650
Bedford	30	Leamington (Warwick)	132
Belfast	550	Leeds	9,000
Birmingham	3,000	Leicester	670
Blackpool	1,500	Liverpool	3,000
Bognor Regis	40	Llandudno, Colwyn Bay & Rhyl	45
Bournemouth	3,000	London (Greater London Area)	196,000
Bradford	170	Luton	550
Brighton & Hove	8,000	Maidenhead (Royal Windsor &)	1,240
Bristol	375	Manchester & Salford	30,000
Cambridge	1,000	Margate & Thanet	200
Canterbury	100	Middlesbrough	65
Cardiff	1,200	Milton Keynes	182
Chatham & Rochester	50	Newcastle upon Tyne	1,100
Chelmsford	145	Newport	10
Cheltenham	70	Northampton	185
Chester	35	Norwich	170
Colchester	100	Nottingham	1,050
Coventry	140	Oxford	700
Crawley	50	Peterborough	105
Darlington	40	Plymouth	100
Dundee	22	Portsmouth	150
East Grinstead	35	Radlett	750
Eastbourne	63	Reading	500
Edinburgh	500	Reigate & Banstead	45
Exeter	150	St. Albans	200
Gateshead	1,430	St. Anne's (Fylde)	500
Glasgow	6,700	Sheffield	650
Grimsby (Great)	40	Solihull	300
Guildford	100	Southampton & Winchester	105
Harlow	190	Southend & Westcliff	4,500
Harrogate	150	Southport (Sefton)	1,350
Hastings	33	Staines & Slough	390

(Table III continued)

Stoke-on-Trent	30
Sunderland	45
Swansea	65
Swindon (Thamesdown)	72
Torquay (Torbay)	20
Wallasey (Wirral)	50
Welwyn (Hatfield)	290
Whitley Bay (Blyth Valley)	20
York	25
Isle of Man	35
Jersey & Guernsey	150

HISTORICAL NOTE ON BRITISH JEWRY

There were probably individual Jews in England in Roman and (though less likely) in Anglo-Saxon times, but the historical records of any organised settlement here start after the Norman Conquest of 1066. Jewish immigrants arrived early in the reign of William the Conqueror and important settlements came to be established in London (at a site still known as Old Jewry), Lincoln and many other centres. In 1190 massacres of Jews occurred in many cities, most notably in York. This medieval settlement was ended by Edward I's expulsion of the Jews in 1290, after which date, with rare and temporary exceptions, only converts to Christianity or secret adherents of Judaism could live here. The Domus Conversorum, the House for Converted Jews (on the site of the former Public Record Office in Chancery Lane, London) had been established in 1232. Perhaps the most notable Jews in medieval England were the financier, Aaron of Lincoln (d.c. 1186), and Elijah Menahem of London (d. 1284), financier, physician and Talmudist.

After the expulsion of the Jews from Spain in 1492 a secret Marrano community became established in London, but the present Anglo-Jewish community dates in practice from the period of the Commonwealth. In 1650 Menasseh ben Israel, of Amsterdam, began to champion the cause of Jewish readmission to England, and in 1655 he led a mission to London for this purpose. A conference was convened at Whitehall and a petition was presented to Oliver Cromwell. Though no formal decision was then recorded, in 1656 the Spanish and Portuguese Congregation in London was organised. It was followed towards the end of the seventeenth century by the establishment of an Ashkenazi community, which increased rapidly inside London as well as throwing out offshoots before long to a number of provincial centres and seaports. The London community, has, however, always comprised numerically the preponderant part of British Jewry.

Britain has the distinction of being one of the few countries in Europe where during the course of the past three centuries there have been no serious outbreaks of violence against Jews and in which the ghetto system never obtained a footing, though in 1753 the passage through Parliament of a Bill to facilitate the naturalisation of foreign-born Jews caused such an outcry that it was repealed in the following year. A short-lived outbreak of anti-semitism in 1772, associated with the so-called 'Chelsea murders' is also notable for its rarity.

Although Jews in Britain had achieved a virtual economic and social emancipation by the early nineteenth century they had not yet gained 'political emancipation'. Minor Jewish disabilities were progressively removed and Jews were admitted to municipal rights and began to win distinction in the professions. The movement for the removal of Jewish political disabilities became an issue after the final removal of political disabilities from Protestant dissenters and then Roman Catholics (1829), and a Bill with that object was first introduced into the House of Commons in 1830. Among the advocates of Jewish emancipation were Macaulay, Lord John Russell, Gladstone (from 1847) and Disraeli. The latter, who was a Christian of Jewish birth, entered Parliament in 1837. Jewish MPs were repeatedly elected from 1847 onwards, but were prevented from taking their seats by the nature of the various oaths required from all new members. Owing to the opposition in the House of Lords it was not until 1858 that a Jew (Lionel de Rothschild) was formally admitted to Parliament, this being followed in 1885 by the elevation of his son (Sir Nathaniel de Rothschild) to the Peerage. Meanwhile, in 1835, David Salomons was the first Jew to become Sheriff of London, and in 1855 Lord Mayor of London (Bart. 1869). The first to be a member of the government was Sir George Jessel, who became Solicitor-General in 1871, and the first Jewish Cabinet Minister was Herbert Samuel in 1909.

During the 19th century British Jews spread out from those callings which had hitherto been regarded as characteristic of the Jews. A further mark of the organisational consolidation of the community can be seen in the growth and strength of many of the communal institutions mentioned elsewhere in this book, such as the Board of Deputies (founded 1760), the Board of Guardians (founded 1859), and the United Synagogue (founded 1870), as well as the development of the office of Chief Rabbi and the longevity of the Jewish Chronicle which marked its 150th anniversary in 1991. Equally significant by the middle of the century was the appearance of a number of newer Jewish communities which had been formed in many of the new industrial centres in the North of England and the Midlands, the intellectual activities and the overseas connections of which received thereby a powerful impetus.

There has always been a steady stream of immigration into Britain from Jewish communities in Europe, originally from the Iberian Penninsula and Northern Italy, later from Western and Central Europe. The community was radically transformed by the large influx of refugees which occurred between 1881 and 1914, the result of the intensified persecution of Jews in the Russian Empire. The Jewish population rose from about 25,000 in the middle of the 19th century to nearly 350,000 by 1914. It also became far more dispersed geographically. The last two decades of the nineteenth century saw a substantial growth in the number of communities both in England and in Scotland, and in consequence the 'provinces' became more significant both in numbers and in the influence upon the community as a whole. The impact of this immigration on the Anglo-Jewish community was intensified because very many of the Jews who left Eastern Europe on their way to North America or South Africa passed through Britain. From 1933 a new emigration of Jews commenced, this time from Nazi persecution, and again many settled in this country. Since the end of the Second World War and notably since 1956, smaller numbers of refugees have come from Egypt, Iran, Iraq and Hungary whose fertility is currently giving demographic figures such growth as there is in some localities. There is, also, a large Israeli 'diaspora' in certain areas.

One of the main features of the years after 1914 was the gradual transfer of the leadership of the community from the representatives of the older establishment of Anglo-Jewry to the children and grandchildren of the newer wave of immigrants. Another feature was the growth of Zionist movements, firstly the Chovevei Zion (Lovers of Zion) and later, under the inspiration of Theodore Herzl, the English Zionist Federation. Under the leadership of Chaim Weizmann and his colleagues in this country, the Zionist Movement obtained, in 1917, the historic Balfour Declaration from the British Government. In 1920 the first British High Commissioner in Mandate Palestine was Sir Herbert Samuel. It was after the withdrawal of the British Government from the Mandate that the State of Israel was proclaimed in 1948.

A mark of British Jewry's full participation in public life is reflected in the number of Jewish signatories to the proclamation of accession of Queen Elizabeth II in 1952 which included seven Jewish Privy Councillors. At the Jubilee there were twenty-one. In the highest offices of the State, in Parliamentary and municipal life, in the Civil and Armed Services, in the judiciary and the universities, in all professions and occupations, the Jewish subjects of the Crown – both at home and overseas – play their full part as inheritors of the political and civic emancipation that was achieved in the mid-nineteenth century. There were 21 Jewish Members in the House of Commons elected on June 7, 2001. There are, however, no Jews among the hereditary peers in the Reformed House of Lords and no Jewish members of the Scottish Parliament. Five Jews serve as Chancellors of British universities.

In its internal life and organisation, British Jewry has constructed the complex fabric of religious, social and philanthropic institutions enumerated in this book. The Jews in Britain are now estimated to number about 285,000 (see the relevant note in the statistical tables) of whom some 196,000 reside in Greater London and the remainder are spread in some 80 regional communities.

UNITED KINGDOM LEGISLATION CONCERNING JEWS

(Prepared (1996) by His Honour Judge Aron Owen. Rev. 2002)

HISTORICAL BACKGROUND

In the Middle Ages, hostility towards Jews was a common feature in many European countries. In England, during the reign of Edward I (1272–1307), the *Statutum de Judeismo* was passed in 1275. This statute forbade usury and included an order continuing to oblige Jews to wear a distinguishing badge and imposing upon them an annual poll tax.

In 1290, Edward personally decreed the expulsion of Jews from England. During the reign of Charles I (1625–49) the number of Jews in England steadily increased. Menasseh ben Israel (1604–57) of Amsterdam made a direct appeal to Cromwell to authorize readmission. His 'Humble Addresses' presented to the Lord Protector in October 1655 urged the revocation of the edict of 1290 and entreated that the Jews be accorded the right of public worship and the right to trade freely. No formal announcement was ever made of the Jews' 're-admission' but, from about 1657, the edict of 1290 ceased to have effect.

The Religious Disabilities Act 1846 extended to Jews the provisions of the Toleration Act 1688. Under the 1846 Act, British subjects professing the Jewish religion were to be subject to the same laws in respect of their schools, places for religious worship, education and charitable purposes, and the property held with them, as Protestant dissenters from the Church of England.

PRESENT POSITION

Today, English Law does not regard Jews as a separate nationality or as different from any other British citizen. They have no special status except in so far as they constitute a dissenting religious denomination.

Provision for that special religious position of Jews has, from time to time, been made in legislation (see, for example, the 1846 Act mentioned above). A discussion of the subject will be found in Halsbury's *Laws of England*, fourth edition 1975, Volume 14, paragraphs 1423 to 1432.

Some of the various statutory provisions in force today are set out briefly below. Further information and details can be obtained from the Board of Deputies 6 Bloomsbury Square, London, WC1A 2LP. ☎ 020-7543 5400). Legal advice should be sought by those wishing to know the impact of specific legislation upon their own particular circumstances.

1. The *Representation of the People Act 1983* (which is a consolidation of several previous Acts) enables a voter in a parliamentary of local election, 'who declares that he is a Jew' and objects on religious grounds to marking the ballot paper on the Jewish Sabbath, to have, if the poll is taken on a Saturday, his vote recorded by the presiding officer. This right does not apply to Jewish Holy-days other than the Sabbath. A person unable by reason of 'religious observance' to go in person to the polling station may apply to be treated as an absent voter and to be given a postal vote for a particular parliamentary or local election.

2. The *Education Act 1994* permits Jewish parents to have their children attending state or state-aided voluntary schools withdrawn from any period of religious instruction and/or worship where such instruction or worship is not in the Jewish faith. In order to take advantage of these provisions of the Act, a written request must be submitted to the head teacher of the school.

3. The *Oaths Act 1978*. A Jew may take an oath (in England, Wales or Northern Ireland) by holding the Old Testament in his uplifted hand, and saying or repeating after the officer administering the oath the words: 'I swear by Almighty God that ...' followed by the words of the oath prescribed by law. The officer will administer the oath in that form and manner without question, unless the person about to take the oath voluntarily objects thereto or is physically incapable of so taking the oath.

Any person who objects to being sworn (whether in that way or in the form and manner usually administered in Scotland) is at liberty instead to make a *solemn affirmation* which will have the same force and effect as an oath. The form of the affirmation is as follows: 'I ... do solemnly, sincerely and truly declare and affirm that ...' followed by the words of the oath prescribed by law. The form of affirmation omits any words of imprecation or calling to witness.

4. *Marriage Act 1949*. English law expressly recognizes the validity of marriages by Jews in England if the ceremonies of the Jewish religion have been complied with.

The Secretary of a synagogue has statutory powers and duties in regard to keeping the marriage register books, and the due registration of marriages between persons professing the Jewish religion under the provisions of the Marriage Act 1949. He has no authority unless and until he has been certified in writing to be the Secretary of a synagogue in England of persons professing the Jewish religion by the President of the Board of Deputies.

When the West London Synagogue was established, acting on the advice of the Chief Rabbi and other recognized Jewish ecclesiastical authorities, the President of the Board of Deputies refused to certify the secretary of the new congregation. Accordingly, by the Marriage Act 1949, it is enacted that the Secretary of the West London Synagogue of British Jews, if certified in writing to the Registrar-General by twenty householders being members of that synagogue, shall be entitled to the same privileges as if he had been certified by the President of the Board of Deputies. These privileges are also accorded to a person whom the Secretary of the West London Synagogue certifies in writing to be the secretary of some other synagogue of not less than twenty householders professing the Jewish religion, if it is connected with the West London Synagogue and has been established for not less than one year.

The Marriages (Secretaries of Synagogues) Act 1959 gives similar rights to Liberal Jewish synagogues.

5. The *Family Law Act 1996* contained important specific provisions in relation to Jewish religious divorce.

Section 9, subsections (3) and (4) provide as follows:

'(3) if the parties –

(a) were married to each other with usages of a kind mentioned in Section 26(1) of the Marriage Act 1949 (marriages which may be solemnized on authority of superintendent registrar's certificate), and

(b) are required to co-operate if the marriage is to be dissolved in accordance with those usages.

the court may, on the application of either party, direct that there must also be produced to the court a declaration by both parties that they have taken such steps as are required to dissolve the marriage in accordance with those usages.

(4) A direction under subsection (3) –

(a) may be given only if the court is satisfied that in all the circumstances of the case it is just and reasonable to give it; and
(b) may be revoked by the court at any time.'

The effect of these provisions is that where parties, who have been married in accordance with the usages of Jewish law (i.e., *Chuppah* and *Kiddushin*), seek a divorce then, before such a Jewish husband and wife would be granted the civil decree of divorce by the English court, they could be required to declare that there has been a *Get*, i.e., the Jewish religious divorce. There would thus be a barrier to such a Jewish husband or wife obtaining a civil divorce and being able to remarry unless and until there has been a prior *Get*.

It is hoped that these new statutory provisions will go some way towards alleviating the plight of an *Agunah*. The usual case of an *Agunah* (literally 'a chained woman') is that of a wife whose husband refuses to give her a *Get* so that she is unable to remarry in accordance with orthodox Jewish law. Under the above provisions of the Family Law Act 1996 such a husband would himself be unable to obtain a civil decree of divorce and remarry.

This legislation, not passed before Parliament, was prorogued. A new Act – the *Divorce (Religious Marriages) Act 2002* – containing similar provisions received the Royal Assent on 24 July 2002.

6. *Shechita*. Animals and birds slaughtered by the Jewish method (*shechita*) for the food of Jews by a Jew duly licensed by the Rabbinical Commission constituted for the purpose do not come within the provision of the Slaughterhouses Act 1974 or the Slaughter of Poultry Act 1967 relating to the methods of slaughter of animals and birds. The right to practice *shechita* is thus preserved.

In March 1995 both Acts (the Slaughterhouses Act 1974 and the Slaughter of Poultry Act 1967) were repealed and replaced by secondary legislation in the form of a Statutory Instrument. This implements the European Community's Directive (93/119/EC) on the protection of animals at the time of slaughter. There is specific provision that the requirement for animals and poultry to be stunned before slaughter or killed instantaneously does not apply in the case of animals subject to particular methods of slaughter required by certain religious rites. *Shechita* is accordingly safeguarded.

7. The *Sunday Trading Act*, which came into operation on 26 August 1994, has removed many of the difficulties caused by the Shops Act 1950. All shops with a selling and display area of less than 280 square metres may be open at any time on Sundays. Shops with a selling and display area of 280 square metres or more are still subject to some restriction, with an opening time limited to a continuous period of six hours between 10 a.m. and 6 p.m.

There is, however, a special exemption for 'persons observing the Jewish Sabbath' who are occupiers of these 'large' shops. Provided such an individual (and there are parallel conditions for partnerships and companies) gives a signed notice to the Local Authority that he is a person of the Jewish religion and intends to keep the shop closed for the serving of customers on the Jewish Sabbath, he may open it as and when he wishes on a Sunday.

The notice given to the Local Authority must be accompanied by a statement from the minister of the shopkeeper's synagogue or the secretary for marriages of that synagogue or a person designated by the President of the Board of Deputies, that the shopkeeper is a person of the Jewish religion. There are severe penalties for any false statements made in connection with this intention to trade.

Large shops which were previously registered under Section 53 of the Shops Act 1950 may continue to trade on Sundays without new notification. But occupiers of food stores and kosher meat shops over 280 square metres who, even if closed on Shabbat, did not previously require exemption, may well have formally to notify their Local Authority that their premises will be closed on Shabbat to enable them to open on Sunday.

Jewish shopkeepers who close their premises for the 25 hours of Shabbat may open after Shabbat.

8. Discrimination against a person on account of his being a Jew is unlawful under the *Race Relations Act 1976*.

9. *Friendly Societies Act 1974*. A Friendly Society may be registered for the purpose, *inter alia*, of ensuring that money is paid to persons of the Jewish persuasion during *Shiva* (referred to in the Act as 'the period of confined mourning').

10. By the *Places of Worship Registration Act 1855*, as amended by the *Charities Act 1960*, the Registrar-General may certify a synagogue. The effect of Certification is freedom from uninvited interference by the Charity Commissioners and, if exclusively appropriate to public worship, from general and special rates.

11. By the *Juries Act 1870*, the minister of a synagogue who has been certified, is free from liability to serve on a jury, provided he follows no secular occupation except that of a schoolmaster.

THE SCOTTISH POSITION

(Prepared by Sheriff Sir G. H. Gordon, CBE, QC, LL.D)

Jews do not appear in Scots legislation as a unique group, except in relation to United Kingdom statutes which treat them as such, of which the only one still in force is the Representation of the People Act 1983. European Regulations apply in Scotland as they do in England.

The Education (Scotland) Act 1944 provides by section 9 that every public and grant-aided school shall be open to all denominations, and that any pupil may be withdrawn by his parents from instruction in religious subjects and from any religious observance in any such school.

The oath is administered by the judge in Scots courts, and the witness repeats the words (which begin 'I swear by Almighty God') after him with his right hand upraised. No books are used. A Jewish witness is in practice allowed to cover his head if he wishes to do so. Anyone who indicates a wish to affirm is allowed to do so.

Section 8 of the Marriages (Scotland) Act 1977 provides that a religious marriage may be solemnized by the minister or clergyman of any religious body prescribed by Regulations, or by any person recognized by such a body as entitled to solemnize marriages. The bodies prescribed by the Marriage (Prescription of Religious Bodies) (Scotland) (Regulations) 1977 (S.I.No. 1670) include 'The Hebrew Congregation', whatever that denotes. In practice Orthodox marriages are solemnized by ministers authorized to do so by the Board of Deputies.

The Law Reform (Miscellaneous Provisions) (Scotland) Act 1980 includes regular ministers of any religious denomination among those persons who although eligible for jury service are entitled to be excused therefrom as of right.

The Race Relations Act 1976 applies to Scotland, but the Sunday Trading Act 1994 does not, nor does the Places of Worship Registration Act 1855.

LISTED SYNAGOGUES, FORMER SYNAGOGUES AND OTHER JEWISH SITES IN THE UK

The following list has been compiled by the Working Party on Jewish Monuments in the UK and Ireland and the Survey of the Jewish Built Heritage and includes upgrades announced in 2000 (see p.5).

LONDON

Grade I

Bevis Marks, EC3 (Joseph Avis 1699–1701)

Grade II*

New West End, St Petersburgh Place, W2 (George Audsley in association with N.S. Joseph 1877–79)
Hampstead, Dennington Park Road, NW6 (Delissa Joseph 1892–1901)

Former synagogues:
Princelet Street, E1 (former synagogue 1870, behind Huguenot house 1719. Hudson 1870. Remodelled by Lewis Solomon 1893. Museum of Immigration)

Grade II

In use as synagogues:
Sandy's Row, E1 (former chapel 1766. Converted into synagogue 1867. Remodelled by N.S. Joseph 1870)
West London Reform, Upper Berkeley Street, W1 (Davis & Emanuel 1870)
New London, 33 Abbey Road, NW8 (formerly St John's Wood United Synagogue. H.H. Collins 1882)
Spanish & Portuguese, Lauderdale Road, W9 (Davis & Emanuel 1896)

Former synagogues:
Spitalfields Great, 23 Brick Lane/Fournier Street, E1 (former chapel 1743. Converted into synagogue 1897–98. Mosque)
East London, Rectory Square, E1 (Davis & Emanuel 1876–77. Flats)
New, Egerton Road, N16 and attached school (Ernest Joseph 1915. Interior reconstructed from Great St Helen's, Bishopsgate by John Davies 1838)
Dollis Hill, Parkside, NW2 (Sir Owen Williams 1936–38. Torah Temimah Primary School)

Other building types:
Soup Kitchen for the Jewish Poor, Brune Street, E1 (Lewis Solomon 1902. Façade only. Flats)
Stepney Jewish Schools, Stepney Green, E1 (Davis & Emanuel 1906)

Cemeteries:
Velho (Spanish & Portuguese), 253 Mile End Road, E1 (1657)
Alderney Road (Ashkenazi), E1 (1696–97)

ENGLISH REGIONS

Grade II*

Birmingham, Singers Hill, Blucher Street, B1 (H. Yeoville Thomason 1855–56)
Brighton, Middle Street, BN1 (Thomas Lainson 1874–75)
Cheltenham, St James's Square, GL50 (W.H. Knight 1837–39)
Exeter, Mary Arches Street, EX4 (1763–64)
Liverpool, Old Hebrew Congregation, Princes Road, L8 (W&G Audsley 1874)
Manchester, Spanish & Portuguese, 190 Cheetham Hill Road, M8 (Edward Salomons 1873–74. Manchester Jewish Museum)
Plymouth, Catherine Street, PL1 (1762)
Ramsgate, Montefiore Synagogue, Honeysuckle Road, CT11 (David Mocatta 1831–33)

Grade II

Blackpool, Leamington Road, FY1 (R.B. Mather 1916)
Bradford, Bowland Street Reform, BD1 (T.H. & F. Healey 1880–81)
Brighton, Sassoon Mausoleum, Paston Place (1898)
Bristol, Jacob's Well (possible medieval *mikveh*)
Carmel College, Mongewell Park, Crowmarsh, Wallingford, OX10; Synagogue (Thomas Hancock 1963); Amphitheatre (Thomas Hancock 1965); Julius Gottlieb Gallery/ Boathouse (Sir Basil Spence, Bonnington & Collins 1968–70, Grade II*)
Chatham Memorial Synagogue, High Street, Rochester, ME1 (H.H. Collins 1865–70)
Grimsby, Sir Moses Montefiore Synagogue, Heneage Road, DN32 – and *mikveh* (B.S. Jacobs 1885–88, *mikveh* 1915–16)
Leicester, Synagogue, Highfield Street (A. Waberley 1897–98)
Liverpool, Greenbank Drive, L17 (Alfred Shennan 1936)
Manchester, Higher Crumpsall, Bury Old Road, Salford, M7 (Pendleton & Dickinson 1928–29.)
Manchester, South Manchester, Wilbraham Road, M14 (Joseph Sunlight 1912–13)
Manchester, Withington Spanish & Portuguese, 8 Queenston Road, West Didsbury, M20 (Delissa Joseph 1925–27, with Joseph Sunlight 'supervising architect')
Nottingham, Shakespeare Street, NG1 (built as chapel 1854. Converted to synagogue 1954)
Ramsgate, Montefiore Mausoleum (1862) and Gateway to Judith, Lady Montefiore College, Hereson Road, CT11 (Henry David Davis 1865–69) (main building demolished)
Reading, Goldsmid Road, RG1 (W.G. Lewton 1900)
Sunderland, Ryhope Road, SR2 (Marcus K. Glass 1928)

Former synagogues:
Brighton, 37–39 Devonshire Place, BN2 (1837–38. Remodelled by David Mocatta. Gym)
Canterbury, King Street, CT1 – and *mikveh* (H. Marshall 1847–48, *mikveh* 1851. King's School music and rehearsal rooms)
Falmouth, Smithick Hill, TR11 (1808. Studio)
Hull, The Western, Linneaus Street (B.S. Jacobs 1902. Judeo-Christian Study Centre)
Leeds, New, Louis Street/Chapeltown Road, LS7 (J. Stanley Wright 1932. Northern School of Contemporary Dance)
Newcastle upon Tyne, Leazes Park, NE1 (J. Johnstone 1879–80. Flats)
Sheffield, Wilson Road, S11 – and *succah* (Rawcliffe & Ogden 1929–30. Being converted into church)

Cemeteries:
Bristol, Barton Road, St Philips, BS2 (listed boundary wall. Earliest stone 1762)
Exeter, Magdelen Street, Bull Meadow, EX2 (1757; listed boundary wall 1807?)
Liverpool, Deane Road, L7 (1836. Screen wall and railings)
Southampton, The Old Jewish Cemetery, The Common Cemetery, Cemetery Road, SO15. Earliest burial 1854 (Parks and Gardens Register)

WALES
Grade II
Former synagogues:
Cardiff, Cathedral Road, CF11 (Delissa Joseph 1896–97. Demolished behind façade. Offices)
Merthyr Tydfil, Bryntirion Road, Thomastown, CF47 (1877. Gym)

SCOTLAND
B List
Edinburgh, 4 Salisbury Road, Newington, EH16 (James Miller 1929–32)
Glasgow, Garnethill, 127 Hill Street, G3 (John McLeod in association with N.S. Joseph 1877–79)
Glasgow, Queen's Park, 4 Falloch Road, G42 (Ninian MacWhannel 1927)

Cemeteries:
A List
Glasgow Necropolis, Cathedral Square (opened 1833 – including 'façade of Jews' Enclosure' – column and gateway by John Bryce 1836)

B List
Edinburgh, Sciennes House Place (Braid Place), Causewayside (1820)

PRE-EXPULSION SITES (with possible Jewish associations; all Grade 1)
Bury St Edmunds, Moyses Hall, IP33 (*ca.* 1180)
Lincoln, Aaron the Jews' House (the Norman House), 47 Steep Hill;
Jew's House and Jews' Court, 2-3 Steep Hill, LN2 (*ca.* 1170)
Norwich, the Music House or Jurnet's House, Wensum Lodge, King Street, NR1 (*ca.* 1175)
York, Clifford's Tower, YO1 (the wooden structure destroyed in 1190 rebuilt in stone; scheduled Ancient Monument)

PRIVY COUNSELLORS, PEERS, MPs, etc.

PRIVY COUNSELLORS

Barnett, Lord
Brittan, Lord, QC
Clinton-Davis, Lord
Cowen, Sir Zelman, AK, GCMG GCVO, QC
Diamond, Lord
Dyson, Sir John
Freeson, Reginald
Goldsmith, Lord
Hayman, Baroness
Howard, Michael, MP, QC
Kaufman, Gerald B., MP
Lawson, Lord
Letwin, Oliver, MP
Millett, Lord
Oppenheim-Barnes, Baroness
Rifkind, Sir Malcolm, QC
Rix, Sir Bernard (Lord Justice)
Sedley, Sir Stephen (Lord Justice)
Sheldon, Lord Robert E.
Woolf, Lord Chief Justice
Young, Lord

PEERS

Bearsted of Maidstone, 5th Viscount
Greenhill of Townhead, 3rd Baron, MD
Marks of Broughton, 3rd Baron
Morris of Kenwood, 2nd Baron
Nathan, 2nd Baron
Rothschild, 4th Baron, OM, MA (Oxon)
Samuel of Mt Carmel & Toxteth, 3rd Viscount
Swaythling, 5th Baron

LIFE PEERS

Barnett of Heywood & Royton, Baron, PC
Brittan, Baron, PC, QC
Carlile, Baron
Clinton-Davis of Hackney, Baron, PC
Dubs, Baron of Battersea
Diamond of Gloucester, Baron, PC
Ezra of Horsham, Baron, MBE
Goldsmith, Baron, PC, QC
Grabiner, Baron, QC
Greengross, Baroness
Hoffman, Lord Justice, PC
Haskel of Higher Broughton, Baron
Hayman of Dartmouth Park, Baroness, PC
Jacobs of Belgravia, Baron
Janner of Braunstone, Baron, QC
Joffe, Baron
Lawson of Blaby, Baron, PC
Lester of Herne Hill, Baron, QC
Levene of Portsoken, Baron
Levy of Mill Hill, Baron
Miller of Hendon, Baroness
Millett, Baron of St Marylebone, PC (Lord of Appeal)
Mishcon of Lambeth, Baron, DL
Moser, Baron of Regent's Park, FBA
Oppenheim-Barnes of Gloucester, Baroness, PC
Peston of Mile End, Baron
Puttnam, Baron of Queensgate, CBE
Rayne of Prince's Meadow, Baron
Saatchi of Staplefield, Baron
Serota of Hampstead, Baroness, DBE
Sheldon, Baron, PC
Sterling of Plaistow, Baron, CBE
Stern, Baroness
Stone of Blackheath, Baron
Weidenfeld of Chelsea, Baron
Wigoder of Cheetham, Baron, QC
Winston of Hammersmith, Baron
Wolfson of Marylebone, Baron
Wolfson of Sunningdale, Baron
Woolf of Barnes, Baron, Lord Chief Justice, PC
Young of Graffham, Baron, PC

MEMBERS OF PARLIAMENT

Bercow, John (C.), Buckingham
Bradley, Peter (Lab.), The Wrekin
Caplin, Ivor (Lab.), Hove
Cohen, Harry (Lab.), Leyton
Djanogly, Jonathan S. (C.), Huntingdon
Ellman, Louise (Lab.), Liverpool Riverside
Fabrikant, Michael (C.), Lichfield
Hamilton, Fabian (Lab.), Leeds North East
Harris, Dr Evan (Lib.), Oxford West & Abingdon
Hodge, Margaret (Lab.), Barking
Howard, Rt. Hon. Michael, PC, QC (C.), Folkestone & Hythe
Kaufman, Rt. Hon. Gerald, PC (Lab.), Manchester, Gorton
King, Oona (Lab.), Bethnal Green and Bow

Letwin, Rt Hon. Oliver, PC (C.), Dorset West
Lewis, Ivor (Lab.), Bury South
Lewis, Dr Julian (C.), New Forest East
Merron, Gillian (Lab.), Lincoln
Roche, Barbara (Lab.), Hornsey & Wood Green
Steen, Anthony (C.), Totnes
Steinberg, Gerry (Lab.), Durham City
Winnick, David (Lab.), Walsall North

MEMBER OF EUROPEAN PARLIAMENT

Sumberg, David (C.)

BARONETS

Cahn, Sir Albert Jonas
Jessel, Sir Charles John
Richardson, Sir Anthony Lewis
Tuck, Sir Bruce A. R.
Waley-Cohen, Sir Stephen

KNIGHTS

Abeles, Sir Peter, AC
Alliance, Sir David
Beecham, Sir Jeremy
Berman, Sir Franklin
Blank, Sir Victor
Blom-Cooper, Sir Louis
Bondi, Sir Hermann, KCB, FRS
Brown, Sir Simon (the Hon. Lord Justice)
Burgen, Sir Arnold, FRS
Burnton, Sir Stanley (the Hon. Mr Justice)
Burton, Sir Michael (the Hon. Mr Justice)
Calne, Sir Roy, FRS
Caro, Sir Anthony, OM
Chinn, Sir Trevor, CVO
Cohen, Sir Edward
Cohen, Sir Ivor Harold
Cohen, Prof. Sir Philip
Cohen, Sir Ronald
Collins, Sir Laurence (the Hon. Mr Justice)
Colman, Sir Anthony (the Hon. Mr Justice)
Copisarow, Sir Alcon
Cowen, Sir Zelman, AK, CGMC, GCVO
Djanogly, Sir Harry
Dyson, Sir John (Lord Justice), PC
Elton, Sir Arnold
Elyan, Sir Isadore Victor
Epstein, Sir Anthony, FRS
Etherton, Sir Terence (the Hon. Mr Justice)
Falk, Sir Roger Salis
Feldman, Sir Basil
Fox, Sir Paul
Freud, Sir Clement
Gainsford, Sir Ian
Gilbert, Sir Martin, CBE
Goldberg, Sir Abraham, FRSE
Goldberg, Prof. Sir David
Golding, Sir John
Goldman, Sir Samuel, KCB
Goode, Prof. Sir Roy
Gordon, Sir Gerald Henry, CBE, QC
Green, Sir Allan, KCB
Greengross, Sir Alan
Grierson, Sir Ronald
Halpern, Sir Ralph
Harris, Sir William Woolf, OBE
Hatter, Sir Maurice
Henriques, Sir Richard (the Hon. Mr Justice)
Hirsch, Sir Peter Bernhard, FRS
Hoffenberg, Prof. Sir Raymond
Isaacs, Sir Jeremy
Japhet, Ernest I., Hon. KBE
Jordan, Sir Gerald
Kalms, Sir Stanley
Katz, Prof. Sir Bernard, FRS
Kingsland, Sir Richard, AO, CBE, DFC
Klug, Sir Aaron, FRS, OM
Kornberg, Prof. Sir Hans Leo, FRS
Krusin, Sir Stanley Marks, CB
Laddie, Sir Hugh (the Hon. Mr Justice)
Landau, Sir Dennis
Lauterpacht, Prof. Sir Elihu
Lawrence, Sir Ivan
Leigh, Sir Geoffrey
Levine, Sir Montague
Lewando, Sir Jan Alfred, CBE
Lightman, Sir Gavin (the Hon. Mr Justice)
Lipton, Sir Stuart
Lipworth, Sir Sydney
Lyons, Sir Isidore Jack, CBE
Marmot, Prof. Sir Michael
Miller, Sir Jonathan
Neuberger, Sir David (the Hon. Mr Justice)
Ognall, Sir Harry Henry (the Hon. Mr Justice)
Oppenheim, Sir Alexander, OBE
Phillips, Sir Henry Ellis Isidore, CMG, MBE

Phillips, Sir Horace
Porter, Sir Leslie
Rieger, Sir Clarence Oscar, CBE
Rifkind, Sir Malcolm, PC
Rix, Sir Bernard (Lord Justice), PC
Robinson, Sir Albert EP
Rodley, Prof. Sir Nigel
Rotblat, Sir Joseph, CBE, FRS
Roth, Prof. Sir Martin, FRS
Rothschild, Sir Evelyn de
Samuelson, Sir Sydney W., CBE
Schreier, Sir Bernard
Sedley, Sir Stephen (Lord Justice), PC
Seligman, Sir Peter Wendel, CBE
Serota, Sir Nicholas
Shaffer, Sir Peter
Sher, Sir Anthony
Sherman, Sir Alfred
Sherman, Sir Lou, OBE
Shields, Sir Neil Stanley, MC
Shock, Sir Maurice
Sieff, Sir David
Silber, Sir Stephen (the Hon. Mr Justice)
Singer, Sir Hans
Smith, Sir David, AK, CVO, AO
Solomon, Sir Harry
Sorrell, Sir Martin
Sternberg, Sir Sigmund
Stoppard, Sir Tom, OM
Sugar, Sir Alan
Tumim, Judge Sir Stephen
Turnberg, Sir Leslie
Weinberg, Sir Mark
Wolfson, Sir Brian
Zissman, Sir Bernard
Zunz, Sir Jack

DAMES

Duffield, Dame Vivien, DBE
Heilbron, Dame Rose, DBE
Markova, Dame Alicia, DBE
Porter, Dame Shirley, DBE
Prendergast, Dame Simone, DBE, JP, DL
Rothschild, the Hon. Dame Miriam, DBE

FELLOWS OF THE ROYAL SOCIETY

Anderson, Prof. Ephraim Saul, CBE
Bondi, Prof. Sir Hermann, KCB
Born, Prof. Gustav Victor Rudolf
Brenner, Prof. Sydney, CH
Burgen, Sir Arnold
Calne, Sir Roy
Cohen, Prof. Sydney, CBE
Devons, Prof. Samuel
Domb, Prof. Cyril
Dunitz, Prof. Jack David
Dwek, Raymond
Epstein, Sir Michael Anthony (Vice-President, 1986–91)
Fersht, Prof. Alan
Glynn, Prof. Ian Michael
Goldstone, Prof. Jeffrey
Grant, Ian Philip
Hirsch, Prof. Sir Peter Bernhard
Horn, Prof. Gabriel
Huppert, Dr Herbert
Josephson, Prof. Brian David
Kalmus, George Ernest
Katz, Prof. Sir Bernard (Vice-President 1965 and 1968–76)
Kennard, Dr Olga, OBE
Klug, Sir Aaron, OM (President 1995–2000)
Kornberg, Prof. Sir Hans Leo
Mahler, Prof. Kurt
Mandelstam, Prof. Joel
Mandelstam, Prof. Stanley
Mestel, Prof. Leon
Nabarro, Prof. F. R. Nunes
Neumann, Prof. Bernard H.
Orgel, Prof. L. E.
Orowan, Prof. Egon
Pepper, Dr Michael
Roitt, Prof. Ivan
Rotblat, Sir Joseph, KCMG, CBE
Roth, Sir Martin
Rothschild, Dame Dr Miriam, CBE, DBE
Sciama, Dr Denis
Segal, Dr Anthony Walter
Shoenberg, Prof. David, MBE
Sondheimer, Prof. Franz
Tabor, Prof. David
Weinberg, Prof. Felix
Weiskrantz, Prof. Lawrence
Woolfson, Prof. Michael Mark
Young, Prof. Alec David, OBE

Foreign Members

Bethe, Hans
Calvin, Prof. Melvin
Katzir, Prof. Ephraim, form. President of Israel
Kornberg, Prof. Arthur

FELLOWS OF THE BRITISH ACADEMY

Bogdanor, Prof. Vernon, CBE
Cohen, Prof. Gerald Allan
Cohen, Laurence Jonathan
Cohn, Prof. Norman
Genn, Prof. Hazel, CBE
Goodman, Prof. Martin
Hajnal, Prof. John
Hobsbawm, Prof. Eric John, CH
Israel, Prof. Jonathan Irvine
Josipovici, Prof. Gabriel David
Koerner, Prof. Stephan
Lewis, Prof. Bernard
Lewis, Prof. Geoffrey, CMG
Lukes, Prof. Steven
Marks, Prof. Shula
Moser, Lord, KCB, CBE
Prais, Sigbert J.
Prawer, Prof. Siegbert Salomon
Schapera, Prof. Isaac
Segal, Prof. Judah Benzion, MC
Steiner, Prof. George
Supple, Prof. Barry, CBE
Ullendorff, Prof. Edward (Vice-President 1980–82)
Vermes, Prof. Geza
Yamey, Prof. Basil Selig, CBE

Corresponding Fellows

Blau, Prof. J.
Levi-Strauss, Prof. Claude
Samuelson, Prof. Paul Antony

VICTORIA CROSS

Lieutenant Frank Alexander De Pass*
Captain Robert Gee, M.C.*
Leonard Keysor*
Acting Corporal Issy Smith*
Jack White*
Lieut.-Cmdr. Thomas William Gould, RNVR*

GEORGE CROSS

Errington, Harry
Lewin, Sgt. Raymond M., RAF*
Latutin, Capt. Simmon*
Newgass, Lieutenant-Commander Harold Reginald, RNVR*

ORDER OF MERIT

Caro, Sir Anthony
Freud, Lucian, CH
Klug, Sir Aaron, FRS
Rothschild, Lord
Stoppard, Sir Tom

COMPANIONS OF HONOUR

Brenner, Prof. Sydney, FRS
Freud, Lucian, OM
Hobsbawm, Prof. Eric John Ernest, FBA
Pinter, Harold

NOBEL PRIZE WINNERS

Peace

Tobias Asser*; Alfred Fried*; Rene Cassin*; Henry Kissinger; Menachem Begin*; Elie Wiesel; Yitzhak Rabin*; Shimon Peres; Joseph Rotblat.

Physics

Albert Abraham Michelson*; Gabriel Lippmann*; Albert Einstein*; Niels Bohr*; Enrico Fermi*; James Franck*; Gustav Herts*; Otto Stern*; Isidor Isaac Rabi*; Felix Bloch*; Max Born*; Igor Tamm*; Emilio Segre*; Donald A. Glaser; Robert Hofstadter*; Lev Davidovic Landau*; Richard Feynman*; Julian Schwinger; Hans Bethe; Murray Gell-Mann; Dennis Gabor*; Brian Josephson; Ben R. Mottelson; Aage Bohr; Burton Richter; Arno Penzias; Sheldon Glashow; Steven Weinberg; Leon Lederman; Melvin Schwartz; Jack Steinberger; Georges Charpak.

Chemistry

Adolph Baeyer*; Henri Moissan*; Otto Wallach*; Richard Willstatter*; Fritz Haber*; George de Hevesy*; Melvin Calvin; Max Ferdinand Perutz*; William Stein*; Herbert Brown; Paul Berg; Walter Gilbert; Roald Hoffmann; Aaron Klug; Dudley Herschebach; Herbert Hauptman; Sidney Altman; Rudolf Marcus; Walter Kohn.

Medicine

Paul Ehrlich*; Elias Metchnikoff*; Robert Barany*; Otto Meyerhoff*; Karl Landsteiner*; Otto Warburg*; Otto Loewi*; Joseph Erlanger*; Sir Ernst B. Chain*; Herbert Gasser*; Hermann Joseph Muller*; Tadeus Reichstein*; Selman Abraham Waksman*; Sir Hans A. Krebs*; Fritz Albert Lipmann*; Joshua Lederberg; Arthur Kornberg; Konrad Bloch; Francois Jacob-Andre Lwoff*; George Wald; Marshall W. Nirenberg; Salvador Luria*; Sir Bernard Katz; Julius Axelrod; Gerald Maurice Edelman;

David Baltimore; Howard Martin Temin; Baruch S. Blumberg; Rosalyn Yalow; David Nathans; Baruj Benacerraf; Cesar Milstein; Joseph L. Goldstein; Michael Brown; Rita Levi-Montalcini; Stanley Cohen; Gertrude Aeilion; Harold Vermus; Gary Becker; Gunter Blobel; H. Robert Horvitz; Sydney Brenner.

Literature

Paul Heyse*; Henri Bergson*; Boris Pasternak*; Shmuel Yosef Agnon*; Nelly Sachs*; Saul Bellow; Isaac Bashevis Singer*; Elias Canetti*; Jaroslav Seifert*; Joseph Brodsky*; Nadine Gordimer, Imre Kertész.

Economics

Paul Samuelson; Simon Kuznets*; Kenneth Arrow; Leonid Kantorovich*; Milton Friedman; Herbert Simon*; Lawrence Klein; Franco Modigliani; Robert Solow; Daniel Kahneman.

* Deceased.

Who's Who

AARON, Martin, MBA, FSCA, MI Mgt, FRSA; b. London, Jan. 25, 1937; Fdr. and Hon. President, Jewish Assoc. for the Mentally Ill; form. Adv. M., All-Party Parliamentary Group on Mental Health; Tr., Ravenswood Foundation; Fdr. and Hon. President, Jewish Soc. for the Mentally Handicapped; form. Memb. Council of CONCERN for the Mentally Ill; form. Adv. C., MENCAP; form. Adv. C. MIND. Ad.: c/o JAMI, 16a North End Rd., London NW11 7PH. ☎ 020-8458 2223.

ABIS, Barrington Gerald, JP; b. Ipswich Nov. 28, 1939; Regional Dir. UJIA (1998–); form. Exec. Off, Leeds Jewish Rep. C. (1985-98); Admin. Sec., Leeds Kashrut Authority (1985-98), Beth Din, Admin. Dir., Leeds Judean Club; and S. H. Lyons Tr. (1982-98); Form. Com. Rel. C., Weetwood & Chapeltown North Police Com. Forums; P/Pres. B'nai B'rith Men's Lodge 1055; Ad.: Balfour House, 399 Street Lane, Leeds LS17 6HQ. ☎ 0113-269 3136. Fax 0113-269 3961. E-mail barryabis@ujia.org.

ABRAHAMSON, Hon. Abraham Eliezer, BA; b. Bulawayo, Oct. 13, 1922, m. Anita née Rabinovitz; MP (Bulawayo East, 1953-64); Min. of Treasury, Local Govt. and Housing (1958), Min. of Labour, Social Welfare and Housing (1958-62); H.L.P. (President 1956-58, 64-79) Central African Jew BoD, Life Member C.A.Z.O. (1989-); Member World Exec. WJC, served on Nat. Exec. S.A. Jewish BoD (1991-); Chairman, S.A.Z. Fed. (1991-94), President (1994-98), Hon. Life P. (1998-); Exec., S.A.Z. Fed (1986); V. Chairman 1988-90. Ad.: 4 Oxford Gdns., 188 Oxford Rd., Illovo 2196, Johannesburg. ☎ 880 1964. Fax 447 2596. E-mail abita@hixnet.co.za.

ABRAMSKY, Chimen, B.A. (Jerusalem), MA (Oxon); b. Minsk, Mar. 5, 1917; form. President, Jewish Hist. Soc. of England; form. Goldsmid Prof. of Heb. and Jewish Studies; form. Reader in Jewish hist., Univ. Coll., London; Sr. Fel., St. Antony's Coll., Oxford. Publ.: Karl Marx and the Engl. Labour Movement (jt. auth.); Essays in honour of E. H. Carr (ed.), two Prague Haggadot (auth.), First Illustrated Grace After Meals, Jews in Poland (jt ed.), many articles and monographs on modern Jewish hist., etc. Ad: 5 Hillway, N6 6QB. ☎ 020-8340 8302.

ABRAMSON, Glenda (née Melzer), BA, MA, PhD (Rand), Hon. D.Litt (HUC); b. Johannesburg, Nov. 16, 1940; m. David; Academic; Cowley Lect. Post-Biblical Hebrew, Oxford (1989-); form. Schreiber Fell. Modern Jewish Studies, Oxford Centre for Hebrew and Jewish Studies (1981); form. Sen. Lect., Univ. Witwatersrand (1970–78); Edr. Journal of Modern Jewish Studies. Publ.: Modern Hebrew Drama (1979); The Writing of Yehuda Amichai (1989); Hebrew in Three Months (1993, repr. 1998); Drama and Ideology in Modern Israel (1998); Ed.: Essays in Honour of Salo Rappaport (1985); The Blackwell Companion to Jewish Culture (1989); Jewish Education and Learning (1994, with T. Parfitt); Tradition and Trauma (1995, with D. Patterson); The Oxford Book of Hebrew Short Stories (1996); The Experienced Soul: Studies in Amichai (1997); Modern Jewish Mythologies (2000). Ad.: Oriental Institute, Pusey Lane, Oxford OX1 2LE. ☎ 01865-278 200. Fax 01865-278 190. E-mail glenda.abramson@stx.ox.ac.uk.

ABSE, Dannie, FRSL, MRCS, LRCP; b. Cardiff, Sept. 22, 1923; writer (poems and novels) and physician. Ad.: Green Hollows, Craig-yr-Eos Rd., Ogmore by-Sea, Glamorgan.

ABSE, Leo; b. Cardiff, Apr. 22, 1917; Solicitor; V. President Inst. for Study and

Treatment of Delinquency (1998-); form. M.P. (Lab.) for Torfaen (1983-87), Pontypool (1958-83). Sponsor or co-sponsor of Private Member's Acts relating to divorce, homosexuality, family planning, legitimacy, widow's damages, industrial injuries, congenital disabilities and relief from forfeiture; sponsored Children's Bill (1973), later taken over by Govt to become Children's Act (1975); sponsored Divorce Bill (1983), later taken over by Govt to become Matrimonial and Family Proceedings Act (1985); initiated first Commons debates on genetic engineering, Windscale, in vitro pregnancies. P. Nat. C. for the Divorced and Separated (1974-92); Member of C. Univ. of Wales (1981-87); Ord. of Brilliant Star (China) (1988). Publ.: Private Member: a psychoanalytically oriented study of contemporary politics (1973); (contrib.) In Vitro Fertilisation: past, present and future (1986); Margaret, daughter of Beatrice: a psychobiography of Margaret Thatcher (1989); Wotan my enemy (1994) (awarded JQ Literary prize for non-fiction, etc. 1994); Fellatio, Masochism, Politics and Love (2000); Tony Blair: The Man Behind the Smile (2001). Ad.: 54 Strand-on-the-Green, W4 3PD. ☎ 020-8994 1166. Fax 020-8742 0032.

ABULAFIA, David Samuel Harvard, MA, PhD, Litt.D, FRHistS; b. Twickenham, Dec. 12, 1949; m. Anna née Sapir; Historian; Prof., Mediterranean History, Cambridge; Fellow, Gonville & Caius College (1974-). Publ.: The Two Italies (1977); Italy, Sicily and the Mediterranean (1987); Frederick II (1988); Commerce and Conquest in the Mediterranean (1993); A Mediterranean Emporium (1994); The French Descent into Renaissance Italy (ed.) (1995); En las Costas del Mediterráneo occidental (ed.) (1998); Cambridge Medieval History, vol. 5, 1198-1300 (ed.) (1999); The Western Mediterranean Kingdoms (1997); Mediterranean Encounters (2000); Medieval Frontiers (ed.) (2002). Ad.: Gonville & Caius College, Cambridge CB2 1TA. ☎ 01233-332473. Email dsa1000@hermes.cam.ac.uk.

ALDERMAN, Geoffrey, MA, D.Phil (Oxon), FRHistS, FRSA, FICPO, MIQA, MIMgt; b. Hampton Court, Middx., Feb. 10, 1944, m. Marion née Freed; Pro.-V.-C. & Prof. Middlesex University (1994–); form. Prof of Politics & Contemporary History, Royal Holloway Coll. (Lond. Univ.), Senior Associate, Oxford Hebrew Centre; Publ.: British Elections: Myth and Reality, The Railway Interest, The Jewish Vote in Great Britain since 1945, The Jewish Community in British Politics, Pressure Groups and Government in Britain, Modern Britain 1700-1983, The Federation of Synagogues 1887-1987, London Jewry & London Politics, 1889-1986; Modern British Jewry. Ad.: 172 Colindeep Lane, London NW9.

ALONY, Dayan Zalman Joseph, b. Penza, Russia, Oct. 10, 1915; Emer.Rosh Beth Din. Fed. of Syns., Lond; form. Dayan, Jewish Coms., Ireland; Chairman, Shechita. Kashrus Cttee., Eire; President, Assn of Jewish Clergy and Teachers. Publ.: Degel Yosef on Law and Ethics (1949), etc.

ALVAREZ, Alfred, MA (Oxon), Hon. D.Litt (East London); b. London, Aug. 5, 1929; poet, author and critic; Hon. Fell. Corpus Christi College, Oxford; poetry critic and editor, The Observer (1956-66), Gauss Seminarian, Princeton Univ. (1958); Vis. Prof., Brandeis Univ. (1960-61), State Univ. of NY, Buffalo (1966). Publ.: The Shaping Spirit, The School of Donne, Under Pressure, Beyond All This Fiddle, Beckett, The Savage God (lit.crit.); Life after Marriage, The Biggest Game in Town, Offshore, Feeding the Rat, Rain Forest, Night, Where Did It All Go Right?, Poker: Bets, Bluffs and Bad Beats (non-fiction); Lost, Apparition, Penguin Modern Poets 18, Autumn to Autumn (poems); New and Selected Poems; Hers, Hunt, Day of Atonement (novels); The New Poetry, Faber Book of Modern European Poetry (anthologies). Ad.: c/o Gillon Aitken Associates, 29 Fernshaw Rd., SW10 0TG. ☎ 020-7351 3594. Fax 020-7376 3594.

AMIAS, Rev. Saul, MBE; b. London, Mar. 9, 1907; M. Emer. Edgware Syn.; Fdr.,

H. Princ., Rosh Pinah Jewish Primary Schs.; Fdr. & President, Jewish Assn. of Cultural Socs.; Life President, Ajex Edgw. Br.: Member, BoD, AJA, JMC, Nat. C. for Soviet Jewry, CCJ, President, CCJ Edgw. Br. V. President Nat. Peace C.; V. President, United Nats. Assn., Edgw. & Stanmore Br.; Emer. Brigade Chaplain, Jewish Lads' & Girls' Bde.; Chaplain, Royal Masonic Hospital; form. Chaplain to Forces, broadcaster; form. President, Union of Anglo-Jewish Preachers. Ad.: 34 Mowbray Rd., Edgware, Middx. HA8 8JQ. ☎ 020-8958 9969.

ANDERSON, Michael John Howard, MA (Oxon.), MEd(L'pool), Dip. Soc. Work (B'ham), CQSW; b. Sheffield, May 7, 1948; Form. Dir., Manchester Jewish Soc. Services (1986-91); Sec. Regional Jewish Welfare Fed.; Head, Soc. Work Courses, Manch. Poly. (1985-87); Sr. Lect., Social Work. L'pool Poly. (1977-85). Ad.: 31 Woodland Loop, Edgewater, Western Australia 6027.

APPLE, Rabbi Raymond, AM, RFD, MLitt, BA, LLB; b. Melbourne, Dec. 27, 1935; Sr. Rabbi, Great Syn., Sydney (1972-); Sr. Rabbi. Australian Defence Force; Dayan, Sydney Beth Din; H.V. President, New South Wales Bd. of Jewish Educ.; Jt. Master Mandelbaum House, Sydney Univ.; Lect. in Judaic Studies, Sydney Univ.; Lect., Jewish Law, NSW Univ.; President, Assn. of Rabbis & Mins. of Australia & New Zealand (1980-84; 1988-1992); Jt.P., Australian Council of Christians & Jews (1996-); President, Australian Jewish Hist. Soc.(1985-89); M., Bayswater Syn. (1960-65), Hampstead Syn. (1965-1972); form. Rel. Dir., AJY. Publ.: The Hampstead Syn., 1892-1967; Making Australian Society: The Jews; Francis Lyon Cohen – the Passionate Patriot; The Jewish Way, etc. Ad.: The Great Syn., 166 Castlereagh St., Sydney 2000, N.S.W., Australia. ☎ (02) 9267 2477. Fax (02) 9264 8871. E-mail rabbi@greatsynagogue.org.au.

ARKUSH, Rabbi Shmuel; b. Birmingham May 5, 1951; Rabbi, Birmingham Jewish Community Care (2000-); Dir. Lubavitch in the Midlands; Dir. Operation Judaism; H.T. B.J.E.B. Talmud Torah; Chaplain of the Midlands Region Chaplaincy Bd. (1980-85). Ad.: 95 Willows Rd., Birmingham B12 9QF. ☎ 0121-440 6673; Fax 0121-446 4199.

AUERBACH, Mrs. Geraldine Yvonne (née Kretzmar), M.B.E., BA(Rand), STC (UCT); b. Kimberly, South Africa; Fd. Dir. Jewish Music Institute (1999-); Founding Festival Dir. Bnai Brith Jewish Music Festival (1984); Founding Chairman The Jewish Music Heritage Trust Ltd. (1989); Founder and MD Jewish Music Heritage Recordings (1984); Founder and former MD (1984-1991) Jewish Music Distribution. Ad.: PO Box 232, Harrow, Middx. HA1 2NN. ☎ 020-8909 2445. Fax 020-8909 1030. E-mail geraldine@jmi.org.uk.

AVIDAN, Rabbi Hillel, M.A.; b. London, July 16, 1933, m. Ruth; M., Bet David Reform Cong. (1992- (Johannesburg); Chairman Southern African Assoc. Progressive Rabbis (1995–99); F.M., West Central Lib. Syn. (1985-92); M. Ealing Lib. Syn. (1986-92); and Chairman, ULPS Rabbinic Conference (1990-92), form. M., Wimbledon & Distr. Ref Syn. (1974-81), Chairman, RSGB Assembly of Rabbis, (1978-80), Teacher Reali High Sch., Haifa; Libr. Haifa Univ. Publ.: Feasts and Fasts of Israel, (Contrib) Judaism & ecology; Renewing the vision. Ad.: Bet David, PO Box 78189, Sandton, 2146, South Africa. ☎ 783-7117. Fax 883-8991. Email BetDavid@icon.co.za.

BAKER, Adrienne, PhD, BSc; b. Manchester, Feb. 15, 1936; Family Therapist & University Lecturer; Senior Lect: School of Psychotherapy, Regent's College, London; Publ.: The Jewish Woman in Contemporary Society: Transitions and Traditions (1993). Ad: 16 Sheldon Ave., Highgate, London N6 4JT. ☎ 020-8340 5970 (home), 020-7487 7406 (college).

BAKER, William, BA (Hons), M.Phil, PhD, MLS; b. Shipston-on-Stour, Warwicks., July 6, 1944; Form. Housemaster, Polack's House, Clifton Coll., Lect. in English, Ben-Gurion Univ. (1971-77), Hebrew Univ., Jerusalem (1973-75); Vis. Prof., Pitzer Coll., Claremont, Ca. (1981-82); Sr. Lect., West Midlands Coll. (1978-85); Edr., George Eliot-G. H. Lewes Newsletter; Publ.: George Eliot and Judaism,

Harold Pinter (co. auth.), Some George Eliot Notebooks, Vols. I-IV, The George Eliot-G. H. Lewes Library, The libraries of G. Eliot and G. Lewes, Antony & Cleopatra. The Merchant of Venice. Ad:

BALCOMBE, Andrew David, BA (Com), MBA (Harvard); b. Adlington, Cheshire, Aug. 4, 1942; m. Jean née Steinberg; Chief Exec. of Armour Trust plc (1970-98); Chairman M@tchnet plc (1998-99); Chairman NetVest.com plc (1999-); Dir. Tecc-15 plc (2000-); Chairman, National Council for Soviet Jewry (1980-82); Founder member of Conscience interdenominational committee for the release of Soviet Jewry (1973-95); Exec. Ctte. Board of Deputies (1980-82); Mem. National Council Zionist Fed. UK (2000-); Tr. Metropolitan Charitable Fd. (1975-2002); Dep. Chairman Ben Uri Art Society (2000). Ad.: 4 Elm Walk, London NW3 7UP. ☎ 020-8455 9974. Fax 020-8209 0416. E-mail andrewbalcombe@ aol.com.

BAND, David; b. Lond., April 8, 1931; HM, Michael Sobell Sinai (Primary) Sch. (1981-90); HM, Solomon Wolfson Bayswater Jewish Sch. (1969-81); Educ. Adviser, Provincial Synagogue Hebrew Classes (under Jewish Memorial C. auspices). Ad.: 23 Woodhill Crescent, Kenton, Middx HA3 0LU.

BARAK, Ehud, MK, BSc (HU), MSc (Stanford), DSM; b. Mishmar Hasharon, 1942; Prime Minister of Israel and Minister of Defence (1999-); MK (1996-); Min. Foreign Affairs (1995-96); Chairman Israel Labour Party (1996-); formed One Israel Party (1999); Lt. General, Chief of General Staff, IDF (1991); involved in negotiations with Jordan and Peace Treaty (1994); involved in negotiations with Syria. Ad:

BARNETT, Rt. Hon. Baron of Heywood & Royton, (Life Peer) **(Joel Barnett)**, PC, JP; b. Manchester, Oct. 14, 1923, m. Lilian née Goldstone; Accountant and Chairman/Dirs. of Companies; form. V. Chairman B.B.C. Govs.; Mem. European Union Select Cttee.; Chairman European Union Sub. Cttee. on Finance, Trade & Industry; Tr. Victoria & Albert Museum; Chairman Educ. Broadcasting Society Tr.; Chairman, Public Accounts Cttee.; House of Commons (1979-83); Chief Sec. to H.M. Treasury (1974-79), Member of Cabinet (1977-79), form. Chairman, form. Mem Public Exp. Cttee., M.P (Lab.) for Heywood & Royton (1964-83); Gov., Birkbeck Coll., Lond. Univ., Fel., Centre for Study of Public Pol., Strathclyde Univ., Hon. Doctorate, Strathclyde, Member, Halle Cttee. Publ.: Inside the Treasury. Ad.: 7 Hillingdon Rd., Whitefield, Manchester, M45 7QQ; Flat 92, 24 John Islip St., SW1.

BARON COHEN, Gerald, BA, FCA; b. Lond., July 13, 1932, m. Daniella née Weiser; Chartered Acct.; President, First Lodge of England, B'nai B'rith, Nat. T., B'nai B'rith, Distr. 15, V. President Hillel Foundation; V. Chairman, U.J.S.; Edr., Mosaic; Dep. Edr., New Middle East, Chairman Bamah-Forum for Jewish Dialogue (Jewish Unity Working Group). Ad.: 70 Wildwood Rd., NW11 6UJ. ☎ 020-8458 1552. Fax 020-8455 1693.

BARRON, Rabbi Moshe, MA; b. Manchester Oct. 24, 1946; M. Richmond Synagogue; M. Bayswater and Maida Vale Synagogue (1976-84) M. South Eastern Hebrew Congregation Johannesburg; Founder Lecturer/Tutor Jewish Students University Programme Johannesburg (1972-76) Ad.: 67 Houblon Rd., Richmond, Surrey TW10 6DB. ☎ 020-8948 1977.

BAUM, Derek, MBE; b. Westcliff-on-Sea, Essex, June 9, 1927; m. Nannette née Sharpe; Ret. Co. Chairman Estate Agents/Property Developers. M. Consultant & Adv. and Exec. Cttees Chief Rabbinate C.; H. Life-President, Southend & Westcliff Hebrew Cong. (1997-); T. (1968-82); Pres. (1982-97); Pres. Southend & Distr. AJEX. (since 1966); Chairman S. & D. Jewish Rep. Council (since 1997); T. (1986-97); H. Sec. Southend & Distr. Council of Christians & Jews (1999-); V.Pres. S & D Jewish Youth Centre; V.Pres. & T. Royal British Legion (S. & D.). Chairman Bd. Govs Herzlia Day School. (1984-88); H.Sec. Nat. AJEX (1964-70); Nat. V.Chairman AJEX (1970-74); Found. AJEX Housing

Assn.; AJEX Gold Badge (1997); Chairman Southend AJEX (1960-62), (1964-66); Member BoD (1968-80) RAF (1945-48). Ad.: Flat 1, 33 Clifftown Parade, Southend-on-Sea, Essex SS1 1DL. ☎ (01702) 343789.

BAYFIELD, Rabbi Anthony Michael, MA (Cantab); b. Ilford, July 4, 1946; Chief Exec. Reform Synagogues of Great Britain; Dir. Reform Foundation Trust; Dir., Sternberg Centre for Judaism; Dir. Manor House Trust; form. Chairman, C., Ref & Lib. Rabbis; Tr., Michael Goulston Educ. Fnd., Lect., Leo Baeck Coll.; Edr., 'Manna'; Rabbi, North-West Surrey Syn. (1972-82); Chairman, Assembly of Rabbis, RSGB (1980-81). Publ.: Churban, The Murder of the Jews of Europe (1981); Dialogue with a Difference (Ed. with Marcus Braybrooke) (1992); Sinai, Law & Responsible Autonomy (1993); He Kissed Him and They Wept (Ed. with Sidney Brichto and Eugene Fisher, 2001). Ad: The Sternberg Centre for Judaism, 80, East End Road, N3 2SY. ☎ 020-8349 5645. Fax 020-8349 5699. E-mail admin@reformjudaism.org.uk.

BEECHAM, Sir Jeremy Hugh, MA, DCL, DL, H. Fellow, Northumbria University; b. Leicester, Nov. 11, 1944; m. Brenda Elizabeth née Woolf; Solicitor; Newcastle City Councillor (1967-); Leader Newcastle City Council (1977-94); Chairman, Assn. Metropolitan Auth. (1991-97); Chairman, Local Govt. Assn. (1997-); Com., English Heritage (1983-87); President, British Urban Regeneration Assn. (1996-). Ad.: 7 Collingwood Street, Newcastle upon Tyne NE1 1JE.

BELLOS, Vivienne, LRAM, ARCM; b. Southend-on-Sea, Apr. 3, 1951; Musician; Director of Music North Western Reform Synagogue; Musical Director, Zemel Choir, Alyth Choral Society, Jewish Heritage Youth Choir. ☎ 07956 912567. E-mail vivienne.bellos@btinternet.com.

BELLOW, Saul; b. Lachine, Canada, June 10, 1915; novelist; Nobel Prize for Lit. (1976); Publ.: Him with His Foot in His Mouth, The Adventures of Augie March, Henderson the Rain King, Herzog, Mr. Sammler's Planet, Humboldt's Gift, To Jerusalem and Back, The Dean's December, The Victim, Mosby's Memoirs and other stories, Ravelstein, etc. Ad.: University Professors, Boston University, 745 Commonwealth Ave., Boston, MA 02215, USA.

BENADY, S., CBE, QC, MA (Cantab); b. Gibraltar, May 21, 1905; barrister; Life President (President, 1956-73) Gibraltar Jewish Com.; Fd. & L.President Gibraltar Oxford & Cambridge Assoc.; Leader, Gib. Bar; Sqdn.-Leader; RAF, Second World War. Ad.: 124 Main St., Gibraltar. ☎ 78549.

BENARROCH, Rev. Halfon, BA; b. Tangiers, Apr. 12, 1939; m. Delia née Sabah; Minister; M. Bevis Marks; Senior Hazan; Spanish & Portuguese Jews' Cong. Ad.: 23 Lauderdale Tower, Barbican, London EC2Y 8DY. ☎ 020-7638 5100. Email broch@onetel.net.uk.

BENEDICTUS, David Henry, BA (Oxon); b. London, Sept. 16, 1938; Author, playwright, theatre dir., Ed. Readings BBC Radio (1989-94) plus Radio 3 Drama from 1992; Commissioning Ed., Channel 4 (1984-86); Judith E. Wilson Vis. Fell., Cambridge Univ. (1981-82); Producer 'Something Understood' (with Mark Tully); Berkoff's Macbeth for BBC Radio 4. Publ.: The Fourth of June, You're a Big Boy Now, This Animal is Mischievous, Hump, or Bone by Bone Alive, The Guru and the Golf Club, A World of Windows, The Rabbi's Wife, Junk, A Twentieth Century Man, The Antique Collector's Guide, Lloyd George, Whose Life is it Anyway?, Who Killed the Prince Consort?, Local Hero, The Essential London Guide, Floating Down to Camelot, The Streets of London, The Absolutely Essential London Guide, Little Sir Nicholas, The Odyssey of a Scientist, Sunny Intervals and Showers, The Stamp Collector, How to Cope when the Money Runs Out, Poets for Pleasure (audio books). Ad.: 95D Talfourd Rd., London SE15 5NN.

BENZIMRA, Maurice; b. Gibraltar, Feb. 21, 1928; Form. Sec., Spanish and Portuguese Jews. Cong., London. Ad.: 119 Poynter House, St. Anne's Rd., W11 4TB. ☎ 020-8603 3255.

BERCOW, John, BA, MP; b. Edgware, Jan. 19, 1963; Public Affairs Consultant; MP for Buckingham; Lambeth Councillor (1986-90); Special Adviser to Treasury Ministers (1995), to National Heritage Secretary (1995-96). Ad.: House of Commons, SW1A 0AA. ☎ 020-7219 3000.

van den BERGH, Rabbi Martin, B.Ed., M.A.; b. Hilversum, Holland, Dec. 2, 1952; M. Wembley Synagogue; Senior Hospital Chaplain Visitation Cttee (1995-); Hon. Sec. Rabbinical Council of the U.S.; Memb. Chief Rabbi's Cabinet; form. M., Withington Cong., Span. & Port. Jews, Manchester; Tr., S. Manch. Teenage Centre; Chairman Manchester Jewish Visitation Board, (1990-94); Asst. M., Withington Cong. (1974-77), Sheffield United Hebrew Cong. (1977-78) Fdr. Chairman & H. President, Span. & Port. Cong., Israel (1981-83). Ad.: Wembley Synagogue, Forty Lane, Wembley HA9 8JW. ☎ 020-8904 7407.

BERKOVITCH, Rev. Mordechai, BA (Ed), Dip. Counselling, FIBA; b. Sunderland, Feb. 15, 1934; Dir., Jewish Studies, Carmel Coll. (1984-92); H. Vis. M., Nightingale House (Home for Aged Jews); M., Kingston, Surbiton & Distr. Syn. (1972-84); Hon. Dir. Welfare Chief Rabbi's Cabinet (1980-1985), Penylan Syn., Cardiff (1968-72), Central Syn., Birmingham (1956-68). Ad.: 2/2 Harosmarin, Gilo, Jerusalem 93758. ☎ 026764 341. Fax 026768 169. E-mail motisali@012.net.il.

BERKOVITS, Rabbi Berel, LLB; b. London, June 3, 1949; (1990-); Dayan of Federation of Synagogues, form. Registrar Lond. Beth Din; Lect., Law Dept., Buckingham Univ. (1977-83). Publ.: Commentary of Ramban on Torah, Vols. 2-4 (Edr. & Translator), Talmud Torah, Oxford Dictionary of Law (Contrib.). Pesach in the Modern Home. Ad.: 65 Watford Way, NW4 3AQ. ☎ 020-8202 2263.

BINSTOCK, Dayan Ivan Alan, BSc; b. London, Oct. 27, 1950; Dayan London Beth Din; Rabbi, St. Johns Wood Syn. (1996-); form. Rabbi, Golders Green Syn.; Princ. North West London Jewish Day School; M. New Syn. (1978-80), Finsbury Pk Syn. (1974-78), R. South-east London Distr. Syn. (1972-74). Ad.: 2 Vale Close, Maida Vale, London W9 1RR. ☎/Fax 020-7289 6229.

BIRAN, Mrs. Jane, JP, BA, MIPM (née Dillon); b. Lond., Sept. 10, 1938, m. Yoav Biran; Dep. Dir, Overseas Dev. Dept., Dir. U.K. Desk Jerusalem Fd.; form. Dir., Bipac; form. Edr., Zionist Year Book; V. President, Brit. Na'amat; Publ.: Anglo-Jewry An Analysis; Effectiveness of Fringe Benefits in Industry, The Violent Society (contrib.). Ad.: The Jerusalem Foundation, 11 Rivka St., Jerusalem 91012. ☎ 02 675 1706.

BIRK, Ellis Samuel, BA (Cantab); b. Newcastle upon Tyne, Oct. 30, 1915; form. Solicitor; V.P. Jewish Care; Gov., Hebrew Univ., Exec., Frs. of Hebrew Univ; Member C., IJPR; Jt. President, Redbridge Jewish Youth and Com. Centre. Ad.: Flat 1, 34 Bryanston Sq., London W1H 7LQ. ☎ 020-7402 4532.

BLACK, Gerald David, LLB, PhD, FRHistS; b. Montreal, Jan 9, 1928; m. Anita, née Abrahams; Chairman Balfour Society for Children (1964-); Member of Council of JHSE (1992-), President (1998-2000), Hon. Sec. (2000-); Tr. of London Museum of Jewish Life and Jewish Museum (1983-). Publ.: Lender to the Lords, Giver to the Poor (1992); Living up West: Jewish Life in London's West End (1994); JFS: The History of the Jews' Free School (1997), Lord Rothschild and the Barber (2000). Ad.: 54 St. Johns Ct., Finchley Rd., London NW3 6LE. ☎ 020-7624 8320. Fax 020-7372 9015. E-mail gblack4455@aol.com.

BLANK, Sir (Maurice) Victor, MA (Oxon), HonFRCOG, CIMgt; b. Manchester, 1942; m. Sylvia Helen née Richford; Company Chairman; Chairman GUS plc, Trinity Mirror plc; Deputy Chairman Coats plc; Non-Exec. Dir. Chubb plc; Mem. C. University of Oxford; Chairman Industrial Development Advisory Bd.; Chairman, WellBeing (RCOG Health Research Charity); Mem. Israel Britain Business C.; Gov. Tel Aviv University; Chairman, Bd. Dir. UJS/Hillel; Mem Bd.,

UJIA. Publ. Weinberg and Blank on Takeovers and Mergers. Ad.: GUS plc, One Stanhope Gate, London W1K 1AF. ☎ 020-7318 6209. Fax 020-7318 6233.

BLASHKI, Arnold Roy, OBE, AMM, BA, LLB (Melb); b. St. Kilda, May 26 1918; Barrister-at-Law, State P. and Nat. President, Australian Legion of Ex-Servicemen; form. H. Sec., Victorian Jewish BoD, H. Sec. Victorian Branch AJA; President, Mt. Scopus Coll. Assn.; form T. Australian Legion of Ex-Service Men and Women; form. H. Sec., Exec. C. of Australian Jewry; Fed P, Victorian Jew Ex-Service Assn.; Chairman Australian Veterans and Services Assoc. (Victims). Ad.: 44A Clendon Rd., Toorak, Vic. 3181. ☎ 03 98221694.

BLOM-COOPER, Sir Louis, QC, Dr. Jur. (Amsterdam), LLB (Lond); Hon. D. Litt. (Loughborough), Hon. D. Litt. (Ulster), Hon. D. Litt (UEA); b. London, March 27, 1926; Judge, Courts of Appeal, Jersey & Guernsey (1989-96); Chairman, Mental Health Act Commission (1987-94); Independent Commissioner for the Holding Centres (NI) (1993-2000); National Chairman Victim Support (1994-97). Ad.: 1 Southgate Road, London N1 3JP. ☎ 020-7704 1514. Fax 020-7226 5457. E-mail blomcoopers@aol.com.

BLUE, Rabbi Lionel, OBE, BA, MA, DU (Oxon); b. London, Feb. 6, 1930; Lect., Leo Baeck Coll., form. Convener Beth Din, RSGB; Hon. V. President RSGB; V. Chairman, Standing Conference Jews, Christians, Moslems in Europe, form. Rel. Dir. (Europe) World Union for Progressive Judaism; Chairman Assembly of Rabbis RSGB, M., St George's Settlement Syn., Middlesex New Syn. Templeton Prize 1993. Publ.: Funeral Service, Forms of Prayer, Vol. I Daily and Sabbath Prayer Book (co-ed.); Vol. III, Days of Awe Prayer Book (co-ed.); Vol.II Shavuoth, Passover & Succoth (co-ed.); To Heaven with Scribes and Pharisees; Bright Blue, A Backdoor to Heaven; Kitchen Blues, Bolts from the Blue, Blue Heaven; The Blue Guide to the Here and Hereafter (co-auth), Blue Horizons; Bedside Manna: How to get up when life gets you down (co-auth.); Tales of body and soul; My affair with Christianity. Ad: c/o Leo Baeck College, Sternberg Centre, 80 East End Rd., London N3 2SY.

BLUMENFELD, Jeffery, OBE, BA (Hons), MA; b. London, Dec. 1949; Hd. Jewish Studies, Deputy Hd. Rosh Pinah Primary School (2000-); Director, Jewish Marriage C. (1984-2002) Mem. Govt. Adv. Gp., Marriage and Relationship Support (1997-2002); Chairman Chief Rabbi's Steering Group on Social and Moral Education (1994-); Act-Chairman JMC Legal Group (1993-); form. Dir. US Youth & Com Services Dept.; Edr., Resources Bulletin, Sch. Assemblies C. (1978-80). Ad.: 41 Holders Hill Crescent, London NW4 1NE. ☎ 020-8203 1458. Email blumen@dircon.co.uk.

BLUMENFELD, Simon; b. London, Nov. 25, 1907; author and journalist. Publ.: Jew Boy, Phineas Kahn, Doctor of the Lost, etc. Ad.

BOGDANOR, Vernon, MA, FBA, CBE, FRSA; b. London, July 16, 1943; Academic; Professor of Government, Oxford University; Hon. Fell. Society for Advanced Legal Studies. Publ.: Devolution in the United Kingdom (1999); The Monarchy and the Constitution (1995); The People and the Party System (1981). Ad.: Brasenose College, Oxford, OX1 4AD. ☎ 01845 277830. Fax. 01865 277822.

BONDI, Sir Hermann, KCB, MA, FRS; b. Vienna Nov. 1, 1919; Master, Churchill Coll., Cambridge (1983-90); Chairman, Natural Environment Res. C. (1980-84), Chief Scientist Dept of Energy (1977-80); Chief Scientific Adv., Min. of Defence (1971-77); form Dir.-Gen. European Space Research Org.; Prof. of Applied Maths, King's Coll., Lond. Univ., form. Chairman, Nat. Cttee for Astronomy; form. Sec., Royal Astronomical Soc., (1956-64); President, IMA (1974-75), President, Brit Humanist Assn. (since 1982); G. D. Birla International Award for Humanism, New Delhi, 1990. Publ.: Scientific works, Science Churchill and Me (autobiography). Ad.: Churchill College, Cambridge CB3 0DS.

BOWER, Marcus H., MA, LLM (Cantab); b. Belfast, Aug. 22, 1918; Barrister; Chairman, Leo Baeck College (1992-96); V. Chairman, European Board of World Union for Progressive Judaism (1990-96); Chairman RSGB (1987-90); form. Dir., Northern Engineering Industries plc.; Dir., Port of Tyne Auth. Chairman, Northern Counties Inst. of Dirs., Mem. Gov. Body, Newcastle Univ.; Mem. BBC Regional Adv. Council; Ad.: 14 Camelot Cl., SW19 7EA. ☎ 020-8947 5173.

BRICHTO, Rabbi Sidney, MA, DD; b. Philadelphia, July 21, 1936; Sr. V. President ULPS, Chairman Adv. Com. Israel Diaspora Tr; Bd. Dir. IJPR; Vis. Lect. and Gov. Oxford Centre for Hebrew & Jewish Studies; Hon. Sec. European J. Publ. Soc.; form. Exec. V. President & Dir. ULPS (1964-89); form. Chairman, C. of Ref. and Lib. Rabbis; M., Lib. Jewish Syn. (1961-64). Translator for The People's Bible: Genesis, Samuel I & II, etc. Publ. Funny You Don't Look Jewish: Guide to Jews and Jewish Life (1994); Ritual Slaughter: Growing Up Jewish in America (2001), etc. Ad.: ULPS, 21 Maple Street, London W1T 4BE. ☎ 020-7580 1663.

BRICKMAN, Rev. Stanley Ivan, b. London, March 29, 1939; Cantor, Hampstead Synagogue (1987-); Chairman Assn. of Ministers (Chazanim); London Regional V. President, Cantorial Council of America (1994-); Cantor: Gt. Synagogue, Sheffield (1960-65); Ilford Synagogue (1966-69); New London Synagogue (1969-71); Singers Hill Synagogue, Birmingham (1971-83); Great Synagogue, Cape Town (1983-86); Publ.: Friday evening service with Zemirot for children (Birmingham 1976); Recording; Synagogue Liturgy Music with Singers Hill Choir, 1981. Ad.: 9 Marlborough Mans., Cannon Hill, Hampstead, London NW6 1JP. ☎ 020-7431 0575.

BRIER, Norma, BA(Hons), MSc, CQSW; b. London, Dec. 23, 1949; Chief Exec. Norwood (1997-); Exec. Dir. Ravenswood Foundation (1989-96); Dir. of Com. Services – Ravenswood and Jewish Society for Mental Handicap (1985); Lect. in Soc. and Soc. Work/Counselling (Harrow College) (1982); Psychiatric Soc. Worker (1972); Soc. Worker (Camden) (1968). Ad.: Norwood, Broadway House, 80-82 The Broadway, Stanmore, Middx HA7 4HB. ☎ 020-8954 4555. Fax 020-8420 6800.

BRIER, Sam, PhD, MA; b. London, July 19, 1946; Chief Exec., KIDS; form. Exec. Dir. (Resources), Norwood Ravenswood. Ad.: KIDS, 6 Aztec Row, Berners Road, London N1 0PW. ☎ 020-7359 3635. Fax 020-7359 8238. Email s.brier@kids-online.org.uk.

BRITTAN, Baron, PC, QC, MA (Cantab), Hon. DCL, Newcastle, Durham, Hon. LLD, Hull, Edinburgh, Bradford, Bath, D.Econ., Korea; b. London, Sept. 25, 1939; Vice-President Commissioner of the European Communities (1989-); MP (Con) for Cleveland and Whitby (1974-83); MP (Con) for Richmond, North Yorkshire (1983-88); Vice-Chairman, Employment Cttee. of Parl. Conservative Party (1974-76); Minister of State, Home Office (1979-81); Chief Sec. to the T. (1981-83); Home Sec. (1983-85); Sec. of State for Trade and Industry (1985-86); President, Cambridge Union (1960); Chairman, Bow Group (1964-65); Editor of Crossbow (1966-67); Distinguished Visiting Fellow at Policy Studies Instit. (1988); Bencher of the Inner Temple (1983). Publ.: The Conservative Opportunity (contributions), Millstones for the Sixties (jointly), Rough Justice, Infancy and the Law, How to Save your Schools, A New Deal for Health Care (1988), Defence and Arms Control in a Changing Era (1988), Europe: Our Sort of Community (1989 Granada Guildhall Lecture), Discussions on Policy (1989), Monetary Union: the issues and the impact (1989), Hersch Lauterpacht Memorial Lectures, University of Cambridge (1990), European Competition Policy (1992), Europe: the Europe we need (1994), The 1997 Rede Lecture. Ad.: Commission des Communautés Européens, rue de la Loi 200, 1049 Brussels, Belgium.

BROCH, Mrs. Hazel (née Rubinstein); b. Dublin, Jan. 29, 1936; H. Life V.

President (form. P.) Leeds Jewish Rep. C.; H.V. President, Tzfia Goren Emunah; Fdr. Chairman, Leeds Ladies Com. Chevra Kadisha (Chairman 1996/7); HLP Leeds Joint Chevra Kadisha; HLP Yorkshire and Humberside Chaplaincy Board; Northern Jewish woman of the year 1989. Ad.: 48/8 Shlomo Hamelach, Netanya 42268. ☎ (09) 8342653.

BRODER, Rabbi Gavin, BA (Hons), MA (Lond.); b. Uitenhage, South Africa, April 17, 1963; Chief Rabbi of Ireland (1996-); Form. Newbury Park Syn. (1990-96), Staines Hebrew Cong. (1988-90); Governor Avigdor Primary School. Ad.: Herzog House, 1 Zion Rd., Rathgar, Dublin 6. ☎ 4923751. Fax 4924680.

BRODIE, Rev. Gabriel, b. Bratislava, July 7, 1924; M., Manchester Great & New Syn.; Sec. Manch. Yeshiva; Chairman Jerusalem Academy Study Gps.; Hon. Chaplain Jewish Meals on Wheels, 45 Aid Society. Ad.: 43 Stanley Rd., Salford M7 4FR. ☎ 0161-740 2506.

BRODIE, Jeffrey, BA (Hons); b. Manchester, Oct. 3, 1950; Admin., Manch Kashrus Authority; Registrar, Manch. Beth Din; Tr., Keren L'David Educ. Tr. Ad.: 56 Stanley Rd., Salford, 7.

BROOKES, Kenneth Joseph Alban, Eur.Ing., BSc (Eng) Met., C. Eng., FIM, FCIJ; b. London, Aug. 5, 1928; Technical Consultant, Author & Journalist; Past-P., Chartered Inst. of Journalists; Vice Chairman, CI of J, Freelance Div.; News Edr., Internat. Journal of Refractory Metals and Hard Materials; Editor, CIoJ International; Consultant Edr., Metal Powder Report; UK Edr., Metal Times. Publ.: World Directory and Handbook of Hardmetals and other Hard Materials etc. Ad.: 33 Oakhurst Ave., East Barnet, Herts. EN4 8DN. ☎ 020-8368 4997. Fax 020-8368 4997. Email kenbrookes@interearb.org.

BROWN, Malcolm Denis, MA; b. Fulwood, March 24, 1936; m. Barbara née Langford; Research historian; Chairman, Exec. Cttee and V. President JHSE (1999-), President (1996-98); form. Asst. Keeper of Manuscripts, British Museum; Archivist, Anglo-Jewish Archives (1965-66); Asst. ed. Jnl of Warburg and Courtauld Insts (1962-64); Lect. Extra-Mural Dept., Univ. of London (1969-81). Publ.: David Salomons House: Catalogues of Mementoes, Commemorative Medals and Ballooniana (1968, 1969 and 1970). Ad.: c/o The Jewish Historical Society of England, 33 Seymour Place, London W1H 5AP. ☎ 020-7723 5852. E-mail jhse@dircon.co.uk.

BROWN, Rabbi Dr. Solomon, OBE, BA, PhD, HCF; b. London, 1921; Sr M., (Ret.) United Heb Cong., Leeds, M., Hornsey and Wood Green Syn. (1943-47); HM, Redmans Rd. Talmud Torah (1942-47); Sr Jewish Chaplain in Germany, Austria and Trieste (1947-50). Publ.: Waters of Life. Ad.: Donisthorpe Hall, Shadwell Lane, Leeds LS17. ☎ 0113 2685320.

BULL, John, JP, DL, Commandeur de l'Ordre National du Mérite; b. London, Nov. 8, 1927, m. Helene née Baran; Antique Dealer; Lord Mayor, City of Westminster (1984-85), form. Councillor (1971-2002); V. President, Chairman, Trades Adv. C.; V. President, North London C.F.I. (1976); B.o.D; Freeman, City of London; Fel., Instit. Dirs.; Gen. C. of Income Tax (1976). Ad.: 85 Mayflower Lodge, Regent's Park Rd., N3 3HX; ☎ 020-8346 6657.

BURMAN, Michael Alfred, BSc (Hons), PGCE, FRGS; b. Southport Sept. 20, 1944; m. Barbara née Schiltzer; Admin. Dir. ULPS; Chair Gov. Clore Shalom School; Gov. Akiva School; Educ. Consultant, Progressive Jewish Day Schools; OFSTED Inspector; Memb. Jewish Community Schools Adv. Board. Ad: The Montagu Centre, 21 Maple Street, London W1T 4BE. ☎ 020-7580 1663. Fax 020-7436 4184. E-mail m.burman@ulps.org.

BURMAN, Rickie Amanda, MA (Cantab), MPhil; b, Liverpool, July 5, 1955, m. Daniel Miller; Director, Jewish Museum (1995-); Curator London Museum of Jewish Life (1984-95); Res. Fell. in Jewish History; Manchester Polytechnic (1979-84); Museum Co-ord., Manchester Jewish Museum (1981-84). Publ. on history of Jewish women in England, and museum studies. Ad.: The Jewish

Museum, Raymond Burton House, 129-131 Albert St., London NW1 7NB. ☎ 020-7284 1997. Fax 020-7267-9008.

BURTON, Raymond Montague, CBE, MA (Cantab), FRSA, D. Univ. York; b. Leeds, 1917; P. Burton Group, p.l.c. (1978-84), Jt. President Jewish Museum; V. President, Weizmann Instit Foundation; C., CCJ; Master Worshipful Comp. of Loriners (1976); Major, R.A. (1945). Ad.: c/o Trustee Management Ltd., 19 Cookridge St., Leeds LS2 3AG.

CALLMAN, His Honour, Clive Vernon, BSc (Econ); b. June 21, 1927; Circuit Judge, South-Eastern Circuit (1973-2000), Dep. High Court Judge, Royal Courts of Justice (1975-2000); Dir. Frank Cass & Co. Ltd; Dir. Vallentine Mitchell & Co. Ltd.; Senator, London Univ. (1978-94), Gov. Council (1994-); Member Careers Adv. Bd. (1979-92), Gov., Birkbeck Coll. (1982-2001); Gov. LSE (1990-), C., AJA (1956); BoD (1998); Gov. Hebrew Univ. of Jerusalem (since 1992); Court City Univ. (1991-), C., West London Syn. (1981-87); Member, Adv. Cttee. for Magistrates' Courses (1979-); Edr. Bd., Media Law & Practice (1980-95); Professional Negligence (1985); Journal of Child Law (1988-94), Child and Family Law Q. (1995-); Exec., Soc. of Labour Lawyers (1958), Chairman, St Marylebone Lab. Party (1960-62). Ad.: 11 Constable Close, NW11 6UA. ☎ 020-8458 3010.

CANNON, Raymond; b. London. Nov. 13, 1933; Solicitor; First Chairman, US Educ. Bd.; form. Chairman, Govs., J.F.S. Comprehensive Sch.; form. T., US Burial Soc.; V.Chairman, Lond. Bd. Jew Rel. Educ., Foundation Chairman, Govs. Michael Sobell Sinai Sch., Chairman, Govs. Solomon Wolfson Jewish Sch; Gov., llford Primary Sch. Ad.: 2 Harewood Pl., Hanover Sq. W1R 9HB. ☎ 020-7629 7991. Fax 020-7499 6792.

CANSINO, H. Manuel, MBE; b. Manchester, July 12, 1914; V. President, London Bd. of Shechita; V. P. Bd. Elders, Span. and Port. Cong.; C. AJA, C., Jewish Lads' & Girls' Brigade; C., Adv. Cttee., Jew Eccl. Officers; C., Jew Autistic Soc. Ad.: 117a Hamilton Terr., NW8 9QU. ☎ 020-7624 5050.

CAPLAN, Leonard, QC; b. Merthyr Tydfil, June 28, 1909; Master of Bench, Gray's Inn; T., Gray's Inn (1979); Member, Senate of Inns of Court and Bar (1976-82); Sometime Dep. High Court Judge, President, Medico-Legal Soc. (1979-81); Chairman, Coll Hall (Univ. of London) (1956-67); C., AJA; form. Chairman, Mental Health Review Tribunal, S.E. Region. Publ.: The Great Experiment. Ad.: 1 Pump Court, Temple, E.C.4. ☎ 020-7353 9332.

CAPLAN, The Hon. Lord (Philip Isaac), QC, LLD (Hon) (Glasgow), FRPS, AFIAP; b. Glasgow, Feb. 24, 1929, m. Joyce née Stone; Senator of the College of Justice, Scotland (1989-2000); Sheriff Princ., North Strathclyde (1983-1989); Member, Sheriff Courts Rules C. (1983-1989) Memb. Advi. Coun. on Messengers-At-Arms, and Sheriff Officers (1987-88); Com., Northern Lighthouse Bd. (1983-1989); Hon. V. President, Scottish Assn. for Study of Delinquency; Hon. President, Family Mediation Scotland (1994-); Sheriff, Lothian & Borders, Edinburgh (1979-83); V. President, Sheriffs' Assn. (1982-83); Chairman, Plant Variety & Seeds Tribunal (Scotland) (1978-79). Chairman James Powell, U.K. Trust, (1992-); Gov. UK College of Family Mediators (1996-). Ad.: Court of Session, Parliament House, Edinburgh.

CAPLAN, Simon, MA (Oxon), PGCE; b. Hamburg (Brit. Army Hospital), Apr. 28, 1955; Community Consultant; Jerusalem Fellow (1990-93); Dir., Jews' College (1985-90); Dir., Jewish Educ. Development Tr. (1985-90); Jerusalem Fellow (1990-93); Adv. to Ashdown Trust (1994); Res. Fellow, Carmel Institute (1999-2002); Director, Westbury Research Unit (2002-). Ad.: Rehov Zeev Bacher 10/9, Jerusalem 93119.

CAPLIN, Ivor Keith, MP; b. Brighton, Nov. 8, 1958, m. Maureen née Whelan; MP for Hove & Portslade (1997-); PPS (1998-2001); Govt. Whip (2001-); Leader, Hove B.C. (1995-97); Dep. Leader Brighton & Hove UA (1996-98). Ad.: House of Commons, SW1 1AA. ☎ 020-7219 2146, or 01273 292933 (constituency).

CAPLIN, Maxwell, OBE, FRCP; b. Lond., Feb. 6, 1917, m. Nancy née Leverson; Ret. Consultant Physician; Lond Chest Hospital (1983); Consultant in Occupational Health, Royal Brompton Nat. Heart and Lung Hospitals and Nat. Heart & Lung Instit. (1983-1991); Honorary Senior Lecturer, Univ. of Lond. (1979-83); Consultant Member Lond. Medical Appeal Tribunal (1977-89); Medical Referee Dept. of Health (1979-90); Chairman Lond. N E Cttee. for Employment of Disabled People (1980-86); Patron, form. Chairman, later President, Greater Lond. Assn. of Disabled People (1982-89). Other professional and vol. offices. Publs: Medical Writings. Ad: 498 Finchley Rd, NW11 8DE. ☎ 020-8455 3314.

CARLEBACH, Rabbi Felix F., MA; b. Lübeck, Apr. 15, 1911; form. M., S. Manchester Syn, (1946-86); Dep. to HM, Jew Secondary Sch, Leipzig (1933-39); Asst. M. Adass Yisroel Syn., Hendon (1939-41); M&HM, Palmers Green and Southgate Syn. (1941-46). Ad: 2A Elm Rd., Manchester, 20. ☎ 0161-445 5716.

CARLOWE, Melvyn, OBE, B.Soc. Sci. (Hons); b. Abingdon, Oxon., April 13, 1941; form. Chief Exec. Jewish Care (1990-2000); form. Chief Exec. Jewish Welfare Board (1972-89); form. Hon. Sec. Central Council for Jewish Communal Service (1972-2000); Tr. Third Sector Trust, North London Hospice, Institute of Jewish Policy Research, National Council of Voluntary Organisations, Jewish Community Ombudsman Service, Jewish Chronicle Trust; mem. Beacon Selection Panel for the office of Deputy Prime Minister (2000-); mem. King's Fund Inquiry on Care Workers (2000-2). ☎/Fax 020-8364 6686. Email karlatsky@aol.com (Melvyn Carlowe).

CARTER, Emmanuel, B.Com., FCCA, FTII; b. London, May 18, 1925; Elder US form. V. President, US; Exec., Chief Rabbinate C.; Financial Adv. Chief Rabbi; Dir. US Trs. Ltd; Fel., Chartered Assn.; Certified Accts., form. Lect., Accounting, LSE. Ad.: 37 Deansway, N2 ONF. ☎ 020-8883 7759. Fax 020-8883 9983.

CASS, Frank, b. London, July 11, 1930, m. Audrey née Steele; Publisher; Chairman, Vallentine Mitchell; Chairman, Frank Cass & Co. Ltd.; Chairman of British Jerusalem Book Fair Committee (1979-); Friends of Jerusalem Award (1989). Ad.: Crown House, 47 Chase Side, Southgate, London N14 5BP. ☎ 020-8920 2100. Fax 020-8447 8548. E-mail info@frankcass.com.

CESARANI, David, D.Phil; b. London, Nov. 13, 1956; Prof. Modern Jewish History and Dir. AHRB Parkes Centre for the Study of Jewish/non-Jewish Relations, University of Southampton (2000-); Dr., Inst. of Contemporary History and Wiener Library (1993-95, 1996-2000); Parkes-Wiener Prof. of 20th Century Jewish History and Culture (1996-2000); Alliance Prof. of Modern J. Studies, Univ. Manchester (1995-96); Montague Burton Fel. in Jewish Studies, Univ. of Leeds, (1983-86); Barnett Shine Senior Res. Fel., Queen Mary College, Univ. of London, (1986-89). Publ.: ed. Making of Modern Anglo-Jewry (1990); Justice Delayed (1992); co-ed. The Internment of Aliens in Twentieth Century Britain (1993); ed. The Final Solution (1994); The Jewish Chronicle and Anglo Jewry, 1841-1991 (1994); co-ed. Citizenship, Nationality and Migration in Europe (1996); ed. 'Lest We Forget', CD-ROM Interactive History of the Holocaust; ed. Genocide and Rescue: the Holocaust in Hungary 1944 (1997); Arthur Koestler: the homeless mind (1998); Bystanders at the Holocaust (co.ed. 2002). Ad.: History Dept., University of Southampton, Highfield, Southampton SO17 1BJ.

CHARING, Rabbi Douglas Stephen; b. London, Nov. 16, 1945; Dir., Jewish Educ. Bureau, Leeds; Tutor, Geneva Theological Coll., Adv., Theol. & Rel. Studies Bd., Dir. Concord MultiFaith/Multi-Cultural Res. Centre (Leeds), Inter-Euro. Com. on Church & Sch, form. Gov. Centre for Study of Rel. & Educ. (Salford); Vis. Lect. Northern Ordination College; M., Sinai Syn., Leeds; Vis. Rabbi, Bradford Syn.; C. for Nat. Academic Awards; Lect., Leeds Univ., Manchester Police Coll.

Member Brd. of Dir. British Friends of the Anne Frank Centre; Exec. M. Coun. for Religious Freedom; Publ.: Glimpses of Jewish Leeds; Comparative Religions (co-auth.), The Jewish World Visiting a Synagogue, Modern Judaism (audio-visual), Jewish Contrib., The Junior R.E. Handbook, World Faiths in Education, Praying Their Faith (contributor), Religion in Leeds (contributor), A Dictionary of Religious Education In the Beginning (Audiovisual), The Torah, etc. Ad.: 8 Westcombe Ave., Leeds LS8 2BS. ☎ 0870 787 1876. Fax 0870 787 1875. E-mail charing@ cwctv.net.

CHERNETT, Jaclyn, ALCM, MPhil; b. St. Neots, June 16, 1941; m. Brian Chernett; Dir. Masorti Assoc. (1984-86); Co-chairman, Assembly of Masorti Synagogues (1992-95); Hon. Life President, Edgware Masorti Synagogue; Vice President Assembly of Masorti Synagogues; V. President, World Council of Synagogues. Publ.: Conference papers. Ad.: 4 Brockley Close, Stanmore, Middx. HA7 4QL. ☎ 020-8958 5090. Fax 020-8958 7651. E-mail jaclyn.chernett@ virgin.net.

CHEYETTE, Bryan, PhD; b. Leicester, Jan. 15, 1959; m. Susan Cooklin; Prof. Twentieth Century Literature, Univ. Southampton (1999-); form. Reader in English Literature, School of English and Drama, Queen Mary and Westfield College, University of London (1992-99); British Academy Postdoctoral Fellow, School of English, University of Leeds (1989-92); Montague Burton Fellow in Jewish Studies, School of English, University of Leeds (1986-89); editorial board, Jewish Quarterly and Patterns of Prejudice. Publ. Constructions of 'the Jew' in English Literature and Society: Racial Representations, 1875-1945 (1993); (editor), Between 'Race' and Culture: Representations of 'the Jew' in English and American Literature (1996); (editor), H. G. Wells, 'Tono-Bungay' (1997); published widely on British-Jewish Literature. Ad.: Dept of English, Univ. Southampton, Highfield, Southampton SO17 1BJ. ☎ 023-80593409. Fax 023-80592859. E-mail bhc@soton.ac.uk.

CHINN, Sir Trevor, CVO; b. London, July 24, 1935; President, Lex Service PLC; P., UJIA; President Norwood; V.Pres., Jewish Assoc. for Business Ethics; Hon.V. President RSGB; Hon.V. President, Z. Fed.; Dep. Ch., Royal Academy Trust; Tr., Community Security Tr. Ad.: 17 Connaught Pl., London W2 2EL. ☎ 020-7705 1212. Fax 020-7723 5501.

CLINTON-DAVIS, Baron of Hackney (Life Peer), (**Stanley Clinton Clinton-Davis**), PC, LLB; b. London, Dec. 6, 1928; Solicitor; Min. State for Trade (1997-98); Pres. British Airline Pilots' Assoc. (BALPA); M.P. (Lab.), Hackney Central (1970-83); Parl. Under Sec. for Companies, Aviation and Shipping, Dept. of Trade (1974-79); Cllr., Hackney Bor. (1959-71), Mayor (1968-69); President, Assoc. of the Metropolitan Authorities (1992); President, UK Pilots (Marine) (1991-98); Honorary Member of the Council of Justice (1989-); Order of Leopold II for Services to EC, 1990; Fel. of Queen Mary and Westfield College and King's College, London Univ.; H. D., Polytechnical Univ. of Bucharest (1993); Fel. of the Royal Society of Arts (1993). Publ., Good Neighbours? Nicaragua, Central America and the United States (jt. auth.). Ad.: House of Lords, London SW1A 1AA. ☎ 020-7533 2222. Fax 020-7533 2000.

COCKS, Lady Valerie (née Davis); b. London, July 10, 1932; Dir., Labour Friends of Israel and Trade Union Friends of Israel (1978-88); Chairman Parliamentary Wives for Soviet Jewry; Hon. Sec. All-Party Friends of Israel Group (H of Lords). Ad.: 162 South Block, County Hall, London SE1 7GE. ☎ 020-7787 2539.

COFNAS, Rabbi Mordechai Leib; b. Birmingham, Dec. 9, 1943; Senior Rabbi, Liverpool, Rabbi, Childwall Syn., Liverpool; Princ. L'pool Yeshiva & Midrasha; Rav, L'pool Kashrut Comm.; form. Chairman Rabbinical Council of the Provinces; form. Sr. M., Cardiff United Syn.; M., Sunderland Hebrew Cong. Ad.: Childwall Synagogue, Dunbabin Rd., Liverpool, L15 6XL. ☎ 0151-722 2079.

COHEN, Arnold Judah, FCA, ATII; b. London, Dec. 17, 1936; m. Sara née Kaminski; Chartered Accountant; Life President, form. President, Fed. of Synagogues (1989-2001); form. Tr. Fed. of Synagogues. Publ.: An Introduction to Jewish Civil Law (1991). Ad.: 807 Finchley Rd., NW11 8DP. ☎ 020-8458 2720. ☎ 020-8458 2720.

COHEN, (Bernard) Martin; b. London, Jan. 31, 1933; Administrator, Lobbyist; Chairman, Jewish Defence & Group Relations Cttee., BoD (1991-94); form. Member, United Synagogue Council; Harrow Councillor (1962-68, 1971-80); Chairman, Public Works & Services Cttee. (1971-74); Gen. Sec., Labour Friends of Israel (1972-80); V. Chairman, Jewish Defence & Group Relations Cttee. (1988-91). Ad.: 486 Kenton Road, Kenton, Harrow, Middlesex HA3 9DL. ☎ 020-8204 6300.

COHEN, David Mayer, LL B, CA, MBA; b. Glasgow, April 18, 1949; m. Smadar née Karni; Company Director, Technology Services; Chairman UJIA Bd. (2000-). Ad.: Flat 9, 32 Onslow Square, London SW7 3NS. ☎ 020-7584 9066. E-mail davidcohen@ps.net.

COHEN, Rabbi Isaac, BA, PhD; b. Llanelli, 1914; Chief Rabbi, Jewish Coms. in Ireland and Ab Beth Din (1958-79) now engaged in research in Talmudic law in Jerusalem; Jt. P. Union of Immigrant Western Rabbis; President, Frs., Hesder Yeshiva, Shiloh, Member of Standing Cttee., Conf of European Rabbis, and Exec. of Israel Assoc. for the Conference; Edr., Irish Jewish Year Book; Rabbi, Edinburgh Hebrew Cong.; M., United Hebrew Cong. Leeds; Harrow & Kenton Cong; and Off. Chaplain to HM Forces. Ad.: 1 Epstein St., Kiryat Ha Yovel, Jerusalem, 96664. ☎ 02-6412536.

COHEN, Isaac Norman, MBE, BA, BCom, BSc (Econ); b. Cardiff, Oct. 30 1924, m. Naomi née Cohen; Tr. Machzike Hadath Comm.; form. Sr. W., Penylan Syn., Cardiff; Member, Chief Rabbinate C.; Gov. Body, Univ. of Wales; form. Chairman, Cardiff JIA Cttee. Ad.: 17 Riverside Drive, 300 Golders Green Rd., London NW11 9PU. ☎ 020-8 381 4305. Fax 020-8381 4302.

COHEN, Rabbi Jeffrey M., BA, MPhil, AJC, PhD; b. Manchester, Feb. 19, 1940; m. Gloria née Goldberg, M., Stanmore & Canon's Pk. Syn.; Chief Examiner, Mod. Hebrew, Jt. Matric Bd. (1973-1987), Lect., Liturg. Studies, Jews' Coll. (1980-1992), Rabbinical Adv. and Gov., Immanuel College; member, Chief Rabbi's cabinet, Chaplain to Mayor of Harrow (1994-95); Scholar-in-Residence, U.S.A. (1998); form. M. Kenton Syn.; Sr. M., Newton Mearns Syn., Glasgow; Lect. in Hebrew, Glasg. Univ., Princ. Glasg. Heb Coll., Dir. Glasg. Bd. of Jewish Educ.; Dir., Jew Educ., King David Schs., Manchester; Member, Rev. Cttee., Singers Prayer Bk; Publ.: Understanding The Synagogue Service, A Samaritan Chronicle, Festival Adventure, Understanding the High Holyday Services, Yizkor, Horizons of Jewish Prayer, Moments of Insight, Blessed Are You, (Contrib. ed., Judaism section) Penguin Encyclopedia of Religions, Prayer & Penitence, Dear Chief Rabbi (ed.); 1001 Questions on Pesach, Following the Synagogue Service, 1001 Questions and Answers on Rosh Hashanah and Yom Kippur, Issues of the Day, Abridged Haggadah for Rusty Readers, Let My People Go: Insights into Pesach and the Haggadah; The Bedside Companion for Jewish Patients. Ad.: Stanmore & Canon's Pk. Synagogue, London Rd., Stanmore, Middx. HA7 4NS. ☎ 020-8954 2210. Fax 020-8385 7124. E-mail jeffrey@eurobell.co.uk.

COHEN, Joseph, BA; b. London Oct. 1, 1920; Exec. Dir., Brit. Technion Soc. (1957-1986); Chairman Friends of Bikur Cholim Hospital, Jerusalem. Ad.: 10 Leeside Cres., NW11 0DB. ☎ 020-8455 0738.

COHEN, Laurence Jonathan, MA, D.Litt, FBA; b. London, May 7, 1923; m. Gillian née Slee; Emeritus Fel., form. Fel, and Sr Tutor, Queen's Coll., Oxford; form. Brit. Academy Reader in Humanities, Oxford (1982–84), Radcliffe Fell. (1971–73); form. Vis. Prof., Columbia, Yale, Northwestern Univs.; form. Vis. Lect., Hebrew Univ.; form. Vis. Fel. Australian Nat. Univ.; Corr. Mem. Hellenic

Society for Philosophical St. (1975-); Hon. Prof. North-West Univ. Xian, China (1987-); form. President, Internat. Union of History and Philos. of Science; Sec. General, Int. Council of Scientific Unions (1993-96); form. President, British Soc for Philos. of Science. Publ: Principles of World Citizenship; Diversity of Meaning; The Implications of Induction; The Probable and the Provable; The Dialogue of Reason; Introduction to the Philosophy of Induction and Probability; An Essay on Belief and Acceptance; Knowledge and Language, etc.; articles in learned journals. Ad.: Queen's Coll., Oxford, OX1 4AW. ☎ 01865 279120.

COHEN, The Hon. Leonard Harold Lionel, OBE, MA (Oxon.); b. London, Jan. 1, 1922; m. Eleanor née Henriques; Barrister-at-Law; form. Chairman Jewish Chronicle Trust Ltd (1995-2000); Bencher of Lincoln's Inn; Fell. Royal Free Hospital School of Medicine (1998-); High Sheriff, Berks. (1986-87); Dir.-Gen. Accepting Houses Cttee. (1976-82); Chairman, Community Trust for Berkshire (1988-94); form. President, JWB (1961-66) and JCA Charitable Foundation (1976-92); form. Master, Skinners Company; form. H. Colonel 39th (City of London) Signals Regiment (Volunteers); Chairman, C., Royal Free Hospital Med. Sch. (1982-92). Ad.: Dovecote House, Swallowfield Pk., Reading, RG7 ITG. ☎ 01189-884775.

COHEN, Marion (née Mendelssohn), BA (Hons), MPhil; b. Prestwich, Lancs., May 8, 1945; m. David J. Cohen; form. Chairman, Jewish Book Council (1992-2002); Chairman, Friends of Hillel Lecture Committee (1988-91); Tr. Jewish Literary Trust; Co-admin. Jewish Quarterly/H. H. Wingate Literary Awards; Instigator and Admin. Porjes Award for Hebrew-English Translation. Ad.: Jewish Book Council, PO Box 20513, London NW8 6ZS. ☎/Fax 020-7483 2092. E-mail info@ jewishbookweek.org.uk. Website www.jewishbookweek.com.

COHEN, Michael, BA, MPhil, Cert. Ed.; b. Oxford, Nov. 3, 1941; Teacher Training Co-ord. (London Borough of Hackney); Educ. Consultant to Stratford College, Dublin, Tiferes Shlomo School, London, American Endowment School (Budapest), Prague Jewish Community; Consultant to Broughton Jewish Cassel Fox Primary School, Manchester (1996-98); Principal of Leibler Yavneh College, Melbourne (1993-95); form. Exec. Dir. United Synagogue Bd of Religious Education, London (1980-92); form. Headmaster Mount Scopus Memorial College, Melbourne (1975-80); form. Dir. Jewish Studies, North-West London Jewish Day School (1969-75). Ad.: 50 Princes Park Ave., NW11 0JT ☎ 020-8458 4537. Fax 020-8201 9396.

COHEN, Lieut-Colonel Mordaunt, TD, DL, FRSA; b. Sunderland, Aug. 6, 1916; Solicitor; Reg. Chairman, Industrial Tribunals (1976-89); Chairman (1974-76); Dep. Lieut., Tyne & Wear; Chairman, Provincial Cttee., BoD (1985-91); H. Dir., Central Enquiry Desk (1990-2000), BoD (1964-); H. Life President, Sunderland Hebrew Cong. (1988-); form. Member, Chief Rabbinate C., Tr. Ajex Charitable Tr.; Tr. AJEX Charitable Foundation; V. President, and Nat. Chairman AJEX (1993-95); Chairman Edgware School (1991-96); H. Life President, Sunderland Ajex; Tr. Colwyn Bay Synagogue Trust, Alderman Sunderland Co. Borough C. (1967-74); Cllr., Tyne & Wear County C. (1973-74), Chairman Sund. Educ. Cttee. (1970-72), Ch. Govs., Sund. Polytechnic (1969-72), Court, Newcastle upon Tyne Univ. (1968-72); Chairman, Mental Health Review Tribunal (1967-76); Dep. Chairman, Northern Traffic Coms. (1972-74), President, Sund. Law Soc. (1970); War service, RA (1940-46) (dispatches, Burma campaign), TA (1947-55), CO 463 (M) HAA Regt. (1954-55); Territorial Decoration (1954). Ad.: 1, Peters Lodge, 2 Stonegrove, Edgware, Middlesex HA8 7TY .

COHEN, Mrs Ruth (née Goodman); b. London, July 11, 1936; Pres. World Union for Progressive Judaism; V. Pres. (form. chairman) Reform Synagogues of Great Britain. Ad.: 80 East End Rd., London N3 2SY. ☎ 020-8349 4731. Fax 020-8343 0901. E-mail shalva43@ aol.com.

COHEN, Shimon David; b. Cardiff, May 24, 1960; CEO Bell Pottinger Public Relations Ltd; Dir. Jewish Chronicle Newspaper Ltd; Dir. IJPR; FRSA; Mem. IPR; Mem. BAFTA; form. Senior Cons. Bell Pottinger Consultants (1990-2000); form. Dir. Andrew Lloyd Webber's office (1995–97); form. Exec. Dir. Office of the Chief Rabbi (1983-90); form. Youth Officer, Stanmore Syn. (1981-83); Jewish Youth Leader of the Year (1979). Ad.: 20-22 Stukeley St., London WC2B 5LR. ☎ 020-7430 2276. Fax 020-7405 6812. E-mail scohen@bell-pottinger.co.uk.

COHEN, Sydney, CBE, MD, PhD, FRC Path, FRS; b. Johannesburg, S. Africa, Sept. 18, 1921; Emer. Prof, Chemical Pathology, Guy's Hospital Med. Sch.; H. Consultant, Chemical Pathologist, Guy's Hospital; Chairman, Malaria Immunology Cttee., WHO (1978-83); Med. Res. C. (1974-76); Chairman, Tropical Med. Res. Bd. (1974-76). Publ.: Immunology of Parasitic Infections. Ad.: 11, Knole Wood, Ascot, SL5 9QR.

COHEN, Mrs. Zina (née Masie); b. London; form. Chairman Shechita Cttee., BoD (1986-91); Central Enquiry Desk, BoD. (1981-). Ad.: Jewish Community Information, Board of Deputies. ☎ 020-7543 5421/2.

COHN, Norman, MA (Oxon), D.Litt (Glas), FBA. b. London, Jan. 12, 1915, m. Vera Broido; Prof., Sussex Univ., and Dir., Columbus Centre (1966-80), form. Prof of French, Univ. of Durham. Publ.: The Pursuit of the Millennium, Warrant for Genocide, Europe's Inner Demons, Cosmos, chaos and the world to come, Noah's Flood. Ad.: Orchard Cottage, Wood End, Ardeley, Herts. SG2 7AZ. ☎ 01438 869247.

COHN-SHERBOK, Dan, BA, BHL, MA, MLitt, PhD(Cantab), DD; b. Denver, Col., Feb. 1, 1945; Prof. Judaism, Univ. Wales (Lampeter) (1997-); Form. Rabbi in synagogues in the USA, England, S. Africa, Australia (1971-75); University Lect. in Theology, Univ. of Kent (1975-); Chairman, Dept. of Theology, Univ. of Kent (1980-2); Vis. Prof., Univ. of Essex (1993-94); Vis. Prof. Univ. Middlesex (1994-), Lampeter (1994-96), Vilnius (2000). Publ.: The Jews of Canterbury (1984); Jewish Petitionary Prayer (1989); Rabbinic Perspectives on the New Testament (1990); Issues in Contemporary Judaism (1990); Islam in a World of Diverse Faiths (ed.) (1990); The Salman Rushdie Controversy in Interreligious Perspective (ed.) (1990); Tradition and Unity: Essays in Honour of Robert Runcie (ed.) (1991); A Traditional Quest: Essays in Honour of Louis Jacobs (ed.) (1991); Dictionary of Judaism and Christianity (1991); The Blackwell Dictionary of Judaica (1992); Israel: The History of an Idea (1992); The Crucified Jew: Twenty Centuries of Christian Anti-Semitism (1992); Atlas of Jewish History (1993); Judaism and other Faiths (1994); Jewish and Christian Mysticism (1995); Beyond Death (ed.) (1995); A Short History of Judaism (1995); Jewish Mysticism (1995); A Popular Dictionary of Judaism (1995); Modern Judaism (1996); The Hebrew Bible (1996); Fifty Key Jewish Thinkers (1996); Medieval Jewish Philosophy (1996); The Jewish Messiah (1997); A Concise Encyclopaedia of Judaism (1998); Jews, Christians and Religious Pluralism (1999); The Future of Jewish-Christian Dialogue (ed.); Understanding the Holocaust (1999); The Future of Religion, ed. (2000); Messianic Judaism (2000); Wisdom of Judaism (2000); The Palestine–Israeli Conflict (2001); Interfaith Theology (2001); Holocaust Theology: A Reader (2001), etc. Ad.: Dept. of Theology and Religious Studies, Dept. of Theology and Religious Studies, Lampeter SA48 7ED. ☎ 01570 424708.

COLEMAN, Rabbi Dr Shalom, CBE, MA, BLitt, PhD, JP, AM (Order of Australia), Hon. LLD (Univ. W. Australia); b. Liverpool, Dec. 5, 1918; Rabbi Emer., Perth Hebrew Cong., H. Life President, Assn. of Rabbis & Mins. of Australian & N. Zealand; H. President, Maimonides Coll., Toronto, form. M. South Head Syn., Sydney; United Heb Inst., Bloemfontein. Publ.: Hosea Concepts in Midrash and Talmud, What Every Jew Should Know, What is a Jewish Home? What is a

Synagogue? Life is a Corridor (An Autobiography) 1992; etc. Ad.: Unit 1, 72 Spencer Ave., Yokine, Western Australia 6060. ☎ 618-9375 3222; E-mail scoleman@iinet.net.au.

COLLINS, John Morris, MA (Oxon); b. Leeds, June 25, 1931; Barrister and Head of Chambers (1966-2002); HL V. President, Leeds Jewish Rep. C. (form. P., 1986-89); Crown Courts Recorder (1980-98); Dep. Circuit Judge (1970-80); Called to the Bar, Middle Temple (1956); past P. Leeds Lodge, B'nai B'rith; BoD (1971-93); President, Beth Hamedrash Hagadol Syn., Leeds (1992-95). Publ.: Summary Justice (1963). Ad.: 14 Sandhill Oval, Leeds, LS17 8EA. ☎ 0113 2686008.

COLLINS, Kenneth Edward, Dr MBChB, MRCGP, MPhil, PhD; b. Glasgow, Dec. 23, 1947; Chairman Scottish Council of Jewish Communities; Chairman: Scottish Jewish Archives Cttee., Glasgow Bd. of Jewish Educ. (1989-93); President Glasgow Jewish Rep. C. (1995-98); Chairman Glasgow Yeshiva. Publ.: Aspects of Scottish Jewry (ed.) (1987); Go and Learn (1988); Second City Jewry (1990); Glasgow Jewry (1994); Scotland's Jews (1999); Be Well: Jewish Immigrant Health and Welfare in Glasgow (2001). Ad.: 3 Glenburn Road, Giffnock, Glasgow G46 6RE. ☎ 0141-638 7462.

CONNICK, (Harold) Ivor, LLB; b. London, Jan. 25, 1927; Consultant, Dir., Land Securities plc (1987-98), and A. Beckman plc (1990-98); V. P. Brit. ORT; Chairman, Central Board World ORT Union (1993-2000); Pres. Westminster Syn. (1990-2000); Board JIA (1985-93); Chairman, Professions Div., JIA (1979-83); Dep. Chairman UDS Group PLC (1983), Director (1975-83). Ad.: 54 Fairacres, Roehampton La., SW15 5LY. ☎ 020-8876 7188. Fax 020-8878 6198.

COOPER, Rabbi Chaim Joshua, MA, PhD; b. London, Aug. 9, 1912; Rabbi Emet. Hull Hebrew Cong; form. Com. Rabbi, Hull; Chief M., Adelaide Hebrew Cong. (1958-59); M., Kingsbury Distr. Syn. (1951-57). Ad.: 36 Parkfield Dr., Hull, HU3 6TB. ☎ 01482-561180.

COPISAROW, Sir Alcon Charles; b. St. Annes-on-Sea, Lancs., June 25, 1920; Council IJPR and AJA; Lieut. Royal Navy (1943-47); Min. of Defence (1947-54), British Embassy, Paris (1954-60); Chief Scientific Officer, Min. of Technology (1964-66), Senior Partner McKinsey and Co Inc. (1966-76); Subsequently: Chairman Tr., The Prince's Youth Business Trust; Tr. The Eden Project; Tr., Duke of Edinburgh's Award; C. Royal Jubilee Trusts; Eden Trust; Press Council, Gov., Benenden School; Dep. Chairman G. English Speaking Union; Patron, Conseil National des Ingénieurs et des Scientifiques de France; Chairman & Man. Tr., The Athenaeum; form. Chairman Humanitarian Trust of Hebrew Univ. Ad.: 25 Launceston Place, London W8 5RN.

CORNEY, Hyam, BA (Hons); b. Lond., May 20, 1938; Deputy Edr, Jewish Chronicle (1991-2002); form. Foreign edr. Home News edr. Exec. Dir., Publ. Rel., Israel & Foreign Affairs Cttees., BoD; Lond. Corres 'Jerusalem Post'; Edr., 'Jewish Observer & Middle East Review', Information Dir., JNF Ad.: Netanya, Israel.

COROB, Sidney, DSc Tech (hc) CBE; b. London, May 2, 1928; Chairman, Corob Holdings Ltd.; Dir., EJPS; Dir. Jewish Assoc. Business Ethics; H.V. President, Frs. of the Sick; V. President Magen David Adom in Brit.; V. President CCJ; T., Westmount Housing Assn.; H.T., Westmount Charitable Tr.; V. Chairman Central C for Jewish Soc. Service; Chairman Int. Centre for Learning Potential, Jerusalem. Ad.: 62 Grosvenor St., London W1K 3JF.

CORREN, Asher, MIBM; b. Warsaw, Nov. 2, 1932; form. Director, Central C. Jewish Community Services; Tr. Richmond, the American International University in London; form. Exec. Dir. Nightingale House; form. Member of Wandsworth Health Authority; form. Member of Exec. Cttee, Alzheimer's Disease Soc.; Member of Adv. Cttee., St Wilfrid's Home for Aged, Chelsea. Email patricia.corren@virgin.net.

COSGROVE, The Honourable Lady, QC, LLB, Hon. LLD (Napier), Hon. LLD (Strathclyde), Hon. LLD (Glasgow) (née Hazel Josephine Aronson); b. Glasgow, Jan. 12, 1946; m. John A. Cosgrove; Senator of the College of Justice, Scotland; Dep. Chairman of the Boundary Commission for Scotland; Sheriff of Lothian & Borders at Edinburgh (1983-96); President Scottish Friends of Alyn; Chairman, Mental Welfare Commission for Scotland (1991-96); Mem., Parole Board for Scotland (1998-91); Sheriff of Glasgow & Strathkelvin (1979-83); Advocate, Scottish Bar (1968-79); Jr. Counsel, Dept. of Trade (1977-79); Hon. Fellow, Harris Manchester College, Oxford. Ad.: Parliament House, Edinburgh EH1 1RQ.

COSGROVE, John Allan, BDS (Glasgow); b. Carmarthen, S. Wales, Dec. 5, 1943; m. The Honourable Lady Cosgrove (Hazel Aronson); Dental Surgeon; President Edinburgh Hebrew Congregation (1986-90), currently Hon. V. President; Chairman Edinburgh Hillel Cttee; Co-opted Mem. Scottish Council of Jewish Communities; regular contributor Thought for the Day, BBC Radio Scotland; Scottish representative Chief Rabbinate selection committee (1989-91). Ad.: 14 Gordon Terrace, Edinburgh EH16 5QR. ☎ 0131-667 8955. Fax 0131-667 6684. E-mail john_cosgrove@blueyonder.co.uk.

COWEN, The Rt Hon. Sir Zelman, PC, AK, GCMG, GCVO KStJ, GCOMRI (Italy); QC, BA, LLM (Melbourne), MA, DCL (Oxon), LLD Hon. (HK, Queensland, Melbourne, Australian Nat Univ, West Australia, Tasmania, Turin, Victoria Univ. Technology), D.Litt Hon. (New England, Sydney, James Cook Univ of N Queensland, Oxford); DHL Hon. (Hebrew Union Coll, Cincinnati, Redlands Univ, Calif), D Univ Hon. (Newcastle, Griffith Univ), Southern Cross (Queensland), PhD Hon. (Hebrew Univ, Jerusalem, Tel Aviv Univ); b. Melbourne, Oct. 7, 1919; m. Anna née Wittner; Chairman Australian National Academy of Music (1995-2000); Nat. President, Australia-Brit. Assn. (1993-95); P. Order of Australia Association (1992-95); Dir., Sir Robert Menzies Memorial Foundation (Aus.) Ltd. (1991-); Hon. Professor Griffith Univ., Queensland (1991-); Professorial Assoc., Univ. of Melbourne (1990-); Member Bd. of Gov. Weizmann Inst. (1990-); Provost, Oriel Coll., Oxford (1982-90); Pro-V. Chancellor, Univ. of Oxford (1988-90); Tr. Winston Churchill Memorial Tr. (UK) (1987-89); Lee Kuan Yew Distinguished Visitor Singapore (1987); Sir Robert Menzies Memorial Tr. (UK) (1984-); Gov.-Gen. of Australia (1977-82), V. Chancellor Queensland Univ. (1970-77); V. Chancellor, New England Univ., NSW (1967-70); H. Fellowships at Oxford, Dublin, Univ. of New England, Univ. Qld, Australian Nat. Univ.; H. Master of Bench, Gray's Inn; Academic Gov., Bd. of Govs., Hebrew Univ., Tel Aviv Univ.; Chairman, Australian V. Chancellors' Cttee. (1977). Knight, Order of Australia; Knight Grand Cross, Order of St Michael and St. George; Knight Grand Cross, Royal Victorian Order; Assoc. Knight, Order of St. John; Knight Grand Cross Order of Merit of Italian Republic, Knight Bachelor. Publ.: Dicey Conflict of Laws; (with P. B. Carter) Essays in the Law of Evidence; (with L. Zines) Federal Jurisdiction in Australia; (with D. M. da Costa) Matrimonial Causes Jurisdiction; The British Commonwealth of Nations in a Changing World; Isaac Isaacs; Individual Liberty and the Law; The Virginia Lectures, Reflections on Medicine, Biotechnology and the Law; A Touch of Healing; Australia and the United States: Some Legal Comparisons; American-Australian Private International Law; The Private Man (ABC Boyer Lectures); etc. Ad.: 4 Treasury Place, East Melbourne, Victoria 3002, Australia. ☎ 61-3-96500299. Fax 61-3-96500301.

CRAFT, Maurice, BSc (Econ) PhD, D.Litt; b. London, May 4, 1932; Emer. Prof., Univ. Nottingham; Visiting Prof. of Education, Goldsmiths Coll., Univ. London (1997-2002); Res. Prof of Education, Univ. Greenwich (1993-97). Foundation Dean of Humanities & Social Science, Hong Kong Univ. of Science and Technology (1989-93); Prof of Educ. Nottingham Univ. (Dean of Faculty of

Education, and Pro-Vice-Chancellor) (1980-89); Goldsmiths' Prof of Educ., London Univ. (1976-80); Prof of Educ., La Trobe Univ., Melbourne (1974-75), Sr. Lect. in Educ., Exeter Univ (1967-73); Publ. include: Teacher Education in Plural Societies (Edr.); Ethnic Relations and Schooling (Jt. Edr.); Change in Teacher Education (Jt. Edr.); Education and Cultural Pluralism (Edr.); Teaching in a Multicultural Society: the Task for Teacher Education (Edr.); Linking Home and School (Jt. Edr.); Ad.: Dept. of Educational Studies, Goldsmiths' College, New Cross, London SE14 6NW. ☎/Fax 020-8852 7611.

CREEGER, Morton. b. Luton, Beds., Sept 22, 1941; Partner Zangwills Charity and Fundraising Consultants (2000-); Dir. Brit. ORT (1973-85); form. Dir. Ronson Foundation (1985-95); Governor, Charles Kalms Henry Ronson Immanuel College (1990-95); Governor, King Solomon High School, Redbridge (1991-); Dir. King Solomon High School, Redbridge Ltd (1993-97); Vice-Chairman, and Non-Exec. Director, Camden and Islington Community Services NHS Trust (1992-95); Council Member, Association for Research into Stammering in Childhood (1994-97); Fellow, Institute of Charity Fund-raising Managers (1994-). Ad.: Zangwills, 1st Floor, 18 North End Rd., London NW11 7PH. ☎ 020-8958 1917. Fax 020-7935 7257.

CREWE, Ivor Martin, D.Litt (Salford); b. Manchester, Dec. 15, 1945; Univ. teacher; Vice-Chancellor (1995-), Pro V. Chancellor (Academic) (1992-95) Univ. of Essex; Prof. of Government, Univ. of Essex; Hon. Fell. Exeter College, Oxford; Memb. Exec. Cttee and UK Council, Universities UK; Dir. SSRC Data Archive (1974-82); Ed./co-ed. British Journal of Political Science (1977-82, 1984-92); Chairman, Dept. of Govemment (1985-89). Publ.: Survey of Higher Civil Service (HMSO 1969) (with A. H. Halsey), Decade of Dealignment (CUP 1983) (with Bo Särlvik); SDP: The Birth, Life and Death of the Social Democratic Party (with Tony King), etc. Ad.: Vice Chancellor's Office, Univ. of Essex, Colchester, Essex CO4 3SQ.

CRIVAN, Harry Edward, MBE, BSc; FEIS; b. Edinburgh, Nov. 9, 1907; Member C. Langside College, Glasgow (1991-94), President, Glasgow Jewish Rep. C. (1971-74); Co.-Chairman, CCJ, Scotland (1979-85); Ex. Comm. Scottish Refugee C.; T., Scottish C. for Racial Equality (since 1982); Exec., Strathclyde Com. Rel. C. (since 1973); President, Scottish Rtd. Teachers' Assn. (since 1979); C., Strathclyde Univ. Graduates Assn. (since 1978). Publ.: Casting of Steel, Iron & Steel for Operatives (Consulting Edr.). Ad.: Flat 5, Homeglen House, Maryville Ave., Giffnock, Glasgow, G46 7NF. ☎ 0141-638 8153.

CUTLER, Rabbi Shlomo, b. Liverpool, Dec. 21, 1927; form. Rav. Kol Yakov, Edgware (1997-2001); M., Mill Hill Syn. (1959-93); form. M., Luton Syn. Ad.: 38 Selvage Lane, NW7. ☎ 020-8959 6131.

DAICHES, David, CBE, MA (Edin), MA and D.Phil (Oxon), Docteur h.c. (Sorbonne), D.Litt (Edin., Sussex, Glasgow), D. Univ. (Stirling), Dottore ad honorem (Bologna), etc.; b. Sunderland, Sept. 2, 1912; Dir., Instit. for Advanced Studies in the Humanities, Edinburgh Univ. (1980-86); Prof of Eng., Univ. of Sussex (1961-77); Dean of School of Eng. and Amer. Studies, Univ. of Sussex (1961-68); form. Lect. in English, Univ. of Cambridge, and Fellow of Jesus Coll.; form. Prof of English, Cornell Univ.; form. Fellow of Balliol Coll., Oxford; Second Sec. British Embassy, Washington (1944-46). Publ.: The Authorised Version of the Bible, a study of its origins and sources, A Study of Literature, Robert Burns, Literary Essays, Two Worlds, Milton, A Critical History of English Literature, Was: a Pastime from Time Past, Moses, Glasgow, Edinburgh, God and the Poets, A Weekly Scotsman and other poems, etc. Ad.: 22 Belgrave Crescent, Edinburgh EH4 3AL.

DAN, David, PhD; b. Bucarest, May 23, 1929; m. Gabriela née Fleischman; Company Director; Chairman, Photome International plc (1992-); Man. Dir. Dedem Automaticas RL, Italy (1962-92); Man. Dir. Fomalto, Israel (1961-62);

Art/Press Photography (1953-60). Ad.: Photome, Church Road, Bookham, Surrey KT23 3EU. ☎ 0778 522 3761. Email ddavid@dedem.com.

DANGOOR, Naim Eliahou, BSc (London); b. Baghdad, 1914; Company Chairman; editor and publisher – The Scribe, Journal of Babylonian Jewry; Fd. Exilarch's Foundation. Ad.: 4 Carlos Place, London W1K 3AW.

DAVIDSON, Lionel, b. Hull, Mar. 31, 1922; author. Publ.: The Night of Wenceslas, The Rose of Tibet, A Long Way to Shiloh, Making Good Again, Smith's Gazelle, The Sun Chemist, The Chelsea Murders, Under Plum Lake, Kolymsky Heights. Ad: c/o Curtis Brown Ltd., 28-29 Haymarket, London SW1Y 4SP.

DAVIS, Sydney, OBE; b. London, Nov. 8, 1921; Vice President, Ajex; form. Nat. Chairman, Ajex; form. Gen. Sec., Ajex; form. Gen. Sec. Ajex Charitable Trust; Tr. Ajex 1984 Trust; Nat. Exec, C.C.J. Ad.: Ajex House, East Bank, N16 SRT. ☎ 020-8800 2844.

DEECH, Dame Ruth Lynn (née Fraenkel), DBE, MA (Oxon), MA (Brandeis); Barrister; b. London, April 29, 1943, m. Dr John Deech; Principal, St Anne's College, Oxford; Mem. European Academy of Sciences and the Arts; Chairman, UK Human Fertilisation & Embryology Authority (1994-2002); Pro-Vice Chancellor, Oxford University (2001); Lecturer in Law, Oxford University (1970–91); Member, Commission on the Representation of the Interests of the British Jewish Community (1998-2000); Governor, UJIA (1997-99); Governor, Oxford Centre for Hebrew and Jewish Studies (1994-2000); Chairman, Stuart Young Foundation Academic Panel (1991-); Senior Proctor, Oxford University (1985-86); Vice-Principal, St Anne's College (1988-91); Non-executive Director, Oxon Health Authority (1993-94); Governor, Carmel College (1980-90); Member, Committee of Inquiry into Equal Opportunities on the Bar Vocational Course (1993-94); Hon. Bencher, Inner Temple (1996); Rhodes Trustee (1996). Ad.: St Anne's College, Oxford, OX2 6HS. ☎ 01865 274800. Fax 01865 274895.

DEMMY, Lawrence, MBE; b. Manchester, Nov. 7, 1931; Comp. Dir. C. Internat. Skating Union. Ad.: Oak Cottage, 112 Beverley Rd., Kirkella, Hull. ☎ 01482 650232.

DIAMOND, Aubrey Lionel, LLM, DCL, QC; b. London, Dec. 28, 1923; Solicitor, H. Fel., Lond. Sch. of Economics; H. Fel., Queen Mary and Westfield Coll.; Hon. DCL, City Univ., Hon. MRCP, Prof. of Law Notre Dame Univ. (1988-99, now Emer.); Dir., Instit. of Advanced Legal Studies, Lond. Univ. & Prof. of Law (1976-86, now Emer.); Law Com. (1971-76); LSE (1957-66). Publ.: The Consumer, Society and the Law (with Lord Borrie), Introduction to Hire Purchase Law, Instalment Credit (ed.) Sutton and Shannon on Contracts, 7th ed. (co-ed.), Commercial and Consumer Credit, A Review of Security Interests in Property (HMSO). Ad.: 1 Suffolk St., London SW1Y 4HG. ☎ 020-7484 7800.

DIAMOND, Rt. Hon. Baron of Gloucester (Life Peer), **(John Diamond)**, PC, FCA, LL.D. (h.c.); b. Leeds, April 30, 1907; Chartered Accountant Dep. Chairman of Cttees., House of Lords (1974); Chairman, Royal Comm. on the Distrib. of Income and Wealth (1974-79), Chairman, Industry and Parliament Trust (1976-81); Tr. SDP (1981-82); House of Lords, SDP Leader (since 1982); Leader, Parl. Del. to Israel (1984); MP for Gloucester (Lab.) (1957-70), Chief Sec., H.M. Treasury (1964-70); Privy Counsellor 1965; Member of Cabinet, (1968-70); form. M.P. for Blackley, Manchester (Lab.) (1945-51); form. Parl. Pte. Sec. to M. of Works; form Member of Gen. Nursing C. and Chairman of its Finance Cttee. (1947-53); form. Chairman, Cambridge and Bethnal Green Boys' Club; form. T., Fabian Soc.; form. Dir., Sadler's Wells Trust. Publ.: Public Expenditure in Practice. Ad.: 'Aynhoe', Doggetts Wood La., Chalfont-St.-Giles, Bucks. HP8 4TH. ☎ 01494 3229.

DJANOGLY, Jonathan Simon, MP; b. London, June 3, 1965; m. Rebecca, née Silk; Solicitor, S. J. Berwin (1990-); MP Huntingdon (2001-); form. Cllr. Westminster CC (1994-2001). Ad.: House of Commons, London SW1A 0AA.

DJANOGLY, Rabbi Saul, BA (Hons); b. London, Aug. 8, 1961; m. Anne; Dir. Sephardi Centre (1998-). Ad.: Sephardi Centre, 2 Ashworth Rd., London W9 1JY. ☎ 020-7266 3682. Fax 020-7289 5957.

DOMB, Cyril, MA, PhD (Cantab), MA (Oxon), FRS; Em. Prof. of Physics. Bar-Ilan Univ. (since 1989); Academic President, Jerusalem Coll. of Tech (1985-94); form. Prof. of Theoretical Physics, King's Coll., Lond. Univ. (1954-81); ICI Fel. Clarendon Lab., Oxford; Univ. Lect. in Maths, Cambridge; President, Assn. of Orthodox Jewish Sci. Professionals. Publ.: Scientific writings, Clerk Maxwell and Modern Science (ed.), Phase Transitions and Critical Phenomena Vols. 1-3, 5, 6 (ed. with M. S. Green), Vols. 7-20 (ed. with J. L. Lebowitz), The Critical Point (1996), Memories of Kopul Rosen (ed.), Challenge, Torah Views on Science and its problems (ed. with A. Carmell), Maaser Kesafim, Giving a Tenth to Charity (ed.). Ad.: Physics Dept., Bar-Ilan Univ., Ramat Gan, 52900, Israel. ☎ (03) 5137928. Fax (03) 5353298.

DOMB, Risa, PhD; b. Israel, Mar. 16, 1937; m. Richard Arnold Domb; University Lecturer; Director of the Centre for Modern Hebrew Studies, U. of Cambridge; Fell. Girton College. Publ.: The Arab in Hebrew Prose (1982); Home Thoughts from Abroad (1995); New Women's Writing from Israel (1996). Ad.: Faculty of Oriental Studies, Sidgwick Ave, Cambridge CB3 9DA.

DOVER, Dr Oskar, MB, ChB, MRCGP; b. Danzig, Oct. 31, 1929; m. Marlene née Levinson; Hon. Life Vice President, Merseyside Jewish Rep. C.; Tr., Liverpool Jew Youth & Com. Centre; form. Chairman & Foundation Gov., now Tr. King David High Sch., L'pool; form. Chairman, Harold House C. Ad.: 153 Menlove Ave., Liverpool L18 3EE.

DU PARC BRAHAM, Donald Samuel, FRGS, IRRV, ACIArb, FRSA; b. London, June 29, 1928; Lord Mayor, city of Westminster (1980-81); Master of Guild of Freeman of City of London (1989/90); Master of Worshipful Comp. of Horners (1991/1992); President, Regent's Park & Kensington North Conservative Assoc. (1996-); Chairman, London Central European Constituency C. (1988-93); Chairman, Central London Valuation Trib. (1977-); Chairman, Parkinson's Disease Soc. (1990-1991); Pat., Central London Br. Parkinson's Disease Soc. of UK; Member Nat. Exec., CCJ; Member, Bd. Man. W. Hampstead Syn.; Member, Jewish Cttee for H.M. Forces; Member, Wiener Library Endowment Appeal Cttee., Member, C. of the Anglo-Jewish Assoc.; Nepalese Order of Gorkha Dakshina Bahu. Ad.: 11 Jerusalem Passage, St. John's Sq., London EC1V 4JP.

DUNITZ, Alfred Abraham, JP, CC; b. London, May 15, 1917; form. Tr. of the Burial Soc. (1978-87); Chairman Burial Soc. (US), (1987-88); Member Exec. Hillel House, Exec. Jewish Memorial Council of AJA; Tr. Jewish Cttee. HM Forces; Chairman The Friends of Jewish Servicemen; Worshipful Company of Carmen (Livery Company); The Court of Common Council City of London; Gov. Guildhall School of Music and Drama (1990-2001); Freeman, City of London; Chairman Friends of Ramat Gan (1990-94); Exec. of the JWB (1983-85); restored Exeter Synagogue (fd. 1763) (1980); rest. Aberdeen Syn. (1982); Chairman of the House Committee of the JWB Homes at Hemel Hempstead (1978-85); Eastern Region Council of the C.B.I. (1973-76); restored and maintains disused cemeteries; recipient of Inst. of Waste Management Medal (1999). Ad.: 14 Sherwood Rd., Hendon, NW4 1AD. ☎ 020-8203 0658.

DUNITZ, Prof. Jack David, FRS, BSc, PhD (Glasgow), Hon. DSc (Technion, Haifa), Hon. DSc (Glasgow), Hon. PhD (Weizmann Instit.), b. Glasgow, March 29, 1923; m. Barbara née Steuer; Scientist and teacher; Hon. Fell. Royal Society of Chemistry; Prof. Chemical Crystallography at the Swiss Federal Inst of Technology (ETH), Zurich, Switzerland (1957-90); Member Academia Europaea, Foreign Member Royal Netherlands Acad. of Arts and Sciences, Foreign Associate, US National Academy of Science, Member Leopoldina Academy; Member Academia Scientarium Artium Europaea; Foreign Member

American Philosophical Society; Foreign Hon. Member American Academy of Arts and Sciences; numerous visiting professorships. Publ.: X-ray Analysis and the Structure of Organic Molecules (1979), Reflections on Symmetry in Chemistry ... and Elsewhere (with E. Heilbronner), (1993). Ad.: Obere Heslibachstr. 77, CH-8700 Küsnacht, Switzerland.

DUNNER, Abraham Moses, MCIJ; b. Konigsberg, Germany, Nov. 13, 1937; m. Miriam née Cohen; Sec. Gen. Community Relations, Conference of European Rabbis; Exec. Dir. Community Centres for Israel Org. (1958-60); Exec. Dir. European Union of Orthodox Hebrew Cong. (1958-60); Dir. Keren Hatorah Education Cttee (1960-71); Sec. Gen. Agudath Israel Org. of Great Britain (1967-71); Ed. Jewish Jewish Tribune (1967-71); Ed. Haderech (1962-70); Hon. Mem. Anglo-Zaire Chamber of Commerce (1987-); Mem. West African Advisory Group to the Foreign Office (1988-90); Chairman, N.W. London Police Liaison Cttee; Tr. Beth Jacobs Schools Israel (1988-); Chairman Lakewood Alumni Assn. (1995-); Bd. of Dirs. Simon Wiesenthal Centre UK (1997-); Special Adviser to the Russian Jews Congress (1998-); Cllr. London Borough of Barnet (1998-). Ad.: 87 Hodford Rd., London NW11 8NH. ☎ 020-8455 9960. Fax 020-8455 4968.

DUNNER, Rabbi Josef Hirsch; b. Cologne, Jan. 4, 1913; Rav., Adath Yisroel Syn., Rav Ab Beth Din, Union of Orthodox Hebrew Congs.; Princ., Beth Jacob Teachers' Training Seminary, form Rav., Königsberg Hebrew Cong. Ad.: 25A Schonfeld Sq., London, N16. ☎ 020-8800 3347.

DUNNER, Rabbi Pinchas Eliezer (Pini), BA Hons; b. London, Sept. 25, 1970; m. Sabine née Ackerman; M. 'The Saatchi Synagogue', Maida Vale (1998-); Asst. Rabbi, Moscow Choral Synagogue (1991-92); Rabbi, Notting Hill Synagogue (1992-93); Producer/Presenter, 'Jewish Spectrum', Spectrum Radio (1996-98). Ad.: 21 Andover Place, London NW6 5ED. ☎ 020-7625 2266. Fax: 020-7625 2277.

DUNNETT, Jack, MA, LLM (Cantab); b. Glasgow, June 24, 1922; Solicitor; MP (Lab.) for Nottingham East (1974-83), Central Nottingham (1964-74), form. PPS, Min. of Transport and Foreign Office; form. Cllr., MCC and GLC, and Ald., Enfield Borough C.; Chairman, Notts. County F.C. (1968-87); Football League Man. Cttee. (1977-89), Football Assn. (1977-89); P. Football League, (1981-86 and 1988-9); V. President Football Assn. (1988-89). Ad.: Whitehall Ct., SW1A 2EP. ☎ 020-7839 6962.

DWEK, Joseph Claude (Joe), CBE, BSc, BA, AMCT, FTI, Hon. DSc UMIST; b. Brussels, May 1, 1940; Exec. Chairman Worthington Group (1999-); Chairman, Bodycote Internat. Plc. (1972-98), Penmarric Plc; Dir. Manchester Federal School of Business & Management; Court of Manchester Univ. and UMIST; Chairman, Healthy Waterways Trust. Ad.: Suite One, Courthill House, 66 Water Lane, Wilmslow, Cheshire SK9 5AP. ☎ 01625-549081. Fax 01625-530791. E-mail penjcdwek@aol.com.

EBAN, Abba, MA (Cantab), LittD, LLD (Hon); b. Cape Town, 1915; Chairman Knesset Foreign Affairs & Defence Cttee. (1984-88); Foreign Min., State of Israel (1966-74); Dep. Prime Min. (1963-66), Educ. Min. (1960-63), P. Weizmann Inst. of Science, Rehovot (1958-66); Israeli Amb. to US (1950-59); Perm. Rep. of Israel at United Nations (1949-59); Browne Res. Fel. (Oriental Languages), Pembroke Coll., Cambridge (1938); Vis. Prof, Columbia Univ. (1974); Fel., Instit. Advanced Study, Princeton (1978). Publ.: Maze of Justice, Voice of Israel, My People, My Country; An Autobiography, The New Diplomacy, Heritage: Civilization and the Jews, etc. Ad.: Bet Berl, Kfar Sava, nr. Tel Aviv, Israel.

EHRENTREU, Dayan Chanoch; b. Frankfurt-am-Main, Dec. 27, 1932; Rosh Beth Din, Lond. Beth Din; Av Beth Din, Manchester Beth Din (1979-84); Princ., Sunderland Kolel (1960-79). Ad.: London Beth Din. ☎ 020-8343 6270. Fax 020-8343 6257.

EILON, Samuel, DSc (Eng), PhD, DIC, FIMechE, FIEE, FR Eng; b. Tel Aviv, Oct. 13, 1923; Emeritus Prof., Univ. London; form. Chief Ed., Omega, The Int Jl. of Management Science; form. Member, Monopolies and Mergers Comm.; form Prof of Man. Science, and Hd of Dept., Imperial Coll., Lond.; form. Dir. of ARC, Compari Int., Spencer Stuart and Associates; management consultant to many industrial companies; form. Assoc. Prof, Technion, Haifa. Publ.: 300 scientific papers, 16 books. Ad.: 1 Meadway Close, London NW11 7BA. ☎ 020-8458 6650.

EIMER, Rabbi Colin, BSc (Econ); b. Lond., March 8, 1945; Co. Chair Assembly of Rabbis, RSGB (1999-2001); M., Southgate & Distr. Reform Syn., Finchley Reform Syn.; Chairman, Assembly of Rabbis, RSGB (1981-83, 1999-2001); Lect., Hebrew and Practical Rabbinics, Leo Baeck Coll., form. M., Bushey Ref. Syn., Lib. Jew Union Syn., Paris. Ad.: Southgate & District Reform Synagogue, 120 Oakleigh Road North, London N20 9EZ. ☎ 020-8445 3400. E-mail colineimer@aol.com.

EISENBERG, Paul Chaim, BHL; b. Vienna, June 26, 1950; m. Annette née Liebman; Chief Rabbi of Vienna and of the Federation of Jewish Communities in Austria. Ad.: A-1010 Vienna, Seitenstetteng. 4. ☎ 43-1-5310416. Fax 43-1-533 15 77.

EKER, Mrs Rita (née Shapiro), MBE; b. London, Oct. 15, 1938; Co-Chairman, Women's Campaign for Soviet Jewry (the 35s); Co-Chairman of One to One and organiser of the One to One Treks in Israel; Project Dir. One to One Children's Fund. Ad.: Carradine House, 237 Regents Park Road, London N3 3LF. ☎ 020-8343 4156. Fax 020-8343 2119. Email rita@one-to-one.org.

ELLENBOGEN, Gershon, M.A. (Cantab.) F.C.I. Arb.; b. Liverpool, Jan. 7, 1917; Barrister; V. President & Hon. M. The Maccabaeans; C., Frs. of Hebrew Univ.; C., AJA; former Deputy Circuit judge. Publ.: Legal Works. Ad.: 9 Montagu Sq., W1H 1RB.

ELLENBOGEN, Myrtle Ruth Franklin (née Sebag-Montefiore, former widow of David E. Franklin); b. London, Oct. 18, 1923; form. Chairman, Children's Central Rescue Fund, Gov. and Hon. Fel. of Hebrew Univ. of Jerusalem, President, Women Frs. (since 1984), Brit. Frs., Hebrew Univ.; form. Gov., now Fel. of the Purcell Sch. for Musically Gifted Children (1968-88); Alice Model Nursery (Chairman 1984-87; 1958-66); Member, ILEA (1967-73); Chairman, Union of Jewish Women's Loan Fund (1966-72), Chairman, Hampstead & St. John's Wood Group, form. Chairman, Imp. Cancer R.F. (1987-89); V. Chairman, AJA Educ. Cttee. (1990-93). Publ.: Sir Moses Montefiore 1784 to 1885 (with Michael Bor). Ad.: Flat 83, Apsley House, 23-29 Finchley Rd., London NW8 0NZ. ☎ 020-7586 0464.

ELLIS, Harold, CBE, MA, DM, MCh, FRCS; b. London, Jan. 13, 1926; Emer. Prof. of Surgery, Lond. Univ.; Prof. & Chairman, Surgery Dept. Charing Cross & Westminster Med. Sch Form. V. President, Royal Coll. of Surgeons; Consultant Surgeon to the Army, resident surgical posts in Oxford, Sheffield & Lond. (1948-62). Publ.: Clinical Anatomy (10th ed.), Maingot's Abdominal Operations (9th ed.), Famous Operations, etc. Ad.: Dept. of Anatomy, King's College London (Guy's Campus), Hodgkin Building, London Bridge, SE1 1UL.

ELYAN, Sir (Isadore) Victor, MA, LLB; b. Dublin, Sept. 5, 1909; Barrister, Sr. Magistrate and Judge; Colonial Legal Service, Gold Coast (1946-54); High Court Judge and Judge of Appeal; Basutoland, Bechuanaland, Swaziland (1955-64); Chief Justice of Swaziland (1964-70); Prof of Law, Dean of Law Faculty, Durban-Westville Univ. (1973-76). Publ.: High Commission Territories Law Reports 1955-60 (ed.) Ad.: P.O.B. 22001 Fish Hoek, Cape, South Africa.

EMANUEL, Aaron, CMG, BSc (Econ); b. London, Feb. 11, 1912; form. Asst. Under-Sec. of State Dept of the Environment; Chairman, W. Midlands Econ. Planning Bd. (1968-72) Consultant, O.E.C.D. (1972-81). Ad.: 119 Salisbury Rd., Birmingham, B13 8LA. ☎ 0121-449 5553.

EMANUEL, Rabbi Dr Charles, BA, MHL, DD (HUC); b. New York, Dec. 15, 1944; M., North Western Ref. Syn.; form M., Sinai Syn., Leeds. Ad.: North Western Reform Synagogue, Alyth Gdns., NW11 7EN. ☎ 020-8455 6763. Fax 020-8458 2469. Email mail@alyth.org.

ENGEL, Ian, MA, FCA; b. Lond., March 24, 1931; Chartered Accountant; V. President (1993-) (Life Gov. 1966-), Ravenswood Norwood; Tr. & Exec. the Sir Georg Solti Music and Arts Fund; Tr. The Karten Alpha CTEC; Exec. British ORT. Ad.: 95 Elizabeth Court, 1 Palgrave Gardens, London NW1 6EJ.

EPSTEIN, Trude Scarlett (née Gruenwald), Dip. Economics and Political Science (Oxon), Dip. Industrial Administration, PhD (Manchester), b. Vienna, July 13, 1922; Social Assessment Consultant; Senior Fel. Research School of Pacific Studies, ANU Canberra (1966-72); Research Prof., Sussex (1972-84). Publ.: Economic Development and Social Change in S. India (1962); Capitalism, Primitive and Modern (1968); South India: Yesterday, Today and Tomorrow (1973); The Paradox of Poverty (1975); The Feasibility of Fertility Planning (1977); The Endless Day: Some Case Material on Asian Rural Women (1981); Urban Food Marketing and Third World Rural Development (1982); Women, Work and Family (1986); A Manual for Culturally Adapated Market Research in the Development Process (1988); A Manual for Development Market Research Investigators (1991); Village Voices – Forty Years of Rural Transformation in S. India (1998); A Manual for Culturally Adapted Social Marketing (1999). Ad.: 5 Viceroy Lodge, Kingsway, Hove BN3 4RA. ☎ 01273-735151. Fax 01273-735151. Email scarlett@epstein.nu.

EZRA, Baron of Horsham (Life Peer), **(Sir Derek Ezra)**, MBE; b. Feb. 23, 1919; Chairman, Nat. Coal Bd. (1971-82). Ad.: House of Lords, SW1.

FAITH, Mrs Sheila (née Book), J.P.; b. Newcastle upon Tyne, June 3, 1928, m. Dennis Faith; Dental Surgeon; Member Parole Bd., (1991-94); MEP (Conservative) for Cumbria and Lancashire North (1984-89) Memb. Euro Parl. Transport Cttee (1984-87), Energy Res. & Technological Cttee (1987-89); MP (C.) for Belper (1979-83) Memb. House of Commons Select Cttee on Health and Social Servs (1979-83), Memb. Exec. Cttee Cons Med. Soc. (1981-84); Sec. Cons Backbench Health and Social Servs Cttee (1982-83); Northumberland C.C. (1970-74); Memb. Health and Social Services Cttees, LEA rep on S. Northumberland Youth Employment Bd; Vice-Ch Jt Consult Cttee on Educ, Newcastle (1973-74); Memb. Newcastle City C. (1975-77), (Memb. Educ Cttee); JP: Northumberland (1972-74), Newcastle (1974-78), Inner London (1978-); President Cumbria and Lancashire N. Cons Euro Constitutency C. (1989-95); Memb. Newcastle upon Tyne CAB, served as Chairman of several sch. governing bodies and mangr. of community homes. Ad.: 52 Moor Ct., Westfield, Gosforth, Newcastle-upon-Tyne NE3 7JL. ☎ 0191-285 4438. Fax 0191-285 4483.

FARHI, Musa Moris, MBE, FRSL; b. Ankara, July 5, 1935; m. Nina Ruth née Gould; Writer; Vice-President, International PEN (2001-); Chairman, International PEN Writers in Prison Cttee (1997-2001); Chairman, English PEN Writers in Prison Cttee (1994-97); M. Edr. Bd., Jewish Quarterly. Publ.: The Pleasure of Your Death (1972); The Last of Days (1983); Journey Through the Wilderness (1989); Children of the Rainbow (1999). Ad.: 11 North Square, London NW11 7AB. ☎ 020-8455 5329. Fax 020-8731 6109. Email farhi@clara.net.

FASS, Richard Andrew, FCA; b. London, Sept. 24, 1945; Chartered Accountant; Man. Dir. Jewish Chronicle Ltd; Member Kessler Fdn.; Non-Exec. Dir. Central and North West London Mental Health NHS Trust. Ad.: Jewish Chronicle, 25 Furnival St., London EC4A 1JT. ☎ 020-7415 1500. Fax 020-7405 0278.

FEIGENBAUM, Clive Harold, FBOA, FSMC; b St. Albans, Sept. 6, 1939; Company Dir.; Jt. Chairman, Herut Org., Gt. Brit., BoD. Ad.: St. Margarets, Mount Park Rd., Harrow, Middx. HA1 3JP. ☎ 020-8422 1231.

FEINSTEIN, Mrs. Elaine (née Cooklin), MA (Cantab), HonD.Litt (Leic.), FRSL; b. Bootle, Oct. 24, 1930; m. Dr Arnold Feinstein; Writer; Cholmondley Prize for Poetry (1990). Publ.: The Circle; The Amberstone Exit; The Crystal Garden; Children of the Rose; The Ecstasy of Dr. Miriam Garner; Some Unease and Angels (poems); The Shadow Master; The Silent Areas; Selected Poems of Marina Tsvetayeva; The Survivors; The Border; Bessie Smith (biog.); A Captive Lion: a life of Marina Tsvetayeva; Badlands (poems); Mother's Girl; All you need; Loving Brecht (novel); Lawrence's Women (biog.); Dreamers (novel); Selected poems; Daylight (poems); Pushkin (biography); Ted Hughes: The Life of a Poet; Collected Poems. Ad.: c/o Gill Coleridge & White, 20 Powis Mews, W11. ☎ 020-8221 3717.

FELDMAN, David Maurice, MA, PhD; b. Lond., Feb. 16, 1957; Historian; Senior Lecturer in History Birkbeck Coll., (1993-); form. Lecturer in Economic & Social History Univ. of Bristol, form. Lect. & Fell., Christ's Coll., Cambridge (1987-90), Junior Res. Fell., Churchill Coll., Cambridge (1983-87); Publ.: Englishmen and Jews, Social relations and political culture 1840-1914 (1993), Metropolis London (ed. with G. Stedman Jones). Ad.: 44 Victoria Park, Cambridge CB4 3EL. ☎ 01223 312272.

FELDMAN, Rabbi Hyman Israel; b. Llanelli, March 28, 1930; Rav, Golders Green Beth Hamedrash, H. Princ., Menorah Primary Sch. Menoral Foundation Sch.; Edr., Kashrus News; Princ., Gateshead Jewish Boarding Sch. (1960-63). Ad.: 125 The Ridgeway, London NW11 9RX. ☎ 020-8455 5068.

FELSENSTEIN, Denis R., B.A. (Hons), PGCE (Distinction), Ac. Dip., M.A (Ed), ACIArb.; b. London, May 16, 1927; form. Hd. Immanuel Coll., form. Dep. Hd. J.F.S.; Hd.Brooke House, Div. Inspector Camden/Westminster and Senior Staff Inspector (Secondary), ILEA. Publ.: Comprehensive Achievement 1987, part-author Combatting Absenteeism 1986, numerous articles. Ad.: 27 Chessington Court, Charter Way, London N3 3DT. ☎ 020-8346 2096.

FELSENSTEIN, Frank, BA (Hons), PhD; b. Westminster, July 28, 1944; m. Carole; Prof. Humanities, Ball State Univ. (2002-); Dir., Honors Program, Yeshiva College, NY; form. Reader in English, Univ. of Leeds; Vis. Prof., Vanderbilt Univ., USA (1989-90). Publ.: Anti-Semitic Stereotypes: A Paradigm of Otherness in English Popular Culture, 1660-1830 (1995); The Jew as Other: A Century of English Caricature, 1730-1830, exhibition catalogue (Jewish Theological Seminary, New York, 1995); Hebraica and Judaica from the Cecil Roth Collection, exhibition catalogue (Brotherton Library, 1997); English Trader, Indian Maid: Representing Gender, Race and Slavery in the New World (1999). Ad.: 8 Manor Drive, Morristown, NJ 07960-2611, USA. ☎ 973-889-1323. Fax 973-889-1423; Dept. English, Ball State University, Muncie, IN 47306. ☎ (765) 285-8580. Fax (765) 285-3765. E-mail felsenstein@bsu.edu.

FERSHT, Alan Roy, MA, PhD, FRS; b. Lond., Apr. 21, 1943; m. Marilyn née Persell; Herchel Smith Prof., Organic Chem., Cambridge; Dir., Cambridge C. for Protein Eng.; Fel., Gonville & Caius Coll.; Prof., Biological Chem., Imperial Coll., Lond. and Wolfson Res. Prof. Royal Soc., (1978-88); Scientific Staff, MRC Lab., Molecular Biology, Cambridge (1969-77). Publ.: Enzyme Structure and Mechanism; Structure and Mechanism in Protein Science. Ad.: University Chemical Laboratory, Lensfield Road, Cambridge, CB2 1EW. ☎ 01223 336341. Fax 01223 336445.

FINE, Rabbi Yisroel, BA; b. Swansea, Nov. 11, 1948; M., Cockfosters and N. Southgate Syn., form. M., Wembley Syn., United Hebrew Cong., Newcastle upon Tyne; form. Chairman of the Rabbinical C. of the United Synagogue; Hon. Princ. Wolfson Hillel Primary Sch.; Educ. Portfolio, Chief Rabbi's Cabinet. Ad.: 274 Chase Side, N14 4PR. ☎ 020-8449 1750.

FINESTEIN, Israel, QC, MA (Cantab); Hon. LLD Hull; b. Hull, April 29, 1921, m. Marion née Oster; P. BoD (1991-94), V. President (1988-91), Mem. (1945-

72); form. Crown Court Judge (1972-87); Mem, President of Israel's Standing Conference on Israel and Diaspora (1976-90); Hon. Life President, Hillel Foundation, P. (1981-94); Chairman of Hillel Union of Jewish Students Educ. Cttee. (1981-91); form. Exec. Cttee. of C.C.J. (1980-95); V. President, Central C. for Jewish Soc. Services; Chairman, Kessler Foundation (1985-91); form. Mem. Exec. Cttee Memorial Foundation for Jewish Culture; Council United Synagogue and Jewish Chaplaincy Bd.; Jewish Memorial Council, Fdr. Member of Yad Vashem Cttee.; V. President, AJY; V. President, Jewish Museum, London and form. Chairman (1989-92) and V. President, Jewish Historical Soc. and form. P. (1973-75, 1993-4); V. President, Conference J. Material Claims Against Germany (1991-94); V. President, World Jewish Congress (1991-94); form. V. President, European Jewish Congress; Exec. Cttees. of London Bd. and Central Bd. of Jewish Religious Educ.; Cttee. of British ORT and JWB. Publ.: James Picciotto's Sketches of Anglo-Jewish History (edr.); Short History of Anglo-Jewry; Jewish Society in Victorian England; Anglo-Jewry in Changing Times: Studies in Diversity, 1840-1914; Scenes and Personalities in Anglo-Jewry, 1800-2000. Ad.: 18 Buttermere Ct., Boundary Rd., NW8 6NR.

FINKELSTEIN, Ludwik, OBE, MA, DSc, Dr. Univ. hc, DCLhc, FREng, FIEE, C. Phys, FInstP, Hon. FInstMC; b. Lwow, Dec. 6, 1929; Prof. Emer. of Measurement & Instrumentation, City Univ.; form. Pro-V. Chancellor; form. Prof of Instrument & Control Engineering, City Univ.; form Dean, School of Engineering, City Univ. Scientific Staff NCB; President, Instit. of Measurement & Control (1980), Hartley Medallist; Res. Fel. Jewish History and Thought, Leo Baeck Coll.; Publ.: Works in Mathematical Modelling, Measurement, etc. Ad.: City University, Northampton Sq., EC1V 0HB. ☎ 020-7040-8139. Fax 020-7040 8568.

FISHER, Dayan Michael; b. Grodno, Poland, Aug. 11, 1912; Rav Rashi (ret.), Fed. of Syns.; V. President, Mizrachi Fed. Ad.: C/o Federation of Synagogues, 65 Watford Way NW4 3AQ. ☎ 020-8202 2263.

FISHMAN, William J., BSc (Econ), Dip. Lit.; DSc (Econ) (London); b. London, April 1, 1921; Barnett Shine Sr. Res. Fel. in Labour Studies, Queen Mary and Westfield Coll, London Univ. (1972-86), & Vis. Prof. (1986); Princ., Tower Hamlets Coll. for Further Educ. (1955-69); Vis. Fel., Balliol Coll., Oxford Univ. (1965), Vis. Prof., Columbia Univ. (1967), Wisc Univ. (1969-70). Publ.: The Insurrectionists, East End Jewish Radicals, Streets of East London, East End 1888, East End and Docklands; Recordings – CDs. Ad.: 42 Willowcourt Ave., Kenton, Harrow, Middx. HA3 8ES. ☎ 020-8907 5166.

FIXMAN, Sydney; b. Manchester, Apr. 5, 1935; Dir., Instit. for Jewish Music Studies & Performance; Music Lect., Lond. Univ. Instit. of Educ.; Fdr., Conductor, Ben Uri Chamber Orchestra, Jewish Youth Orchestra, Music Dir., West Lond. Syn.; form. Guest Conductor, leading orchestras in Brit. & abroad (seasons in Israel: 1976-89); Conductor, B.B.C. (TV & Radio). Publ.: (ed.) Psaume Tehillim (Markevitch); Recordings, CDs. Ad.: 5 Bradby House, Hamilton Tce., NW8 9XE.

FORSTER, Donald, CBE; b. London, Dec. 18, 1920; President Soc. Jewish Golf Captains (1994-); Man. Dir. & Chairman B. Forster & Co. Ltd. (1946-85); Chairman, Merseyside Development Corp. (1984-87); Chairman Warrington/Runcorn Devel. Corp (1981-85), President, Manchester JIA (1981-83); President, Assn. Jewish Golf Clubs & Socs. (1973-83), HLP Whitefield Golf Club; Pilot (Flt.-Lieut.) RAF (1940-45); Rep. England, 1954 Maccabiah (tennis). Ad.: The Dingle, South Downs Drive, Hale, Cheshire WA14 3HR.

FRANKEL, William, CBE, LLB; b. London, 1917; Barrister-at-Law; Edr., 'Jewish Chronicle' (1958-77); Director Jewish Chronicle Ltd. (1959-94), Chairman (1991-94); Emer. Gov., Oxford Centre for Hebrew Studies; Gov. Cambridge Centre for Modern Hebrew Studies; Hon. President New Israel Fund (UK); Vice

President, IJPR; Tr. Israel Diaspora Trust; London Museum of Jewish Life; New London Synagogue; Hon. Fellow, Girton College. Publ.: Friday Nights (ed.), Israel Observed. Ad.: 30 Montagu Square, W1H 2LQ. Fax 020-7935 3052. Email frankelond@aol.com.

FRANKENBERG, Ronald Jonas, AcSS, BA (Hons Cantab), MA (Econ), PhD (Manchester), Hon. DSocSci (Brunel), Hon. D.Litt (Keele); b. Cricklewood, London, Oct. 20, 1929; m. Pauline née Hunt; Founding Academician, Academy of Social Sciences (1999); Fell. Keele University, Emer. Professor of Sociology and Social Anthropology; Hon. Fellow, Centre for Jewish Studies, Univ. Manchester; form. Dir. Centre for Medical Social Anthropology, Keele; Prof.Assoc., Hum. Sci., Brunel; Dean and Prof. Zambia University (1966–68); Reader, Manchester; Education Officer NUMineworkers. Publ.: Village on The Border, Communities in Britain, Custom and Conflict in British Society, Time, Health & Medicine. Ad.: 19 Keele Rd., Newcastle-u-Lyme, Staffs. ST5 2JT. ☎ 01782 628498. E-mail RFrank1251@aol.com.

FRANSES, Rabbi Simon J.; b. Larissa, Greece, May 25, 1943; M., Middlesex New Syn., Chairman of the Assembly of Rabbis RSGB (1989-91); Asst. M., Edgware & Dist. Reform Syn. (1971-74); M., Glasgow New Syn. (1974-87); Member of Children's Panel for Strathclyde Region (1977-87). Ad.: 39 Bessborough Rd., Harrow, Middx. HA1 3BS. ☎ 020-8864 0133. Email rabbi@mns.org.uk.

FREEDLAND, Jonathan; b. London, Feb. 25, 1967; m. Sarah née Peter; Journalist; Editorial writer and Columnist, The Guardian (1997-); Columnist, The Jewish Chronicle (1998); Washington Correspondent, The Guardian (1993-97). Publ.: Bring Home the Revolution: The Case for a British Republic (1998). Ad.: The Guardian, 119 Farringdon Road, London EC1R 3ER. ☎ 020-7278 2332.

FREEDLAND, Michael Rodney; b. London, Dec. 18, 1934; journalist and broadcaster, contributor to national press; Exec. Ed. & Presenter (BBC and LBC), 'You Don't Have to be Jewish' (1971-94). Publ.: Al Jolson; Irving Berlin; James Cagney; Fred Astaire; Sophie; Jerome Kern; Errol Flynn; Gregory Peck; Maurice Chevalier; Peter O'Toole; The Warner Brothers; Katharine Hepburn; So Let's Hear the Applause – The Story of the Jewish Entertainer; Jack Lemmon; The Secret Life of Danny Kaye; Shirley MacLaine; Leonard Bernstein; The Goldwyn Touch: A Biography of Sam Goldwyn; Jane Fonda; Liza With A Z; Dustin Hoffman; Kenneth Williams: A Biography; Andre Previn: Music Man; Sean Connery: A Biography; All the Way: A Biography of Frank Sinatra; Bob Hope; Bing Crosby; Michael Caine; Doris Day; (with Morecambe and Wise) There's No Answer To That; (with Walter Scharf) Composed and Conducted by Walter Scharf. Ad.: Bays Hill Lodge, Barnet Lane, Elstree, Herts. WD6 3QU. ☎ 020-8953 3000; 020-8953 7599.

FREEDMAN, Harry, PhD, MA (London), BA; b. London 1950; form. Chief Exec., Assembly of Masorti Synagogues (1994-2000); European Rep., Masorti; Lay minister Exeter Synagogue (1981-87); Dir. & Lecturer Masorti Academy (1994-2001); Editorial Advisory Committee, Jewish Bible Quarterly, Judaism Today. Publ.: The Halacha in Targum Pseudo-Jonathan (1999). Ad.: Career Energy, 100 Pall Mall, London SW1Y 5HP. ☎ 020-7664 8990. Email harry@careerenergy.co.uk.

FREEDMAN, Jeromé David, FCA; b. Brighton, 1935; m. Louise née Hershman; Chartered Accountant; Vice President ULPS, form. Chairman (1995-2001); form. Hon. Tr. (1990-95); Board of Management, Chartered Accountants' Benevolent Association (CABA); Director, CABA Trustees Ltd. Ad.: 5 Thanescroft Gardens, Croydon, Surrey CR0 5JR. ☎ 020-8688 2250. Fax 020-8680 4631. E-mail jerome@freedman.org.

FREESON, Rt. Hon. Reginald, PC; b. London, Feb. 24, 1926; Journalist; Urban renewal and housing consultant; Member National Planning & Housing C.;

Labour Party (1948-); form. Lab. M.P., Willesden and Brent East (1964-87); Member Town & Country Planning Assn.; Member Labour Finance & Industry Group; Fabian Soc.; Labour Campaign for Electoral Reform; Centre for Social Policy Studies in Israel UK Advisory Group; Commonwealth Parl. Assoc.; Life Memb. National Tr. & Youth Hostels Assoc.; Memb. Friends of Kew Gardens, Globe Theatre; Dir. Labour & Trade Union Friends of Israel (1992-94); Pol. Sec. Poale Zion (1987-94); Editor, 'Jewish Vanguard' (1988-); Chairman, DOE inner area studies (1974-77); Journ; M.P. (Lab.) for Willesden & Brent East (1964-87); Chairman, House of Commons Select Cttee. on the Environment (1981-83); Parl. Assembly C. of Europe (1983-87); Exec. Member Jewish Welfare Board (1970-74); Dir. JBG Housing Society (1982-83); BoD Inner City Study Gp. (1990); Jewish Orphanage (1931-41); President Norwood Old Scholars Assoc. (1972-). Ad.: 159 Chevening Rd., NW6 6DZ. ☎/Fax 020-8969 7407. Email charlottefreeson @compuserve.com.

FRIEDLANDER, Rabbi Albert Hoschander, OBE, PhD, DD, MHL, PhB; b. Berlin, May 10, 1927; President CCJ (2000-); Landesrabbiner, Niedersachsen; M. Emer. Westminster Syn., Dean and Sr. Lect., Leo Baeck Coll.; Vis. Fel. Berlin Institute of Higher Studies; Ed., European Judaism (periodical); f.PEN; International Hon. President, World Conference of Religions for Peace, F. Exec., Leo Baeck Inst.; form. M., Wembley & District Prog. Synagogue; Jewish Chaplain, Columbia Univ. and M., East Hampton and Wilkes-Barre; Ed. in Chief, The Collected Works of Leo Baeck. Publ.: Out of the Whirlwind, Six Days of Destruction (with E. Wiesel), Five Scrolls, Thread of Gold, Riders Towards the Dawn, etc. Ad.: Kent House, Rutland Gardens, SW7 IBX. ☎ 020-7584 2754. Email albert.friedlander@virgin.net.

FRIEDLANDER, Evelyn (née Philipp), ARCM, Order of Merit (Germany); b. London, June 22, 1940; m. Albert Hoschander Friedlander; Executive Director, Hidden Legacy Foundation; Tr. Czech Memorial Scrolls Trust. Publ.: Ich Will nach Hause, aber ich war noch nie da (1996); Mappot ... The Band of Jewish Tradition (1997, co-ed.); The Jews of Devon and Cornwall (2000). Ad.: Kent House, Rutland Gardens, London SW7 1BX. ☎ 020-7584 2754. Fax 020-7584 6896.

FRIEDMAN, Milton, BA, MA, PhD; b. Brooklyn, July 31, 1912; Economist; Nobel Prize in Economics, (1976); Sr. Res. Fel., Hoover Instit. Stanford Univ.; Paul Snowden Russell Distinguished Service Prof. Emer., Chicago Univ.; many honorary degrees. Publ.: Writings on economics. Ad.: Hoover Institution, Stanford, California 94305-6010 USA. ☎ (650) 723-0580.

FRIEDMAN, Rosemary (née Tibber); b. London, Feb. 5, 1929; m. Dennis Friedman, FRCpsych; Writer. Exec. Cttee Society of Authors (1989-92); Exec. Cttee P.E.N. (1993-). Sole judge, Authors' Club First Novel Award 1989; Judge, Betty Trask Fiction Award 1991; Chair of judges, Jewish Quarterly Literary Prizes 1993 and Macmillan Silver Pen Award 1996. Publ.: The Writing Game, Vintage, Golden Boy, An Eligible Man, To Live in Peace, A Second Wife, Rose of Jericho, A Loving Mistress, Proofs of Affection, The Long Hot Summer, The Life Situation, The Ideal Jewish Woman and Contemporary Society (Confrontations with Judaism, Ed. Philip Logworth); Home Truths (play, UK tour 1997); Juvenile: Aristide, Aristide in Paris; Works before 1975 with pen name Robert Tibber: Practice Makes Perfect, The General Practice, The Commonplace Day, The Fraternity, Patients of a Saint, We All Fall Down, Love on My List, No White Coat, Intensive Care. Ad.: 5, 3 Cambridge Gate, London NW1 4JX. ☎ 020-7935 6252. Fax 020-7486 2398. E-mail rosemaryfriedman@hotmail.com.

FRIEND, John, BSc, PhD (Liv), PhD (Cantab), FIBiol; b. Liverpool, May 31, 1931; m. Carol née Loofe; President Hull Jewish Representative Council (1999-); Emer. Prof. of Plant Biology, Hull Univ.; Prof. of Plant Biology, Hull

Univ. (1969-97); Pro-V. Chancellor, Hull Univ. (1983-87); Vis. Prof. Hebrew Univ. of Jerusalem (1974); Vis. Fel. Wolfson College, Cambridge (1988). Publ.: Biochemical Aspects of Plant-Parasite Relations (with D. R. Threlfall, 1976); Recent Advances in the Biochemistry of Fruit and Vegetables (with MJC Rhodes, 1983). Ad.: 9 Allanhall Way, Kirkella, Hull HU10 7QU. ☎ 01482-658930. Fax 01482-656394. E-mail j.friend@hull.ac.uk.

FROSH, Sidney, JP; b. London, Aug. 22, 1923; President, US (1987-92), Chairman, Beth Hamedrash & Beth Din. Man. Bd., Chairman, Chief Rabbinate C. (1987-92); Chairman, Min. Placement Cttee., Chairman, Singer's Prayer Book Publ. Cttee. (1987-92); VP Norwood Ravenswood; V. President, Cen. C. for Jewish Comm. Services; Chief Rabbinate C.; V. Chairman & T., Lond. Bd. of Jewish Rel. Educ. (1968-78), Gov., J.F.S. Ad.: 50 Lodge Close, Edgware, Middx. HA8 7RL. ☎ 020-8952 9097. Fax 020-8951 0823.

GABAY, Isaac, MBE; b. Gibraltar, May 14, 1931; Exec. Head Chef, House of Commons; Head Chef, Hurlingham Club, (1954-62); Head Chef, Army and Navy Club (1962-72). Ad.: 119 Preston Hill, Harrow, Middlesex HA3 9SN. ☎ 020-8204 1943.

GAFFIN, Jean (née Silver), OBE, JP, MSc, BSc (Econ); b. London, Aug. 1, 1936; m. Alexander; Chair, Brent Primary Care NHS Trust (2002-); Non. Exec. Dir. Harrow & Hillingdon Healthcare NHS Trust (1998-2002); Memb. Consumer Panel Financial Services Auth. (1999-); Exec. Dir. National Hospice Council (1991-98); Chief Exec. Arthritis Care (1988-91); Exec. Sec., British Paediatric Assoc. (1982-87); Organising Sec., Child Accident Prevention Cttee (1979-82); Lecturer II/Senior Lecturer, Social Policy and Administration, Polytechnic of the South Bank (1973-79); Chairman, OFTEL's Advisory Committee on Telecommunications for Disabled and Elderly People – DIEL (1993-99); Hon. Sec. Royal Society of Medicine (1997-2001); Mem. UK Xeno-Transplantation Interim Regulatory Authority (1997-); Magistrate, Harrow Bench (1981-). Publ. include: (Editor) The Nurse and the Welfare State (1981); with D. Thoms, Caring and Sharing: the Centenary History of the Co-operative Women's Guild (1983, second ed. 1993); Women's Co-operative Guild 1884-1914, in Women in the Labour Movement, ed. L. Middleton (1977). Ad.: 509 Kenton Rd., Harrow, Middx HA3 0UL. ☎ 020-8206 0327. E-mail agaffin@csi.com.

GAINSFORD, Doreen; b. London, May 9, 1937; Public & Press Relations Off.; form. Chairman, 35's (Women's Campaign for Soviet Jewry). Emigrated to Israel, March, 1978, Coord, JIA Project Renewal, Ashkelon; Founder, 35's Israel Campaign for Soviet Jewry; Dir., TAL Mini Gifts (Israel). Ad.: Yehoshua Ben Nun 2, Herzlia Pituach, Israel 46763. ☎ 09-9507011. Fax 03-9226108.

GAINSFORD, Sir Ian Derek, BDS, DDS, FDSRCS Eng, FDSRCS Edin., FICD, FACD, FKC, DDS (Hons) Toronto; b. Twickenham, June 24, 1930; m. Carmel née Liebster; Dental Surgeon; President, Maccabaeans (2000-); Regent, Royal College of Surgeons, Edinburgh (2002-); President, Western Marble Arch Synagogue (1998-2000); Dean, King's College School of Medicine & Dentistry (1988-97); Vice-Principal, King's College, London (1994-97); Hon. President, British Friends of Magen David Adom (1995-); Hon. Chairman, British Friends of Bet Morasha (1999-). Ad.: 31 York Terrace East, London NW1 4PT. ☎ 020-7935 8659.

GALE, Rev. Norman Eric, BA, PhD; b. Leeds, Nov. 9, 1929; Mem. Prison Religious Advisory Service Group; form. M., Hampstead Syn. (1988-95); M., Ealing Syn. (1968-88); M., Harrogate Hebrew Cong. (1958-68); form. Chairman, US Rabbinical C.; Memb. Chief Rabbi's Cabinet (Welfare Portfolio 1990-93); form. H. Chaplain, Nat. Assn. of Jewish Friendship Clubs; H. Dir., Jewish Prison Chaplaincy; Chaplain, Wormwood Scrubs Prison. Ad.: Flat 6, Orford Ct., Marsh Lane, Stanmore, Middx HA7 4TQ. ☎ 020-8954 3843.

GARAI, George, PhD (Lond); b. Budapest, Aug. 31, 1926; Journalist; Gen. Sec., Z.

Fed. of Gt. Brit. & Ireland (1982-92); Dir., Public Rel., Z. Fed. (1975-82); Edr. Staff, 'Jewish Chronicle' (1966-75); Edr., 'Australian Jewish Times' (1960-66). Ad.: Balfour House, 741 High Rd., London N12 0BQ.

GARBACZ, Bernard, FCA; b. Westcliff, Dec. 30, 1932; W., Kingsbury Syn. (1965-72); President, B'nai B'rith First Lodge of England (1976-78); Fdr. Tr, Jewish Education Development Tr. (1980-91); Receiver and Manager, Jewish Secondary Schools Movement (1979-82); Chairman, Bd. of Govs., Hasmonean Boys' Grammar Sch. (1979-82); Chairman, J. Marriage C. (1989-91), T. then V.-Chairman, Brit-Israel Chamber of Commerce (1980-92); T., Jews Coll. (1971-84); V.Chairman, Hillel Foundation (1980-92); H. President, Univ. Jewish Chaplaincy Bd.; Chairman, London Jewish Chaplaincy Bd. (1997-2000); Dir., Central Middlesex Hospital N.H.S. Tr. (1991-96); Chairman, Black's Leisure Gp. Plc (1986-90), Dmatek Ltd. (1995-96). Publ.: Anglo Jewry Research Project 1985 (Garbacz Report on Communal Funding). Ad.: 2 Beatrice Court, 15 Queens Road, London NW4 2TL. ☎ 020-8203 5807. Fax 020-8203 5824. E-mail bgarbacz@AOL.com.

GASTWIRTH, Rabbi Ephraim Levy, BA, MLitt; b. London, 1920; Ret. Rabbi & Chaplain, Heathlands, Manchester; M., Sale Hebrew Cong. (1979-82), Blackpool Hebrew Cong. (1976-79); Princ., Judith Lady Montefiore Coll (1968-76); Dir. of Jewish Studies, Carmel Coll. (1964-66); M., Sunderland Hebrew Cong. (1960-64); M., S. Hampstead Syn. (1956-60). Ad.: 3 Falcon Ct., Park St., Salford, M7 4WH. ☎ 0161-792 4239.

GEE, George Maxwell, FRSA, JP; b. Gillingham, Jan. 12, 1921; P. US (1981-84), V. President (1973-81), US Jt. T. (1961-73), Elder U.S. (1984-); Chairman, Affil. Syns. Cttee. (1973-77); Mem U.S. Placement Cttee. (and form. Chairman); Mem (form. Chairman and Jt. T.) Chief Rabbinate C. (1961-); Mem of Chief Rabbinate Conf. (1966 and 1990); Singer's Prayer Book Publ. Cttee. (since 1983); President, Jewish Deaf Assn. (1979-); President Cttee. for Jewish H.M. Forces (1999-), (Chairman 1971-99); T., Frs., Jewish Servicemen & Women (1971-99); Tr., Nathan & Adolph Haendler Char.; C., World Conf of Syns. & Kehillot (1981-84); Shechita Bd. (1971-77); Kashrus Com. (1971-81); BoD; Freeman, City of Lond. (1953); P.M., Worshipful Comp. Glaziers & Painters of Glass; form. Chairman, Glaziers Tr for preserv. & restor. of glass of hist. interest (1976-84); Chairman of Trustees, London Stained Glass Repository (1989-2002); L. Member, Royal Engineers OCA. Ad.: 23 Denewood Rd., N6 4AQ. ☎ 020-8340 0863. Fax 020-8348 8797.

GELLER, Markham Judah, b. Corpus Christi, Texas, Jan. 2, 1949; University Lecturer; Prof. of Semitic Languages, Dept. of Hebrew and Jewish Studies, University College London; Dir. Institute of Jewish Studies, University College London. Ad.: Dept of Hebrew and Jewish Studies, UCL, Gower St., London WC1E 6BT. ☎ 020-7679 3588. Fax 020-7209 1026. Email m.geller@ucl.ac.uk; 30 Gilling Court, London NW3 4XA. ☎ 020-7586 9693.

GILBERT, Andrew, BSc; b. London, May 31, 1959; Managing Dir., Henry Bertrand Silk Fabrics; Chairman, RSGB (2002-), Chairman, External Board (1998-2000), Chairman, Synagogue Support Board (2000-2); Chairperson, Limmud (1990-97); Exec. Mem. BoD (1994-97); Chairman, BoD Education, Youth & Information Committee (1994-97); Chairperson, Jewish Youth Service Partners Group (1994-98); Chairperson, European Hanhallah, CAJE Israel Conference (1996); Exec. Mem., UJIA Jewish Renewal (1998-) and Chair, Israel Experience Policy Group (1998-2002); Mem. Lay Leadership Task Force, Jewish Continuity. Ad.: 52 Holmes Rd., London NW5 3AB. ☎ 020-7424 7002. Fax 020-7424 7001. Email silk@compuserve.com.

GILBERT, Sir Martin, CBE, D.Litt; b. London, Oct. 25, 1936; historian; Official Biographer of Winston Churchill (since 1968); Fel., Merton Col., Oxford; Vis. Prof, Hebrew Univ. (1980, 1995-98); Vis. Prof., Tel Aviv Univ. (1979); Vis. Prof.

UCL (1995-6). Publ.: Winston S. Churchill (6 vols.); Churchill, A Life; The Appeasers (with Richard Gott); Britain and Germany Between the Wars; The European Powers 1900-1945; The Roots of Appeasement; Exile and Return: A Study in the Emergence of Jewish Statehood; The Holocaust – the Jewish Tragedy; Churchill, A Photographic Portrait; In Search of Churchill; Auschwitz and the Allies; The Jews of Hope; The Plight of Soviet Jewry Today; Shcharansky, Portrait of a Hero; Jerusalem – Rebirth of a City; Jerusalem in the Twentieth Century; First World War; Second World War; The Day the War Ended; The Boys – Triumph over Adversity; Israel, A History; A History of the Twentieth Century (3 vols); Letters to Aunt Fiori: 5,000 Year History of the Jewish People and Their Faith; The Righteous: The Unsung Heroes of the Holocaust; and other historical works; 12 history atlases, including the Jewish History Atlas, Jerusalem Illustrated History Atlas and the Atlas of the Holocaust. Ad.: Merton College, Oxford.

GINSBURG, Major the Rev. Alec., Hon. CF; b. Aberavon, Aug. 21, 1920; Chaplain to HM Forces; form Sr. M. & Braham Lect., Old Hebrew Cong. Liverpool; form. M., Hove Hebrew Cong., St. Annes, Terenure and Plymouth Syns.; Lect. Classical Hebrew & Semitics Exeter Univ. (1964-74); Lect., Jew Homilies. Irish Sch. Ecumenics, Dublin (1974-76); (perm.) Ecumenical Panel, King Edward VII Hospital, Midhurst, Sussex; Jew Chaplain Hq. CMF (Udine. Italy), CF (J) Hq. British Troops (Klagenfurt) Austria, 1947, Sr. Jewish Chaplain, Hq. Brit. Troops, Egypt & Middle East (1947-50), Jewish Chaplain, Hq. BAOR (1950-55), UK Hq. Lond. Distr. (1956-62); Mentioned: London Gazette, 8 Jan. 1961 on promotion 3rd Class, 8 June, 1962 as Hon. Chaplain Third Class; Rank: Major on retirement; Chap., Dartmoor, Exeter Prisons (1962-74), H.T., Dublin Univ Jewish Soc. Publ.: Judaism and Freemasonry. Ad.: 15 Courtenay Gate, Kingsway, Hove, E. Sussex, BN3 2WJ. ☎ 01273-739440

GINSBURG David, MA; b. London, Mar. 18, 1921; Comp. Dir., Economist Market and Marketing Res. Consultant; Broadcaster; Fel., Royal Soc. of Med.; M.P. (Lab. 1959-81, SDP 1981-83 Dewsbury), Sec., Research Dept. Labour Party(1952-59); Sr. Research Off., Govt. Social Survey (1946-52). Ad.: 3 Bell Moor, East Heath Rd., NW3 1DY. ☎ 020-8435 8700.

GINSBURY, Rabbi Mordechai Shlomo; b. London, May 10, 1960; m. Judy née Burns; M., Hendon United Synagogue (1999-); M., Prestwich Hebrew Congregation, Manchester (1985-99); Chairman, Rabbinical Council of the Provinces (1997-98). Ad.: Hendon United Synagogue, 18 Raleigh Close, London NW4 2TA. ☎ 020-8202 6924 (main office), 020-8203 7762 (direct line, off.). Fax 020-8202 1720.

GINSBURY, Rabbi Philip Norman, MA; b. London, Mar. 26, 1936; M., South London Syn.; form. M., Streatham Distr. Syn., Brixton Syn.; Chairman South London Rabbinical Council. Publ. Jewish Faith in Action (1995). Ad.: 146 Downton Ave., SW2 3TT. ☎/Fax 020-8674 7451. E-mail p.ginsbury@aol.com

GLANVILLE, Brian Lester, b. London, Sept. 24, 1931; writer. Publ.: Along the Arno, A Bad Streak, The Bankrupts, Diamond, etc. Ad.: 160 Holland Park Ave.,W11.

GLATTER, Robert, FCA; b. Antwerp, Belgium, Mar. 14, 1937; Chartered Accountant, Non-Exec. Director Bank Leumi (UK) plc; Chairman, Bank Leumi Pension Fund; Non-Exec. Director CP Holdings Ltd; V-Pres. Bnai Brith Hillel Foundation; Council Mem. Weizmann Institute Foundation; President, Maccabi Union GB; Tr. Maccabi Fd., Tr. Arbib Lucas Charity; V-Pres. Akiva School; Member, Maccabi World Union; Form. Tr. Volcani Fnd.; Gov. Tr. Carmel College; Ch. NW Reform Syn.; Chairman, RSGB Cttee for Ed. and Youth; Ch. RSGB Israel Action Ct.; V-Ch., Ch., Tr., V-Press. Maccabi Union GB; Dep. Ch. Maccabi Europe; Ch. and Dep. Ch. Maccabiah Organ. Cttee; Tr. Bd for Jewish Sport; Tr. Manor House Trustees; Ch., Funders Cttee, Assn. Jewish Sixth Formers. Ad.: 12 York Gate, London NW1 4QS.

GLINERT, Lewis H., BA (Oxon), PhD; b. London, June 17, 1950; m. Joan née Abraham; University Lecturer; Prof. of Hebraic Studies and Linguistics, Dartmouth College; form. Prof. of Hebrew, Univ. of London (School of Oriental and African Studies, 1979-97); Dir. Centre for Jewish Studies, SOAS; Vis. Prof. of Hebrew Studies, Chicago U. (1987/8); Asst. Prof. of Hebrew Linguistics, Haifa U. (1974-77). Publ.: The Grammar of Modern Hebrew (1989); The Joys of Hebrew (1992); Hebrew in Ashkenaz (1993); Modern Hebrew: An Essential Grammar (1994); Mamma Dear (1997). Ad.: Dartmouth College, 6191 Bartlett Hall, Hanover, N.H. 03755, USA. ☎ 603 646 0364. Fax 617 244 4011. E-mail Lewis.Glinert@Dartmouth.edu.

GOLD, Sir Arthur Abraham, CBE; b. Lond., Jan. 10, 1917; Engineer; President, European Athletic Assn.; V.President, Commonwealth Games C. for England; Chairman, Drug Abuse Adv. Group, Sports C.; P. Counties Athletic Union; Life V. President (H.Sec., 1962-77) Brit. Amateur Athletic Bd.; President, Amateur Ath. Assn.; V.President Brit. Olympic Assn.; Member, Sports C.; Exec. Central C. of Physical Recreation; Athletics Team Leader, Olympic Games, Mexico 1968, Munich 1972, Montreal 1976; Commandant, C'wealth Games Team Brisbane 1982, Edinburgh 1986, Auckland 1990; British Olympic Team 1988, 1992; President, Lond. Ath. Club (1962-63); President, Middlesex CAAA (1963 and 1993). Ad.: 49 Friern Mount Drive, N20 9DJ. ☎ 020-8445 2848.

GOLD, Rev. Sidney, BA; b. London Dec. 6, 1919; Emer. M (Chief M., 1960-85) Birmingham Hebrew Cong., form. M., Highgate Syn., Regent's Park & Belsize Park Syn., Bayswater Syn., Member Chief Rabbi's Cabinet (1979-83); P. Union of Anglo-Jewish Preachers (1977-78), form. V.Chairman B'ham C.C.J.; Chairman B'ham Inter-Faith C.; President, B'ham JIA Cttee. Publ.: Children's Prayer Book for High Festivals (jt. author). Ad.: 12 Dean Park Mans., 27 Dean Park Rd., Bournemouth BH1 1JA ☎ 01202 551578.

GOLDBERG, Sir Abraham, MD, DSc, FRCP, FRSE; b. Edinburgh, Dec. 7, 1923; Regius Prof (Materia Med., 1970-78), Emer. Regius Prof. Practice of Med., Glasgow Univ. (1978-89); Chairman, Cttee. on Safety of Medicines (1980-86); Chairman, Biological Res. Cttee., Scottish Home & Health Dept., Glasg. (1978-83); H. Consultant, Western Infirmary, Glasg.; Chairman, Grants Cttee., Med. Res. C. (1972-76), Fdn. P. Faculty of Pharmaceutical Medicine of Royal Colleges of Physicians (UK), (1989-91); Vis. Prof, Tel Hashomer Hospital, Israel (1966), Henry Cohen Lect., Hebrew Univ. (1973); Lord Provost's Award for Public Service to Glasgow (1989); Chairman Glasgow Friends of Shaare Zedek Hospital, Jerusalem. Publ.: Diseases of Porphyrin Metabolism (jt. auth.), Recent Advances in Haematology (jt. edr.). Ad.: 16 Birnam Cres., Bearsden, Glasgow G61 2AU.

GOLDBERG, Rabbi David J., MA (Oxon), DD (Hons), Manchester; b. London, Feb. 25, 1939; Sr. Rabbi, Liberal Jewish Syn.; Interfaith Gold Medallion (1999); Premio Iglesias (1999); M. Wembley & Dist. Lib. Syn. (1971-75); Associate Rabbi L.J.S. (1975-87); Chairman, ULPS Rabbinic Conference (1981-83, 1996-98). Publ.: The Jewish People: Their History and their Religion (with John D. Rayner); To the Promised Land: A History of Zionist Thought; On the Vistula Facing East (ed.); Progressive Judaism Today (gen. ed.). Ad.: Liberal Jewish Synagogue, 28 St. John's Wood Rd., NW8 7HA. ☎ 020-7286 5181.

GOLDBERG, David Jonathan, MA (Jewish Communal Service) Brandeis; Cert. Youth and Community Studies, London; b. London, June 27, 1961; Dir. Israel Experience UK/UJIA/JAFI (1998-); Exec. Director, Zionist Fed. of Great Britain & Ireland (1992-98); H. Chair, Association of Jewish Communal Professionals (1992-98); Senior Youth and Community Work, Redbridge JYCC (1983-90). Ad. 18 Chiltern Avenue, Bushey, Herts WD2 3QA. ☎ 020-8950 0080. E-mail dgng@globalnet.co.uk.

GOLDMAN, William; b. London, April 4, 1910; Novelist. Publ.: A Start in Life,

A Tent of Blue, East End My Cradle, In England and in English, A Saint in the Making, The Light in the Dust, Some Blind Hand, The Forgotten Word, etc. Ad.: 12 Quintock House, Broomfield Rd., Kew Gdns., Richmond, Surrey TW9 3HT. ☎ 020-8948 4798.

GOLDREIN, Neville Clive, CBE, MA (Cantab.); b. Hull; m. Sonia née Sumner; Solicitor; Mem. Int. Assoc. Jewish Lawyers and Jurists; Mem. BAJS; Tr. Southport J. Rep. Council (1999-); form. Dep. Circuit Judge; form. Member (Leader, 1980-81, V. Chairman, 1977-80) Merseyside County C. (1973-86); Leader, Conservative Group (1980-86); Lancashire County Council (1965-74); Crosby Borough C. (1957-71); Mayor of Crosby (1966-67); Dep. Mayor (1967-68); North-West Economic Planning C. (1972-74); Gov. Merchant Taylors' Schools, Crosby (1965-74); Area President, St. John Amb., Sefton (1965-87); C., L'pool Univ. (1977-81); Vice-President, Crosby MENCAP (1966-89); C. L'pool Chamber of Commerce (1986-); Chairman Environment and Energy Cttee (1993-); British Assoc. of Chambers of Commerce, Mem. Local & Regional Aff. Cttee (1994-97); Chairman L'pool Royal Court Theatre Foundation; Chairman, Crosby Conservative Association (1986-89); Chairman (Appeals), Crosby Hall Educ. Trust (1989-91); BoD (1965-85, and 1992-2001); Sr.W., L'pool Old Hebrew Cong. (1968-71). Ad.: Torreno, St Andrew's Rd., Blundellsands, Liverpool L23 7UR. ☎/Fax 0151-924 2065. E-mail goldrein@aol.com.

GOLDSMITH, Lord (Peter Henry), PC, QC, MA (Cantab), LLM (London); b. Liverpool, Jan. 5, 1950; m. Joy née Elterman; Barrister; H.M. Attorney-General (2001-); President (2001-), Chairman, Bar Pro Bono Unit (1996-2000); Chairman, Financial Reporting Review Panel (1997-2000); Co-Chairman, Human Rights Institute of International Bar Assoc. (1998-2001); Chairman, Bar of England and Wales (1995). Publ.: contr. to Common Values, Common Law, Common Bond (2000). Ad.: House of Lords, London SW1A.

GOLDSMITH, Walter Kenneth, FCA CiMgt, FRSA; b. London, Jan. 19, 1938; Chairman PremiSys Technologies plc (1998-); Chairman ULPS Centenary Committee 2002 (1999-); Chairman (1987-91), V. President (1992-) Brit Overseas Trade Group for Israel; Dir.-Gen. Inst. of Dirs. (1979-84); Co-founder and Tr. Israel Diaspora Tr. (1982-92); Treasurer Leo Baeck College (1987-89); Dir. Bank Leumi (UK) plc (1984-); Chairman Wembley & Distr. Lib Syn (1974-76); C. and Exec. ULPS (1956-66); Chairman Youth Section World Union for Progressive Judaism (1960-61). Ad.: c/o Glenmore Investments Ltd, 52 Queen Anne Street, London W1M 9LA. ☎ 020-7935 0100. Fax 020-7935 7787.

GOLDSTEIN, Rabbi Andrew, PhD; b. Warwick, Aug. 12, 1943; M., Northwood and Pinner Liberal Syn. (1970-); Vice-Chair, European Region, World Univ. for Progressive Judaism (2001-); Vice-Chair, Hillingdon Branch LCCJ (2001-); Chairman, ULPS Rabbinic Conf (1979-81); Chairman, ULPS Educ. Cttee. (1970-88); Dir., Kadimah Holiday School, (1970-89); Chairman ULPS Prayerbook Editorial Cttee; Co-ed. ULPS Machzor (1998-); Consultant Rabbi Liberal congregations in Brno and Bratislava. Publ.: My Jewish Home, Jerusalem, Tradition Roots, Britain and Israel, Mishnah Kadimah, Exploring the Bible, Parts 1 & 2. Ad.: 10 Hallowell Rd., Northwood, Middx. HA6 1DW. ☎ 01923 822818. Fax 01923 824454. E-mail admin@npls.org.uk.

GOLDSTEIN, Rabbi Henry; b. London, March 10, 1936; Rabbi Emeritus, South-West Essex and Settlement Reform Syn. (2001-), M. (1973-2001); M., Finchley Reform Syn. (1967-73); Ch, RSGB Rabbis' Assembly (1973-75); Convenor Redbridge Jewish Vegetarian Soc. Ad.: 15 Chichester Gardens, Ilford, Essex, IG1 3NB. ☎ 020-8554 2297.

GOLDSTEIN, Michael, MBE; b. London, April 5, 1919; form. Gen. Sec., AJY (1951-77); form. Chairman, Greater Lond. Conf of Vol. Youth Orgs. Ad.: Flat 12, Broadway Close, Woodford Green, Essex, IG8 OHD. ☎ 020-8504 2304.

GOLDSTONE, Richard Joseph, BA, LLB (Witwatersrand), Hon.DL (Cape Town,

Witwatersrand, Natal, Hebrew University, Notre Dame, Maryland, Wilfred Laurier, Glasgow, Catholic University, Brabant, Calgary, Emory University; b. Boksburg, Oct. 26, 1938; m. Noleen Joy née Behrman; Justice of the Constitutional Court of South Africa (1994-); Chair, Int. Task Force on Terrorism (International Bar Association) (2001-); Chair, Commission of Inquiry, Public Violence and Intimidation (Goldstone Commission) (1991-94); Chief Prosecutor, UN International Criminal Tribunals for the former Yugoslavia and Rwanda (1994-96); Chair, Valencia Declaration (1999-2001); Chancellor University of the Witwatersrand (1995-); Mem., School of Law, Gov., Hebrew U. (1980-); President, World ORT; Mem. Gp. Adv. International Committee on the Red Cross (2000-); Hon. Bencher, Inner Temple; Hon. Fell., St John's College (Cambridge). Publ: For Humanity: Reflections of a War Crimes Investigator. Ad.: Constitutional Court of South Africa, Forum II, Braampark, 33 Hoofd Street, Braamfontein, Johannesburg 2001; Private Bag X32, Braamfontein, Johannesburg 2017. ☎ (011) 359 7407. Fax (011) 403 9131. Email goldstone@concourt.org.za.

GOLDWATER, Raymond, LLB; b. Hove, Sept. 28, 1918; Solicitor; Elder, US; V. President, AJY; form. Ch, Rel Adv. Cttee., AJY; form Chairman, London Student Counsellor Bd.; form C., Jews' Coll.; form. Lond. Bd., Jewish Rel. Educ.; form. Chairman, Youth & Com. Services Dept. & Jt. T., Bequests & Tr. Funds, US; Chairman, I.U.J.F. & Lond. Jewish Graduates' Assn. Publ.: Jewish Philosophy and Philosophers (Edr.). Ad.: 451 West End Ave., Apt 5E, New York, NY 10024. ☎ 212-873-8221.

GOLOMBOK, Ezra, BSc, PhD; b. Glasgow, Aug. 22, 1922; Dir. Israel Information Office, Glasgow; Edr., Jewish Echo; Edr., Scottish Nat. Orchestra Scene; form. Convener, Public Relations Cttee., Glasgow Jewish Rep. C. Ad.: 222 Fenwick Rd., Giffnock, Glasgow G46 6UE. ☎ 0141-577 8240. Fax 0141-577 8241. E-mail ezra@isrinfo.demon.co.uk. Website www.isrinfo.demon.co.uk

GOODMAN, Martin David, MA, D.Phil (Oxon) FBA; b. Aug. 1, 1953; m. Sarah Jane née Lock; Professor of Jewish Studies, University of Oxford; Fellow of the Oxford Centre for Hebrew and Jewish Studies and Wolfson College; Lecturer in Ancient History, University of Birmingham (1977-86); Fellow of Oxford Centre for Hebrew and Jewish Studies (1986-); Senior Research Fellow, St Cross College (1986-91); Reader in Jewish Studies, University of Oxford (1991-96); President, British Association for Jewish Studies (1995); Sec. European Association for Jewish Studies (1995-98); Joint Editor of Journal of Jewish Studies (1995-99). Publ.: State and Society in Roman Galilee, A.D. 132-212 (1983, 2nd ed. 2000); Johann Reuchlin, On the Art of the Kabbalah (translation with S.J. Goodman) (1983 and 1993); E. Schürer, The History of the Jewish People in the Age of Jesus Christ, rev. ed. (with G. Vermes and F.G.B. Millar), volume 3 (1986 [part 1], 1987 [part 2]); The Ruling Class of Judaea: the origins of the Jewish Revolt against Rome, A.D. 66-70 (1987); The Essenes according to the Classical Sources (with Geza Vermes) (1989); Mission and Conversion: proselytizing in the religious history of the Roman Empire (1994); The Roman World 44BC-AD180 (1997); Jews in a Graeco-Roman World (ed. 1998); Apologetics in the Roman Empire (jt. ed. 1999). Ad.: Oriental Institute, Pusey Lane, Oxford, OX1 2LE. ☎ 01865-278208. Fax 01865-278190. Email martin.goodman@orinst.ox.ac.uk.

GOODMAN, Mervyn, MPhil, MRCS (Eng.), LRCP (Lond), FRCGP, FRSH, DObstRCOG; b. Liverpool, Jan. 8, 1928; Freeman, City of London; Fel., BMA; Fel. Roy. Soc. Med.; Mem. Court of Univ. of L'pool (1988-2002); form. General Medical Practitioner, Clinical Teacher, Dept Gen. Pract., Univ. of L'pool; P. (now Hon. Life V.P.) Merseyside Jewish Rep. C. (1973–76); P. L'pool Z. Cent. (1970–73); C. L'pool Jew. Graduates Soc. (1958); C. Merseyside Cttee for Adult Jew. Educ. (1966-73); C. M'side Amalgamated Talmud Torah (1976-81); Gov. King David Primary School (1971-86); C. L'pool Branch, Jewish Historical Society of England (1989-99); Mem. BoD (1975-2000); Gov. Norman Pannell School (1960-2000); P. Mersey Reg. C., BMA (1984-94); Mem. Exec. L'pool Div. BMA (1961-2000, P. 1974, 1985); Mem. L'pool Local Med. Cttee (1969-2000, C. 1987-90); Mem. L'pool Area Med. Cttee (1974-90, C. 1982-84); Council Cameron Fund (1971-2000, T. 1979-88, V.C. 1988-95); Mem. Gen. Med. Serv. Cttee, BMA (1967-90); Council BMA (1980-92); Tr. BMA Charitable Trust (1977-99). Publ.: The Merseyside Jewish Representative Council (1985); From Toxteth to Tel Aviv (2000). Ad.: Flat 2, 5 St Winifred's Road, Meyrick Park, Bournemouth BH2 6NY. ☎ 01202 310859. Fax 01202 291 399. E-mail mervyn@mgoodman.demon.co.uk.

GOODMAN, Mrs Vera (née Appleberg); b. London; BoD (1973-94), Exec. Cttee. (1985-91), form Chairman, Publ. Rel. Cttee.; Bd. of Elders, Span. & Port Jews' Cong. (1977-80; 1990-94); Life V. President (Chairman, 1976-79) Richmond Park Conservative Women's Constit. Cttee.; Nat. C. for Soviet Jewry (1977-80); Greater Lond. Conservative Women's Gen. Purposes Cttee. (1979-85); Conservative Rep., Nat. C. of Women (1974-79); form. Central Lond. C., Conservative Frs. of Israel; Rep., Union of Jewish Women at U.N.A.; Central C., Conservative Party; Conservative Women's Nat. Cttee, Exec.; European Union of Women (Brit. Section); Chairman, Sephardi Women's Guild; Brit. C., World Sephardi Fed., V. Chairman, Govs., Russell Sch., Petersham (1974-82). Ad.: 87 Ashburnham Rd., Ham, Richmond, Surrey, TW10 7NN. ☎ 020-8948 1060.

GORDIMER, Nadine; b. Springs, S. Africa, Nov. 20, 1923; Author; Nobel Prize for Literature (1991); W. H. Smith Literary Award (1961), James Tait Black Member Prize (1972), Booker Prize (1974), Grand Aigle d'Or (1975), Premio Maleparte (1985), Nelly Sachs Prize (1985), Bennett Award, New York (1986). Publ.: Soft Voice of the Serpent, The Lying Days, Six Feet of the Country, A World of Strangers, Friday's Footprint, Occasion for Loving, Not for Publication, The Late Bourgeois World, A Guest of Honour, Livingstone's Companions, The Conservationist, Burger's Daughter, A Soldier's Embrace, July's People, Something Out There, A Sport of Nature (1990), My Son's Story, Jump (1991), None to Accompany Me (1994), The House Gun (1998), The Essential Gesture (1988 non-fiction), Writing and Being (1995, essays), Living in Hope and History (1999, essays), The Pick Up (2001), etc. Ad.: c/o A. P. Watt Ltd, 20 John St., London WC1N 2DR. ☎ 020-7405 6774. Fax 020-7831 2154.

GORDON, Sir Gerald Henry, CBE, QC, MA, LLB, PhD (Glasgow), LLD (Edinburgh), LLD (Hon, Glasgow), Hon. FRSE; b. Glasgow, June 17, 1929; Sheriff of Glasgow and Strathkelvin (1977-99); Temp. Judge Ct. Session and High Ct. of Justiciary (1992-); Memb. Scottish Criminal Cases Review Cttee. (1978-99); Personal Professor of Criminal Law (1969-72), Professor of Scots Law (1972-76), Dean of Faculty of Law (1970-73), all at University of Edinburgh. Publ. Criminal Law of Scotland (1st ed. 1968; 2nd ed. 1978), with Second Cumulative Supplement, 1992; Renton & Brown's Criminal Procedure (ed.) (4th ed. 1972, 5th ed., 1983, 6th ed. 1996). Ad.:

GORDON, Lionel Lawrence, BSc (Econ); b. London, Aug. 31, 1933; Market Research Dir.; form. Chairman, Jewish Chronicle Ltd.; Dir. Jewish Chronicle Trust Ltd; Chairman Jewish Renaissance. Ad.: The Hyde, 5 Orchard Gate, Esher, Surrey, KT10 8HY. ☎ 020-8398 5774. Fax 020-8398 1866.

GOULD, Samuel Julius, MA (Oxon); b. Liverpool, Oct. 13, 1924; Prof. of Sociology, Nottingham Univ. (1964-82); form R., Social Instits., Lond. Sch. of Econ. & Pol. Sci.; Chairman, Trs., Social Affairs Unit, Lond. (since 1981); Res. Dir., Instit. for Pol. Res. (1983-85), Bd. of Dirs., Centre for Pol. Studies; Res. Bd. & Pol. Planning Group, IJA; BoD. Publ.: Dictionary of the Social Sciences (jt edr.), Jewish Life in Modern Britain (jt edr.), The Attack on Higher Education Jewish Commitment: A study in London. Ad.: c/o The Reform Club, Pall Mall, London SW1.

GOULDEN, Simon Charles, BSc (Eng), DMS, CEng, MICE, MIM; b. London, Mar. 1, 1949; Dir. Community Services Group United Synagogue and Chief Exec. Agency for Jewish Education; form. Exec. Dir., Jews' College; Acting Chairman, United Synagogue Bd. of Religious Educ.; Member, Ecumenical Standing Conference on Disability; Princ. Engineer London Borough Haringey (1976-1986). Ad.: Bet Meir, 44a Albert Road, London NW14 2SJ. ☎ 020-8457 9700. Fax 020-8457 9707. E-mail simon@aje.org.uk.

GOURGEY, Percy Sassoon, MBE, FRSA; b. Bombay, June 2, 1923; Journalist; form. Nat. Chairman, Poale Zion; V. Pres. Z Fed.; Chairman Socialist Societies Section of the Labour Party.; Exec. Cttee., BoD, V. Chairman, Erets Israel Cttee., BoD; Chairman, Jews in Arab Lands Cttee., Z. Fed.; Hon. Fel. WZO (1996); form. ed. Jewish Advocate, Bombay; Co-Fdr. and first ed. The Scribe (London), ex-Lieutenant RINVR; Parl. C.; Member, Royal Instit. of International Affairs, Chatham House, London, Contr. to Encyclopaedia Judaica, etc. Publ.: The Jew and his Mission, Ideals, India, Israel in Asia, Indian Jews and the Indian Freedom Struggle, The Indian Naval Revolt of 1946, etc. Ad.: 4 Poplar Ct., Richmond Rd., E. Twickenham, Middx. TW1 2DS. ☎ 020-8892 8498.

GRAHAM, Stewart David, QC, MA, BCL (Oxon), FRSA; b. Leeds, Feb. 27, 1934; Barrister; form. Chairman, Law, Parl. & Gen. Purposes Cttee., BoD; form. Member, Insolvency Rules Adv. Cttee.; form. Mem., C. & Exec. Cttee. of Justice; Senior Vis. Fellow, Centre for Commercial Law Studies, QMW College; form. Member C. Insurance Ombudsman Bureau; Assoc. Memb. British & Irish Ombudsman Assoc. Publ.: Works on bankruptcy and insolvency. Ad.: 6 Grosvenor Lodge, Dennis Lane, Stanmore, Middx., HA7 4JE. ☎ 020-8954 3783.

GRANT, Linda, BA, MA; b. Liverpool, Feb. 15, 1951; Writer. Publ.: (fiction) The Cast Iron Shore (1996); When I Lived in Modern Times (2000); Still Here (2002); (non-fiction) Sexing the Millenium: A Political History of the Sexual Revolution (1993); Remind Me Who I Am Again (1998). Ad.: c/o A.P. Watt, Literary Agents, 20 John Street, London WC1N 2DR.

GRAUS, Eric; b. Bratislava, April 22, 1927; President, Likud-Herut Movement of Gt Britain; Vice Chairman, World Likud Movement; Jt. Chairman, Nat. Z. C. Ad.: 143/5 Brondesbury Pk, NW2 5JL. ☎ 020-8451 0002/3.

GREEN, Sir Allan David, KCB, QC, (KCB 1991); b. March 1, 1935; Form. Dir. of Pub. Prosecutions, First Sr. Treasury Counsel, Central Criminal Court. (1985-87), Sr. Prosecuting Counsel (1979-85), Jr. Prosecuting Counsel (1977-79); Bencher, Inner Temple (1985); Q.C. (1987), Member, Legal Group Tel Aviv Univ. Tr.; Served RN (1953-55). Ad.: 2, Hare Court, Temple, EC4Y 7BH.

GREENBAT, Alan, OBE, JP, b. London, April 1929; Hon. Consultant, Office of the Chief Rabbi; Sec. Rabbinical Commission for the Licensing of Shochetim; Memb. Inner London Youth Courts (1964-99); Exec. & V.Chairman National Council of Voluntary Youth Services (1981-91); Exec. Dir. Office of the Chief Rabbi (1990-91); Dir. Assoc. for Jewish Youth (1980-89); Dir. Victoria Community Centre (1961-80); V.Pres. AJY (1989-96); V.Pres. London Union of Youth Clubs (1984-94); V.Principal Norwood Home for Jewish Children (1955-61). Ad.: Adler House, 735 High Road, London N12 0US. ☎ 020-8343 6301. Fax 020-8343 6310.

GREENBERG, Rabbi Philip T., BA, MPhil, FJC; b. Liverpool, June 28, 1937; Emer. Rabbi, Giffnock & Newlands Syn., Glasgow; Rav. Glasgow Shechita Bd. (1993-99); Chairman Va'ad HaRabbonim, Glasgow; H. Chaplain, Calderwood Lodge Jewish Sch., Glasg.; M., Nottingham Syn. (1968-72), Highams Park & Chingford Syn. (1959-68); Head, Mishna Stream, Hasmonean Boys' Sch. (1972-81). Ad.: 72 Bridge Lane, Golders Green, London NW11 0EJ. ☎/Fax 020-8455 5685.

GREENGROSS, Dr Wendy, MB, BS (Lond), LRCP, MRCS, DObst, RCOG; Dip. Med. Law & Eth.; b. London, Apr. 29, 1925; Medical Practitioner; Broadcaster;

Medical Consultant; Marriage Guidance C.; V. President, AJY Fel., Leo Baeck Coll.; Tr., Leonard Cheshire Foundation; President, Ranulf Assn.; Member Govt. Enquiry into human fertilisation and embryology; Chairman, Ethics Cttee, Wellington Humana Hospital Publ.: Sex in the Middle Years, Sex in Early Marriage; Marriage, Sex and Arthritis; The Health of Women; Entitled to Love; Jewish and Homosexual; Living, Loving and Aging. Ad.: 2 Willifield Way, NW11 7XT. ☎ 020-8455 1153.

GREENWOOD, Jeffrey Michael, MA, LLM; b. London, Apr. 21, 1935; Solicitor; Chairman Wigmore Property Investment Tr. plc; Stow Securities plc; Senior Partner Nabarro Nathanson (1987-95); Chairman Central Council for Education and Training in Social Work (1993-98); V. President Jewish Care; Exec., Anglo-Israel Assn.; Tr & Exec., English Frs., Jerusalem Coll. of Tech (1980-98); Dir., Bank Leumi (UK) plc; Dep. Chairman Jewish Chronicle Ltd.; Chairman, Jewish Literary Trust (2001-); M. Council JHSE. Ad.: 5 Spencer Walk, Hampstead High Street, London NW3 1QZ. ☎ 020-7794 5281. Fax 020-7794 0094. E-mail jeff@thegreenwoods.org.

GROSBERG, Percy, MSc, PhD; b. Cape Town, Apr. 5, 1925; m. Queenie née Fisch; Sr. Res. Off, S. African Wool Textile Res. Instit.(1949-55); Res. Prof., Chair of Textile Engineering, Leeds Univ., (1960-90); Member Bd. Gov. and currently Marcus Sieff Prof. Shenkar School of Engineering and Design, Ramat Gan; Form. Chairman, Leeds Frs., Bar-Ilan Univ. Publ.: Scientific writings. Ad.: Apt 25, 55 Shlomo Hamelech, Netanya 42267. ☎ 09-8628652. Fax 09-8871534.

GROSS, Solomon Joseph, CMG; b. London, Sept. 3, 1920; Ret., Dir., British Steel (1978-90), Plc and other comps.; Dir., Reg. Affairs, B.T.G. (1983-84); Under-Sec., Dept. of Industry (1974-80); Min., Brit. Embassy, Pretoria (1969-73); Brit. Dep. High Com. in Ghana (1966-67). Ad.: 38 Barnes Ct., Station Rd., New Barnet, Herts EN5 1QY.

GRUNEWALD, Rabbi Hans Isaac; b. Frankfurt-am-Main, March 15, 1914; Com. Rabbi of Munich (ret.); Member, Standing Cttee., Conf of European Rab. Union of Orth. Jewish Congs. of Continental Europe, form. Chief Rabbi, Hamburg, Niedersachsen and Schleswig Holstein; President, B'nai B'rith Hebraica Lodge, Munich, President, B'nai B'rith Bialik Lodge, Tel Aviv; President, Z. Org., Munich; Jt. Chairman, C., CCJ, Munich. Publ.: Die Lehre Israels, (1970); Einblicke, (1989). Ad.: 36 Monarch Ct., Lyttelton Rd., N2 0RA. ☎/Fax 020-8455 0811.

GRUNEWALD, Rabbi Jacob Ezekiel, BA; b. Tel Aviv, Oct. 26, 1945; M., Pinner Syn. Ad.: 65 Cecil Park, Pinner, Middx., HA5 5HL. ☎ 020-8933 7045.

GRUNWALD, Henry Cyril, LLB (Hons); b. London, Aug. 8, 1949; m. Alison née Appleton; Barrister, Queen's Counsel; Bencher, Hon. Society of Gray's Inn (2002-); Sen. Vice President BoD (2000-), V. President (1997-2000); Warden, Hampstead Synagogue (1997-); Tr. North London Relate (1995-); Chairman, Pikuach Bd. Gov. (2000-); Mem. Hillel Bd. Dir. (2000-). Ad.: 2 Tudor Street, London EC4Y 0AA. ☎ 020-7797 7111. Fax 020-7797 7120. E-mail h.grunwald@btinternet.com.

GUBBAY, Lucien Ezra, MA (Oxon), MICE; b. Buenos Aires, 1931, m. Joyce née Shammah; Consulting Engineer; President of the Board of Elders, Spanish & Portuguese Jews' Congregation London (1996-2000); Tr. Montefiore Endowment; Mem. Exec. Jewish Memorial Council; form. Warden S & P Synagogue; form. Warden Beth Holim; form. Dir. Industrial Dwellings Society (1885) Ltd; Flg. Off. RAF (1952-54). Publ: Ages of Man (1985), The Jewish Book of Why and What (1987), Origins (1989), Quest for the Messiah (1990), You Can Beat Arthritis (1992), The Sephardim (1992), Sunlight and Shadow: Jewish Experience of Islam (1999). Ad.: 26 Linden Lea, London N2 0RG. ☎ 020-8458 3385.

GUTERMAN, Henry, MBE, MLIA (Dip), AMCT; b. Berlin, Jan. 22, 1926; President, Jewish Rep. C. Greater Manchester & Region, (1986-89), Vice-President and Mem. BoD. (1992-98); Chairman, Def. & Publ. Rel. Cttee. (1978-86, 1997-); Exec., Manch. C. for Com. Rel.; Bd., Com. Rel. Housing Assn.; Mem. Coleyhurst Police Com. Action Group, N. Manch. Crime Prevention Cttee; V. President Disabled Living (1986-); Exec., Manch. Zionist Central Council (1986-); Vice-Chairman CCJ Manch. Branch (1994-); Co. Chair Indian Jewish Ass. (Manch.) (1998-); Co. Chair Black Jewish Forum (1999-2001); V. Chair Manch. Multi-Faith. C. (2000-); Memb. Standing Adv. C. for Religious Education, Manch. (1986-), Trafford (1988-); Bd., South-east Lancashire Housing Ass. Ltd. (SELHAL); Exec., Outreach for Jew Youth; Bd., Heathlands Jewish Homes for Aged; V.-Chairman Manch. Action Cttee. on Health Care for Ethnic Minorities (M.A.C.H.E.M.) (1984-2001); Mem. N. Manch. Jewish Youth Project (1995-). Ad.: 42 Lidgate Grove, Didsbury, Manchester, M20 6TS. ☎ 0161-434 4019; 0161-228 2321 (off.). Fax 0161-236 5976. Email henry@lidgate42.freeserve.co.uk.

HALBAN, Peter Francis, BA (Princeton); b. New York, June 1 1946; Book Publisher; Dir., Peter Halban Publishers Ltd. (1986-); C. European Jewish Publication Soc. (1994-); Memb. Exec. Institute for Jewish Policy Research (1994-). Ad.: Peter Halban Publishers, 22 Golden Square, London W1F 9JW. ☎ 020-7437 9300. Fax 020-7437 9512. Email books@halbanpublishers.com.

HAMILTON, Fabian, BA, MP; b. April 12, 1955; m. Rosemary née Ratcliffe; MP, Leeds North-East (1997-); Leeds City Councillor (1987-98); Chair Edcu. Cttee. (1996-97); Chair Economic Development Cttee (1994-96); Chair Race Equality Cttee (1988-94). Ad.: House of Commons, SW1A 0AA. ☎ 020-7219 3493. Fax 020-7219 4945.

HANDLER, Arieh L.; b. Brun, May 27, 1915; Financial. Consultant; Jewish Agency C. & Member Z. Actions Cttee., P. Mizrachi Fed.; Chairman, Bachad Fellowship (Friends of B'nai Akiva); Chairman, Adv. Body, Torah Dept., Jewish Agency; BoD (form. Chairman, Israel Cttee.); Exec. Jewish Child's Day, Youth Aliyah, (form Dir., Y.A.); Exec WZO; V.Chairman, Brit Frs., Boy's Town, Jerusalem, V. President (form. Chairman) Nat. C. for Soviet Jewry; Montefiore Found.; Jewish Colonial Tr. C.; President, Brit. Frs., Israel Aged, Edr., Jewish Review World Exec. Religious Zionist Movement, T. Mifal Hatorah Aid Foundation; Patron, Jerusalem Institute for the Blind; President, Midreshet Eretz Yisrael; Member, Instit. of Bankers; Fel., Instit. of Dirs.; form. Dir., Hapoel Hamizrachi World Org; form. Man. Dir., Migdal London, Man. Dir. JCB, London. Ad.: c/o Reform Club, SW1.

HARDMAN, Rev. Leslie Henry, MBE, MA, HCF; b. Glynneath, Wales, Feb. 18, 1913; Emer. M., Hendon Syn., V. President, Herut Org.; H. President, NW Lond. Jewish Ex-Servicemen's Assn.; Chaplain, Edgware Hospital Psychiatric Unit. Publ.: The Survivors. Awards: BBC 'Hearts of Gold', 1993; Simon Wiesenthal Museum of Tolerance, 1995. Ad.: 20 St. Peter's Ct., Queens Rd., NW4 2HG. ☎ 020-8202 6977.

HARMATZ, Joseph; b. Rokishkis, Lithuania, Jan. 23, 1925; Dir.-Gen. ORT Israel (1966-79); Dir.-Gen. World ORT (1980-93); Publ.: From the Wings (1998); Life with ORT (2002). Ad.: 36 Yehuda Hanassi Str., Tel Aviv 69206. ☎/Fax 972 3 642 5463.

HARRIS, Rabbi Cyril K., BA, MPhil; b. Glasgow, Sept. 19, 1936; m. Ann née Boyars; Chief Rabbi of South Africa; H. President S.A. Jewish Board of Educ.; H.V.-P. S.A. Zionist Fed., H. P. Mizrachi Org.; H. President S.A. Rabbinical Assoc.; Co-President, Tikkun (Black Upliftment and Empowerment Projects); Distinguished Leadership Award of the South African Jewish Board of Deputies (1997); Commonwealth Jewish Council Award (2000) with Mrs Harris; form. M., Kenton Syn. (1958-72), Edgware Syn. (1975-78), St. John's Wood Syn. (1979-87); Sr. Jewish Chap. to H.M. Forces (1966-71). Publ.: Jewish Obligation to the Non-Jew

(1996); For Heaven's Sake – the Chief Rabbi's Diary (2000). Ad.: c/o Union of Orthodox Synagogues of South Africa, 58 Oaklands Rd., Orchards 2192, Johannesburg, S. Africa. ☎ 485-4865. Fax 485-1497. E-mail chief@uos.co.za.

HARRIS, Dr Evan, MP, BA, BM, BS; b. Sheffield, Oct. 21, 1965; Registrar in Public Health Medicine (1994-97); MP (Lib.Dem.) Oxford West and Abingdon (1997-); Health Spokesman (2001-); Hon. Assoc. National Secular Soc. (2000-). Ad.: House of Commons, London SW1A 0AA.☎ 020-7219 3614; 32a North Hinksey Village, Oxford OX2 8NA. ☎ 01865-250424.

HARRIS, Michael; b. London, Aug. 8, 1928; Public Relations Adviser; London repr. Delamere Forest School; form. Dir. United Kingdom Jewish Aid; form. Insurance Manager; Freeman of City of London (1976); AJY Exec (1953-94), V. Pres. (1981-), Chairman (1989-93); AJA Council (1960-); Tr. Sutton AJEX (1990-99); BoD Mem. (for AJY 1958-73, for Sutton & Cheam 1973-); Central J. Lect. Cttee (1982-94), V.C. (1988-91), Chairman (1991-94), Exec. Cttee (1991-94), Educ. Cttee (V.C. 1994-97); United Syn. Council (1984-); World Confed. JCC's V.P. (1990-96); BoD Heritage Group (1996-); Assn. Jewish Friendship Clubs (Jt. Hon. Tr. 1994-); Imperial Cancer Research Fund, Life Gov. (1985); Jewish Youth Fund, Adv. Cttee. (1989-95); Nat. Assoc Boys Clubs C. (1988-99); Sutton Synagogue, H. Sec. (1978-84), Warden (1984-88); H. Tr. South London Comm. C. (1990-99); North West Jewish Boys Club, H. Sec. (1956-66). Ad.: 63 Lodge Close, Edgware, Middx HA8 7RL. ☎ 020-8952 8863.

HARRIS, Rabbi Michael Jacob, MA (Cantab), MA (Jerusalem), PhD (SOAS); b. London, Feb. 17, 1964; Rabbi, Hampstead Synagogue (1995-); Lecturer in Jewish Law, Jews' College, London (1995-97); form. Rabbi, Southend and Westcliff Hebrew Cong. (1992-95). Ad.: The Hampstead Synagogue, Dennington Park Rd., London NW6 1AX. ☎/Fax 020-7435 1518. Fax 020-7431 8368. E-mail rabbi.michael@talk21.com.

HASKEL, Lord; b. Kaunas, Oct. 9, 1934; m. Carole Lewis; Life Peer; Deputy Speaker, House of Lords; President, IJPR (2002-). Ad.: House of Lords, London SW1A 0PW. ☎ 020-7219 4076. Email haskel@compuserve.com.

HASS, Rev. Simon, LLCM; b. Poland, May 2, 1927; Cantor Central Syn. Gt Portland St., London,W.l. (since 1951); Composer Musical Arranger. Publ.: Many Recordings of Jewish liturgical and classical music. Ad.: "Beit Shirah", 2A Allandale Ave., N3 3PJ.

HAYMAN, Baroness Helene of Dartmouth Park (née Middleweek), PC, MA (Cantab); b. Wolverhampton, March 26, 1949; m. Martin Hayman; Chairman, Cancer Research UK (2001-); Min. State, Agriculture (1999-2001); Parlt Under Sec. of State, Dept. of Environment, Transport and the Regions (1997-98); PPS Dept. of Health (1998-99); Labour Mem. of Parliament (1974-79); Chairman, Whittington Hospital (1992-97). Ad.: House of Lords, SW1A 0PW.

HEILBRON, Dame Rose, DBE, LLB, LLM, Hon. LLD (Liverpool), Hon. LLD (Warwick), Hon. LLD (Manchester); Hon. LLD (CNAA); b. Liverpool, Aug. 19, 1914; Judge of the High Court' Family Division (1974-88); Tr., Gray's lnn (1985); Presiding Judge, Northern Circuit (1979-82); form. Leader, Northern Circuit Recorder and H. Recorder of Burnley; Tr., Gray's Inn (1985); H. Fel., Lady Margaret Hall, Oxford; H.Fel., Manch. Univ. Instit. of Sci. & Tech.

HELFGOTT, Ben, MBE; b. Pabianice, Poland, Nov. 22, 1929; Chairman, '45 Aid Soc. (1963–70, 1975–); Chairman, Yad Vashem Cttee., BoD; Chairman C., Promotion of Yiddish & Yiddish Culture; C., Jewish Youth Fund; Exec., Wiener Libr.; Chairman, Polin-Inst. for Polish Jewish Studies; Vice Chairman, Claims Conference; form. Jt. T., CBF-WJR; Brit. Weightlifting Champion & Record Holder; competed in Olympic Games (1956; 1960); Bronze Medal, Commonwealth Games (1958); Gold Medals, Maccabiah (1950, 1953, 1957). Ad.: 46 Amery Rd., Harrow, Middx. HA1 3UG. ☎ 020-8422 1512.

HELLNER, Rabbi Frank, BA, BHL, MA, DD (Hon); b. Philadelphia, Pa., Jan. 1,

1935; Emer. Rabbi Finchley Progressive Syn.; Exec., Barnet Com. Rel. C.; Gov., Akiva Sch.; Mem. Jewish Community Schools Adv. Board; V. President, Finchley CCJ, Member Leo Baeck Coll. Comp.; Extra-Mural Lect. Birkbeck Coll. (Pt.-time); Chairman, ULPS Rabbinic Conference (1970-71); Edr., ULPS News (1978-86); Chaplain to Mayor of L. B. Barnet (1993-94). Publ.: I Promise I Will Try not to Kick My Sister and Other Sermons. Ad.: Finchley Progressive Synagogue, 54 Hutton Grove, N12 8DR. Tel/Fax 020-8446 4063.

HENIG, Stanley, MA, (Oxford); Hon. RNCM, (Royal Northern College of Music); b. Leicester, July 7, 1939; Prof. (Emeritus) of Politics, University of Central Lancashire; Leader, Lancaster City Council (1991-); M.P. (Lancaster) (1966-70) Chairman, RNCM (1986-89); Secretary Labour Group, Local Government Association (1997-99). Publ.: Uniting of Europe (1997, 2nd ed. 2002) and other books on political parties and on European Union; Enrico Caruso: Recollections and Retrospectives; Modernising Britain. Ad.: 10 Yealand Drive, Lancaster LA1 4EW. ☎ 01524 69624.

HERTZBERG, Rabbi Arthur, PhD; b. Lubaczow, Poland; Rabbi Emer., Temple Emanuel of Englewood; form. President, American Jewish Cong.; Hon. V. President, World Jewish Cong.; Prof. of Religion Emer., Dartmouth Coll., Adjunct Prof of Hist. Columbia Univ, Prof of Hist., Hebrew Univ. (1970-71); Fel. Instit. Advanced Studies, Hebrew Univ. (1982); Vis. Prof. of the Humanities, New York Univ. Publ.: The Zionist Idea, Judaism, The French Enlightenment and the Jews, Being Jewish in America, The Jews in America (1989), Judaism, 2nd ed. (1991), Jewish Polemics (1992), Jews, the Essence and Character of a People (jt.auth., 1998). Ad.: 83 Glenwood Rd., Englewood, New Jersey 07631, USA. ☎ 201-568-3259.

HILL, Brad Sabin, AB, FRAS; b. New York, Nov. 2, 1953; Librarian and Fel. in Hebrew Bibliography, Oxford Centre for Hebrew and Jewish Studies; form. Hd., Hebrew Section, The British Library (1989-96); Curator of Rare Hebraica, National Library of Canada, Ottawa (1979-89). Publ.: Incunabula, Hebraica & Judaica (1981); Hebraica from the Valmadonna Trust (1989); (ed.) Miscellanea Hebraica Bibliographica (1995). Ad.: 119 Banbury Road, Oxford OX2 6LB.

HILTON, Rabbi Michael, MA, D.Phil, PGCE; b. London, Feb. 27, 1951; M. Kol Chai Hatch End Jewish Community (2001-); M. North London Progressive Synagogue (1999-2001); M. Cheshire Reform Congregation (1987-98); Hon. Res. Fel. Centre for Jewish Studies, University of Manchester (1998-); Homeless Persons off., L.B. Hammersmith & Fulham (1980-82). Publ.: The Gospels and Rabbinic Judaism (with G. Marshall, 1988.), The Christian Effect on Jewish Life (1994). Ad.: Hatch End Jewish Community, 434 Uxbridge Road, Pinner, Middx HA5 4RG. ☎ 020-8906 8241. Email greystar@zetnet.co.uk.

HOBSBAWM, Eric John Ernest, CH, FBA, MA, PhD; b. Alexandria, Egypt, June 9, 1917; Emer. Prof of Econ. and Soc. Hist., Birkbeck Coll., Lond. Univ.; H. Fel., King's Coll., Cambridge. Publ.: Primitive Rebels, The Jazz Scene, The Age of Revolution, Labouring Men, Industry and Empire, Nations and Nationalism, The Age of Extremes, 1914-1991, Uncommon People, Interesting Times: A Twentieth-Century Life (2002), etc. Ad.: Birkbeck College, Malet St., WC1E 7HX. ☎ 020-7631 6000.

HOCHHAUSER, Dr Daniel, MA, D.Phil, FRCP; b. London, July 18, 1957; m. Joanne née Garland; Senior Lecturer and Consultant in Medical Oncology, Royal Free and University College Medical School. Publ.: articles on treatment of gastrointestinal cancer and new agents for treating cancer. Ad.: Royal Free Hospital, Rowland Hill Street, London NW3 2QE. ☎ 020-7830 2601. Fax 020-7794 3341. E-mail d.hochhauser@ucl.uk.

HOCHHAUSER, Victor, CBE; b. Kosice, Czechoslovakia, Mar. 27, 1923; Impresario for internat. artists orchestras, ballet companies, etc. Ad.: 4 Oak Hill Way, NW3 7LR. ☎ 020-7794 0987. Fax 020-7431 2531.

HOWARD, Michael, PC, QC, MP; b. Gorseinon, Wales, July 7, 1941; M.P. (Cons) for Folkestone and Hythe; Shadow Chancellor (2001-); form. Home Secretary (1993-97); Secretary of State for the Environment (1992-93); Chairman, Conservative Bow Group (1970-71); form. President, Cambridge Union. Ad.: House of Commons, SW1A 0AA.

HUBERT, Walter I., FRSA, F. Inst. Dir.; b. Schluechtern, Germany, Aug. 13, 1932; First Chairman, Gateshead Foundation for Torah, IJA; Patron, Didsbury Jewish Primary Sch.; H. Life V. President, Brit. Cttee., Peylim of Israel; Gov., Global Bd., & H. Fel., Bar-Ilan Univ.; Gov., Ben Gurion Univ.; V. President, Cancer Res. Cttee.; Dir. State of Israel Bonds (UK); V.P., British Herut; form. Chairman, Blackburn Rovers F.C.; First Recipient (1981) Bank Hapoalim Silver Rose Award for new Israeli industry; Jerusalem Educ. Medal (1974); Zurich Jewish Secondary Schs., 'Man of Year' Gold Medal (1978); assoc. with many educ. and charitable instit. in Brit., Israel, Switzerland, US and Argentina. Ad.: 24 King David Gdns., 27 King David St., Jerusalem, Israel. ☎ 02 241754.

HURST, Alex; b. Liverpool, Jan. 6, 1935; form. Admin., Merseyside Jewish Welfare C.; form. Sec., L'pool Jewish Housing Assn. Ad.: 440 Allerton Rd., Liverpool L18 3JX. ☎ 0151-427 7377.

HYMAN, Barry S., MIPR; b. Scotland, June 24, 1941, m. Judith; Public Relations and Media Consultant, Broadcaster, Writer; PR consultant and newsletter editor to RSGB (1995-2002); Hon. Vice President Radlett and Bushey Reform Syn (2000-); BoD Public Relations Cttee (1988-97); Member of the Institute of Public Relations (1987-); Head of Corporate Affairs, Media Relations, Community Affairs and Company Archive, Marks and Spencer (1984-94). Publ.: Young in Herts (1996), a history of the Radlett and Bushey Reform Synagogue; A Job for a Jewish Girl ... or Boy? The Rabbinate as a Career (2000); (Ed.) Reform Judaism News (1996-2002). Ad.: Radlett & Bushey Reform Syn., 118 Watling Street, Radlett, Herts. WD7 7AA. ☎ 01923 856110. Fax 01923 818444. Email barry@hypeople.freeserve.co.uk.

HYMAN, Mrs. Marguerite Grete (née De Jongh); b. London, Mar. 26, 1913; V. President (form. Fin. Sec.) Union of Lib. & Progr. Syns.. Ad.: 14 The Cedars, St. Stephen's Rd., W13 8JF. ☎ 020-8997 8258.

INGRAM, Rabbi Chaim Nota, BA (Hons); b. London, May 14, 1952; Assoc. Rabbi, The Central Synagogue, Sydney; M., Leicester Hebrew Cong. (1986-92); M./R., United Hebrew Cong., Newcastle Upon Tyne (1982-96); R., Cricklewood Syn, London (1979-82). Publ.: Renana Song Book. Ad: 196 Old South Head Road, Bellevue Hill, Sydney, NSW 2023. ☎/Fax 02-9365 5716. E-mail judaism @matra.com.au.

ISRAEL, Jonathan Irvine, MA, D.Phil. FRHS, FBA; b. London, Jan. 22, 1946; Professor, Dutch Hist. & Instits., Lond. Univ., Univ. Coll.; H. Sec., JHSE (1974-79); Wolfson Hist. Prize (1986); Ed. Littman Library of Jewish Civilization (1990-). Publ.: European Jewry in the Age of Mercantilism, 1550-1750, The Dutch Republic and the Hispanic World, 1606-61, Race, Class and Politics in Colonial Mexico, 1610-70, Dutch Primacy in World Trade (1585-1740), Empires and Entrepots: the Dutch, the Spanish Monarchy and the Jews, 1585-1713, Anglo-Dutch moment: essays on the Glorious Revolution and its world impact, The Dutch Republic, its rise, greatness and fall, 1477-1806 (1995); Conflicts of Empires: Spain, the Low Countries and the Struggle for World Supremacy, 1585-1713 (1997). Ad.: 48 Parkside Dr., Edgware, Middx. HA8 8JX. ☎ 020-8958 6069.

ISSERLIN, Benedikt Sigmund Johannes, M.A. (Edin.), M.A., B.Litt., D.Phil. (Oxon.); b. Munich, Feb. 25, 1916; form. Reader and Head of Dept. Semitic Studies, Leeds Univ.; Kennicott Hebrew Fellowship (Oxford, 1947); form. H. Sec., Anglo-Israel Archaeological Soc.; President, Brit. Assn. for Jewish Studies (1982). Publ.: The Israelites (1998); Writings on Near Eastern Studies, incl. A

Hebrew Work Book for Beginners; Ch. on Israelite Art in C. Roth, Jewish Art; Motya, a Phoenician and Carthaginian City in Sicily, I (with J. du Plat Taylor); A Study of Contemporary Dialectal Maltese, I (with J. Aquilina); Das Volk der Bibel (2001); Contr. Times Atlas of the Bible, and O. Tufnell, Lachish IV. Ad.: c/o Dept. of Arabic and Middle Eastern Studies, Leeds Univ., Leeds, LS2 9JT. ☎ 0113 2751576.

JACKSON, Bernard Stuart, LLB (Hons), D.Phil, LLD, DHL (h.c.); b. Liverpool, Nov. 16, 1944; Barrister; Alliance Professor of Modern Jewish Studies, Co-Dir. Centre for Jewish Studies, Univ. Manchester (1997-); President BAJS (1993); Edr., Jewish Law Annual (1978-97); Sec., J. Law Publ. Fund (1980-). Publ.: Theft in Early Jewish Law, Essays in Jewish and Comparative Legal Hist., Semiotics and Legal Theory, Law, Fact and Narrative Coherence, Making Sense in Law, Making Sense in Jurisprudence, Studies in the Semiotics of Biblical Law, (edr.) Studies in Jewish Legal Hist. in Hon. of David Daube, Modern Research in Jewish Law, Jewish Law in Legal Hist. and the Modern World, Semiotics, Law and Social Science (with D. Carzo), The Touro Conference Volume (Jew. Law Assn. Studies I), The Jerusalem Conference Volume (Jew. Law Assn. Studies II), The Boston Conference Volume (Jew. Law Assn. Studies IV), The Halakhic Thought of R. Isaac Herzog (Jew. Law Assn. Studies V), The Jerusalem 1990 Conference Volume (Jew. Law Assn. Studies VI) (with S. M. Passamaneck); Legal Visions of the New Europe (with D. McGoldrick); Legal Semiotics and the Sociology of Law; Introduction to the History and Sources of Jewish Law (with N. Hecht and others). Ad.: Centre for Jewish Studies, Dept. of Religions and Theology, Arts Building, Univ. Manchester, Oxford Rd., M13 9PL. Fax 0161-729 0371. E-mail bernard. jackson@man.ac.uk.

JACOBI, Rabbi Harry Martin, BA Hons; b. Berlin, Oct. 19, 1925; Chairman, Rabbinic Bd, ULPS; form. M. South Bucks Jewish Community, Zurich Lib. Syn., Wembley Lib. Syn., Southgate Progressive Syn.; President, Southgate B'nai B'rith Ben-Gurion Lodge (1974-75). Ad.: 1 Walton Court, Lyonsdown Road, New Barnet, EN5 1JW. ☎ 020-8440 1261.

JACOBS, David; b. Manchester, 1951; m. Hannah Rose née Noorden; Dir. Syn. Support, Reform Synagogues of Great Britain; Vice President, Jewish Genealogical Society of GB; Mem. C. JHSE; Co-fdr. Jewish East End Project (1977); Co-fdr. London Museum of Jewish Life (1983); RSGB Youth Development Off. (1975-79); Dir. Victoria Com. Centre (1988-91). Ad.: RSGB, The Sternberg Centre for Judaism, 80 East End Road, Finchley, N3 2SY. ☎ 020-8349 5643. Email david.jacobs@reformjudaism.org.uk.

JACOBS, David Lewis, CBE, DL, Hon. D. Kingston Univ.; b. London, May 19, 1926; Broadcaster; host and Chairman of BBC radio and television programmes; Dep. Lieutenant for Greater London; High Steward, Royal Borough of Kingston upon Thames; V. President, Stars Org. for Spastics; form. Chairman, Think British Campaign; V. President, R. Star and Garter Home, Richmond; Past President, Nat. Children's Orchestra; form. V. Chairman, R.S.P.C.A.; President, Kingston Upon Thames Royal British Legion; V. President, Wimbledon Girls Choir; Chairman, Kingston Theatre Trust; Life Governor Imperial Cancer Research Fd.; Jt. Pres. Thames Community Tr.; Pres. S.W. London Area SSAFFA; Chairman Thames FM; Pres. T.S. Steadfast; Patron Age Resource; Patron Kingston Bereavement Tr.; Pres. Kingston Alcohol Service. Publ.: Jacobs' Ladder (autobiog.), Caroline, Any Questions (with Michael Bowen). Ad.: 203 Pavilion Rd., SW1X 0BJ.

JACOBS, David Michael, b. Bristol, June 4, 1930, m. Marion née Davis; Exec. (form. Gen. Sec.), AJA; Exec. Dir. Likud-Herut GB; Chairman Jewish Affiliates of the United Nations Assoc.; Vice-P., form. Chairman Guild of Jewish Journalists; H.V. President Chiltern Progressive Syn.; form. Chairman, Beds.-Herts. Progressive Jewish Cong.; form. BoD, Press Officer; Brit. Z. Fed. Publ.:

Israel (World in Colour series) 1968, Research & writing for Jewish Communities of the World, (Ed. A. Lerman) 1989. Ad.: 56 Normandy Rd., St. Albans, Herts AL3 5PW. ☎ /Fax 01727-858454.

JACOBS, Rabbi Irving, BA, PhD (Lond); b. London, Aug. 2, 1938; Princ. Jews, College (1990-93); Res. Fell, (1966-69), Lect. (1969-84); Dean (1984-90); First Incumbent, Sir Israel Brodie Chair in Bible Studies; Dir., Midrashah Instit. for Israel Studies (1980-82); form. Min., Sutton and District Hebrew Cong. Publ.: The Midrashic Process. Ad.: 28 Elmstead Ave., Wembley, Middx. ☎ 020-8248 5777.

JACOBS, Rabbi Julian Godfrey, MA, PhD (Lond), PGCE; b. London, March 6, 1934; m. Margaret née Harris; form. M., Ealing Syn.; Chap., Thames Valley Univ.; Chap., Heathrow Airport; M. of Chief Rabbi's Cabinet; Exec. cttee Interfaith Network; form. M., Liverpool Old Hebrew Cong.; M., Blackpool United Hebrew Cong.; Barking & Becontree Syn.; West Hackney Syn.; Richmond Syn. Chap. to Mayor of Ealing (1992-93); Publ.: The Ship has a Captain, From Week to Week, Judaism looks at Modern Issues, A Haftara Companion. Ad.: Rehov Shaulson 30/7, Har Nof, Jerusalem 95400. ☎ 6541859.

JACOBS, June Ruth (née Caller); b. London, June 1, 1930; Professional Volunteer; Immediate Past President, Int. Council of Jewish Women; V. Chairman, Jewish Council for Racial Equality and Jewish Black Forum; Co-Chairman, International Executive, International Centre for Peace in Middle East; Life Mem. League, Jewish Women; L. President, Jewish Child's Day; Trustee, Kessler Foundation; Exec. Mem., Council for Jewish Palestinian Dialogue; BoD; Mem. of International Board and UK Board, New Israel Fund; Bd. Mem., IJPR; Vice President, Memorial Foundation for Jewish Culture; Exec. European Jewish Congress; Exec. World J. Congress. Ad.: 13 Modbury Gardens, London NW5 3QE. ☎ 020-7485 6027. Fax 020-7284 2809.

JACOBS, Rabbi Louis, CBE, BA, PhD, HDHL (Chicago, New York, Cincinnati), HLiD (Lancaster); b. Manchester, July 17, 1920; Founder Rabbi and form. M., New London Syn. (1964-2000); Vis. Prof, Lancaster Univ.; form. H. Dir., Soc. for Study of Jewish Theology; form. Tutor and Lect., Jews, Coll. (1959-62), form. Minister-Preacher, New West End Syn., London (1954-59); and Rab., Manchester Central Syn. Publ: Jewish Prayer, We Have Reason to Believe, Jewish Values, Principles of the Jewish Faith, A Jewish Theology, Teyku, The Talmudic Argument, A Tree of Life, Helping with Enquiries, Holy Living; God, Torah and Israel, Structure and Form of the Babylonian Talmud, Religion and the Individual, The Jewish religion: a companion, Beyond Reasonable Doubt, Ask the Rabbi, Concise Companion to the Jewish Religion, etc. Ad.: 27 Clifton Hill, NW8 0QE ☎ 020-7624 1299.

JACOBS, Myrna (née Appleton); b. London, Aug. 18, 1940; m. Laurance D. Jacobs; Headteacher of Immanuel College (1995-2000); Head of Languages, Anna Head High, Berkeley, California (1962-66); Lecturer, Univ. of California Extension (Berkeley & San Francisco) (1964-66); Head of Language Faculty in Borough of Brent, consecutively Brondesbury & Kilburn, John Kelly Girls, Preston Manor (1973-89).

JACOBSON, Dan, BA, DLitt (Hons); b. Johannesburg, March 7, 1929; Novelist and univ. Prof. Emer., Univ. Coll. London (1994-); Publ.: A Dance in the Sun, The Beginners, The Rape of Tamar, The Story of Stories: the Chosen People and its God, Her Story, Heshel's Kingdom, etc. Ad.: c/o A. M. Heath & Co., 79 St. Martin's La., WC2N 4AA ☎ 020-7836 4271.

JACOBSON, Howard, MA (Cantab); b. Manchester, Aug. 25, 1942; Novelist and critic; JQ/Wingate Prize for Fiction, 2001; Senior Lect., Wolverhampton Polytechnic (1974-80); Supervisor in English Studies, Selwyn College (1968-72); Lect., English Literature, University of Sydney (1965-67). Publ.: Shakespeare's Magnanimity (with Wilbur Sanders, 1978); Coming from Behind (1983);

Peeping Tom (1984); Redback (1986); In the Land of Oz (1987); The Very Model of a Man (1992); Roots Schmoots (1993); Seriously Funny: An Argument for Comedy (1996); No More Mister Nice Guy (1998); The Mighty Walzer (1999); Who's Sorry Now? (2002). Ad.: c/o Peter Fraser & Dunlop, Drury House, 34-43 Russell Street, London WC2B 5HA. ☎ 020-7344 1000.

JAKOBOVITS, Lady, Amelie (née Munk), PhD (Hon); b. Ansbach, May 31, 1928; Fdr. and President, Assoc. of US Women; V. President, Emunah Women's Org.; President, Jewish Marriage C., Dir. of Jewish Care; Fdr. and Patron of Chai Lifeline, L.P. JIA Women's Division; Life V. President, League of Jewish Women; Patron of Dysautonomia Foundation; V. President, Wizo; P. Ladies, Visitation Cttee., US; V. President, Youth Aliyah; Patron 'J' Link; President, 'Chen'. Ad.: 44a Albert Rd., London NW4 2SJ.

JANNER, Baron of Braunstone (Life Peer) (Hon., Greville Ewan), MA (Cantab), Hon. PhD (Haifa), Hon. LLD (De Montfort), QC; b. Cardiff, July 11, 1928; Barrister-at-law; form. MP (Lab.) for Leicester West (1970-97); President Inter Party Council Against Anti-Semitism; Chairman, Select Cttee. on Employment (1993-96); Dir., Ladbroke plc (1986-95); Chairman, JSB Group Ltd., including Effective Presentational Skills (1984-97); President, BoD (1979-85); P. Commonwealth Jewish C.; Hon. V. President, WJC; Fdr. and V. Chairman, All-Party Parl. Cttee. for Jews from the FSU; V. Chairman, Brit.-Israel Parl. Group, H. Sec., All-Party Parl. War Crimes Group; Chairman, Holocaust Educ. Tr.; President, Maimonides Foundation; Member Magic Circle and International Brotherhood of Magicians; Sec., Parl. Cttee. for East European Jewry (1993-97); Chairman, All-Party Parl. Industrial Safety Group (1975-97); P. Ret. Execs. Action Group (REACH); form. President, Jewish Museum; Bd. Dirs., UJIA; Tr., Elsie & Barnett Janner Tr.; Exec., Lab. Frs. of Israel; V. President, AJY, Ajex; Fel., Inst. of Personnel and Development; Member NUJ; H. Member, Nat. Union Mineworkers (Leics. Br.); form. President, WJC (Europe); form. President, Nat. C. for Soviet Jewry; form. Tr., Jewish Chronicle, form. Dir., Jewish Chronicle; President, Camb. Union & Fdr. & Chairman, The Bridge in Britain; Chairman, Camb. Univ. Lab. Club; form. Chairman, Brady Boys, Club. Lect., contrib. and author 68 books. Ad.: House of Lords, London SW1A 0PW.

JAQUE, Sidney, JP; b. Toledo, Ohio, USA, June 23, 1912; Ret. Solicitor; form. Mayor of Holborn (1958), H.L. Patron (form. Chairman), Camden (form. Holborn) Chamber of Commerce; form. Chairman, Camden Commercial Ratepayers Group (since 1979); Past President, now Hon. Life President Western Marble Arch Syn. (form. Western Syn.); Chairman, Western Charitable Foundation; form. Gov., St. Nicholas Montessori Instit.; form. Gov., J.F.S.; form. Dep. Chairman, West Central Magistrates, Div.; V. President (form. President), Holborn & St. Pancras Conservative Assn.; Patron Frs., Royal Lond. Homoeopathic Hospital, Vice-P., London Youth Tr. Publ.: The Western Synagogue, 1961-1991 (1998). Ad.: 56 Sheringham, St. Johns Wood Park, NW8 6RA. ☎ 020-7722 3671. Fax 020-7722 9317.

JEUDA, Basil Simon; b. Manchester, Sept. 17, 1938; m. Laura née Madden; Chartered Accountant; Chairman, Manchester Jewish Museum (2001-), Tr. (1997-); Chairman, Mersey Regional Ambulance Service, NHS Trust (1999-); form. Leader, Cheshire County Council (1981-85). Publ.: History of Churnet Valley Railway, 1849-1999; History of Rudyard Lake, 1797-1997; The Knotty: An Illustrated History of the North Staffordshire Railway. Ad.: 305 Buxton Road, Macclesfield, Cheshire SK11 7ET. ☎ 01625-426740. E-mail bjeuda@ aol.com.

JOSEPH, Dr Anthony Peter, MBBChir (Cantab), MRCGP, FSG; b. Birmingham, April 23, 1937; form. GP; Post-graduate tutor in paediatrics, Univ. of Birmingham (1986-91); form. President JHSE (1994-96); President, Jewish Genealogical Society of Gt. Britain (1997-); Chairman, Birmingham Branch of JHSE (1969-);

Corresponding member for Great Britain, Australian Jewish Historical Society (1965-); UK rep. of Society of Australian Genealogists (1965-95); Dir. Int. Assoc. Jewish Genealogical Societies (2000-); Contributor on Jewish Genealogy to Blackwell Companion to Jewish Culture; Author of papers in many different genealogical publications, including JHSE. Ad.: 25 Westbourne Road, Edgbaston, Birmingham B15 3TX. ☎ 0121-454 0408. Fax 0121-454 9758.

JOSEPH, John Michael; b. London, 11 Feb. 1939; Chairman, GET Group Plc; Chairman, Jewish Blind & Disabled; Chairman, Cavendish Housing Trust Ltd. Ad.: 24 Rosslyn Hill, London NW3.

JOSIPOVICI, Prof. Gabriel David, FRSL, FBA; b. Nice, France, Oct. 8, 1940; Writer; Univ. Teacher; Prof. of English, School of European Studies, Univ. of Sussex; Asst. Lect. in English, School of European Studies, Univ. of Sussex (1963-5); Lect. in English (1965-73); Reader in English (1973-85); Lord Weidenfeld Vis. Prof., Oxford (1996-97). Publ.: The Inventory, Words, The Present, Migrations, The Air We Breathe, Conversations in Another Room, Contre-Jour, The Big Glass, In a Hotel Garden, Moo Pak, Now, The World and the Book, The Lessons of Modernism, The Book of God, Text and Voice, Touch, On Trust, A Life, Goldberg Variations. Ad.: 60 Prince Edward's Rd., Lewes, Sussex BN7 1BH.

JULIUS, Anthony Robert, MA (Cantab), PhD (London); b. London, July 16, 1956; m. Dina née Rabinovitch; Solicitor; Partner, Mishcon de Reya (1984-98), Hd. Litigation (1988-98); Consultant; Vice President, Diana, Princess of Wales Mem. Fd. (2002-), Chairman (1997-99), T. (1997-2002); Chairman, Law Panel, IJPR (1997-), reporting on Holocaust Denial Legislation; Mem. Appeals Cttee., Dermatrust (1999-); Chairman, Management Bd., Centre for Cultural Analysis, Theory and History, University of Leeds (2001-). Publ.: T.S. Eliot, Anti-semitism and Literary Form (1995); Idolizing Pictures (2001); Transgressions: The Offences of Art (2002). Ad.: Mishcon de Reya, Summit House, 12 Red Lion Square, London WC1R 4QD. ☎ 020-7440 7000. E-mail anthony.julius@mishcon.co.uk.

JUST, Rabbi Mayer; b. Wignitz, Aug. 15, 1912; President Chief Rabbinate of Holland; Ad.: Frans Van Mierisstraat 77, 107 1 RN Amsterdam.

KALMS, Lady Pamela, MBE; b. London, July 29, 1931; form. Vol. Services Co-ordinator, Edgware Gen. Hospital; form. Deputy Chairman, form. NHS Wellhouse Tr. (Barnet and Edgware Gen. Hospitals); form. Mem. Exec. Jewish Marriage Council; Tr. and Dir., Ravenswood Foundation; Exec. Director, Literary Manager, New End Theatre. Ad.: 29 Farm Street, London W1J 5RL. ☎ 020-7499 3494. Fax 020-7499 3436.

KALMS, Sir Stanley, Hon. FCGI (1991), Hon. DLitt CNAA/ University of London (1991), Hon. D. Univ. North London (1994), Hon. Fellow London Business School (1995), Hon. D. Econ. Richmond (1996), Hon. D.Litt, Sheffield (2002), Hon. Degree, Buckingham (2002); b. London Nov. 21, 1931; m. Pamela née; Chairman Dixons Group plc; Tr., Conservative Party (2001-); Dir. Centre for Policy Studies (1991-2002); Vis. Prof., Business Sch., Univ. of North London (1991-); Mem. of Bd. of Funding Agency for Schs – Chairman of the Agency's Finance Cttee (1994-97); Gov., Dixons Bradford City Technology Coll. (1988-); Tr. Industry in Educn. Ltd. (1993-); Gov. of National Institute of Economic & Social Research (1995-2001); Dir. Business for Sterling (1998-2002); Tr., The Economic Education Tr. (1993); F. and Sponsor of Centre for Applied Jewish Ethics in Business and the Professions, Jerusalem; Fd. of Stanley Kalms Foundation; Co-Fd. and Sponsor of Immanuel College; form. Chairman, Jewish Educational Development Tr. (1978-89) and Jews' College (1983-89); Non-Exec. Dir., British Gas (1987-97); Chairman King's Healthcare NHS Trust (1993-96). Publ.: A Time for Change (1992). Ad.: 29 Farm Street, London W1J 5RL. ☎ 020-7499 3494. Fax 020-7499 3436.

KARPF, Anne, BA Oxon, MA Oxon, MSc; b. June 8, 1950; Journalist and writer; Radio critic, the Guardian (1993-); columnist, Jewish Chronicle (1999-). Publ.: Doctoring the Media: The Reporting of Health and Medicine (1988); The War After: Living with the Holocaust (1996). Ad.: c/o The Guardian, 119 Farringdon Road, London EC1R 3ER.

KATSAV, Moshe, BA (HU), BEd (HU), DU (Hon) Nebraska, George Washington U., University of Hertford, Yeshivah University; b. Iran, 1945, Aliyah 1951; m. Gila; 8th President of Israel (2000-); MK (1977-2000); Dep. Prime Minister and Minister of Tourism (1996-99); Mayor, Kiryat Malachi (1969, 1974-81). Ad.: Presidency, Jerusalem.

KATTEN, Brenda (née Rosenblit), b. London, Sept. 8, 1936; Chairperson of Public Affairs & NGO Dept. World WIZO (Israel); Exec. Mem. Israel, Britain and the Commonwealth Assoc. (Israel); form. Chairperson Bnai Brith Hillel Fd; Chairperson UK National Cttee Jerusalem 3000 (1995-96); form. Mem. JC Tr. Ltd; H.Vice-Pres. Zionist Fed. of Great Britain & Ireland (Chair 1990-94); Jt. H. Pres. British WIZO (Chair 1981-87). Ad.: c/o World WIZO, 38 David Hamelech Blvd, Tel Aviv 64237. ☎ 00 972 3 6923729. Fax 00 972 3 6958267. Email brendak@wizo.org.

KATZ, Agi (née Rojko); b. Budapest, Oct. 29, 1937; m. Peter Katz; Art curator; Exhibition organiser with special knowledge of Anglo-Jewish artists of the 20th century; Dir. Boundary Gallery (1986-); Curator, Ben Uri Gallery (1979-85); Asst. to Chief Economist, Temple Press (1961-63); Economic Intelligence Off., Monsanto UK (1963-65). Publ.: catalogues on Epstein, Brodzky, Herman, Kestelman and Koenig. Ad.: Boundary Gallery, 98 Boundary Rd., London NW8 0RH. ☎ 020-7624 1126. Fax 020-7681 7663. E-mail boundary@agikatz.demon.co.uk.

KATZ, Sir Bernard, MD, DSc, FRS; b. March 26, 1911; Prof. and Head of Biophysics Dept., Univ. Coll., London (1952-78); Nobel Prize for Medicine (1970), V. President, Royal Society (1968-76); Asst. Dir. of Biophysics Res. Lond. Univ.; Res. Fel., Royal Soc. (1946-50) Reader in Physiology (1950-51). Publ.: Scientific writings. Ad.: University Coll., WC1E 8BT. ☎ 020-7387 7050.

KATZ, Dovid, BA (Columbia), PhD (Lond); b. New York, May 9, 1956; Founder of Yiddish Studies at Oxford University; Yiddish linguist and author; form. Dir., Oxford Programme in Yiddish at the Oxford Centre for Postgraduate Hebrew Studies (1978-95); Director, Oxford Institute for Yiddish Studies (1994-97); Founder, Vilnius Programme in Yiddish, Vilnius University (1998); Vis. Prof. in Yiddish Studies, Yale (1998-99); Prof. Yiddish Language, Literature and Culture and Dir. of the Centre for Stateless Cultures, Vilnius University (1999-); Academic Dir. Vilnius Yiddish Institute (2001-). Publ.: Grammar of the Yiddish Language (1987); ed. Origins of the Yiddish Language (1987); ed. Dialects of the Yiddish Language (1988); ed. Oxford Yiddish (vol. 1, 1990; vol. 2, 1991; vol. 3, 1995); Klal-takones fun yidishn oysleyg [Code of Yiddish Spelling] (1992); Tikney takones: fragn fun yidisher stilistik [Amended Amendments: Issues in Yiddish Stylistics] (1993); founder and ed. Yiddish Pen (literary and academic monthly) (1994-97); columnist, Yiddish Forward (1993-); Yiddish fiction under pseudonym of Heershadovid Menkes: Edra Don (1992); Der flakher shpits [The Flat Peak] (1993); Misnagdishe mayses fun vilner gubernye [Tales of the Misnagdim of Vilna Province] (1996). Awards: John Marshall Medal in Comparative Philology, University College London (1980). Awards for Yiddish Literature: Israel Marshak, Canada (1979); Sholem Aleichem, Tel Aviv (1988); Hirsh Rosenfeld, Montreal (1994); Chaim Grade, New York (1995); Zhitlovsky, New York (1996); Manger Prize, Tel Aviv (1997); Y.Y. Sigal, Montreal (1999); Guggenheim Fellowship for Yiddish fiction (2001-02). Ad.: 2 Bryn Aber, Fairy Glen Road, Capelulo, Gwynedd LL34 6YU. ☎ 01492-622315. E-mail info@yiddish.vilnius.com.

KATZ, Rabbi Steven Anthony, BA (Hons); b. London, Dec. 18, 1948; M., Hendon Ref. Syn., H. Sec. RSGB Assembly of Rabbis; Chaplain, Univ., Coll. Hospital, London. Ad.: Hendon Reform Synagogue, Danescroft Ave., NW4 2NA. ☎ 020-8203 4168.

KATZIR (Katchalski), Professor Ephraim; b. Kiev, May 16, 1916; Fourth President, State of Israel (1973-78); Chief Scientist, Israel Def. Forces (1966-68); Prof, Weizmann Instit. of Science; Prof Emer., Tel Aviv Univ.; Foreign Member, Royal Society Lond.; Hon. Member, The Royal Institution of Great Britain (1989); Foreign Assoc. Nat. Acad. of Sciences USA; Foreign Hon. Member, Amer Acad. of Arts & Sciences. Many honorary doctorates, honours prizes, medals and awards. Publ.: Papers & reviews in scientific journals & books. Ad.: Weizmann Instit., Rehovot 76100, Israel. ☎ 972-8-9343947. Fax 972-8-9468256.

KAUFMAN, Rt. Hon. Gerald Bernard, MA, PC, MP; b. Leeds, June 21, 1930; Journalist; Labour Party Parl. Cttee (1980-92); Opposition Spokesman for Foreign Affairs (1987-92); Member, Nat. Exec. Cttee. of the Labour Party (1991-1992), Chairman, House of Commons Nat. Heritage Cttee (1992-); Opp. Spokesman for Home Affairs (1983-87); form. Min. of State, Dept of Industry; Parl. Under-Sec., Industry; Parl. Under-Sec., Environment; MP (Lab.) for Ardwick (1970-83) for Gorton, Manchester (since 1983); Parl. Press Liaison Off, Labour Party (1965-70); Pol. Corr., New Statesman, (1964-65); Pol. Staff, Daily Mirror, (1955-64), Asst. Gen. Sec., Fabian Society (1954-55). Publ.: How to be a Minister, To Build the Promised Land, How to live under Labour (co-author), My Life in the Silver Screen, Inside the Promised Land, Meet me in St Louis, The Left (ed.), Renewal (ed). Ad.: 87 Charlbert Ct., Eamont St., London NW8 7DA. ☎ 020-7219 5145. Fax 020-7219 6825.

KAUFMANN, Flo (née Israel), JP, BA; b. Berkamsted, Aug. 3, 1942, m. Aubrey Kaufmann; Hon. Tr., Magistrates' Assoc. (2001-); Board of Deputies: Vice-Chairman Israel Cttee. (1989-94), Chairman (1994-97), Chairman, Finance & Organisation Div. (1997-), Tr., Hon. Off. (1997-); Chairman, NW West London Valuation Tribunal (1996-). Ad.: Board of Deputies, 6 Bloomsbury Square, London WC1A 2LP.

KAUFMANN, Georgia Louise, BA, MSc, D.Phil; b. Edgware, Middx, Jan. 10, 1961; form. Council Member of Edgware Masorti Synagogue and the Assembly of Masorti Synagogues (1998-2000); BoD (2000-2); Dir. UKJAID (UK Jewish Aid and International Development) (1996-97); Fellow at the Institute of Development Studies at the University of Sussex (1992-95); Bell-MacArthur Fellow at the Harvard Center for Population & Development Studies (1994-95). Ad.: 3 Rochester Terrace, London NW1 9JN. ☎ 020-7485 1689. E-mail Georgiak@btinternet.com.

KAY, Rabbi Sidney, b. Manchester, Oct. 25, 1920; M., Southport New Syn. (1976-84), Emer. Rabbi (since 1985). Ad.: 4 Westhill, Lord St. West, Southport, PR8 2BJ. ☎ 01704 541344. Fax 01704-514059. Email ravkay@aol.com.

KEDOURIE, Sylvia (née Haim), MA, PhD (Edin); b. Baghdad, Iraq; Independent scholar; Ed. Middle Eastern Studies. Publ.: Arab Nationalism: An Anthology (1962, 1967, 1975). Ad.: 75 Lawn Rd., London NW3 2XB. ☎/Fax 020-7722 0901.

KEMPNER GLASMAN, Mrs. Sheila (née Goldstein); b. London, May 22, 1933; Chairman BoD Women's Issues Action Gp. (1995-99); UK Vice-President. Int. Council of Jewish Women (2002-); Memb. Thames Customer Service Cttee OFWAT (1993-96); form. President, League of Jewish Women; V. Chairman, Hillingdon Com. Health C. (1974-82); Member Hillingdon Dist. Health Auth. (1983-87); Member, Women's Nat. Com. (1990-94). Ad.: 10 Ashurst Close, Northwood, Middx. HA6 1EL.

KERSHEN, Anne Jacqueline (née Rothenberg), BA, MPhil, PhD, FRSA; b. London, June 8, 1942; Historian; Barnett Shine Res. Fell. Queen Mary &

Westfield Coll. Univ. of London (1990-); Director Centre for the Study of Migration, QMW (1994-); Memb. Faculty Leo Baeck Coll. (1992-); Memb. C. JHSE; Council Memb Jewish Museum. Publ.: A Question of Identity (1998); London, the Promised Land? (1997); Uniting the Tailors (1995); 150 years progressive Judaism (ed.) (1990); Off-the-peg: Story of Women's Wholesale Clothing Industry (ed.) (1988); Trade Unionism amongst Jewish Tailors in London, 1872-1915 (1988); (with Jonathan Romain) Tradition and Change: The History of Reform Judaism in Britain, 1840-1995 (1995); Language, Labour and Migration (2000); Food in the Migrant Experience (2002). Ad.: Dept. of Politics, Queen Mary & Westfield College, Mile End Rd., E1 4NS. ☎ 020-7975 5003. Email a.kershen@qmw.ac.uk.

KESTENBAUM, Jonathan, BA (Hons), MA, MBA; b. Tokyo, Japan, Aug. 5, 1959; Chief Exec., UJIA; form. Ex. Dir. Office of the Chief Rabbi; Mazkir, Bnei Akiva London (1982-83); IDF, Outstanding Soldier Award (1983); Jerusalem Fellows Researcher (1985-87). Ad.: Balfour House, 741 High Rd., Finchley N12 0BQ.

KING, Oona, MP; b. Sheffield, Oct. 22, 1967; m. Tiberio Santomarco; MP for Bethnal Green & Bow (Lab.) (1997-). Ad.: House of Commons, SW1A 0AA.

KING-HAMILTON, His Honour Myer Alan Barry, QC, MA; b. London, Dec. 9, 1904; Judge, Central Criminal Court (1964-79); Chairman, Jt. Standing Cttee. of RSGB and ULPS; President, West Lond. Syn. (1977-83 and 1965-72), Hon. Life President (1994-); President, Maccabaeans (1967-75); Leader Oxford Circuit (1961-64); Recorder of Wolverhampton (1961-64), Gloucester (1956-61), Hereford (1955-56); Dep. Chairman. Oxford Qrt. Sessions (1956-64); Bencher, Middle Temple (1961); V. President, World Cong. of Faiths (since 1970); President, Westlon Hsg. Trust (1970-95), Hon. Life President (1995); London J.; Hsg. Cttee. (1975-); President, Birnbeck Hsg. Assoc. (1995-97), and Hon. Life President (1997-); Chairman, Pornography and Violence Research Trust (form. Mary Whitehouse, etc.) (1986-96); Master, Worshipful Comp. of Needlemakers (1969-70); Freeman of the City of London (1945); form. President, Cambridge Union Soc.; Squadron Leader RAF Publ.: And Nothing But The Truth (autobiog.) Ad.: 33 Seymour Place, W1H 6AP.

KINGSLAND, Sir Richard, AO, CBE, DFC; b. Moree, New South Wales, Australia, Oct. 19, 1916, m. Kathleen J. Adams; President Barnardos Canberra (1995-); Dir. Sir Edward Dunlop Medical Res. Fd. (1995-); Chairman, A.C.T. Health Promotion Fund (1990-94); Tr., Canberra Festival (1988-92); Life Gov. Sir Moses Montefiore Jewish Home, Sydney; Sec., Australian Veterans Affairs Dept. (1970-81); Chairman, Repatriation Com. (1970-81); Sec., Interior Dept. (1963-70); Nat. Dir., Australian Bicentennial Auth. (1983-89); President, Man. Bd., Goodwin Retirement Villages (1984-88); Nat. C., Australian Opera (1983-96); Chairman, Uranium Adv. C. (1982-84); H. Nat. Sec., Nat. Heart Foundation (1976-90); Member at Large since 1990; form. Chairman, Commonwealth Films Review Bd.; First Chairman, Canberra Sch. of Art (1975-84); First Chairman, ACT Arts Development Bd. (1981-84); Tr., Australian War Memorial (1966-76); Man. Sydney Airport (1948-49); Dir.-Gen., Org., RAAF Hq. (1946-48); Dir., RAAF Intelligence (1944-45); Cdr., RAAF Base, Rathmines, NSW (1942-43); Cdr., No. 11 Sqdn. RAAF Papua New Guinea (1941-42); No. 10 Sqdn. RAAF, Brit. (1939-41). Ad.: 36 Vasey Cresc., Campbell, ACT 2612, Australia. ☎ (02) 624 78502.

KLAUSNER, Menny; b. Frankfurt, Sept. 19, 1926; Comp. Dir.; Chairman, Mizrachi–Hapoel Hamizrachi Fed., UK & Ireland; Chairman, Israel Cttee., BoD; CoChairman, Nat. Z.C.; President, Hendon Adath Yisroel Cong.; T., N.W. Lond. Com. Mikva, T., Mifal Hatora Med. Aid Fund; Gov., Hasmonean Prep. Sch., Hendon; Chairman, Frs. of Ariel Instits., Israel; Netiv Meir Sch., Jerusalem; Actions Cttee., WZO, Adv. Bd., Torah Dept. Youth Aff. Com., World Mizrachi Exec.; Chairman, Mizrachi Fed. (1972-76); V. Chairman & T., Jewish Review,

(1966-71); V.Chairman, Tora Vavoda (1948-52). Ad.: 1 Edgeworth Ave., NW4 4EX. ☎ 020-8202 9220, 020-7286 9141.

KLINER, Stephen Ivor, MA, LLB, NP; b. Glasgow April 15, 1953; m. Barbara née Mitchell; Solicitor (Partner), Vallance Kliner and Associates, Glasgow; President Glasgow Jewish Representative Council (2001-); V. President National Executive Habonim-Dror (1993-); Chairman Habonim-Dror Glasgow (1990-2002); H. Sec. Giffnock and Newlands Hebrew Congregation (1995-98). Ad.: 1 Eglinton Drive, Giffnock, Glasgow, G46 7NQ. ☎ 0141-638 6602. Fax 0141-332 5332. E-mail stephen@intlworld.com.

KLUG, Sir Aaron, OM, ScD, FRS; b. Aug. 11, 1926, m. Liebe née Bobrow; President of the Royal Society (1995-2000); Nobel Prize for chemistry (1982); Med. Res. C. Laboratory of Molecular Biology, Cambridge; Hon. Fel., Peterhouse, Cambridge; form. Nuffield Fel., Birkbeck Col., Lond.; Lect., Cambridge Univ., Cape Town Univ. Publ.: Papers in scientific journals. Ad.: Peterhouse, Cambridge, CB2 1RD.

KNAPP, Alexander Victor, MA (Hons), MusB (Cantab), Hon. ARAM, LRAM, ARCM, Churchill Fellow; b. London, May 13, 1945; Joe Loss Lecturer in Jewish Music, SOAS (1999-); City Univ. (1992-99); Vis. Scholar Wolfson College, Cambridge (1983-86); Assistant Dir. of Studies, Royal College of Music, London (1977-83). Publ.: Four Sephardi Songs (1993); Anthology of Essays on Jewish Music (in Chinese) (1998). Ad.: Music Department, SOAS, Thornhaugh St., London WC1H 0XG. ☎ 020-7898 4688. E-mail ak42@soas.ac.uk.

KNOBIL, Henry Eric, FTI; b. Vienna, Nov. 27, 1932; V. President British-Israel Chamber of Commerce; Bd. Gov. Immanuel Coll.; President Western Marble Arch Synagogue; Bd. Govs., Carmel Coll. (1980-87). Ad.: Apt. 78, Harley House, Marylebone Rd., London NW1 5HN. ☎ 020-7224 4005. Fax 020-7224 0875.

KNORPEL, Henry, CB, QC, BCL, MA (Oxon).; b. London, Aug. 18, 1924, m. Brenda née Sterling; Barrister; Bencher, Inner Temple; Counsel to the Speaker, House of Commons (1985-95); Solicitor to D.H.S.S. (1978-85); Princ. Asst. Solicitor (1971-78); form. Chairman Sutton and District Syn.; V. President Epsom Syn. Ad.: Conway, 32 Sunnybank, Woodcote Grn., Epsom, Surrey KT18 7DX. ☎ 01372 721394.

KOCHAN, Lionel, BA, MA (Cantab), PhD (Lond), FR Hist Soc; b. London, Aug. 20, 1922; Bearsted Reader in Jewish Hist., Warwick Univ. (1968-87); form. Reader, Mod. Hist., East Anglia Univ.; P. Jew Hist. Soc. (1980-82); President, Society for Jewish Study (2001-). Publ.: Russia and Weimar Republic, Pogrom - November 10, 1938, Making of Modern Russia, Struggle for Germany 1914-45, The Jews in Soviet Russia Since 1917 (ed.), The Jew and His History, Jews Idols and Messiahs - The Challenge from History (1990), The Jewish Renaissance and some of its discontents (1992), Beyond the graven image. Ad.: 237 Woodstock Rd., Oxford OX2 7AD. ☎ 01865 558435.

KOPELOWITZ, Lionel, MA (Cantab), MRCS, LRCP, MRCGP, JP; b. Newcastle upon Tyne, Dec. 9, 1926; President, BoD (1985-91); Chairman, London Regional Council, BMA (2001-); Exec. Cttee, Friends of Hebrew Univ. (1998-); C. Initiation Soc. (1993-); V. President, Trades Adv. C.; V. President, Conf J. Material Claims against Germany; Member, Gen. Med. C. (1984-94); C., BMA (1982-94), Fel. (1980); President, WJC Europe (1988-90), World Exec. WJC (1986); C., AJA; President, Nat. C., Soviet Jewry (1985-91); President, Rep. C., Newc. Jewry (1967-73); First President, United Hebrew Cong. Newc. (1973-76); Life President (President 1964-74), Newc. JWB; V. President, British Friends Shaare Zedek Hospital Medical Centre; President, Old Cliftonian Soc. (1991-93); Council, United Synagogue (1991-96); Chairman, St Marylebone Division BMA (1992-); Mem. Bd. Gov., Clifton Coll., Bristol; Mem. C., Royal Coll. General Practitioners (1995-99). Ad.: 10 Cumberland House, Clifton Gardens,

W9 1DX. ☎ 020-7289 6375; 145 Barrack Lane, Aldwick, West Sussex PO21 4ED. ☎ 01243 268134.

KOPS, Bernard; b. London, 1926; Writer; C., Day Lewis Fellowship (1980-83). Pub.: Yes; From No Man's Land, The Dissent of Dominick Shapiro, By the Waters of Whitechapel, The Passionate Past of Gloria Gaye, Settle Down Simon Katz, Partners, On Margate Sands (novels), Collected Plays, The Hamlet of Stepney Green (play), Erica I Want to Read You Something, For the Record (poetry), Barricades In West Hampstead (poetry), The World is a Wedding (autobiography), Plays One (collection), Plays Two (collection), Plays Three (collection), Shalom Bomb (autobiography continued), Neither Your Honey Nor Your Sting (history), Grandchildren and other poems, Playing Sinatra (play), Dreams of Anne Frank (play), Green Rabbi (play), Cafe Zeitgeist (play), River change (play), etc. Ad.: 41B Canfield Gdns., London NW6 3JL. ☎ 020-7624 2940.

KORNBERG, Sir Hans (Leo), MA, DSc (Oxon), ScD (Cantab), Hon. ScD (Cincinnati), Hon. DSc (Warwick, Leicester, Sheffield, Bath, Strathclyde, Leeds, La Trobe), Hon. DU (Essex), Dr Med, hc (Leipzig), Hon. LLD (Dundee), PhD (Sheffield), FRS, Hon. FRCP, FlBiol, FRSA; b. Herford, Germany, Jan. 14, 1928; Sir W. Dunn Prof of Biochemistry, Cambridge Univ. (1974-95); Master, Christ's Coll. Cambridge (1982-95); H.Fel., Brasenose and Worcester Colls., Oxford, Wolfson Coll., Cambridge; Member, German Acad. Sciences 'Leopoldina', For. Assoc., Nat. Acad. Sci., US; For. H. Member, Amer. Acad. Arts & Sciences; H. Member, Amer. Soc. Biochem. & Mol. Biol.; Japanese Biochem. Soc., German Soc. Biol. Chem. (Warburg Medallist); The Biochem. Soc. (UK), Brit. Assn. Adv. Sci.; Fel., Amer. Acad. Microbiol.; Mem. Academia Europea; Accademia Nazionale dei Lincei; American Philosophical Soc.; Hon. Mem. Phi Beta Kappa; President, Brit. Assn. Adv. Sci. (1984-85); Chairman, Brit. Nat. Cttee. for Problems of Environment (1982-87); P. Internat. Union of Biochem. & Mol. Biol. (1991-1994); President, Biochemical Soc. (1990-95); Ch, Adv. Cttee. on Genetic Modification (1986-95); Dir., UK Nirex Ltd (1986-95); Chairman, Kurt Hahn Trust (U. of Camb.) (1990-95); Member, Science Res. C. (1967-72) and Chairman, Science Bd. (1969-72). Publ.: Scientific writings. Ad.: The University Professors, Boston University, 745 Commonwealth Ave., Boston, MA 02215. Fax (617) 353-5084.

KOSKY, Mark, JP; b. London, Jan. 5, 1923; m. Susan née Corrick; Company Chairman; Chairman, Westminster Br., AJEX (2000-2); form. Jt. Tr., United Synagogue Burial Soc.; form. President London Bd. for Shechita; form. Vice-President National Shechita C.; Exec. Kashrus Comm.; form. Hon. Sec. Hon. Tr., London Bd., Religious Education (1968-78); form. Gov., JFS; Chief Rabbinate C.; Exec. Bd., BoD; Vice-Chairman Mizrachi; Chairman British Aliyah M. (1983-84); Gen. Commissioner for Income Tax. Ad.: Flat 51, Century Ct., Grove End Road, London NW8 9LD. ☎ 020-7286 2791. Fax 020-7286 8958. Email ssperber@tiscali.co.uk.

KOSMIN, Barry A., BA, MA, D.Phil; b. London, Oct. 11, 1946; m. Helen; Professor of Sociology; Exec. Dir. JPR (2000-); Exec. Dir. Research Unit, Board of Deputies of British Jews (1974-86); Fellow, Institute for Advanced Studies, Hebrew University (1980-81); Founding Dir., North American Jewish Data Bank, The Graduate School and University Center of The City University of New York (1986-96); Dir. of Research, Council of Jewish Federations, NY (1986-96); Dir. CUNY National Survey of Religious Identification (1989); Dir. CJF 1990 US National Jewish Population Survey (1990). Publ.: Majuta: A History of the Jews in Zimbabwe (1981); British Jewry in the Eighties: A Statistical and Geographical Guide (1986); Highlights of the CJF 1990 National Jewish Research Population Survey (with S. Goldstein, J. Waksberg, N. Lerer, and A. Keysar) (1991); Contemporary Jewish Philanthropy in America (Jt. Ed. with P.

Ritterband (1991); One Nation Under God: Religion in Contemporary American Society (with S. Lachman) (1993). Ad.: JPR, 79 Wimpole Street, London W1G 1RY. ☎ 020-7935 8266.

KOSSOWSKY, Rabbi Zalman, MEd, PhD; b. Teheran, Dec. 15, 1940; Rabbi Israelitische Cultusgemeinde, Zurich; form. Rabbi, Kenton Syn. (1986-91); Chaplain, US Naval Reserve; Rabbi, Sydenham Highlands N. Hebrew Cong., Johannesburg (1978-86); Admin., Colorado Kosher Meats, Colorado Springs, US (1974-78), Rabbi, Young Israel, Greater Miami Florida (1972-74); Assoc. Dean, Talmudic Res. Instit., Colorado (1967-72). Publ.: Prayer Book for Friday Evening and Festivals, Prayer Book for the House of Mourning, The Modern Kosher Home. Ad.: Lavaterstrasse 33, CH-8027 Zürich, Switzerland. ☎ 01283-2245. Fax 01283-2223. E-mail rabbi@icz.org.

KRAIS, Anthony, JP; b. Lond., May 3, 1938; Assoc. Ch. Exec., Jewish Care (1990-97); Exec. Dir. Jewish Blind Society (1980-89); Ch. British Frs. Israel Guide Dog Centre for the Blind; Dep. Ch. Resources for Autism; Member The Appeals Service; General Commissioner of Taxes. Ad.: 14 Mayflower Lodge, Regents Park Rd., London N3 3HU ☎/Fax 020-8349 0337. E-mail alk@aikrais.free-online.co.uk

KRAMER, Lotte Karoline (née Wertheimer); b. Mainz, Germany, Oct., 22, 1923; m. Frederic Kramer; Poet. Publ.: Ice Break (1980); Family Arrivals (1981, 1992); A Lifelong House (1983); The Shoemaker's Wife (1987); The Desecration of Trees (1994); Earthquake and Other Poems (1994); Selected and New Poems 1980-1997; Heimweh/Homesick (German/English ed., 1999); The Phantom Lane (2000). Ad.: 4 Apsley Way, Longthorpe, Peterborough PE3 9NE. ☎ 01733-264378.

KRAUSZ, Ernest, MSc, PhD; b. Romania, Aug. 13, 1931; Prof. Emer (1999-), Rector, Bar-Ilan Univ. (1986-89), Prof. of Soc. (Dean, Soc. Sci. Faculty (1973-76) Bar-Ilan Univ.; Reader in Sociology, City Univ. Lond. (1971-72); Vis. Prof, Dept. of Social Studies, Newcastle Univ. (1976-77); LSE (1981-82); C., Higher Educ, Israel (1979-81), Planning and Grants Cttee. C. Higher Educ. (1990-96); Mem.C. Israel Science Fd. (1994-2001); Mem. British Association for the Advancement of Science (1998-); American Assoc. for the Advancement of Science (2000-); Edr., Studies of Israeli Society (1979-2000); Dir., Sociological Instit. for Community Studies, Bar-Ilan Univ. (1990-99), Senior Res. Fell. (1999-). Publs.: Leeds Jewry, Sociology in Britain, Jews in a London Suburb, Ethnic Minorities in Britain, Key Variables in Social Research, Social Research Design, On Ethnic and Religious Diversity in Israel, Sociological Research - A Philosophy of Science Perspective, The Limits of Science, Co-ed. Sociological Papers (1992-), Starting the XXIst Century (2001). Ad.: Dept. of Sociology Bar-Ilan Univ., Ramat Gan 52900, Israel. ☎ (03) 5344449. Fax (03) 6350422.

KRITZ, Simon Gedaliah, b. Lond., Sept. 17, 1919; Gen. Sec., Mizrachi Fed. Reg., Midrashah Instit. for Israel Studies Asst. Edr., Jewish Review; Sec., Frs. of Mifal Hatorah; Sec., Mizrachi Palestine Fund Charitable Tr., Sec., Brit. Frs. of Ariel; Gen. Sec., Nat. Z. C.; W., Willesden & Brondesbury Syn., Exec. & C., US; form. Fin. Rep., Willesden Syn.; Central Jewish Lect. & Information Cttee., BoD. Ad.:

KUPFERMANN, Jeannette Anne, B.A. (Hons.), M.Phil. Anthropology, (née Weitz); b. Woking, March 28, 1941; Anthropologist, Feature writer for The Sunday Times, Broadcaster Columnist, The Daily Telegraph, TV Critic, Daily Mail, TV writer: The Quest for Beauty (Channel 4); Everyman Film on Edith Stein (BBC). Publ.: The Mistaken Body, When the Crying's Done: A Journey through Widowhood. Ad.: c/o Sunday Times, 1 Pennington St, E1.

KUSHNER, Tony, PhD; b. Manchester, May 30, 1960; University Lecturer; Marcus Sieff Professor, Dept of History, and Director Parkes Institute for the Study of Jewish/Non-Jewish Relations, University of Southampton; Historian at Manchester Jewish Museum (1985-86); Member of C., JHSE; Tr., Anne Frank

Educ. Trust, UK; Tr. Searchlight Educ. Trust, UK; President, BAJS (2002). Publ.: The Persistence of Prejudice: Antisemitism in British Society During the Second World War (1989); (jt. ed.) Traditions of Intolerance (1989); (jt. ed.) The Politics of Marginality (1990); (ed.) Jewish Heritage in British History: Englishness and Jewishness (1992); (jt. ed.) The Internment of Aliens in Twentieth Century Britain (1993); The Holocaust and the Liberal Imagination (1994); (jt. col.) Belsen in History and Memory (1997); (jt. ed.) Cultures of Ambivalence and Contempt (1998); Refugees in an Age of Genocide (1999); Remembering Cable Street (jt. ed., 1999); Disraeli's Jewishness (jt. ed., 2002). Ad.: Dept. of History, The University, Southampton SO17 1BJ. ☎ 02380-592211.

KUSTOW, Michael David, b. London Nov. 18, 1939; Writer, Theatre Dir.; Literary Dir., Amer. Repertory Theatre (1980-82); Associate Dir., Nat. Theatre (1975-80), Dir., Instit. of Contemporary Arts (1968-71); Member, Ed. Cttee, Jewish Quarterly. Publ.: Tank, an Autobiographical Fiction. Ad.: c/o Tim Corrie, The Chambers, Chelsea Harbour, Lots Rd., London SW10 0XF.

LAMM, Rabbi Norman, PhD; b. Brooklyn, NY, Dec. 19, 1927; President, Yeshiva Univ. & President, Rabbi Isaac Elchanan Theol. Semin., New York (since 1976); Erna and Jakob Michael Prof of Jewish Philosophy, Yeshiva Univ. (since 1966); Fdr. Edr., Tradition; Edr., The Library of Jewish Law and Ethics (14 vols.); Rabbi, Cong. Kodimoh, Springfield, Mass. (1954-58); Rabbi, The Jewish Center, New York (1958-76). Publ. A Hedge of Roses, The Royal Reach; Faith and Doubt, Torah Lishmah, The Good Society, Torah Umadda, Halakhot ve'Halikhot, Shema, The Religious Thought of Hasidism. Ad.: Yeshiva Univ., 500 W. 185th St., New York, NY 10033. ☎ (212) 960 5280.

LANGDON, Harold S., B.Com; b. Lond. April 22, 1916; Economist; Chairman, Public Rel. Cttee. (1979-85), BoD; Exec., BoD (1974-91); Life Vice-President, Leo Baeck College (2002-), Governor (1978-2001), Chairman (1975-78); Chairman, RSGB (1967-70); North Western Reform Syn. (1960-61). Publ.: Contr., A Genuine Search (ed. Dow Marmur). Ad.: 24 Hoop Lane, NW11 8BU.

de LANGE, Rabbi Nicholas, RM, MA, DPhil, DD; b. Nottingham, Aug. 7, 1944; Professor of Hebrew & Jewish Studies, Cambridge Univ; C., Jewish Hist. Soc. of England; Fel., Wolfson Coll., Cambridge. Publ.: Judaism, Apocrypha Jewish Literature of the Hellenistic Age, Atlas of the Jewish World, Illustrated History of the Jewish People, An Introduction to Judaism, various specialised works and literary translations. Ad.: Faculty of Divinity, West Road, Cambridge CB3 9BS. ☎ 01223 763019. Fax 01223 763003.

LAPPIN, Elena, b. Moscow, Dec. 16, 1954; form. Editor, "Jewish Quarterly". Freelance editor & author, New York (1990-94); English (ESL) instructor, Technion, Haifa, Israel (1986-90). Publ.: Jewish Voices, German Words: Growing up Jewish in Postwar Germany and Austria (1994), Daylight in Nightclub Inferno: New Fiction from the Post-Kundera Generation (1997). Ad.:

LAQUEUR, Walter; b. Breslau, May 26, 1921; Dir., Wiener Library (1964-1992); Edr., Journal of Contemporary History; Chairman, Research C., Centre for Strategic and International Studies, Washington, USA.; Several honorary degrees. Publ.: Communism and Nationalism in the Middle East, Young Germany, Russia and Germany, The Road to War - 1967, Europe since Hitler, A History of Zionism, Holocaust Encyclopedia (Edr. 2001), etc. Ad.: CSlS, 1800 K St., Washington D.C. 20006, USA. Fax (202) 686-0048.

LASKY, Melvin J., MA; b. New York, Jan. 15, 1920; Co-Edr., Encounter Magazine (Lond.) (since 1958); Edr., Dir., Library Press, New York; Publ., Alcove Press Lond.; Edr. & Publ., Der Monat (Berlin); Dist. Alumnus Award, New York City Univ. (1978); Michigan Univ. Sesquicentennial Award (1967); US Combat Historian, France & Gemany (1944-45). Publ.: Utopia and Revolution, Festschrift for Raymond Aron, Sprache und Politik, New Paths in American

History, The Hungarian Revolution (ed.), Africa for Beginners. Ad.: Encounter, 59 St Martins La., WC2N 4JS. ☎ 020-7836 4194.

LAUTERPACHT, Sir Elihu, CBE, QC, MA, LLB; b. London, July 13, 1928; International Lawyer; Fel., Trinity Coll., Cambridge; Hon. Prof. International Law; Reader, Internat. Law (1980-88); Dir., Res. Centre for lnternat. Law, Cambridge Univ. (1983-95); Chairman, East African Common Market Tribunal (1972-75); Dir. of Research, Hague Academy of Internat. Law (1959-60); Legal Adv. to Australian Dept. of Foreign Affairs (1975-77); Consultant, Central Policy Review Staff (1978-80; 1972-74); Member, World Bank Admin. Tribunal (1979-98), President (1995-98); Chairman, Asian Development Bank Admin. Tribunal(1993-95); Judge ad hoc, Int. Court of Justice (1993-); Chairman, Dispute Settlement Panel, US-Canada NAFTA (1996), US-Mexico (1997-), US-Costa Rica (1997-), US-Ukraine (1998-); Member Institut de Droit International; Bencher, Gray's Inn (1983); H. Fel., Hebrew Univ. of Jerusalem, 1989; H. Member, Amer. Soc. of Internat. Law, (1993). Publ.: Aspects of the Administration of International Justice (1991); Jerusalem and the Holy Places (1968), The Development of the Law of International Organisations; Ed. International Law Reports. Ad.: Lauterpacht Research Centre for Internat. Law, 5 Cranmer Road, Cambridge CB3 9BP. ☎ 01223 335358. Fax 01223-300406.

LAWRENCE, Sir Ivan, MA (Oxon), QC; b. Brighton, Dec. 24, 1936; Barrister; Mem. of BoD; Sec. of Holocaust Educational Trust; Mem. of Commonwealth Jewish Council; form. MP (C.) for Burton (1974-97); Bencher, Inner Temple (1990); Recorder of the Crown Courts (1983); Exec. Mem. Society of Conservative Lawyers; form. Chairman Conservative Friends of Israel; form. Mem. of Policy Planning Gp. of IJA; form. Vice Chairman Inter-Parlt. Cttee for the Release of Soviet Jewry. Ad.: Dunally Cottage, Walton Lane, Shepperton, Middx. TW17 8LH.

LAWTON, Clive Allen, JP, BA, MA, MEd, MSc, Cert. Ed., ADB (Ed); b. London, July 14, 1951; Educ. and organisational consultant; Exec. Dir. Limmud; Chair North Middlesex University Hospital NHS Trust; UJIA Fellow in Jewish Education, LSJS; Chair Tzedek; form. V. Chair Anne Frank Educ. Trust; form. Ch. Exec. Jewish Continuity (1993-96); form. Dep. Dir., Liverpool City Local Educ. Auth.; Member RS Cttee., School's Examination and Assessment Council (SEAC); form. Exec., AJY; Chairman, Shap Working Party on World Rels. in Educ.; Edr., Shap Calendar of World Rel. Festivals; Fdr., Limmud Conf; form. HM, King David High Sch., L'pool; Exec. Dir., Central Jewish Lect. & Information Cttee. & Educ. Off, BoD; Coordinator, Vietnam Working Party; Educ. Off., Yad Vashem Cttee., Exec. C. CCJ; form. V. Chairman, IUJF. Publ.: The Jewish People – Some Questions Answered; The Seder Handbook; I am a Jew; Passport to Israel; Religion Through Festivals; Celebrating Cultures: Islam; Ethics in Six Traditions; The Story of the Holocaust; The Web of Insights; Auschwitz. Ad.: 363 Alexandra Rd., London N10 2ET. E-mail clive@calawton. freeserve.co.uk.

LEDERBERG, Joshua, BA, PhD, LittD, MD(hc), ScD(hc) Tel Aviv Univ. (1991); b. New Jersey, May 23, 1925; Sackler Foundation Scholar at Rockefeller U. (1990-); President, The Rockefeller Univ. (1978-90); Prof., Stanford U. (1959-78); Nobel Prize for Medicine (1958); US Nat. Medal of Science (1989); Gov. Bd., Weizmann Inst. Publ.: Scientific works. Ad.: The Rockefeller Univ., 1230 York Ave., New York, NY 10021 ☎ (212) 327 7809. Email lederberg@mail. rockefeller.edu.

LEE, Arnold, b. London, Aug. 31, 1920; Solicitor; form. Chairman, Jews, Coll. Ad.: 47 Orchard Court, Portman Sq., W1H 9PD. ☎ 020-7486 8918.

LEE, John Robert Louis, b. Manchester, June 2, 1942; MP (Cons.), Pendle, (1983-92) and for Nelson & Colne (1979-83); FCA, Fdn. Dir., Chancery Consolidated Ltd., Investment Bankers; Dir., Paterson Zochonis (UK) Ltd., (1975-76); V. Chairman NW Conciliation Cttee., Race Relations Bd. (1976-77); Political Sec. to

Rt. Hon. Robert Carr, (1974); Chairman Council, Nat. Youth Bureau, (1980-83); Jt. Sec., Conservative Back Bench Industry Cttee., (1979-80); PPS to Minister of State for Industry (1981-83); to Sec.of State for Trade & lndustry, (1983); Parly. Under Sec. of State MOD, (1983-86); Dept. of Employment, (1986-89); Minister for Tourism, (1987-89); Non-exec.; Chairman, Country Holidays Ltd. (1989); Non-exec. Dir., P. S. Turner (Holdings) Ltd (1989); Non-exec. Dir., Paterson Zochonis, (1990-); Chairman, ALVA (1990-). Ad.:

LEGUM, Colin, LLD (Rhodes), PhD, LittD (Univ. of South Africa); b. South Africa, Jan. 3, 1919; m. Margaret née Roberts; Journalist, author, broadcaster, lect.; Hon. Life President Royal Africa Soc. (UK); Edr., The Africa Contemporary Record; Assoc. Edr., The Middle East Contemporary Survey; Edr., Third World Reports; Assoc. Edr. and Commonwealth Corresp., The Observer, (1949-81); Gen. Sec., S.A. Lab. Party (1946-48); Edr., The Forward and Illustrated Bulletin (Johannesburg); Political Corr. Sunday Express (Johannesburg); Political Asst S.A. Zionist Fed.; Exec. Memb. Poale Zion (SA); SA Jewish BoD (1938-47); Member of Johannesburg City C., (1941-47). Publ.: Books on Africa, Middle East and Third World; Africa since Independence. Ad.: Kob Cottage, 12 Harris Rd., Kalk Bay, Cape 7975, RSA. ☎/Fax (012) 788 8455.

LEHMAN, Rabbi Israel Otto, MA, BLitt, DPhil, FRAS; b. 1912; Adjunct Prof. of Jewish Studies, Miami Univ.; Assoc. Oxford Centre for PostGraduate Hebrew Studies; Hon. Fel. of the John F. Kennedy Library; form. Lect., Leo Baeck Coll.; Curator of Manuscripts Emer., Hebrew Union Coll., form. Assist. Keeper, Bodleian Library (1947-56); Fdr., Oxford B.B. Lodge, OUJS Library. Publ.: Translation of Chief Rabbi's Pentat. into Germ., 'Moses', (ed.), Handbook of Hebrew and Aramaic Manuscripts. etc. Ad.: 3101 Clifton Ave., Cincinnati, Ohio, USA. ☎ 45220-2488.

LEIBLER, Isi Joseph, AO, CBE, BA (Hons); D.Litt (Hon), Deakin University; b. Antwerp, Belgium, Oct. 9, 1934; m. Naomi née Porush; Chairman and Chief Exec. Leibler Investments Ltd. (1997-); fd. Chairman and Chief Exec., Jetset Tours Pty Ltd. (1965-); Chairman, Governing Bd World Jewish Congress (1995-2001); V.P World Jewish Congress (1988-1991); President, Asia Pacific Region, World Jewish Congress (1981-2001); Chairman, Asia Pacific Jewish Assoc. (1980-2001); Chairman, Australian Institute of Jewish Affairs (1983-), President, Exec. Council of Australian Jewry (1978-1980), (1982-1985), (1987-1989), (1992-95); Member Exec. and Gov. Bd., World Jewish Congress (1978-), Bd. of Gov., Memorial Foundation for Jewish Culture (1979-); Board of Gov., Tel Aviv University (1990-); Dir. and Member, Exec. Cttee., Conference on Jewish Claims Against Germany (1979-). Publ.: Soviet Jewry and Human Rights (1963) Soviet Jewry and the Australian Communist Party (1964), The Case for Israel (1972), The Contemporary Condition of World Jewry (1990), Jewish Religious Extremism: a Threat to the Future of the Jewish people. (1991), The Israel-Diaspora Identity Crisis: A looming disaster (1994), Is the Dream Ending? Post Zionism and Its Discontents (2001). Ad.: 8 Ahad Ha'am St., 92151 Jerusalem. ☎ (02) 561 2241. Fax (02) 561 2243. E-mail ileibler@leibler.com.

LERMAN, Antony, BA Hons; b. London, Mar. 11, 1946; Dir. European Programmes, Yad Hanadiv (2000-); Chief Exec. Hanadiv Charitable Fd. (2000-); Exec. Dir. Inst. for Jewish Policy Research (1991-99); Memb. Imperial War Museum Holocaust Exhibition Advisory Cttee; Memb. Runnymede Trust Commission on the Future of Multi-Ethnic Britain (1998-2000); Memb. Jewish Memorial Foundation Think-Tank on the Holocaust (1996-99); Jt. Ed., Patterns of Prejudice (1983-99); Chairman Jewish Council for Com. Relations (1992-94); Assist Ed., Survey of Jewish Affairs (1982-91); form. Ed., Jewish Quarterly (1985-86). Publ.: Ed., The Jewish Communities of the World (1989), Jt. Gen. Ed. Antisemitism World Report (1992-98). Ad.: The Dairy, Queen Street,

Waddesdon, Bucks HP18 0JW. ☎ 01296 653250. E-mail tony.lerman@hanadiv.org.uk.

LEVENE, Baron of Portsoken (Life Peer), **(Peter)** KBE; b. Pinner, Middlesex, December 8, 1941; Lord Mayor of London (1998–99); Chairman & Chief Exec. Canary Wharf Ltd; Prime Minister's Adviser on Efficiency & Effectiveness; Deputy Chairman & Managing Dir. Wasserstein Perella & Co. Ltd; Alderman, City of London (Portsoken) (1984-); form. Managing Dir. United Scientific Holdings plc (1968-85); Chairman (1981-85); Chief of Defence Procurement, Ministry of Defence (1985-91); Chairman Docklands Light Railway Ltd. (1991-94). Ad.: One Canada Square, Canary Wharf, London E14 5AB. ☎ 020-7418 2250. Fax 020-7418 2082.

LEVY, Rabbi Abraham, Knight Commander (Encomienda) Order of Civil Merit (Spain), BA, PhD, FJC; b. Gibraltar, July 16, 1939; m. Estelle née Nahum; Com. Rabbi, Spiritual Head, S. & P. Cong., Lond.; M., Lauderdale Rd. Syn.; Jt. Eccl. Auth. BoD; Dep.P., Jews Coll.; Founder and Dir., The Sephardi Centre; form. Dir. Young Jewish Leadership Instit.; Founder and H. Princ., Naima Jewish Preparatory Sch.; Gov., Carmel Coll.; President, Union Anglo-Jewish Preachers (1973-75); V. President, AJA. Publ.: The Sephardim – A Problem of Survival; Ages of Man (jt. auth.); The Sephardim (jt. auth.). Ad.: 2 Ashworth Road, London W9 1JY. ☎ 020-7289 2573. Fax 020-7289 5957.

LEVY, David, B.A. (Com.), FCA, b. Manchester, June 27, 1942; Chart. Accountant; Dir., Zone Corporation Ltd.; Chief Exec. Brideoak Associates, Management Consultants; Mem., Worshipful Comp. of Chartered Accountants; Freeman, City of London. Ad.: 6, The Mews, Gatley, Cheadle, Cheshire SK8 4PS. ☎ 0161-428 7708/0161-707 6465 (off.).

LEVY, Elkan David, BA (Hons), MHL; b. Preston, Lancs, March 29, 1943; m. Celia, née Fisher; Solicitor; Mem. Exec. BoD (2000-); Dir. Moorfields Eye Hospital NHS Trust (2001-); President, United Synagogue (1996-99); form. Chairman, Chief Rabbinate Conference; Chairman, Singers Prayer Book Publication Cttee.; Jt. Chairman, Stanmore Council of Christians and Jews; form. Minister, Belmont Synagogue (1969-73); Warden, Stanmore Synagogue (1980-90); Chairman US Burial Society (1992-96); Mem. United Synagogue Council (1980-92); Officer, United Grand Lodge of England and Grand Lodge of the State of Israel. Ad.: United Synagogue, Adler House, 735 Finchley Road, N12 0US. E-mail elkan.levy@easynet.co.uk.

LEVY, Rabbi Emanuel, BA, b. Manchester, July 31, 1948; M., Palmers Grn. & Southgate Syn.; Vice-Chairman Rabbinical Council of the United Synagogue; Fd. Gov. JFS; Memb. Borough of Enfield Educ. Cttee.; Chaplain to Whittington Hospital; Form. Hon. Principal, Herzlia Jewish Day School, Westcliff-on-Sea; form. Rabbi, Southend & Westcliff Hebrew Cong.; Chief Rabbi's Cabinet, Reg. Affairs, to Chief Rabbi's Cabinet Education Portfolio; J. Rep. to Standing Advisory Council for Religious Education (SACRE) for Borough of Enfield: form. Chaplain to Mayor of Southend (1981-82, 1983-84); form. Rabbi, Langside Hebrew Cong., Glasgow; Rabbi, South Broughton Syn, Manchester; Chairman, Rabbinical Council of the Provinces (1986-88); F.P. Southend Community Relations Council, (1986-88). Ad.: 11, Morton Crescent, Southgate, London N14 7AH. ☎ 020-8882-2943.

LEVY, Rev. Isaac, OBE, TD, BA, PhD (Lond); b. London, Sept. 14, 1910; form. Dir., JNF in Britain; form. M. Hampstead Syn., Hampstead Gdn. Suburb Syn. and Bayswater Syn.; form. Sr. Jewish Chaplain to H.M. Forces and Middle East Forces and Brit. Army of the Rhine, V.Pres. CCJ; Emer. Chaplain to Ajex. Publ.: Daiches Memorial Volume (jt Edr.), Guide to Passover, The Synagogue Its History and Function, Journeys of the Children of Israel, All About Israel, Now I Can Tell, Witness to Evil-Belsen 1945. Ad.: 25 Lyndale Ave., NW2 2QB. ☎ 020-7435 6803.

LEVY, John David Ashley, BA (Hon) Sociology; b. Lond., Sept. 10, 1947; Dir. Frs. of Israel Educ. Tr.; Exec. Dir., Academic Study Group on Israel & Middle East; Hon. Co-ord. UK Society for the Protection of Nature in Israel; form. Information Dir., Z. Fed.; Social Worker, Lond. Borough of Lambeth Ad.: POB 7545, London NW2 2QZ. ☎ 020-7435 6803. Fax 020-7794 0291. Email info@foi-asg.org.

LEVY, Baron of Mill Hill (Life Peer) (Michael Abraham), FCA, HonD (Middx); b. London, July 11, 1944; Comp. Chairman; President of Jewish Care (1998-); Mem. Exec. Cttee., Chai-Lifeline (2001-); Patron, Simon Marks Jewish Primary School Tr. (2002-); Chairman Bd. Trustees of New Policy Network (2000-); Trustee of the Holocaust Educational Trust (1998-); Patron of Friends of Israel Educational Trust (1998-); President of CSV (Community Service Volunteers) (1998-); Patron of the British Music Industry Awards (1995-); Member of the Advisory Council to the Foreign Policy Centre (1997-); Patron of the Prostate Cancer Charitable Trust (1997-); Member of the International Board of Governors of the Peres Center for Peace (1997-); Hon. President UJIA; Chairman Fd. for Education; Chairman, Chief Rabbinate Awards for Excellence (1992-); Hon. President JFS School (1995-2001), President (2001-); V. Chairman Central Council for Jewish Social Services; Member of World Commission on Israel-Diaspora Relations (1995-); Member, National Council for Voluntary Organisations Advisory Council (1998-); Member, Community Legal Service Champions Panel (1999-); Patron, Save a Child's Heart Foundation (2000-); Mem. Hon. Cttee Israel, Britain and the Commonwealth Association (2000-); recipient of B'nai B'rith First Lodge Award (1994); Scopus Award Friends of the Hebrew University (1998); form. Member of the World Board of Gov. of the Jewish Agency – representing Great Britain; form. Chairman of the Youth Aliyah Cttee. of the Jewish Agency Board of Govs.; form. V. President, JIA; form. Nat. Campaign Chairman JIA; form. Chairman, JIA Kol Nidre Appeal; form. V. Chairman British Phonographic Industry; form. V. Chairman Phonographic Performance Limited. Ad.: House of Lords, London SW1A 0PW.

LEVY, Peter Lawrence, OBE, BSc, FRICS; b. Lond., Nov. 10, 1939; Chartered Surveyor; Chairman, Shaftesbury PLC; Chairman IJPR; Hon. Vice President RSGB; Vice Chairman and Tr. Dementia Relief Tr.; President, Akiva Sch.; Tr., Frs. of Israel Educ. Tr.; V. President Cystic Fibrosis Tr.; V. President, London Youth; V. Chairman, JIA (1979-81); Chairman, Young Leadership JIA (1973-77); Professional Div. JIA (1977-79). Ad.: 52 Springfield Rd., NW8 0QN. ☎ 020-7333 8118. Fax 020-7333 0660.

LEW, Jonathan Michael, BCom, ACMA; b. London, Nov. 23, 1937; Hon. Off., United Synagogue (1984-85); Chief Exec., United Synagogue (1986-98). Ad.: 41 Eyre Court, Finchley Road, London NW8 9TG. ☎ 020-7722 6255. E-mail jonathanlew@41eyre.freeserve.co.uk.

LEWIN, Mrs. Sylvia Rose (née Goldschmidt), BA (Log), (Rand), RSA Dip.Sp.L.D.; b. Johannesburg; Speech and Dyslexia Therapist; Chairman, Leadership, Training and Development, B'nai B'rith, UK; H. President (Nat. President 1982-86, 1988) Bnai Brith UK; past Chairman Jewish Music Heritage Trust. Ad.: White Gables, 156 Totteridge Lane, N20 8JJ. ☎ 020-8446 0404. Fax 020-8445 8732. E-mail sylvialewin@bigfoot.com.

LEWIS, Bernard, BA, PhD, FBA, FR Hist. S., Hon. Dr. (Hebrew Univ, Tel Aviv Univ., HUC, Univ. Pennsylvania, SUNY, Univ. Haifa, Yeshiva Univ., Brandeis, Bar-Ilan Univ., Ben Gurion Univ., Ankara Univ., New School Univ., NY, Princeton Univ.; b. London, May 31, 1916; Cleveland E. Dodge, Prof. of Near Eastern Studies Princeton Univ. (1974-86), now Emer.; Mem. American Philosophical Soc.; American Academy of Arts & Sciences; Corr. Mem. Institut de France, Académie des Inscriptions et Belles-Lettres. Member, Instit. for Advanced Study, Princeton (1974-86); Prof. Near & Middle East Hist., Lond. Univ. (1949-74); Army (1940-41), attached to a Foreign Office dept. (1941-45). Publ.: The Jews of Islam; Semites and Anti-Semites; The Political Language of Islam; books on Turkish and Arabic Studies; Race and Slavery in the Middle East; Islam and the West; Cultures in Conflict; The Middle East: Two Thousand Years of History; The Future of the Middle East; The Multiple Identities of the Middle East (1998); A Middle East Mosaic: Fragments of Life, Letters and History; Music of a Distant Drum (2001); What Went Wrong? Western Impact and Middle Eastern Response (2002). Ad.: Near Eastern Studies Dept., 110 Jones Hall, Princeton University, Princeton, NJ, 08544, USA. ☎ (609) 258 5489. Fax (609) 258 1242.

LEWIS, D. Jerry, BA (Econ) (Hons, Manchester); b. Surrey, June 12, 1949; Parlt. Lobby Journalist and Broadcaster; Vice-President, Board of Deputies (2000-), Chairman, Communal Issues Div. (2000–), Vice-Chairman Law, Parlt. and General Purposes Cttee (1994-97), Constitution Standing Cttee (1981-97), etc.; National Council Poale Zion; form. Mem. Exec. Cttee, ZF, Nat. Council for Soviet Jewry; Mem. Foreign Press Assoc.; London correspondent Israel Radio, Yediot Ahronot, Jewish Telegraph; contr. BBC World TV, BBC News 24, BBC World Service, BBC Radio 5 Live, Sky News, Jewish Chronicle. Ad.: 9 Weech Hall, Fortune Green Road, London NW6 1DJ. ☎ 020-7794 0044; 020-7794 3512 (off.). Fax 020-7431 6450.

LEWIS, Geoffrey Lewis, CMG, FBA, MA, D.Phil (Oxon), D. Univ. Istanbul and Bosphorus Universities, Order of Merit of the Turkish Republic; b. June 14, 1920, London; m. Raphaela née Bale Seideman; University teacher (retired); Lecturer in Turkish, University of Oxford (1950-54), Senior Lecturer in Islamic Studies (1954-64), Senior Lecturer in Turkish (1964-86), Professor of Turkish (1986); Fell. St Antony's College (1961-87), now Emeritus; Hon. Fell. St John's College, Oxford (2000-), Mem. British–Turkish Mixed Commission (1975-94). Publ.: Teach Yourself Turkish (1953, 2nd ed. 1988), Plotiniana Arabica (1959), Albucasis on Surgery and Instruments (with M.S. Spink) (1973), Modern Turkey (1974), The Book of Dede Korkut (1974), Turkish Grammar (1974, revised and enlarged ed. 2000), The Atatürk I Knew (1981), The Turkish Language Reform: A Catastrophic Success (1999). Ad.: 93 Woodstock Road, Oxford OX2 6HL. ☎ 01865 557150. Fax 01865 513532. E-mail geoffreyllewis@aol.com.

LEWIS, Ivan, b. Manchester, March 4, 1967; m. Juliette née Fox; M.P. (Lab.), Bury South (1997-); Parlt. Under Sec. for Adult Skills (2002-); PPS Sec. State of Trade and Industry (1997-2001); Tr. of Holocaust Educ. Tr. (1998-); V. Chairman, Inter-Parliamentary Council Against Anti-semitism (1998-); V. Chairman, Labour Friends of Israel (1998); member Exec. Cttee of the Commonwealth Jewish Council (1998-); Member Health Select Cttee (1998-99); Chairman All-Party Parliamentary Group for Parenting (1999-); Chief Exec. Jewish Social Services, Greater Manchester (1992-97); Coordinator, Contact Community Care Group (1986-89). Ad.: House of Commons, London SW1A 0AA. ☎ 020-7219 6404.

LEWIS, Dr Julian Murray, b. Swansea, Sept. 26, 1951; MP (Con.), New Forest East (1997-); Historian, researcher and campaigner; Opposition Whip (2001-); Jt. Sec. Cons Parlt. Defence Cttee (1997-2001); Vice Chairman Cons. Parlt. Foreign Affairs and Europe Cttees (2000-1); Member Select Cttee on Defence (2000-1); Member Select Cttee on Welsh Affairs (1998-2001); Dep. Dir. Conservative Research Dept. (1990-96); Dir., Policy Research Associates (1985); Research Dir. and Dir., Coalition for Peace Through Security (1981-85). Publ.: Changing Direction: British Military Planning for Post-War Strategic Defence, 1942-1947 (1988); Who's Left? An Index of Labour MPs and Left-wing Causes, 1985-1992 (1992); What's Liberal? Liberal Democrat Quotations and Facts (1996). Ad.: House of Commons, London SW1A 0AA. ☎ 020-7219 3000.

LIBESKIND, Daniel, BArch, MA, BDA; b. Łodz, May 12, 1946; m. Nina née Lewis; Architect; Principal, Studio Daniel Libeskind (1989-); Prof., Hochschule für Gestaltung, Karlsruhe; Cret Chair of Architecture, Univ. of Pennsylvania; Frank O. Grety Chair, Univ. of Toronto. Architectural projects include: Imperial War

Museum North (Manchester, 2002), University of North London Graduate School (2003), The Spiral, Victoria & Albert Museum (London), Felix-Nusbaum-House (Osnabrück, 1998), Jewish Museum (Berlin, 2001), Maurice Wohl Convention Centre (Bar Ilan University, 2003), Jewish Museum (San Francisco), Danish Jewish Museum (Copenhagen, 2003). Publ.: Between Zero and Infinity (1981); Chamber Works (1983); Theatrum Mundi (1985); Line of Fire (1988); Marking City Boundaries (1990); Countersign (1992); El Croquis: Daniel Liberskind (1996); Unfolding (with Cecil Balmond, 1997); Fishing from the Pavement (1997); Radix: Matrix: Works and Writings (1997); The Space of Encounter (2001). Ad.: Studio Daniel Libeskind, Windscheidstr. 18, 10627 Berlin, Germany. ☎ 30-3277820. Fax 30-32778299. Email info@daniel-libeskind.com.

LICHFIELD, Nathaniel, BSc, PhD, FRICS; b. Lond., Feb. 29, 1916; Emer. Prof. of Economics of Environmental Planning, Lond. Univ.; Fdr. Partner, Nathaniel Lichfield & Part. (1962-92); Partner, Lichfield Planning (1992-); Vis. Prof. Berkeley (1959-60, 1968), Hebrew Univ. (1980-2000); Consultant to Mins., internat. orgs., cities in Britain and overseas. Publ.: Israel's New Towns: A Strategy for their Future (with A. Berler and Samuel Shaked), etc. Ad.: 13 Chalcot Gdns., Englands Lane, NW3 4YB. ☎ 020-7586 0461.

LIGHTMAN, Sir Gavin Anthony, b. London, Dec. 20, 1939; Justice of the High Court, Chancery Division (1994-); Fellow, Univ. College London (2002); QC (1980-94); Bencher of Lincolns Inn (1987); Deputy President of AJA (1986-92); Chairman of Education Cttee of AJA (1988-94); V. President, AJA (1994-); Chairman Education Cttee of Hillel (1992-94), Vice-President (1994-); Chairman, Legal Friends of Univ. Haifa (1986-); Chairman Commonwealth J. Assoc. (1999-); Patron, The Hammerson Home (1995-); Chairman, The Bar Adv. Bd. of the College of Law (1996-99); Chairman, Sainer Legal Fd. (1999-). Publ.: (with G. Battersby) Cases and Statutes on the Law of Real Property (1965); (with G. Moss) Law of Receivers of Companies (3rd ed. 2000). Ad.: Royal Courts of Justice, Strand, London WC2A 2LL. ☎ 020-7947 6671. Fax 020-7947 6291.

LIGHTMAN, Sidney, FIL; b. Lond. Apr. 5, 1924; journalist, translator; Sec., British & European Machal Assoc.; form. (1981-89) Asst. Foreign Edr., Jewish Chronicle; form. (1966-89) Edr., Jewish Travel Guide. Ad.: 5 West Heath Ct., North End Rd., NW11 7RE. ☎ 020-8455 1673.

LIPMAN, Maureen Diane (Mrs Jack Rosenthal), CBE, Hon. MA, Hon. D.Litt; b. Hull, May 10, 1946; Actress/Writer. Films: 'Solomon & Gaenor' (1998), Discovery of Heaven, The Pianist (2000/1). TV: 'Eskimo Day' (1996), 'Cold Enough for Snow' (1997), 'Flight 'n Fancy', 'Coronation Street'. Theatre: Oklahoma! (National Theatre, 1998), Peggy for You, The Vagina Monologues, Sitting Pretty. Seventh book: Lip Reading. Ad.: c/o Conway Ven Gelder, 18/21 Jermyn Street, SW1Y 6HP. ☎ 020-7287 0077.

LITHMAN-IMBER, Mrs. Ethel; b. London; P. (form. Nat. Chairman), Brit. Olim Relatives Assn.; Hadassah Medal for services to Israel (1967-); Staff Off, Brit. Red Cross, Second World War; form. Cttee., Guild Jewish Journs.; form. Member, Norfolk County Council SACRE; President Norwich Hebrew Cong. (1997-2000); V. President Norwich Hebrew Congregation (1996, 2000-); form. Act. Chairman, Norwich CCJ. Publ.: The Man Who Wrote Hatikvah. Ad.: c/o BORA, Balfour House, 741 High Road, N12 0BQ. ☎ 01379-674400.

LIVINGSTON, Edward Colin, MBE, MB, BS (Lond.), JP; b. London, Mar. 22, 1925; Med. Prac.; Barrister; form. Ombudsman, Central C. for Jewish Community Services; Medical Examiner, Medical Fnd. for Care of Victims of Torture; P/T Chairman, Soc Sec. Appeal Trib., Harrow; V. President, Harrow Com. Tr; Liveryman. Soc. of Apothecaries; Freeman, City of Lond.; Flt./Lieut (Med. Br.) R.A.F.V.R. (1948-50); form. P/T Chairman, Disability Appeal

Tribunal, South East Region. Ad.: Wyck Cottage, Barrow Point La., Pinner, Middx. HA5 3DH.

LIVINGSTONE, Rabbi Reuben, BA, LLB, MA, LLM, PgDipCPsych, PgDipLaw, JD; b. Johannesburg, South Africa, July 3, 1959; m. Esther née Koenigsberg; Rabbi, Lecturer (barrister/solicitor, non-practising); Rabbi, Hampstead Garden Suburb Synagogue (1999-); Programme Dir., Jewish Cultural Centre, Manchester (1983-85); Rabbi, Sale and District Hebrew Congregation (1985-88); Rabbi, Ilford Federation Synagogue (1988-99); Lecturer in Jewish and Comparative Law, Jews' College, London (1990-98); Corob Lecturer in Jewish Studies, Jews' College, London (1994-95). Publ: Contract in the Law of Obligations: A Comparative Analysis of Jewish Law and English Common Law (1994). Ad.: Hampstead Garden Suburb Synagogue, Norrice Lea, London N2 0RE.

LOBENSTEIN, Josef H., MBE; b. Hanover, Apr. 27, 1927; Mayor, London Borough of Hackney (1997-2001); Hon. Freeman L. B. Hackney; President, Adath Yisroel Syn. and Burial Soc.; Chairman, N. London Jewish Liaison Cttee.; Vice-President; Union of Orth. Hebrew Cong and Chairman External Affairs Cttee; Exec. Kedassia Kashruth Cttee.; Exec., Agudath Israel World Org.; V. Chairman, Agudath Israel of Great Britain; Executive, National Shechita C.; Governor, Avigdor Primary School, Craven Park Primary School; President Hackney North Conservative Assn.; form. Gen. Sec., Agudath Israel of Great Britain; Member, BoD; Tr. Jewish Secondary School Movement; Conservative Opposition Leader L. B. Hackney (1974-97); Councillor Metropolitan Borough of Stoke Newington (1962-65); Hon. President Hackney and Tower Hamlets Chamber of Commerce. Ad.: 27 Fairholt Rd., N16 5EW. ☎ 020-8800 4746. Fax 020-7502 0985.

LOEWE, Raphael James, MC, MA (Cantab), FSA; b. Calcutta, Apr. 16, 1919; form. Goldsmid Prof. of Hebrew (form. Dir., Instit. of Jewish Studies), Univ. Coll., Lond.; form. S. A. Cook Fellow, Caius Coll., Cambridge; form. Lect. in Hebrew, Leeds Univ.; Vis. Prof in Judaica, Brown Univ. Providence, R.I. (1963-64); C. (form. P.), JHSE; C., Soc. for Jew Study; C. BAJS (former P.); Seatonian Prize for Sacred Poem, Cambridge (2000); form. Elder and Warden, Span. & Port. Jews, Cong., London; War service, Suffolk Regt., Royal Armoured Corps. Publ.: Women in Judaism, Omar Khayyam (Hebr.), The Rylands Sephardi Haggadah, Ibn Gabirol, etc. Ad.: 50 Gurney Dr., N2 0DE. ☎/Fax 020-8455 5379.

LUCAS, Gerald Ephraim, b. London, Oct. 20, 1946; m. Angela née Daltroff; Exec. Dir., B'nai B'rith Hillel Foundation (1993-). Ad.: Hillel House, 1/2 Endsleigh Street, London WC1H 0DS. ☎ 020-7388 0801. Fax 020-7916 3973. Email info@hillel.co.uk.

LUCAS, Mrs Stella (née Waldman), JP; b. London, July 30, 1916; V. President Jewish Care; Chairman, Stepney Girls' Club and Settlement; President, First Women's Lodge B'nai B'rith (1975-77), V. President Assn. of US Women; President, Dollis Hill Ladies, Guild; V. President (Chairman, 1978-84); Frs. of Hebrew Univ. (Women's Group); Exec. Off., Internat. C. of Jewish Women (1963-66); Chairman, Union of Jewish Women (1966-72); Chairman, Women Frs. of Jewis, Coll. (1957-66); Central Council for Jewish Soc. Services; BoD; Chairman, Brodie Instit.; Convenor BoD Central Enquiry Desk; Fdr. 'All Aboard Shops'. Ad.: 51 Wellington Ct., Wellington Rd., NW8 9TB. ☎ 020-7586 3030.

LYONS, Bernard, CBE, JP, DL, Hon. LLD (Leeds); b. Leeds, Mar. 30, 1913, m. Lucy; Chairman 1972-82 U.D.S. Group plc; L.P. Leeds Jewish Rep. C.; Chairman, Yorks. & N.E. Conciliation Cttee.; Race Rel. Bd (1968-70); Community Rel. Com. (1970-72); Dep. Lieutenant Yorks., W. Riding (1971); Leeds City C (1951-65). Publ.: The Thread is Strong; The Narrow Edge; The Adventures of Jimmie Jupiter; Tombola. Ad.: Upton Wood, Black Park Rd., Fulmer, Bucks. SL3 6JJ. ☎ 01753-662404. Fax 01753-662413.

LYONS, Edward, QC, LLB (Leeds); b. Glasgow, May 17, 1926, m. Barbara née Katz; Recorder (1972-98); M.P. (SDP) Bradford West (1981-83); M.P. (Lab.) Bradford West (1974-81); Bradford East (1966-74); Parl. Pr. Sec. Treasury (1969-70); Bencher, Lincoln's Inn; Nat. Cttee., SDP (1984-89). Ad.: 4 Primley Park Lane, Leeds, LS17 7JR. ☎ 0113 2685351 and 59 Westminster Gardens, Marsham Street, SW1P 4JG. ☎ 020-7834 1960.

LYONS, Sir Isidore Jack, CBE, Hon. D.Univ. (York); b. Leeds, Feb. 1, 1916; Life V. President, JIA; Dep. Chairman, Youth Aliyah; Member of Court, York Univ.; H.V. President, Leeds Musical Festival; Ch of Trs., London Symphony Orchestra; Life Tr. Shakespeare Birthplace Trust; Chairman, Henry Wood Rehearsal Hall; H. Fel., Royal Acad. of Music; Chairman, Foreign and Commonwealth Office US Bicentennial sub-cttee.

MACCOBY, Hyam Zoundell, MA (Oxon), D. Univ. (Open U.); b. Sunderland, March 20, 1924; Emer. Fellow Leo Baeck Coll., Lond.; Res. Prof. Centre for Jewish Studies, Leeds (1998); Edr. Bd., European Judaism; Publ.: Revolution in Judaea, Judaism on Trial, The Sacred Executioner, The Mythmaker, Early Rabbinic Writings, Judas Iscariot and the myth of Jewish evil (awarded Wingate Prize 1992-3), Paul and Hellenism, The Disputation (TV & Stage play), A Pariah People, Ritual and Morality, etc. Ad.: Centre for Jewish Studies, University of Leeds, LS2 9JT. ☎ 01113-268 1972.

MAGONET, Rabbi Professor Dr Jonathan David, MB, BS, PhD (Heid.), FRSA; b. London, Aug. 2, 1942; Princ., Leo Baeck Coll.; V. President, World Union for Progressive Judaism; Guest Prof. Univ. Oldenburg (1999); Chairman, Yth Section, WUPJ (1964-66); Co-Editor European Judaism (1992-). Publ.: Returning: Exercises in Repentance, Forms of Prayer, Vol. I, Daily and Sabbath (co-ed.); Vol. II, Pilgrim Festivals (co-ed.); Vol. III, Days of Awe Prayerbook (co-ed.); Form and Meaning – Studies in Literary Techniques in the Book of Jonah, Guide to the Here and Hereafter (co-ed.); A Rabbi's Bible (1991); Bible Lives (1992); How To Get Up When Life Gets You Down (1993) (co-ed.); The Little Blue Book Of Prayer (1993) (co-ed.); A Rabbi Reads the Psalms (1994); Kindred Spirits (co-ed. 1995); Jewish Explorations of Sexuality (ed. 1995); The Subversive Bible (1997); The Explorer's Guide to Judaism (1998); Sun, Sand and Soul (co-ed. 1999); Abraham–Jesus–Mohammed: Interreligiöser Dialog aus Jüdischer Perspektiv (2000); From Autumn to Summer: A Biblical Journey through the Jewish Year (2000). Ad.: 18 Wellfield Ave., N10 2EA. ☎ 020-8444 3025.

MAILER, Norman, b. Long Branch, NJ, Jan. 31, 1923; Writer; Pulitzer Prize for non-fiction and Nat. Book Award for Arts and Letters (1969), Ed., Dissent, (1953-69). Publ.: The Naked and the Dead, Barbary Shore, The Deer Park, Advertisements for Myself, Deaths for the Ladies, The Presidential Papers, The Armies of the Night, Existential Errands, Marilyn, The Fight, The Executioner's Song, Of Women and Their Elegance, Pieces and Pontifications, Ancient Evenings, Tough Guys Don't Dance, Harlot's Ghost, Oswald's Tale, Portrait of Picasso as a Young Man, The Gospel According to the Son, The Time of Our Time, etc. Ad.: c/o Rembar, 19 W. 44th St., New York, NY 10036, USA.

MALITS, Rabbi Malcolm Henry, MBE, MA, D.Litt; b. Birmingham, Jan. 26, 1919; Emer. R.; M., Allerton Hebrew Cong. Liverpool (1964-90); Chaplain Ajex; (Masonic), Past Prov. Grand Chap. for West Lancashire. Ad.: 12 Glenside, Liverpool L18 9UJ. ☎ 0151-724 1967.

MARCUS, Mark Hyman, BA (Com); b. Manchester, Feb. 22, 1933; Vice-Chairman London Bureau of Int. Affairs; form. Exec. Dir., B'nai B'rith Distr. 15 (1984-98); Dir. Provincial & London Divisions, JIA. Ad.: B'nai B'rith Hillel House, 1-2 Endsleigh St., WC1H ODS. ☎ 020-7383 0442. Fax 020-7387 8014. E-mail mark@bbuk.org.

MARGOLYES, Miriam, BA (Cantab), LGSM&D; b. Oxford, May 18, 1941;

Actress. Ad.: c/o Jonathan Altaras Associates Ltd, 2 Goodwins Court, WC2N 4LL ☎ 020-7497 8878. Fax.: 020-7497 8876.

MARINER, Rabbi Rodney John, BA (Hons), Dip. Ed.; b. Melbourne, Australia, May 29, 1941; m. Susan; M., Belsize Sq. Syn.; Convener, Beth Din, RSGB; Assoc. M., Edgware & Distr. Ref. Syn. (1979-82); Asst. M., North Westem Ref Syn. (1976-79). Publ.: Prayers For All The Year: Part 1, Shabbat; Part 2, Festivals; Part 3, New Year; Part 4, Atonement; Part 5, Evening Prayers. Ad.: 92 North Road, London N6 4AA.

MARKOVA, Dame Alicia, DBE, Hon. DMus (Leics. and East Anglia Univs.); b. London, Dec. 1, 1910; Prima Ballerina Assoluta; P.: English National Ballet (since 1989); V. President, Royal Academy of Dancing (since 1958); Dir., Metrop. Opera Ballet, New York (1963-69), Gov., Royal Ballet, Prof. of Ballet and Performing Arts., Univ. of Cincinnati; President, Lond. Ballet Circle (since 1981), President, All England Dance Competition (1983); President, Arts Educ. Schs (1984); Lond. Festival Ballet (1986). Publ.: Giselle and I, Markova Remembers. Ad.: c/o Barclays Bank, P.O. Box 40, SW3 1QB.

MARKS, John Henry, MD, FRCGP, DObst, RCOG; b. London, May 30, 1925; m. Shirley, née Nathan; Chairman, C. BMA (1984-90); Chairman, Rep. Body BMA (1981-84); Gen. Med. C. (1979-84, 1989-94); V. President, Lond. Jewish Med. Soc. (1983-84, 1999-2000). Publ.: The Conference of Local Medical Committees and its Executive: An Historical Review. Ad.: Brown Gables, Barnet La., Elstree, Herts., WD6 3RQ. ☎ 020-8953 7687.

MARKS, Kenneth Anthony, b. London, July 28, 1931; Company Director; Non-Exec. Dir. Focus DIY; Non-Exec. Dir., Courts plc; Dir., Sheridan Australia (UK); V. President British-Israel Chamber of Commerce. Ad.: 279 Dover House Rd, Roehampton, SW15 5BP.

MARKS, Shula Eta (née Winokur), OBE, FBA, BA (UCT), Ph.D.(London), Hon. DLitt (UCT), Hon. D.Soc.Sci. (Natal), Distinguished Africanist Award, African Studies Assoc. (UK) (2002); b. Cape Town, Oct. 14, 1936; m. Isaac Meyer Marks; Historian; Emer. Prof. History of Southern Africa, SOAS (2001-), Prof. (1993-2001); Dir. Institute of Commonwealth Studies, Univ. of London (1983-93); Lecturer and Reader, History of Southern Africa, Jointly SOAS and ICS (1963-83); Mem. Arts and Humanities Research Bd. (1998-2000); Chair, Council for Assisting Refugee Academics (CARA); Chair International Records Management Tr. (1995). Publ.: Reluctant Rebellion: The 1906-1908 Disturbances in Natal (1970); The Ambiguities of Dependence in South Africa (1986); Not Either an Experimental Doll: The Separate Lives of Three South African Women (1987); Divided Sisterhood: Class, Race and Gender in the South African Nursing Profession (1944). Ad.: Dept. of History, School of Oriental and African Studies, Thornhaugh St., WC1H 0XG. ☎ 020-8699 3661. Email smarks@aol.com.

MARMUR, Rabbi Dow, b. Sosnowiec, Poland, Feb. 24, 1935; Rabbi-Emer., Holy Blossom Temple, Toronto; form. President, Toronto Board of Rabbis; form. Chairman, C. of Reform and Lib. Rabbis; M., North Western Reform Syn. (1969-83); South-West Essex Reform Syn. (1962-69). Publ.: Beyond Survival; The Star of Return; Walking Toward Elijah; On being a Jew; Reform Judaism (Edr.); A Genuine Search (Edr.); Choose Life. Ad.: 1950 Bathurst St., Toronto, Ontario, M5P 3K9, Canada. ☎ (416) 789 3291. Fax (416) 789 9697.

MAY, Michael, MSc (econ.); b. Jerusalem, Dec. 16, 1945; Exec. Director, European Council of Jewish Communities; Form. Dir., Institute of Jewish Affairs, London; Dir. Jewish Film Fdn.; form. Assoc. Ed., J. Quarterly; Member BoD Foreign Affairs Cttee.; Member Adv. C., STIBA (Dutch) Foundation for the Fight Against Anti-Semitism; Member Adv. Bd., Intern. Centre for Holocaust Studies, NY; former Dir. Jewish Book Council; Member Gov. Bd., World Jewish Congress (1983-91); Dir., Jewish Literary Trust (1984-91); Co.-Fdr. & Tr.

Limmud Conf. (1980-84). Ad.: 74 Gloucester Place, W1H 3HN. ☎ 020-7224 3445. Fax 020-7224 3446. E-mail ecjc@ort.org.

MAYER, Daniel, b. Paris, April 29, 1909; Member (President, 1983) French Constitutional C.; form. M. of Labour, War-time Member of C.N.R. (Resistance Nat. C.); Deputy for Seine; Sec.-Gen.; Socialist Party, S.F.I.O.; President, Internat. Fedn. of Human Rights; Conseil Supérieur de la Magistrature; President, Ligue des Droits de l'Homme. Ad.: Conseil Constitutionnel, 2 rue de Montpensier, Paris, 1e.

MELINEK, Rabbi A., BA, PhD; b. London, Sept. 15, 1912; form. Edr., L'Eylah; form. M., Willesden, Brondesbury, Stoke Newington Syns.; fom. Lect. Jews, Coll., Member, Court of the Univ. of Kent. Publ.: Life and Times of Abarbanel. Ad.: 6 Elm Close, NW4 2PH. ☎ 020-8202 9826.

MENCER, DAVID, BA; b. London, May 15, 1972; Director, Labour Friends of Israel; Labour Party agent and official (1995-97). Ad.: LFI, BM LFI, London WC1N 3XX. ☎ 020-7222 4323. Fax 020-7222 4324. Email david@lfi.org.uk.

MENDELSOHN, Jon, b. London, Dec. 30, 1966; m. Nicola née Clyne; Company Director; Chairman, Labour Friends of Israel (2002-). Ad.: LLM Communications, Bugle House, 21a Noel Street, London W1F 8GR.

MICHAELS, Leslie David, FCA, MBA; b. London, July 14, 1943; m. Lesley née Stern; Dir. Time Products plc; form. Chairman Ben Uri Art Gallery and Society. Ad.: 23 Grosvenor Street, London W1X 9FE. ☎ 020-7343 7215. E-mail ldmichaels@ timeproducts.co.uk.

MICHAELS, Rabbi Maurice Arnold, MA; b. Woolmer's Park, Herts., Aug. 31, 1941; Rabbi, South West Essex and Settlement Reform Syn.; Chairman Govs. Clore Tikva School; Hon. Life Vice-President LBC-CJE; Hon. Tr. RSGB Assembly of Rabbis; Previous: Chairman and V. President, RSGB; Chairman, Leo Baeck Coll.; Chairman, S. W. Essex Reform Syn.; Chairman, Redbridge Business Educ. Partnership; Gov. of Redbridge Coll.; Gov. of Akiva School; Gov. of Jewish Joint Bur. Soc.; Tr., Redbridge Racial Equality Council; Tr., Limmud; Member, World Union for Progressive Judaism Gov. Body; Member, Redbridge Jewish Community Cttee; Council Member, Redbridge Campaign Against Racism and Fascism; Dir., Harlow Enterprise Agency; Man. Cttee., West Essex Business Educ. Partnership; V. Chairman, Harlow & Dist. Employers' Group; Member, BoD; Member, Nat. Council Zionist Fed.; Member, Nat. Council Soviet Jewry. Ad.: 18 Exeter Gardens, Ilford, Essex IG1 3LA. ☎ 020-8554 2812. E-mail ramaby@mamichaels.fsnet.co.uk.

MIDDLEBURGH, Rabbi Charles H., BA Hons, PhD, FRSA; b. Hove, Oct. 2, 1956. Minister, Kingston Liberal Synagogue (1977-83); Rabbi, Harrow and Wembley Progressive Synagogue (1983-97); Exec. Dir. Union of Liberal and Progressive Synagogues (1997-2002); Assoc. Ed. Siddur Lev Chadash (1989-95); Co-Ed., Mahzor Ruach Chadashah (1996-); Chairman, ULPS Rabbinic Conference (1988-90, 1993-95); Lect. and Principal, ULPS Evening Institute (1980-92); Lect. Aramaic, Bible, Practical Rabbinics, Leo Baeck College (1985-2001); Fell. Zoological Soc., London; Vice-President, Voluntary Euthanasia Society; Mem., Int. Adv. Bd., CHAI. Ad.: The Montagu Centre, 21 Maple St., W1P 6DS. ☎ 020-7580 1663. Fax 020-8436 4184.

MILLER, Arthur, b. New York, Oct. 17, 1915; Novelist and Playwright; President, Internat. PEN Publ.: Focus, All My Sons, Death of a Salesman, After the Fall, A View from the Bridge, The Crucible, Incident at Vichy, The Price, The American Clock, Playing for Time, Timebends, The Ride down Mount Morgan, Mr Peter's Connections, etc. Ad.: c/o Kay Brown, ICM, 40 West 57th St., New York, NY.

MILLER, Harold, b. London, 1917; Member BoD; form. Chairman, ZF; V. President, form. Chairman, Brit Poale Zion; Elected to Fel. of WZO, 1993; Member of Board of Deputies. Ad.: 71 Francklyn Gdns., Edgware, Middlesex. ☎ 020-8958 5418.

MILLER, Rabbi Israel, MA, DD (Yeshiva Univ.); b. Baltimore, Md., April 6, 1918; Sr. V. President Emeritus, Yeshiva Univ.; H. President, Amer. Z. Fed.; President, Conference Jewish Material Claims against Germany; V. President, Amer.-Israel. Publ Affairs Cttee. (1983-90); Sec., Memorial Foundation for Jewish Culture; V.P , Jewish Com. Relations C. of New York; V. President, Nat. Jewish Welfare Bd. (1970-78); Chairmam., Conf of Presidents. of Major Amer. Jewish Orgs. (1974-76); Chairman, Amer. Jewish Conference on Soviet Jewry (1965-67); Chairman, Com. on Jewish Chaplaincy, NJWB (1962-65). Ad.: 11/3 Rehov Brand, Har Nof, Jerusalem. Fax 02-6512273.

MILLER, Dr Jack Elius, OBE, FRCGP, JP, OSTJ; b. Glasgow, March 7, 1918; form. Treasury Med. Off.; H.V.P (President 1968-71), Glasg. Jewish Rep. C.; H. V. President, Garnethill Syn.; Chairman, Soviet Jewry Com. (1968-78); Chairman, WJC Scotland (1954-63); H. President (Chairman 1950-57, 1960-65), Ajex Scotland (1997); BoD (1979-88), Nat.T. BMA (1972-81); Fel., BMA, Royal Soc. of Med, Royal Coll. of G.Ps.; Gold Medallist, BMA; Freeman of the City of London; Chairman, Scottish Gen. Med. Services Cttee (1969-72); Gen. Med. Services Com.; H. V. President, Scottish Marriage Guidance C. & Glasg. MGC; Race Rel. Bd., Scottish Conciliation Cttee. (1968-75); H. V. President, Prince and Princess of Wales Hospice, Glasg.; Chairman, Epilepsy Assn. of Scotland, Strathclyde Br. (1983-88); Chairman, Working Party on Priorities of the National Health Service; (1985-87); Sharpen, Report (1988); Edr., Glasg. Doctors, Handbook. Ad.: 38 Fruin Ave. Newton Mearns, Glasgow G77 6HJ. ☎ 0141-639 7869.

MILLER, Maurice Solomon, MBChB, JP; b. Glasgow, Aug. 16, 1920; Med. practitioner; MP (Lab.) for East Kilbride (1974-87); MP for Kelvingrove (Glasgow) (1964-74), form. H.Sec., Lab. Frs. of Israel, Parl. Br. Publ.: Window on Russia. Ad.:

MILLETT, The Rt. Hon. The Lord Millett, Baron Millett of St. Marylebone, PC, MA (Cantab), Hon. DL (QMW), Hon. DLL (Univ. London); b. London, June 23, 1932; Lord of Appeal in Ordinary (1998-); Member, Court of Appeal (1994-98); Judge of the High Court Chancery Div. (1986-94); QC (1973-86), Member, Insolvency Law Review Cttee. (1976-82); Stndg. Jr. Counsel, Trade & Industry Dept. (1967-73); Bencher, Lincoln's lnn, Called to Bar, Middle Temple; form. Chairman, Lewis Hammerson Home (1981-1991); President, West London Syn. (1991-95); Hon. Fel. Trinity Hall (1994). Publ.: (contrib.) Halsbury's Law of England; Ed-in-Chief: Encyclopaedia of Forms and Precedents. Ad.: 18 Portman Cl., W1H 9HJ. ☎ 020-7935 1152.

MIRVIS, Rabbi Ephraim Yitzchak, BA: b. Johannesburg, Sept. 7, 1956; Rabbi Finchley Synagogue (1996-); Chairman Rabbinical Council of the US (1999-2002); Member, Chief Rabbi's Cabinet; Edr. Daf Hashavua; Hon. Sec. LSJS; Member St. Cttee of Conference of European Rabbis; Religious Adv. to the Jewish Marriage Council; M. Western Marble Arch Syn. (1992-96); form. Chief Rabbi, Jewish Coms. of Ireland (1984-92); M. Dublin Hebrew Cong. (1982-84); Lect. MacHon. Meir, Jerusalem (1980-82). Ad.: 69 Lichfield Grove, London N3 2JJ. ☎/Fax 020-8346 3773. E-mail mirvis@mirvis.homechoice.co.uk.

MISHCON, Baron of Lambeth (Life Peer) (Victor Mishcon), DL, QC; b. London Aug. 14, 1915; Solicitor; Official Opposition Spokesman in House of Lords on Legal Affairs (1983-92); Dep. Lieut. for Greater Lond.; Chairman, LCC (1954-55); form. Chairman, Gen. Purposes Cttee., GLC, LCC and various LCC Cttees., Member, Govt. Com. of Inquiry into Lond. Transport (1953-54), Member Dept. Cttee. of Inquiry into Homosexual Offences and Prostitution (1954-57); Member, Nat. Theatre Bd. (1965-90) and South Bank Theatre Bd.; President Brit. C. of Shaare Zedek Hospital, Jerusalem; H. President, Brit. Technion Cttee; V. President, (form. P), AJY; Hon. Solicitor, JIA; Patron, and (1968-88) Chairman, Instit. of Jewish Studies; V. Chairman, CCJ (1977-79); form. V.

President, BoD.; Cdr., Royal Swedish Order of North Star, Star of Ethiopia; Star of Jordan; LL.D (Hon.) Birmingham Univ. 1991; Hon. Fellow, UCL; QC (Hon) 1992. Ad.: House of Lords, SW1A 0PW.

MISHON, Philip, OBE, b. London, March 23, 1924; Comp. Dir.; Chairman, Trs., UK Frs. for Further Educ. in Israel; Tr. Royal Free Hospital Breast Cancer Tr. (2000-); V. President (Nat. Chairman, 1966-68) AJEX. Appointed Tr. 1993; Council, CCJ; JLGB; President, Ajex Golf Soc. Ad.: 53 Bolsover St., W1P 7HL. ☎ 020-7387 6404. Fax 020-7722 3354.

MITCHELL, Mrs Eva (née Rose); b. Munster, June 14, 1929; Life V. President, West Lond. Syn. of Brit. Jews (1994-); Exec. Dir., CBFWJR (1979-89); form. Chairman, V. President Chairman, RSGB (1973-76); form. Chairman, Assn. of Jew Women's Orgs. in UK; form. V. Chairman; Nat. C. for Soviet Jewry. Ad.:.

MOCKTON, Rev. Leslie, b. Manchester Aug. 5, 1928; form. M., Waltham Forest Hebrew Cong.; Mayor's Chaplain, Lond. Borough Waltham Forest (1981-82); Hospital Chaplain Forest. Health Care Trust (1992-96); form. M., Highams Pk. & Chingford Syn. (1969-87); form. M. Bradford Hebrew Cong. (1965-69); West End Gt. Syn. (1958-65); Barking & Becontree Hebrew Cong. (1955-58). Ad.: 36 Halleswelle Rd., London NW11 0DJ.

MONTAGUE, Lee, b. Bow, London, Oct. 16, 1927; Actor; many leading roles including Shakespeare and Chekhov, title-role Leon in The Workshop, Raymond Chandler in Private Dick, O'Connor in Cause Célèbre (London 1977), Ed in Entertaining Mr. Sloane (New York 1965); Court in the Act (London 1987); films include Moulin Rouge, Mahler, Brass Target, London Affair, Silver Dream Racer, Lady Jane, Madame Sousatzka, Enigma; Television appearances include Holocaust, Thank You Comrades, Tussy Marx, Parsons Pleasure, The Workshop, Passing Through, Sharing Time, Kim, Dr. Sakharov, Bird of Prey, Much Ado About Nothing, Countdown to War, Incident in Judaea, House of Elliott, Casualty. Best TV Actor of the Year 1960. Ad.: c/o Joyce Edwards, 275 Kennington Rd., London SE11 6BY.

MONTEFIORE, Alan Claude Robin Goldsmid, MA (Oxon); b. London Dec. 29, 1926; Emer. Fellow, form. Fellow and Tutor in Philosophy, Balliol College, Oxford; Vis. Prof. Middlesex Univ.; form. Sr. Lect. in Moral & Political Philosophy, Keele Univ.; President, Wiener Libr.; President Forum for European Philosophy. Publ.: A Modern Introduction to Moral Philosophy, British Analytic Philosophy (co-ed.), Neutrality and Impartiality, The University and Political Commitment (ed.), French Philosophy Today (ed.), Goals, No-Goals and Own Goals: A Debate on Goal Directed and Intentional Behaviour (co-ed.), The Political Responsibility of Intellectuals (co-ed.), Integrity in the Public and Private Domains (co-ed.), etc. Ad.: 34 Scarsdale Villas, W8 6PR. ☎ 020-7937 7708. Fax 020-7938 4257.

MONTY, Mrs Regina Joy (née Dixon); b. London, Sept. 19, 1935; Hon. President, Fed. Women Zionists (Brit. WIZO); form. Chairman, V. Chairman and Membership Chairman, British WIZO. Ad.: 107 Gloucester Pl., W1U 6BY.

MOONMAN, Eric, OBE; b. Liverpool, Apr. 29, 1929; m. Gillian Louise née Mayer; President Zionist Federation (2001-); M.P. (Lab.) for Basildon (1974-79), for Billericay (1966-70); Chair, ERG Group of Radio Stations (1991-2002); V. President, BoD (1994-2000); Sr. V. President, BoD (1985-91); Chairman, Media Network; Chairman City of Liverpool Continuing Care Cttee (1996-); Prof Health Management, City Univ., London; Chairman, Academic Response to Racism & Antisemitism (1994-); Bd. Memb. IRC, Potomac Inst. for Policy Studies; Consultant, ICRC (Africa) (1992-95); Director Natural History Museum Development Trust (1989-91); (seconded) Chairman, WJC Europe Br. Cttee. on Antisemitism (1985-92, 1998-); Chairman Community Research Unit, (1985-96); Chairman, Z. Fed. (1975-80); President, Friends of Union of Jewish Students; Co.-Chairman, Nat. Jewish Solidarity Cttee. (1975-79); form. Parl. Pte. Sec. to Sec. of State for Educ. and Science; form. Sr. Res. Fel., Manch. Univ.;

form. Leader, Stepney Borough C.; Sr. Adv., Brit. Instit. of Management (1956-62); European Adv. WJC (1973-76); Chairman, Nat. Aliyah and Volunteers C.; Chairman, P.R. Cttee., Z.F. (1983-85; 1972-75); Trustee, Balfour Tr.; CRE Award for Multi Racial Service (1996). Publ.: The Alternative Government, The Manager and the Organisation, Reluctant Partnership, European Science and Technology, etc. Ad.: 1 Beacon Hill, N7 9LY.

MORGAN, Rabbi Fred; b. New York City, March 18, 1948, m. Susan Sinclair; Sen. M. Temple Beth Israel, Melbourne, Australia; Chairman, C. Progressive Rabbis of Australia & N.Z. (2000); Hon. Assoc. Rabbi Sim Shalom Jewish Community Budapest; M. North West Surrey Synagogue (1984-97); Lect. in Midrash and Jewish Thought Leo Baeck Rabbinical College (1987-97); V.-Chairman Assembly of Reform Rabbis (1996-97); Lect. in Judaism, Roehampton Institute (1989-92); Lect. in Religious Studies, Univ. of Bristol (1973-79); Vis. Prof. Eotvos Lorand Univ., Budapest (1992-94). Ad.: Temple Beth Israel, 76-82 Alma Road, St Kilda 3182, Victoria, Australia. ☎ 61-3-9510 1488. Fax 61-3-9521 1229. E-mail rabbi.fred.morgan@tbi.org.au.

MORITZ, Ludwig Alfred, MA, D.Phil (Oxon.); b. Munich, May 11, 1921, m. Doris née Rath; retd.; form. V. Princ. (Admin.) and Reg., Univ. Coll., Cardiff (1971-87); Lect., Bedford Coll., Lond. (1950-53), Univ. Coll. Cardiff (1953-60); Prof. of Classics, Univ. Coll. of Ghana (1959-60), Univ Coll., Cardiff (1960-71); Chairman Cardiff New Syn. (1991-95). Publ.: Classical studies. Ad.: 1 Llanedeyrn Rd., Penylan, Cardiff CF23 9DT. ☎/Fax 029 2048 5065. E-mail lamoritz-99@yahoo.com.

MORRIS, Henry, b. London Mar. 5, 1921; Curator, AJEX Military Museum; form. Chairman, Jewish Defence & Group Rel Cttee., BoD; V. President (Nat.Chairman 1979-81) Ajex. Publ.: We Will Remember Them (1989 and Addendum 1994); The AJEX Chronicles: A History of the Association (2000). Ad.: 4 Ashbrook, Stonegrove, Edgware, Middx HA8 7SU. ☎ 020-8958 7154.

MORRIS, Norman Harold, FRSA; b. London, June 8, 1932; Principal N.M. Consultants; form. Exec. Dir., Balfour Diamond Jubilee Tr. (Consult. 1995-); Exec. Consultant Scopus Jewish Educational Tr. (1995-); Freeman, City of Lond.; form. Exec. Sec. Z. Fed.; Dep. Provincial Dir., Z. Fed.; J.P.A.; Printing & Publ. Cttee., Brit.-Israel Chamber of Commerce; Sec., Eastern Cape Z. C. Ad.: Balfour House, 741 High Rd., N12 0BQ. ☎ 020-8343 8196. Fax 020-8347 7283.

MORRIS OF KENWOOD, Philip Geoffrey, 2nd Baron, JP; b. Sheffield, June 18, 1928; form. P. Hotel Caterers and Allied Trades Aid for Israel Cttee.; President, JNF Bridge Tournament. Ad.: 35 Fitzjohn's Ave., London NW3 5JY. ☎ 020-7431 6332.

MORRIS OF KENWOOD, Lady Ruth (née Janner); b. London, Sept. 21, 1932; Solicitor; President, Nat. Cttee., Va'ad Lema'an Habonim; H. Solicitor, various youth orgs.; Dir., WOYL; Tr. Jewish Youth Fund; Tr. Brady Maccabi; Memb. Allocations Cttee UJIA; Tr. Elsie & Barnett Janner Charitable Tr.; Dir. Womankind worldwide; form. Man., Brady Girls' Club; form. exec. Member, Victoria Boys' and Girls' Club; Tr., Rowan Educ.; Tr.; form. Member, Gen. Adv. C., Independent Broadcasting Auth. (I.B.A.). Chairman DSS Appeals Tribunal. Ad.: 35 Fitzjohn's Ave., London NW3 5JY. ☎ 020-7431 6332.

MOSER, Lord, Baron of Regent's Park, KCB, CBE, FBA, BSc (Econ), Hon. D. (Southampton, Leeds, Surrey, Sussex, York, Keele, City, Wales, Edinburgh, Liverpool London, Brunel, Brighton, Hull, Heriot-Watt, Northumbria, South Bank Univs); b. Berlin, Nov. 24, 1922; Chancellor, Keele Univ. (1986-2002); Tr. British Museum (1988-); Chairman British Museum Dev. Trust (1994-); Chancellor Open University Israel (1994-), Hon. Fellow; Warden, Wadham Coll., Oxford (1984-93); Chairman, Holt Ltd. (1990-2002); Chairman Basic Skills Agency (1998-2002); Dir., V. Chairman, CBF-WJR. Publ.: Writings on statistics. Ad.: 3 Regent's Park Tce., NW1 7EE. ☎ 020-7485 1619.

NABARRO, Eric John Nunes, JP, FCA; b. London, April 5, 1917; m. Cecily née Orenstein; Chartered accountant; P. of Elders, Spanish and Portuguese Jews, Cong., London (1984-88; 1994-96); T., Heshaim (Beth Hamidrash) (1984-94); H. Member, Nat. Shechita C.; Tr., Ravenswood Foundation (1986-92), Chairman, Sephardi Kashrut Auth. (1968-84); President, Sephardi Welfare Bd. (1979-87); T., BoD (1973-79); V. President (T. 1947-72), Victoria Com. Centre; Capt., Jewish Brigade (1945); T., London Bd. for Shechita (1949-63); Chairman, Kosher School Meals Service (1966-73). Ad.: 61 William Ct., 6 Hall Rd., London NW8 9PB. ☎ 020-7266 3787.

NABARRO, Frank Reginald Nunes, MBE, MA, BSc (Oxon), DSc (Birmingham), DSc (Hon.) (Witwatersrand, Natal, Cape Town), FRS, Hon. FRSSAf; b. London March 7, 1916; P. Roy. Soc. S. Africa (1988-92); H. Prof Res. Fel., Physics Dept. Witwatersrand Univ., Johannesburg; Fell. S. African CSIR; Dep. V. Chancellor (1978-80), form. Dean, Faculty of Science; Fd. Mem., S.A. Acad. Sci.; Foreign Assoc. US Nat. Acad. Eng. Publ.: Theory of Crystal Dislocations; Physics of Creep (with H. L. de Villiers). Ad.: 32 Cookham Rd., Auckland Park, Johannesburg 2092, S. Africa. ☎ (11) 726 7745. Fax (11) 717 6879. E-mail dobson@physnet.phys.wits.ac.za.

NAGLER, Neville Anthony, MA (Cantab); b. London, Jan. 2, 1945; m. Judy née Mordant; Director General BoD; Exec. Cttee, Interfaith Network for the UK; Certificate in Public Services Management (2000); form. Asst. Sec. Home Office (1980-91); UK Representative to UN Narcotics Comm., (1983-88); Chairman, Council of Europe Drug Co-op Group (1984-88); Haldane Essay Prize (1979); Princ. H.M. Treasury; Pte. Sec. Chancellor of Exchequer (1971); Fin. Rep. and Warden, Pinner Syn. (1979-91). Ad.: Board of Deputies ☎ 020-7543 5400. Fax 020-7543 0100. E-mail info@bod.org.uk.

NATHAN, Clemens Neumann, CTexFTI, FRAI, Officers' Cross, Austria; Cavalieri, al Merito della Repub. Italiana; b. Hamburg, Aug. 24, 1933; Comp. Dir., P. (T., 1965-71) Anglo-Jewish Assn.; V. President (President 1983-89); Jt. Chairman Consultant C. of Jewish Orgs. (Non-Govt. Org. at United Nations); Chairman, Centre for Christian–Jewish Studies, Cambridge (1998-); Claims Conf, Memorial Foundation for Jewish Culture; Mem, Jewish Memorial C.; Hon. Fell. Shenkar Coll., Israel; Hon. Fell. SSEES, Univ. London; Director Sephardi Centre; CCJ, Fdr. Member, Internat. Cttee. for Human Rights in Soviet Union (1966); BoD (1979-85); Soc. of Heshaim, Span. & Port. Jews, Cong., Lond. (1979-), Bd. of Elders (1977-83); Chairman, Sha'are Tikva Cttee. (1975-81); form. V. President, Textile Instit.; Textile Institute Medal for services to the Industry and Institute. Publ.: Technological and marketing works. Ad.: 2 Ellerdale Cl., NW3 6BE. ☎ 020-7794 6537.

NATHAN, Roger Carol Michael, 2nd Baron; Hon. LLD (Sussex); b. London, Dec. 5, 1922; H. President (Chairman 1971-77) CBF-WJR (since 1977); President, JWB (1967-71); V. Chairman, Cancer Res. Campaign (Chairman Ex. Cttee. 1970-75); Chairman Cttee. on Energy and the Environment (1974); V. Chairman Cttee. on Charity Law and Practice (1976); Member Royal Com. on Environmental Pollution (1979-89); Memb. House of Lords Select Cttee on Science & Technology (1994-); Member House of Lords Select Cttee. on European Com.; Chairman, Sub-Cttee. (Environment) (1983-87, 1989-92); Chairman, House of Lords Select Cttee. on Murder and Life Imprison-ment (1988-89); Chairman Cttee. on Effectiveness and the Voluntary Sector (1989-90); Sol; V. President (Chairman 1975-77); Royal Society of Arts; Fel., Soc. of Antiquaries; Fel., Royal Geographical Soc.; Chairman, Sussex Downs Conservation Board (1992-97); President Weald & Downland Open Air Museum (1994-97). Master, Worshipful Co. of Gardeners (1964); Capt., 17/21 Lancers (Ment. in Dispatches). Ad.: House of Lords, SW1 0PW.

NAVON, Yitzhak, b. Jerusalem, April 9, 1921; form. Israeli Dep. Prime Min. and

Educ & Culture Min.; Fifth President, State of Israel (1978-83); Member, Knesset (1965-78; since 1984); form. Chairman, Knesset Foreign Affairs and Defence Cttee.; Dir., Office of Prime Minister (Ben-Gurion) (1952-63); form. Chairman, World Zionist Council. Publ.: Bustan Sephardi, Six Days and Seven Gates. Ad.: 31 Haneviim St., Jerusalem.

NEUBERGER, Rabbi Julia Babette Sarah (née Schwab), MA (Cantab), Hon. Doctorates Univ. Humberside, Ulster, City, Stirling, Oxford Brookes, Teesside, Nottingham, Open U., Queens, Sheffield Hallam, Aberdeen; b. London, Feb. 27, 1950, m. Anthony; Tr. Imperial War Museum (1999-); Civil Service Commissioner (2001-2); Mem., Cttee on Standards in Public Life (Wicks Committee) (2001-); Mem. Cttee to Review Funding of the BBC (1999); Chancellor Univ. Ulster (1994-2000); Chief Exec. The King's Fund (1997-); Council Mem. Save the Children Fund (1994-98); Mem. General Medical Council (1993-2000); Mem. Medical Res. C. (1995-2000); Lect., Leo Baeck Coll.; Harkness Fel. Harvard University (1991-92); Mem. Human Fertilisation and Embryology Authority (1990-95); T., Runnymede Trust (1990-97); Rabbi, S. Lond. Lib. Syn. (1977-89); Assoc., Newnham Coll., Cambridge; Presenter, Choices, BBC-1 (1986-87). Publ.: Women in Judaism: The Fact and the Fiction (in Women's Religious Experience, ed. Pat Holden); The Story of Judaism (for children); Judaism (in Spiritual Care in Nursing, ed. McGilloway and Myco); Days of Decision, Vols. I-IV (ed.); Women's Policy, Defence and Disarmament; Bill of Rights and Freedom of Information; Privatisation; Caring for Dying Patients of Different Faiths (Lisa Sainsbury Foundation, 2nd ed. 1994); ed. (with Canon John White), A Necessary End (1991); Whatever's Happening to Women (1991); Ethics and Healthcare: The role of research ethics committees in the UK (Kings's Fund 1992); (ed.) The Things that Matter (1993); On Being Jewish (1995); Dying Well: A Guide to Enabling a Good Death (1999); Hidden Assets: Decision Making in the NHS (jt. ed., 2002). Ad.: 28 Regents Park Rd., London NW1 7TR. ☎ 020-7428 9895. Fax 020-7813 2030.

NEWMAN, Aubrey Norris, MA (Glasgow), MA, D.Phil (Oxon), FRHistS; b. London, Dec. 14, 1927; m. Bernice Freda née Gould; Prof. (Emeritus) of History, Leicester Univ.; President, Jewish Hist. Soc. (1977-79, 1992-93). Publ.: The United Synagogue, 1870-1970 (1977); The History of the Board of Deputies (1985); The Stanhopes of Chevening (1970); The Parliamentary Diary of Sir Edward Knatchbull (1966); (ed.) Migration and Settlement (1971); (ed.) Provincial Jewry in Victorian Britain (1975); (ed.) The Jewish East End, 1840-1939 (1981); (joint ed.) Patterns of Migration, 1850-1914 (1996). Ad.: 33 Stanley Road, Stoneygate, Leicester, LE2 1RF. ☎ (0116) 270 4065 (home), (0116) 252 2802 (university). Fax. (0116) 252 3986. E-mail new@leicester.ac.uk.

NEWMAN, Eddy, b. Liverpool, May 14, 1953. Manchester City Councillor (1979-85); Labour MEP for Greater Manchester Central (1984-99); Member of the European Parliament's Delegation for Relations with Israel and the Knesset (1994-99); V. Chairman, European Parliament Regional Policy ad Regional Planning Cttee (1984-87); Chairman, European Parliament Cttee on Petitions (1994-97); V. Chairman, Cttee on Petitions (1997-). Publ.: Respect for Human Rights in the European Union', a report of the European Parliament Committee on Civil Liberties, 1994. Ad.: 234 Ryebank Rd., Manchester M21 9LU. ☎ 0161-881 9641.

NEWMAN, Rabbi Isaac, MPhil, PGCE, Dip. Counselling; b. London, Apr. 3, 1924; form. Chairman, Rabbis for Human Rights (Israel); M. Retd., Barnet Syn.; Sr. Lect., Judaica, & Chaplain, Middlesex Polytechnic, Trent Park; form. H.Sec., Rabbinical C., United Synagogue; Chaplain to RAF Publ.: Talmudic Discipleship. Ad.: 90 Sderot Herzl, Jerusalem. ☎ 02 6525763.

NEWMAN, Rabbi Jeffrey, MA (Oxon.); b. Reading, Dec. 26 1941; m. Bracha;

Minister Finchley Reform Synagogue (1973-); form. Chairman Rabbinic In-service training, Leo Baeck Rabbinical College (LBC); form. Chairman, Pastoral Skills and Counselling Department LBC; Chairman of Tr. Israel Palestine Centre for Research and Information; Ed. Living Judaism (1969-73); Lect. in Heimler Training. Contributor to various journals on Judaism, Psychology and Spirituality. Ad.: Finchley Reform Synagogue, Fallowcourt Avenue, N12 0BE. ☎ 020-8446 3244. Fax 020-8446 5980.

NEWMAN, Lotte Therese, CBE, MB, BS, LRCP, MRCS, FRCGP; b. Frankfurt am Main, Jan. 22, 1929; m. Norman Aronsohn; General practitioner; Mem. GMC (1984-98); Chairman, Registration Committee, General Medical Council (1997-98); Gov. PPP Medical Trust (1996-99); President, London Jewish Medical Society (1998-99); President Royal College General Practitioners (1994-97); Freeman, City of London; Mem. Hampstead Synagogue Bd of Management (1999-); Mem. BoD (1999-); Mem. Defence Group Relations Cttee and Chairman of Circumcision Working Group (1999-); Medical Adv. St John Ambulance (1999-). Publ.: Papers on medical, health and training topics. Ad.: The White House, 1 Ardwick Rd., London NW2 2BX. ☎ 020-7436 6630. Fax 020-7435 6672. E-mail JH44@dial.pipex.com.

OPPENHEIM, Jeremy, b. June 6, 1955; m. Karen née Tanner; Chief Exec. Jewish Care (2000-); form. Dir. Social Services, London Borough of Hackney (1997-99); Hd. Children's Services, London Borough of Barking and Dagenham (1993-97); London Borough of Haringey: Service Man., Child Care (1989-93), Team Man. (1986-89), Social Worker (1983-86); Senior Social Worker, Jewish Welfare Board (1980-83); Social Worker, Jewish Welfare Board (1977-79). Ad.: Jewish Care, Stuart Young House, 221 Golders Green Road, London NW11 9DQ. ☎ 020-8922 2000. Fax 020-8922 1998. E-mail joppenheim@jcare.org.

OPPENHEIM-BARNES, Baroness of Gloucester (Life Peer) (Sally), PC; b. Dublin, July 1930; Mem. Shadow Cabinet (2001-); MP (Conservative) for Gloucester (1970-87); form. Chairman, Conservative Party Parl. Prices and Consumer Protection Cttee.; form Nat. V. President, Nat. Union of Townswomen's Guilds; form. Nat. V. President, ROSPA; Chairman, Nat. Consumer C. (1987-89); Dir. (non-exec.) Robert Fleming (1989-97); Non-Exec. Director. HFC Bank (1989-98). Ad.: House of Lords.

OPPENHEIMER, Peter Morris, MA; b. London, Apr 16, 1938; President, Oxford Centre for Hebrew and Jewish Studies; Student (Fel.) Christ Church Oxford; Chairman Jewish Chronicle Ltd.; Dir. Dixons plc (1987-93); Delbanco, Meyer & Co. Ltd. (1987-2001); Chief Economist, Shell Internat. Petroleum Co. (1985-86). Ad.: Christ Church, Oxford OX1 1DP. ☎ 01865 558226. Fax 01865-516834.

ORGEL, Leslie Eleazer, DPhil, FRS; b. London, Jan 12, 1927; m. Hassia Alice née Levinson; Sr. Fellow & Res. Prof., Salk Instit. and Adjunct Prof., Univ. of California, San Diego; Member Nat Acad. Sci., form. Fellow of Peterhouse, Cambridge Univ. Publ.: Scientific work. Ad.: The Salk Institute, 10010 North Torrey Pines Road, La Jolla, CA 92037-1099, USA. ☎ 858-453 4100, ext 1321. Fax 858-550 9959. E-mail orgel@salk.edu.

ORLINSKY, Harry M., BA, PhD; b. Owen Sound, Ont., Can, Mar 14, 1908; Prof. of Bible. HUC-JIR, New York (since 1943); Ed., Library of Biblical Studies, President, Soc. of Biblical Lit. (1969-70); Centennial Award for Biblical Scholarship; President, Amer. Friends of Israel Exploration Soc. (1951-79); President, Internat. Org. for Masoretic Studies; President, Internat. Org. for Septuagint and Cognate Studies (1969-75), President, Amer. Acad. for Jewish Res.; Fel. Guggenheim Form. Soc. of Scholars, Johns Hopkins Univ. (1982); form. Vis. Prof., Hebrew Univ.; Acad. Cttee., Annenberg Res. Instit. (since 1987). Publ.: Works of Bible, lit. and hist., The Pentateuch A Linear Translation, 5 vols.; Revised Standard Version, Old Testament; The Torah, Edr.-in-chief of J.P.S.

trans. (1963); The Prophets; The Writings; The So-called Servant of the Lord and Suffering Servant in Second Isaiah; Ancient Israel; Understanding the Bible; The Bible as Law; Tanakh; Essays in Biblical Culture and Bible Translation, etc. Ad.: 1 West 4th St., New York 10012. ☎ 212-674 5300.

OWEN, His Honour Judge Aron, BA, PhD (Wales); b. Tredegar, Gwent, Feb. 16, 1919, m. Rose née Fishman; Circuit Judge, South-East Circuit (1980-94); Dep. High Court Judge, Family Division; Freeman, City of Lond; C. JHSE; Patron, Jewish Marriage Co. Publ.: Social History of Jews in Thirteenth-Century Europe, Amos and Hosea, Rashi. Ad.: 44 Brampton Grove, NW4 4AQ. ☎ 020-8202 8151.

OZIN, Malcolm John; b. London, Nov. 14, 1934; Managing Dir., Investment & Securities Trust Ltd.; Hon. Chief Exec. Jewish Blind & Disabled; Tr. Cecil Rosen Found.; Hon. Sec. Cavendish Housing Trust Ltd. Ad.: 118 Seymour Place, W1H 1NP. ☎ 020-7262 2003. E-mail mjo@jbd.org.

PAISNER, Martin David, MA (Oxon), LLM (Ann Arbor, Michigan); b. Windsor, Berkshire, Sept. 1, 1943; m. Susan Sarah née Spence; solicitor; Chairman, The Jerusalem Foundation (1997-); Hon. Fellow, Queen Mary College, London; Governor, Weizmann Institute of Science, Ben Gurion Univ.; Bd Mem./Tr. Oxford Centre for Hebrew and Jewish Studies, Jewish Care, Weizmann Institute Foundation, European Jewish Publication Society, Holocaust Educational Trust and The Royal Free Cancerkin Breast Cancer Trust. Ad.: 4 Heath Drive, Hampstead, London NW3 7SY.

PASCAL, Julia, BA (Hons) (Lond.); b. Manchester, Nov. 15, 1949; m. Alain Carpentier; Playwright/Theatre director; Theatre Dir., National Theatre (1978); Assoc. Dir., Orange Tree Theatre (1979); Artistic Dir., Pascal Theatre Co. (1983-2003); Prima Ballerina Assoluta in Virago's 'Truth, Dare or Promise' and Boxtree's 'Memoirs of a Jewish Childhood'. Plays include Theresa (1990), The Dybbuk (1992), Year Zero (1995), The Yiddish Queen Lear (1999), London Continental (2000), 20/20 for Amici Dance Theatre (2000), Woman in the Moon (2001); Radio Plays: The Road to Paradise (1997), The Golem (2002), Crossing Jerusalem (2002). Publ.: The Holocaust Trilogy; The Yiddish Queen Lear and Woman in the Moon; The Golem and Crossing Jerusalem. Ad.: 35 Flaxman Court, Flaxman Terrace, London WC1H 9AR. ☎ 020-7383 0920. Fax 020-7419 9798. E-mail pascal7038@aol.com.

PATTERSON, David, MA, PhD, DHL (Hon) (Balt.), DHL (Hon) (HUC; b. Liverpool, June 10, 1922; Cowley Lect. in Post-Biblical Hebrew, Univ. of Oxford (1956-89); Emeritus President & H. Fel., Oxford Centre for Hebrew & Jewish Studies; Emeritus Fel. St. Cross Coll., Oxford; Vis. Prof. (Scholar in Residence 1981) Northwestern Univ. (1983, 1985, 1993); Fel., Soc. Humanities (Vis. Prof. 1966-71), Cornell Univ. (1983); Fel., Humanities Res. Centre, Canberra (1979); Prof. Jewish Studies, Mt. Holyoke Coll., Mass. (1987-88); Scholar in Res., Vis. Prof. (1993) Hebrew Union Coll., Cincinnati (1982); Vis. Prof., Univ. of Sydney (1993); Vis. Prof. Smith Coll., Mass. (1994-95); Vis. Prof. Hampshire College, Mass. (1996); H.Res. Fel. Centre for J. Studies, Manchester (1998-); Lect. in Modern Hebrew, Manchester Univ. (1953–56); Fel., Jew. Academy of Arts and Sciences, USA; Brotherhood Award, Nat. Conf., Christians and Jews, USA; Stiller Prize, Baltimore Hebrew Univ (1988); Webber Prize for translation of Hebrew Literature (1989); Mem. Senate of the Hochschule für Jüdische Studien, Heidelberg (1990-99). Publ.: Abraham Mapu, The Hebrew Novel in Czarist Russia, A Phoenix in Fetters, Tradition and Trauma (with G. Abramson, eds), Random Harvest (transl.), etc. Ad.: 35 Hayward Rd., Oxford, OX2 8LN. ☎/Fax 01865 559003.

PAUL, Geoffrey D., OBE, FRSA; b. Liverpool, March 26, 1929; Director, Anglo-Israel Assoc. (2001-); Ed. (1977-1990) Jewish Chronicle, American Affairs Ed.

(1991-96). Ad.: 1 Carlton Close, West Heath Rd., NW3 7UA. ☎/Fax 020-8458 6948. E-mail infoman@btinternet.com.

PEPPER, Michael, BSc, MA, PhD, ScD, FRS; b. London, Aug. 10, 1942, m. Jeannette; Physics Prof, Cambridge Univ., Fel., Trinity Coll.; Warren Res. Fel., Royal Soc. (1978-86); Vis. Prof Bar-Ilan Univ. (1984). Ad.: Cavendish Laboratory, Madingley Rd., Cambridge, CB3 0HE. ☎ 01223 337330.

PERES, Shimon, Nobel Peace Laureate; b. Vishniev, Belarus, Aug. 16, 1923; m. Sonia née Gelman; Deputy Prime Minister of Israel and Minister of Foreign Affairs (2001-); Minister for Regional Cooperation (1999-2001); Fd. Peres Center for Peace (1997); Prime Minister and Minister of Defense (1995-96); Minister of Foreign Affairs (1992-95); Chairman of the Labour Party (1977-92, 1995-97); M.K. (1959-). Publ.: In Between Hatred and Neighbourhood (1961), The Next Phase (1965), David's Sling (1970), Entebbe Diary (1991), The New Middle East (1993), Battling for Peace (1995), For the Future of Israel (1997), New Genesis (1998), The Imaginary Voyage (1999). Ad. Foreign Ministry, Jerusalem.

PERSOFF, Meir, JP, MA (Lond), FRSA; b. Letchworth, Aug. 25, 1941; Judaism Edr., Saleroom corr. (1981-2000), News Edr. (1974-76), Arts Edr. (1980-85), Features Edr. (1976-90), Jewish Chronicle; President, Israel-Judaica Philatelic Soc.; form. Cttee., Jewish Book C.; form. Publ. Cttee., Jewish Marriage C.; Silver Medallist, internat. philatelic exhibitions, Jerusalem, London, Stockholm, Pretoria, Paris, Madrid. Publ.: The Running Stag: The Stamps and Postal History of Israel, ed., Jewish Living, The Hasmonean, Immanuel Jacobovits: A Prophet in Israel, etc. Ad.: 20 Hill Close, Stanmore, Middx HA7 3BS. ☎ 020-8420 6472.

PINNER, Hayim, OBE, FRSA; Commander Order of Civil Merit (Spain); b. London, May 25, 1925; Dir., Sternberg Charitable Trust; Hon. Sec. CCJ; form. Sec.-Gen., BoD (1977-1991); H.V. President, Z.F.; V. President, Labour Z. Movt.; form Dir B'nai Brith (1957-77); form Exec., TAC; Lab. Frs. of Israel; Exec., CCJ; Member, Adv. C., World Congress of Faiths, Inter-Faith Network; Central Campaign; Exec., JIA; Chairman, Belsen Commemoration Cttee., Imperial War Museum; Freeman, City of Lond.; Hillel Foundation C.; BoD Defence & Eretz Israel Cttee.; World Zion. "Actions Cttee."; Jewish Agency Assembly; Chairman, Poale Zion; P. Z. Del., Lab. Party Confs.; Edr., Jewish Vanguard, Jewish Labour News, B'nai B'rith Journal. Ad.: 62 Grosvenor St., W1X 9DA. ☎ 020-7485 2538.

PINNICK, Jeffrey, FCA; b. London Dec. 6, 1935; T., BoD; Chairman, Fin. Cttee., BoD (V. Chairman, 1982-85); V.Chairman, Frs., Boys Town, Jerusalem, Ad.: 5th Floor, Commonwealth House, 1-19 Oxford St., London WC1A 1NF.

PINTER, Harold, CBE; b. London, Oct. 10, 1930; Playwright. Publ.: The Birthday Party, The Caretaker, The Homecoming, Old Times, No Man's Land, Moonlight, Betrayal, and other plays. Ad.: Judy Daish Associates Ltd., 2 St Charles Place, W10 6EG. ☎ 020-8964 8811. Fax 020-8964 8966.

PLANCEY, Rabbi Alan; b. Edinburgh, Oct. 30, 1941; M., Borehamwood & Elstree Syn.; Chairman, Rabbin. C. US (1987-94); Member Chief Rabbi's Cabinet; H. V.-President & Rel Adv., Jewish Care; Area Chaplain Herts. Police; Hon. Chaplain Jewish Police Association; Hon. Chaplain Jewish Scouting Adv. Cttee.; Freeman of the City of London; M., Luton Syn. (1965-69); Youth M., Hampstead Garden Sub. Syn. (1970-76). Ad.: 98 Anthony Rd., Borehamwood, Herts., WD6 4NB. ☎ 020-8207 3759. Fax 020-8207 0568.

PLASKOW, Rev. Michael Lionel, MBE, LTSC, ALCM; b. Palestine, July 8, 1936; Chairman, Hard of Hearing Assoc., Netanya; Emer. R., Woodside Park Syn.; Chaplain to the Mayor of Barnet (1999-2000); Chairman Central Found. School, Jewish Old Boys Group; Norman B. Spencer award 1992 for research into Freemasonry; Freeman City of London (1994). Publ. The Story of a

Community: Woodside Park 1937-1987. Ad.: 4/4 Nitza Boulevard, 42262 Netanya. ☎ (09) 832-9592.

POLONSKY, Antony, BA (Rand), MA, D.Phil (Oxon), Knight's Cross of the Order of Merit, Poland; b. Johannesburg, Sept. 23, 1940, m. Arlene née Glickman; Albert Abramson Professor of Holocaust Studies at the United States Holocaust Memorial Museum and Brandeis University; Vice-president, Institute for Polish-Jewish Studies, Oxford; Vice-president, American Association for Polish-Jewish Studies, Cambridge, MA; Member Exec Ctte, National Polish American-Jewish American Council; Ed., Polin: A Journal of Polish-Jewish Studies. Publ. Politics in Independent Poland (1972), The Little Dictators (1973), The Great Powers and the Polish Question (1976), The Beginnings of Communist Rule in Poland (1981), (ed.) The Jews in Poland (1986), (ed.) A Cup of Tears (1989), (ed.) Recent Polish Debates about the Holocaust (1990), (ed.) Polish Paradoxes (1990), (ed.) The Jews of Warsaw (1991), (ed.) The Jews in Old Poland (1992), Contemporary Jewish Writing in Poland (ed.) (2001). Ad.: 322 Harvard Street, Cambridge, MA 02139. ☎ (617) 492 9788, 736 2980, Fax (617) 736 2070 E-mail polonsky@brandeis.edu.

PORTER, Sir Leslie, PhD (Hon) (Tel Aviv Univ.) OStJ; b. July 10, 1920; President, Tesco plc (1970-1985); Companion, Brit., Instit. of Management; V. President, Nat. Playing Fields Assn.; Member, Lloyd's; President, Instit., Grocery Distribution (1977-80); Chancellor, Tel Aviv Univ. Ad.: Seymour Pierce Advisory Services Ltd., 79 Mount Street, London W1K 2SN.

PORTER, Dame Shirley (née Cohen), DBE, FRSA, HonPhD (Tel Aviv); b. Nov. 29, 1930; Form. Leader, Westminster City C. (1983-91); Lord Mayor (1991); V. President London Union of Youth Clubs; Past Master Worshipful Co. Environmental Cleaners; Freeman of the City of London; form. Dep. Ch., London Festival Ballet. Publ.: A Minister for London, Efficiency in Local Government. Ad.: Seymour Pierce Advisory Services Ltd., 79 Mount Street, London W1K 2SN. ☎ 020-7616 4700.

POSEN, Felix, BA (John Hopkins Univ.), D.Phil. (Hon., Hebrew Univ.); b. Berlin, Oct. 24, 1928; m. Jane née Levy; Gov. Emer. and Hon. Fellow Oxford Centre for Hebrew and Jewish Studies; Gov. Hebrew University; Tr. Institute of Archaeo-metallurgical Studies, University of London; Member of the Bd of Alma Hebrew College, Tel Aviv; Member of the Bd of the College of Pluralistic Judaism, Jerusalem; Council member of the JPR; Member Cttee Interfaith Mission for Christians, Muslims and Jews. Ad.: 24 Kensington Gate, London W8 5NA. ☎ 020-7584 0914. Fax 020-7584 0904. E-mail nesop@ dircon.co.uk.

PRAG, Derek Nathan, MA (Cantab), HD.Litt (Univ. Herts), Hon. MEP; b. Merthyr Tydfil, Aug. 6, 1923; m. Dora née Weiner; MEP (Cons), for Hertfordshire (1979-94); Mem. European Parl. Delegation for Relations with Israel (1989-94); Chairman, All-Party Disablement Group (1980-94); V. Chairman, European Parl.-Israel Intergroup (1990-94); Commander of the Order of Leopold II, Belgium (1996); Silver Medal of European Merit, Luxembourg (1974); H. Dir., EEC Com. (1974). Publ.: Businessman's Guide to the Common Market (1973), Europe's International Strategy (1978), Democracy in the European Union (1998), etc. Ad.: Pine Hill, 47 New Rd., Digswell, Herts., AL6 0AQ. ☎ 01438-715686. Fax 01438-840422.

PRAIS, Sigbert J., M. Com, PhD, ScD (Cantab), Hon. D.Litt (City), FBA; b. Frankfurt am Main, Dec. 19, 1928; Economist; Sr. Res. Fel., Nat. Instit. of Econ. and Social Res., London; form. Edr. Adv. Bd., Jewish Journal of Soc.; Vis. Prof. of Econometrics, City Univ.; form. H. Consultant, BoD Statistical and Demographic Res. Unit; Economist, Internat. Monetary Fund; Adv. on Statistics, Govt. of Israel; Lect., Cambridge Univ. Publ.: Productivity and Industrial Structure; The Evolution of Giant Firms; Analysis of Family Budgets;

Productivity, Education and Training, etc. Ad.: 83 West Heath Rd., NW3 7TN. ☎ 020-8458 4428.

PRAWER, Siegbert Salomon, MA, D.Litt (Oxon.), MA, LittD (Cantab), PhD, HonD.Litt (Birmingham), D.Phil hc. (Cologne), FBA; b. Cologne, Feb. 15, 1925; Member of the German Academy of Languages and Literature; Taylor Prof of German, Emer., Oxford Univ.; Hon. Fel. Jesus College, Cambridge; Hon. Fel. Queen's Coll.. Oxford; Hon. Fel., form. President, Brit. Comparative Lit. Assn.; H.Fel., form. H. Dir., Lond. Univ. Instit. of Germanic Studies; Hon. Member of the Modern Language Association of America; V. President of the English Goethe Soc. (1994-), President (1991-94); Memb. of the London Bd. of the Leo Baeck Inst. (1969-96); form. Prof of German, Lond. Univ. and Head of German Dept., Westfield Coll.; Sr. Lect. Birmingham Univ.; Vis. Prof, City Coll., New York, Chicago, Harvard, Hamburg, California, Pittsburgh, Otago (New Zealand), Australian Nat. Univ., Canberra, Brandeis; C., Leo Baeck Instit.; Goethe Medal (1973); Isaac Deutscher Prize (1977); Friedrich Gundolf Prize (1986); Gold Medal of the Goethe Gesellschaft 1995. Publ.: Writings on German, English, Jewish and Comparative Literature. Ad.: The Queen's Coll., Oxford OX1 4AW.

PRENDERGAST, Dame Simone Ruth (née Laski), DBE, JP, DL, OStJ; b. Manchester, July 2, 1930;, President CBF World Jewish Relief; Solicitors' Disciplinary Tribunal (1986-2002); Vice-Chairman, Age Concern Westminster (1989-2002); Chairman, Jewish Refugees Cttee. (1981-1991); Pt. time Commissioner for Commission for Racial Equality (1996-98); Commandant JLGB (1986-2000); Co. Patron Fed. Women Zionists; Chairman, Blond McIndoe Centre for Med Res.; Chairman, Westminster Children's Soc. (1980-90); Court of Patrons, Royal Coll. of Surgeons; Chairman, Greater London Area Conservative & Unionist Assns. (1984-87), Solicitors Disciplinary Tribunal (1986-); Lord Chancellors Advisory Cttee. (Inner London) (1981-91); V. Chairman, Age Concern Westminster (1989-); Member East London & Bethnal Green Housing Assoc. (1990); Tr., Camperdown House Trust (1990-). Ad.: 52 Warwick Sq., SW1V 2AJ.

PRESTON, Rosalind (née Morris), OBE; b. London, Dec. 29, 1935; Professional Volunteer; Tr. Jewish Chronicle (2000-); Chair Nightingale House (1999-); Hon. Vice-President British WIZO (1993-); Jt. Hon. Sec. CCJ (1997-); Co. Chair Interfaith Network, UK; form. V. President, BoD; form. President, The National Council of Women of G.B. (1988-90). Ad.: 7 Woodside Close, Stanmore, Middx. HA7 3AJ. ☎ 020-8954 1411. Fax 020-8954 6898. Email ros.p@dial.pipex.com.

PULZER, Peter George Julius, MA, B.Sc.(Econ.), PhD; b. Vienna, May 20, 1929; Gladstone Prof, Government & Publ. Admin., Fel. All Souls, Oxford (1985-96); Official Student (Fel.) in Politics, Christ Church, Oxford (1962-84). Publ.: The Rise of Political Antisemitism in Germany and Austria, Political Representation and Elections in Britain, Jews and the German State: The Political History of a Minority (1848-1933); German Politics 1945-1995; Germany 1870-1945: Politics, State Formation and War; contr. German Jewish History in Modern Times (ed. M. Meyer). Ad.: All Souls College, Oxford, OX1 4AL. ☎ 01865 279379. Fax 01865 279299. Email peter.pulzer@all-souls.ox. ac.uk.

RABINOVITCH, Rabbi Nachum L., BSc, MA, PhD, b. Montreal, Apr 30, 1928; Rosh Yeshiva, Maale Adumim; form. Princ., Jews, College; Rab., Clanton Park Syn., Toronto. Publ.: Hadar Itamar, Probability and Statistical Inference in Ancient and Medieval Jewish Literature; Critical Edn. of Rambam's Mishneh Torah with comprehensive commentary, Yad P'shutah, 10 vols. Ad.: 72 Mizpe Nevo St., Maale Adumim, Israel 98410. ☎ (02) 5353655. Fax (02) 535 3947. Email y-bm@moreshet.co.il.

RABINOWITZ, Rabbi Benjamin, BA, M.Phil, AJC; b. Newcastle upon Tyne June 21, 1945; M., Edgware Syn.; Tr., Co-Chairman Edgware CCJ (1982-); form. M. Yeshurun Heb Cong., Gatley; Blackpoo1 Hebrew Cong. Ad.: 14 Ashcombe

Gdns., Edgware, Middx. HA8 8HS. ☎ 020-8958 5320/6126 (Synagogue office). Fax 020-8958 7684. Email benrab@shalom.bayyit.demon.co.uk.

RABINOWITZ, Rabbi Lippa, b. Manchester, Nov. 15, 1930; Rav, Vine St Syn., Manch.; Princ., Manch. Jewish Grammar Sch., form. Princ. Judith Lady Montefiore Coll., Ramsgate; Lect., Etz Haim Yeshiva, Tangier. Publ.: Eleph Lamateh Chidushim on Sugioth (Israel). Ad.: 57 Waterpark Rd., Salford.

RABSON, Ronald Jeffery, MA; Dipl. Arch. FRIBA; b. Lond, March 3, 1928; Chartered Architect; form. Chairman & Jt. H. Sec., Lond. Bd. Jewish Rel. Educ.; form. Chairman & Gov., JFS Comp. Sch.; form. Chairman, Instit. of Jewish Educ.; form. Gov., Michael Sobell Sinai Sch.; Life M., C., US. Ad.: 16 Broadfields Ave., Edgware, Middx, HA8 8PG. ☎ 020-8958 9035. Fax 020-8905 4035.

RADOMSKY, Rabbi David, BA, MA, NPQH; b. East London, South Africa, Sept. 4, 1956; H.T. Hasmonean High School (2000-); form. Deputy H.T. and Head of Jewish Studies at Immanuel Coll.; Lect., Jews, Coll., (1991-93); form. M., Wembley Syn.; Com. M. Jewish Com. in Eire (1985-88); Talmud Lect., Midrashiat Noam Yeshiva High Sch. Pardes Hanna, Israel (1982-85). Ad.: 27 Windsor Ave, Edgware, Middx. HA8 8SR. ☎ 020-8958 3879.

RAJAK, Tessa, née Goldsmith, MA, D.Phil; b. London, Aug. 2, 1946, m. Harry; Scholar and University Teacher; Prof. Ancient History, Univ. Reading; Assoc. Dir., AHRB Research Centre for the Study of Jewish/Non-Jewish Relations; Edr Journal of Jewish Studies; Grinfield Lect. in the Septuagint, Oxford (1994-96). Publ.: Josephus, the Historian and his Society, The Jews among Pagans and Christians in the Roman Empire (jt. ed); The Jewish Dialogue with Greece and Rome. Ad.: 64 Talbot Rd., N6 4RA.

RAPHAEL, David Daiches, D.Phil, MA, Hon. FIC; b. Liverpool, Jan. 25, 1916; Emer. Prof of Philosophy, Lond. Univ.; Chairman, Westminster Syn. (1987-89); form. Head Humanities Dept., Imperial Coll.; Prof. Phil., Reading Univ.; Prof. Pol. & Soc. Phil., Glasgow Univ.; Sr. Lect., Moral Phil., Glasgow Univ.; Prof., Phil., Otago Univ., Dunedin; form. Princ. Off M. of Lab. and Nat. Service. Publ.: The Moral Sense, Richard Price's Review of Morals, Moral Judgement, The Paradox of Tragedy, Political Theory and the Rights of Man, British Moralists 1650-1800, Problems of Political Philosophy, Adam Smith's Theory of Moral Sentiments (Jt. Edr.), Hobbes: Morals and Politics, Adam Smith's Lectures on Jurisprudence (Jt. Edr.), Adam Smith's Essays on Philosophical Subjects, (Jt. Edr.), Justice and Liberty, Moral Philosophy, Adam Smith, Concepts of Justice, etc. Ad.: Humanities Programme, Imperial College, SW7 2BX.

RAPHAEL, Frederic Michael, MA (Cantab), FRSL; b. Chicago, Aug. 14, 1931; Writer. Publ.: Novels, Obbligato, The Earlsdon Way, The Limits of Love, The Graduate Wife, The Trouble with England, Lindmann, Darling, Orchestra and Beginners, Who Were You With Last Night?, Like Men Betrayed, April June and November, California Time, The Glittering Prizes, Heaven and Earth, After The War, The Hidden I, A Double Life, Old Scores, Coast to Coast; Short stories, Sleeps Six, Oxbridge Blues, Think of England, The Latin Lover, All His Sons; Non-fiction: Byron, Somerset Maugham, Cracks in the Ice, Of Gods and Men, France: the Four Seasons, The Necessity of Anti-Semitism, Popper: Historicism and its Poverty, Eyes Wide Open, The Benefits of Doubt (essays), A Spoilt Boy (autobiography); Published Screenplays and Drama: Two for the Road, Darling, Oxbridge Blues, Eyes Wide Shut (with Stanley Kubrick); Translations: The Satyrica of Petronius, The Poems of Catullus (with Kenneth McLeish), The Oresteia of Aeschylus, Sophocles' Aias, Euripides' Medea, Bacchae and Hippolytus. Ad.: c/o Rogers, Coleridge and White, 20, Powis Mews, W11 1JN.

RAPOPORT-ALBERT, Ada, BA, PhD; b. Tel Aviv; Reader in Jewish History, University College London. Publ.: Hasidism Reappraised (ed., 1996); Essays in Jewish Historiography (1988/1991). Ad.: Dept. of Hebrew & Jewish Studies,

University College, Gower Street, London WC1E 6BT. ☎ 020-7679 3591. Email uclhara@ucl.ac.uk.

RASMINSKY, Louis, CC, CBE, LLD, DCL, DHL; b. Montreal, Feb. 1, 1908; Gov., Bank of Canada (1961-73); President, Industrial Development Bank (1961-73); H. Fel., Lond. Sch. of Economics. Ad.: 1006-20 Driveway, Ottawa, Ontario, K2P 1C8, Canada. ☎ 613-594-0150.

RAYNE, Baron, of Prince's Meadow (Life Peer) (Sir Max Rayne), Hon. LLD (London); b. Feb. 8, 1918; Dir. of Companies; Life President (2000-), Chairman (1960-2000) London Merchant Securities, plc.; Chairman, Nat. Theatre Bd. (1971-88); Special Tr., St. Thomas' Hospital; Gen. C., King Edward VII's Hospital Fund for Lond.; Chairman, Lond. Festival Ballet Tr. (1967-75); Fdr. Patron, The Rayne Fdn.; H.V. President, Jewish Care. H.Fel., Univ. Coll., Lond., Darwin Coll., Cambridge, Univ. Col., Oxford, Lond. Sch. of Economics; Royal Coll. of Psychiatrists; King's Coll. Hospital Med. School; King's College London; Westminster School; Officier, Legion d'Honneur, 1987 (Chevalier, 1973); Hon. Fel., UMDS, 1992; Hon. FRCP 1992. Ad.: 33 Robert Adam St., W1U 3HR. 020-7935 3555.

RAYNER, Rabbi John D., CBE, MA, DD (Hon); b. Berlin, May 30, 1924; Hon. Life President, Union of Liberal and Progressive Synagogues, M. Emer. (Sr. M. 1961-89), Lib. Jewish Syn.; M., South London Lib. Syn. (1953-57); Chairman, C., Reform and Lib. Rabbis (1969-71, 82-84, 1989-92); V. President and Lect., Leo Baeck Coll.; Co-President, Lond. Soc. of Jews & Christians. Publ.: Guide to Jewish Marriage; Gate of Repentance (co-ed.), Judaism for Today (co-author), Passover Haggadah (ed.), The Jewish People: Their History and Their Religion (co-author), Siddur Lev Chadash (co-ed), An Understanding of Judaism, A Jewish Understanding of the World, Jewish Religious Law: A Progressive Perspective, Principles of Jewish Ethics. Ad.: 37 Walmington Fold, N12 7LD. ☎/Fax 020-8446 6196.

REIF, Stefan, BA, PhD (Lond.), LittD (Cantab); b. Edinburgh, Jan. 21, 1944; m. Shulamit; Dir., Taylor-Schechter Genizah Research Unit and Head of Oriental Div., Cambridge Univ. Library; Professor of Medieval Hebrew Studies, Faculty of Oriental Studies, Cambridge Univ.; Fellow St John's College, Cambridge; President JHSE (1991-92); President Brit. Assoc. for Jewish Studies (1992); Hon. Fel., Mekize Nirdamim Society, Jerusalem; T., Cambridge Traditional Jewish Cong.; Lect., Hebrew and Semitics, Glasgow Univ. (1968-72); Princ., Glasgow Hebrew Coll. (1970-72); Asst. Prof., Hebrew Language and Lit., Dropsie Coll. (1972-73). Publ.: Shabbethai Sofer and His Prayer Book; Judaism and Hebrew Prayer; Hebrew Manuscripts at Cambridge University Library; A Jewish Archive from Old Cairo, Why Medieval Hebrew Studies?; (ed.) Interpreting the Hebrew Bible, Genizah Research after Ninety Years, The Cambridge Genizah Collections, Cambridge Univ. Library Genizah Series, etc. Ad.: Cambridge University Library, CB3 9DR. ☎ 01223 333000. Fax 01223333160. E-mail scr3@cam.ac.uk.

REISS, Simon, b. Berlin, Dec. 31, 1923; Comp. Dir.; V. President Zionist Fed.; Hon. Life and form. President Western Marble Arch Syn.; Mem. BoD; Chairman Jt. Cttee., Youth Aff; Co-Chairman and Tr. Balfour Diamond Jubilee Trust; Vice-Chairman and Tr., Yad Vashem Cttee., BoD; Hon. President Int. Fur Trade Fed. Ad.: Fax 020-7409 7410.

RICHARDSON, Montague, MA, (Cantab); b. London, July 4, 1918; Patron Jewish Museum; form. Welfare & Youth Off., US & Welfare Off., Jewish After-Care Assn.; form. Chairman, Tower Hamlets Soc.; form. V. Chairman Tower H. Soc. Service C.; Chaplain: Blantyre House, Canterbury, Cookham Wood Elmley, E. Sutton Park, Maidstone, Stanford Hill, Swaleside Prisons & Rochester Youth Custody Centre; V. President (form. Chairman) AJY; Tr. and form. Chairman, Tower Hamlets Old People's Welfare Trust; form. Tr., London Museum of Jewish Life; form. Tr., Children's Aid Cttee. Charitable Fund; form. Chairman, Brady Boys' Club; form. V. Chairman Tower H. Adult Educ. Instit.; form. Chairman,

Soc. Security Appeal Tribunal; form Exec., Tower H. Racial Equality C.; Chairman, Zekeinim Club. Ad.: Flat 1, 12 Belsize Sq., NW3 4HT. ☎ 020-7794 9684.

RICKAYZEN, Gerald, BSc, PhD, FInstP, CPhys; b. London, Oct. 16, 1929; Physicist; Chairman Canterbury Jewish Community (1998-2000); Prof. of Theoretical Physics, Univ. of Kent (1965-98), Emeritus (1998-); Pro-Vice-Chancellor (1980-90), Deputy V. Chancellor (1984-90). Publ.: Theory of Superconductivity (1965); Green's Functions and Condensed Matter Physics (1980). Ad: The Physics Laboratory, The University, Canterbury CT2 7NR. ☎ 020-8866 5589. Email gerald.rickayzen@physics.org.

RIETTI, Robert, Cavaliere Ufficiale, OMRI, Officer-Knight of the Italian Republic; b. London, Feb. 8, 1923; Actor, broadcaster, writer, director, editor of Drama Quarterly GAMBIT; BAFTA nomination for Special Award (1993). Publ.: English translations of the entire dramatic works of Luigi Pirandello (John Calder); Look up and dream (1999). Ad.: 40 Old Church Lane, NW9 8TA. ☎ 020-8205 3024. Fax 020-8200 4688.

RIFKIND, Rt. Hon. Sir Malcolm, QC, PC; b. Edinburgh, June 21, 1946; form. M.P. for Edinburgh, Pentlands (Con.) (1974-97); Foreign Secretary (1995-97), Min. of Defence (1992-95), Min. of Transport (1990-92); Sec. of State for Scotland (1986-90), Min. of State Foreign & Commonwealth Office (1983-86); Parl. Under-Sec. of State, FCO (1982-83); Parl. Under-Sec. of State, Scottish Office (1979-82); H. President, Scottish Young Conservatives (1976-77); H.Sec., Conservative Frs. of Israel Parl. Group (1974-79); Sec. Conservative Parl. Foreign & Commonwealth Affairs Group (1977-79); Opposition Spokesman on Scottish Affairs (1975-76); Select Cttee. on Overseas Development (1978-79); Edinburgh Town C. (1970-74). Ad.: Pentland Conservative Assoc., Edinburgh.

RIGAL, Mrs. Margaret H., (née Lazarus); b. London, Nov. 28, 1932; Co.-Chairman, Women's Campaign for Soviet Jewry (the 35s), H.Sec., Jewish Aged Needy Pension Soc.; Chairman Jewish Aid Cttee; Hon. Sec. London Society of Jews and Christians. Ad.: 14 Pembridge Place, W2 4XB. ☎ 020-7229 8845. Fax 020-7221 7302.

ROBERG, Rabbi Meir, BA (Hons), MPhil, DipEd; b. Wurzburg Germany, June 25, 1937; HM, Hasmonean High Sch.; Chairman, Academic Cttee. Massoret Instit.; Chairman, Assoc. of Head Teachers of Orthodox Jewish Schls.; form. HM Middlesex Reg. Centre; Dep. HM, Yavneh Grammar Sch. Ad.: 34 Green Lane, NW4 2NG. ☎ 020-8203 2632.

ROBINS, Ruth, BA, TTHD; Headteacher JFS. Ad.: 175 Camden Road, London NW1 9HD. ☎ 020-7485 9416. Fax 020-7284 3948.

ROBSON, Jeremy, b. Llandudno, Sept. 5, 1939; Publisher, Robson Books. Publ.: 33 Poems, In Focus (poetry), Poetry anthologies, incl. The Young British Poets (ed.), Poems from Poetry and Jazz in Concert (ed.). Ad.: Robson Books, 29 Pattison Road, London NW2 2HL. ☎ 020-7700 7444.

ROCHE, Barbara Maureen (née Margolis), BA (Oxon); b. London, April 13, 1954; Barrister; MP, Hornsey and Wood Green (Lab. 1992-); Cabinet Office (2001-2); Office of Prime Minister (2002-); Min. State Home Office (1999-2001); Parlt. Under-Sec. of State for Small Firms, Trade and Industry (1997-99); Financial Sec. at the Treasury (1999); Min. State at the Home Office (1999-2001). Ad.: House of Commons, London SW1. ☎ 020-7219 3000.

ROITT, Ivan Maurice, MA, DSc (Oxon), FRCPath, FRS, Hon. FRCP; b. Lond., Sept. 30, 1927; Emer. Prof. Immunology UCL. Publ.: Essential Immunology. Ad.: Windeyer Building, UCL., Cleveland Street, W1P 6DB. ☎ 020-7679 9360. Fax 020-7679 9400.

ROMAIN, Rabbi Jonathan Anidjar, BA; PhD; b. London, Aug. 24, 1954; m. Sybil Sheridan; M., Maidenhead Syn.; Director, Jewish Information and Media Service; Chairman, Youth Assn. of Syns. in Gt. Brit. (1972-74); form. M., Barkingside

Progressive Syn. Publ.: The Open and Closed Paragraphs of the Pentateuch, In a Strange Land, Signs and Wonders, The Jews of England, Faith and Practice, I'm Jewish, My Partner Isn't, Tradition and Change, Till Faith Us Do Part, Renewing the Vision, Your God Shall Be My God. Ad.: Grenfell Lodge, Ray Park Road, Maidenhead, Berks. SL6 8QX. ☎ 01628 671058. Fax 01628 625536.

ROSE, Rabbi Abraham Maurice, MA; b. Birmingham, Sept. 7, 1925; Exec. Dir., C. of Young Israel Syn. (Israel) (1975-90); Adm. Dir. & Lect., Jerusalem Academy of Jewish Studies (1973-74); Exec. Dir., Office of the Chief Rabbi (1962-73); Exec. Dir., Conf. of Europ. Rabbis; form. M., Sutton Syn. (1952-62), Derby Syn. (1948-52). Ad.: Rechov Machal 30/2, Jerusalem 97763. ☎ 5812859. Fax 5810080. E-mail rose-nm@netvision.net.il.

ROSE, Aubrey, CBE, D. Univ. (Hon), FRSA; b. London, Nov. 1, 1926; Solicitor; Senior V. President, BoD (1991, 1994); Commissioner & Dep. Chairman Commission for Racial Equality (CRE); Dep. Chairman British Caribbean Assoc.; Tr. Project Fullemploy; Tr. Commonwealth Human Rights Initiative; Member, Working Group Commonwealth Jewish Coun.; form. Chairman, Defence and Group Rel. Cttee. BoD; Chairman, Working Group on Environment BoD, Publ.: Jewish Communities in the Commonwealth (CJT); Judaism and Ecology (1992); Journey into Immortality, the Story of David Rose (1997); Brief Encounters of a Legal Kind (1997). Ad.: 14 Pagitts Grove, Hadley Wood, Herts EN4 0NT. ☎ 020-8449 2166. Fax 020-8449 1469. E-mail as.rose@virgin.net.

ROSE, Jeffery Samuel, BDS, FDS, D.Orth. RCS; b. Harrow, Middx., Dec. 22, 1924; Ret. Consultant Orthodontist, Royal London Hospital (1967-90); Hon. Vice-President RSGB (1999-); Chairman Reform Foundation Tr. (1996-99); President Brit. Orthodontic Soc. (1994-95); V. President World Union Progressive Judaism (1995-99); form. Chairman, Leo Baeck Coll. (1985-88); Life Gov. (1988); Hon. Fellow (1988); Chairman, Euro. Region, World Union Prog Judaism (1990-95); form. V. President & Chairman RSGB; form. V. President & Chairman, North Western Reform Syn.; President, Brit. Paedontic Soc. (1964-65); President, Brit. Soc. for the Study of Orthodontics (1972-73). President, British Assoc. of Orthodontists (1991-94). Ad.: 17 Broadlands Lodge, 18 Broadlands Road, London N6 4AW. ☎ 020-8340 8836. Fax 020-8374 4355.

ROSE, Mrs. Joyce Dora Hester (née Woolf), CBE, JP, DL (Herts); m. Cyril Rose, b. London, August 14, 1929; Hertfordshire Family Mediation Service (1996-); S.W. Hertfordshire Hospice Charitable Trust (The Peace Hospice) (1996-); Chairman, Nat. Exec. and Council, Magistrate Assn. (1990-93); Mem. Bd. Dir. Apex Tr. (1994-); Herts Care Tr. (1995-99); V. President Magistrates Assn. and V. President Hertfordshire Branch; H. D. Laws, Univ. of Hertfordshire (1992); form. P. (1979-80), Chairman (1982-83), Lib. Party; President, S.W. Herts Const. L.D.; form. Chairman, Watford (Herts.) Bench (1990-94); Dep. Chairman, Family Proceedings Panel; P. & Chairman, Women's Liberal Fed. (1972-73); V. Chairman, UK Cttee. for Unicef (1968-70). Ad.: 2 Oak House, 101 Ducks Hill Road, Northwood, Middx HA6 2WQ. ☎ 01923 821385. Fax 01923 840515.

ROSEN, Clive H., FCOptom.; b. London Apr. 15, 1938; City Univ. 1963; Dip. Sports Vision, UMIST (1997); Freeman, City of London 1964; Designer of Judaica commemorative covers and lecturer on Judaica and Masonic philately; Chairman ZF Fund-Raising Cttee. (1996-98); Hon. Sec. ZF (2002-); Cttee Mem., Sports Vision Assoc. (2002-); Hon. Sports Vision Consult. to Leyton Orient FC (1997-); Hon. Tr. East London and the City Health Authority L.O.C. (1994-); Chairman, Menorah JNF Committee (1974-1985); Hon. Off. JNF (1979-81, 1983-90); Memb. Zionist Federation National Council, (1989-); Hon. Tr. ZF (1994-96); Founding memb. Israel-Judaica Stamp Club; Chairman, I-JSC (1990-); jt. ed. The Israel Judaica Collector Journal; Dir. David Elliott

(Opticians) Ltd. (1965-). Ad.: 152 Morton Way, London N14 7AL. ☎ 020-8886 9331. Fax 020-8886 5116.

ROSEN, Rabbi Jeremy, MA (Cantab), PhD; b. Sept. 11, 1942; Dir. Yakar Foundation (1999-); Rabbi Western Syn. (1985-91); Rabbi, Western Marble Arch Syn. (1991-92); Chief Rabbi's Cabinet advisor Interfaith (1987-90); Prof., Jewish Studies F.V.G. Antwerp. (1991-); Tr., Yakar Foundation; Princ., Carmel Coll. (1971-84); Rabbi, Giffnock & Newlands Syn., Glasgow (1968-71). Publ.: Exploding Myths that Jews Believe (2001). Ad.: c/o Yakar, 2 Egerton Gardens, London NW4 4BA. ☎ 020-8202 5551. E-mail jeremyrosen@msn.com.

ROSENBERG, Mrs. Rosita (née Gould); b. London, Sept. 2, 1933; V. President, form. Dir., ULPS. Ad.: The Montagu Centre, 21, Maple St., W1P 6DS. ☎ 020-7580 1663. Fax 020-7436 4184.

ROSENTHAL, Jack (Morris), CBE, BA, MA (Hon), D.Litt (Hon); b. Manchester, Sept. 8, 1931; m. Maureen née Lipman; Writer; Brit. Academy of Film and Television Arts Writers Award, 1976; Royal Television Society Writers' Award, 1976, Royal Television Society Hall of Fame (1993). TV plays include: The Evacuees, Ready When You Are, Mr McGill; Barmitzvah Boy (also stage musical), Auntie's Niece; Spend, Spend, Spend; The Knowledge; And A Nightingale Sang; Bag Lady; P'Tang, Yang, Kipperbang, Day to Remember, Wide-Eyed And Legless, London's Burning; Bye, Bye, Baby; Eskimo Day; Cold Enough for Snow; Lucky Jim, etc. Feature films include: Yentl (co. writer), The Chain. Ad.: c/o Casarotto Ramsay Ltd., 60-66 Wardour St., W1V 4ND.

ROTBLAT, Sir Joseph, KCMG, CBE, MA, DSc (Warsaw), PhD (Liverpool), DSc (Lond.), FInstP, FRS; b. Warsaw, Nov. 4, 1908; President Pugwash Conferences on Science and World Affairs (1988-97); Prof. of Physics in the Univ. of London at St. Bartholomew's Hospital Med. Coll. (1950-76), now Emer.; Asst. Dir., Atomic Physics Instit., Free Univ. of Poland (1937-39); Lect., Liverpool Univ. (1940-49); Dir. of Research in Nuclear Physics, Univ. of Liverpool (1945-49); V. President, Atomic Scientists, Assn. (1952-59). Publ.: Scientific works. Ad.: 8 Asmara Rd., NW2 3ST. ☎ 020-7435 1471.

ROTH, Sir Martin, FRS. FMedSci; b. Budapest, Nov. 6, 1917, m. Constance née Heller; Prof. Emer. of Psychiatry Cambridge Univ.; Fel., Trinity Coll. Cambridge; Mems. WHO Steering Cttee for Epidemiological Studies of Alzheimer Disease; form. Prof. of Psychological Medicine, Newcastle Univ.; first P. Royal Coll. of Psychiatry (1971-75); Member, Medical Research C. (1964-68). Publ.: Clinical Psychiatry (with E. Slater); The Reality of Mental Illness (with J. Kroll, 1986), Handbook of Anxiety, vols. 1-5 (Ed. with R. Noyes & G. Burrows 1990-93), Alzheimer Disease and related disorders (with L. Iversen 1986), Psychiatry, human rights and the law (with R. Bluglass, 1985). Ad.: Trinity College, Cambridge. ☎ 01223-242106. Fax 01223-412193.

ROTHSCHILD, Edmund Leopold de, CBE, TD, Hon. DSc (Salford Univ.); b. London, Jan. 2, 1916; Hon. LLD (Univ. of Newfoundland); Hon. V. President, CBF, World Jewish Relief; V. President, CCJ; President, Ajex; Bd. Govs., Technical Univ., Nova Scotia; form. Major, Royal Artillery, 1939-46, (Commanded P. Battery, Jewish Field Regt.). Publ.: Window on the World; A gilt-edged life: a memoir. Ad.: New Court, St. Swithin's Lane, EC4P 4DU.

ROTHSCHILD, Sir Evelyn de; b. Aug. 29, 1931; Merchant Banker; Dir., Industrial Dwellings Soc. Ltd.; form. President, JBS Ad.: New Court, St. Swithin's Lane, EC4P 4DU. ☎ 020-7280 5000.

ROTHSCHILD, Leopold David de, CBE; b. London, May 12, 1927; Dir., N. M. Rothschild & Sons; Investment Adv. Cttee., JWB; Jt. President Jewish Music Institute. Ad.: New Court, St. Swithin's Lane, EC4P 4DU. ☎ 020-7280 5000.

ROTHSCHILD, Hon. Dame Miriam (Hon. Mrs Miriam Lane), DBE, Defence Medal, FRS, Hon. Doc. (Oxford, Cambridge, Hull, Göteburg, North-Western Univ., Chicago Leicester, Essex, Open University); b. Ashton, Peterborough.,

Aug. 5, 1908; d. of the late Hon. N. Charles Rothschild and aunt of Lord Rothschild; zoologist and farmer; Tr. Brit. Museum; H. Fellow, St. Hugh's Coll., Oxford; Romanes Lect. (1985); Vis. Prof, Lond. Univ.; Wigglesworth Medal, RHS Victorian Medal of Honour; Med. Soc. Chem. Oecology; Linnean Soc.; Mendel Award. Publ.: Catalogue of Fleas in the Rothschild and British Museum Collection, Fleas, Flukes, and Cuckoos, and 300 other zoolog. works; Biography of 2nd Lord Rothschild The Butterfly Gardener, Atlas of Insect Tissues, Animals and Man, Butterfly Cooing like a Dove, Rothschild Gardens, Rothschild's Reserves. Ad.: Ashton Wold, Peterborough, PE8 5LZ.

ROTHSCHILD, Nathaniel Charles Jacob, Lord, OM, MA (Oxon); b. Cambridge, Apr. 29, 1936; Chairman RIT Capital Partners plc; President St. James's Place Capital plc; Chairman of the J. Rothschild Group; President IJPR (1992-); Chairman of the Tr. of the National Gallery (1985-91); Chairman of the Tr. of the National Heritage Memorial Fund (1992-98); C., Weizmann Instit. Foundation; Tr., Jerusalem Foundation. Ad.: 27 St. James's Pl., SW1A 1NR. ☎ 020-7493 8111. Fax 020-7493 5765.

ROTHSCHILD, Rabbi Sylvia Helen Fay, BSc; b. Bradford, West Yorkshire, Nov. 21, 1957; m. Martin Fischer; M. Wimbledon Syn. (2002-); M. Bromley and District Reform Synagogue (1987-2002); Co-Chair Assembly of Rabbis (1998-2000), Chair (2000-). Publ.: Co-ed. Taking up the Timbrel (2000). Ad.: c/o Assembly of Rabbis, RSGB, 80 East End Road, London N3 2SY.

RUBEN, David-Hillel, BA, PhD; b. Chicago, July 25, 1943; Dir., New York Univ. in London (2000-); form. Dir., London School of Jewish Studies (1998-99); Professor of Philosophy, London School of Economics (1984-97); University of Glasgow, Lecturer in Philosophy (1970-75); University of Essex, Lecturer in Philosophy (1975-79); The City University, London, Senior Lecturer in Philosophy (1979-84). Publ.: Marxism and Materialism (1979); The Metaphysics of the Social World (1985); Explaining Explanation (1990); Explanation, editor (1993). Ad.: NYU in London, 6 Bedford Square, London WC1B 3RA. ☎ 020-7907 3201. E-mail ruben@hendon.u-net.com.

RUBENS, Bernice Ruth, Hon. D.Litt Univ. Wales, FRSL; b. Cardiff, July 26, 1926; author; film dir.; Fel. Univ. Coll. Cardiff; Hon. V. President English PEN. Publ.: The Elected Member (Booker Prize, 1970), Brothers, Mr. Wakefield's Crusade, Our Father, A Solitary Grief, Mother Russia, Autobiopsy (1993) etc. Ad.: 213A Goldhurst Terrace, London NW6 3ER. ☎ 020-7625 4845.

RUBENS, Kenneth David, OBE, FRICS, FRSA; b. Lond., Oct. 10, 1929; Chartered Surveyor; Chairman, Jewish Museum, London., Chairman, ORT Trust.; L. Elder Span. & Port. Jews, Cong.; Past Chairman, C. World Jewish Relief; Past Master, Worshipful Company, Painter-Stainers.; Hon. Life Mem., Brit. Property Fed. Ad.: 5 Clarke's Mews, London W1G 6QN. ☎ 020-7486 1884. Email kenneth@rubens.org.

RUBINSTEIN, William David, BA, PhD, FAHA, FASSA, FRHistS; b. New York, Aug. 12, 1946; m. Hilary L. Rubinstein; Prof. of History, The University of Wales, Aberystwyth (1995-); President, JHSE (2002-), Mem. Council (1996-); Prof. of Social and Economic History, Deakin University, Australia (1987-95); Ed., Journal of the Australian Jewish Historical Society (1988-95); President, Australian Association for Jewish Studies (1989-91); Member, Committee of Management, Executive Council of Australian Jewry (1983-95). Publ.: Men of Property: The Very Wealthy in Britain Since the Industrial Revolution (1981); The Jews in Australia: A Thematic History (with Hilary L. Rubinstein) (1991); Capitalism, Culture, and Decline in Britain, 1750-1990 (1993); A History of the Jews in the English-Speaking World: Great Britain (1996); The Myth of Rescue (1997); Britain's Century: A Political and Social History 1815-1905 (1998); Philosemitism: Admiration and Support in the English-speaking World for Jews 1840-1939 (with Hilary L. Rubinstein, 1999); The Jews in the Modern World:

A History since 1750 (co-author, 2002). Ad.: Department of History, University of Wales, Aberystwyth, Penglais, Ceredigion SY23 3DY. ☎ 01970 622661. Fax 01970 622676. E-mail wdr@aber. ac.uk.

RUDMAN, Michael Edward, MA (Oxon), BA (Oberlin Coll.); b. Tyler, Texas, USA, Feb. 14, 1939; Artistic Director, Sheffield Theatres (1992-94); Dir. Chichester Festival Theatre (1989-90); Assoc. Dir., Nat. Theatre, (1979-88); Dir. Lyttelton Theatre (1979-81), Bd. Dirs. Art. Dir.; Hampstead Theatre (1973-78); Art. Dir., Traverse Theatre Club (1970-73). Ad.: c/o Peter Murphy, Curtis Brown Group, 4th Floor, 28/29 Haymarket, SW1Y 4SP. ☎ 020-7396 6600. Fax 020-7396 0110.

RUDOLF, Anthony, BA (Cantab); b. London, Sept. 6, 1942; Writer, Publisher/ Translator; Visiting Lect. in Humanities, University of North London; Ad. Ed. Modern Poetry in Translation; Ad. Ed., Jerusalem Review; Adam Lecturer, Kings Coll. London (1990); Ed./Literary Ed. of European Judaism (1970-75). Publ.: The Arithmetic of Memory (1999); Piotr Rawicz and Blood from the Sky (1996); The Diary of Jerzy Urman (1991); Primo Levi's War against Oblivion (1990); After the Dream (1979). Ad.: 8 The Oaks, Woodside Av., N12 8AR. ☎/Fax 020-8446 5571.

RUSSELL, Cllr. Mrs. Theresa Science, OBE, JP, DCL (Hon) FRSA; b. Hull; Rotary Intl. Paul Harris Fel. (1989); Lord Mayor (1965-66), form. Lady Mayoress and Sheriff's Lady, Newcastle upon Tyne; Chairman, N. East Emunah; Chairman, Newc. Inf & Publicity Cttee.; Chairman, North-East Diocesan After-Care Cttee.; Brit. President, Internat. Friendship Force; Gov., Royal Grammar Sch.; Reg. Hospital Area Health Auth.; Fdr. President, B'nai B'rith Lodge; B.B.C. Appeals Cttee. Newcastle B.B.C. Radio Cttee.; Vis. Magistrate; Low Newton Prison, Exec., Northumbria Tourist Bd.; Jewish Woman of Distinction Award (1977); Chairman, Newcastle Children in Danger. Ad.:

SACERDOTI, Cesare David Salomone; b. Florence, Feb. 24, 1938; m. Judith née Margulies; Publisher, Company Director; Man. Dir. H. Karnac (Books) Ltd (1984-99); Consultant, Publishing Int. Psychoanalytical Assoc. (2002-); Tr. Winnicott Clinic of Psychotherapy Charitable Tr. (1999-) President, Bd. of Elders, Spanish & Portuguese Jews' Cong., and Thesoureiro (2000-), V. President (1996-2000); Parnas Heshaim (1995-2000); Dir. Sephardi Centre Ltd (1997-). Ad.: 25 Manor House Drive, London NW6 7DE. ☎ 020-8459 2012. Fax 020-8451 8829. E-mail cesare@sacerdoti.com.

SACKER, Anthony (Tony); b. London, March 2, 1940; m. Frances née Maister; Solicitor; V. President BoD (2000-); Chairman, City of London Law Society (1998-2001); Chairperson, Union of Lib. and Prog. Syns. (1990-95); T. ULPS (1988-90); Vice-Chairman, LBC-CJE; Freeman of City of London. Publ.: Practical Partnership Agreements (1995). Ad.: 18 Montagu Street, London W1H 7EX. ☎ 020-7262 6993. Fax 020-7224 9926. E-mail tony@sacker.co.uk.

SACKS, Chief Rabbi Jonathan Henry, MA (Cantab), PhD, DD (Lambeth), Hon. DD (Camb), Hon. DD (King's Coll., Lond.), Hon. D. Univ. (Middx.), Hon. D. Univ (Glasgow); b. London, March 8, 1948; m. Elaine née Taylor; Chief Rabbi of the United Hebrew Congregations of the Commonwealth (1991-); Assoc. President, Conf. European Rabbis (1999-); Vis. Prof. Philosophy Hebrew Univ.; Vis. Prof. Theology and Religious Studies, King's College, London; Vis. Prof. Philosophy, Univ. Essex (1989-90); form. Princ., Jews College and holder of the Lord Jakobovits Chair (1984-1990); M. Marble Arch Syn. (1983-1990); M., Golders Green Syn. (1978-1982); BBC Reith Lect. (1990); Ed. L'Eylah (1984-1990); Hon. Fell. Gonville and Caius Coll. Cambridge (1993-). Publ.: Torah Studies (1986); Tradition and Transition (1986); Traditional Alternatives (1989); Tradition in an Untraditional Age (1990); The Persistence of Faith (1991); Arguments for the Sake of Heaven (1991); Orthodoxy Confronts Modernity (1991); Crisis and Covenant (1992); One People: Tradition Modernity and

Jewish Unity (1993); Will We Have Jewish Grandchildren? (1994); Faith in the Future (1995); Community of Faith (1995); The Politics of Hope (1997); Morals and Markets (1999); Radical Then, Radical Now (2000); A Letter in the Scroll (2000); Celebrating Life (2000); The Dignity of Difference (2002). Ad.: Office of the Chief Rabbi, 735 High Road, London N12 0US. ☎ 020-8343 6301. Fax 020-8343 6310. E-mail info@chiefrabbi.org www.chiefrabbi.org.

SAFRAN, Rabbi Alexander, PhD (Vienna); b. Bacau, Romania, Sept. 12, 1910; Chief Rabbi of Geneva (1948-); Lect. in Jewish Thought at Univ. of Geneva; form. Chief Rabbi of Romania and Member of Romanian Senate. Publ.: La Cabale, Israel dans le Temps et dans l'Espace, etc. Ad.: 1 rue Crespin, CH 1206 Geneva. ☎ 346-66-97. Fax 346-6739.

SAIDEMAN, Seymour Geoffrey, FCA; b. London, April 5, 1939; Consultant; President B'nai B'rith Europe; Mem. Bd. Gov. B'nai B'rith Int.; Mem. Adv. Cttee Three Faiths Forum; form. President, United Syn. (1992-96); Chairman, Chief Rabbinate Council (1992-96); form. Chairman, London Board of Jewish Rel. Educ. (1984-87); form. Chairman, Governors JFS Comprehensive Sch. (1984-87). Ad.: 36 Rue Dautzenberg, B-1050 Brussels, Belgium. ☎ +32-2-646.92.98. Fax +32-2-646.89.49. E-mail bb_europe@compuserve.com.

SALAMAN, Esther, ARAM, LRAM, (Mrs Paul Hamburger); b. Barley, Herts; Singing Consultant, Trinity Coll. Music; form. Prof, Guildhall School of Music and Drama; Prof. singer & teacher of Voice, form. Hon. Org., Jewish Inst. Sunday Concerts; Recitals and Talks on BBC Radio 3; form. Consultant Teacher for Nat. Opera Studio. Master Classes and Demonstrations England and Overseas; H. Music Adv., Spiro Instit. Publ.: Unlocking your Voice, freedom to sing (1989; 2nd. 1999). Ad.: 114 Priory Gdns., N6 5QT. ☎ 020-8340 3042.

SALAMON, Rabbi Thomas; b. Kosice, May 10, 1948; Rabbi/Solicitor; m. Renée née Heffes; M., Westminster Syn. (1997-); M., Hampstead Ref. Jewish Com. (1988-90); M., Hertsmere Progressive Syn. (1980-88); Assoc. M., West London Syn. (1972-75); Exec. Dir., Norwood Child Care (1975-80). Ad.: Westminster Synagogue, Kent House, Rutland Gardens, London SW7 1BX. ☎ 020-7584 3953. Fax 020-7581 8012.

SALASNIK, Rabbi Eli; b. Old City of Jerusalem; Rav. in London since 1950 Chairman, Rabbin. C., East Lond. and West Essex; District Rav Lond. Bd. for Shechita. Ad.: 8 The Lindens, Prospect Hill, Waltham Forest, London E17 3EJ.

SALASNIK, Rabbi Zorach Meir, BA, FJC; b. Lond., July 29, 1951; M., Bushey & Distr. Syn.; Sec., Chief Rabbi's Cabinet; Chairman Rabbin. C., U.S.; Community Development Programme, US; Central Services Cttee US; Chaplain, RisHon. Multiple Sclerosis Aid Gp.; Cttee., Michael Sobell Sinai School; Rabbinical Adv., Agency for Jewish Education; form. M., Notting Hill Syn., Leytonstone & Wanstead Syn. Ad.: 8 Richfield Rd., Bushey Heath, Herts., WD23 4LQ. ☎ 020-8950-6453. Fax 020-8421 8267.

SAMUEL, David Herbert, 3rd Viscount, of Mount Carmel and Toxteth, OBE, MA (Oxon), PhD (Jerusalem), CChem, FRSC (UK); b. Jerusalem, July 8, 1922; m. Eve née Black; Scientist, Prof. Emeritus, Weizmann Inst. of Science, Rehovot; President, Shenkar Coll. of Textile Tech. and Fashion, Ramat Gan (1987-94); Dir., Centre for Neurosciences and Behavioural Res., Weizmann Inst. of Science (1978-87); Dean, Faculty of Chemistry (1971-73); Dep. Chairman, Scientific C. (1963-65); Postdoctoral Fel., Chemistry Depts, Univ. Coll., London (1956); Harvard Univ. (1957-58); Biodynamics Lab., Univ. of California at Berkeley (1965-66); Visiting Prof. MRC Neuroimmunology Unit, Univ. Coll. London (1974-75); Dept of Pharmacology, Yale University Medical School (1983-84); McLaughlin Visiting Prof. Life Sciences, McMaster Univ., Canada (1984); Visiting Prof. Chem. Dept, Univ. of York (1996-97); served in British Army (UK, India, Burma, Sumatra) (mentioned in Despatches) (1942-46); IDF (1948-49); Scopus Award (2000), Hebrew University, Tercentenary Medal (2001), Yale University, Hon. Fellowship,

Shenker College. Publ.: The Aging of the Brain (D. Samuel et al, edrs, 1983); Memory: how we use it, lose it and can improve it (1999), and over 300 scientific articles. Ad.: Weizmann Institute, Rehovot, Israel. ☎ (972)-89344229; 99553242 (home). Fax (972)-99552511. E-mail eveblack@netvision.net.il.

SAMUEL, Edgar Roy, BA (Hons), M.Phil, FRHistS, FSMC, DCLP; b. London, 1928; m. Louise Hillman; Chairman Publ. Cttee JHSE; Past Dir., Jewish Museum (1983-95); Past President, JHSE (1988-90), Records & Treasures Cttee., Span. & Port. Cong., Lond. Publ.: Contribs. to Transactions of Jewish Hist. Soc.; The Portuguese Jewish Community in London, 1656-1830 (1992). Ad.: 5 Hollyview Close, Hendon, NW4 3SZ. ☎ 020-8203 7712.

SAMUELSON, Sir Sydney Wylie, CBE, Hon. D. Sheffield Hallam U.; b. Paddington, London, Dec. 7, 1925, m. Doris née Magen; British Film Commissioner (1991-97); Fel. British Film Institute (1997); Fd., Chairman & Chief Exec., Samuelson Group PLC (1954-1990); Trustee and Fellow, British Academy of Film and Television Arts (1973-); Chairman (1965-85), President (1985-), Israel Association for the Mentally Handicapped (AKIM); Mem., Exec. Cttee, Inter-Parliamentary Council Against Antisemitism; Mem., Beth Hatefutsoth. Ad.: 31 West Heath Ave., NW11 7QJ. ☎ 020-8455 6696.

SANDLER, Merton, MD, FRCP, FRCPath, FRCPsych, CBiol, FIBiol; b. Salford, Mar. 28, 1926; m. Lorna née Grenby; Emeritus Prof. of Chemical Pathology, Royal Postgraduate Med. Sch., Instit. of Obstetrics & Gynaecology, London Univ.; H. Consultant, Chemical Pathologist, Queen Charlotte's and Chelsea Hospital. Publ.: Scientific writings. Ad.: 33 Park Rd., East Twickenham, Middx. TW1 2QD. ☎ 020-8892 9085. Fax 020-8891 5370. E-mail m.sandler @ic.ac.uk.

SARAH, Rabbi Elizabeth Tikvah, BSc (Soc.); b. 1955; Semichah Leo Baeck Coll. (1989); Rabbi Brighton and Hove Progressive Synagogue (2001-); Rabbi, Leicester Progressive J. Cong. (1998-2000); Buckhurst Hill Reform Syn. (1989-94); Dir. Programmes RSGB, Deputy Dir. Sternberg Centre (1994-97); Pt. time Lect. Leo Baeck College (1997-). Publ.: Co-ed., Learning to Lose – Sexism and Education (1980), On the Problem of Men (1982); ed., Reassessments of First Wave Feminism (1982); researcher into Rabbi Regina Jonas, 1902-44; contr. to Hear our Voice – Women Rabbis Tell their Stories (1994), Jewish Explorations of Sexuality (1995), The Dybbuk of Delight (1995), Renewing the Vision (1996); Taking up the Timbrel (2000); Mem. Edr. Bd., Manna (1994-); Int. Edr. Adv. Bd., Nashim (1998-). Ad.: LBC, The Sternberg Centre for Judaism, 80 East End Road, N3 2SY.

SARNA, Nahum Mattathias, MA, (Lond.), PhD, Hon. DHL, Baltimore; b. Lond., March 27, 1923; Gimbelstob Eminent Scholar and Prof. Judaica (2000-), Eminent Scholar of Judaica (1999-), Florida Atlantic Univ.; Dora Golding Prof. Emeritus, Dept. of Near Eastern and Judaic Studies, Brandeis; President, Assn. for Jewish Studies (1983-85); ed., translator, Jewish Publ. Soc. Bible; ed., Proc. of the American Academy for Jewish Research (1990); Gen. Ed., Jewish Publ. Soc. Bible Commentary Series; Minister's diploma, Jews' Coll. Lond. Publ.: Understanding Genesis, Exploring Exodus; Commentary on the Book of Exodus; Commentary on the Book of Genesis; A New Translation of the Book of Psalms (co-auth.); (contribs.) Encyclopaedia Britannica, Encyclopaedia Judaica, Encyclopaedia Hebraica, Encyclopaedia of Religion, Anchor Bible Dictionary, An Introduction to the Book of Psalms, Songs of the Heart, Oxford Companion to the Bible; (co-author) A New Translation of the Book of Job; Entry in Who's Who in America, etc. Ad.: 7886 Chula Vista Crescent, Boca Raton, Fl. 33433. ☎ (561) 395 0486. Fax (561) 395 7289.

SAXTON, Robert Louis Alfred, MA (Cantab), DMus (Oxon), FGSM; b. London, Oct. 10, 1953; Composer and Univ. Lect.; Fel. and Tutor in Music, Worcester College, Oxford (1999-); Hd. Composition, RAM (1998-99); Hd. Composition, GSMD (1991-97). Publ.: Over 50 compositions; 20 commercial recordings;

articles. Ad.: Worcester College, Oxford OX1 2HB. Email robert.saxton@music.ox.uk.

SCHAMA, Simon Michael, CBE, PhD; b. London, Feb. 13, 1945; m. Virginia Papaidannou; Writer and Broadcaster; Univ. Prof., Dept. of History, Columbia University. Presented BBC TV series: History of Britain. Publ.: Patriots and Liberators: Revolution in the Netherlands, 1780-1813; Two Rothschilds in the Land of Israel; The Embarrassment of Riches: An Interpretation of Dutch Culture in the Golden Age; Citizens: A Chronicle of the French Revolution; Dead Certainties (Unwarranted Speculations); Landscape and Memory; Rembrandt's Eyes. Ad.: Dept. of History, Columbia University, 1180 Amsterdam Avenue, MC 2533, New York, NY 10027.

SCHLESINGER, John Richard, CBE, MA (Oxon); b. London, Feb 16, 1926; Film Dir., Princ. Films directed: Terminus, A Kind of Loving, Billy Liar, Darling, Far from the Madding Crowd, Midnight Cowboy, Sunday Bloody Sunday, The Day of the Locust, MaratHon. Man, Yanks, Honky Tonk Freeway, Separate Tables (HBO & HTV), An Englishman Abroad (BBC), The Falcon and the Snowman, The Believers, Madame Sousatzka, Pacific Heights, Cold Comfort Farm, The Innocent, A Question of Attribution (BBC), Eye for an Eye, Sweeney Todd, The Next Best Thing. Plays: No, Why, Timon of Athens, I and Albert, Heartbreak House, Julius Caesar, True West. Operas: Les Contes d'Hoffmann, Der Rosenkavalier, Un Ballo in Maschera, Peter Grimes. Ad.: Duncan Heath, ICM, 76 Oxford St., W1R 1RB.

SCHMOOL, Marlena (née Lee), B.oc. Sc; b. Leeds, 1941; Dir. Community Issues Divison, BoD; European V. President, World Council of Jewish Communal Service (1988-); Exec. Cttee, Association of Jewish Communal Professionals (1988-96); Exec. Cttee, European Israel Forum (1990-97). Publ.: Women in the Jewish Community (with S.H. Miller) (1994); A Profile of British Jewry (with F. Cohen) (1998); various statistical publications. Ad.: Board of Deputies, 6 Bloomsbury Square, London WC1A 2LP. ☎ 020-7543 5400. Fax 020-7543 0010. Email marlena.schmool@bod.org.uk.

SCIAMA, Dennis William Siahou, MA, PhD, FRS; b. Manchester, Nov. 18, 1926; Prof., Astrophysics, Internat Sch. for Advanced Studies, Trieste; Consultant, Internat. Centre for Theoretical Physics, Trieste; form. Physics Prof, Texas Univ.; Maths. Lect., Cambridge Univ.; Jr. Res. Fel., Trinity Coll., Cambridge; Sr. Res. Fel. All Souls Coll., Oxford; Extraord. Fel., Churchill Coll. Cambridge. Publ.: The Physical Foundations of General Relativity, Modern Cosmology, The Unity of the Universe, Modern cosmology and the dark matter problem. Ad.: 7 Park Town, Oxford OX2 6SN. ☎ 01865 559441.

SEBAG-MONTEFIORE, Harold, MA (Cantab); b. Dec. 5, 1924; m. Harriet née Paley; Barrister at Law, President, AJA (1965-71), Dep. Circuit Judge (1973-83); Tr., Royal Nat. Theatre Fdn.; Jt. President, Barkingside Jewish Youth Centre (1988-94); Freeman City of London, Chevalier Legion d'Honneur. Ad.: 4 Breams Buildings, London EC4. ☎ 020-7353 5835.

SECHER, Paul, LLB; b. Whitehaven, March 1, 1951; Man. Dir., JSB Group (Training, Consultancy and Publishing); Mem. Employment Tribunal; Vice-President Commonwealth Jewish C. Publ.: Co-author, books and video manuals on employment law and communication skills; Ed., Employment Lawletter, Employment Law Bulletin. Ad.: Dove House, Arcadia Avenue, London N3 2JU. ☎ 020-8371 7000. Fax 020-8371 7001. Email paul.secher@jsbtrainingandconsulting.com.

SEGAL, Anthony Walter, MB, ChB, MD, MSc, PhD, DSc, FRCP, FMedSci, FRS; b. Johannesburg, Feb. 24, 1944; Charles Dent Prof. of Med. Lond. Univ., attached Univ. Coll. & Middlesex Hospital Med. Sch. Ad.: 48B Regents Park Rd., NW1 7SX. ☎ 020-7586 8745.

SEGAL, Judah Benzion, MC, MA (Cantab), D.Phil (Oxon), FBA, b. Newcastle,

June 21, 1912; V. President, RSGB (1985-91); Emer. Prof. of Semitic Languages Sch. of Oriental & African Studies, London Univ.; President, form. Princ., Leo Baeck Coll.; President, NorthWestem Reform Syn.; V. President, Anglo-Israel Archaeological Soc; Lect. in Aramaic, Ain Shams Univ., Cairo (1979); form. with Sudan Gov. (1939-41); Intelligence Off, M.E.F. (1942-44); Capt, Brit. Mil. Admin., Tripolitania (1945-46). Publ.: Hebrew Passover, History of the Jews of Cochin and other Orientalist studies Ad. 17 Hillersdon Ave., Edgware, Middx. HA8 7SG. ☎ 020-8958 4993.

SELBY, The Hon. David Mayer, AM, ED, QC, BA, LLB, Hon. D. Sydney Univ. (1991), Lieut-Col. (R.); b. Melbourne Mar. 13 1906; Justice of the Supreme Court of N.S W. (1962-76); Dep. Chancellor, (1971-87); Fel. Senate, Sydney Univ. (1964-89); President, N.S.W Medico-Legal Soc.; V. President, N.S.W. Marriage Guidance C. (1964-89); form. O.C., Rabaul A/A Battery (1941-42; Chief Legal Off., Eastern Command, Acting Justice Supreme Court, Territory of Papua & New Guinea (1961-62), Life Member, Australian Red Cross Soc. (1990); Hon. Dr. Syd. Univ. 1991. Publ.: Hell and High Fever, Itambu. Ad.: 19 Pibrac Ave., Warrawee NSW, 2074.

SHAHAR, Tovia, B.A. (Hebrew Univ.); b. Lond., Sept. 14, 1927; form. Sr. Educ. Officer, London Bd. of Jewish Religious Education; Registrar, Central Exam. Bd., Jews' Coll.; Dir., Faculty for Training of Teachers; Lect., Hebrew Grammar, Jerusalem Teachers Coll.; HM, Moriah Coll., Sydney; Dir., Jewish Studies, Mt. Scopus Coll., Melbourne. Publ.: Medinatenu. Ad.: 9 Durley Rd., N16 5JW. ☎ 020-8800 2603.

SHAMIR, Yitzhak; b. Ruzinoy, Poland, 1915; form. Prime Min., State of Israel (June 1990-June 1992; Oct. 1983-Sept 1984; Oct. 1986-Mar. 1990); Vice-Premier (1984-86), Foreign Min. (1980-86); Herut Leader; M. K. (1973-96); Member, Betar in Poland emigrated Palestine 1935; joined Irgun Zvai Leumi (1937); later helped reorganise Central Cttee., Lohamei Herut Yisrael. Publ.: Summing Up (1994). Ad.: Beit Amot Misphat, 8 Shaul HaMelech Blvd., Tel Aviv. ☎ Tel Aviv 695-1166.

SHARON, Ariel, LLB (HU); b. Kfar Malal, 1928; Prime Minister of Israel (2001-); Career officer in the IDF (1948-72); M.K. (1974-); Minister of Agriculture (1977-81); Minister of Defence (1981-83); Minister of Industry and Trade (1984-90); Minister of National Infrastructure (1996-98); Minister of Foreign Affairs (1998-99); Chairman of Likud Party (1999-2001). Publ.: Warrior. Ad.: Prime Minister's Office, 3 Kaplan St., POB 187, Kiryat Ben Gurion, Jerusalem 91919. ☎ (02)-670-5555. Fax (02) 670-5475.

SHATZKES, Pamela Joy, BA, MA, PhD; b. New York, June 12, 1949; m. Jerry Shatzkes; Historian; Lecturer, Dept., International History, LSE (1998-2002); Lect., Holocaust Studies, LSJS (2001); Chair, International Orthodox Forum, LSJS (1999-2000); Lect., Spiro Institute (1989-1992). Publ.: Holocaust and Rescue: Impotent or Indifferent? Anglo-Jewry, 1938-1945 (2002). Ad.: 13 Danescroft Gardens, London NW4 2ND. ☎ 020-8203 2166. Fax 020-8201 5252. Email p.j.shatzkes@lse.ac.uk.

SHAW, Martin, BA; b. London, Aug. 16, 1949; Consultant, Variety Club of Great Britain (2002-), Gen. Man. (2001-2); Senior Consult, Charity Recruitment (1999-2001); Ind. Consult, Action Planning (1995-99); Exec. Dir. of the Assoc. for Jewish Youth (1989-95), Senior Youth Off., London Borough of Ealing (1986-89); Sen. Youth Off., ILEA (1983-86); Project Dir. Nat. C. for Voluntary Youth Services (1979-82). Publ.: Young People and Decision. Ad.: 64 The Grove, Edgware, Middx. HA8 9QB. ☎ 020-8958 6885. Email mshaw@dircon.co.uk.

SHAW, Peter; b. Lond., Dec. 17, 1935, m. Leila; Sec., Jewish Youth Fund; Exec. Dir., Jewish Child's Day; Clerk, Finnart House School Trust; Bd. Memb. (Chief Exec. 1971-77) Redbridge Jewish Youth & Com. Centre; Exec. C., Bernhard Baron St. George's Jewish Settlement (1990-98); Tr., The Duveen Trust Org.

(1990-96); Sec., Stamford Hill Assoc. Clubs (1959-71); Dep. Dir., Youth & Hechalutz Dept., WZO (1977-80); Exec. Dir., Norwood Child Care (1980-84); form. Chairman, Jewish Assn. of Professionals in Soc. Work, Chairman, Assn. of Execs. of Jewish Com. Orgs. (1982-84); Chairman, Jewish Programme Materials Project (1980-84). Ad.: 2 Lodge Close, Canons Drive, Edgware, Middx HA8 7RL. ☎ 020-8381 2894. Fax 020-8446 7370.

SHEFF, Mrs Sylvia Claire (née Glickman), MBE, JP, BA; b. Manchester, Nov. 9, 1935; Ret. Teacher; Concert and events promoter (2002-); Asst. Nat. Dir. (Nat. Projects Dir., 1974-85), Conservative Frs. of Israel (1985-89); Fdr. & Dir., Friendship with Israel, Group (European Parl.) (1979-90); P. (Fdr. Chairman, 1972-80), Manch. 35 Group Women's Campaign for Soviet Jewry (1980-); H. Sec., Nat. C. for Soviet Jewry (1987-89); Assoc. Dir. Jewish Cultural & Leisure Centre (1990-93); Del. BoD (1987-). Int. Co-ord. Yeled Yafeh Fellowship of Children of Chernobyl (1990-93). Magistrate (1976). Ad.: 6, The Meadows, Old Hall La., Whitefield, Manchester M45 7RZ. ☎/Fax 0161-766 4391.

SHELDON, Peter, JP, FA; b. Chesterfield, June 11, 1941; m. Judith Marion née Grunberger; International Business Consultant; Chairman Bat M Advanced Communications Ltd; President United Synagogue (1999-), Hon. Officer (1996-99); Chairman Kashrut Division London Beth Din (1996-99); Chairman Kerem Schools (1976-88); Council Mem. Friends of Bnei Akivah (1985-92). Ad.: 34 Fairholme Gardens, London N3 3EB. ☎ 020-8349 9462. Fax 020-8349 9473. E-mail sheld@btinternet.com.

SHELDON, Rt. Hon. Lord Robert Edward, PC; b. Sept. 13, 1923; M.P. (Lab.) for Ashton-under-Lyne (1964–2001); form. Chairman, Public Accounts Cttee; form. Fin. Sec., Treasury. Ad.: 27 Darley Ave., West Didsbury, Manchester M20 8ZD.

SHELLEY, Ronald Charles, FCA; b. London, March 27, 1929; T., BoD (1991-97); V. President (Nat. Chairman, 1975-77) Ajex; Chairman, Ajex Housing Assn. (1987-91); Tr., London Museum of Jewish Life. Ad.: Second Floor, 45 Mortimer St., W1W 8HJ. ☎ 020-7323 6626. Fax 020-7255 1203.

SHERIDAN, Rabbi Sybil Ann, MA (Cantab); b. Bolton, Lancs., Sept. 27, 1953; m. Jonathan Romain; M., Thames Valley Progressive J. Community, Reading; Lect. Leo Baeck College; Publ.: Stories from the Jewish World (1987, 1998), Creating the Old Testament (contr. 1994), Hear Our Voice (ed) (1994), Christian-Jewish Dialogue (1996, contr.), Renewing the Vision (1996, contr.), Taking up the Timbrel (ed., 2000), Feminist Perspectives on History and Religion (2001, contr.). Ad.: 2 Church Street, Reading RG1 2SB. ☎ 01628 781971. Fax 01628 625536. E-mail sybilsheri@aol.com.

SHIELDS, Sir Neil (Stanley) MC; b. London, Sept. 7, 1919; Chairman, Com. for New Towns (1982-95); Bd., Lond. Transport (1986-93), Chairman, (1988-89) Dep. Chairman (1989-93); Chairman, Lond. Transport Property Bd. (1986-95); Dep. Leader (1952-61), Hampstead Bor C.; Nat. Exec. Chairman London area (1961-63), Conservative Party; C., AJA. Ad.: 12 London House, Avenue Rd., NW8 7PX.

SHINDLER, Colin, BSc, MSc DipEd (Further Education), PhD; b. Hackney, London, Sept. 3, 1946; Fellow in Hebrew and Israel Studies, SOAS; Assoc. Lect. in Chemistry, Open U.; Ed., Judaism Today (1994-2000); Political Affairs Sec., World Union of Jewish Students (1970-72); Ed., Jews in the USSR, (1972-75). Ed. Jewish Quarterly (1985-94); Dir. European Jewish Publication Soc. (1995-). Publ.: All Party Parl. Exhibition on Soviet Jewry (1974), Exit Visa: Detente, Human Rights and the Jewish Emigration Movement in the USSR (1978), The Raoul Wallenburg Exhibition (1982), Ploughshares into Swords? Israelis and Jews in the Shadow of the Intifada (1991), Israel, Likud and the Zionist Dream (1995), The Land Beyond Promise (2002). Ad.: 80 Stanhope Ave., London N3 3NA. ☎ 020-8349 1264.

SHINE, Rabbi Cyril, BA; b. London, Jan. 24, 1923; M., Central Syn. (1955-90);

Domestic Chaplain to Lord Mayor of London (1960-61); Westminster C. Com. Rel. Cttee.; Chairman Central JIA Cttee.; Chaplain, Pentonville Prison; form. M., N. Finchley & Woodside Park Syn., Walthamstow & Leyton Syn. and Peterborough. Ad.: Suite R, 82 Portland Pl., W1N 3DH ☎ 020-7636 3195.

SHIPTON, Sidney Lawrence, LLB, MBA, FRSA, FIMgt; b. London, Jul. 25, 1929; Solicitor; Freeman of the City of London; Co-ord. The Three Faiths Forum; Council, JHSE; Member, Royal Instit. of Internat. Affairs; Mem. of the Praesidium of the WZO Zionist General Council; Memb. Bd. Gov. Comptrollers Cttee of the Jewish Agency for Israel; Mem. Int. Adv. Cttee Inter-religious Co-ordinating Council in Israel; form. M., Exec. Bnai Brith UK; President Leo Baeck (London) Lodge of Bnai Brith; Hon. V. President Zionist Federation of Great Britain; Hon. V. President Federation of Zionist Youth; Hon. President Hanoar Hazioni; form. Exec. Dir. World Movement for a United Israel (Ta'ali); Exec. Dir., Sephardi Fed. of Brit. & C'wlth; Exec. Dir., WOJAC (British Section); Exec. Member, Council of Christians and Jews; Chairman, Israel Cttee. BoD; Exec. Scopus J. Educ. Tr.; Chairman, Simon Marks Jewish Day Sch.; Exec. The Network; Chairman, Assoc. Execs. of Jewish Com. Orgs.; Gen. Sec., Chairman, H. Sec. and H.T. Z. Fed.; Dir., JNF; Man. Dir., K.K.L. Executor & Tr. Co. Ltd. Ad.: 82 Hurstwood Rd., NW11 0AU. ☎/Fax 020-8455 0987.

SHIRE, Michael, BA (Hons), MA, PhD (Hebrew Union Coll. LA); Rabbinic ordination at Leo Baeck Coll. (1996); b. 1957; Vice-Principal Leo Baeck College – Centre for Jewish Education; Assoc. Memb. Int. Seminar on Religon and Values; Dir. of Education, Temple Beth Hillel, Hollywood (1983-88); Gov., Akiva School (1990-). Publ.: Ed. Cons. Illustrated Atlas of Jewish Civilization, The Illuminated Haggadah (1998), L'Chaim! (2000), The Jewish Prophet (2002). Ad.: Leo Baeck College, 80 East End Road, Finchley N3 2SY.

SHOMBROT, Jeffrey, OBE, BSc (Eng), FICE; b. London, Apr. 30, 1915; Ret. Consult, form. Supt. Eng. Admiralty and Environment Dept. Ad. Holly Lodge, 7 Aylmer Dr., Stanmore HA7 3EJ. ☎ 020-8954 4316.

SHORT, Mrs. Renee; b. Apr., 1916; MP (Lab.) for Wolverhampton, North-East (1964-87); Member, NEC Lab. Party; form. Chairman, Educ. Cttee.; Chairman, Parl. Select Cttee. for Soc. Services; Patron, Chiropractic Advancement Assn.; President, Nat. Campaign for Nursery Educ; Member, Med. Res. C. (1988) Ethics Cttee. Royal Coll. Physicians; BMA Invitro Fertilisation Ethics Cttee.; P, Action for Newborn; Chairman, CO-ORD; C., NSPCC; Hon. Life Member; Inst. Medical Ethics; Working Party on Aids; Hon. Fel., Wolverhampton Polytechnic (1987); Hon. Fel. Royal Coll. Psychiatrists (1988); Hon. MRCP (1989); Ch. Celebrities Guild (1989-92); Member BoD Community Res. Cttee; V. President, Health Visitors Assn.; V. President, Womens National Cancer Control Campaign (WNCCC); V. President, Parl. Scientific Cttee. Publ.: The Care of Long Term Prisoners. Ad: 70 Westminster Gdns., Marsham St., SW1P 4JG.

SHRANK, Paul Stephen, MA (Cantab); b. March 15, 1947; Solicitor; Co-Chairman, Assembly of Masorti Synagogues (1998-); Chairman, New North London Synagogue (1994-98); Mem. BoD, form. V. Chairman Finance Cttee; Tr. Ruth Schneider Memorial Trust; form. Tr. Jewish Aids Trust, Home In My Mind and Manor House Centre for Psychotherapy and Counselling. Ad.: 33 Northway, London NW11 6PB.

SHTAUBER, Zvi (H.E. Ambassador of Israel); b. July 15, 1947; m. Nitza; Ambassador (2001-); Senior Foreign Policy Advisor to Ehud Barak (1999-2000); form. V. President Ben Gurion University (1996-99); form. Military Intelligence Officer; participant in the Oslo Peace Negotiations; Gen. (Ret.) IDF (1970-95). Ad.: Israel Embassy, 2 Palace Green, London W8 4QB. ☎ 020-7957 9500. Fax 020-7957 9555. E-mail isr-info@dircon.co.uk.

SHUKMAN, Harold, BA (Nottingham), MA, D.Phil (Oxon); b. London, March 23, 1931; Emer. Fel., St. Antony's Coll., Oxford; Chairman Edr. Bd., East

European Jewish Affairs. Publ.: Lenin and the Russian Revolution; Ed. Blackwell's Encyclopedia of the Russian Revolution; trans. Children of the Arbat, by A. Rybakov; Ed. & trans. Memories by Andrey Gromyko; Ed. & trans. Stalin: Triumph & Tragedy by Dmitri Volkogonov; Ed. Stalin's Generals; trans. Lenin (D. Volkogonov); Ed. & trans. Trotsky, The Rise and Fall of the Soviet Empire; Rasputin; The Russian Revolution; Stalin; (Ed.) Agents for Change: Intelligence Services in the 21st Century; Stalin and the Soviet–Finnish War (Ed.). Ad.: St. Antony's Coll., Oxford, OX2 6JF. ☎ 01865 554147.

SHULMAN, Milton, BA, LLB; b. Toronto; Writer and critic; Evening Standard, theatre and television critic (1948-97); IPC Critic of the Year Award, 1966; Evening Standard, and Daily Express, film critic (1948-58); Film Critic, Vogue, (1975-87); Social and Political Columnist Evening Standard (1958-96); Regular Member, BBC Radio 4 Stop the Week; Exec. Producer, Granada TV (1958-62); Asst. Controller of Programmes, Rediffusion TV (1962-64); Served in Canada Army (Major, mentioned in dispatches). Publ.: Defeat in the West, How to be a Celebrity, Kill 3, The Ravenous Eye, The Least Worst Television in the World, Marilyn, Hitler and Me; Voltaire, Goldberg and Others; It Takes All Sorts; Preep; Preep in Paris; Preep and the Queen, etc. Ad.: Flat G, 51 Eaton Sq., SW1. ☎ 020-7235 7162.

SHULMAN, Rabbi Nisson E., BA, MA, DHL; Capt. CHC, USNR, Ret.; b. New York, Dec. 12, 1931; m. Rywka née Kossowsky; Faculty, IBC, Yeshiva Univ. (1999-); Dir., Dept. of Rabbinic Services, RIETS, Yeshiva Univ. (1994-99); Rabbi St John's Wood Syn., London (1988-94); Rabbi, Central Syn., Sydney, Dayan Sydney Beth Din (1985-88); Rabbi, Fifth Ave. Syn., New York (1978-85); Rabbi Cong. Shaarei Tefila and Dean, Yavneh Hebrew Academy, Los Angeles (1971-77); Rabbi and Educ. Dir., Cong. Sons of Israel, Yonkers, N.Y. (1962-71); Chaplain, US Naval Reserve, Ready (1956-88); Co-Chairman, Com. of Med. Ethics, Fellowship of Jewish Doctors, New South Wales (1985-88); Edr., Proc. of the 1987 Sydney Med. Ethics Conf.; Mem. Med. Ethics Commission, Fed. of Jewish Philanthropies, N.Y. (1971-78); Edr., Yearbook of Med. Ethics, Jews College, London (1993); Proc. Sydney Conf. on Bioethics (1987). Publ.: Authority and Community: 16th Century Polish Jewry (1986); Jewish Answers to Medical Ethics Questions (1988). Ad.: 383 Grand St., Apt. 207, New York City 10002. USA. ☎/Fax 212 505-3432.

SILK, Donald, MA (Oxon); b. Lond., 1928; Solicitor; H.V. President, Z. Fed.; Chairman, Fed. Z. Youth (1953-55), Tr. Chichester Festival Theatre. Ad.: 69 Charlbury Rd., Oxford OX2 6UX. ☎ 01865 513881.

SILVERMAN, Rabbi Robert Malcolm (Reuven), BA, PhD; b. Oxford, July 26, 1947; m. Dr Isobel Braidman; M., Manchester Reform Syn.; Hon. Fel., Middle Eastern Studies Dept. and Centre for Jewish Studies, Univ. Manchester; Chairman, Assembly of Rabbis, RSGB (1991-93); Anglo-Israel Friendship League, Manch.; Chaplain, Progressive Jew. Students, Manch.; form. Second M., Edgware Reform Syn.; M., Mikve Israel Emanuel, Curacao. Publ: Baruch Spinoza. Ad.: 26 Daylesford Rd., Cheadle, Cheshire, SK8 1LF. Fax 0161-834 0415 or 0161-839 4865.

SINCLAIR, Clive John, BA, PhD (East Anglia Univ.), FRSL; b. Lond., Feb 19, 1948; British Library Penguin Writers Fellow (1996); form. Lit. Edr., Jewish Chronicle; Writer-in-Residence Uppsala Univ., 1988; Prizes: Somerset Maugham Award (1981); Jewish Quarterly Award for Fiction (1997); PEN Silver Pen for Fiction (1997). Publ.: The Brothers Singer, Bedbugs, Hearts of Gold, Bibliosexuality, Blood Libels, Diaspora Blues, Cosmetic Effects, Augustus Rex, The Lady with the Laptop, A Soap Opera from Hell, Meet the Wife. Ad.: 22 Church St., St Albans, Herts. AL3 5NQ.

SINCLAIR, Rabbi Dr Daniel Bernard, LLB, LLM, LLD; b. London, June 30, 1950; Prof. Jewish Law and Comparative Biomedical Law, Tel Aviv College of

Management Law School; Principal, Jews' College (1994-97); Lect. in Jewish Law, Gold College, Jerusalem (1978-84); Research Fellow, Institute for Research in Jewish Law, Hebrew University, Jerusalem (1978-84); Tutor in Jewish Law, Hebrew University, Jerusalem (1980-84); Visiting Research Associate, Centre for Criminology and the Social and Philosophical Study of Law, Edinburgh University (1984-87); M. of the Edinburgh Hebrew Congregation, Edinburgh (1984-87); Tutor in Jurisprudence, Faculty of Law, Edinburgh University, Edinburgh (1985-87); Senior Research Fellow, Institute for Research in Jewish Law, Jerusalem (1987-); Lect. in Jewish Law and Comparative Biomedical Law, Tel Aviv University (1988-); Lect. in Jewish Law and Philosophy of Halakhah, Pardes Institute, Jerusalem (1988-90); Lecturer in Jewish and Comparative Bioethics, Hebrew University, Jerusalem (1991); Jacob Herzog Memorial Prize, 1980; Asst. Ed. Jewish Law Annual (1990). Publ: Selected Topics in Jewish Law, vols. 4-5 (1994), Law, Judicial Policy and Jewish Identity in the State of Israel (2000). Ad.: 3/21 Ben Tabbai St., Jerusalem 93591. ☎ (02) 6784268.

SINCLAIR, Dr Michael J.; b. London, Dec. 20, 1942, m. Penny; Chairman, Sinclair Montrose Trust Ltd.; Partner, Atlantic Medical Partners USA; Vice Chairman UJIA; Mem. Bd. Gov. Jewish Agency for Israel; Chairman Exec. Bd. World Council of Torah Education; Chairman of Management Cttee, Sidney and Ruza Last Foundation Home; Member of Council The Caldecott Community; Tr. Jewish Outreach Network; Tr. Schools J-Link. Ad.: Yoomedia Plc, 166 College Road, Harrow, Middx. HA1 1BH. ☎ 020-8515 2800. Fax 020-8515 2801.

SINGER, Malcolm John, b. London, July 13, 1953; m. Sara née Nathan; Composer and Conductor; Director of Music, Yehudi Menuhin School (1998-). Ad.: Yehudi Menuhin School, Stoke D'Abernon, Cobham, Surrey KT11 3QQ.

SINGER, Norbert, CBE, BSc, PhD, Hon. DSc (Greenwich), C.Chem., FRSC; b. Vienna May 3, 1931; Physical Chemist; Fellow Queen Mary & Westfield College; Fellow Nene College; Vis. Prof. Univ. Westminster (1996-); Chairman, Bexley Dist. Health Auth. (1993-94); Chairman Oxleas NHS Tr. (1994-2001); Chairman Rose Bruford College Gov. Body (1994-99); V. Chanc., Univ. Greenwich (1992-93); Dir., Thames Polytechnic (1978-92); Res. Chemist, Morgan Crucibles Co. Ltd. (1954-57); Lect. and eventually Dep. Hd. of Dept. of Chemistry Northern Polytechnic (1958-70); Hd. of Dept. of Life Sciences & Prof., Polytechnic of Central London (1971-1974); Assist. then Dep. Dir., Polytechnic of North London (1974-78); Member of C.N.A.A. & Cttees. (1982-93). Ad.: Croft Lodge, Bayhall Rd.; Tunbridge Wells, Kent TN2 4TP. ☎ 01892 523821.

SITRUK, Rabbi Joseph, b. Tunis, 1944; Chief Rabbi of France; Chief Rabbi Marseilles (1975-87); Rabbi, Strassbourg (1970-75). Ad.: 19 rue St. Georges, 75009 Paris. ☎ 14970 8800.

SKELKER, Philip David, MA (Oxon), FRSA; b. Sept. 7, 1946; H.M. Immanuel College (2000-); Educational Leadership Dir., UJIA (1998-2000); English master, Eton College (1997-98); form. HM, Carmel Coll, HM, King David High Sch., Liverpool (1981-84). Ad.: 4 Broadhurst Ave., Edgware, Middx. HA8 8TR.

SKLAN, Alexander, BSc, Soc. Sci, MSc Econ, CQSW; b. London Jan. 13, 1947; Chief Exec. Jewish Care, Dir. of Quality Assurance; Dir. of Social Services Jewish Welfare Board (1979-90); Dir. of Social Services Jewish Care (1990-96); Jt. Chairman, Assembly of Masorti Synagogues (1996-2000); Dir. of Clinical Services, Medical Foundation for Care of Victims of Torture (1997-). Ad.: 96-98 Grafton Rd., London NW5 3EJ. ☎ 020-7813 7777. Fax 020-7813 0059. E-mail alex@mf.torturecare.org.uk.

SMITH, Rabbi Amnon Daniel, MA; b. Hadera, Israel, Oct. 10, 1949; Sr. M., Edgware & Dist. Reform Syn.; form. Chairman RSGB Assembly of Rabbis; form. M., Wimbledon & Dist. Syn.; form. Assoc. M., West Lond. Syn.; Fdr. Chairman, Raphael Centre – a Jewish counselling service. Ad.: 118 Stonegrove, Edgware, HA8 8AB.

SOBER, Phillip, FCA, FRSA; b. London, April 1, 1931; m. Vivien; Chartered Accountant; form. Dir. Liberty International plc Mem. C. Univ. London (1998); Mem. Finance Cttee Univ. London (1999); form. Dir. Capital & Counties plc (1993-); form. Dir. Capital Shopping Centres plc (Chairman Audit Cttee.) (1994-); Consultant, BDO Stoy Hayward, Chartered Accountants (1990); Gov. and Chairman of Audit Cttee., London Institute Higher Education Corporation (1994); form. Tr. Jewish Assoc. of Business Ethics; Chairman, Central Council for Jewish Community Services; form. Jt. Tr., Ravenswood; Partner, Stoy Hayward, Chartered Accountants (1958-90); Fell. of the Inst. of Chartered Accountants (1963-); International Partner and Member of Management Cttee., Stoy Hayward, Chartered Accountants (1974-90); Chairman, Accounting Standards Cttee., British Property Federation (1976-83); Member Council, UK Central Council for Nursing, Midwifery and Health Visiting (1980-83); Crown Estate Commissioner (1983-94); Senior Partner, Stoy Hayward, Chatered Accountants (1985-90); Tr., Royal Opera House Tr. (1985-91); President, Norwood Child Care (1989-94); European Regional Dir., Horwath International (1990-94); Consult. Hunting Gate Group Ltd. (1992-95). Publ.: Articles in professional press on various subjects but primarily on property company accounting. Ad.: 10 Duchess of Bedford House, Duchess of Bedford Walk, London W8 7QL. ☎ 020-7937 8217. Office BDO Stoy Hayward, 8 Baker Street, W1M 1DA. ☎ 020-7486 5888. Fax 020-7487 4585.

SOETENDORP, Rabbi David Menachem Baruch; b. Amsterdam, July 1, 1945; Rabbi, Bournemouth Reform Syn; V. President, B'mouth Br., CCJ; Chairman Exodus 2000; J. Chaplain, Bournemouth Univ.; Counsellor, Headway House Day Centre, Poole; Contrib., local radio, TV; Contr. 'Renewing the Vision', SPC London; Chairman, AFETUK; Rabbi, South Hants Reform Cong. Publ.: Op Weg Naar Het Verleden. Ad.: 25 De Lisle Rd., Bournemouth, BH3 7NF. ☎ 01202 514788. Email soetendorp@britishlibrary.net.

SOFER, Mark, b. London, Sept. 29, 1954; m. Sara née Giladi; Diplomat; Ambassador of Israel to Dublin (1999-); Policy adviser to the Ministry of Foreign Affairs, Jerusalem (1993-96); form. Dep. Consul-General, Israeli Consulate, New York (1991-93). Ad.: 121 Pembroke Road, Ballsbridge, Dublin 4, Ireland. ☎ 230-9400. Fax 230-9446.

SOLOMON, Sir Harry, KB, FRCP (Hon); b. Middlesbrough, March 20, 1937; Company Chairman; Hillsdown Holdings plc (1975-1993): Chairman (1987-1993); Non-Exec. Dir. (1993-97); Fel. of the Royal Coll. of Physicians (Hon.). Ad.: Hillsdown House, 32 Hampstead High St., London NW3 1QD. ☎ 020-7431 7739.

SOLOMON, Rabbi Norman, PhD (Manc), MA (Cantab.), BMus (Lond.); b. Cardiff, May 31, 1933; Fellow, Oxford Centre for Hebrew and Jewish Studies (1995-2001); form. Lect. Faculty of Theology, Univ. Oxford; form. Dir., Centre for Study of Judaism & Jewish Christian Relations, Selly Oak Colls.; President BAJS (1994); Edr., Christian Jewish Relations (1986-91); form. M., Birmingham Central Syn., Hampstead Syn., Lond., Greenbank Drive Syn., Liverpool, Whitefield Hebrew Cong., Manchester. Publ: Judaism and World Religion (1991); The Analytic Movement (1993); A Very Short Introduction to Judaism (1996); Historical Dictionary of Judaism (1998). Ad.: 5 Phoebe Court, Bainton Rd., Oxford OX2 7AQ. ☎ 01865-437952.

SPENCER, Charles Samuel, b. Lond. Aug. 26, 1920; Fine Art and Theatre Lect.; Exhibition organiser; Lond. correspondent art publ. in Italy, Germany, Greece, etc.; form. Sec., AJA, Maccabi Union, Brady Clubs, Edr., Art and Artists; Member Jewish Relief Unit (1944-47). Publ.: Erté; The Aesthetic Movement: A Decade of Print Making, Leon Bakst and the Ballets Russes, The World of Serge Diaghilev, Cecil Beaton, Film and Stage Designs. Ad.: 24A Ashworth Rd., W9 1JY. ☎ 020-7286 9396. Fax 020-7286 1759.

SPIRO, Nitza (née Lieberman), M.Phil. (Oxon); b. Jerusalem, Nov. 1937; m.

Robin; Dir. The Spiro Ark, an educational, languages and cultural institute for adults (1978-98); Org. national and international Jewish tours and cultural events; Deputy Dir. Ulpan Akiva Netanya, Israel (1959-68); Lect. in Hebrew and Hebrew Literature, Univ. Oxford (1976-83); Exec. Dir. Spiro Inst. (1983-98); teaching of Hebrew on radio. Publ.: Hebrew Correspondence Course (1987); Hebrew Accelerated Learning Course (Suggestopedia course co-author); weekly Hebrew column London Jewish News. Ad.: 43 St John's Wood Ct., St John's Wood Rd., London NW8 8QR. ☎ 020-8286 4671. Fax 020-7289 6825. E-mail spiroark@aol.com. Website www.spiroark.org.

SPIRO, Robin Myer, MA (Oxon), M.Phil (Oxon), FCA; b. London, Feb. 9, 1931; m. Nitza née Lieberman; Dir. Property Companies (1961-78); Creator and developer of St Christopher's Place, off London's Oxford St. (W1); Founding Dir. and part-time lecturer in Jewish History at Spiro Institute (1978-98); Jt. Founding Dir., Spiro Ark (1999-); regular lecturer in Jewish History at Florida Atlantic University, Boca Raton, USA. Contributor, The Jewish Enigma. Ad.: 43/44 St. John's Wood Court, St. John's Wood Rd., London NW8 8QR.

STEEN, Anthony, MP; b. London, July 22, 1939; Barrister, social worker, youth ldr., law lect; MP (Con.) for Totnes (1997-), South Hams (1983-97), Liverpool, Wavertree (1974-83); Party Cttees: Sec. to 1922 Cttee (2001-); Public Admin. (2001-2); Chairman, Urban & Inner City Cttee (1987-93); Chairman Deregulation Cttee (1994-97); European Scrutiny (1997-); Chairman Sane Planning; V. Chairman, Health & Soc. Services (1979-80); Chairman 1974 Conservative MPs Gp; Sec., Parl. Brit. Caribbean Gp; Race Rel. (1974-79); Select Cttee. Environment (1991-). Publ.: New Life for Old Cities (1981), Tested Ideas for Political Success (rev. 1991), Public Land Utilisation Management Schemes (PLUMS) (1988). Ad.: House of Commons, SW1A 0AA. ☎ 020-7219 5045. Email steena@parliament.uk.

STEINBERG, Gerry, MP; b. Durham Apr. 20, 1945; MP (Lab.) for Durham City; Mem. Parl. Public Accounts Cttee; Durham Distr. Cllr. (1976-87); form. HM, Spennymoor Special Sch., Durham. Ad.: House of Commons, SW1 0AA. ☎ 020-7219 6909.

STEINER, Prof. George, FBA, MA, D.Phil; Hon. D.Litt: East Anglia, 1976; Louvain, 1980; Mount Holyoke Coll., USA, 1983; Bristol, 1989; Glasgow, 1990; Liège, 1990; Ulster, 1993; Kenyon College, 1995; Trinity College, Dublin, 1995; b. Apr. 23, 1929; m. Zara née Shakow; Member, staff of the Economist, in London (1952-56); Extraordinary Fellow, Churchill College, Cambridge (1969); RA (Hon); Weidenfeld Professor of Comparative Literature, and Hon. Fellow of Balliol College, Oxford (1995-); Hon. Fellow St. Anne's College, Oxford; Inst. for Advanced Study, Princeton (1956-58); Gauss Lect., Princeton Univ. (1959-60); Fellow of Churchill Coll., Cambridge (1961-); Prof. of English and Comparative Literature, Univ. of Geneva (1974-94). Lectures: Massey (1974); Leslie Stephen, Cambridge (1986); W. P. Ker (1986), Gifford (1990), Univ. of Glasgow; Page-Barbour, Univ. of Viriginia (1987). Fulbright Professorship (1959-69); Vis. Prof., Collège de France (1992). O. Henry Short Story Award (1958); Guggenheim Fellowship (1971-72); Zabel Award of Nat. Inst. of Arts and Letters of the US (1970); Faulkner Stipend for Fiction, PEN (1983); Pres., English Assoc., 1975; Corresp. Mem., (Federal) German Acad. of Literature (1981); Hon. Mem., Amer. Acad. of Arts and Sciences (1989); FRSL (1964). PEN Macmillan Fiction Prize, 1993. Chevalier de la Légion d'Honneur (1984). Publ: Tolstoy or Dostoevsky, 1958; The Death of Tragedy, 1960; Anno Domini, 1964; Language and Silence, 1967; Extraterritorial, 1971; In Bluebeard's Castle, 1971; The Sporting Scene: White Knights in Reykjavik, 1973; After Babel, 1975 (adapted for TV as The Tongues of Men, 1977); Heidegger, 1978; On Difficulty and Other Essays, 1978; The Portage to San Cristobel of A.H., 1981; Antigones, 1984; George Steiner: a reader, 1984; Real Presences: is there anything in what we say?, 1989; Proofs and

Three Parables, 1992; No Passion Spent, 1996; The Deeps of the Sea, 1996; Homer in English (ed.), 1996; Errata: an Examined Life, 1997. Ad: 32 Barrow Rd., Cambridge CB2 2AS. ☎ 01223 61200.

STEPHENS, Judge Martin, QC, MA (Oxon); b. Swansea, June 26, 1939; Circuit Judge (since 1986); Recorder (1979-86); form. Chairman, Cardiff Jewish Rep. C. (1986-95). Member Parole Bd (1995-2000); Member Main Bd., Judicial St. Bd. (1997-2000). Ad.: c/o Central Criminal Court, City of London, London EC4M 7EH.

STERLING, Baron of Plaistow (Life Peer) (Jeffrey Maurice), CBE; Hon. DBA (Nottingham Trent Univ.); Hon. DCL (Durham), Kt., Order of St John 1998; b. Dec. 27, 1934; m. Dorothy Ann née Ssmith; Paul Schweder and Co. (Stock Exchange (1955-57); G. Eberstadt & Co. (1957-62); Fin. Dir. Gen. Guarantee Corp. (1962-64); Mng. Dir., Gula Investments Ltd. (1964-69); Chairman Sterling Guarantee Trust plc (1969-) (merging with P&O 1985); The Peninsular and Oriental Steam Navigation Company (1980-, Chairman, 1983-); Chairman, orgn. cttee. World ORT Union (1969-73), Mem. Exec. (1966-), Tech. svcs. (1974-), V. President Brit. ORT (1978-); Dep. Chairman and Hon. Tr. London Celebrations Cttee. Queen's Silver Jubilee (1975-83); Chairman Young Vic Co. (1975-83); V. Chairman and Chairman of the Exec. Motability (1977-); Bd. Dirs. British Airways (1979-82); Spl Adv. Sec. of State for Industry (1982-83) and to Sec. of State for Trade & Industry (1983-90); Chairman Govs. Royal Ballet Sch. (1983-99); Gov. Royal Ballet (1986-99); Chairman P&O Princess Cruises (2000); President of the General Council of British Shipping (1990-91); President, European Community Shipowners' Associations (1992-94); Freeman of the City of London; Hon. Captain Royal Naval Reserve (1991); Elder Brother Trinity House (1991); Hon. Fellow Institute of Marine Engineers (1991); Hon. Fellow Institute of Chartered Shipbrokers (1992); Hon. Member Institute of Chartered Surveyors (1993); Fellow of the ISVA (1995); Hon. Fellow R. Institute of Naval Architects (1997); Chairman, Queen's Golden Jubilee Weekend Tr. (2002). Ad. Office: 79 Pall Mall, SW1Y 5EJ. ☎ 020-7930 4343.

STERN, David, JP, FRIBA, MIPI; b. London, July 18, 1920; Architect; Dir., Lynne Development Co. Ltd.; H. President, B.B. Distr. 15. Ad.: 9 Willowdene, View Rd., N6 4DE. ☎ 020-8348 0261. Fax 020-8348 1063.

STERNBERG, Sir Sigmund, Kt (1976), KCSG, JP; b. Hungary, June 2, 1921; m. Hazel née Everett Jones; Chairman Martin Slowe Estates (1971-); Paul Harris Fell., Rotary Internat. Award of Honour; Officer Brother of the Order of St. John; Patron International Council of Christians and Jews; Mem. Board of Deputies of British Jews; Gov. Hebrew Univ. of Jerusalem; Life President Sternberg Centre for Judaism (1996-); Pres. RSGB (1998-); Founder Three Faiths Forum; Fell. Leo Baeck College; Vis. Prof. Moderna Univ. (Lisbon) (1998); DU Essex (1996); DU Open (1998); DU Hebrew Union College (2000); Templeton Prize for Progress in Religion (1998); Comdr., Order of Honour (Greece); Commander's Cross Order of Merit (Germany); Cmdr., Royal Order of Polar Star (Sweden) (1997); Wilhelm Leuschner Medal (Wiesbaden) (1998); Order of Commandatore of the Italian Republic (Italy) (1999); The Commander's Cross with a Star of the Order of Merit (Poland) (1999); Order of Bernardo O'Higgins Gran Cruz (Chile, 1999); Order of Ukraine for Public Services (2001); Order of Merit (Portugal, 2002); Co-ord. Relgious Comp. World Economic Forum (2002-); Hon. President Royal College Speech & Language Therapists (2002-). Ad.: 80 East End Rd., N3 2SY. Fax 020-7485 4512.

STONE, Baron of Blackheath (Andrew Zelig), Hon. LLD (Oxford Brookes), FRSA; b. Sept. 9, 1942; m. Vivienne née Lee; Company Director; Dir. Marks and Spencer plc (1990-), form. Jt. Managing Dir. (1994-2000); Tr. Jewish Association for Business Ethics; Gov. Weizmann Institute; Gov. Tel Aviv

University; Tr. Maimonides Fd.; Patron RSGB; Mem. Council Royal Institution. Ad.: House of Lords, London SW1A 0PW.

SUDAK, Rabbi Nachman, OBE; b. Feb. 3, 1936; Princ., Lubavitch Foundation (1959-); Lubavitcher Rebbe's Emissary in Britain. Ad.: 37 Portland Ave., N16 6HD. ☎ (H.) 020-8800 6432; (O.) 020-8800 0022.

SUMBERG, David Anthony Gerald, MEP; b. Stoke-on-Trent, June 2, 1941, m. Carolyn née Franks; Solicitor; Dir. Anglo-Israel Association (1997-2001); form. M.P. (Cons) for Bury South (1983-97); Parl. Pte. Sec., Attorney Gen. (1986-90); Jt. H.Sec., Parl. Group, Conservative Frs. of Israel, V.Chairman, All-Party Cttee., Release of Soviet Jewry; V. Chairman, All-Party War Crimes Group; Memb. Home Affairs Select Cttee. of the House of Commons, (1991-92); Memb. Foreign Affairs Select Cttee. House of Commons (1992-97); Mem. Lord Chancellor's Adv. Cttee. on Public Records (1992); Tr. Holocaust Educ. Tr. Ad.: 42 Camden Sq., London NW1 9XA. ☎ 020-7267 9590.

SUMRAY, Monty, CBE, FINSTD, FCFI, FRSA; b. London, Oct. 12, 1918; m. Kitty née); Dir. of FIBI Bank (UK) Plc; V.-P., British-Israel Chamber of Commerce; Chairman, British Footwear Manufacturers Federation Project Survival Cttee.; V. President, Jewish Care; V -P., Stamford Hill branch of AJEX; Member of the Anti-Boycott Co-ordination Cttee.; Fel. of the Clothing & Footwear Instit.; Fel. of the Instit. of Dir.; Pres. London Footwear Manufacturers Assoc; Member of the Footwear Industry Study Steering Group, and Chairman of its Home Working Cttee.; President, British Footwear Manufacturers Federation (1976-77); Mem., Footwear Economic Development Cttee. Chairman, British-Israel Chamber of Commerce; Captain Royal Berkshire Regiment (1939-46); Served in Burma. Ad.: 6 Inverforth House, North End Way, London NW3 7EU. ☎ 020-8458 2788.

SUZMAN, Janet; b. Johannesburg, Feb. 9, 1939; Actress/Director; V. President C. of LAMDA; Hon. MA (Open University); Hon. D.Litt (Warwick Univ., Leicester Univ., QMW, London Univ., Southampton Univ.); Hon. Assoc. Artist, RSC. Publ.: Acting with Shakespeare (1996); Commentary on Antony and Cleopatra (2001); Free State: A South African Response to the Cherry Orchard (2000). Ad.: c/o Steve Kenis & Co, Royalty House, 72-74 Dean Street, London W1D 3SG. ☎ 020-7354 6001. Fax 020-7287 6328.

TABACHNIK, Eldred, Q.C., B.A., LL.B. (Cape Town), LL.M. (London); b. Cape Town, Nov. 5, 1943; m. Jennifer; President Board of Deputies (1994–2000); President European Jewish Congress (1994-98); Hon. Officer (Warden), Richmond Syn. (1980-94); Chairman, British Friends of Boys Town, Jerusalem. Ad.: Board of Deputies, Commonwealth House, 1-19 New Oxford Street, London WC1A 1NF.

TABICK, Rabbi Jacqueline Hazel (née Acker), BA (Hons.), Dip. Ed.; b. Dublin, Oct. 8, 1948; Rabbi North West Surrey Syngogue; Chairman, World Congress of Faiths; V. President RSGB; Past Chairman, Assembly of Rabbis, RSGB; Past Chairman, Central Educ Cttee., R.S.G.B; Council of Reform & Liberal Rabbis. Ad.: Horvath Close, Weybridge, Surrey KT13 9QZ. ☎ 01932-85444.

TABICK, Rabbi Larry Alan, BA, MA; b. Brooklyn, NY, Nov. 24, 1947; Rabbi, Hampstead Ref. Jewish Com. (1976-81, 1990-); Rabbi Leicester Progressive Jewish Community (1994-98); Assoc. Rabbi, Edgware & Dist. Ref. Syn. (1986-90); Asst. Rabbi, Middlesex New Syn. (1981-86). Ad.: 1 Ashbourne Grove, Mill Hill, NW7 3RS. ☎ 020-8959 3129. E-mail rabtab@tabick.abel.co.uk. Website www.tabick.abel.co.uk.

TABOR, David, ScD (Cantab) Hon. DSc (Bath), FRS; b. London, Oct. 23, 1913; Fellow, Gonville and Caius Coll., Emer. Prof., Dept. of Physics, Cambridge Univ. Publ.: Scientific works. Ad.: 3 Westberry Court, Grange Road, Cambridge, CB3 9BG. ☎ 01223-304585.

TANKEL, Henry Isidore, OBE, MD, FRCS; b. Glasgow, Jan. 14, 1926; surgeon;

Non-Exec. Dir., Southern Gen. Hosp. NHS Trust (1993-97); Chairman W. of Scotland Branch CCJ (1998-2001); Chairman, Glasgow J. Hsng. Assoc. (1996-2001); H.V. President Glasgow Jew. Rep. C.; Sec. Glasgow and West of Scotland Kashruth Commission; Chairman, Scottish Joint Consultants Cttee. (1989-92); Member Scottish Health Service Advisory Cttee. (1989-92); Jt. Con. Cttee. (UK) (1989-92); Chairman, Youth Liaison Cttee.- Glasgow Hospital Med. Services Cttee; Scottish Hospital Med. Services Cttee. Books: Gastroenterology – an intergrated course (contrib 1983); Cancer in the Elderly (contrib 1990). Ad.: 26 Dalziel Drive, Glasgow, G41 4PI . ☎ 0141-423 5830. Fax 0141-424 3648.

TANN, Rabbi Leonard, BA, MA; b. London, Apr. 20, 1945; Chief M., Birmingham Hebrew Cong.; M., Sutton (Surrey) Syn. (1972-82); Hale Syn. (Manch.) (1982-86). Ad.: 61 Wheeleys Rd., Birmingham B15 2LL. ☎ 0121-440 8375.

TANNENBAUM, Mrs. Bernice Salpeter; b. New York City; Liaison Hadassah Foundation; form. Chairman Hadassah Magazine; Sec. Jewish Telegraphic Agency; Mem. Bd. Trustees, United Jewish Appeal; form. Chairman, Amer. Section, WZO; form. Nat. Chairman, Hadassah International; Nat. President, Hadassah (1976-80); Exec. Nat. Conference on Soviet Jewry; Life Tr., United Israel Appeal; Exec., WJC Amer. Section; Exec. Bd., Jewish Agency; Hon. President, World Confed., United Zionists; Gov. Bd., Hebrew Univ.; Bd., U.I.A. Publ.: It Takes a Dream, The Story of Hadassah; The Hadassah Idea (co.-ed.). Ad.: Hadassah, 50 W 58 Street, N.Y., 10019. ☎ (212) 303-8081.

TAUSKÝ, Vilém, CBE, FGSM; b. Prerov, Czechoslovakia, July 20, 1910; Composer & Conductor; Dir. of Opera & Head of Conducting Course, Guildhall Sch. of Music; Freeman, City of Lond.; Czechoslovak MC & Order of Merit; form. Conductor, BBC; Mus. Dir. Carl Rosa Opera (1945-49); National School of Opera (1951-67). Publ.: Vilém Tauský Tells His Story (1979); Leos Janácek: Leaves from His Life (1982). Ad.: Ivor Newton House, 10-12 Edward Rd., Sundridge Park, Bromley, Kent BR1 3NQ. ☎ 020-8466 5112.

TEMERLIES, Marc Stephen, ACA, BSc, ALCM; b. Hove; m. Idit née Herstik; Chartered Accountant & Investment Banker; Conductor, Choirmaster, Arranger and Pianist; Fd and Conductor, Ne'imah Singers (1993-); Choirmaster, St John's Wood Syn. (1996-); Chazan, Hove Hebrew Congregation (1991-92). Ad.: 21 Holders Hill Drive, London NW4 1NL. ☎ 020-8202 2924; 07973-909384. Email marc.temerlies@citigroup.com.

TEMKO, Edward J.; b. Washington, DC, USA, Nov. 5, 1952; Journalist, Ed. Jewish Chronicle (1991-); Foreign Corr. United Press International (1976); Associated Press (1977-78), The Christian Science Monitor (1978-1988); World Monitor Television (1984-90). Publ.: To Win or To Die (Biography of Menachem Begin, 1987). Ad.: 25 Furnival St., EC4A 1JT.

TERRET, Norman Harold, JP; Compagnon d'Europe; FInstD, MBA; b. Ayr, Scotland, Jan. 10, 1951; President, CITS Group Hounslow, Middx.; SITA V. President, Marketing; Tr., British Israel Educ. Tr. Ad.: SITA, Lampton House, Lampton Road, Hounslow, Middx. TW3 4ED.

TIBBER, Judge Anthony Harris; b. London, June 23, 1926; Circuit Judge; Ad: c/o Edmonton County Court, Fore St., N18 2TN. ☎ 020-8807 1666.

TILSON THOMAS, Michael; b. Dec. 21, 1944; Conductor; Musical Director, San Francisco S.; Artistic Director, New World S.; Princ. Guest Conductor, London Symphony Orchestra; Artistic Director, Pacific Music Festival, Sapporo. Ad: c/o Columbia Artists Management Inc., 165 W. 57th Street, New York, NY 10019.

TOLEDANO, Dayan Pinchas, BA, PhD; b. Meknes, Morocco, Oct. 12, 1939; Ab Beth Din Sephardi Communities of GB; Rabbi, Wembley Sephardi Cong.; Eccl. Auth., Lond. Bd. of Shechita; V. President, Mizrachi Fed.; V. President, Herut, Gt. Brit., Patron, Mentally Handicapped Soc., Patron, Massoret; Edr., SRIDIM (Standing Cttee., Conf of European Rabbis). Publ.: Rinah-oo-Tefillah (co-Edr),

Fountain of Blessings, Blessings: Code of Jewish Law, Home Ceremonies, Sha'alou - Le Baruch, Rabbinic response (co-edr.) Ad.: 17 Barn Hill, Wembley Park, Middlesex, HA9 9LA. ☎ 020-8904 7658. Fax 020-7289 2709.

TRAVIS, Anthony Selwyn; b. Cardiff, June 9, 1932; Emeritus Prof. of Planning - Univ. of Birmingham; late Visiting Prof. in Tourism - Glasgow Caledonian Univ.; Director, East-West Tourism Consultancy; form. Programme Co-ordinator EEC PHARE. Tourism Programme for Poland; Dir. Research, Newcastle City Planning Dept. (1962-64); Prof. of Planning, Heriot Watt Univ., Edinburgh (1967-73); Prof and Dir., Centre for Urban and Regional Studies, Univ. of Birmingham. Publ.: 300, including Recreation Planning for the Clyde (1970), Realising Tourism Potential of the S. Wales Valleys (1985). Ad.: 20 Mead Rise, Birmingham B15 3SD. ☎/Fax 0121-454 1215. E-mail tony@e-w-tourism.demon.co.uk.

TROPP, Asher, BSc (Econ), MA, PhD; b. Johannesburg, Jan. 2, 1925; Prof. of Sociology, University of Surrey (1967-1987). Publ.: The School Teachers (1957); Jews in the Professions in Great Britain 1891-1991 (1991). Ad.: 162 Goldhurst Terrace, NW6 3HP. ☎ 020-7372 6662.

TUCKMAN, Fred, OBE; b. Magdeburg, June 9, 1922; Management Consultant; President, AJA (1989-95); MEP (1979-89), Conservative Spokesman, Soc. & Employment Affairs (1984-89); Cllr., Lond. Borough of Camden (1965-71); H.Sec., Conservative Bow Group (1958-9); Commanders Cross of the German Order of Merit 1990. Ad.: 6 Cumberland Rd., London SW13 9LY ☎ 020-8748 2392. Fax 020-8746 3918.

TURNER, Rev. Reuben; b. Karlsruhe, Jan. 8, 1924; Min., Finsbury Park Syn. (1948-50); Reader, Brixton Syn. (1950-68), Dir. Zion. Fed Syn C. (1967-70); Gen. Sec., Mizrachi-Hapoel Hamizrachi Fed. of Gt. Britain (1970-73). Director JNF Educ. Dept. (1973-91). Publ.: Jewish Living, The Popular Jewish Bible Atlas; Producer, The Four Brothers Kusevitsky (CD), The Master Chazanim Collection. Ad.: 13 St Peter's Court, NW4 2HG. ☎ 020-8202 7023.

ULLENDORFF, Edward, MA (Jerusalem), D.Phil (Oxford), Hon. D.Litt (St Andrews), Hon. Dr Phil (Hamburg); Hon. Fell. SOAS, Hon. Fellow Oxford Hebrew Centre, FBA; b. Jan. 25, 1920; Prof Emer., Semitic Languages Lond. Univ. (since 1982); Prof. of Ethiopian Studies (1964-79); form. Prof. of Semitic Languages and Literatures, Manchester Univ. (1959-64); Jt. Edr., Journal of Semitic Studies; V. President, Brit. Academy (1980-82), Schweich Lect. (1967); V. President, Royal Asiatic Soc. (1981-85; 1975-79); Foreign Fell. Accademia Lincei, Rome; served in Brit. Mil. Govt , Eritrea and Ethiopia (1942-46); Asst. Sec. Palestine Govt (1947-48); Res. officer, Inst. Colonial Studies Oxford (1948-49); Reader in Semitic Languages, St. Andrews Univ. (1950-59); Chairman, Assn. of Brit. Orientalists (1963-64); Chairman, Anglo-Ethiopian Soc. (1965-68); Haile Selassie intern. prize for Ethiopian studies (1972). Publ.: The Semitic Languages of Ethiopia, The Ethiopians, Comp. Grammar of the Semitic Languages, Ethiopia and the Bible, Studies in Semitic Languages & Civilizations, The Hebrew Letters of Prester John, The Two Zions, From the Bible to Enrico Cerulli, H. J. Polotsky 1905-91, From Emperor Haile Selassie to H. J. Polotsky, 1995, etc. Ad.: 4 Bladon Close, Oxford, OX2 8AD.

UNTERMAN, Rev. Alan, BA, B.Phil, PhD; b. Bushey, Herts., May 31, 1942; M., Yeshurun Syn., Gatley, Cheshire; form. Lect., Comparative Rel. & Chaplain to Jewish Students, Manchester Univ.; Lect., Jerusalem Academy of Jewish Studies; Hillel Dir., Victoria, Australia. Publ: Encyclopaedia Judaica (Contribs), Wisdom of the Jewish Mystics, Jews their Religious Beliefs and Practices, Judaism, Penguin Dictionary of Religion (Contribs. on Judaism and Hinduism), Penguin Handbook of Living Religions (Contrib. Judaism), Dictionary of Jewish Lore and Legend. Ad.: 13 South Park Rd., Gatley, Cheshire, SK8 4AL. ☎ 0161-428 8469. E-mail alannechama@unterman.freeserve.co.uk.

URIS, Leon M.; b. Baltimore Aug. 3, 1924; Writer. Publ.: Exodus, Mila 18, and other novels, screenplays and essays. Ad.: c/o Doubleday Publ. Co, 245 Park Ave., New York, 11530, USA.

VEIL, Mme. Simone (née Jacob), Hon. DBE; b. Nice, July 13, 1927; deported to Auschwitz and Bergen-Bergen Nazi concentration camps (1944-45); m. 1946 Antoine Veil, Inspecteur des Finances. Educ.: Lycée de Nice; Lic. en Droit, dipl. de l'Institut d'Etudes Politiques, Paris; qualified as Magistrate, 1956; Sec. Gen. Superior Coucil of the Magistrature (1970-74); Cons. Adm. ORTF (1972-74); French Health Min. (1974-76), Health and Social Security Min. (1976-79); Member Europ. Parliament (1979-93), President (1979-82); Chairman Liberal Group (1984-89); State Min. Social Affairs, Health and Urban (1993-95); President Haut Conseil à l'Intégration (1997); Memb. Constitutional Council (1998); Chevalier de l'Ordre National du Mérite; Médaille Pénitentiaire; Médaille de l'Education surveillée. Dr (h.c.) Universities: Princeton, USA; Weizman Institute, Israel; Bar Ilan, Israel; Yale, USA; Cambridge, GB; Edinburgh, GB; Georgetown, USA; Urbino, Italy; Yeshiva Univ., NY, USA; Sussex, GB; Universitié Libre de Bruxelles, Belgium; Brandeis, USA; Glasgow, GB; Pennsylvania, USA. Recipient of honours and prizes from many countries including France, Israel, Germany, Spain, Brazil, Luxembourg, Greece, Ivory Coast, Morocco, Senegal, Venezuela, Sweden, USA, Italy. Publ.: Les Données Psycho-sociologiques de l'Adoption (with Prof. Launay and Dr Soule). Ad : 10 rue de Rome, 75008 Paris. ☎ 01 42 93 00 60.

VERMES, Geza, MA, D.Litt (Oxon), Hon. DD (Edinburgh, Durham), Hon. D.Litt (Sheffield), FBA, W. Bacher Medallist, Hungarian Academy of Sciences, Fellow, European Academy of Arts, Sciences and Humanities; b. Mako, June 22, 1924; Prof. of Jew. Studies, Oxford Univ. (1989-91), now Emeritus; Dir. Forum for Qumran Research, Oxford Centre for Hebrew and Jewish Studies (1991-); R. in Jew. Studies, Oxford (1965-91), Fel. of Wolfson Coll. (1965-91), now Emer.; President, British Assn. for Jew. Studies (1975, 1988); President, European Assn. for Jew. Studies (1981-84); Edr. Journal of Jew. Studies (1971-); Vis. Prof. Rel. Studies, Brown Univ. (1971); Riddell Memorial Lect., Newcastle Univ. (1981). Publ.: Discovery in the Judean Desert, Scripture and Tradition in Judaism, The Dead Sea Scrolls in English, Jesus the Jew, Postbiblical Jewish Studies, The Dead Sea Scrolls: Qumran in Perspective, The Gospel of Jesus the Jew, Jesus and the World of Judaism, History of the Jewish People in the Age of Jesus Christ by E. Schürer (co-ed. and reviser), The Essenes According to the Classical Sources (co-author), The Religion of Jesus the Jew, The Complete Dead Sea Scrolls in English, Providential Accidents: An Autobiography; Discovery in the Judean Desert XXVI (co-editor): An Introduction to the Complete Dead Sea Scrolls; The Changing Faces of Jesus. Ad.: West Wood Cottage, Foxcombe Lane, Boars Hill, Oxford, OX1 5DH. ☎ 01865 735384. Fax 01865 735 034.

VOGEL, Rabbi Shraga Faivish; b. Salford, Lancs, April 22, 1936; Dir., Lubavitch Foundation Ad.: 15 Paget Rd, N16. ☎ 020-8800 7355.

WAGERMAN, Mrs. Josephine Miriam (née Barbanel), OBE, BA (Hons.), PGCE, Ac. Dip., MA (Ed); b. London, Sept. 17, 1933, m. Peter; President BoD (2000-), Senior Vice-President (1997-2000); Inner Cities Religious C. (Dept. of the Environment) (1994-); Mem. Academic Panel, Stuart Young Awards (1990-); Advisor to the Trustees, Pierre and Maniusia Gildesgame Trust (1996-99); Trustee of the Central Foundation Schools London (1996); Jewish Care Woman of Distinction (1996); Mem. Bd. of Dir. UJIA/Continuity (1997-); Chief Exec. Lennox Lewis College (1994-96); Memb.C. Centre for Study of Jewish Christian Relations Selly Oak Colleges (1995-98); form. Headteacher, JFS (1985-93); Member BoD, V. President (1994-), Senior Vice-President (1997-); President, Lond. AMMA (1982-83); form. Member, ILEA Standing Jt. Adv. Cttee., Working Party on Teachers Service Conditions, Hist. & Soc. Studies Adv. Cttee;

Independent Assessor NHS Non-Exec. Appointments Panel (1998-). Ad.: 38 Crespigny Rd., London NW4 3DX. ☎/Fax 020-8203 7471.

WAGNER, Leslie, CBE, MA (Econ.); b. Manchester, Feb. 21, 1943, m. Jennifer; Professor, Vice-Chancellor, Leeds Metropolitan Univ. (1994-); Chairman, University Vocational Awards C.; V. Chanc. & Chief Exec. University of North London (1987-93); Dep. Sec., Nat. Adv. Body, Publ. Sector Higher Educ. (1982-87); Prof. & Dean, Sch. of Soc. Sciences & Business Studies Central Lond. Poly. (1976-82); Lect. The Open Univ. (1970-76); V. President, United Syn., (1992-93); Member, C., US M. Exec. Comm. of Chief Rabbinate C.; Mem. Universities UK; Chairman, Society for Research into Higher Education (1994-96); Chairman, Higher Education for Capability (1994-98); Chairman, Yorkshire and Humberside Universities Association (1996-99); Mem. Council for Industry and Higher Education; Chair, Universities UK Wider Participation and Lifelong Learning Gp; Chair, Leeds Common Purpose Advisory Gp; Dir. Leeds Business Services Ltd; Mem. Leeds Cares Leadership Gp (2000-1); Dir. Leeds TEC Ltd (1997-2001); Mem. National Skills Task Force (1998-2000); Chairman Jewish Community Allocation Bd. (1994-96); Tr. Jewish Chronicle. Publ.: Choosing to Learn: Mature Students in Education (with others), The Economics of Educational Media, Agenda for Institutional Change in Higher Education (Edr.), Readings in Applied Microeconomics (Edr.). Ad.: Leeds Metropolitan University, Calverley Street, Leeds LS1 3HE. ☎ 0113 283 3100.

WALD, George, PhD; b. New York City, Nov. 18, 1906; Emer. Prof. (Higgins Prof of Biology 1968-77), Harvard Univ., Nobel Prize for Medicine (1967). Publ: General Education in a Free Society (co-author), Twenty-Six Afternoons of Biology (Addison Wesley). Ad: 21 Lakeview Ave., Cambridge, Massachusetts, 02138, USA. ☎ (617) 868 7748.

WALSH, David, LLB (Hons); b. Leeds, May 21, 1937; m. Jenny, née Cronin, Solicitor, Director, Peek Plc, Carlisle Group Plc; Mem. Bd. of J.I.A.; form. Chairman, RSGB, now Vice President; form. Chairman, West London Synagogue (1981-85); President, West London Synagogue (1988-91). Ad.: 82 North Gate, Prince Albert Road, London NW8 7EJ. ☎ 020-7586 1118. Fax 020-7483 2598.

WASSERSTEIN, Bernard Mano Julius, MA, D.Phil, D.Litt, FRHistS; b. London, Jan. 22, 1948; Prof. History, Univ. Glasgow (2000-2); President JHSE (2000-2); President Oxford Centre for Hebrew & Jewish Studies (1996-2000); form. Prof. of Hist., Brandeis Univ. (Dean of Graduate Sch. of Arts and Sciences, 1990-92) (1982-96); Lect., Modern Hist., Sheffield Univ. (1976-80); Vis. Lect., Hist. Hebrew Univ. (1979-80); form. Res. Fel., Nuffield Coll., Oxford. Publ.: The British in Palestine, Britain and the Jews of Europe 1939-1945, The Secret Lives of Trebitsch Lincoln, Herbert Samuel, Vanishing Diaspora, Secret War in Shanghai, Divided Jerusalem. Ad.: History Dept., Univ. of Glasgow, 2 University Gardens, Glasgow G12 8QQ. ☎ 0141-330 5907. Fax 0141-330 5000. E-mail b.wasserstein@ modhist.arts.gla.ac.uk.

WASSERSTEIN, David John, MA, D.Phil, FRHistS, FRAS; b. London, Sept. 21, 1951; Academic; Asst. Lecturer (later College Lecturer) Semitic Langs. Dept. University College, Dublin (1978-90), Tel Aviv University (1990-94), Associate Professor (1994-), Professor of Islamic History (1994-). Publ.: The Rise and Fall of the Party-Kings: Politics and Society in Islamic Spain 1002–1086 (1985); The Caliphate in the West: An Islamic Political Institution in the Iberian Peninsula (1993). Ad.: Dept. of Middle Eastern and African History, Tel Aviv University, Ramat Aviv, 69978 Tel Aviv, Israel. ☎ +972-3-640-93-39. Fax +972-3-640-69-34. E-mail wassers@post.tau.ac.il.

WATERMAN, Stanley, PhD; b. Dublin, Jan. 27, 1945; m. Vivien née Lee; Professor Dept. of Geography, Univ. Haifa (1972-); Dir. Research, IJPR; Vis. Assoc. Prof., University of Toronto (1977-78); Acad. Vis. LSE (1984-86), Queen Mary College (1995-97). Publ.: Pluralism and Political Geography (with N.

Kliot, 1983); The Political Geography of Conflict and Peace (with N. Kliot, 1990); British Jewry in the Eighties (with Barry Kosmin, 1986); Jews in an Outer London Borough: Barnet (1989); Cultural Politics and European Jewry (1999). Ad.: 79 Wimpole Street, London W1G 9RY. ☎ 020-7935 8266. Fax 020-7935 3252. Email s.waterman@jpr.org.uk.

WEBBER, Alan, MSc, PhD, FRICS; b. London, Sept. 5, 1933; m. Sylvia née Barnett; Managing Director, Brymore Group; Deputy Chairman, B'nai B'rith Hillel Foundation Executive (2001-); Chairman, B'nai B'rith Hillel Foundation (1998-2001); Chairman of Governors, St. Margaret's School, Hampstead (1990-2001); form. Hon. Sec. B'nai B'rith Hillel Foundation (1990-98); President First Lodge, B'nai B'rith (1995-97); Chairman, Jewish Community Information (1994-97); Hon. Officer Hampstead Synagogue (1970-76); Hon. Officer St. John's Wood Synagogue (1990-91); Jt. Ed. (with Sylvia Webber) of Hampstead (1960-70) and St. John's Wood (1986-97) synagogue magazines. Publ.: The B'nai B'rith Hillel Foundation – 1953-1993; B'nai B'rith – 150 years of service to the community. Ad.: c/o Brymore Group, 8 Tavistock Court, Tavistock Rd., Croydon CR9 2ED. ☎ 020-8680 5585. Fax 020-8688 6979. E-mail alanwebber@brymore.co.uk.

WEBBER, Anne, BSc (Hons.); b. Manchester; Documentary film-maker; Chairman Jewish Book Council (2002-); Fd. and Co-Chair Commission for Looted Art in Europe (1999-); Dir. Central Registry of Information on Looted Cultural Property, 1933-1945 (2001-); Mem. European Council of Jewish Communities Restitution Cttee (2000-); Mem. European Council of Jewish Communities Policy Unit (2001-); Dir. Legend Films (1994-); Producer BBC Features Dept. (1992-94); Senior Producer Yorkshire Television Documentaries Dept. (1987-92); Producer BBC Documentaries Dept. (1980-97). Ad.: 76 Gloucester Place, London W1U 6HJ. ☎ 020-7487 3401. Fax 020-7487 4211. E-mail annewebber@compuserve.com.

WEBER, Harry, CBE; b. Nov. 10, 1899; form Princ. Exec. Off , Min. of Educ.; V. President, N W. Lond. Jew. Boys, & Girls, Clubs & V. President Old Boys, Assn. Ad.: Sunridge Ct., 76 The Ridgeway, NW11 8PG ☎ 020-8209 1743.

WEIDENFELD, Baron of Chelsea (Life Peer) (Sir George Weidenfeld), Hon. MA (Oxon), Hon. PhD, Ben Gurion Univ., D.Litt, Exeter; Holder of the Knight Commander's Cross (Badge & Star) of the German Order of Merit; Holder of the Golden Knight's Cross with Star of the Austrian Order of Merit, Chevalier de l'Ordre National de la Légion d'Honneur, France, Charlemagne Medal for European Media; b. Vienna, Sept. 13, 1919; Publisher; Chairman, Weidenfeld & Nicolson, Lond.; Hon. Fell. St. Peter's College, Oxford (1992), St. Anne's College, Oxford (1993); Member Bd. Gov Institute of Human Science, Vienna; Political adv. to President Weizmann of Israel (1949-50); Chairman, Bd of Govs, Ben Gurion Univ. of Negev; Gov., Weizmann Instit. of Science; Gov., Tel Aviv Univ.; Tr., Jerusalem Foundation; Hon. Senator, Univ. Bonn (1996); Freeman City of London, etc. Publ.: The Goebbels Experiment, Remembering My Good Friends (auto). Ad.: 9 Chelsea Embankment, SW3 4LE. ☎ 020-7351 0042.

WEIL (Breuer-Weil), George; b. Vienna July 7, 1938; Sculptor, painter, jeweller, exhibited UK, US, Israel, Tokyo, Switzerland, South Africa etc.; portrait busts Ben-Gurion, Churchill, General de Gaulle, etc., Specialist in Judaica, including Bar-Ilan collection shown in Mann Auditorium, Tel Aviv; collections in Brit. Museum, Antwerp Museum, Royal Museum of Scotland, etc. H. Mem., Japanese Art Carvers Soc. (1986), only Western Artist so honoured. Ad.: 93 Ha Eshel Street, Herzlia Pituach, Israel.

WEINER, Rabbi Chaim, BA (Hebrew Univ. of Jerusalem), M.A. (Hebrew Univ. of Jerusalem), Rabbinical Ordination (Seminary of Judaic Studies Jerusalem (Masorti); b. Sydney, Nova Scotia, Nov. 11, 1958; m. Judy; Rabbi New London Synagogue (2000-); form. M. Edgware Masorti Synagogue (1991-98); Jerusalem

Fellow (1998-2000); National Dir. of Noam, Masorti Youth Movement, Israel (1987-91); Dir. Gesher, Masorti Teenage Centre, London (1991-96). Ad.: New London Synagogue, 33 Abbey Road, London NW8 0AT. ☎ 020-7328 1026. E-mail weiner@masorti.org.uk.

WEISMAN, Malcolm, OBE, MA (Oxon), OCF; Barrister-at-Law; Recorder, S.E. Circuit; Special Adjudicator, Immigration Appeals (1998-); Hon. President Birmingham J. Graduates Assoc. (1995-96); Chief Rabbi's Award for Excellence (1993); B'nai B'rith Award for Community Service (1980); Asst. Com., Parl. Boundaries (1976-85), Rel. Adv. to Small Coms; Member, Chief Rabbi's Cabinet; Chaplain, Oxford Univ. & new univs.; Fell. Centre for the Study of Theology, Univ. of Essex; Hillel Nat. Student Cllr.; Sr. Jew. Chaplain to H.M. Forces; Hon. V. President, Monash Branch of Roy. Brit. Legion; Tr. Jewish Music Institute; Tr. International Multi-Faith Centre, Univ. Derby; US Jewish Chaplaincy Special Award (2000); I.C.C.J. Gold Medallion (2001); National Hon. Chaplain AJEX (2000-); form. Gov. Carmel College (1996-98); Edr. Menorah, Chairman and Sec.Gen., Sr. Allied Air Force Chaplains (1980-1992) President (1993); Chaplain Award U.S. Airforce Jewish Chaplain Council; Sec. Allied Air Forces Chaplain Cttee.; Member, Council of Selly Oak Coll. Birmingham (1992), Chaplain to Lord Mayor of Westminster (1992-93), Mayor of Barnet (1994-95); Member, Min. of Def. Advisory Cttee on Chaplaincy; Chaplain R.A.F. Univs. Jew Chaplaincy Bd., Progr. Jewish Students Chaplaincy; Nat. Exec., Mizrachi Fed.; Nat. Exec. Council of Christians and Jews; Cttee, Three Faiths Forum; Ct., Lancaster, East Anglia, Kent, Warwick, Sussex and Essex Univs.; Exec. United States Military Chaplains Assoc.; form. JWB, Ajex Exec.; Jewish Youth Fund; President, Univ. Coll. Jew. Soc.; form. H. Sec., IUJF; form. V. President, Torah V'avodah Org., Provincial Exec., JIA. Ad.: 25 Enford St., W1H 1DW. ☎ 020-7724 7778.

WEITZMAN, Peter David Jacob, MA, MSc, D.Phil (Oxon), DSc (Bath), FIBiol, FRSA, FRSC; b. London, Sept. 22, 1935; m. Avis née Galinski; Higher Education consultant; Emer. Prof. Univ. Wales; Dir. of Academic Affairs, Univ. Wales Inst., Cardiff (1988-93); Prof. of Biochemistry, Univ. Bath (1979-88); President, Penylan House Jewish Retirement Home, Cardiff (1991-99); Chairman, South Wales Jewish Representative Council (1997-). Publ.: Scientific writings. Ad.: 41 Hollybush Road, Cardiff CF23 6SY. ☎ 029-2075 2277.

WEIZMAN, Ezer; b. Tel Aviv, 1924; Seventh President of Israel (1993-2000); Science and Technology Min., State of Israel, Defence Min. (1977-80); Transport Min. (1969-70); Served as fighter pilot in World War II and Israel War of Independence Commander of Israel Air Force 1958-66; Head of General Staff Branch/GHQ (1966-69). Publ.: On Eagles' Wings (autobiog.), The Battle for Peace. Ad.:

WESKER, Arnold, FRSL, D.Litt (Hon. UEA), DHL (Denison Univ.), Hon. Fell. Queen Mary & Westfield Coll., London; b. London, May 24, 1932, m. Dusty Bicker; CoP, Internat. Playwrights Cttee. (1980-83); Chairman, Brit. Section, Internat. Theatre Instit. (1978-83); Dir. Centre 42 (1960-70). Publ. include: Chicken Soup with Barley (1959); I'm Talking about Jerusalem (1960); The Wesker Trilogy (1960); The Kitchen (1961); Chips with Everything (1962); The Four Seasons (1966); Their Very Own and Golden City (1966); The Friends (1970); Fears of Fragmentation (essays) (1971); Six Sundays in January (1971); The Old Ones (1972); The Journalists (1974) (in Dialog; repr. 1975); Love Letters on Blue Paper (stories) (1974), 2nd edn 1990; (with John Allin) Say Goodbye! You May Never See Them Again (1974); Words – as definitions of experience (1976); The Wedding Feast (1977); Journey into Journalism (1977); Said the Old Man to the Young Man (stories) (1978); The Merchant (1978); Fatlips (for young people) (1978); The Journalists, a triptych (with Journey into Journalism and A Diary of the Writing of The Journalists) (1979); Caritas

(1981); Shylock (form. The Merchant) (1983); Distinctions (1985); Yardsale (1987); Whatever Happened to Betty Lemon (1987); Little Old Lady (1988); Shoeshine (1989); Collected Plays (vols. 1 and 5, 1989, vols. 2, 3, 4 and 6, 1990, vol. 7), As Much As I Dare (autobiog.) (1994); Circles of Perception (1996); Denial (1997); Break, My Heart (1997); The Birth of Shylock and the Death of Zero Mostel (1997); The King's Daughters (1998); Letter to a Daughter (1998). Film scripts: Lady Othello (1980); Homage to Catalonia (1990). Television: (first play) Menace (1963); Breakfast (1981); (adapted) Thieves in the Night, by A. Koestler (1984); (adapted) Diary of Jane Somers, by Doris Lessing (1989); Maudie (1995); Barabbas (2000). Radio: Yardsdale (1984); Bluey (Eur. Radio Commn.) (Cologne Radio, 1984, BBC Radio 3, 1985), Groupie (2001). Complete list, 'Catching up with Wesker', available from David Higham Associates, 5 Lower John St., Golden Square, London W1F 4HA. Ad.: Hay-on-Wye, Hereford HR3 5RJ. Fax 01497-821 005. Website www. arnoldwesker.com.

WHITESON, Adrian Leon, OBE, MBBS (Hons.), MRCS, LRCP; b. London, Dec. 12, 1934, m. Myrna; Med. Practitioner; President of the Brit. Paralympic Assoc., Chairman, World Boxing Council and European Boxing Union Med. Commission; Chief Med. Off., Brit. Boxing Board of Control; Chairman, The Teenage Cancer Tr.; Member, Govt. Review Body for Sport for People with Disabilities. Ad.: Pender Lodge, 6 Oakleigh Park North, Whetstone, London, N20 9AR. ☎ 020-7580 3637. Fax 020-7487 2504. 58a Wimpole St., W1M 7DE. ☎ 020-7935 3351.

WIESEL, Elie, D.Lett (hc), D.Hum.Lett (hc), D.Hebrew.Lett. (hc), PhD (hc), DL (hc), etc.; b. Sighet, Sept. 30, 1928; m. Marion; Survivor of Auschwitz and Buchenwald; Fd. Elie Wiesel Foundation for Humanity; Andrew W. Mellon Prof. in the Humanities, Boston Univ.; Dist. Prof., Judaic Studies, City Univ , N.Y. (1972-76); Chairman, US President's Com. on Holocaust (1979-80); Chairman, US Holocaust Memorial C. (1980-86); Bd. Dirs., Internat. Rescue Cttee., Grand-Croix, Legion of Honour; US Congress Gold Medal (1986); Presidential Medal of Freedom (1992); Nobel Peace Prize (1986); Internat. Peace Prize Royal Belgian Acad. Publ.: Night, Dawn, The Jews of Silence, A Beggar in Jerusalem, etc.; Ani Maamin, a cantata (music by D. Milhaud), Zalmen, or the Madness of God, A Jew Today, Messengers of God, Souls on Fire, The Trial of God (play), The Testament (novel), Five Biblical Portraits, Somewhere a Master, Paroles d'Etranger, The Golem, The Fifth Son, Signes D'Exode, Against Silence (3 vols.), Twilight, L'oublié, From the Kingdom of Memory, Reminiscences, The Forgotten, Memoirs: All Rivers Run to the Sea; Vol.II: And the Sea is Never Full (1999), etc. Ad.: Boston University, 745 Commonwealth Ave., Boston, Mass., 02215. ☎ (617) 353 4566.

WIGODER, Baron of Cheetham (Life Peer) (Basil Thomas Wigoder), QC, MA; b. Manchester, Feb. 12, 1921; Barrister; Recorder, Crown Court. Ad.: House of Lords, SW1A 0PW.

WINE, Judge Hubert, MA, LLB, TCD; b. Dublin, April 3, 1922; Dublin district judge (1976-), H. President, Jewish Rep. C. of Ireland; Act. President Dublin Hebrew Cong.; Cllr., HLP, Dublin Hebrew Cong.; H. President, C. of Ireland for Soviet Jewry; Patron, Criminal Lawyers, Assn., Gt. Brit. & Ireland; Patron, Jewish Adoption Soc., Great Britain & Ireland, H. L. P. Dublin Maccabi Assn., Patron, Irish Frs. of Hebrew Univ.; Patron Israel-Ireland Friendship League; Patron Irish Penal Reform Tr.; Patron Irish Rape Crisis Centre; Tr. Irish Legal Research and Education Tr.; form. Irish Internat. Table Tennis player & Irish champion; form. Capt., Edmondstown Golf Club. Ad.: 19 Merrion Village, Merrion Rd., Dublin, 4. ☎ Dublin 269 5895.

WINER, Rabbi Dr Mark L., PhD, DD; b. Logan, Utah, Dec. 12, 1942; m. Suellen née Mark; Senior Rabbi West London Synagogue (1998-); President National C. of Synagogues (1995-98); V. President, Synagogue C. of America (1993-94);

Mem., International Jewish Committee for Interreligious Consultations (1987-). Publ.: Papers for the American Jewish Committee, articles in Reform Judaism, etc. Ad.: West London Synagogue, 33 Seymour Place, London W1H 5AU. ☎ 020-7723 4404. Fax 020-7224 8258.

WINNICK, David, MP; b. Brighton, June, 1933; MP (Lab.), for Walsall North (1979-), Croydon South (1966-70). Ad.: House of Commons, SW1A 0AA.

WINSTON, Clive Noel, BA (Cantab); b. London, April 20, 1925; m. Beatrice Jeannette née Lawton; V. President (form. Chairman) ULPS; form. Tr., European Bd. of WUPJ; form., Dep. Solicitor, Metropolitan Police. Ad.: 2 Bournwell Cl., Cockfosters, Herts. EN4 0JX. ☎ 020-8449 5963.

WINSTON, Baron of Hammersmith (Life Peer) (Robert Maurice Lipson), MB, BS, LRCP, MRCS, FRCOG; b. London, July 15, 1940; Prof., Fertility Studies, Obstetrics & Gynaecology Instit., Lond. Univ.; Chairman Science & Technology Select Cttee, House of Lords (1999-); Chancellor, Sheffield Hallam University (2001-); Dean, Institute of Obstetrics & Gynaecology (1995-); Consultant Obstetrician & Gynaecologist, Hammersmith Hospital, Lond., Prof. of Gynaecology, Texas Univ. (1980-81); Vis. Prof., Leuven Univ., Belgium (1976-77); Chief Rabbi's Open Award for Contribution to Society (1993). Publ.: Reversibility of Female Sterilization, Tubal lnfertility, Infertility: a Sympathetic Approach; Scientific writings on aspects of reproduction. Ad.: 11 Denman Dr., London NW11. ☎ 020-8455 7475.

WINSTON-FOX, Mrs. Ruth (née Lipson), MBE, JP, BSc; b. London, Sept. 12, 1912; form. Mayor & Ald., Lond. Borough of Southgate; V. President, Internat C. of Jewish Women (1974-81); Chairman, Inter-Affilliate Travel Cttee. (1975-81); Chairman, Status of Women Cttee. (since 1984, 1970-78); Chairman, ICJW Cttee., Women in Judaism; form. President, League of Jewish Women; Member Exec. Cttee, Jewish Commonwealth C. (1980-); President, B'nai B'rith First Women's Lodge; Co-Chairman, Women's Nat. Com.; Member BoD (1960-); Member of Exec. BoD (since 1982); Chairman, Educ. Cttee. (1974-80); Fdr., H. Org., Jewish Way of Life Exhibition, sponsored by BoD in many parts of Brit. (1978-); V. President, Southgate Old People's Welfare Cttee., Fdr., Ruth Winston House, Southgate Old People's Centre, the first comprehensive day centre in Brit.; Chairman, Jewish Com. Exhibition Centre; P. Relate (Enfield Marriage Guidance C.) (1985-); Lond. Rent Assessment Panel (1976-83) Herts. Adoptions Consultant (1949-77) Ad.: 4 Morton Cres., London N14 7AH. ☎ 020-8886 5056.

WISTRICH, Robert Solomon, BA, MA (Cantab, 1970), PhD (London, 1974); b. Lenger (USSR), April 7, 1945; Univ Prof.; First Holder of the Jewish Chronicle Chair in Jewish Studies, University Coll., London; Neuberger Chair of Modern Jewish History, Hebrew University of Jerusalem (1985-); Dir., Vidal Sassoon International Centre for the Study of Antisemitism (2002-). Awards: James Parkes Prize (1984); H.H. Wingate/Jewish Quarterly Prize for Non-Fiction (1992); Austrian State Prize for Danubian History (1992). Publ.: Revolutionary Jews from Marx to Trotsky (1976); Trotsky (1979); Socialism and the Jews (1982), Who's Who in Nazi Germany (1982), Hitler's Apocalypse (1985); The Jews of Vienna in the Age of Franz Joseph (1989); Between Redemption and Perdition (1990); Antisemitism: The Longest Hatred (1991); Weekend in Munich (1995); Co-maker, Understanding the Holocaust (film, 1997); Demonizing the Other: Antisemitism, Racism and Xenophobia (1999); Hitler and the Holocaust (2001). Ad.: 63 Woodstock Road, NW11. ☎ 020-8455 6949.

WITTENBERG, Rabbi Jonathan, MA, PGCE; b. Glasgow, Sept. 17, 1957; m. Nicola Solomon; Rabbi, New North London Masorti Synagogue (1987-); Coord., Multi-faith Chaplaincy of the North London Hospice (1996-); Publ.: The Three Pillars of Judaism: A Search for Faith and Values (1996); The Laws of Life: A Guide to Traditional Jewish Practice in Times of Bereavement (1997); A

High Holiday Companion (ed. and co-auth., 1996); A Pesach Companion (ed. and co-auth., 1997); The Eternal Journey: Meditations on the Jewish Year (2001). Ad.: 10 Amberden Ave., London N3 3BJ. ☎ 020-8343 3927. Fax 020-8346 1914. E-mail wittenberg@masorti.org.uk.

WOLFF, Rabbi William, b. Berlin; Landersrabbiner Mecklenburg-Nieder Pommern (2002-); M. Wimbledon Reform Syn. (1997-2002); M. Brighton & Hove Progressive Syn. (1993-97); Chairman, C. Reform and Liberal Rabbis (1994-97); Gov. Akiva School; form. Journalist, Daily Mirror (1963-75), Evening News (1976-80), Glasgow Sunday Mail (1980-89). Ad.: c/o Montagu Centre, 21 Maple St., London W1P 6DS. ☎ 0049 385550 7345. Fax 0049 385593 60989.

WOLFSON, Dianna (née Sherry), BA, DCE; b. Birmingham, June 29, 1938; Head Teacher (retd.); Head Teacher, Calderwood Lodge Jewish Primary School (1976-98); President, Glasgow Jewish Representative Council (1998-2001), Hon. President (2001-); Chairman, West of Scotland Council of Christians and Jews (1992-95). Ad.: 22 Park Court, Giffnock, Glasgow G46 7PB. ☎/Fax 0141-620 0650. E-mail d.wolfson@tinyworld.co.uk.

WOLFSON, Baron of Marylebone in the City of Westminster (Life Peer) (Leonard Gordon Wolfson Kt. 1977), 2nd Bart 1991, Hon. Fel. St. Catherine's Coll. Oxford; Wolfson Coll., Cambridge, Wolfson Coll., Oxford; Worcester Coll., Somerville College, Oxon; UCL; LSHTM, 1985; Queen Mary Coll., 1985; Poly. of Central London, 1991; Imperial CoD., 1985; Patron Royal College of Surgeons, 1976; Hon. FRCP, 1977; Hon. FRCS, 1988; Hon. FBA, 1986; Hon. DCL, Oxon, 1972; East Anglia, 1986; Hon. LLD, Strathclyde, 1972; Dundee, 1979; Cantab, 1982; London, 1982; Hon. DSC, Hull, 1977; Wales, 1984; D. Univ. Surrey, 1990; Hon. D. Medicine, Birmingham, 1992; Hon. PhD, Tel Aviv, 1971; Hebrew Univ., 1978; Weitzmann Inst., 1988; Hon. DHL, Bar-Ilan Univ., 1983; Winston Churchill award British Technion Society, 1989; b. London, Nov. 11, 1927; m. Estelle Jackson; Chairman, Wolfson Fdn (1972-); Chairman, Great Universal Stores (1981-96) (Man. Dir., 1962, Dir., 1952); Burberrys Ltd. (1978-96); Tr. Imperial War Museum (1988-94); Pr. of Jewish Welfare Bd. (1972-82); Fellow, Israel Museum (2001-); Hon. Fellow, Institute of Education, U. London (2001-); Hon. Fellow, Royal Institution (2002-). Ad.: 8 Queen Anne St., London W1G 9LD.

WOLFSON, Rev. M., b. Liverpool Feb. 22, 1908; Emer. M., Childwall Cong. Ad.: 9 Sinclair Drive, Liverpool, L18 0HN. ☎ 0151-722 5618.

WOOLF, The Lord, The Rt. Hon. Harry, PC, LLB, Hon. FBA, DLL (Hon.), Buckingham 1992, Bristol 1992, Lond. 1993, Anglia 1994, Manchester Metropolitan 1995, LLD Hon., Cranfield 2001, Hull 2001, Richmond 2001, Cambridge 2002, Exeter 2002, Birmingham 2002, Wolverhampton 2002; b. Newcastle-upon-Tyne, May 2, 1933; Lord Chief Justice (2000-); Master of the Rolls (1996-2000); Lord of Appeal in Ordinary (1992-96); Lord Justice (1985-92); High Court Judge (1979-85); Presiding Judge S.E. Circuit (1981-85), Member, Senate Bench & Bar; Master of the Bench, Inner Temple; Pro-Chancellor, Univ. London (1994-); Tr. Jewish Chronicle Trust (1994-, Chairman 2000-); Tr. Jewish Continuity (1994-2000); Fel. Univ. Coll., Lond.; First Counsel to Treasury (Common Law) (1974-79); Jnr. Counsel to Inland Revenue (1973-74), Recorder of the Crown Court (1972-9); Chairman, Bd. of Man., Instit. of Advanced Legal Studies (1987-94), H. President, Assn. of Law Teachers, (1985-89); Instit. of Jewish Affairs Legal Section; Int. Jewish Lawyers Assoc. (1993-); Anglo-Jewish Archives (1985-89), Tel Aviv Univ. Tr. (Legal Section) (1995); Chairman, Lord Chancellor's Adv. Cttee. on Legal Educ. (1987-90); President, UK Frs., Magen David Adam (1987-); President, Central C. for Jewish Soc. Services (1987-99); Gov. of the Oxford Centre for Hebrew & Jewish Studies (1989-93); Chairman, Bar & Bench Cttee., J.P.A. (1974-76); 15/19th Hussars

(1954-56) Captain (1955). Publ.: Protecting the Public: The New Challenge (Hamlyn Lectures, 1989), Zamir and Woolf, Declaring Judgement (3rd edn, 2002), Appointed to Inquire into Prison Disturbances (1990), Civil Procedure of Access to Justice (1994); Judicial Review of Administrative Action, 5th edn (1995, jt. ed.). Ad.: Royal Courts of Justice, Strand, WC2A 2LL. ☎ 020-7947 6776.

WOOLFSON, Michael Mark, MA, PhD, DSc, FRS, FRAS, FInstP; b. London, Jan. 9, 1927; Emer. Prof., Theoretical Physics York Univ., form. Reader in Physics, Manchester Instit. of Sci. & Tech. Publ.: Direct Methods in Crystallography; An Introduction to X-Ray Crystallography; The Origin of the Solar System; Physical and Non-physical Methods of Solving Crystal Structures; An Introduction to Computer Simulation, The Origin and Evolution of the Solar System, Planetary Science. Ad.: Physics Dept., Univ. York, York, YO10 5DD.☎ 01904-432230.

WORMS, Fred Simon, OBE, FCA; b. Frankfurt, Nov. 21, 1920; Hon. Fell. Israel Museum; Hon. Fell. Hebrew University; President, B'nai B'rith Hillel Foundation; Chairman, B'nai B'rith Foundation; Chairman, European Jewish Publication Society; Chairman, B'nai B'rith Housing Tr.; Hon. President, B'nai B'rith First Lodge of England; Hon. President, B'nai B'rith Gt. Britain & N.I.; Life President, Union of Jewish Students; President, formerly Chairman, Network of Jewish Housing Associations; President, B'nai B'rith JBG Housing Assoc.; Hon. President, formerly President, Maccabi World Union; Gov. Hebrew University; Council, Tel Aviv Museum; Chairman of Tr. B'nai B'rith World Centre; Council, IJPR; Founder Gov., Immanuel College; Vice-President, British-Israel Chamber of Commerce; Bd. of Regents, International Cttee for Teaching of Jewish Civilisation; form. Dir. Bank Leumi (UK) PLC and Union Bank of Israel. Awards: B'nai B'rith Award for Communal Services; The Jerusalem Medal (builder of Jerusalem); The Samuel Rothberg Prize in Jewish Education (Hebrew University); Int. Jewish Sports Hall of Fame, Lifetime Achievement Award. Publ.: A Life in Three Cities (1996). Ad.: 23 Highpoint, North Hill, Highgate, N6 4BA. ☎ 020-8458 1181. Fax 020-8458 6045.

WOUK, Herman, BA, Columbia U., 1934; LHD (Hon.), Yeshiva Univ.; LLD (Hon.), Clark U.; DLitt (Hon.), American International College; PhD (Hon.), Bar-Ilan Univ., Hebrew Univ.; DLitt (Hon.) Trinity College; DLitt George Washington Univ.; b. New York, May 27, 1915; Writer. Publ.: Non-fiction: This is My God; The Will to Live On; Novels: Aurora Dawn, Marjorie Morningstar, The Winds of War, War and Remembrance, Youngblood Hawke, Don't Stop the Carnival, The Caine Mutiny, Inside, Outside, City Boy, The Hope, The Glory. Plays: The Caine Mutiny Court-Martial, etc. TV Screenplays: The Winds of War, War and Remembrance. Ad.: c/o B.S.W. Literary Agency, 3255 N. St. N.W., Washington, D.C., 20007, 2845.

WRIGHT, Rabbi Alexandra (née Levitt), BA, PGCE; b. London, Dec. 10, 1956; m. Roderick Wright; Rabbi, Radlett and Bushey Reform Synagogue; Co-chair Assembly of Rabbis; Assoc. M. Liberal Jewish Synagogue (1986-89); Lecturer in Classical Hebrew Leo Baeck College (1987-97). Publ.: 'An approach to feminist theology' in Hear Our Voice (1994); 'Judaism' in Women in Religion (1994). Ad.: 90 The Ridgeway, London NW11 9RU. ☎ 020-8455 5305.

WRIGHT, Rosalind (née Kerstein), CB, LLB (Hons) (London); b. London, Nov. 2, 1942; m. Dr David J.M. Wright; Barrister; Director, Serious Fraud Office (1997-); Head, Prosecutions, Exec. Director, Securities and Futures Authority (1987-97); Asst. Director, Head of Fraud Investigation Group, D.P.P. (1985-87); Tr., Jewish Association for Business Ethics. Ad.: Serious Fraud Office, 10-16 Elm Street, London WC1X 0BJ. ☎ 020-7239 7272. Fax 020-7837 1689. E-mail public.enquiries@sfo.gsi.gov.uk.

WURZBURGER, Rabbi Walter S.; b. Munich Mar. 29, 1920; m. Naomi née Rabinowitz; form. President, Syn. C. of Amer.; form President, Rab. C. of Amer.

Rabbi, Emer. Cong. Shaaray Tefila, Lawrence N.Y., Adjunct Prof. of Philosophy Yeshiva Univ.; Edr., Tradition, (1962-87), Co-Edr., A Treasury of Tradition. Publ.: Ethics of responsibility (1994); God is Proof Enough (2000). Ad.: 138 Hards La., Lawrence, New York, NY 11559, USA. ☎ 516-2397181. Fax 516-239 7413.

YAMEY, Basil Selig, CBE, BCom, FBA; b. Cape Town, May 4, 1919, m. Demetra Georgakopoulou; Emer. Prof., Lond. Univ.; form. Economics Prof., Lond. Sch. of Economics; Member, Monopolies and Mergers Com. (1966-78); Tr., National Gallery (1974-81); Tr., Tate Gallery (1978-81), Museums & Galleries Com (1983-85); Tr., Instit. of Econ. Aff (1986-91). Publ.: Economics of Resale Price Maintenance, Economics of Underdeveloped Countries (part auth.), The Restrictive Practices Court (part auth.), Economics of Futures Trading (part auth.), Essays on the History of Accounting, Arte e Contabilità, Art & Accounting. Ad.: London Sch. of Economics, Houghton Street, London WC2A 2AE. ☎ 020-7405 7686.

YOUNG, Rt. Hon. Baron of Graffham (Life Peer) (David Ivor Young), PC, LLB (Hons.); b. London, Feb. 27, 1932; Solicitor; Dep. Chairman, Conservative Party (1989-90); President, Jewish Care (1990-); Chairman Oxford Centre for Hebrew and Jewish Studies (1989-92); Exec. Chairman, Cable & Wireless plc (1990-); Dir. Salomon Inc. (1990-); Sec. of State for Trade and Industry (1987-89); Sec. of State for Employment (1985-87), Min. without Portfolio, Min. in Cabinet (1984-85); Chairman, Manpower Services Com. (1982-84), Nat. Economic Development Org (1982-89); Chairman, Admin. Cttee., World ORT Union (1980-84), Gov., Oxford Centre for Post-Graduate Heb Studies; form. President, Brit. ORT; Dir., Centre for Policy Studies (1979-82), Chairman Internat. C., Jewish Soc. & Welfare Services (1982-83). Publ.: The Enterprise Years, A Businessman in the Cabinet (1990). Ad.: 88 Brook St., W1A 4NF.

YOUNG, Emanuel, ARCM; b. Brighton, Feb. 12, 1918; Conductor, Royal Ballet, Royal Opera House Lond. Guest Conductor, concerts, TV recordings, etc.; form. Cond., Royal Opera House, New Lond. Opera Company. Ad.: 16 Selborne Rd., N14 7DH. ☎ 020-8886 1144.

YUDKIN, Leon Israel, D.Litt (Lond); b. Northampton, Sept. 8, 1939; m. Meirah (Mickey) née Goss; University Lecturer, Hebrew Dept., UCL (1996-) and Author; Vis. Prof. Univ. Paris VIII (2000-); Univ. Lect., University of Manchester (1966-96). Publ.: Isaac Lamdan: A Study in Twentieth-Century Hebrew Poetry (1971); Escape into Siege: A Survey of Israeli Literature Today (1974); Jewish Writing and Identity in the Twentieth Century (1982); 1984 and After: Aspects of Israeli Fiction (1984); On the Poetry of Uri Zvi Greenberg (in Hebrew, 1987); Else Lasker-Schueler: A Study in German Jewish Literature (1991); Beyond Sequence: Current Israeli Fiction and its Context (1992); A Home Within: Varieties of Jewish Expression in Modern Fiction (1996); Public Crisis and Literary Response: The Adjustment of Modern Jewish Literature (2001); Ed. Modern Hebrew Literature in English Translation (1987); Agnon: Texts and Contexts in English Translation (1988); Hebrew Literature in the Wake of the Holocaust (1993); Israeli Writers Consider the 'Outsider' (1993); Co-edited (with Benjamin Tammuz) Meetings with the Angel: Seven Stories from Israel (1973); Ed. of the monograph series 'Jews in Modern Culture'. Ad.: 51 Hillside Court, 409 Finchley Rd., London NW3 6HQ. ☎ 020-7435 5777. Fax 020-7209 1026. E-mail l.yudkin@ucl.ac.uk.

ZALUD, Rabbi Norman, APhS, FRSA; b. Liverpool, Oct. 5, 1932; M., Liverpool Progressive Syn.; also Minister at Sha'arei Shalom Syn., Manchester, and Blackpool Reform Jewish Cong.; Jewish Chaplain to H.M. Prisons. Ad.: 265 Woolton Rd., L16 8NB. ☎ 0151-722 4389; 0151-733 5871.

ZEIDMAN, His Honour Judge Martyn, QC, LLB; b. Cardiff May 30, 1952; m. Verity née Owen; Circuit Judge (2001-); Recorder (1995); President of Mental Health Tribunal (1999-); Cttee Mem. UK Association of Jewish Lawers and

Jurists (2001-); Get Advisory Cttee, Jewish Marriage Council, Exec. C. (2001-). Publ.: A Short Guide to the Landlord & Tenant Act 1987 (1987); A Short Guide to the Housing Act 1988 (1988); Steps to Possession (1989); A Short Guide to the Courts & Legal Services Act 1990 (1990); A Short Guide to the Road Traffic Act 1991 (1991); Making Sense of the Leasehold Reform Housing & Urban Development Act 1993 (1994). Ad.: The Crown Court at Snaresbrook, The Court House, Hollybush Hill, London E11 1QW ☎ 020-8982 5500. Fax 020-8989 1371.

ZELLICK, Graham John., MA, PhD (Cantab), Hon. LHD (NYU), AcSS, FRSA, FRSM, FInstD, Hon. FSALS, FICPD, Hon. FBS; b. London, Aug. 12, 1948; Barrister; Assoc. Mem. Chambers (Gray's Inn); Princ., Queen Mary & Westfield Coll., Univ. of London (1991-98); Vice-Chancellor and President Univ. London (1997-2003), Dep. V. Chancellor (1994-97); Prof. of Law, Univ. of London (1982-98), Emer. Prof. (1998-); Hon. Fellow Gonville & Caius Coll., Cambridge (2001-); Gov. Tel Aviv Univ. (2000-); Mem. Criminal Injuries Compensation Appeals Panel (2000-); Electoral Commissioner (2001-); Master of the Bench, Middle Temple (2001); Mem. Competition Commission Appeal Tribunals (2000-); Mem. of the Court, Drapers' Company (2000-); Patron, London Jewish Cultural Centre (2001-); Freeman, City of London; President West London Syn. (2000-); Member of Council Cttee. of Vice-Chancellors & Principals (1993-97); Hd. of Law Dept., Queen Mary Coll , Lond. (1984-90); Dean of Laws Faculty, Lond. Univ. (1986-88); Chairman Cttee. of Heads of Univ. Law Schs. (1988-90); V. Chairman Nat. Adv. Council, Acad. Studies Group for Israel & The Middle East. Publ.: (contrib.) Halsbury's Laws of England, 4th edn., etc. Ad.: Senate House, University of London, Malet St., London WC1E 7HU. ☎ 020-7862 8004. Fax 020-7862 8008.

ZERMANSKY, Victor David, LLB (Hon.); b. Leeds, Dec. 28, 1931, m. Anita née Levison; Solicitor; Past P. Leeds Law Soc. (1988-9), form. Asst. Recorder; H. L. V-P (President, 1974-77), Leeds Jewish Rep. C.; Life President, Leeds Z.C.; form. Chairman Leeds Kashrut Auth., Beth Din Admin. Cttee., form. Immigration Appeals Adjudicator (1970-78). Ad.: 52 Alwoodley Lane, Leeds, LS17 7PT. ☎/Fax 0113 2673523.

ZIPPERSTEIN, Steven J., BA, MA, PhD (UCLA); b. Los Angeles, Dec. 11, 1950; m. Sally, née Goodis; Daniel E. Koshland Prof. in Jewish Culture and History, Stanford University; Co.-Dir. Taube Centre for Jewish Studies; Vice-President, Assoc. Jewish Social Studies; Fellow, Academy Jewish Research; Ed. Jewish Social Studies; Prof. Stanford University (1991-); Assoc. Prof. UCLA (1987-91); Frank Green Fellow in Modern Jewish History, Oxford Centre for Postgraduate Hebrew Studies (1981-87); Research Fellow, Wolfson College, Oxford (1983-87). Publ.: Imagining Russian Jewry: Memory, History, Identity (1999); Elusive Prophet: Ahad Ha'am and the Origins of Zionism (1993), awarded National Jewish Book Award; Assimilation and Community: The Jews in Nineteenth-Century Europe, jnt. ed. (1992); The Jews of Odessa: A Cultural History (1985), awarded Smilen Prize in Jewish History. Ad.: Dept. of History, Stanford University, Building 200, Room 11, Stanford, CA 94305. ☎ (650) 725-5660. Fax (650) 725-0597.

ZISSMAN, Sir Bernard Philip, Hon. LLD (B'ham), Hon. D. (UCE), FRSA; b. Birmingham, Dec. 11, 1934; Chairman, Good Hope Hospital NHS Tr. (1998-); Dir. BRMB (1995-2000); C. Mem. Birmingham, Chamber of Commerce & Industry; Lord Mayor, City of Birmingham (1990-91); Freeman of the City of London (1991); Leader, Conservative Group, Birmingham City Council (1992-95); Hon. Alderman, City of Birmingham (1995); Tr. City of Birmingham Symphony Orchestra (1992-); Chairman, Representative Council of Birmingham & Midland Jewry (1992-2000); Chairman, Alexandra Theatre (Birmingham) Ltd (1986-93); Chairman, Cttee to establish Birmingham International

Convention Centre/Symphony Hall (1982-86); Mem. Birmingham City Council (1965-95); Chairman, Millennium Point Partnership (1995-99); President Council Birmingham Hebrew Congregation (1999-). Ad.: 4 Petersham Place, Richmond Hill Rd., Birmingham B15 3RY. ☎/Fax 0121-454 1751.

ZNEIMER, Rabbi Saul, MA (Oxon); b. Wokingham, Berkshire, Oct. 12, 1960; m. Elizabeth née Colman; Chief Executive of the United Synagogue (2001-); Dir. of Youth Programme, Yakar (1984-86); Dir. Informal Education, United Synagogue Board of Religious Education (1992); Rabbinic Liaison Officer, Office of the Chief Rabbi (1993-94); Chief Rabbi's Cabinet (1994-); Rabbi, Kenton United Synagogue (1994-2000); Dir. Jewish Outreach Network (1999-2001). Ad.: United Synagogue, Adler House, 735 High Road, North Finchley, London N12 0US. ☎ 020-8343 8989. Website www.unitedsynagogue.org.uk.

Obituaries, October 2001–September 2002

Full obituary notices may be found in the pages of the *Jewish Chronicle*, *The Times* and *The Independent*, and selective journals in music and the arts.

Alexandrovitch, Mikhail, Tenor, 23 July 1914–4 July 2002
Altschul, Annie, Nurse, 18 February 1919–24 December 2001
Aronsfeld, Caesar C., Historian, 18 July 1910–28 August 2002
Ban, Joseph, Artist, 18 June 1920–24 May 2002
Bard, Basil, Scientist, 14 August 1914–2 February 2002
Bauer, Lord Peter, Economist, 6 November 1915–3 May 2002
Benady, Samuel, Gibraltar Barrister, 21 May 1905–4 February 2002
Berman, Morris, Costumier, 16 February 1912–15 July 2002
Bernstein, Lionel ('Rusty'), Architect and Political Activist, 5 March 1920–23 June 2002
Carvalho, Esther (née Montefiore-Myers), Communal Leader, 10 September 1918–20 March 2002
Cohn, Haim Herman, Lawyer, 11 March 1911–10 April 2002
Dub, Trude, Communal Leader, 12 October 1910–14 February 2002
Epstein, Hans, Scientist, 25 April 1909–1 August 2002
Finklestone, Joseph, Journalist, 6 December 1929–1 January 2002
Frohlich, Albrecht, Mathematician, 22 May 1916–8 November 2001
Gal, Uri, Engineer, 1923–7 September 2002
Glasser, Ralph, Writer, 3 April 1916–6 March 2002
Glatt, Max, Psychiatrist, 26 January 1912–14 May 2002
Glick, Srul Irving, Composer, 8 September 1934–17 April 2002
Gold, Sir Arthur, Sports Administrator, 10 January 1917–25 May 2002
Goldschmidt, Ruth P. (née Lehmann), Librarian, 11 February 1930–5 January 2002
Gombrich, Sir Ernst Hans Josef, Art Historian, 30 March 1909–3 November 2001
Goodman, Lewis, Textile Technologist, 9 December 1926–8 March 2002
Gould, Stephen Jay, Palaeontologist, 10 September 1941–20 May 2002
Gould, Thomas William, Submariner, 28 December 1914–6 December 2001
Gradon, Kenneth, Communal Leader, 20 July 1919–24 May 2002
Grebenik, E. (Eugene), Demographer, 20 July 1919–14 October 2001
Halle, Robert, Technologist, 14 February 1914–20 September 2002.
Heym, Stefan (né Helmut Flieg), Writer, 10 April 1913–16 December 2001
Kashet, Howard, Actor, 26 July 1926–20 January 2002
Kipnis, Igor, Harpsichordist, 27 September 1930–23 January 2002
Kitson, Norma (née Cranko), Political Activist, 18 August 1933–12 June 2002
Kolvin, Israel, Child Psychologist, 5 May 1929–12 March 2002
Kott, Jan, Writer, 27 October 1914–22 December 2001
Labovitch, Neville, Businessman, 20 February 1927–13 April 2002
Lenkiewicz, Robert, Artist, 31 December 1941–5 August 2002
Levinson, Dinora Pines, Psychoanalyst, 30 December 1918–26 February 2002
Lipschitz, Chaim, Communal Leader, 1 February 1906–24 May 2002
Meyer, Klaus, Printmaker, 16 September 1918–7 June 2002
Miller, Rabbi Israel, 6 April 1918–21 March 2002
Milstein, César, Chemist, 8 October 1926–24 March 2002
Peled, Benny (né Benjamin Weidenfeld), Air Force Commander, 1928–July 2002
Perlemuter, Vlado, Pianist, 26 May 1904–4 September 2002
Perutz, Max Ferdinand, Molecular Biologist, 19 May 1914–6 February 2002

Potok, Chaim (né Herman Harold Potok), Author, 17 February 1929–23 July 2002
Rabinowicz, Rabbi Harry Mordka, 8 July 1919–25 January 2002
Rein, Natalie, Campaigner, 5 February 1932–26 November 2001
Richardson, Martin Barrington Newman, Architect, 10 June 1929–1 December 2001
Riegner, Gerhart, Secretary-General, WJC, 12 September 1911–3 December 2001
Rosemarine, Rita, Communal Leader, 19 June 1923–9 March 2002
Rothman, Bennie, Campaigner, 11 June 1911–23 January 2002
Rothstein, Jack, Violinist, 15 December 1925–16 November 2001
Rubin, Leslie Isidore, Politician, 5 August 1909–28 March 2002
Rubinstein, Aniela (née Mlynarski), Society Hostess, 1908–31 December 2001
Rubinstein, Nicolai, Historian, 13 July 1911–19 August 2002
Sandelson, Neville Devonshire, Barrister, 27 November 1923–January 2002
Savitt, Martin, Communal Leader, 18 February 1921–June 2002
Schach, Rabbi Eliezer, 1896?–2 November 2001
Seifert, Richard, Architect, 25 November 1910–26 October 2001
Shenkin, Arthur, Psychiatrist, 1 March 1915–25 January 2002
Sherman, Sir Lou, Taxi-driver, 23 May 1914–16 November 2001
Snowman, A. Kenneth, Jeweller, 26 July 1919–9 July 2002
Sommer, Raphael, Cellist, 21 June 1937–13 November 2001
Spaisman, Zypora, Actor, 2 January 1916–8 May 2002
Temkin, Owsei, Medical Historian, 6 October 1902–18 July 2002
Treuhaft, Robert Edward, Lawyer, 8 August 1912–11 November 2001
Wallach, John, Peace Activist, 18 June 1943–9 July 2002
Warhaftig, Rabbi Zerach, Lawyer, 2 February 1906–26 September 2002
Weinstock, Arnold, Baron Weinstock of Bowden, Industrialist, 29 July 1924–23 July 2002
Weisskopf, Victor Frederick, Physicist, 19 September 1908–21 April 2002
Wilder, Billy (Samuel), Scriptwriter and Film Director, 22 June 1906–27 March 2002
Ze'evi, Rehavan, Politician, 20 June 1926–17 October 2001
Zeidman, Katya Gwenda (Gwenda David), Literary Agent, 2 April 1905–20 March 2002
Zinkin, Maurice, Communal Leader, 4 May 1915–11 May 2002

Events of the Year 2002

Anniversaries
125th St John's Wood Synagogue
100th ULPS
100th JNF
100th Subotica Synagogue
100th Sha'areh Tikvah Synagogue, Lisbon
100th Waltham Forest Hebrew Congregation
100th Jewish Institute for the Blind
80th AJEX
70th Jewish Museum
60th Holocaust telegram
60th AJR
60th Holy Law Higher Broughton
60th Jewish Youth Study Groups
50th Death of Chaim Weizmann
50th Harlow Reform

January
American Peace Negotiator returned to Middle East
Woman 'suicide-bomber' in Jerusalem

February
Service for Queen Mother at Bevis Marks
New Statesman apology for 'Kosher Conspiracy?'
Resignation of Rabbi Dr Weiss, Principal of Jews' College

March
London Conference on Jewish Identity in the 21st Century
Peace Now petition in Jewish Chronicle
Seder Night suicide bomb in Netanya
Beirut Arab Summit
Jewish Culture centre opened in São Paulo

April
Siege of Bethlehem
Ambush of Israeli soldiers in Jenin; Destruction of Jenin
Withdrawal from Ramallah
Vandalism at Finsbury Park Synagogue, Hull cemetery and elsewhere
Bomb at Ghibra Synagogue, Tunisia

May
Solidarity with Israel demonstrations
Fire at Israeli Embassy in Paris
End of siege in Bethlehem

June
Jubilee
European Day of Jewish culture and heritage
Sackings at UMIST

July
Bomb at the Hebrew University
Chief Rabbi delivered Templeton Lecture

August
Eruv in north-west London
Trial of Marwan Barghouti opened
Jacqueline Rose's Channel 4 programme on Israel and America

September
JFS opened at new premises in Kenton
Gerald Kaufman's BBC TV programme on Israel
Mark Gertler Exhibition opened at the new Ben Uri Gallery

October
Muslim Mayor of Birmingham at Civic Service at Singer's Hill
Collapse of Israeli government coalition

November
Amos Gitai's 'Kedma' at London Film Festival
Israel Labour Party leadership election

Publications and Booksellers

The following is a list of notable British and Irish publications of 2001–2002 with paperback reprints, available from Jewish and general bookshops.

Antisemitism

Cohn-Sherbok, D.: Anti-semitism, Sutton, 2002
Iganski, P., ed.: The hate debate: should hate be punished as a crime?, Profile Books, 2002
Kertzer, D.: Unholy war: the Vatican's role in the rise of modern antisemitism, Macmillan, 2002

Bibliography and Archives

Reif, S.C.: The Cambridge Genizah collections: their contents and significance, Cambridge University Press, 2002
Sirat, C.: Hebrew manuscripts of the middle ages, Cambridge University Press, 2002

Bible and Hebrew Studies

Drancy, J.: The divine drama: the Hebrew Old Testament as literature, Lutterworth Press, 2001
Davies, Philip R., *et al.*: The complete world of the Dead Sea Scrolls, Thames & Hudson, 2002
Pleins, J.D.: The social visions of the Hebrew Bible: a theological introduction, Westminster John Knox Press, 2001

Arts

Feaver, W.: Lucian Freud, Tate Publishing, 2002
Foster, P., ed.: Chagall glass at Chichester and Tudelay, with a preface by Jonathan Sacks, University College Chichester, 2002
Lampert, C., *et al.*: Frank Auerbach: paintings and drawings, 1954–2001, Royal Academy of Arts, 2001
Mann, V., ed.: Jewish texts on the visual arts, Cambridge University Press, 2001
Myers, C.: The book decorations of Thomas Lowinskym with a memoir by Katherine Thirkell, Incline Press, 2001

Biography and Autobiography

Angier, C.: The double bond: Primo Levi: a biography, Viking, 2002
Barenboim, D.: A life in music, Weidenfeld & Nicolson, 2002
Brian, D.: The man who took the 'World': Pulitzer: a life, Wiley, 2002
Chesno, V.: Vera: the amazing autobiography of Vera Chesno written at the age of 94, Lennard Publishing, 2002
Drazin, C.: Korda: Britain's only movie mogul, Sidgwick & Jackson, 2002
Endelman, T., and Kushner, T.: Disraeli's Jewishness, Vallentine Mitchell, 2002
Eskin, B.: A life in pieces: the making of Binjamin Wilkomirski, Aurum Press, 2002
Geller, U.: Unorthodox encounters, Robson Books, 2001
Ginsburg, C.: Wooden eye : nine reflections on distance, translated by Martin Ryle and Kate Soper, Verso, 2002
Hobsbawm, E.: Interesting times : a twentieth century life, Viking, 2002
Kessler, E.: An English Jew: the life and writings of Claude Montefiore, Vallentine Mitchell, 2002
Kushner, D.Z.: The Ernest Bloch companion, Greenwood Press, 2002

Landau, J.: Saved by my faith, Mainstream, 2002
Langton, D.: Claude Montefiore, Vallentine Mitchell, 2002
Lee, C.A.: The hidden life of Otto Frank, Viking, 2002
MacDougall, S.: Mark Gertler, John Murray, 2002
Maddox, B.: Rosalind Franklin: the dark lady of DNA, HarperCollins, 2002
Myers, N.: Uncle Magic: the life and times of Norman Myers, Guild, 2001
Nadel, I.: Double act: a life of Tom Stoppard, Methuen, 2002
Raphael, F.: Personal terms, Carcanet Press, 2001
Rose, J.: Daemons and angels: a life of Jacob Epstein, Constable, 2002
Rosenblum, R.: David Sylvester: the private collection at Sotheby's, Sotheby's, 2002
Sacks, O.: Uncle Tungsten: memories of a chemical childhood, Picador, 2001
Schumacher, M.: Family business: Allen and Louis Ginsberg, Bloomsbury, 2002
Sieradzki, M.: By a twist of history: three lives of a Polish Jew, Vallentine Mitchell, 2001
Siner, I.B.: In my father's house, Vintage, 2001
Steinberg, S.: Reflections and shadows, translated from the Italian by John Shepley, Allen Lane/Penguin Press, 2002
Thomson, I.: Primo Levi, Hutchinson, 2002
Volk, P.: Stuffed: growing up in a restaurant family, Bloomsbury, 2002

Current Affairs and Sociological

Arieli, Y.: Totalitarian democracy and after: international colloquium in memory of Jacob Talmon, Frank Cass, 2002
Berkowitz, M., *et al.*, eds: Forging modern Jewish identities, Vallentine Mitchell, 2002
Bevan, J.: The rise and fall of Marks & Spencer, Profile Books, 2001
Gilbert, M.: From the ends of the earth: the Jews in the twentieth century, Cassell, 2001
Gorny, Y.: Between Auschwitz and Jerusalem: Jewish collective identity in crisis, Vallentine Mitchell, 2002
Grenville, J.A.S., ed.: Leo Baeck Institute year book 2001, Berghahn Books, 2002
Hart, R., *et al.*: Jewish education at the crossroads, Board of Deputies of British Jews, Community Research Unit, 2001
Klug, B.: Minding our language: essays on prejudice and discrimination, Vallentine Mitchell, 2002
Malet, M., and Grenville, A., eds: Changing countries: the experience and achievement of the German-speaking exiles from Hitler in Britain from 1933 to today, Libris, 2002
Longley, C.: Chosen people: the big idea that shaped England and America, Hodder & Stoughton, 2002
Reingold, E.M. and Dershowitz, N.: Calendrical tabulations, 1900–2200, Cambridge University Press, 2002
Sacks, J.: Dignity of difference: how to avoid the clash of civilisations, Continuum, 2002
Valins, O.: Facing the future: the provision of long-term care facilities for older Jewish people in the United Kingdom, JPR in association with Profile Books, 2002
Woolf, V., *et al.*: Capturing memories: the art of reminiscing, foreword by Maureen Lipman, Vallentine Mitchell, 2002

Cookery

Spieler, M.: The Jewish heritage cookbook, Anness Publishing, 2002

History

Benjamin, A.F.: Jews of the Dutch Caribbean: exploring ethnic identity in Curaçao, Routledge, 2002
Comay, J.: Who's who in Jewish history, new edn, rev. by Lavinia Cohn-Sherbok, Routledge, 2002
Defries, H.: Conservative Party attitudes to the Jews, 1900–1950, Frank Cass, 2001
Derfler, L.: The Dreyfus Affair, Greenwood Press, 2002
Fishman, W.J.: East End 1888: a year in a London borough among the labouring poor, Peter Halban, 2001
Finestein, I.: Scenes and personalities in Anglo-Jewry, 1800–2000, Vallentine Mitchell, 2002
Freedman, M.: The 'Jewish' schools of Leeds, 1830–1930, Leeds, 2001
García-Ballester, L.: Medicine in a multicultural society: Christian, Jewish and Muslim practitioners in the Spanish kingdoms, 1222–1610, Ashgate, 2001
Gilbert, M.: Letters to Auntie Fiori: the 5000-year history of the Jewish people and their faith, Weidenfeld & Nicolson, 2002
Gilbert, M.: The Routledge atlas of Jewish history, Routledge, 2002
Hyman, T.: The history of the Moor Allerton Golf Club, 2nd upd. edn, Moor Allerton Golf Club Ltd., 2002
Jordan, W.C.: Ideology and royal power in medieval France: kingship, crusades and the Jews, Ashgate, 2001
Khanin, V.: Documents on Ukrainian–Jewish identity and emigration, 1944–1990, Frank Cass, 2002
King, P.J., and Stager, L.E.: Life in Biblical Israel, Westminster John Knox Press, 2002
Longley, C.: Chosen people: the big idea that shaped England and America, Hodder & Stoughton, 2002
Makiya, K.: The rock: a tale of seventh-century Jerusalem, Constable, 2002
Parfitt, T.: The lost tribes of Israel: the history of a myth, Weidenfeld & Nicolson, 2002
Pugliese, S.G.: The most ancient of minorities: the Jews of Italy, Greenwood Press, 2002
Roberts, M.: Nightingale: the story since 1840, Tymsder Publications, 2001
Rubinstein, H.L., *et al.*: The Jews in the modern world: a history since 1750, Arnold, 2002
Schulze, K.E.: The Jews of Lebanon: between co-existence and conflict, Sussex Academic Press, 2001
Seller, M.S.: We built up our lives: education and community among Jewish refugees interned by Britain in World War II, Greenwood Press, 2002
Smith, H.W., ed.: Protestants, Catholics and Jews in Germany, 1800–1914, Berg, 2001
Toch, M.: Peasants and Jews in medieval Germany: studies in cultural, social and economic history, Ashgate, 2002
Vigne, R., and Littleton, C., eds.: From strangers to citizens: the integration of immigrant communities in Britain, Ireland and Colonial America, 1550–1750, Sussex Academic Press, 2001

Holocaust

Albrich, T., and Zweig, R.W., eds: Escape through Austria: Jewish refugees and the Austrian route to Palestine, Frank Cass, 2002
Blatman, D.: The Jewish labour Bund in Poland 1939–1949: for our freedom and yours, Vallentine Mitchell, 2002
Bolkosky, S.M.: Searching for meaning in the holocaust, Greenwood Press, 2002

Bolkovsky, S., and Greenspan, H.: Holocaust survivors and their listeners: testimonies, interviews, encounters, Palgrave, 2002

Cesarani, D., and Levine, P.A., eds: Bystanders at the holocaust: a re-evaluation, Frank Cass, 2002

Chrostowski, W.: The Treblinka death camp, Vallentine Mitchell, 2002

Clendinnan, I.: Reading the holocaust, Cambridge University Press, 2002

Cohn-Sherbok, D.: Holocaust theology: a reader, University of Exeter Press, 2002

Corni, G.: Hitler's ghettos: voices from the beleaguered, 1939–1944, translated from the Italian by Nicola Rudge Ianelli, Arnold, 2002

David, R.: Child of our time: a young girl's flight from the holocaust, I.B. Tauris, 2002

Emanuel, M., and Gissing, V.: Nicolas Winton and the rescued generation, Vallentine Mitchell, 2002

Evans, R.J.: Lying about Hitler: history, holocaust and the David Irving trial, Verso Books, 2002

Friedman, S.: A history of the holocaust, Vallentine Mitchell, 2002

Gilbert, M.: The Routledge atlas of the holocaust: the complete history, Routledge, 2002

Hahn, I.: A life sentence of memories, Vallentine Mitchell, 2001

James, P.: The murderous paradise: German nationalism and the holocaust, Greenwood Press, 2001

Katz, Z.: Our Jewish life: a shtetl, the Gestapo, Siberia, DP camps and Israel, Vallentine Mitchell, 2002

Levy, A.: Nazi hunter: the Wiesenthal file, Robinson, 2002

Lowenheim, B.: Survival in the shadows: seven hidden Jews in Hitler's Berlin, Peter Owen, 2002

Mankowitz, Z.W.: Life between memory and hope: the survivors of the holocaust in Occupied Germany, Cambridge University Press, 2002

Marcuse, H.: Legacies of Dachau: the uses and abuses of a concentration camp, 1933–2001, Cambridge University Press, 2001

Megged, A.: The story of Selvino's children: journey to the Promised Land, translated by Vivian Eden, Vallentine Mitchell, 2002

Michman, D.: Holocaust historiography from a Jewish perspective: conceptualisation, terminology, approaches and fundamental issues, Vallentine Mitchell, 2002

Newman, J.: Refugees and the British West Indies during the Nazi era, Vallentine Mitchell, 2002

Prager, P.: From Berlin to England and back: experiences of a Jewish Berliner, Vallentine Mitchell, 2002

Reading, A.: Gender, culture and memory: reconciling men and women's inheritance of the holocaust, Palgrave, 2002

Roseman, M.: The villa, the lake, the meeting: Wannsee and the final solution, Allen Lane/Penguin Press, 2002

Roth, J.K., Maxwell, E., and Levy, M., eds: Remembering for the future: the holocaust in an age of genocide, Palgrave, 2002

Shatzkes, P.: Holocaust and rescue: impotent or indifferent? Anglo-Jewry 1938–1945, Palgrave, 2002

Snowman, D.: The Hitler emigres: the cultural impact on Britain of refugees from Nazism, Chatto & Windus, 2002

Steinberg, P.: Speak you also, Penguin Books, 2002

Zucker, B-A.: In search of refuge: Jews and US consuls in Nazi Germany, 1933–1941, Vallentine Mitchell, 2001

Zweig, R.W.: The gold train: the destruction of the Jews and the Second World War's most terrible robbery, Allen Lane/Penguin Press, 2002

Israel

Aronson, S.: Israel's nuclear programme: the Six Day War and its ramifications, King's College, 2002.
Ben-Zvi, A.: John F. Kennedy and the politics of arms sales to IsraeL, London: Frank Cass, 2001
Bregman, A.: Israel's wars: from 1947 to the present, Routledge, 2002
Brichta, A.: Political reform in Israel: the quest for stable and effective government, Sussex Academic Press, 2001
Carmel, A.: Old Haifa, I.B. Tauris, 2002
Govrin, Y.: Israeli–Romanian relations at the end of Ceausescu's era, Frank Cass, 2002.
Inbarm, E.: The Israeli–Turkish entente, King's College, 2002
Israeli, R.: Green crescent over Nazareth, Frank Cass, 2002
Israeli, R.: Jerusalem divided: the Armistice regime, 1947–1967, Frank Cass, 2002
Karsh, E., ed.: Israel in the international arena, Frank Cass, 2002.
Karsh, E., ed.: Israeli politics and society since 1948: problems of collective identity, Frank Cass, 2002.
Ma'or, M.: Developments in Israeli public administration, Frank Cass, 2002
Nahmias, D., and Menahem, G., eds: Public policy in Israel, Frank Cass, 2002
Pedhazur, A.: The Israeli response to Jewish extremism and violence: defending democracy, Manchester University Press, 2002
Schindler, C.: The land beyond promise: Israel, Likud and the Zionists, I.B. Tauris, 2001
Shafir, G., and Peled, Y.: Being Israeli: the dynamics of multiple citizenship, Cambridge University Press, 2002
Sheffi, N.: The ring of myths: the Israelis, Wagner and the Nazis, Sussex Academic Press, 2001
Tyler, W.P.N.: State lands and rural development in Mandatory Palestine, 1920–1948, Sussex Academic Press, 2001

Judaism

Buber, M.: Between man and man, Routledge, 2002
Buber, M.: Legend of the Baal-Shem, Routledge, 2002
Buber, M.: Meetings, Routledge, 2002
Buber, M.: The way of man: according to the teachings of Hasidism, Routledge, 2002
Dundas, A.: The shabbat elevator and other Sabbath subterfuges: an unorthodox essay on circumventing custom and Jewish character, Rowman & Littlefield, 2002
Gabriel, R.: Gods of our fathers: the memory of Egypt in Judaism and Christianity, Greenwood Press, 2001
Gellman, J.I.: Abraham! Abraham! Kierkegaard and the Hasidim on the binding of Isaac, Ashgate, 2002
Jakobovits, I.: Companion to the High Holydays prayer book, Reuben Turner, editorial co-ordinator, Vallentine Mitchell, 2002
Katz, S.T., ed.: The Cambridge history of Judaism: Vol 4, The late Roman-Rabbinic period, Cambridge University Press, 2002
Laenen, J.H.: Jewish mysticism: an introduction, Westminster John Knox Press, 2001
Maccoby, H.: The philosophy of the Talmud, Routledge Curzon, 2002
Rapoport, C.: Judaism and homosexuality, Vallentine Mitchell, 2002
The really Jewish food guide: the London Beth Din kashrut guide 2002–5762/3, United Synagogue Kashrut Board, 2002
Rosen, J.: The Talmud and the internet, Continuum, 2001

Samuelson, N.M.: Revelation and the God of Israel, Cambridge University Press, 2002
Sheil, P.: Kierkegaard, Levinas and the subjunctive mood, Ashgate, 2002
Shire, M.: The Jewish prophet: visionary words from Moses to Buber, illustrated with medieval manuscripts from the British Library, Frances Lincoln, 2002
Sicker, M.: Between man and God: issues in Judaic thought, Greenwood Press, 2001
Sicker, M.: The political culture of Judaism, Praeger, 2001

Language & Literature

Abse, D.: The strange case of Dr Simmonds and Dr Glass, Robson Books, 2002
Babel, I.: The complete works of Isaac Babel; edited by Nathalie Babel; translated by Peter Constable, with an introduction by Cynthia Ozick, Picador, 2002
Baraitser, M., and Hoffman, H., eds: Cherries in the icebox: contemporary Hebrew short stories, Loki Books, 2002
Bellow, S.: Collected stories, Penguin, Viking, 2001
Brauner, D.: Post-war Jewish fiction, Palgrave, 2001
Brøgger, S.: The jade cat, translated from the Danish by Anne Born, Harvill, 2002
Brookner, A.: The next big thing, Viking, 2002
Clare, G.: Last walk in Vienna, Pan Books, 2002
Daneshvar, S.: A Persian requiem, translated by Roxane Zand, Peter Halban, 2002
Dawson, P., ed.: Passionate renewal: Jewish poetry in Britain since 1945: an anthology, Five Leaves Press, 2001
De Kat, O.: The figure in the distance, translated from the Dutch, Harvill, 2002
Delany, S.: Chaucer and the Jews: sources, contexts, meanings, Routledge, 2002
Desarthe, A.: Five photos of my wife, translated from the French by Adriana Hunter, Flamingo, 2001
Desarthe, A.: Good intentions, translated from the French by Adriana Hunter, Flamingo, 2002
Edelman, G.: The war, Bloomsbury, 2002
Foer, J.S.: Everything is illuminating: a novel, Hamish Hamilton, 2002
Frister, R.: Impossible love: Asher Lev's longing for Germany, Weidenfeld & Nicolson, 2002
Ginzburg, N.: A place to live: and other essays, selected and translated by Lynne Sharon-Schwartz, Seven Sisters, 2002
Grant, L.: Still here, Little, Brown, 2002
Grossman, D.: Be my knife, Bloomsbury, 2002
Gstrein, N.: The English years, translated from the German by Anthea Bell, Harvill Press, 2002
Gussow, M.: Conversations with Arthur Miller, Nick Hern Books, 2002
Halevi, Yehudah: Poems from the Diwan, translated from the Hebrew by Gabriel Levin, Anvil Press, 2002
Hamberger, R.: The smug bridegroom, Five Leaves Press, 2002
Jacobson, H.: Who's sorry now?, Jonathan Cape, 2002
Josipovici, G.: Goldberg variations, Carcanet Press, 2002
Kerbel, S., ed.: Jewish writers of the 20th century, Fitzroy Dearborn, 2002
Kimhi, A.: Weeping Susannah, translated from the Hebrew by Dalia Bilu, Harvill Press, 2002
Mahon, J.W., and Mahon, E.M., eds: The Merchant of Venice: critical essays, Routledge, 2002
Mail, M.: Coralena, Simon & Schuster, 2002
Miller, A.: Focus, with an afterword: antisemitism then and now, Methuen, 2000
Morris, R.: Take him a nation: a novel of independent Scotland, Iumix, 2002
Nisly, L.L.: Impossible to say: representing religious mystery in fiction by Malamud, Percy, Ozick, and O'Connor, Greenwood Press, 2002

Oz, A.: Fima, translated from the Hebrew by Nicholas de Lange in collaboration with the author, Vintage Books, 2002
Peleg, D.: Miss Fanny's voice, translated from the Hebrew by Michael Sapir in collaboration with the author, Jonathan Cape, 2001
Richler, E.: Sister crazy, Flamingo, 2001
Roth, J.: Collected shorter fiction, translated by Michael Hofmann, Granta, 2001
Rudnor, R.: Tickled pink, Little, Brown, 2002
Sebald, W.G.: Austerlitz, translated from the German by Anthea Bell, Penguin Books, 2002
Sheridan, Y.: From here to obscurity: a novel, Tenterbooks, 2002
Stead, C.K.: The secret history of modernism, Harvill Press, 2001
Szerb, A.: Journey by moonlight, translated from the Hungarian by Len Rix, Pushkin Press, 2001
Taylor, K.: Address unknown, Souvenir Press, 2002
Weiner, S.: Arnost, Starhaven in association with the European Jewish Publication Association, 2001
Wesker, A.: Catching up with Wesker, David Higham Associates, 2002

Middle East

Allan, T.: The Middle East water question: hydropolitics and the global economy, I.B. Tauris, 2002
Almog, O.: Britain, Israel and the US, 1956–1958: beyond Suez, Frank Cass, 2002
Ben-Zvi, A.: John F. Kennedy and the politics of arms sales to Israel, Frank Cass, 2002
Bruce, A.: The last crusade: the Palestine Campaign in the First World War, John Murray, 2002
Gazit, M.: Israeli diplomacy and the Middle East Peace Process, Frank Cass, 2002
Gelber, Y.: Palestine 1948: war, escape and the emergence of the Palestinian refugee problem, Sussex Academic Press, 2001
Ghanem, A.: The Palestinian regime: a 'partial democracy', Sussex Academic Press, 2001
Gilbert, M.: The Routledge atlas of the Arab–Israeli conflict: the complete history of the struggle and efforts to resolve it, Routledge, 2002
Ginat, J., and Perkins, E.J., eds: The Middle East peace process: vision versus reality, foreword by Prince El Hassan bin Talal; preface by David L. Boren, Sussex Academic Press in association with the University of Oklahoma Press, 2002
Goldscheider, C.: Cultures in conflict: the Arab–Israeli conflict, Greenwood Publishing Group, 2001
Israeli, R.: Jerusalem divided: the Armistice regime, 1947–1967, Frank Cass, 2002
Jacoby, T.A., and Sasley, B., eds: Redefining security in the Middle East, Manchester University Press, 2002
Levin, I.: Locked doors: the seizure of Jewish property in Arab countries, translated by Rachel Neiman, Greenwood Publishing Group, 2001
Mishal, S., *et al*.: Investment in peace: the politics of economic cooperation between Israel, Jordan, and the Palestinians, Sussex Academic Press, 2001
Morris, B.: The road to Jerusalem: Glubb Pasha, Palestine and the Jews, I.B. Tauris, 2002
Oren, M.: Six days of war: June 1967 and the making of the modern Middle East, Oxford University Press, 2002
Pappe, I., ed.: The Israel/Palestine question, Routledge, 2002.
Penkower, M.N.: Decision on Palestine deferred: how America and Britain stalled in the Second World War, Frank Cass, 2002
Podeh, E.: The Arab–Israeli conflict in Israeli history textbooks, 1948–2000, Bergin & Garvey, Greenwood Publishing Group, 2001

Rubin, B.: The tragedy of the Middle East, Cambridge University Press, 2002
Shalom, Z.: David Ben-Gurion, the State of Israel, and the Arab world, 1949–1956, Sussex Academic Press, 2002
Stewart, N.: The Royal Navy and the Palestine Patrol, 1945–1949; with a foreword by the First Sea Lord, Frank Cass, 2002
Tal, D., ed.: War and Palestine, 1948: strategy and diplomacy, Frank Cass, 2002

Booksellers

The booksellers listed below specialise in Jewish books. Many also supply religious requisites.

GREATER LONDON

J. Aisenthal, 11 Ashbourne Pde., Finchley Rd., NW11. ☎ 020-8455 0501. Fax 0208-455 0501. E-mail info@aisenthal.co.uk. Website www.aisenthal.co.uk

Blue & White Shop, 439 Cranbrook Road, Ilford, Essex, IG2 6EW. ☎ 020-8518 1982.

Carmel Gifts, 62 Edgware Way, Middx. ☎ 020-8958 7632. Fax: 020-8958 6226.

Daunt Books, Belsize Bookshop, Haverstock Hill, NW3. ☎ 020-7794 4006.

Aubrey Goldstein, 7 Windsor Court, Chase Side, N14 5HT. ☎ 020-8886 4075.

R. Golub & Co. Ltd., 305 Eastern Av., Gants Hill, Ilford, Essex IG2 6NT. ☎ 020-8550 6751.

Hasifria: The Israeli Music & Book Shop of London, Unit 4, Sentinel Square, Brent Street, Hendon, London NW4 2EL. ☎ 020-8202 2118. Fax 020-8203 4914. Email hasifria@ hotmail.com. Website www.hasifria.cwc.net.

Hebrew Book & Gift Centre (M.E. Hochhauser), 24 Amhurst Parade, N16 5AA. ☎/Fax 020-8802 0609.

B. Horwitz–Judaica World, Unit 23, Dollis Hill Estate, 105 Brook Rd., NW2 7BZ. ☎ 07970-018692. Fax 0161-740 5897.

Jerusalem the Golden, 146a Golders Green Rd., NW11 8HE. ☎ 020-8455 4960 or 8458 7011. Fax: 020-8203 7808.

Jewish Memorial Council Bookshop, 25 Enford St., W1H 1DW. ☎ 020-7724 7778. Fax: 020-7706 1710. Email: jmcbookshop@btinternet.com (Mail order only available). Contact: J. Zaltzman, B. Carp.

John Trotter Books, 80 East End Rd., N3 2SY. ☎ 020-8349 9484. Fax: 020-8346 7430. Email jtrotter@freenetname.co.uk; Website www.abebooks.com/home/johntrotter. Rare and second-hand Judaica, Hebraica.

Joseph's Bookstore, 1255-1257 Finchley Rd., NW11 0AD. ☎ 020-8731 7575; Fax 020-8731 6699. Email info@josephsbookstore.com. Website www.josephsbookstore.com.

H. Karnac (Books) Limited, 58 Gloucester Road, SW7 4QY.

Kuperard, 311 Ballards Lane, N12 8LY. ☎ 020-8446 2440. Fax 020-8446 2441. Email kuperard@bravo.clara.net. Website www.kuperard.co.uk (publishers and distributors, mail order, educational suppliers, book fairs, book launches).

Manor House Bookshop, Sternberg Centre, 80 East End Road, N3 2SY. ☎ 020-8349 9484. Fax 020-8346 7430. E-mail jtrotter@freenetname.co.uk.

Menorah Book Centre, 16 Russell Parade, Golders Green Rd., NW11 9NN. ☎ 020-8458 8289.

Mesorah Bookstore, 61 Old Hill St., N16 6LU. ☎ 020-8809 4310.

Muswell Hill Bookshop, 72 Fortis Green Rd., N10 3HN. ☎ 020-8444 7588.

M. Rogosnitzky, 20 The Drive, NW11 9SR. ☎ 020-8455 7645 or 4112.

On Your Doorstep (Sandra E. Breger), 1 Rosecroft Walk, Pinner, Middlesex HA5 1LJ. ☎ 020-8866 6236.

Selfridges Departmental Store, Jewish Section of Book Dept., Oxford St., W1A 1AB. ☎ 020-7629 1234.

Stamford Hill Stationers, 153 Clapton Common, E5 9AE. ☎ 020-8802 5222. Fax 020-8802 5224.

Steimatzky Hasifria, 46 Golders Green Road, NW11 8LL. ☎ 020-8458 9774. Fax 020-8458 3449. Email shirley@hasifria.com. Website www.hasifria.com.

Torah Treasures, 4 Sentinel Sq., NW4 2EL. ☎ 020-8202 3134. Fax 020-8202 3161.

Email torahtreasures@btinternet.com.
WH Smith, Brent Cross Shopping Centre, NW4. ☎ 020-8202 4226.
Waterstone's, 68 Hampstead High St., NW3 1QP. ☎ 020-7794 1098.
Waterstone's, 82 Gower St., WC1E 6EG. ☎ 020-7636 1577.
The Woburn Book Shop, 10 Woburn Walk, WC1H 0JL (near The Place Theatre), ☎ 020-7388 7278.

REGIONS

BIRMINGHAM Lubavitch Bookshop, 95 Willows Rd., B12 9QF. ☎ 0121-440 6673. Fax: 0121-446 4199.

GATESHEAD J. Lehmann Retail: 28-30 Grasmere St. West, NE8 1TS. ☎ 0191-477 3523; Mail order and wholesale: Unit E, Viking Industrial Park, Rolling Mill Road, Jarrow, Tyne & Wear NE32 3DP. ☎ 0191-430 0555. Email info@lehmanns.co.uk.

GLASGOW J. & E. Levingstone, 47 & 55 Sinclair Dr., G42 9PT. ☎ 0141-649 2962. Fax 0141-649 2962.

LEICESTER Bookshop: Com. Centre, Highfield St. LE2 0NQ. Inq.: J. Markham, 74 Wakerley Rd., LE5 6AQ. ☎ 0116 2128920.

LIVERPOOL Jewish Book & Gift Centre, Harold House, Dunbabin Rd., L15 6XL. Sun. only, 11 a.m. to 1 p.m. Orders ☎ 0151-722 5021. Fax 0151 475 2212.

MANCHESTER & SALFORD

J. Goldberg, 11 Parkside Ave., Salford, M7 0HB. ☎ 0161-740 0732.
Hasefer, 18 Merrybower Rd., Salford M7 0HE. ☎ 0161-740 3013.
B. Horwitz (Wholesale & retail Judaica), 20 King Edward Bldgs., Bury Old Rd., M8. ☎ 0161-740 5897, & 2 Kings Rd., Prestwich. ☎ 0161-773 4956.
Jewish Book Centre (Mr Klein), 25 Ashbourne Gr., Salford, M7 4DB. ☎ 0161-792 1253. Fax 0161-661 5505.

OXFORD B. H. Blackwell Ltd., 48-51 Broad St., OX1 3BQ. ☎ 01865 792792. Fax 01865 261 355. Email blackwells.extra@blackwell.co.uk. Has a Jewish book section.

SOUTHEND Dorothy Young, 21 Colchester Rd., SS2 6HW. ☎ 01702 331218 for appointment. Email dorothy@dorothyyoung.co.uk. Website www.dorothyyoung.co.uk.

PRINCIPAL FESTIVALS AND FASTS 2002–2010 (5763–5770)

Festival or Fast	Hebrew Date	5763 2002-03	5764 2003-04	5765 2004-05	5766 2005-06	5767 2006-07	5768 2007-08	5769 2008-09	5770 2009-10
New Year	Tishri 1	Sept. 7	Sept. 27	Sept. 16	Oct. 4	Sept. 23	Sept. 13	Sept. 30	Sept. 19
Day of Atonement	Tishri 10	Sept. 16	Oct. 6	Sept. 25	Oct. 13	Oct. 2	Sept. 22	Oct. 9	Sept. 28
Tabernacles, 1st Day	Tishri 15	Sept. 21	Oct. 11	Sept. 30	Oct. 18	Oct. 7	Sept. 27	Oct.14	Oct. 3
Tabernacles, 8th Day	Tishri 22	Sept. 28	Oct. 18	Oct. 7	Oct. 25	Oct. 14	Oct. 4	Oct. 21	Oct. 10
Rejoicing of the Law	Tishri 23	Sept. 29	Oct. 19	Oct. 8	Oct. 26	Oct. 15	Oct. 5	Oct. 22	Oct. 11
Chanucah	Kislev 25	Nov. 30	Dec. 20	Dec. 8	Dec. 26	Dec. 16	Dec. 5	Dec. 22	Dec. 12
Purim	Adar[1] 14	Mar. 18	Mar. 7	Mar. 25	Mar. 14	Mar. 4	Mar. 21	Mar. 10	Feb. 28
Passover, 1st Day	Nisan 15	Apr. 17	Apr. 6	Apr. 24	Apr. 13	Apr. 3	Apr. 20	Apr. 9	Mar. 30
Passover, 7th Day	Nisan 21	Apr. 23	Apr. 12	Apr. 30	Apr. 19	Apr. 9	Apr. 26	Apr.15	Apr. 5
Israel Indep. Day	Iyar 5[2]	May 7	Apr. 26	May 12	May 3	Apr. 23	May 8	Apr. 29	Apr. 19
Feast of Weeks	Sivan 6	June 6	May 26	June 13	June 2	May 23	June 9	May 29	May 19
Fast of Ab	Ab 9	Aug. 7	July 27	Aug. 14	Aug. 3	July 24	Aug. 10	July 30	July 20

1. Ve-Adar 14 in Leap Years.
2. When this date occurs on Friday or Sabbath, Israel Independence Day is observed on the previous Thursday.

THE JEWISH CALENDAR

The Jewish Calendar is a lunar one, adapted to the solar year by various expedients. The hour is divided into 1,080 portions or *minims*, and the month between one new moon and the next is reckoned as 29 days, 12 hours, 793 minims. The years are grouped in cycles of 19. The present calendar was fixed by the Palestinian Jewish Patriarch, Hillel II, in 358 C.E. In early Talmudic times the new moons were fixed by the actual observation, and were announced from Jerusalem to the surrounding districts and countries by messenger or beacon.

If the time elapsing between one new moon and another were *exactly* 29½ days, the length of the months could be fixed at alternately 29 and 30 days. But there are three corrections to make which disturb this regularity: (1) The excess of 793 minims over the half day, (2) the adjustment to the solar year, (3) the requirement that the incidence of certain Jewish festivals shall not conflict with the Sabbath. To overcome these difficulties the Jewish Calendar recognises six different classes of years; three of them common and three leap. The leap years, which are the 3rd, 6th, 8th, 11th, 14th, 17th, and 19th of the Metyonic cycle of 19 years, are composed of thirteen months, an additional month being added. It is usually stated that this intercalary month is inserted after the month of Adar which in the ordinary year is of 29 days, but in a leap year has 30 days, but in reality the inserted month precedes the ordinary Adar and always has 30 days. Both the common and the leap years may be either regular, "minimal" , or full. The regular year has an alternation of 30 and 29 days. The "minimal" year gives Kislev only 29 days instead of 30, while in a full year Marcheshvan has 30 instead of 29 days.

Besides the lunar cycle of 19 years there is a solar cycle of 28 years, at the beginning of which the *Tekufah* of Nisan (the vernal equinox) returns to the same day and the same hour.

The chief disturbing influence in the arrangement of the Jewish Calendar is to prevent the Day of Atonement (Tishri 10th) from either immediately preceding or immediately succeeding the Sabbath, and Hoshana Rabba (Tishri 21st) from falling on the Sabbath. Consequently the New Year (Tishri Ist) cannot fall upon Sunday, Wednesday or Friday. A further complication of a purely astronomical character is introduced by the consideration that the Jewish day formally commences six hours before midnight. Hence, if the Molad or lunar conjunction for the month of Tishri occurs at noon or later, the new moon will be seen only after 6 p.m. and the Festival is postponed to the next day. When, after paying regard to these and certain other considerations, the days upon which two successive New Year Festivals fall are determined, the number of days in the intervening year is known and the length of Marcheshvan and Kislev is fixed accordingly.

It is customary to describe the character of a Jewish Year by a "Determinative" consisting of three Hebrew letters. The first of these indicates the day of the week upon which the New Year Festival falls, the second whether the year is regular, "minimal", or full, and the third the day of the week upon which Passover occurs. To this "Determinative" is added the Hebrew word for "ordinary" or "leap".

Authorities differ regarding the manner in which the figure employed for the Jewish Era (this year 5763) is arrived at. It is sufficient to describe it as the "Mundane Era" (dating from the Creation of the World) or the "Adamic Era" (dating from the Creation of Man). The chronology is based on Biblical data.

For the beginning of Sabbaths and Festivals, rules were laid down for the latitude of London by David Nieto, Haham of the Sephardi Community (1702-1728). The hours for nightfall given here are based on those fixed by Nathan Marcus Adler, Chief

Rabbi, in accordance with the formula of Michael Friedlander, Principal of Jews' College, but adjusted to take account of the movement of the Jewish population within the Metropolis since their day.

THE JEWISH YEAR

The times in this calendar for the beginning and ending of Sabbaths, Festivals and Fasts are given in Greenwich Mean Time from January 1 to March 29 and October 26 to the end, and in British Summer Time from March 30 to October 25, 2003.

5763

is known as **763** on the short system, and is a full leap year of 13 months, 55 Sabbaths and 385 days. Its first of Tishri is on a Sabbath, and the first day of Passover on a Thursday.

It is the sixth year of the 304th minor or lunar cycle (of 19 years each) since the Era of Creation, and the twenty-third of the 206th major or solar cycle (of 28 years each) since the same epoch.

The year began on Friday evening, September 6, 2002, and concludes on Friday, September 26, 2003.

5764

is known as **764** on the short system, and is a full common year of 12 months, 51 Sabbaths and 355 days. Its first of Tishri is on a Sabbath, and the first day of Passover on a Tuesday.

It is the seventh year of the 304th minor or lunar cycle (of 19 years each) since the Era of Creation, and the twenty-fourth of the 206th major or solar cycle (of 28 years each) since the same epoch.

The year begins on Friday evening, September 26, 2003, and concludes on Wednesday, September 15, 2004.

CALENDAR NOTES

Pent. denotes Pentateuchal readings; **Proph.** denotes Prophetical readings.

Parentheses in either of the above denote Sephardi ritual.

Times for the commencement of the Sabbath during the summer months are, as is the tradition in Britain, given as 20.00. The actual times are given in parentheses.

ABRIDGED JEWISH CALENDAR FOR 2003 (5763-5764)

New Moon Shebat, 5763	Saturday	2003 January 4
New Year for Trees	Saturday	18
New Moon I Adar, 1st day	Sunday	February 2
Minor Purim	Sunday	16
Minor Shushan Purim	Monday	17
New Moon II Adar, 1st day	Tuesday	March 4
Fast of Esther	Monday	17
Purim	Tuesday	18
Shushan Purim	Wednesday	19
New Moon Nisan	Thursday	April 3
Fast of Firstborn	Wednesday	16
First Day Passover	Thursday	17
Second Day Passover	Friday	18
Seventh Day Passover	Wednesday	23
Eighth Day Passover	Thursday	24
Holocaust Memorial Day	Tuesday	29
New Moon Iyar, 1st Day	Friday	May 2
Israel Independence Day	Wednesday	7
Minor Passover	Friday	16
Thirty-third day of the (Lag Ba') Omer	Tuesday	20
Jerusalem Day	Friday	30
New Moon Sivan	Sunday	June 1
First Day Feast of Weeks	Friday	6
Second Day Feast of Weeks	Saturday	7
New Moon Tammuz, 1st day	Monday	30
Fast of Tammuz	Thursday	July 17
New Moon Ab	Wednesday	30
Fast of Ab	Thursday	August 7
Festival of 15th Ab	Wednesday	13
New Moon Elul, 1st day	Thursday	28
First Day New Year, 5764	Saturday	September 27
Second Day New Year	Sunday	28
Fast of Gedaliah	Monday	29
Day of Atonement	Monday	October 6
First Day Tabernacles	Saturday	11
Second Day Tabernacles	Sunday	12
Hoshana Rabba	Friday	17
Eighth Day of Solemn Assembly	Saturday	18
Rejoicing of the Law	Sunday	19
New Moon Marcheshvan, 1st day	Sunday	26
New Moon Kislev, 1st day	Tuesday	November 25
First Day Chanucah	Saturday	December 20
New Moon Tebet, 1st day	Thursday	25

ABRIDGED JEWISH CALENDAR FOR 2004 (5764-5765)

Fast of Tebet, 5764	Sunday	2004 January 4
New Moon Shebat	Saturday	24
New Year for Trees	Saturday	February 7
New Moon Adar, 1st day	Sunday	22
Fast of Esther	Thursday	March 4
Purim	Sunday	7
Shushan Purim	Monday	8
New Moon Nisan	Tuesday	23
Fast of Firstborn	Monday	April 5
First Day Passover	Tuesday	6
Second Day Passover	Wednesday	7
Seventh Day Passover	Monday	12
Eighth Day Passover	Tuesday	13
Holocaust Memorial Day	Sunday	18
New Moon Iyar, 1st day	Wednesday	21
Israel Independence Day	Monday	26
Minor Passover	Wednesday	May 5
Thirty-third day of the (Lag Ba') Omer	Sunday	9
Jerusalem Day	Wednesday	19
New Moon Sivan	Friday	21
First Day Feast of Weeks	Wednesday	26
Second Day Feast of Weeks	Thursday	27
New Moon Tammuz, 1st day	Saturday	June 19
Fast of Tammuz	Tuesday	July 6
New Moon Ab	Monday	19
Fast of Ab	Tuesday	27
Festival of 15th Ab	Monday	August 2
New Moon Elul, 1st day	Tuesday	17
First Day New Year, 5765	Thursday	September 16
Second Day New Year	Friday	17
Fast of Gedaliah	Sunday	19
Day of Atonement	Saturday	25
First Day Tabernacles	Thursday	30
Second Day Tabernacles	Friday	October 1
Hoshana Rabba	Wednesday	6
Eighth Day of Solemn Assembly	Thursday	7
Rejoicing of the Law	Friday	8
New Moon Marcheshvan, 1st day	Friday	15
New Moon Kislev	Sunday	November 14
First Day Chanucah	Wednesday	December 8
New Moon Tebet	Monday	13
Fast of Tebet	Wednesday	22

JANUARY, 2003 — TEBET 27–SHEBAT 28, 5763

Tekufah Mon Jan 6 22.30 — Molad Fri Jan 3 9h 50m 47s

			Tebet
1	W		27
2	Th	Yom Kippur Katan	28
3	F	Sabbath commences 15.49	29
			Shebat
4	**S**	Rosh Chodesh. Sabbath ends 16.59. **Pent** Va'era, Ex **6**, 2-**9** and Num **28**, 9-15. **Proph** Is **66**	**1**
5	S		2
6	M		3
7	T		4
8	W		5
9	Th		6
10	F	Sabbath commences 15.58	7
11	**S**	Sabbath ends 17.07. **Pent** Bo, Ex **10**, 1-**13**, 16. **Proph** Jer **46**, 13-28	**8**
12	S		9
13	M		10
14	T		11
15	W		12
16	Th		13
17	F	Sabbath commences 16.09	14
18	**S**	**New Year for Trees**. Sabbath ends 17.17. **Pent** Beshallach, Shabbat Shirah, Ex **13**, 17-**17**. **Proph** Judges **4**, 4-**5** (**5**, 1-31)	**15**
19	S		16
20	M		17
21	T		18
22	W		19
23	Th		20
24	F	Sabbath commences 16.20	21
25	**S**	Sabbath ends 17.28. **Pent** Yitro, Ex **18-20**. **Proph** Is **6**, 1-**7**, 6 and **9**, 5-6 (**6**, 1-13).	**22**
26	S		23
27	M	Holocaust Day (National)	24
28	T		25
29	W		26
30	Th	Yom Kippur Katan	27
31	F	Sabbath commences 16.33	28

Liturgical notes – Jan 4, Half-Hallel; omit Tsidkatcha Tsedek in Minchah.–Jan 18, omit Tsidkatcha Tsedek in Minchah.

FEBRUARY, 2003 SHEBAT 29–ADAR RISHON 26, 5763

Molad Sat Feb 1 22h 34m 50s

			Shebat
1	**S**	Sabbath ends 17.39. **Pent** Mishpatim, Ex **21-24**. **Proph** Machar Chodesh I Sam **20**, 18-42. Benediction of Adar Rishon.	**29**
2	S	Rosh Chodesh first day. **Pent** Num **28**, 1-15	30
			Adar Rishon
3	M	Rosh Chodesh second day. **Pent** Num **28**, 1-15	1
4	T		2
5	W		3
6	Th		4
7	F	Sabbath commences 16.45	5
8	**S**	Sabbath ends 17.51. **Pent** Terumah, Ex **25**, 1-**27**, 19. **Proph** I Kings **5**, 26-**6**, 13	**6**
9	S		7
10	M		8
11	T		9
12	W		10
13	Th		11
14	F	Sabbath commences 16.58	12
15	**S**	Sabbath ends 18.03. **Pent** Tetsaveh, Ex **27**, 20-**30**, 10. **Proph** Ezek **43**, 10-27	**13**
16	S	Minor Purim.	14
17	M	Minor Shushan Purim.	15
18	T		16
19	W		17
20	Th		18
21	F	Sabbath commences 17.11	19
22	**S**	Sabbath ends 18.15. **Pent** Ki Tissa, Ex **30**, 11-**34**. **Proph** I Kings **18**, 1-39 (20-39).	**20**
23	S		21
24	M		22
25	T		23
26	W		24
27	Th		25
28	F	Sabbath commences 17.24	26

Liturgical notes – Feb 1, omit Tsidkatcha Tsedek in Minchah.–Feb 2 and 3, Half-Hallel.–Feb 15, omit Tsidkatcha Tsedek in Minchah.–Feb 16, omit Tachanun and Lamenatse'ach.–Feb 17, omit Tachanun, El Erech Appayim and Lamenatse'ach.

MARCH, 2003 ADAR RISHON 27–ADAR SHENI 27, 5763

Molad Mon March 3 11h 18m 53s

			Adar Rishon
1	**S**	Sabbath ends 18.26. **Pent** Vayakhel. Parshat Shekalim, Ex **35**, 1-**38**, 20 and **30**, 11-16. Proph II Kings **12**, 1-17 (**11**, 17-**12**, 17). Benediction of Adar Sheni.	**27**
2	S		28
3	M	Yom Kippur Katan	29
4	T	Rosh Chodesh first day. **Pent** Num **28**, 1-15	30
			Adar Sheni
5	W	Rosh Chodesh second day. **Pent** Num **28**, 1-15	1
6	Th		2
7	F	Sabbath commences 17.36	3
8	**S**	Sabbath ends 18.40. **Pent** Pekudei, Ex **38**, 21 to end of book. **Proph** I Kings **7**, 51-**8**, 21 (others **7**, 40-50)	**4**
9	S		5
10	M		6
11	T		7
12	W		8
13	Th		9
14	F	Sabbath commences 17.49	10
15	**S**	Sabbath ends 18.52. **Pent** Vayikra, Parshat Zachor, Lev **1-5** and Deut **25**, 17-19. **Proph** I Sam **15**, 2-34 (**15**, 1-34)	**11**
16	S		12
17	**M**	**Fast of Esther** ends 18.49. **Pent** morning and afternoon Ex **32**, 11-14 and **34**, 1-10. **Proph** afternoon only Is **55**, 6-**56**, 8 (none)	**13**
18	**T**	**Purim. Pent** Ex **17**, 8-16	**14**
19	W	Shushan Purim	15
20	Th		16
21	F	Sabbath commences 18.01	17
22	**S**	Sabbath ends 19.04. **Pent** Tsav, Parshat Parah, Lev **6-8**, and Num **19** **Proph** Ezek **36**, 16-38 (16-36)	**18**
23	S		19
24	M		20
25	T		21
26	W		22
27	Th		23
28	F	Sabbath commences 18.12	24
29	**S**	Sabbath ends 19.16. **Pent** Shemini, Parshat Hachodesh. Lev **9-11** and Ex **12**, 1-20. **Proph** Ezek **45**, 16-**46**, 18 (**45**, 18-**46**, 15). Benediction of Nisan	**25**
30	S		26
31	M		27

Liturgical notes – March 3, omit Tachanun in Minchah.–March 4 and 5, Half-Hallel.–March 17, Selichot, Aneinu; omit Tachanun in Minchah; Al Hannissim is said in Maariv; Book of Esther is read; Half-Shekel is given.–March 18, Al Hannissim said; Book of Esther read in morning; omit Tachanun and Lamenatse'ach.–March 19, omit Tachanun and Lamenatse'ach.

APRIL, 2003 — ADAR SHENI 28–NISAN 28, 5763

Tekufah Tues Apr 8 06.00 — Molad Wed Apr 2 0h 2m 57s

Date	Day	Events	Omer days	Adar Sheni / Nisan
				Adar Sheni
1	T			28
2	W	Yom Kippur Katan		29
				Nisan
3	Th	Rosh Chodesh. **Pent** Num **28**, 1-15		1
4	F	Sabbath commences 19.24		2
5	**S**	Sabbath ends 20.29. Pent Tazria, Lev **12-13**. **Proph** II Kings **4**, 42-**5**, 19		**3**
6	S			4
7	M			5
8	T			6
9	W			7
10	Th			8
11	F	Sabbath commences 19.36		9
12	**S**	Sabbath ends 20.41. **Pent** Metsora, Shabbat Haggadol, Lev **14-15**. **Proph** Mal **3**, 4-24		**10**
13	S			11
14	M			12
15	T			13
16	W	**Fast of Firstborn**. Eruv Tavshilin. Festival commences 19.44. **First Seder** in evening		14
17	**Th**	**Passover first day** ends 20.51. **Second Seder** in evening. **Pent** Ex **12**, 21-51; Num **28**, 16-25. **Proph** Josh **5**, 2-**6**, 1 (and **6**,27).		**15**
18	**F**	**Passover second day**. Sabbath commences 19.48. **Pent** Lev **22**, 26-**23**, 44; Num **28**, 16-25. **Proph** II Kings **23**, 1-9 and 21-25.	1	**16**
19	**S**	Sabbath ends 20.55. **Pent** Ex **33**, 12-**34**, 26; Num **28**, 19-25. **Proph** Ezek **37**, 1-14.	2	**17**
20	S	**Pent** Ex **13**, 1-16; Num **28**, 19-25	3	18
21	M	**Pent** Ex **22**, 24-**23**, 19; Num **28**, 19-25	4	19
22	T	Festival commences 19.54. **Pent** Num **9**, 1-14 and **28**, 19-25	5	20
23	**W**	**Passover seventh day** ends 21.02. **Pent** Ex **13**, 17-**15**, 26; Num **28**, 19-25; **Proph** II Samuel **22**	6	**21**
24	**Th**	**Passover eighth day** ends 21.04. **Pent** Deut **15**, 19-**16**, 17; Num **28**, 19-25. **Proph** Is **10**, 32-**12**, 6	7	**22**
25	F	Issru Chag. Sabbath commences 19.59	8	23
26	**S**	Sabbath ends 21.08. **Pent** Acharei Mot, Lev **16-18**. **Proph** Amos **9**, 7-15 (Ezek. **22**, 1-16) Benediction of Iyar. Ethics 1.	9	**24**
27	S		10	25
28	M		11	26
29	T	**Holocaust Memorial Day**	12	27
30	W		13	28

Liturgical notes – April 2, omit Tachanun in Minchah.–April 3, Half-Hallel.–April 4 to 16, omit Tachanun.–April 5 and 12, omit Tsidkatcha Tsedek in Minchah.–April 12, read from Haggadah and discontinue Barachi Nafshi in Minchah; omit Vihi Noam in Maariv.–April 15, Bedikat Chamets in evening.–April 16, omit Mizmor Letodah and Lamenatse'ach; abstain from Chamets by 10.41; Biur Chamets; discontinue Tal Umatar after Minchah.–April 17, discontinue Mashiv Haruach in Mussaf; in the evening commence counting the Omer.–April 17 and 18, Whole-Hallel.–April 19 to 24, Half-Hallel.–April 19, read Song of Songs; omit Tsidkatcha Tsedek in Minchah and Vihi Noam in Maariv.–April 20 to 22, omit Mizmor Letodah.–April 25 to 30, omit Tachanun.–April 26, omit Tsidkatcha Tsedek in Minchah.

MAY, 2003 — NISAN 29–IYAR 29, 5763

Molad Iyar Thurs May 1 12h 47m 0s
Molad Sivan Sat May 31 1h 31m 3s

			Omer days	Nisan
1	Th		14	29
2	F	Rosh Chodesh first day. Sabbath commences 20.00 (20.11) **Pent** Num **28**, 1-15	15	30
				Iyar
3	**S**	Rosh Chodesh second day. Sabbath ends 21.21 **Pent** Kedoshim, Lev **19-20** and Num **28**, 9-15. **Proph** Is **66**. Ethics 2.	16	**1**
4	S		17	2
5	M		18	3
6	T		19	4
7	**W**	**Yom Ha'atsma'ut – Israel Independence Day**	20	**5**
8	Th		21	6
9	F	Sabbath commences 20.00 (20.22)	22	7
10	**S**	Sabbath ends 21.34. **Pent** Emor, Lev **21-24**. **Proph** Ezek **44**, 15-31. Ethics 3	23	**8**
11	S		24	9
12	M	**First fast day** ends 21.32	25	10
13	T		26	11
14	W		27	12
15	Th	**Second fast day** ends 21.37	28	13
16	F	**Minor Passover**. Sabbath commences 20.00 (20.33)	29	14
17	**S**	Sabbath ends 21.47. **Pent** Behar, Lev **25-26**, 2. **Proph** Jer **32**, 6-27. Ethics 4	30	**15**
18	S		31	16
19	M	**Third fast day** ends 21.44	32	17
20	**T**	**Lag b'Omer–Scholars' festival**	33	**18**
21	W		34	19
22	Th		35	20
23	F	Sabbath commences 20.00 (20.43)	36	21
24	**S**	Sabbath ends 21.59. **Pent** Bechukkotai, Lev **26**, 3 to end of book. **Proph** Jer **16**, 19-**17**, 14. Ethics 5	37	**22**
25	S		38	23
26	M		39	24
27	T		40	25
28	W		41	26
29	Th	Yom Kippur Katan	42	27
30	F	Sabbath commences 20.00 (20.52). **Yom Yerushalayim–Jerusalem Day**	43	28
31	**S**	Sabbath ends 22.10. **Pent** Bemidbar, Num **1-4**, 20. **Proph** Machar Chodesh, I Sam **20**, 18-42. Benediction of Sivan. Ethics 6.	44	**29**

Liturgical notes – May 1, omit Tachanun.–May 2 and 3, Half-Hallel.–May 3, omit Tsidkatcha Tsedek in Minchah.–May 7, see Order of Service and Customs for Israel Independence Day (pubd. Routledge & Kegan Paul, 1964).–May 12, 15 & 19, Selichot are said in some communities and, if there be a Minyan who fast, Vay'chal is read.–May 19, omit Tachanun in Minchah.–May 20, omit Tachanun.–May 31, say Av Harachamim in morning service; omit Tsidkatcha Tsedek in Minchah and Vihi Noam in Maariv.

JUNE, 2003 — SIVAN 1-30, 5763

Molad Tammuz Sun June 29 14h 15m 7s

			Omer days	Sivan
1	S	Rosh Chodesh. **Pent** Num **28**, 1-15	45	1
2	M		46	2
3	T		47	3
4	W		48	4
5	Th	Festival commences 20.00 (20.58). Eruv Tavshilin	49	5
6	**F**	**Feast of Weeks** first day. Sabbath commences 20.00 (20.59) **Pent** Ex **19-20**. Num **28**, 26-31. **Proph** Ezek **1** and **3**, 12		**6**
7	**S**	**Feast of Weeks** second day. Sabbath and Festival end 22.19. **Pent** Deut **14**, 22-**16**, 17; Num **28**, 26-31; **Proph** Habak **2**, 20-**3**, 19		**7**
8	S	Issru Chag		8
9	M			9
10	T			10
11	W			11
12	Th			12
13	F	Sabbath commences 20.00 (21.04)		13
14	**S**	Sabbath ends 22.25. **Pent** Naso, Num **4**, 21-**7**. **Proph** Judges **13**, 2-25. Ethics 1.		**14**
15	S			15
16	M			16
17	T			17
18	W			18
19	Th			19
20	F	Sabbath commences 20.00 (21.07)		20
21	**S**	Sabbath ends 22.28. **Pent** Beha'alotecha, Num **8-12**. **Proph** Zech **2**, 14-**4**, 7 Ethics 2.		**21**
22	S			22
23	M			23
24	T			24
25	W			25
26	Th			26
27	F	Sabbath commences 20.00 (21.08)		27
28	**S**	Sabbath ends 22.27. **Pent** Shelach Lecha, Num **13-15**. **Proph** Joshua **2** Benediction of Tammuz. Ethics 3.		**28**
29	S	Yom Kippur Katan		29
30	M	Rosh Chodesh first day. **Pent** Num **28**, 1-15		30

Liturgical notes – June 1, Half-Hallel.–June 2 to 5, omit Tachanun.–June 6 and 7, Whole-Hallel.–June 7, Book of Ruth is read.–June 8, omit Tachanun.–June 29, omit Tachanun in Minchah.–June 30, Half-Hallel.

JULY, 2003 — TAMMUZ 1–AB 2, 5763

Tekufah Tues July 8 13.30

Molad Ab Tues July 29 2h 59m 10s

			Tammuz
1	T	Rosh Chodesh second day. **Pent** Num **28**, 1-15	1
2	W		2
3	Th		3
4	F	Sabbath commences 20.00 (21.06)	4
5	**S**	Sabbath ends 22.24. **Pent** Korach, Num **16-18**. **Proph** I Sam **11**, 14-**12**, 22. Ethics 4.	**5**
6	S		6
7	M		7
8	T		8
9	W		9
10	Th		10
11	F	Sabbath commences 20.00 (21.01)	11
12	**S**	Sabbath ends 22.17. **Pent** Chukkat-Balak, Num **19-25**, 9. **Proph** Micah **5**, 6-**6**,8. Ethics 5	**12**
13	S		13
14	M		14
15	T		15
16	W		16
17	**Th**	**Fast of Tammuz** ends 22.05. **Pent** Morning and afternoon. Ex **32**, 11-14 and **34**, 1-10. **Proph** Afternoon only Is. **55**, 6-**56**, 8 (none)	**17**
18	F	Sabbath commences 20.00 (20.54)	18
19	**S**	Sabbath ends 22.08. **Pent** Pinchas, Num **25**, 10-**30**, 1. **Proph** Jer **1-2**, 3. Ethics 6	**19**
20	S		20
21	M		21
22	T		22
23	W		23
24	Th		24
25	F	Sabbath commences 20.00 (20.45)	25
26	**S**	Sabbath ends 21.56. **Pent** Mattot-Massei, Num **30**, 2-end of book. **Proph** Jer **2**, 4-28; **3**, 4 (Jer **2**, 4-28; **4**, 1-2) Benediction of Ab. Ethics 1	**26**
27	S		27
28	M		28
29	T	Yom Kippur Katan	29
			Ab
30	W	Rosh Chodesh. **Pent** Num **28**, 1-15	1
31	Th		2

Liturgical notes – July 1, Half-Hallel.–July 17, Selichot, Aneinu.–July 29, omit Tachanun in Minchah.–July 30, Half-Hallel.

AUGUST, 2003 — AB 3–ELUL 3, 5763

Molad Elul Wed Aug 27 15h 43m 13s

			Ab
1	F	Sabbath commences 20.00 (20.35)	3
2	**S**	Sabbath ends 21.43. **Pent** Devarim, Shabbat Chazon, Deut **1**, 1-**3**, 22. **Proph** Is **1**, 1-27. Ethics 2	**4**
3	S		5
4	M		6
5	T		7
6	W	Fast commences 20.40	8
7	**Th**	**Fast of Ab** ends 21.27. **Pent** Morning Deut **4**, 25-40; afternoon: Ex **32**, 11-14 and **34**, 1-10. **Proph** Morning Jer **8**, 13-**9**, 23; afternoon Is **55**, 6-**56**, 8 (Hosea **14**, 2-10 and Micah **7**, 18-20)	**9**
8	F	Sabbath commences 20.00 (20.22)	10
9	**S**	Sabbath ends 21.29. **Pent** Va'etchanan, Shabbat Nachamu, Deut **3**, 23-**7**, 11. **Proph** Is **40**, 1-26. Ethics 3	**11**
10	S		12
11	M		13
12	T		14
13	W	**Festival of Ab**	15
14	Th		16
15	F	Sabbath commences 20.00 (20.09)	17
16	**S**	Sabbath ends 21.13. **Pent** Ekev, Deut **7**, 12-**11**, 25. **Proph** Is **49**, 14-**51**, 3. Ethics 4.	**18**
17	S		19
18	M		20
19	T		21
20	W		22
21	Th		23
22	F	Sabbath commences 19.55	24
23	**S**	Sabbath ends 20.57. **Pent** Re'eh, Deut **11**, 26-**16**, 17. **Proph** Is **54**, 11-**55**, 5 Benediction of Elul. Ethics 5	**25**
24	S		26
25	M		27
26	T		28
27	W	Yom Kippur Katan	29
28	Th	Rosh Chodesh first day. **Pent** Num **28**, 1-15	30
			Elul
29	F	Rosh Chodesh second day. Sabbath commences 19.39. **Pent** Num **28**, 1-15	1
30	**S**	Sabbath ends 20.41. **Pent** Shof'tim, Deut **16**, 18-**21**, 9. **Proph** Is **51**, 12-**52**, 12. Ethics 6	**2**
31	S		3

Liturgical notes – Aug 2, say Av Harachamim in morning service.–Aug 6, omit Tachanun in Minchah; Book of Lamentations is read in Maariv.–Aug 7, read Kinot; omit Tachanun, El Erech Appayim and Lamenatse'ach; say Aneinu and insert Nachem in Minchah.–Aug 12, omit Tachanun in Minchah.–Aug 13, omit Tachanun.–Aug 27, omit Tachanun in Minchah.–Aug 28 and 29, Half-Hallel.–Aug 29 and 31, the Shofar is blown.

SEPTEMBER, 2003 — ELUL 4, 5763–TISHRI 4, 5764

Molad Tishri Fri Sept 26 4h 27m 17s

			Elul
1	M		4
2	T		5
3	W		6
4	Th		7
5	F	Sabbath commences 19.24	8
6	**S**	Sabbath ends 20.24. **Pent** Ki-Tetsei, Deut **21**, 10-**25**. **Proph** Is **54**, 1-10. Ethics 1 and 2	**9**
7	S		10
8	M		11
9	T		12
10	W		13
11	Th		14
12	F	Sabbath commences 19.08	15
13	**S**	Sabbath ends 20.07. **Pent** Ki-Tavo, Deut **26-29**, 8. **Proph** Is **60**. Ethics 3 and 4	**16**
14	S		17
15	M		18
16	T		19
17	W		20
18	Th		21
19	F	Sabbath commences 18.52	22
20	**S**	Sabbath ends 19.51. **Pent** Nitsavim-Vayelech. Deut **29**, 9-**31**. **Proph** Is **61**, 10-**63**, 9. Ethics 5 and 6	**23**
21	S		24
22	M		25
23	T		26
24	W		27
25	Th		28
26	F	Sabbath and Festival commence 18.35	29
			Tishri
27	**S**	**New Year 5764 first day**. Sabbath ends 19.34. **Pent** Gen **21**; Num **29**, 1-6. **Proph** I Sam **1**, 1-**2**, 10	**1**
28	**S**	**New Year second day** ends 19.32. **Pent** Gen **22**; Num **29**, 1-6. **Proph** Jer **31**, 2-20	**2**
29	**M**	**Fast of Gedaliah** ends 19.24. **Pent** Morning and afternoon Ex **32**, 11-14; **34**, 1-10. **Proph** Afternoon only Is **55**, 6-**56**, 8 (none)	**3**
30	T		4

Liturgical notes – Sept 1 to 25, the Shofar is blown on weekdays.–Sept 21 to 26, Selichot.–Sept 26, omit Tachanun.–Sept 28, Tashlich.–Sept 29 and 30, Selichot.–Sept 29, Aneinu.

OCTOBER, 2003 TISHRI 5–MARCHESHVAN 5, 5764

Tekufah Tues Oct 7 21.00 | Molad Sat Oct 25 17h 11m 20s

			Tishri
1	W		5
2	Th		6
3	F	Sabbath commences 18.19	7
4	**S**	Sabbath ends 19.18. **Pent** Ha'azinu, Shabbat Shuvah, Deut **32**. **Proph** Hosea **14**, 2-10; Joel **2**, 15-27 (Hosea **14**, 2-10 and Micah **7**, 18-20)	**8**
5	S	**Fast of Atonement** commences 18.15; service at 18.30	9
6	**M**	**Day of Atonement** ends 19.14. **Pent** Morning Lev **16**; Num **29**, 7-11. Afternoon Lev **18**. **Proph** Morning Is **57**, 14-**58**, 14; Afternoon Book of Jonah and Micah **7**, 18-20	**10**
7	T		11
8	W		12
9	Th		13
10	F	Sabbath and Festival commence 18.04	14
11	**S**	**Tabernacles first day**. Sabbath ends 19.03. **Pent** Lev **22**, 26-**23**, 44; Num **29**, 12-16. **Proph** Zech **14**	**15**
12	**S**	**Tabernacles second day** ends 19.01. **Pent** Lev **22**, 26-**23**, 44; Num **29**, 12-16. **Proph** I Kings **8**, 2-21.	**16**
13	M	**Pent** Num **29**, 17-25	17
14	T	**Pent** Num **29**, 20-28	18
15	W	**Pent** Num **29**, 23-31	19
16	Th	**Pent** Num **29**, 26-34	20
17	F	**Hoshana Rabba**, Sabbath and Festival commence 17.49 **Pent** Num **29**, 26-34	21
18	**S**	**Eighth day of Solemn Assembly**. Sabbath ends 18.48 **Pent** Deut **14**, 22-**16**, 17; Num **29**, 35-**30**, 1. **Proph** I Kings **8**, 54-66	**22**
19	**S**	**Rejoicing of the Law** ends 18.46. **Pent** Deut **33-34**; Gen **1-2**, 3; Num **29**, 35-**30**, 1. **Proph** Joshua **1** (**1**, 1-9)	**23**
20	M	Issru Chag	24
21	T		25
22	W		26
23	Th		27
24	F	Sabbath commences 17.34	28
25	**S**	Sabbath ends 18.35. **Pent** Bereshit, Gen **1-6**, 8. **Proph** Machar Chodesh, I Sam **20**, 18-42. Benediction of Marcheshvan	**29**
26	S	Rosh Chodesh first day. **Pent** Num **28**, 1-15	30
			Marcheshvan
27	M	Rosh Chodesh second day. **Pent** Num **28**, 1-15	1
28	T		2
29	W		3
30	Th		4
31	F	Sabbath commences 16.21	5

Liturgical notes – Oct 1 to 5, Selichot said on weekdays.–Oct 4, omit Vihi Noam in Maariv.–Oct 5, omit Mizmor Letodah, Tachanun and Lamenatse'ach; Vidduy said in Minchah.–Oct 7 to 10, omit Tachanun.–Oct 11 to 19, Whole Hallel.–Hoshanot: Oct 11, Om Netsurah; Oct 12, Lema'an Amitach; Oct 13, E'eroch Shu'i; Oct 14, Even Shetiyah; Oct 15, El Lemoshaot; Oct 16, Adon Hammoshia.–Oct 18, Ecclesiastes is read and Mashiv Haruach commenced in Mussaf.–Oct 20, omit Tachanun.–Oct 25, Barachi Nafshi commenced in Minchah and Tsidkatcha Tsedek omitted therein.–Oct 26 and 27, Half-Hallel.

NOVEMBER, 2003 MARCHESHVAN 6–KISLEV 5, 5764

Molad Mon Nov 24 5h 55m 23s

			Marcheshvan
1	**S**	Sabbath ends 17.22. **Pent** Noach, Gen **6**, 9-**11**. **Proph** Is **54**, 1-**55**, 5 (**54**, 1-10)	**6**
2	S		7
3	M		8
4	T		9
5	W		10
6	Th		11
7	F	Sabbath commences 16.08	12
8	**S**	Sabbath ends 17.11. **Pent** Lech Lecha, Gen **12-17**. **Proph** Is **40**, 27-**41**, 16	**13**
9	S		14
10	M		15
11	T		16
12	W		17
13	Th		18
14	F	Sabbath commences 15.58	19
15	**S**	Sabbath ends 17.02. **Pent** Vayera, Gen **18-22**. **Proph** II Kings **4**, 1-37 (**4**, 1-23)	**20**
16	S		21
17	M	**First Fast Day** ends 16.54	22
18	T		23
19	W		24
20	Th	**Second Fast Day** ends 16.50	25
21	F	Sabbath commences 15.49	26
22	**S**	Sabbath ends 16.54. **Pent** Chayei Sarah, Gen **23-25**, 18. **Proph** I Kings **1**, 1-31 Benediction of Kislev	**27**
23	S		28
24	M	**Third Fast Day** ends 16.47. Yom Kippur Katan	29
25	T	Rosh Chodesh first day. **Pent** Num **28**, 1-15	30
			Kislev
26	W	Rosh Chodesh second day. **Pent** Num **28**, 1-15	1
27	Th		2
28	F	Sabbath commences 15.42	3
29	**S**	Sabbath ends 16.49. **Pent** Tol'dot. Gen **25**, 19-**28**, 9. **Proph** Malachi **1**, 1-**2**, 7	**4**
30	S		5

Liturgical notes – Nov 17, 20 & 24, Selichot are said in some communities and, if there be a Minyan who fast, Vay'chal is read.–Nov 24, omit Tachanun in Minchah.–Nov 25 and 26, Half-Hallel.

DECEMBER, 2003 — KISLEV 6–TEBET 6, 5764

Molad Tues Dec 23 18h 39m 27s

			Kislev
1	M		6
2	T		7
3	W		8
4	Th		9
5	F	Sabbath commences 15.38	10
6	**S**	Sabbath ends 16.46. **Pent** Vayetsei, Gen **28**, 10-**32**, 3. **Proph** Hosea **12**, 13-**14**, 10 (**11**, 7-**12**, 12)	**11**
7	S		12
8	M		13
9	T		14
10	W		15
11	Th		16
12	F	Sabbath commences 15.36	17
13	**S**	Sabbath ends 16.46. **Pent** Vayishlach, Gen **32**, 4-**36**. **Proph** Hosea **11**, 7-**12**, 12 (Others, Book of Obadiah)	**18**
14	S		19
15	M		20
16	T		21
17	W		22
18	Th		23
19	F	First Chanucah Light. Sabbath commences 15.38.	24
20	**S**	**Chanucah first day**. Sabbath ends 16.47. **Pent** Vayeshev, Gen **37-40**; Num **7**, 1-17. **Proph** Zech **2**, 14-**4**, 7. Benediction of Tebet	**25**
21	**S**	**Chanucah second day. Pent** Num **7**, 18-29	**26**
22	**M**	**Chanucah third day. Pent** Num **7**, 24-35	**27**
23	**T**	**Chanucah fourth day. Pent** Num **7**, 30-41	**28**
24	**W**	**Chanucah fifth day. Pent** Num **7**, 36-47	**29**
25	**Th**	Rosh Chodesh. **Chanucah sixth day. Pent** Num **28**, 1-15 and **7**, 42-47	**30**
			Tebet
26	**F**	Rosh Chodesh. **Chanucah seventh day.** Sabbath commences 15.41 **Pent** Num **28**, 1-15 and **7**, 48-53	**1**
27	**S**	**Chanucah eighth day**. Sabbath ends 16.52. **Pent** Mikkets, Gen **41-44**, 17; Num **7**, 54-**8**, 4. **Proph** I Kings **7**, 40-50	**2**
28	S		3
29	M		4
30	T		5
31	W		6

Liturgical notes – Dec 6, Tal Umatar commenced in Maariv.–During Chanucah say Al Hannissim and Whole-Hallel; omit Tachanun, El Erech Appayim and Lamenatse'ach, and on Sabbath Tsidkatcha Tsedek in Minchah.

JANUARY, 2004 — TEBET 7–SHEBAT 8, 5764

Tekufah Wed Jan 7 04.30 — Molad Thurs Jan 22 7h 23m 30s

			Tebet
1	Th		7
2	F	Sabbath commences 15.48	8
3	**S**	Sabbath ends 16.58. **Pent** Vayiggash, Gen **44**, 18-**47**, 27. **Proph** Ezek **37**, 15-28	**9**
4	**S**	**Fast of Tebet** ends 16.53. **Pent** Morning and afternoon Ex **32**, 11-14 and **34**, 1-10, **Proph** Afternoon only Is **55**, 6-**56**, 8 (none)	**10**
5	M		11
6	T		12
7	W		13
8	Th		14
9	F	Sabbath commences 15.57	15
10	**S**	Sabbath ends 17.06. **Pent** Vay'chi, Gen **47**, 28 to end of Book. **Proph** I Kings **2**, 1-12	**16**
11	S		17
12	M		18
13	T		19
14	W		20
15	Th		21
16	F	Sabbath commences 16.07	22
17	**S**	Sabbath ends 17.16. **Pent** Shemot, Ex **1**-**6**, 1. **Proph** Is **27**, 6-**28**, 13; **29**, 22-23 (Jer **1**, 1-**2**, 3) Benediction of Shebat	**23**
18	S		24
19	M		25
20	T		26
21	W		27
22	Th	Yom Kippur Katan	28
23	F	Sabbath commences 16.19	29
			Shebat
24	**S**	Rosh Chodesh. Sabbath ends 17.27. **Pent** Va'era, Ex **6**, 2-**9** and Num **28**, 9-15. **Proph** Is **66**	**1**
25	S		2
26	M		3
27	T	Holocaust Day (National)	4
28	W		5
29	Th		6
30	F	Sabbath commences 16.31	7
31	**S**	Sabbath ends 17.38. **Pent** Bo, Ex **10**, 1-**13**, 16. **Proph** Jer **46**, 13-28	**8**

Liturgical notes – Jan 4, Selichot, Aneinu.–Jan 24, Half-Hallel; omit Tsidkatcha Tsedek in Minchah.

FEBRUARY, 2004 — SHEBAT 9–ADAR 7, 5764

Molad Fri Feb 20 20h 7m 33s

			Shebat
1	S		9
2	M		10
3	T		11
4	W		12
5	Th		13
6	F	Sabbath commences 16.44	14
7	**S**	**New Year for Trees.** Sabbath ends 17.50. **Pent** Beshallach, Shabbat Shirah, Ex **13**, 17-**17**. **Proph** Judges **4**, 4-**5** (**5**, 1-31)	**15**
8	S		16
9	M		17
10	T		18
11	W		19
12	Th		20
13	F	Sabbath commences 16.57	21
14	**S**	Sabbath ends 18.02. **Pent** Yitro, Ex **18-20**. **Proph** Is **6**, 1-**7**, 6 and **9**, 5-6 (**6**, 1-13)	**22**
15	S		23
16	M		24
17	T		25
18	W		26
19	Th	Yom Kippur Katan	27
20	F	Sabbath commences 17.09	28
21	**S**	Sabbath ends 18.14. **Pent** Mishpatim, Parshat Shekalim, Ex **21-24** and **30**, 11-16 **Proph** II Kings **12**, 1-17;(**11**, 17-**12**, 17; I Sam **20**, 18 and 42). Benediction of Adar	**29**
22	S	Rosh Chodesh first day. **Pent** Num **28**, 1-15	30
			Adar
23	M	Rosh Chodesh second day. **Pent** Num **28**, 1-15	1
24	T		2
25	W		3
26	Th		4
27	F	Sabbath commences 17.22	5
28	**S**	Sabbath ends 18.26. **Pent** Terumah, Ex **25**, 1-**27**, 19. **Proph** I Kings **5**, 26-**6**, 13	**6**
29	S		7

Liturgical notes – Feb 7 and 21, omit Tsidkatcha Tsedek in Minchah.–Feb 22 and 23, Half-Hallel.

EVENING TWILIGHT VARIATION FOR REGIONS

This table shows the number of minutes required to be added to, or substracted from, the times for London, in order to determine the time of the termination of Sabbath, Festival, or Fast. For dates between those indicated here, an approximate calculation must be made. Acknowledgement is made to the Royal Greenwich Observatory for valued co-operation in the compilation of this table.

		BIRMINGHAM	BOURNEMOUTH	GLASGOW	LEEDS	LIVERPOOL	MANCHESTER	NEWCASTLE
Jan.	1	+ 9	+15	0	+ 4	+11	+ 8	0
	11	+ 9	+14	+ 1	+ 4	+11	+ 8	0
	21	+ 9	+14	+ 3	+ 5	+12	+ 9	+ 2
	31	+ 9	+13	+ 6	+ 6	+12	+ 9	+ 3
Feb.	10	+ 9	+12	+ 9	+ 7	+13	+10	+ 5
	20	+ 9	+11	+12	+ 8	+14	+11	+ 7
Mar.	2	+10	+10	+16	+10	+16	+13	+10
	12	+10	+ 9	+20	+12	+18	+15	+13
	22	+10	+ 7	+22	+12	+18	+15	+14
Apr.	1	+11	+ 7	+27	+15	+20	+17	+18
	11	+12	+ 7	+31	+17	+22	+19	+22
	21	+13	+ 7	+35	+20	+24	+21	+26
May	1	+16	+ 7	+40	+23	+27	+24	+30
	11	+18	+ 7	+46	+26	+30	+27	+35
	21	+20	+ 7	+52	+30	+34	+31	+42
	31	+23	+ 7	+57	+34	+37	+34	+48
June	10	+25	+ 7	+63	+38	+40	+38	+55
	20	+26	+ 7	+64	+40	+41	+39	+58
	30	+26	+ 7	+62	+38	+40	+38	+55
July	10	+23	+ 7	+57	+35	+38	+35	+50
	20	+21	+ 7	+51	+31	+34	+31	+43
	30	+19	+ 8	+46	+27	+30	+27	+38
Aug.	9	+17	+ 8	+40	+24	+27	+24	+32
	19	+16	+ 8	+35	+20	+25	+22	+27
	29	+16	+ 8	+30	+18	+23	+20	+23
Sept.	8	+14	+ 8	+26	+15	+20	+17	+18
	18	+13	+ 8	+23	+12	+18	+15	+15
	28	+13	+10	+20	+12	+18	+15	+14
Oct.	8	+12	+10	+16	+10	+16	+13	+10
	18	+11	+12	+13	+ 9	+15	+12	+9
	28	+11	+12	+10	+ 8	+14	+11	+6
Nov.	7	+10	+13	+ 7	+ 6	+13	+10	+4
	17	+10	+14	+ 4	+ 5	+12	+ 9	+3
	27	+10	+14	+ 2	+ 4	+11	+ 8	+1
Dec.	7	+10	+15	0	+ 4	+11	+ 8	0
	17	+ 9	+15	0	+ 3	+11	+ 7	- 1
	27	+ 9	+15	0	+ 3	+11	+ 8	- 1
	31	+ 9	+15	0	+ 4	+11	+ 8	0

SIDROT AND HAFTAROT FOR 2004 (5764-5765)

Haftara parentheses indicate Sephardi ritual.

2004		5764		HAFTARA	SIDRA
Jan	3	Tebet	9	Ezekiel **37**, 15-28	*Vayiggash*
	10		16	I Kings **2**, 1-12	*Vay'chi*
	17		23	Isaiah **27**, 6-**28**, 13, and **29**, 22-32 (Jer. **1**, 1-**2**, 3)	*Shemot*
	24	Shebat	1	Isaiah **66**, 1-24	*Va'era (Rosh Chodesh)*
	31		8	Jeremiah **46**, 13-28	*Bo*
Feb.	7		15	Judges **4**, 4-**5**, 31 (**5**, 1-31)	*Beshallach (Shirah)*
	14		22	Isaiah **6**, 1-7, 6; **9**, 5-6 (**6**, 1-13)	*Yitro*
	21		29	II Kings **12**, 1-17 (**11**, 17-**12**, 17; I Sam **20**, 18 and 42)	*Mishpatim (Shekalim)*
	28	Adar	6	I Kings **5**, 26-**6**, 13	*Terumah*
Mar.	6		13	I Samuel **15**, 2-34 (**15**, 1-34)	*Tetsaveh (Zachor)*
	13		20	Ezekiel **36**, 16-38 (16-36)	*Ki Tissa (Parah)*
	20		27	Ezek **45**, 16-**46**, 18 (**45**, 18-**46**, 15)	*Vayakhel-Pekudei (Hachodesh)*
	27	Nisan	5	Isaiah **43**, 21-**44**, 23	*Vayikra*
Apr	3		12	Malachi **3**, 4-24	*Tsav (Haggadol)*
	10		19	Ezekiel **37**, 1-14	*Chol Hamo'ed Pesach*
	17		26	II Samuel **6**, 1-7, 17 (**6**, 1-19)	*Shemini*
	24	Iyar	3	II Kings **7**, 3-20	*Tazria-Metsora*
May	1		10	Amos **9**, 7-15 (Ezek **20**, 2-20)	*Acharei Mot-Kedoshim*
	8		17	Ezekiel **44**, 15-31	*Emor*
	15		24	Jeremiah **16**, 19-**17**, 14	*Behar-Bechukkotai*
	22	Sivan	2	Hosea **2**, 1-22	*Bemidbar*
	29		9	Judges **13**, 2-25	*Naso*
June	5		16	Zechariah **2**, 14-**4**, 7	*Beha'alotecha*
	12		23	Joshua **2**, 1-24	*Shelach Lecha*
	19		30	Isaiah **66**, 1-24 (and I Sam **20**, 18 and 42	*Korach (Rosh Chodesh)*
	26	Tammuz	7	Judges **11**, 1-33	*Chukkat*
July	3		14	Micah **5**, 6-**6**, 8	*Balak*
	10		21	Jeremiah **1**, 1-**2**, 3	*Pinchas*
	17		28	Jeremiah **2**, 4-28 and **3**, 4 (**2**, 4-28 and **4**, 1-2)	*Mattot-Massei*
	24	Ab	6	Isaiah **1**, 1-27	*Devarim (Chazon)*
	31		13	Isaiah **40**, 1-26	*Va'etchanan (Nachamu)*

Sidrot and Haftarot

2004		5764	HAFTARA	SIDRA
Aug. 7	Ab	20	Isaiah **49**, 14-**51**, 3	*Ekev*
14		27	Isaiah **54**, 11-**55**, 5	*Re'eh*
21	Elul	4	Isaiah **51**, 12-**52**, 12	*Shof'tim*
28		11	Isaiah **54**, 1-10	*Ki Tetsei*
Sept. 4		18	Isaiah **60**, 1-22	*Ki Tavo*
11		25	Isaiah **61**, 10-**63**, 9	*Nitsavim-Vayelech*
		5765		
18	Tishri	3	Hosea **14**, 2-10 and Joel **2**, 15-27 (Hosea **14**, 2-10 and Micah **7**, 18-20)	*Ha'azinu (Shuvah)*
25		10	Isaiah **57**, 14-**58**, 14	*Yom Kippur*
Oct. 2		17	Ezekiel **38**, 18-**39**, 16	*Chol Hamoed Succot*
9		24	Isaiah **42**, 5-**43**, 10 (**42**, 5-21)	*Bereshit*
16	Cheshvan	1	Isaiah **66**, 1-24	*Noach (Rosh Chodesh)*
23		8	Isaiah **40**, 27-**41**, 16	*Lech Lecha*
30		15	II Kings **4**, 1-37 (**4**, 1-23)	*Vayera*
Nov. 6		22	I Kings **1**, 1-31	*Chayei Sarah*
13		29	I Samuel **20**, 18-42	*Tol'dot (Machar Chodesh)*
20	Kislev	7	Hosea **12**, 13-**14**, 10 (**11**, 7-**12**, 12)	*Vayetsei*
27		14	Hosea **11**, 7-**12**, 12 (Obadiah)	*Vayishlach*
Dec. 4		21	Amos **2**, 6-**3**, 8	*Vayeshev*
11		28	Zechariah **2**, 14-**4**, 7	*Mikkets (Chanucah)*
18	Tebet	6	Ezekiel **37**, 15-28	*Vayiggash*
25		13	I Kings **2**, 1-12	*Vay'chi*

MARRIAGE REGULATIONS (General)

Marriages may be contracted according to the usage of the Jews between persons *both* professing the Jewish religion, provided that due notice has been given to the Superintendent Registrar and that his certificate (or licence and certificate) has been obtained. There is no restriction regarding the hours within which the marriage may be solemnised, nor the place of marriage, which may be a synagogue, private house, or any other building.

The date and place of the intended marriage having been decided, the parties should consult the Minister or Secretary for Marriages of the synagogue through which the marriage is to be solemnised. He will advise of the necessary preliminary steps and the suitability of the proposed date.

Notice of the intended marriage must be given to the local Superintendent Registrar, and the document or documents obtained from him must be handed to the Synagogue Marriage Secretary in advance of the date appointed. In the case of a marriage in a building other than a synagogue, care should be taken that these documents contain the words "*both* parties being of the Jewish persuasion" following the description of the building.

If the marriage is to be solemnised at or through a synagogue under the jurisdiction of the Chief Rabbi, his Authorisation of Marriage must be presented. The minister of the synagogue will explain how this may be obtained.

No marriage is valid if solemnised between persons who are within the degrees of kindred of affinity (e.g., between uncle and niece) prohibited by English law, even though such a marriage is permissible by Jewish law.

A marriage between Jews must be registered immediately after the ceremony by the Secretary of Marriages of the synagogue of which the husband is a member. If he is not already a member he may become one by paying a membership fee in addition to the marriage charges.

The belief that marriage by licence may be solemnised only by civil ceremony at a Registry Office is erroneous. It may take place in a synagogue, or any other building, provided that the place of solemnisation is stated to the Superintendent Registrar when application is made for his licence.

No marriage between Jews should take place without due notice being given to the Superintendent Registrar, and without being registered in the Marriage Register of a synagogue. Marriages in such circumstances are not necessarily valid in English law. (Outside England and Wales other regulations apply and the Minister of the synagogue should be consulted.)

According to the regulations valid among Orthodox Jews, marriages may not be solemnised on the following dates:

2003		2004
–	Fast of Tebet	4 January
17 March	Fast of Esther	4 March
18 March	Purim	7 March
16 April	Day before Pesach	5 April
17-24 April	Pesach	6-13 April
4-19 May	Sephirah	23 April-7 May
21-31 May	Sephirah	10-20 May
5 June	Day before Shavuot	25 May
6-7 June	Shavuot	26-27 May
17 July-7 August	Three Weeks	6-27 July
26 September	Day before Rosh Hashana	15 September
27-28 September	Rosh Hashana	16-17 September
29 September	Fast of Gedaliah	19 September
5 October	Day before Yom Kippur	24 September
6 October	Yom Kippur	25 September
10 October	Day before Succot	29 September
11-19 October	Succot	30 September-8 October
–	Fast of Tebet	22 December

Nor on any Sabbath

Among Reform Jews, marriages are solemnised during the Sephirah, from the Fast of Tammuz until the Fast of Ab (but not on the Fast of Ab itself), on the days that precede Festivals, on the Second days of Festivals, and on Purim, but not on the other prohibited days mentioned above.

JEWISH CALENDAR FOR THIRTY YEARS

5749–5778

(1988–2018)

INSTRUCTIONS FOR USE

The following Table shows on one line the civil date and the day of the week on which every date of the Jewish year falls during the thirty years which it covers; those dates which occur on Sabbath are printed in *heavier* type. Thus, Tishri 10, 5759, coincided with September 30, 1998, and this was a Wednesday, since September 26 is marked as being Sabbath. The civil dates on which the festivals and fasts (or any other occasion of the Jewish Calendar) occur in any particular year may be ascertained in the same manner. The Table is arranged according to the months of the Hebrew Year, the day of the month being shown in the left-hand column.

YAHRZEIT. – This is always observed on the Jewish date on which the parent died. It has never been customary under the jurisdiction of the Chief Rabbi of the United Hebrew Congregations of the British Commonwealth to observe the Yahrzeit after the death on the anniversary of the burial as is enjoined, in certain circumstances, by some authorities. If the death took place after dark, it must be dated from the next civil day, as the day is reckoned among Jews from sunset to sunset. This date must be located in the Table, according to the month and day, and the civil date of the Yahrzeit in any particular year will be found on the same line in the column beneath the year in question. It should be noted, however, that if a parent died during Adar in an ordinary year, the Yahrzeit is observed in a leap year in the First Adar. (Some people observe it in both Adars.) If the death took place in a leap year the Yahrzeit is observed in a leap year in the same Adar (whether First or Second) during which the death happened. The Yahrzeit begins and the memorial light is kindled on the evening before the civil date thus ascertained.

BARMITZVAH. – A boy attains his Barmitzvah (religious majority) when he reaches his thirteenth birthday, i.e., on the first day of his fourteenth year, this being computed according to the Jewish date on which he was born. The date and year of birth being located in the Table, the corresponding civil date of the first day of his fourteenth year will be found on the same line in the 13th column. If this be a Sabbath, he reads his *Parsha* on that day; if a week-day, he reads it on the following Sabbath. By consulting the Calendar the scriptural portion of the week may be ascertained. It should be noted, however, that if a boy be born in Adar of an ordinary year and become Barmitzvah in a leap year, the celebration falls in the Second Adar. If he were born in a leap year and becomes Barmitzvah in a leap year it is celebrated in that Adar (whether First or Second) during which his birth occurred. If he were born in a leap year and the Barmitzvah is in an ordinary year, it is observed in Adar.

TISHRI (30 days)

	5749	50	51	52	53	54	55	56	57	58	59	60	61	62	63	64	65	66	67	68	69	70	71	72	73	74	75	76	77	78
	1988	89	90	91	92	93	94	95	96	97	98	99	2000	01	02	03	04	05	06	07	08	09	10	11	12	13	14	15	16	17
Tish	Sept-Oct	Sept-Oct	Sept-Oct	Sept-Oct	Sept-Oct	Sept-Oct	Sept-Oct	Sept-Oct	Sept-Oct	-October	Sept-Oct	Sept-Oct	Sept-Oct	Sept-Oct	Sept-Oct	Sept-Oct	Sept-Oct	Oct-Nov	Sept-Oct	Sept-Oct	Sept-Oct	Sept-Oct	Sept-Oct	Sept-Oct	Sept-Oct	Sept-Oct	Sept-Oct	Sept-Oct	Oct-Nov	Sept-Oct
1	12	**30**	20	9	28	16	6	25	**14**	2	21	**11**	**30**	18	**7**	**27**	16	4	**23**	13	30	**19**	9	29	17	5	25	14	3	21
2	13	1	21	10	29	17	7	26	15	3	22	12	1	19	8	28	17	5	24	14	1	20	10	30	18	6	26	15	4	22
3	14	2	**22**	11	30	**18**	8	27	16	**4**	23	13	2	20	9	29	**18**	6	25	**15**	2	21	**11**	**1**	19	**7**	**27**	16	5	**23**
4	15	3	23	12	1	19	9	28	17	5	24	14	3	21	10	30	19	7	26	16	3	22	12	2	20	8	28	17	6	24
5	16	4	24	13	2	20	**10**	29	18	6	25	15	4	**22**	11	1	20	**8**	27	17	**4**	23	13	3	21	9	29	18	7	25
6	**17**	5	25	**14**	**3**	21	11	**30**	19	7	**26**	16	5	23	12	2	21	9	28	18	5	24	14	4	**22**	10	30	**19**	**8**	26
7	18	6	26	15	4	22	12	1	20	8	27	17	6	24	13	3	22	10	29	19	6	25	15	5	23	11	1	20	9	27
8	19	**7**	27	16	5	23	13	2	**21**	9	28	**18**	**7**	25	**14**	**4**	23	11	**30**	20	7	**26**	16	6	24	12	2	21	10	28
9	20	8	28	17	6	24	14	3	22	10	29	19	8	26	15	5	24	12	1	21	8	27	17	7	25	13	3	22	11	29
10	21	9	**29**	18	7	**25**	15	4	23	**11**	30	20	9	27	16	6	**25**	13	2	**22**	9	28	**18**	**8**	26	**14**	**4**	23	12	**30**
11	22	10	30	19	8	26	16	5	24	12	1	21	10	28	17	7	26	14	3	23	10	29	19	9	27	15	5	24	13	1
12	23	11	1	20	9	27	**17**	6	25	13	2	22	11	**29**	18	8	27	**15**	4	24	**11**	30	20	10	28	16	6	25	14	2
13	**24**	12	2	**21**	**10**	28	18	**7**	26	14	**3**	23	12	30	19	9	28	16	5	25	12	1	21	11	**29**	17	7	**26**	**15**	3
14	25	13	3	22	11	29	19	8	27	15	4	24	13	1	20	10	29	17	6	26	13	2	22	12	30	18	8	27	16	4
15	26	**14**	4	23	12	30	20	9	**28**	16	5	**25**	**14**	2	**21**	**11**	30	18	**7**	27	14	**3**	23	13	1	19	9	28	17	5
16	27	15	5	24	13	1	21	10	29	17	6	26	15	3	22	12	1	19	8	28	15	4	24	14	2	20	10	29	18	6
17	28	16	**6**	25	14	**2**	22	11	30	**18**	7	27	16	4	23	13	**2**	20	9	**29**	16	5	**25**	**15**	3	**21**	**11**	30	19	**7**
18	29	17	7	26	15	3	23	12	1	19	8	28	17	5	24	14	3	21	10	30	17	6	26	16	4	22	12	1	20	8
19	30	18	8	27	16	4	**24**	13	2	20	9	29	18	**6**	25	15	4	**22**	11	1	**18**	7	27	17	5	23	13	2	21	9
20	**1**	19	9	**28**	**17**	5	25	**14**	3	21	**10**	30	19	7	26	16	5	23	12	2	19	8	28	18	**6**	24	14	**3**	**22**	10
21	2	20	10	29	18	6	26	15	4	22	11	1	20	8	27	17	6	24	13	3	20	9	29	19	7	25	15	4	23	11
22	3	**21**	11	30	19	7	27	16	**5**	23	12	**2**	**21**	9	**28**	**18**	7	25	**14**	4	21	**10**	30	20	8	26	16	5	24	12
23	4	22	12	1	20	8	28	17	6	24	13	3	22	10	29	19	8	26	15	5	22	11	1	21	9	27	17	6	25	13
24	5	23	**13**	2	21	**9**	29	18	7	**25**	14	4	23	11	30	20	**9**	27	16	**6**	23	12	**2**	**22**	10	**28**	**18**	7	26	**14**
25	6	24	14	3	22	10	30	19	8	26	15	5	24	12	1	21	10	28	17	7	24	13	3	23	11	29	19	8	27	15
26	7	25	15	4	23	11	**1**	20	9	27	16	6	25	**13**	2	22	11	**29**	18	8	**25**	14	4	24	12	30	20	9	28	16
27	**8**	26	16	**5**	**24**	12	2	**21**	10	28	**17**	7	26	14	3	23	12	30	19	9	26	15	5	25	**13**	1	21	**10**	**29**	17
28	9	27	17	6	25	13	3	22	11	29	18	8	27	15	4	24	13	31	20	10	27	16	6	26	14	2	22	11	30	18
29	10	**28**	18	7	26	14	4	23	**12**	30	19	**9**	**28**	16	**5**	**25**	14	1	**21**	11	28	**17**	7	27	15	3	23	12	31	19
30	11	29	19	8	27	15	5	24	13	31	20	10	29	17	6	26	15	2	22	12	29	18	8	28	16	4	24	13	1	20

In the left-hand margin figures in **black type** denote major Holy-days; elsewhere they denote Sabbaths. 1st and 2nd, New Year; 3rd, Fast of Gedaliah (if on Sabbath, postponed to Sunday); 10th, Day of Atonement; 15th to 23rd, Tabernacles, etc.; 30th, First day of New Moon of Marcheshvan.

CHESHVAN or MARCHESHVAN (29 or 30 days)

5749		50	51	52	53	54	55	56	57	58	59	60	61	62	63	64	65	66	67	68	69	70	71	72	73	74	75	76	77	78
1988		89	90	91	92	93	94	95	96	97	98	99	2000	01	02	03	04	05	06	07	08	09	10	11	12	13	14	15	16	17
Chesh	Oct-Nov	Oct-Nov	Oct-Nov	Oct-Nov	Oct-Nov	Oct-Nov	Oct-Nov	Oct-Nov	Oct-Nov	November	Oct-Nov	Oct-Nov	Oct-Nov	Oct-Nov	Oct-Nov	Oct-Nov	Oct-Nov	Nov-Dec	Oct-Nov	Oct-Nov	Oct-Nov	Oct-Nov	Oct-Nov	Oct-Nov	Oct-Nov	Oct-Nov	Oct-Nov	Oct-Nov	November	Oct-Nov
1	12	30	**20**	9	28	**16**	6	25	14	**1**	21	11	30	18	7	27	**16**	3	23	**13**	30	19	**9**	**29**	17	**5**	**25**	14	2	**21**
2	13	31	21	10	29	17	7	26	15	2	22	12	31	19	8	28	17	4	24	14	31	20	10	30	18	6	26	15	3	22
3	14	1	22	11	30	18	**8**	27	16	3	23	13	1	**20**	9	29	18	**5**	25	15	**1**	21	11	31	19	7	27	16	4	23
4	**15**	2	23	**12**	**31**	19	9	**28**	17	4	**24**	14	2	21	10	30	19	6	26	16	2	22	12	1	**20**	8	28	**17**	**5**	24
5	16	3	24	13	1	20	10	29	18	5	25	15	3	22	11	31	20	7	27	17	3	23	13	2	21	9	29	18	6	25
6	17	**4**	25	14	2	21	11	30	**19**	6	26	**16**	**4**	23	**12**	**1**	21	8	**28**	18	4	**24**	14	3	22	10	30	19	7	26
7	18	5	26	15	3	22	12	31	20	7	27	17	5	24	13	2	22	9	29	19	5	25	15	4	23	11	31	20	8	27
8	19	6	**27**	16	4	**23**	13	1	21	**8**	28	18	6	25	14	3	**23**	10	30	**20**	6	26	**16**	**5**	24	**12**	**1**	21	9	**28**
9	20	7	28	17	5	24	14	2	22	9	29	19	7	26	15	4	24	11	31	21	7	27	17	6	25	13	2	22	10	29
10	21	8	29	18	6	25	**15**	3	23	10	30	20	8	**27**	16	5	25	**12**	1	22	**8**	28	18	7	26	14	3	23	11	30
11	**22**	9	30	**19**	**7**	26	16	**4**	24	11	**31**	21	9	28	17	6	26	13	2	23	9	29	19	8	**27**	15	4	**24**	**12**	31
12	23	10	31	20	8	27	17	5	25	12	1	22	10	29	18	7	27	14	3	24	10	30	20	9	28	16	5	25	13	1
13	24	**11**	1	21	9	28	18	6	**26**	13	2	**23**	**11**	30	**19**	**8**	28	15	**4**	25	11	**31**	21	10	29	17	6	26	14	2
14	25	12	2	22	10	29	19	7	27	14	3	24	12	31	20	9	29	16	5	26	12	1	22	11	30	18	7	27	15	3
15	26	13	**3**	23	11	**30**	20	8	28	**15**	4	25	13	1	21	10	**30**	17	6	**27**	13	2	**23**	**12**	31	**19**	**8**	28	16	**4**
16	27	14	4	24	12	31	21	9	29	16	5	26	14	2	22	11	31	18	7	28	14	3	24	13	1	20	9	29	17	5
17	28	15	5	25	13	1	**22**	10	30	17	6	27	15	**3**	23	12	1	**19**	8	29	**15**	4	25	14	2	21	10	30	18	6
18	**29**	16	6	**26**	**14**	2	23	**11**	31	18	**7**	28	16	4	24	13	2	20	9	30	16	5	26	15	**3**	22	11	**31**	**19**	7
19	30	17	7	27	15	3	24	12	1	19	8	29	17	5	25	14	3	21	10	31	17	6	27	16	4	23	12	1	20	8
20	31	**18**	8	28	16	4	25	13	**2**	20	9	**30**	**18**	6	**26**	**15**	4	22	**11**	1	18	**7**	28	17	5	24	13	2	21	9
21	1	19	9	29	17	5	26	14	3	21	10	31	19	7	27	16	5	23	12	2	19	8	29	18	6	25	14	3	22	10
22	2	20	**10**	30	18	**6**	27	15	4	**22**	11	1	20	8	28	17	**6**	24	13	**3**	20	9	**30**	**19**	7	**26**	**15**	4	23	**11**
23	3	21	11	31	19	7	28	16	5	23	12	2	21	9	29	18	7	25	14	4	21	10	31	20	8	27	16	5	24	12
24	4	22	12	1	20	8	**29**	17	6	24	13	3	22	**10**	30	19	8	**26**	15	5	**22**	11	1	21	9	28	17	6	25	13
25	**5**	23	13	**2**	**21**	9	30	**18**	7	25	**14**	4	23	11	31	20	9	27	16	6	23	12	2	22	**10**	29	18	**7**	**26**	14
26	6	24	14	3	22	10	31	19	8	26	15	5	24	12	1	21	10	28	17	7	24	13	3	23	11	30	19	8	27	15
27	7	**25**	15	4	23	11	1	20	**9**	27	16	**6**	**25**	13	**2**	**22**	11	29	**18**	8	25	**14**	4	24	12	31	20	9	28	16
28	8	26	16	5	24	12	2	21	10	28	17	7	26	14	3	23	12	30	19	9	26	15	5	25	13	1	21	10	29	17
29	9	27	**17**	6	25	**13**	3	22	11	**29**	18	8	27	15	424	**13**	1	20		**10**	27	16	**6**	**26**	14	**2**	**22**	11	30	**18**
30	—	28	—	7	—	14	—	23	—	—	19	9	—	—	5	25	—	—	21	—	—	17	7	—	—	3	—	12	—	—

Figures in **black type** denote Sabbaths.
30th, First day of New Moon of Kislev.

KISLEV (29 or 30 days)

Kis	5749	50	51	52	53	54	55	56	57	58	59	60	61	62	63
	1988	89	90	91	92	93	94	95	96	97	98	99	2000	01	02
	Nov-Dec	Nov-Dec	Nov-Dec	Nov-Dec	Nov-Dec	Nov-Dec	Nov-Dec	Nov-Dec	Nov-Dec	Nov-Dec	Nov-Dec	Nov-Dec	Nov-Dec	Nov-Dec	Nov-Dec
1	10	29	18	8	26	15	4	24	12	30	20	10	28	16	6
2	11	30	19	**9**	27	16	**5**	**25**	13	1	**21**	11	29	**17**	7
3	**12**	1	20	10	**28**	17	6	26	14	2	22	12	30	18	8
4	13	**2**	21	11	29	18	7	27	15	3	23	**13**	1	19	**9**
5	14	3	22	12	30	19	8	28	**16**	4	24	14	**2**	20	10
6	15	4	23	13	1	**20**	9	29	17	5	25	15	3	21	11
7	16	5	**24**	14	2	21	10	30	18	**6**	26	16	4	22	12
8	17	6	25	15	3	22	11	1	19	7	27	17	5	23	13
9	18	7	26	**16**	4	23	**12**	**2**	20	8	**28**	18	6	**24**	14
10	**19**	8	27	17	**5**	24	13	3	21	9	29	19	7	25	15
11	20	**9**	28	18	6	25	14	4	22	10	30	**20**	8	26	**16**
12	21	10	29	19	7	26	15	5	**23**	11	1	21	**9**	27	17
13	22	11	30	20	8	**27**	16	6	24	12	2	22	10	28	18
14	23	12	**1**	21	9	28	17	7	25	**13**	3	23	11	29	19
15	24	13	2	22	10	29	18	8	26	14	4	24	12	30	20
16	25	14	3	**23**	11	30	**19**	**9**	27	15	**5**	25	13	**1**	21
17	**26**	15	4	24	**12**	1	20	10	28	16	6	26	14	2	22
18	27	**16**	5	25	13	2	21	11	29	17	7	**27**	15	3	**23**
19	28	17	6	26	14	3	22	12	**30**	18	8	28	**16**	4	24
20	29	18	7	27	15	**4**	23	13	1	19	9	29	17	5	25
21	30	19	**8**	28	16	5	24	14	2	**20**	10	30	18	6	26
22	1	20	9	29	17	6	25	15	3	21	11	1	19	7	27
23	2	21	10	**30**	18	7	**26**	**16**	4	22	**12**	2	20	**8**	28
24	**3**	22	11	1	**19**	8	27	17	5	23	13	3	21	9	29
25	4	**23**	12	2	20	9	28	18	6	24	14	**4**	22	10	**30**
26	5	24	13	3	21	10	29	19	**7**	25	15	5	**23**	11	1
27	6	25	14	4	22	**11**	30	20	8	26	16	6	24	12	2
28	7	26	**15**	5	23	12	1	21	9	**27**	17	7	25	13	3
29	8	27	16	6	24	13	2	22	10	28	18	8	26	14	4
30	—	28	17	**7**	—	14	**3**	**23**	—	29	**19**	9	—	**15**	5

Kis	64	65	66	67	68	69	70	71	72	73	74	75	76	77	78
	03	04	05	06	07	08	09	10	11	12	13	14	15	16	17
	Nov-Dec	Nov-Dec	Dec	Nov-Dec	Nov-Dec	Nov-Dec	Nov-Dec	Nov-Dec	Nov-Dec	Nov-Dec	Nov-Dec	Nov-Dec	Nov-Dec	Dec	Nov-Dec
1	26	14	2	22	11	28	18	8	27	15	4	23	13	1	19
2	27	15	**3**	23	12	**29**	19	9	28	16	5	24	**14**	2	20
3	28	16	4	24	13	30	20	10	29	**17**	6	25	15	**3**	21
4	**29**	17	5	**25**	14	1	**21**	11	30	18	7	26	16	4	22
5	30	18	6	26	15	2	22	12	1	19	8	27	17	5	23
6	1	19	7	27	16	3	23	**13**	2	20	**9**	28	18	6	24
7	2	**20**	8	28	**17**	4	24	14	**3**	21	10	**29**	19	7	**25**
8	3	21	9	29	18	5	25	15	4	22	11	30	20	8	26
9	4	22	**10**	30	19	**6**	26	16	5	23	12	1	**21**	9	27
10	5	23	11	1	20	7	27	17	6	**24**	13	2	22	**10**	28
11	**6**	24	12	**2**	21	8	**28**	18	7	25	14	3	23	11	29
12	7	25	13	3	22	9	29	19	8	26	15	4	24	12	30
13	8	26	14	4	23	10	30	**20**	9	27	**16**	5	25	13	1
14	9	**27**	15	5	**24**	11	1	21	**10**	28	17	**6**	26	14	**2**
15	10	28	16	6	25	12	2	22	11	29	18	7	27	15	3
16	11	29	**17**	7	26	**13**	3	23	12	30	19	8	**28**	16	4
17	12	30	18	8	27	14	4	24	13	**1**	20	9	29	**17**	5
18	**13**	1	19	**9**	28	15	**5**	25	14	2	21	10	30	18	6
19	14	2	20	10	29	16	6	26	15	3	22	11	1	19	7
20	15	3	21	11	30	17	7	**27**	16	4	**23**	12	2	20	8
21	16	**4**	22	12	**1**	18	8	28	**17**	5	24	**13**	3	21	**9**
22	17	5	23	13	2	19	9	29	18	6	25	14	4	22	10
23	18	6	**24**	14	3	**20**	10	30	19	7	26	15	**5**	23	11
24	19	7	25	15	4	21	11	1	20	**8**	27	16	6	**24**	12
25	**20**	8	26	**16**	5	22	**12**	2	21	9	28	17	7	25	13
26	21	9	27	17	6	23	13	3	22	10	29	18	8	26	14
27	22	10	28	18	7	24	14	**4**	23	11	**30**	19	9	27	15
28	23	**11**	29	19	**8**	25	15	5	**24**	12	1	**20**	10	28	**16**
29	24	12	30	20	9	26	16	6	25	13	2	21	11	29	17
30	25	—	**31**	21	—	**27**	17	7	26	—	3	22	**12**	—	18

Figures in **black type** denote Sabbaths.

25th to 29th or 30th, Chanucah (opening days); 30th, First day of New Moon of Tebet.

TEBET (29 days)

	5749	50	51	52	53	54	55	56	57	58	59	60	61	62	63	64	65	66	67	68	69	70	71	72	73	74	75	76	77	78
	1988 1989	89 90	90 91	91 92	92 93	93 94	94 95	95 96	96 97	97 98	98 99	99 2000	2000 01	01 02	02 03	03 04	04 05	06	06 07	07 08	08 09	09 10	10 11	11 12	12 13	13 14	14 15	15 16	16 17	17 18
Teb	Dec-Jan	Dec-Jan	Dec-Jan	Dec-Jan	Dec-Jan	Dec-Jan	Dec-Jan	Dec-Jan	Dec-Jan	Dec-Jan	Dec-Jan	Dec-Jan	Dec-Jan	Dec-Jan	Dec-Jan	Dec-Jan	Dec-Jan	January	Dec-Jan	Dec-Jan	Dec-Jan	Dec-Jan	Dec-Jan	Dec-Jan	Dec-Jan	Dec-Jan	Dec-Jan	Dec-Jan	Dec-Jan	Dec-Jan
1	9	29	18	8	25	15	4	24	11	30	20	10	27	16	6	26	13	1	22	10	28	18	8	27	14	4	23	13	30	19
2	**10**	**30**	19	9	**26**	16	5	25	12	31	21	**11**	28	17	**7**	**27**	14	2	**23**	11	29	**19**	9	28	**15**	5	24	14	**31**	20
3	11	31	20	10	27	17	6	26	13	1	22	12	29	18	8	28	15	3	24	12	30	20	10	29	16	6	25	15	1	21
4	12	1	21	11	28	**18**	7	27	**14**	2	23	13	**30**	19	9	29	16	4	25	13	31	21	**11**	30	17	**7**	26	16	2	22
5	13	2	**22**	12	29	19	8	28	15	**3**	24	14	31	20	10	30	17	5	26	14	1	22	12	**31**	18	8	**27**	17	3	**23**
6	14	3	23	13	30	20	9	29	16	4	25	15	1	21	11	31	**18**	6	27	**15**	2	23	13	1	19	9	28	18	4	24
7	15	4	24	**14**	31	21	**10**	**30**	17	5	**26**	16	2	**22**	12	1	19	**7**	28	16	**3**	24	14	2	20	10	29	**19**	5	25
8	16	5	25	15	1	22	11	31	18	6	27	17	3	23	13	2	20	8	29	17	4	25	15	3	21	11	30	20	6	26
9	**17**	**6**	26	16	**2**	23	12	1	19	7	28	**18**	4	24	**14**	**3**	21	9	**30**	18	5	**26**	16	4	**22**	12	31	21	**7**	27
10	18	7	27	17	3	24	13	2	20	8	29	19	5	25	15	4	22	10	31	19	6	27	17	5	23	13	1	22	8	28
11	19	8	28	18	4	**25**	14	3	**21**	9	30	20	**6**	26	16	5	23	11	1	20	7	28	**18**	6	24	**14**	2	23	9	29
12	20	9	**29**	19	5	26	15	4	22	**10**	31	21	7	27	17	6	24	12	2	21	8	29	19	**7**	25	15	**3**	24	10	**30**
13	21	10	30	20	6	27	16	5	23	11	1	22	8	28	18	7	**25**	13	3	**22**	9	30	20	8	26	16	4	25	11	31
14	22	11	31	**21**	7	28	**17**	**6**	24	12	**2**	23	9	**29**	19	8	26	**14**	4	23	**10**	31	21	9	27	17	5	**26**	12	1
15	23	12	1	22	8	29	18	7	25	13	3	24	10	30	20	9	27	15	5	24	11	1	22	10	28	18	6	27	13	2
16	**24**	**13**	2	23	**9**	30	19	8	26	14	4	**25**	11	31	**21**	**10**	28	16	**6**	25	12	**2**	23	11	**29**	19	7	28	**14**	3
17	25	14	3	24	10	31	20	9	27	15	5	26	12	1	22	11	29	17	7	26	13	3	24	12	30	20	8	29	15	4
18	26	15	4	25	11	**1**	21	10	**28**	16	6	27	**13**	2	23	12	30	18	8	27	14	4	**25**	13	31	**21**	9	30	16	5
19	27	16	**5**	26	12	2	22	11	29	**17**	7	28	14	3	24	13	31	19	9	28	15	5	26	**14**	1	22	**10**	31	17	**6**
20	28	17	6	27	13	3	23	12	30	18	8	29	15	4	25	14	**1**	20	10	**29**	16	6	27	15	2	23	11	1	18	7
21	29	18	7	**28**	14	4	**24**	**13**	31	19	**9**	30	16	**5**	26	15	2	**21**	11	30	**17**	7	28	16	3	24	12	**2**	19	8
22	30	19	8	29	15	5	25	14	1	20	10	31	17	6	27	16	3	22	12	31	18	8	29	17	4	25	13	3	20	9
23	**31**	**20**	9	30	**16**	6	26	15	2	21	11	**1**	18	7	**28**	**17**	4	23	**13**	1	19	**9**	30	18	**5**	26	14	4	**21**	10
24	1	21	10	31	17	7	27	16	3	22	12	2	19	8	29	18	5	24	14	2	20	10	31	19	6	27	15	5	22	11
25	2	22	11	1	18	**8**	28	17	**4**	23	13	3	**20**	9	30	19	6	25	15	3	21	11	**1**	20	7	**28**	16	6	23	12
26	3	23	**12**	2	19	9	29	18	5	**24**	14	4	21	10	31	20	7	26	16	4	22	12	2	**21**	8	29	**17**	7	24	**13**
27	4	24	13	3	20	10	30	19	6	25	15	5	22	11	1	21	**8**	27	17	**5**	23	13	3	22	9	30	18	8	25	14
28	5	25	14	**4**	21	11	**31**	**20**	7	26	**16**	6	23	**12**	2	22	9	**28**	18	6	**24**	14	4	23	10	31	19	**9**	26	15
29	6	26	15	5	22	12	1	21	8	27	17	7	24	13	3	23	10	29	19	7	25	15	5	24	11	1	20	10	27	16

Figures in **black type** denote Sabbaths.
1st to 2nd or 3rd, Chanucah (final days); 10th, Fast of Tebet.

SHEBAT (30 days)

Sheb	5749	50	51	52	53	54	55	56	57	58	59	60	61	62	63
	1989	90	91	92	93	94	95	96	97	98	99	2000	01	02	03
	Jan-Feb	Jan-Feb	Jan-Feb	Jan-Feb	Jan-Feb	Jan-Feb	January	Jan-Feb	Jan-Feb	Jan-Feb	Jan-Feb	Jan-Feb	Jan-Feb	Jan-Feb	Jan-Feb
1	**7**	**27**	16	6	**23**	13	2	22	9	28	18	**8**	25	14	**4**
2	8	28	17	7	24	14	3	23	10	29	19	9	26	15	5
3	9	29	18	8	25	**15**	4	24	**11**	30	20	10	**27**	16	6
4	10	30	**19**	9	26	16	5	25	12	**31**	21	11	28	17	7
5	11	31	20	10	27	17	6	26	13	1	22	12	29	18	8
6	12	1	21	**11**	28	18	**7**	**27**	14	2	**23**	13	30	**19**	9
7	13	2	22	12	29	19	8	28	15	3	24	14	31	20	10
8	**14**	**3**	23	13	**30**	20	9	29	16	4	25	**15**	1	21	**11**
9	15	4	24	14	31	21	10	30	17	5	26	16	2	22	12
10	16	5	25	15	1	**22**	11	31	**18**	6	27	17	**3**	23	13
11	17	6	**26**	16	2	23	12	1	19	**7**	28	18	4	24	14
12	18	7	27	17	3	24	13	2	20	8	29	19	5	25	15
13	19	8	28	**18**	4	25	**14**	**3**	21	9	**30**	20	6	**26**	16
14	20	9	29	19	5	26	15	4	22	10	31	21	7	27	17
15	**21**	**10**	30	20	**6**	27	16	5	23	11	1	**22**	8	28	**18**
16	22	11	31	21	7	28	17	6	24	12	2	23	9	29	19
17	23	12	1	22	8	**29**	18	7	**25**	13	3	24	**10**	30	20
18	24	13	**2**	23	9	30	19	8	26	**14**	4	25	11	31	21
19	25	14	3	24	10	31	20	9	27	15	5	26	12	1	22
20	26	15	4	**25**	11	1	**21**	**10**	28	16	**6**	27	13	**2**	23
21	27	16	5	26	12	2	22	11	29	17	7	28	14	3	24
22	**28**	**17**	6	27	**13**	3	23	12	30	18	8	**29**	15	4	**25**
23	29	18	7	28	14	4	24	13	31	19	9	30	16	5	26
24	30	19	8	29	15	**5**	25	14	**1**	20	10	31	**17**	6	27
25	31	20	**9**	30	16	6	26	15	2	**21**	11	1	18	7	28
26	1	21	10	31	17	7	27	16	3	22	12	2	19	8	29
27	2	22	11	**1**	18	8	**28**	**17**	4	23	**13**	3	20	**9**	30
28	3	23	12	2	19	9	29	18	5	24	14	4	21	10	31
29	**4**	**24**	13	3	**20**	10	30	19	6	25	15	**5**	22	11	**1**
30	5	25	14	4	21	11	31	20	7	26	16	6	23	12	2

Sheb	64	65	66	67	68	69	70	71	72	73	74	75	76	77	78
	04	05	06	07	08	09	10	11	12	13	14	15	16	17	18
	Jan-Feb	Jan-Feb	Jan-Feb	Jan-Feb	Jan-Feb	Jan-Feb	Jan-Feb	Jan-Feb	Jan-Feb	Jan-Feb	January	Jan-Feb	Jan-Feb	Jan-Feb	Jan-Feb
1	**24**	11	30	**20**	8	26	**16**	6	25	**12**	2	21	11	**28**	17
2	25	12	31	21	9	27	17	7	26	13	3	22	12	29	18
3	26	13	1	22	10	28	18	**8**	27	14	**4**	23	13	30	19
4	27	14	2	23	11	29	19	9	**28**	15	5	**24**	14	31	**20**
5	28	**15**	3	24	**12**	30	20	10	29	16	6	25	15	1	21
6	29	16	**4**	25	13	**31**	21	11	30	17	7	26	**16**	2	22
7	30	17	5	26	14	1	22	12	31	18	8	27	17	3	23
8	**31**	18	6	**27**	15	2	**23**	13	1	**19**	9	28	18	**4**	24
9	1	19	7	28	16	3	24	14	2	20	10	29	19	5	25
10	2	20	8	29	17	4	25	**15**	3	21	**11**	30	20	6	26
11	3	21	9	30	18	5	26	16	**4**	22	12	**31**	21	7	**27**
12	4	**22**	10	31	**19**	6	27	17	5	23	13	1	22	8	28
13	5	23	**11**	1	20	**7**	28	18	6	24	14	2	**23**	9	29
14	6	24	12	2	21	8	29	19	7	25	15	3	24	10	30
15	**7**	25	13	**3**	22	9	**30**	20	8	**26**	16	4	25	**11**	31
16	8	26	14	4	23	10	31	21	9	27	17	5	26	12	1
17	9	27	15	5	24	11	1	**22**	10	28	**18**	6	27	13	2
18	10	28	16	6	25	12	2	23	**11**	29	19	**7**	28	14	**3**
19	11	**29**	17	7	**26**	13	3	24	12	30	20	8	29	15	4
20	12	30	**18**	8	27	**14**	4	25	13	31	21	9	**30**	16	5
21	13	31	19	9	28	15	5	26	14	1	22	10	31	17	6
22	**14**	1	20	**10**	29	16	**6**	27	15	**2**	23	11	1	**18**	7
23	15	2	21	11	30	17	7	28	16	3	24	12	2	19	8
24	16	3	22	12	31	18	8	**29**	17	4	**25**	13	3	20	9
25	17	4	23	13	1	19	9	30	**18**	5	26	**14**	4	21	**10**
26	18	**5**	24	14	**2**	20	10	31	19	6	27	15	5	22	11
27	19	6	**25**	15	3	**21**	11	1	20	7	28	16	**6**	23	12
28	20	7	26	16	4	22	12	2	21	8	29	17	7	24	13
29	**21**	8	27	**17**	5	23	**13**	3	22	**9**	30	18	8	**25**	14
30	22	9	28	18	6	24	14	4	23	10	31	19	9	26	15

Figures in **black type** denote Sabbaths.
15th, New Year for Trees; 30th, First day of New Moon of Adar.

ADAR (29 days); in Leap Year, known as ADAR RISHON — 1st ADAR (30 days)

	5749	50	51	52	53	54	55	56	57	58	59	60	61	62	63
	1989	90	91	92	93	94	95	96	97	98	99	2000	01	02	03
Adar	Feb-Mar	Feb-Mar	Feb-Mar	Feb-Mar	Feb-Mar	Feb-Mar	Feb-Mar	Feb-Mar	Feb-Mar	Feb-Mar	Feb-Mar	Feb-Mar	Feb-Mar	Feb-Mar	Feb-Mar
1	6	26	15	5	22	**12**	1	21	**8**	27	17	7	**24**	13	3
2	7	27	**16**	6	23	13	2	22	9	**28**	18	8	25	14	4
3	8	28	17	7	24	14	3	23	10	1	19	9	26	15	5
4	9	1	18	**8**	25	15	**4**	**24**	11	2	**20**	10	27	**16**	6
5	10	2	19	9	26	16	5	25	12	3	21	11	28	17	7
6	**11**	**3**	20	10	**27**	17	6	26	13	4	22	**12**	1	18	**8**
7	12	4	21	11	28	18	7	27	14	5	23	13	2	19	9
8	13	5	22	12	1	**19**	8	28	**15**	6	24	14	**3**	20	10
9	14	6	**23**	13	2	20	9	29	16	**7**	25	15	4	21	11
10	15	7	24	14	3	21	10	1	17	8	26	16	5	22	12
11	16	8	25	**15**	4	22	**11**	**2**	18	9	**27**	17	6	**23**	13
12	17	9	26	16	5	23	12	3	19	10	28	18	7	24	14
13	**18**	**10**	27	17	**6**	24	13	4	20	11	1	**19**	8	25	**15**
14	19	11	28	18	7	25	14	5	21	12	2	20	9	26	16
15	20	12	1	19	8	**26**	15	6	**22**	13	3	21	**10**	27	17
16	21	13	**2**	20	9	27	16	7	23	**14**	4	22	11	28	18
17	22	14	3	21	10	28	17	8	24	15	5	23	12	1	19
18	23	15	4	**22**	11	1	**18**	**9**	25	16	**6**	24	13	**2**	20
19	24	16	5	23	12	2	19	10	26	17	7	25	14	3	21
20	**25**	**17**	6	24	**13**	3	20	11	27	18	8	**26**	15	4	**22**
21	26	18	7	25	14	4	21	12	28	19	9	27	16	5	23
22	27	19	8	26	15	**5**	22	13	**1**	20	10	28	**17**	6	24
23	28	20	**9**	27	16	6	23	14	2	**21**	11	29	18	7	25
24	1	21	10	28	17	7	24	15	3	22	12	1	19	8	26
25	2	22	11	**29**	18	8	**25**	**16**	4	23	**13**	2	20	**9**	27
26	3	23	12	1	19	9	26	17	5	24	14	3	21	10	28
27	**4**	**24**	13	2	**20**	10	27	18	6	25	15	**4**	22	11	**1**
28	5	25	14	3	21	11	28	19	7	26	16	5	23	12	2
29	6	26	15	4	22	**12**	1	20	**8**	27	17	6	**24**	13	3
30	7	—	—	5	—	—	2	—	9	—	—	7	—	—	4
	R			**R**			**R**		**R**			**R**			**R**

	64	65	66	67	68	69	70	71	72	73	74	75	76	77	78
	04	05	06	07	08	09	10	11	12	13	14	15	16	17	18
Adar	Feb-Mar	Feb-Mar	March	Feb-Mar	Feb-Mar	Feb-Mar	Feb-Mar	Feb-Mar	Feb-Mar	Feb-Mar	Feb-Mar	Feb-Mar	Feb-Mar	Feb-Mar	Feb-Mar
1	23	10	1	19	7	25	15	**5**	24	11	**1**	20	10	27	16
2	24	11	2	20	8	26	16	6	**25**	12	2	**21**	11	28	**17**
3	25	**12**	3	21	**9**	27	17	7	26	13	3	22	12	1	18
4	26	13	**4**	22	10	**28**	18	8	27	14	4	23	**13**	2	19
5	27	14	5	23	11	1	19	9	28	15	5	24	14	3	20
6	**28**	15	6	**24**	12	2	**20**	10	29	**16**	6	25	15	**4**	21
7	29	16	7	25	13	3	21	11	1	17	7	26	16	5	22
8	1	17	8	26	14	4	22	**12**	2	18	**8**	27	17	6	23
9	2	18	9	27	15	5	23	13	**3**	19	9	**28**	18	7	**24**
10	3	**19**	10	28	**16**	6	24	14	4	20	10	1	19	8	25
11	4	20	**11**	1	17	**7**	25	15	5	21	11	2	**20**	9	26
12	5	21	12	2	18	8	26	16	6	22	12	3	21	10	27
13	**6**	22	13	**3**	19	9	**27**	17	7	**23**	13	4	22	**11**	28
14	7	23	14	4	20	10	28	18	8	24	14	5	23	12	1
15	8	24	15	5	21	11	1	**19**	9	25	**15**	6	24	13	2
16	9	25	16	6	22	12	2	20	**10**	26	16	**7**	25	14	**3**
17	10	**26**	17	7	**23**	13	3	21	11	27	17	8	26	15	4
18	11	27	**18**	8	24	**14**	4	22	12	28	18	9	**27**	16	5
19	12	28	19	9	25	15	5	23	13	1	19	10	28	17	6
20	**13**	1	20	**10**	26	16	**6**	24	14	**2**	20	11	29	**18**	7
21	14	2	21	11	27	17	7	25	15	3	21	12	1	19	8
22	15	3	22	12	28	18	8	**26**	16	4	**22**	13	2	20	9
23	16	4	23	13	29	19	9	27	**17**	5	23	**14**	3	21	**10**
24	17	**5**	24	14	**1**	20	10	28	18	6	24	15	4	22	11
25	18	6	**25**	15	2	**21**	11	1	19	7	25	16	**5**	23	12
26	19	7	26	16	3	22	12	2	20	8	26	17	6	24	13
27	**20**	8	27	**17**	4	23	**13**	3	21	**9**	27	18	7	**25**	14
28	21	9	28	18	5	24	14	4	22	10	28	19	8	26	15
29	22	10	29	19	6	25	15	**5**	23	11	**1**	20	9	27	16
30	—	11	—	—	7	—	—	6	—	—	2	—	10	—	—
		R			**R**			**R**			**R**		**R**		

Figures in **black type** denote Sabbaths.

13th, Fast of Esther (if on Sabbath, observed the preceding Thursday); 14th, Purim; 15th, Shushan Purim.

NOTE. — In a Jewish leap year, indicated by the letter **R** (for Adar Rishon) at the foot of a column, the above days are observed in 2nd Adar.

In a leap year, 30th day is First day of New Moon of the 2nd Adar.

2nd ADAR — ADAR SHENI, also known as VE-ADAR (29 days)

	5749	50	51	52	53	54	55	56	57	58	59	60	61	62	63	64	65	66	67	68	69	70	71	72	73	74	75	76	77	78
	1989	90	91	92	93	94	95	96	97	98	99	2000	01	02	03	04	05	06	07	08	09	10	11	12	13	14	15	16	17	18
2nd Adar	Mar-Apr			Mar-Apr			March		Mar-Apr			Mar-Apr			Mar-Apr		Mar-Apr			Mar-Apr			Mar-Apr			March		Mar-Apr		
1	8			6			3		10			8			5		**12**			**8**			7			3		11		
2	9			**7**			**4**		11			9			6		13			9			8			4		**12**		
3	10			8			5		12			10			7		14			10			9			5		13		
4	**11**			9			6		13			**11**			**8**		15			11			10			6		14		
5	12			10			7		14			12			9		16			12			11			7		15		
6	13			11			8		**15**			13			10		17			13			**12**			**8**		16		
7	14			12			9		16			14			11		18			14			13			9		17		
8	15			13			10		17			15			12		**19**			**15**			14			10		18		
9	16			**14**			**11**		18			16			13		20			16			15			11		**19**		
10	17			15			12		19			17			14		21			17			16			12		20		
11	**18**			16			13		20			**18**			**15**		22			18			17			13		21		
12	19			17			14		21			19			16		23			19			18			14		22		
13	20			18			15		**22**			20			17		24			20			**19**			**15**		23		
14	21			19			16		23			21			18		25			21			20			16		24		
15	22			20			17		24			22			19		**26**			**22**			21			17		25		
16	23			**21**			**18**		25			23			20		27			23			22			18		**26**		
17	24			22			19		26			24			21		28			24			23			19		27		
18	**25**			23			20		27			**25**			**22**		29			25			24			20		28		
19	26			24			21		28			26			23		30			26			25			21		29		
20	27			25			22		**29**			27			24		31			27			**26**			**22**		30		
21	28			26			23		30			28			25		1			28			27			23		31		
22	29			27			24		31			29			26		**2**			**29**			28			24		1		
23	30			**28**			**25**		1			30			27		3			30			29			25		**2**		
24	31			29			26		2			31			28		4			31			30			26		3		
25	**1**			30			27		3			**1**			**29**		5			1			31			27		4		
26	2			31			28		4			2			30		6			2			1			28		5		
27	3			1			29		**5**			3			31		7			3			**2**			**29**		6		
28	4			2			30		6			4			1		8			4			3			30		7		
29	5			3			31		7			5			2		**9**			**5**			4			31		8		

Figures in **black type** denote Sabbaths.
13th, Fast of Esther (if on Sabbath, observed on the preceding Thurday); 14th, Purim; 15th Shushan Purim.

NISAN (30 days)

	5749	50	51	52	53	54	55	56	57	58	59	60	61	62	63
	1989	90	91	92	93	94	95	96	97	98	99	2000	01	02	03
Nis	Apr-May	Mar-Apr	Mar-Apr	Apr-May	Mar-Apr	Mar-Apr	April	Mar-Apr	Apr-May	Mar-Apr	Mar-Apr	Apr-May	Mar-Apr	Mar-Apr	Apr-May
1	6	27	**16**	**4**	23	13	**1**	21	8	**28**	18	6	25	14	3
2	7	28	17	5	24	14	2	22	9	29	19	7	26	15	4
3	**8**	29	18	6	25	15	3	**23**	10	30	**20**	**8**	27	**16**	**5**
4	9	30	19	7	26	16	4	24	11	31	21	9	28	17	6
5	10	**31**	20	8	**27**	17	5	25	**12**	1	22	10	29	18	7
6	11	1	21	9	28	18	6	26	13	2	23	11	30	19	8
7	12	2	22	10	29	**19**	7	27	14	3	24	12	**31**	20	9
8	13	3	**23**	**11**	30	20	**8**	28	15	**4**	25	13	1	21	10
9	14	4	24	12	31	21	9	29	16	5	26	14	2	22	11
10	**15**	5	25	13	1	22	10	**30**	17	6	**27**	**15**	3	**23**	**12**
11	16	6	26	14	2	23	11	31	18	7	28	16	4	24	13
12	17	**7**	27	15	**3**	24	12	1	**19**	8	29	17	5	25	14
13	18	8	28	16	4	25	13	2	20	9	30	18	6	26	15
14	19	9	29	17	5	**26**	14	3	21	10	31	19	**7**	27	16
15	20	10	**30**	**18**	6	27	**15**	4	22	**11**	1	20	8	28	17
16	21	11	31	19	7	28	16	5	23	12	2	21	9	29	18
17	**22**	12	1	20	8	29	17	**6**	24	13	**3**	**22**	10	**30**	**19**
18	23	13	2	21	9	30	18	7	25	14	4	23	11	31	20
19	24	**14**	3	22	**10**	31	19	8	**26**	15	5	24	12	1	21
20	25	15	4	23	11	1	20	9	27	16	6	25	13	2	22
21	26	16	5	24	12	**2**	21	10	28	17	7	26	**14**	3	23
22	27	17	**6**	**25**	13	3	**22**	11	29	**18**	8	27	15	4	24
23	28	18	7	26	14	4	23	12	30	19	9	28	16	5	25
24	**29**	19	8	27	15	5	24	**13**	1	20	**10**	**29**	17	**6**	**26**
25	30	20	9	28	16	6	25	14	2	21	11	30	18	7	27
26	1	**21**	10	29	**17**	7	26	15	**3**	22	12	1	19	8	28
27	2	22	11	30	18	8	27	16	4	23	13	2	20	9	29
28	3	23	12	1	19	**9**	28	17	5	24	14	3	**21**	10	30
29	4	24	**13**	**2**	20	10	**29**	18	6	**25**	15	4	22	11	1
30	5	25	14	3	21	11	30	19	7	26	16	5	23	12	2

	64	65	66	67	68	69	70	71	72	73	74	75	76	77	78
	04	05	06	07	08	09	10	11	12	13	14	15	16	17	18
Nis	Mar-Apr	Apr-May	Mar-Apr	Mar-Apr	Apr-May	Mar-Apr	Mar-Apr	Apr-May	Mar-Apr	Mar-Apr	April	Mar-Apr	Apr-May	Mar-Apr	Mar-Apr
1	23	10	30	20	6	26	16	5	**24**	12	1	**21**	**9**	28	**17**
2	24	11	31	21	7	27	17	6	25	13	2	22	10	29	18
3	25	12	**1**	22	8	**28**	18	7	26	14	3	23	11	30	19
4	26	13	2	23	9	29	19	8	27	15	4	24	12	31	20
5	**27**	14	3	**24**	10	30	**20**	**9**	28	**16**	**5**	25	13	**1**	21
6	28	15	4	25	11	31	21	10	29	17	6	26	14	2	22
7	29	**16**	5	26	**12**	1	22	11	30	18	7	27	15	3	23
8	30	17	6	27	13	2	23	12	**31**	19	8	**28**	**16**	4	**24**
9	31	18	7	28	14	3	24	13	1	20	9	29	17	5	25
10	1	19	**8**	29	15	**4**	25	14	2	21	10	30	18	6	26
11	2	20	9	30	16	5	26	15	3	22	11	31	19	7	27
12	**3**	21	10	**31**	17	6	**27**	**16**	4	**23**	**12**	1	20	**8**	28
13	4	22	11	1	18	7	28	17	5	24	13	2	21	9	29
14	5	**23**	12	2	**19**	8	29	18	6	25	14	3	22	10	30
15	6	24	13	3	20	9	30	19	**7**	26	15	**4**	**23**	11	**31**
16	7	25	14	4	21	10	31	20	8	27	16	5	24	12	1
17	8	26	**15**	5	22	**11**	1	21	9	28	17	6	25	13	2
18	9	27	16	6	23	12	2	22	10	29	18	7	26	14	3
19	**10**	28	17	**7**	24	13	**3**	**23**	11	**30**	**19**	8	27	**15**	4
20	11	29	18	8	25	14	4	24	12	31	20	9	28	16	5
21	12	**30**	19	9	**26**	15	5	25	13	1	21	10	29	17	6
22	13	1	20	10	27	16	6	26	**14**	2	22	**11**	**30**	18	**7**
23	14	2	21	11	28	17	7	27	15	3	23	12	1	19	8
24	15	3	**22**	12	29	**18**	8	28	16	4	24	13	2	20	9
25	16	4	23	13	30	19	9	29	17	5	25	14	3	21	10
26	**17**	5	24	**14**	1	20	**10**	**30**	18	**6**	**26**	15	4	**22**	11
27	18	6	25	15	2	21	11	1	19	7	27	16	5	23	12
28	19	**7**	26	16	**3**	22	12	2	20	8	28	17	6	24	13
29	20	8	27	17	4	23	13	3	**21**	9	29	**18**	**7**	25	**14**
30	21	9	28	18	5	24	14	4	22	10	30	19	8	26	15

In the left-hand margin figures in **black type** denote major Holy-days; elsewhere they denote Sabbaths.
14th, Fast of the Firstborn (if on Sabbath, observed on the preceding Thursday); 15th to 22nd, Passover;
30th, First day of New Moon of Iyar.

IYAR (29 days)

	5749	50	51	52	53	54	55	56	57	58	59	60	61	62	63	64	65	66	67	68	69	70	71	72	73	74	75	76	77	78
	1989	90	91	92	93	94	95	96	97	98	99	2000	01	02	03	04	05	06	07	08	09	10	11	12	13	14	15	16	17	18
Iyar	May-Jn	Apr-May	Apr-May	May-Jn	Apr-May	Apr-May	May	Apr-May	May-Jn	Apr-May	Apr-May	May-Jn	Apr-May	Apr-May	May	Apr-May	May-Jn	Apr-May	Apr-May	May-Jn	Apr-May	Apr-May	May-Jn	Apr-May	Apr-May	May	Apr-May	May-Jn	Apr-May	Apr-May
1	**6**	26	15	4	22	12	1	**20**	8	27	**17**	**6**	24	**13**	**3**	22	10	**29**	19	6	**25**	15	5	23	11	1	20	9	27	16
2	7	27	16	5	23	13	2	21	9	28	18	7	25	14	4	23	11	30	20	7	26	16	6	24	12	2	21	10	28	17
3	8	**28**	17	6	**24**	14	3	22	**10**	29	19	8	26	15	5	**24**	12	1	**21**	8	27	**17**	**7**	25	**13**	**3**	22	11	**29**	18
4	9	29	18	7	25	15	4	23	11	30	20	9	27	16	6	25	13	2	22	9	28	18	8	26	14	4	23	12	30	19
5	10	30	19	8	26	**16**	5	24	12	1	21	10	**28**	17	7	26	**14**	3	23	**10**	29	19	9	27	15	5	24	13	1	20
6	11	1	**20**	**9**	27	17	**6**	25	13	**2**	22	11	29	18	8	27	15	4	24	11	30	20	10	**28**	16	6	**25**	**14**	2	**21**
7	12	2	21	10	28	18	7	26	14	3	23	12	30	19	9	28	16	5	25	12	1	21	11	29	17	7	26	15	3	22
8	**13**	3	22	11	29	19	8	**27**	15	4	**24**	**13**	1	**20**	**10**	29	17	**6**	26	13	**2**	22	12	30	18	8	27	16	4	23
9	14	4	23	12	30	20	9	28	16	5	25	14	2	21	11	30	18	7	27	14	3	23	13	1	19	9	28	17	5	24
10	15	**5**	24	13	**1**	21	10	29	**17**	6	26	15	3	22	12	**1**	19	8	**28**	15	4	**24**	**14**	2	**20**	**10**	29	18	**6**	25
11	16	6	25	14	2	22	11	30	18	7	27	16	4	23	13	2	20	9	29	16	5	25	15	3	21	11	30	19	7	26
12	17	7	26	15	3	**23**	12	1	19	8	28	17	**5**	24	14	3	**21**	10	30	**17**	6	26	16	4	22	12	1	20	8	27
13	18	8	**27**	**16**	4	24	**13**	2	20	**9**	29	18	6	25	15	4	22	11	1	18	7	27	17	**5**	23	13	**2**	**21**	9	**28**
14	19	9	28	17	5	25	14	3	21	10	30	19	7	26	16	5	23	12	2	19	8	28	18	6	24	14	3	22	10	29
15	**20**	10	29	18	6	26	15	**4**	22	11	**1**	**20**	8	**27**	**17**	6	24	**13**	3	20	**9**	29	19	7	25	15	4	23	11	30
16	21	11	30	19	7	27	16	5	23	12	2	21	9	28	18	7	25	14	4	21	10	30	20	8	26	16	5	24	12	1
17	22	**12**	1	20	**8**	28	17	6	**24**	13	3	22	10	29	19	**8**	26	15	**5**	22	11	**1**	**21**	9	**27**	**17**	6	25	**13**	2
18	23	13	2	21	9	29	18	7	25	14	4	23	11	30	20	9	27	16	6	23	12	2	22	10	28	18	7	26	14	3
19	24	14	3	22	10	**30**	19	8	26	15	5	24	**12**	1	21	10	**28**	17	7	**24**	13	3	23	11	29	19	8	27	15	4
20	25	15	**4**	**23**	11	1	**20**	9	27	**16**	6	25	13	2	22	11	29	18	8	25	14	4	24	**12**	30	20	**9**	**28**	16	**5**
21	26	16	5	24	12	2	21	10	28	17	7	26	14	3	23	12	30	19	9	26	15	5	25	13	1	21	10	29	17	6
22	**27**	17	6	25	13	3	22	**11**	29	18	**8**	**27**	15	**4**	**24**	13	31	**20**	10	27	**16**	6	26	14	2	22	11	30	18	7
23	28	18	7	26	14	4	23	12	30	19	9	28	16	5	25	14	1	21	11	28	17	7	27	15	3	23	12	31	19	8
24	29	**19**	8	27	**15**	5	24	13	**31**	20	10	29	17	6	26	**15**	2	22	**12**	29	18	**8**	**28**	16	**4**	**24**	13	1	**20**	9
25	30	20	9	28	16	6	25	14	1	21	11	30	18	7	27	16	3	23	13	30	19	9	29	17	5	25	14	2	21	10
26	31	21	10	29	17	**7**	26	15	2	22	12	31	**19**	8	28	17	**4**	24	14	**31**	20	10	30	18	6	26	15	3	22	11
27	1	22	**11**	**30**	18	8	**27**	16	3	**23**	13	1	20	9	29	18	5	25	15	1	21	11	31	**19**	7	27	**16**	**4**	23	**12**
28	2	23	12	31	19	9	28	17	4	24	14	2	21	10	30	19	6	26	16	2	22	12	1	20	8	28	17	5	24	13
29	**3**	24	13	1	20	10	29	**18**	5	25	**15**	**3**	22	**11**	**31**	20	7	**27**	17	3	**23**	13	2	21	9	29	18	6	25	14

Figures in **black type** denote Sabbaths.
18th, 33rd Day Omer, Scholars' Festival.

SIVAN (30 days)

	5749	50	51	52	53	54	55	56	57	58	59	60	61	62	63	64	65	66	67	68	69	70	71	72	73	74	75	76	77	78
	1989	90	91	92	93	94	95	96	97	98	99	2000	01	02	03	04	05	06	07	08	09	10	11	12	13	14	15	16	17	18
Sivan	Jn-July	May-Jn	May-Jn	Jn-July	May-Jn	May-Jn	May-Jn	May-Jn	Jn-July	May-Jn	May-Jn	Jn-July	May-Jn	May-Jn	June	May-Jn	Jn-July	May-Jn	May-Jn	Jn-July	May-Jn	May-Jn	Ju-July	May-Jn	May-Jn	May-Jn	May-Jn	Ju-July	May-Jn	May-Jn
1	4	25	14	2	21	11	30	19	6	26	16	4	23	12	1	21	8	28	18	4	24	14	3	22	10	30	19	7	26	15
2	5	**26**	15	3	**22**	12	31	20	**7**	27	17	5	24	13	2	**22**	9	29	**19**	5	25	**15**	**4**	23	**11**	**31**	20	8	**27**	16
3	6	27	16	4	23	13	1	21	8	28	18	6	25	14	3	23	10	30	20	6	26	16	5	24	12	1	21	9	28	17
4	7	28	17	5	24	**14**	2	22	9	29	19	7	**26**	15	4	24	**11**	31	21	**7**	27	17	6	25	13	2	22	10	29	18
5	8	29	**18**	**6**	25	15	**3**	23	10	**30**	20	8	27	16	5	25	12	1	22	8	28	18	7	**26**	14	**3**	**23**	**11**	30	**19**
6	9	30	19	7	26	16	4	24	11	31	21	9	28	17	6	26	13	2	23	9	29	19	8	27	15	4	24	12	31	20
7	**10**	31	20	8	27	17	5	**25**	12	1	**22**	**10**	29	**18**	**7**	27	14	**3**	24	10	**30**	20	9	28	16	5	25	13	1	21
8	11	1	21	9	28	18	6	26	13	2	23	11	30	19	8	28	15	4	25	11	31	21	10	29	17	6	26	14	2	22
9	12	**2**	22	10	**29**	19	7	27	**14**	3	24	12	31	20	9	**29**	16	5	**26**	12	1	**22**	**11**	30	**18**	**7**	27	15	**3**	23
10	13	3	23	11	30	20	8	28	15	4	25	13	1	21	10	30	17	6	27	13	2	23	12	31	19	8	28	16	4	24
11	14	4	24	12	31	**21**	9	29	16	5	26	14	**2**	22	11	31	**18**	7	28	**14**	3	24	13	1	20	9	29	17	5	25
12	15	5	**25**	**13**	1	22	**10**	30	17	**6**	27	15	3	23	12	1	19	8	29	15	4	25	14	**2**	21	10	**30**	**18**	6	**26**
13	16	6	26	14	2	23	11	31	18	7	28	16	4	24	13	2	20	9	30	16	5	26	15	3	22	11	31	19	7	27
14	**17**	7	27	15	3	24	12	**1**	19	8	**29**	**17**	5	**25**	**14**	3	21	**10**	31	17	**6**	27	16	4	23	12	1	20	8	28
15	18	8	28	16	4	25	13	2	20	9	30	18	6	26	15	4	22	11	1	18	7	28	17	5	24	13	2	21	9	29
16	19	**9**	29	17	**5**	26	14	3	**21**	10	31	19	7	27	16	**5**	23	12	**2**	19	8	**29**	**18**	6	**25**	**14**	3	22	**10**	30
17	20	10	30	18	6	27	15	4	22	11	1	20	8	28	17	6	24	13	3	20	9	30	19	7	26	15	4	23	11	31
18	21	11	31	19	7	**28**	16	5	23	12	2	21	**9**	29	18	7	**25**	14	4	**21**	10	31	20	8	27	16	5	24	12	1
19	22	12	**1**	**20**	8	29	**17**	6	24	**13**	3	22	10	30	19	8	26	15	5	22	11	1	21	**9**	28	17	**6**	**25**	13	**2**
20	23	13	2	21	9	30	18	7	25	14	4	23	11	31	20	9	27	16	6	23	12	2	22	10	29	18	7	26	14	3
21	**24**	14	3	22	10	31	19	**8**	26	15	**5**	**24**	12	**1**	**21**	10	28	**17**	7	24	**13**	3	23	11	30	19	8	27	15	4
22	25	15	4	23	11	1	20	9	27	16	6	25	13	2	22	11	29	18	8	25	14	4	24	12	31	20	9	28	16	5
23	26	**16**	5	24	**12**	2	21	10	**28**	17	7	26	14	3	23	**12**	30	19	**9**	26	15	**5**	**25**	13	**1**	**21**	10	29	**17**	6
24	27	17	6	25	13	3	22	11	29	18	8	27	15	4	24	13	1	20	10	27	16	6	26	14	2	22	11	30	18	7
25	28	18	7	26	14	**4**	23	12	30	19	9	28	**16**	5	25	14	**2**	21	11	**28**	17	7	27	15	3	23	12	1	19	8
26	29	19	**8**	**27**	15	5	**24**	13	1	**20**	10	29	17	6	26	15	3	22	12	29	18	8	28	**16**	4	24	**13**	**2**	20	**9**
27	30	20	9	28	16	6	25	14	2	21	11	30	18	7	27	16	4	23	13	30	19	9	29	17	5	25	14	3	21	10
28	**1**	21	10	29	17	7	26	**15**	3	22	**12**	**1**	19	**8**	**28**	17	5	**24**	14	1	**20**	10	30	18	6	26	15	4	22	11
29	2	22	11	30	18	8	27	16	4	23	13	2	20	9	29	18	6	25	15	2	21	11	1	19	7	27	16	5	23	12
30	3	**23**	12	1	**19**	9	28	17	**5**	24	14	3	21	10	30	**19**	7	26	**16**	3	22	**12**	**2**	20	**8**	**28**	17	6	**24**	13

In the left-hand margin figures in **black type** denote major Holy-days; elsewhere they denote Sabbaths.
6th and 7th, Pentecost; 30th, First day of New Moon of Tammuz.

TAMMUZ (29 days)

	5749	50	51	52	53	54	55	56	57	58
	1989	90	91	92	93	94	95	96	97	98
Tam	July-Au	Jn-July	Jn-July	July	Jn-July	Jn-July	Jn-July	Jn-July	July-Au	Jn-July
1	4	24	13	2	20	10	29	18	6	25
2	5	25	14	3	21	**11**	30	19	7	26
3	6	26	**15**	**4**	22	12	**1**	20	8	**27**
4	7	27	16	5	23	13	2	21	9	28
5	**8**	28	17	6	24	14	3	**22**	10	29
6	9	29	18	7	25	15	4	23	11	30
7	10	**30**	19	8	**26**	16	5	24	**12**	1
8	11	1	20	9	27	17	6	25	13	2
9	12	2	21	10	28	**18**	7	26	14	3
10	13	3	**22**	**11**	29	19	**8**	27	15	**4**
11	14	4	23	12	30	20	9	28	16	5
12	**15**	5	24	13	1	21	10	**29**	17	6
13	16	6	25	14	2	22	11	30	18	7
14	17	**7**	26	15	**3**	23	12	1	**19**	8
15	18	8	27	16	4	24	13	2	20	9
16	19	9	28	17	5	**25**	14	3	21	10
17	20	10	**29**	**18**	6	26	**15**	4	22	**11**
18	21	11	30	19	7	27	16	5	23	12
19	**22**	12	1	20	8	28	17	**6**	24	13
20	23	13	2	21	9	29	18	7	25	14
21	24	**14**	3	22	**10**	30	19	8	**26**	15
22	25	15	4	23	11	1	20	9	27	16
23	26	16	5	24	12	**2**	21	10	28	17
24	27	17	**6**	**25**	13	3	**22**	11	29	**18**
25	28	18	7	26	14	4	23	12	30	19
26	**29**	19	8	27	15	5	24	**13**	31	20
27	30	20	9	28	16	6	25	14	1	21
28	31	**21**	10	29	**17**	7	26	15	**2**	22
29	1	22	11	30	18	8	27	16	3	23

	59	60	61	62	63	64	65	66	67	68
	99	2000	01	02	03	04	05	06	07	08
Tam	Jn-July	July-Au	Jn-July	Jn-July	July	Jn-July	July-Au	Jn-July	Jn-July	July-Au
1	15	4	22	11	1	20	8	27	17	4
2	16	5	**23**	12	2	21	**9**	28	18	**5**
3	17	6	24	13	3	22	10	29	19	6
4	18	7	25	14	4	23	11	30	20	7
5	**19**	**8**	26	**15**	**5**	24	12	**1**	21	8
6	20	9	27	16	6	25	13	2	22	9
7	21	10	28	17	7	**26**	14	3	**23**	10
8	22	11	29	18	8	27	15	4	24	11
9	23	12	**30**	19	9	28	**16**	5	25	**12**
10	24	13	1	20	10	29	17	6	26	13
11	25	14	2	21	11	30	18	7	27	14
12	**26**	**15**	3	**22**	**12**	1	19	**8**	28	15
13	27	16	4	23	13	2	20	9	29	16
14	28	17	5	24	14	**3**	21	10	**30**	17
15	29	18	6	25	15	4	22	11	1	18
16	30	19	**7**	26	16	5	**23**	12	2	**19**
17	1	20	8	27	17	6	24	13	3	20
18	2	21	9	28	18	7	25	14	4	21
19	**3**	**22**	10	**29**	**19**	8	26	**15**	5	22
20	4	23	11	30	20	9	27	16	6	23
21	5	24	12	1	21	**10**	28	17	**7**	24
22	6	25	13	2	22	11	29	18	8	25
23	7	26	**14**	3	23	12	**30**	19	9	**26**
24	8	27	15	4	24	13	31	20	10	27
25	9	28	16	5	25	14	1	21	11	28
26	**10**	**29**	17	**6**	**26**	15	2	**22**	12	29
27	11	30	18	7	27	16	3	23	13	30
28	12	31	19	8	28	**17**	4	24	**14**	31
29	13	1	20	9	29	18	5	25	15	1

	69	70	71	72	73	74	75	76	77	78
	09	10	11	12	13	14	15	16	17	18
Tam	Jn-July	Jn-July	July	Ju-July	Ju-July	Ju-July	Ju-July	July-Au	Ju-July	Ju-July
1	23	13	3	21	9	29	18	7	25	14
2	24	14	4	22	10	30	19	8	26	15
3	25	15	5	**23**	11	1	**20**	**9**	27	**16**
4	26	16	6	24	12	2	21	10	28	17
5	**27**	17	7	25	13	3	22	11	29	18
6	28	18	8	26	14	4	23	12	30	19
7	29	**19**	**9**	27	**15**	**5**	24	13	**1**	20
8	30	20	10	28	16	6	25	14	2	21
9	1	21	11	29	17	7	26	15	3	22
10	2	22	12	**30**	18	8	**27**	**16**	4	**23**
11	3	23	13	1	19	9	28	17	5	24
12	**4**	24	14	2	20	10	29	18	6	25
13	5	25	15	3	21	11	30	19	7	26
14	6	**26**	**16**	4	**22**	**12**	1	20	**8**	27
15	7	27	17	5	23	13	2	21	9	28
16	8	28	18	6	24	14	3	22	10	29
17	9	29	19	**7**	25	15	**4**	**23**	11	**30**
18	10	30	20	8	26	16	5	24	12	1
19	**11**	1	21	9	27	17	6	25	13	2
20	12	2	22	10	28	18	7	26	14	3
21	13	**3**	**23**	11	**29**	**19**	8	27	**15**	4
22	14	4	24	12	30	20	9	28	16	5
23	15	5	25	13	1	21	10	29	17	6
24	16	6	26	**14**	2	22	**11**	**30**	18	**7**
25	17	7	27	15	3	23	12	31	19	8
26	**18**	8	28	16	4	24	13	1	20	9
27	19	9	29	17	5	25	14	2	21	10
28	20	**10**	**30**	18	**6**	**26**	15	3	**22**	11
29	21	11	31	19	7	27	16	4	23	12

Figures in **black type** denote Sabbaths.
17th, Fast of Tammuz (if on Sabbath, postponed to Sunday).

AB (30 days)

	5749	50	51	52	53	54	55	56	57	58	59	60	61	62	63	64	65	66	67	68	69	70	71	72	73	74	75	76	77	78
	1989	90	91	92	93	94	95	96	97	98	99	2000	01	02	03	04	05	06	07	08	09	10	11	12	13	14	15	16	17	18
Ab	August	July-Au	July-Au	July-Au	July-Au	July-Au	July-Au	July-Au	Au-Sep	July-Au	July-Au	August	July-Au	July-Au	July-Au	July-Au	Au-Sep	July-Au	July-Au	August	July-Au	July-Au	August	July-Au	July-Au	July-Au	July-Au	Au-Sep	July-Au	July-Au
1	2	23	12	31	19	**9**	28	17	4	24	14	2	**21**	10	30	19	**6**	26	16	**2**	22	12	1	20	8	28	17	5	24	13
2	3	24	**13**	**1**	20	10	**29**	18	5	**25**	15	3	22	11	31	20	7	27	17	3	23	13	2	**21**	9	29	**18**	**6**	25	**14**
3	4	25	14	2	21	11	30	19	6	26	16	4	23	12	1	21	8	28	18	4	24	14	3	22	10	30	19	7	26	15
4	**5**	26	15	3	22	12	31	**20**	7	27	**17**	**5**	24	**13**	**2**	22	9	**29**	19	5	**25**	15	4	23	11	31	20	8	27	16
5	6	27	16	4	23	13	1	21	8	28	18	6	25	14	3	23	10	30	20	6	26	16	5	24	12	1	21	9	28	17
6	7	**28**	17	5	**24**	14	2	22	**9**	29	19	7	26	15	4	**24**	11	31	**21**	7	27	**17**	**6**	25	**13**	**2**	22	10	**29**	18
7	8	29	18	6	25	15	3	23	10	30	20	8	27	16	5	25	12	1	22	8	28	18	7	26	14	3	23	11	30	19
8	9	30	19	7	26	**16**	4	24	11	31	21	9	**28**	17	6	26	**13**	2	23	**9**	29	19	8	27	15	4	24	12	31	20
9	10	31	**20**	**8**	27	17	**5**	25	12	**1**	22	10	29	18	7	27	14	3	24	10	30	20	9	**28**	16	5	**25**	**13**	1	**21**
10	11	1	21	9	28	18	6	26	13	2	23	11	30	19	8	28	15	4	25	11	31	21	10	29	17	6	26	14	2	22
11	**12**	2	22	10	29	19	7	**27**	14	3	**24**	**12**	31	**20**	**9**	29	16	**5**	26	12	**1**	22	11	30	18	7	27	15	3	23
12	13	3	23	11	30	20	8	28	15	4	25	13	1	21	10	30	17	6	27	13	2	23	12	31	19	8	28	16	4	24
13	14	**4**	24	12	**31**	21	9	29	**16**	5	26	14	2	22	11	**31**	18	7	**28**	14	3	**24**	**13**	1	**20**	**9**	29	17	**5**	25
14	15	5	25	13	1	22	10	30	17	6	27	15	3	23	12	1	19	8	29	15	4	25	14	2	21	10	30	18	6	26
15	16	6	26	14	2	**23**	11	31	18	7	28	16	**4**	24	13	2	**20**	9	30	**16**	5	26	15	3	22	11	31	19	7	27
16	17	7	**27**	**15**	3	24	**12**	1	19	**8**	29	17	5	25	14	3	21	10	31	17	6	27	16	**4**	23	12	**1**	**20**	8	**28**
17	18	8	28	16	4	25	13	2	20	9	30	18	6	26	15	4	22	11	1	18	7	28	17	5	24	13	2	21	9	29
18	**19**	9	29	17	5	26	14	**3**	21	10	**31**	**19**	7	**27**	**16**	5	23	**12**	2	19	**8**	29	18	6	25	14	3	22	10	30
19	20	10	30	18	6	27	15	4	22	11	1	20	8	28	17	6	24	13	3	20	9	30	19	7	26	15	4	23	11	31
20	21	**11**	31	19	**7**	28	16	5	**23**	12	2	21	9	29	18	**7**	25	14	**4**	21	10	**31**	**20**	8	**27**	**16**	5	24	**12**	1
21	22	12	1	20	8	29	17	6	24	13	3	22	10	30	19	8	26	15	5	22	11	1	21	9	28	17	6	25	13	2
22	23	13	2	21	9	**30**	18	7	25	14	4	23	**11**	31	20	9	**27**	16	6	**23**	12	2	22	10	29	18	7	26	14	3
23	24	14	**3**	**22**	10	31	**19**	8	26	**15**	5	24	12	1	21	10	28	17	7	24	13	3	23	**11**	30	19	**8**	**27**	15	**4**
24	25	15	4	23	11	1	20	9	27	16	6	25	13	2	22	11	29	18	8	25	14	4	24	12	31	20	9	28	16	5
25	**26**	16	5	24	12	2	21	**10**	28	17	**7**	**26**	14	**3**	**23**	12	30	**19**	9	26	**15**	5	25	13	1	21	10	29	17	6
26	27	17	6	25	13	3	22	11	29	18	8	27	15	4	24	13	31	20	10	27	16	6	26	14	2	22	11	30	18	7
27	28	**18**	7	26	**14**	4	23	12	**30**	19	9	28	16	5	25	**14**	1	21	**11**	28	17	**7**	**27**	15	**3**	**23**	12	31	**19**	8
28	29	19	8	27	15	5	24	13	31	20	10	29	17	6	26	15	2	22	12	29	18	8	28	16	4	24	13	1	20	9
29	30	20	9	28	16	**6**	25	14	1	21	11	30	**18**	7	27	16	**3**	23	13	**30**	19	9	29	17	5	25	14	2	21	10
30	31	21	**10**	**29**	17	7	**26**	15	2	**22**	12	31	19	8	28	17	4	24	14	31	20	10	30	**18**	6	26	**15**	**3**	22	**11**

Figures in **black type** denote Sabbaths.
9th, Fast of Ab (if on Sabbath, postponed to Sunday); 30th, First Day of New Moon of Elul.

ELUL (29 days)

	5749	50	51	52	53	54	55	56	57	58	59	60	61	62	63	64	65	66	67	68	69	70	71	72	73	74	75	76	77	78
	1989	90	91	92	93	94	95	96	97	98	99	2000	01	02	03	04	05	06	07	08	09	10	11	12	13	14	15	16	17	18
Elul	Sept	Au-Sep	Au-Sep	Au-Sep	Au-Sep	Au-Sep	Au-Sep	Au-Sep	Sep-Oct	Au-Sep	Au-Sep	Sept	Au-Sep	Au-Sep	Au-Sep	Au-Sep	Sep-Oct	Au-Sep	Au-Sep	Sept	Au-Sep	Au-Sep	Au-Sep	Au-Sep	Au-Sep	Au-Sep	Au-Sep	Sep-Oct	Au-Sep	Au-Sep
1	1	22	11	30	18	8	27	16	3	23	13	1	20	9	29	18	5	25	15	1	21	11	31	19	7	27	16	4	23	12
2	**2**	23	12	31	19	9	28	**17**	4	24	**14**	**2**	21	**10**	**30**	19	6	**26**	16	2	**22**	12	1	20	8	28	17	5	24	13
3	3	24	13	1	20	10	29	18	5	25	15	3	22	11	31	20	7	27	17	3	23	13	2	21	9	29	18	6	25	14
4	4	**25**	14	2	**21**	11	30	19	**6**	26	16	4	23	12	1	**21**	8	28	**18**	4	24	**14**	**3**	22	**10**	**30**	19	7	**26**	15
5	5	26	15	3	22	12	31	20	7	27	17	5	24	13	2	22	9	29	19	5	25	15	4	23	11	31	20	8	27	16
6	6	27	16	4	23	**13**	1	21	8	28	18	6	**25**	14	3	23	**10**	30	20	**6**	26	16	5	24	12	1	21	9	28	17
7	7	28	**17**	**5**	24	14	**2**	22	9	**29**	19	7	26	15	4	24	11	31	21	7	27	17	6	**25**	13	2	**22**	**10**	29	**18**
8	8	29	18	6	25	15	3	23	10	30	20	8	27	16	5	25	12	1	22	8	28	18	7	26	14	3	23	11	30	19
9	**9**	30	19	7	26	16	4	**24**	11	31	**21**	**9**	28	**17**	**6**	26	13	**2**	23	9	**29**	19	8	27	15	4	24	12	31	20
10	10	31	20	8	27	17	5	25	12	1	22	10	29	18	7	27	14	3	24	10	30	20	9	28	16	5	25	13	1	21
11	11	**1**	21	9	**28**	18	6	26	**13**	2	23	11	30	19	8	**28**	15	4	**25**	11	31	**21**	**10**	29	**17**	**6**	26	14	**2**	22
12	12	2	22	10	29	19	7	27	14	3	24	12	31	20	9	29	16	5	26	12	1	22	11	30	18	7	27	15	3	23
13	13	3	23	11	30	**20**	8	28	15	4	25	13	**1**	21	10	30	**17**	6	27	**13**	2	23	12	31	19	8	28	16	4	24
14	14	4	**24**	**12**	31	21	**9**	29	16	**5**	26	14	2	22	11	31	18	7	28	14	3	24	13	**1**	20	9	**29**	**17**	5	**25**
15	15	5	25	13	1	22	10	30	17	6	27	15	3	23	12	1	19	8	29	15	4	25	14	2	21	10	30	18	6	26
16	**16**	6	26	14	2	23	11	**31**	18	7	**28**	**16**	4	**24**	**13**	2	20	**9**	30	16	**5**	26	15	3	22	11	31	19	7	27
17	17	7	27	15	3	24	12	1	19	8	29	17	5	25	14	3	21	10	31	17	6	27	16	4	23	12	1	20	8	28
18	18	**8**	28	16	**4**	25	13	2	**20**	9	30	18	6	26	15	**4**	22	11	**1**	18	7	**28**	**17**	5	**24**	**13**	2	21	**9**	29
19	19	9	29	17	5	26	14	3	21	10	31	19	7	27	16	5	23	12	2	19	8	29	18	6	25	14	3	22	10	30
20	20	10	30	18	6	**27**	15	4	22	11	1	20	**8**	28	17	6	**24**	13	3	**20**	9	30	19	7	26	15	4	23	11	31
21	21	11	**31**	**19**	7	28	**16**	5	23	**12**	2	21	9	29	18	7	25	14	4	21	10	31	20	**8**	27	16	**5**	**24**	12	**1**
22	22	12	1	20	8	29	17	6	24	13	3	22	10	30	19	8	26	15	5	22	11	1	21	9	28	17	6	25	13	2
23	**23**	13	2	21	9	30	18	**7**	25	14	**4**	**23**	11	**31**	**20**	9	27	**16**	6	23	**12**	2	22	10	29	18	7	26	14	3
24	24	14	3	22	10	31	19	8	26	15	5	24	12	1	21	10	28	17	7	24	13	3	23	11	30	19	8	27	15	4
25	25	**15**	4	23	**11**	1	20	9	**27**	16	6	25	13	2	22	**11**	29	18	**8**	25	14	**4**	**24**	12	**31**	**20**	9	28	**16**	5
26	26	16	5	24	12	2	21	10	28	17	7	26	14	3	23	12	30	19	9	26	15	5	25	13	1	21	10	29	17	6
27	27	17	6	25	13	**3**	22	11	29	18	8	27	**15**	4	24	13	**1**	20	10	**27**	16	6	26	14	2	22	11	30	18	7
28	28	18	**7**	**26**	14	4	**23**	12	30	**19**	9	28	16	5	25	14	2	21	11	28	17	7	27	**15**	3	23	**12**	**1**	19	**8**
29	29	19	8	27	15	5	24	13	1	20	10	29	17	6	26	15	3	22	12	29	18	8	28	16	4	24	13	2	20	9

Figures in **black type** denote Sabbaths.

INDEX

A

B

C

J

K

L

T

Y

Z

PUBLISHER'S REQUEST

Update for Jewish Year Book 2004

Readers are asked kindly to draw attention to any omissions or errors. If errors are discovered, it would be appreciated if you could give up-to-date information, referring to the appropriate page, and send this form to the Editor at the address given below. Alternatively, you can email us.

With reference to the following entry:

Page:

Country:

Entry should read:

Kindly list on separate sheet if preferred.

Signed: ______________________ Date: __________

Name (BLOCK CAPITALS) ______________________

Address: ______________________

____

Telephone: ______________________

SEND TO:

The Editor

Jewish Year Book

Vallentine Mitchell & Co. Ltd.

Crown House, 47 Chase Side,

Southgate, London N14 5BP

Fax: + 44(0)20-8447 8548. E-mail: jtg@vmbooks.com

THE JEWISH YEAR BOOK 2004

ADVERTISING RATES

Advertising Rates for the

Jewish Year Book 2004

Full Page	**£550**	**182 x 113 mm**
Half Page	**£275**	**88 x 113 mm**
Quarter Page	**£165**	**44 x 54 mm**

Special positions are available by arrangement

(Please note the above rates are subject to VAT)

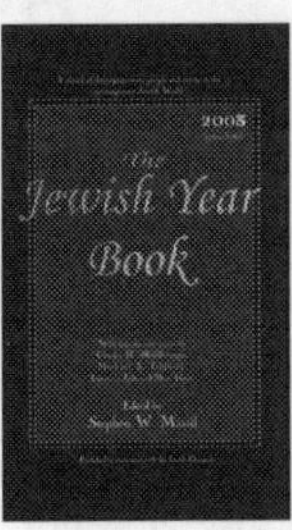

A record of the organisations, people and events in the contemporary Jewish world.

'*... With a cast of thousands, a meandering plot and telephone numbers and addresses to die for, the Jewish Year Book is essential reading.*'

***Anna Charin*, Jewish Chronicle**

'*... All in all ... a worthy reference companion that will help in traversing the particulars of the Jewish world.*'

***Elli Wohlgelernter*, Jerusalem Post**

'*... The Year Book is undoubtedly a vital tool for all communal workers and others who need to be in contact with Jewish organisations throughout the world.*'

***I. Selig*, Belfast Jewish Record**

- **FREE** copy of The **Jewish Year Book 2004** for all advertisers.
- **The Jewish Year Book** is updated each year.

- Visit our website: www.vmbooks.com
- Don't forget to complete and return the advertisement order form on the reverse.

To: The Advertising Department

The Jewish Year Book

VALLENTINE MITCHELL

Crown House, 47 Chase Side, Southgate, London N14 5BP, England

Tel: +44 (0)20 8920 2100 *Fax:* +44 (0)20 8447 8548

E-mail: jyb@vmbooks.com *Website:* www.vmbooks.com

THE JEWISH YEAR BOOK 2004
Advertising Order Form

☐ Please insert the attached copy
If setting is required a 10% setting charge will be made.)

☐ Copy will be forwarded from our Advertising Agents (*see below*)

☐ I enclose a cheque for £_________made payable to Vallentine Mitchell

Please charge my ☐ Visa ☐ Mastercard ☐ American Express

Card Number____________________________________Expiry Date___________

All advertisements set by the publisher will only be included if the proofs have been signed and approved by the advertiser

Contact Name: ______________________________

Advertisers Name: ______________________________

Address: ______________________________

____

Tel: ______________ Fax: ______________

Signed: ______________ Title: ______________

VAT No: ______________ Date: ______________

Agency Name (if applicable: ______________________________

Address: ______________________________

____

____

Tel: ______________ Fax: ______________

To: The Advertising Department

The Jewish Year Book

VALLENTINE MITCHELL

Crown House, 47 Chase Side, Southgate, London N14 5BP, England
Tel: +44 (0)20 8920 2100 *Fax:* +44 (0)20 8447 8548
E-mail: jyb@vmbooks.com *Website:* www.vmbooks.com

FrankCass publishers

JOURNALS

The Journal of Holocaust Education
Editors: **Dr Jo Reilly** and **Dr Donald Bloxham**, *University of Southampton*

ISSN 1359-1371 Volume 11 2003
Three issues per year: Summer, Autumn, Winter
Individuals £32/$45 Institutions £95/$145
New individual introductory subscriber rate £25/$36

East European Jewish Affairs
Managing Editor: **Howard Spier**
Editors: **Robert Brown**, *University of Toronto*, **Gennady Estraikh**, *Oxford Institute for Yiddish Studies and School of Oriental and African Studies*, **Zvi Gitelman**, *University of Michigan*, **John Klier**, *University College London* and **Mikhail Krutikov**, *Oxford Institute for Yiddish Studies*

ISSN 1350-1674 Volume 33 2003 Two issues per year: Summer, Winter
Individuals £35.00/$52.00 Institutions £85.00/$125.00
New individual subscriber introductory rate £28.00/$41.00

Jewish Culture and History
Editor: **Nadia Valman**, *University of Southampton*
Deputy Editor: **Tony Kushner**, *University of Southampton*
Reviews Editor: **Daniel Langton**, *University of Manchester*

ISSN 1462-169X Volume 5 2003 Two issues per year: Summer, Winter
Individuals £32.00/$42.00 Institutions £95.00/$130.00
New individual subscriber introductory rate £25.00/$33.00

The Journal of Israeli History
Editors: **Anita Shapira**, *Tel Aviv University* and *Chaim Weizmann Institute for the Study of Zionism* and **Derek J. Penslar**, *University of Toronto*

ISSN 1353-1042 Volume 22 2003 Twice a year: Spring, Autumn
Individuals £35.00/$48.00 Institutions £130.00/$185.00
New individual subscriber introductory rate £28.00/$38.00

Israel Affairs
Editor: **Efraim Karsh**, *King's College, London*
Associate Editor: Inari Karsh

ISSN 1353-7121 Volume 9 2003 Quarterly: Autumn, Winter, Spring, Summer
Individuals £48.00/$65.00 Institutions £195.00/$280.00
New individual subscriber introductory rate £38.00/$52.00

Middle Eastern Studies
Founding Editor: **Elie Kedourie**
Editor: **Sylvia Kedourie**

ISSN 0026-3206 Volume 39 2003 Quarterly: January, April, July, October
Individuals £52.00/$74.00 Institutions £260.00/$350.00
New individual subscriber introductory rate £41.00/$59.00

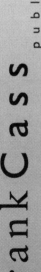

UK: Crown House, 47 Chase Side, Southgate, London N14 5BP.
Tel: +44 (0)20 8920 2100 Fax: +44 (0)20 8447 8548

North America: 5824 NE Hassalo Street, Portland, OR 97213 3644
Tel: 800 944 6190 Fax: 503 280 8832

Website: www.frankcass.com E-mail: sales@frankcass.com

The Companion to the High Holydays Prayer Book

Lord Jakobovits, *Emeritus Chief Rabbi* and
Reverend Reuben Turner, *Co-ordinating Editor*

Provides introductory notes and self-contained essays on a wide range of subjects related to the text of the Machzor, and presents some basic Jewish concepts. It aims to help the reader to use the holiest moments of their life to gain a deeper appreciation of Jewish values and virtues, turning the renewal of each year into the renewal of the Jewish spirit.

200 pages 2002 0 85303 434 6 paper £8.50/$12.50

Immanual Jacobovits: A Prophet in Israel

Meir Persoff

Offers a fascinating kaleidoscope of the life and achievements of Immanual Jacobovits as mirrored in his writings, speeches and activities, drawing on his private papers and scrapbooks. It also includes previously unpublished autobiographical chapters and specially written contributions by Nobel Peace Laureate Elie Wiesel and British Chief Rabbi Jonathan Sacks.

448 pages 2002 0 85303 4443 cloth £19.50/$27.50

Lord Jacobovits in Conversation

Michael Shashar

Presents Rabbi Jakobovits' views as they emerged from conversations with the journalist Michael Shashar, on a multitude of topics. The subjects covered include opinions about contemporary issues such as Jerusalem, the sanctity of the family, interreligious dialogue, Israel and the Territories, Who is a Jew, medical ethics, Church and State, as well as very current topics such as Nazi gold and the new British government.

256 pages 2000 0 85303 377 3 cloth £19.50/$29.95

UK: Crown House, 47 Chase Side, Southgate, London N14 5BP.
Tel: +44 (0)20 8920 2100 Fax: +44 (0)20 8447 8548

North America: 5824 NE Hassalo Street, Portland, OR 97213 3644
Tel: 800 944 6190 Fax: 503 280 8832

Website: www.vmbooks.com

Vallentine Mitchell

Drugsline
CHABAD

A FREE & CONFIDENTIAL SERVICE

Freephone: 0800 731 0713
(24-hour answer phone)

Helpline and drop-in service for people with drug and alcohol related problems, their families and friends.

Education and prevention programmes for schools, youth clubs and other organisations.

SUNDAY
10.00am-1.00pm

MONDAY
7.00pm-10.30pm

TUESDAY
7.00pm-10.30pm

THURSDAY
7.00pm-10.30pm

395 Eastern Avenue, Gants Hill, Ilford, Essex IG2 6LR
General enquiries: 020 8554 3220
Registered Charity No. 1067573

Jewish AIDS Trust

Registered Charity No. 327936

Jewish teaching tells us ...
- To respect our fellow human beings
- To care for the needs of the sick
- To be responsible for each other
- To endeavour to understand the lifestyle of others

The **Jewish AIDS Trust** was set up in 1988 to provide the Jewish community with HIV/AIDS education, counselling and support.

How does JAT help?
Education – We tailor HIV prevention workshops and activities to individuals and groups, including youth groups and workers, teachers, schools, students, rabbis and welfare organisations.

Counselling – Our qualified and experienced counsellors provide confidential counselling for people with HIV, their partners, family and friends.

Support – We provide a wide range of support to people with HIV and carers. This includes: visiting; shopping; outings; and a monthly drop-in bagel brunch.

You can contact the Jewish AIDS Trust by telephoning 020 8446 8228 or by writing to: Jewish AIDS Trust, Walsingham House, 1331 High Road, London N20 9HR

We rely on your donations for our important work.

IMMANUEL COLLEGE

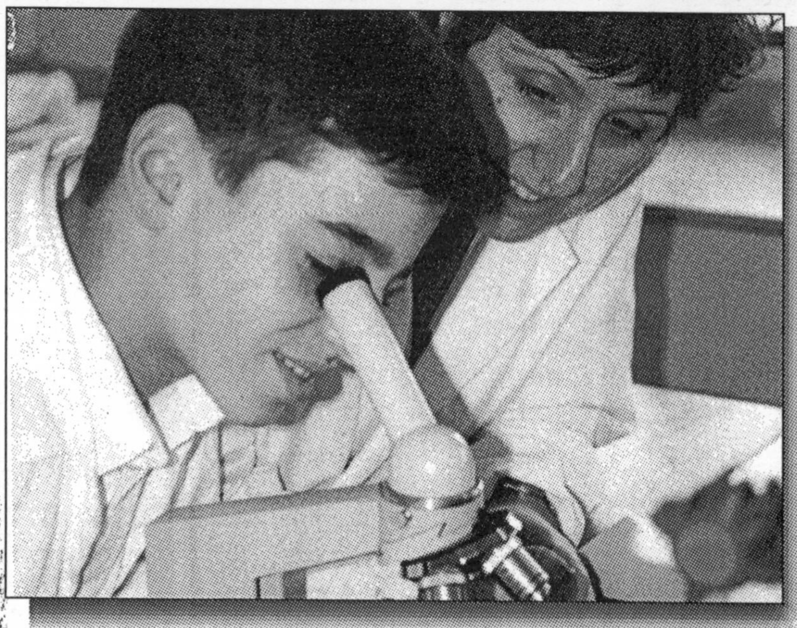

An independent selective co-educational modern Orthodox day school, Immanuel College aims to prepare its pupils (aged 11-18) to live loyal and knowledgeable Jewish lives in the modern World.

The College ethos is characterised by attentiveness to individual pupils' progress, high academic achievement and the integration of Jewish and secular learning.

Parental visits are encouraged throughout the school year.

To request the prospectus and further information and to arrange a visit, please telephone the Admissions Secretary,
Mrs Denise Rodgers, on 020 8955 8938.

87/91 Elstree Road, Bushey Herts, WD23 4BE
Tel: 020 8950 9604 Bursar 020 8950 8462 Fax: 020 8950 8687

HILL SYNAGOGUE LIBRARY